Abstracts
of
Tennessee
Death Records
for
Carter County

1908-1925

Eddie M. Nikazy

HERITAGE BOOKS
2007

HERITAGE BOOKS
AN IMPRINT OF HERITAGE BOOKS, INC.

Books, CDs, and more—Worldwide

For our listing of thousands of titles see our website at
www.HeritageBooks.com

Published 2007 by
HERITAGE BOOKS, INC.
Publishing Division
65 East Main Street
Westminster, Maryland 21157-5026

Copyright © 1992 Eddie M. Nikazy

Other books by the author:

Abstracts of Death Records for Johnson County, Tennessee, 1908 to 1941

Carter County, Tennessee Deaths, 1926-1934

Carter County, Tennessee Record Abstracts, Marriages, 1871-1920

Forgotten Soldiers: History of the 2nd Tennessee Volunteer Infantry Regiment (USA), 1861-1865

Forgotten Soldiers: History of the 4th Tennessee Volunteer Infantry Regiment (USA), 1863-1865

Greene County, Tennessee Death Record Abstracts, 1908-1918

Sullivan County, Tennessee Death Records, 1908-1918, Volume 1

Sullivan County, Tennessee Death Records, 1919-1925, Volume 2

Unicoi County, Tennessee Death Record Abstracts, 1908-1936

Washington County, Tennessee Death Record Abstracts, 1908-1916

All rights reserved. No part of this book may be reproduced or transmitted in any form or by any means, electronic or mechanical, including photocopying, recording or by any information storage and retrieval system without written permission from the author, except for the inclusion of brief quotations in a review.

International Standard Book Number: 978-1-55613-738-9

Foreword

This volume contains abstracts of Tennessee death records for Carter County, Tennessee. Death records are available for rural Tennessee counties beginning in 1908. Currently records of 1908 through 1941, with the exception of 1913, are available for public access in the Tennessee State Library and Archives.

The area of Carter County was an early and important eastern Tennessee county which served as a major migration center.

In this compilation of Carter County death records:

1.) Where the reported place of birth is different from the local county, the place of birth is stated.

2.) Name spelling variations have been preserved. When looking for a particular surname, it is may be necessary to check other possible spelling variations.

3.) Where possible, the cause of death is quoted as it appears in the record.

4.) Parenthetical entries following parents names indicate the reported place of the parents birth.

5.) Parenthetical entries following the informants name indicate place of residence.

6.) Record numbers correspond with the official death record numbers on file in the Tennessee State Library and Archives.

Cora PERRY, age 3 months, died: 6 Jul 1909, record (1908-1912) #: 6444.
Lizzie PERRY, age 28 years, born in Sullivan County, TN, married: died: date not stated, record (1908-1912) #: 6445.
M.C. DAVIS, age 47 years, female, married, cause of death: cancer, died: 18 Nov 1908, record (1908-1912) #: 6446.
Martha MORRIS, age 20 days, cause of death: not stated, died: 20 Jan 1909, record (1908-1912) #: 6447.
J.T. LANE, age 1 year, cause of death: "bronchitis", died: 22 Aug 1908.
Dan DAVIS, age 56 years, married, cause of death: not stated, died: 22 Aug 1908, record (1908-1912) #: 6449.
Jessie DANIELS, age 5 years, cause of death: "pneumonia", died: 1 Nov 1908, record (1908-1912) #: 6450.
Lottie VAUGHN, age 64 years, born in Sullivan County, TN, married, cause of death: "heart trouble", died: 20 Dec 1908, record (1908-1912) #: 6451.
Luvenia CULBERT, age 41 years, cause of death: "consumption", died: 6 Jun 1909, record (1908-1912) #: 6452.
Garfield CLEMENS, age 8 months, cause of death: "whooping cough:, died: 27 Dec 1908, record (1908-1912) #: 6453.
Marry SMITH, age 85 years, married, cause of death: "heart trouble", died: 17 Jan 1909, record (1908-1912) #: 6454.
G.F.L. SMITH, age 61 years, married, cause of death: not stated, died: 27 May 1909, record (1908-1912) #: 6455.
Maggie SLAGLE, age 41 years, married, cause of death: "consumption", died: 7 Apr 1909, record (1908-1912) #: 6456.
John LIVINGSTON, age 73 years, born in North Carolina, cause of death: "dropsy", died: 12 Oct 1909, record (1908-1912) #: 6457.
Beckey MORRIS, age 66 years, born at Jonesboro, TN, cause of death: "general break down", died: 27 Apr 1910, record (1908-1912) #: 6458.
Daniel SIMERLY, age 1 month and 1 day, cause of death: "throat trouble", died: 30 Jun 1910, record (1908-1912) #: 6459.
Mattie SIMERLY, age 39 years, cause of death: "hart trouble", died: 16 Aug 1909, record (1908-1912) #: 6460.

Mandie HENIGER, age 10 days, cause of death: "sutten", died: 26 May 1910, record (1908-1912) #: 6461.

Grant CAMPBELL, age 21 years, born in North Carolina, cause of death: "train accident at Sunbrite, Virginia", died: 17 Mar 1910, record (1908-1912) #: 6462.

Liza TREADWAY, age 65 years, married, cause of death: "fever", died: 20 Jun 1910, record (1908-1912) #: 6463.

Jacob TREADWAY, age 73 years, married, cause of death: "general breakdown", died: 5 May 1910, record (1908-1912) #: 6464.

Abe HATHAWAY, age 79 years, married, cause of death: "old age", died: 3 Jul 1909, record (1908-1912) #: 6465.

Matilda HART, age 42 years, married, cause of death: "consumption", died: 20 Jun 1910, record (1908-1912) #: 6466.

J.A. CURTIS, age 36 years, single, cause of death: "blood poison", died: 28 May 1910, record (1908-1912) #: 6468.

Ira HART, age 3 years, cause of death: "sp miningeus", died: 8 May 1910, record (1908-1912) #: 6467.

Belle SHELL, age 20 years, married, born in Johnson City, TN, cause of death: "consumption", died: 5 Dec 1909, record (1908-1912) #: 6469.

Samuel Jacob THOMPSON, age 2 years, cause of death: "memberence croup", died: 4 May 1910, record (1908-1912) #: 6470.

Susie GREENWAY, age 3 years, death cause: "diabetes", died: 15 Jun 1910, record (1908-1912) #: 6471.

Charles OLIVER, age 3 years, cause of death: "stomach trouble", died: 10 Feb 1910, record (1908-1912) #: 6472.

Harret COLE, age 59 years, married, cause of death: "scroflow", died: 21 Aug 1909, record (1908-1912) #: 6473.

D.C. GARLAND, age 71 years, married, cause of death: "paralysis", died: 24 Oct 1909, record (1908-1912) #: 6474.

Zoh PIERCE, age 50 years, single, death cause: not recorded, died: 31 Jul 1909, record (1908-1912) #: 6475.

Infant WELLS, male, cause of death: not stated, born/died: 27 Dec 1909, record (1908-1912) #: 6476.

Robert NIDIFFER, age 84 years, single, cause of death: "laryninx resperation", died: 20 Sep 1909, record (1908-1912) #: 6477.

Eliza COLE, age 72 years, married, born in Sullivan Co., TN, cause of death: "liver trouble", died: 1 Dec 1909, record (1908-1912) #: 6478.
Infant STOUT, female, cause of death: not stated, born/died: 20 Mar 1910, record (1908-1912) #: 6479.
Infant PIERCE, female, born: 27 May 1910, cause of death: not stated, died: 30 May 1910, record (1908-1912) #: 6480.
Gorda CARRIER, age 6 months, cause of death: "croup", died: 30 Mar 1910, record (1908-1912) #: 6481.
Eveline ESTIS, age 63 years, born in North Carolina, married, cause of death: "pluracy", died: 16 Aug 1909, record (1908-1912) #: 6482.
Connie ARNOLD, age 11 months, cause of death: "dierrier", died: 30 Jul 1909, record (1908-1912) #: 6483.
Nancy WILSON, age 6 years, cause of death: "dipthara", died: 18 Sep 1909, record (1908-1912) #: 6484.
Nancy WILSON, age about 82, widow, cause of death: "old age", died: 27 Jul 1909, record (1908-1912) #: 6485.
Ellen MARKLAND, age 19 years, married, cause of death: "tifoid fever", died: 7 Aug 1909, record (1908-1912) #: 6486.
Luvice TAYLOR, age 64 years, married, cause of death: "paralysis", died: 12 Feb 1910, record (1908-1912) #: 6487.
Dorthia ESTEP, age 56 years, married, cause of death: "paralysis" died: 16 Jan 1910, record (1908-1912) #: 6488.
Luvenia GARLAND, age 58 years, born in Johnson Co., TN, married, cause of death: "dropsy", died: 22 Dec 1910, record (1908-1912) #: 6489.
Frank N. LITTLE, age not stated, married, preacher, born in Wilkes Co., NC, cause of death: not recorded, died: 15 Apr 1909, record (1908-1912) #: 6490.
Thomas WATSON, black, age 37 years, single, born in North Carolina, cause of death: "consumption, died: 23 Dec 1908, record (1908-1912) #: 6491.
Mama WATSON, black, age 33 years, married, born in North Carolina, cause of death: "consumption", died: 8 Dec 1908, record (1908-1912) #: 6492.
Thomas ERWIN, black, age 65 years, single, born in North Carolina, cause of death: "pneumonia", died: 27 Dec 1908, record (1908-1912) #: 6493.
Lank DAVIS, black, age 68 years, married, cause of death: "consumption", died: 8 May 1909, record (1908-1912) #: 6494.

Bessie DAVIS, black, age 16 years, cause of death: not stated, died: 12 Jun 1909, record (1908-1912) #: 6495.
Mollie MARLER, black, age 41 years, married, cause of death: "consumption", died: 25 Aug 1908, record (1908-1912) #: 6496.
Pleasant PRESTON, black, age about 78, born in North Carolina, single, cause of death: not recorded, died: 8 Jul 1908, record (1908-1912) #: 6497.
Nat SAT.. (illegible), age 55 years, married, cause of death: illegible, died: 6 Jun 1908, record (1908-1912) #: 6498.
Ladima GORDEN, age about 100 years, born at "Wilx Co., NC, single, cause of death: "old age", died: 24 Mar 1909, record (1908-1912) #: 6499.
Unnamed INFANT, female, born: 24 May 1909, cause of death: "don't no", died: 27 May 1909, record (1908-1912) #: 6500.
Unnamed INFANT, female, black, cause of death: not stated, born/died: 25 Apr 1909, record (1908-1912) #: 6501.
Dicy A. HOLLOWAY, age 43 years, 10 months and 8 days, married, cause of death: "typhoid fever", died: 3 Oct 1910, record (1908-1912) #: 6502.
Nancy CHEEK, age 81 years, married, cause of death: "general break down", died: 6 Aug 1910, record (1908-1912) #: 6503.
Mary BLEVINS, age 82 years, born in Washington County, married, cause of death: "consumption", died: 22 Jun 1911, record (1908-1912) #: 6504.
Pansy E. HINKLE, died at birth, born/died: 5 Apr 1911, record (1908-1912) #: 6505.
Guy Buteir PIERCE, male, age 1 month, cause of death: "pneumonia fever", died: 3 Dec 1910, record (1908-1912) #: 6506.
David Spencer BERRY, age 1 month and 15 days, cause of death: "liver trouble", died: 24 May 1911, record (1908-1912) #: 6507.
Hi HAZLEWOOD, age 30 years, single, cause of death: "consumption", died: 9 Feb 1911, record (1908-1912) #: 6508.
Gaines HAZLEWOOD, age: "somewhere near 7 years, cause of death: "typhoid fever", died: 9 Feb 1911, record (1908-1912) #: 6509.
Nathan TIMBS, age: "near 18 years", cause of death: "shot", died: 29 Dec 1910, record (1908-1912) #: 6510.
Unnamed INFANT, male, died at birth, born/died: 6 Jun 1911, record (1908-1912) #: 6511.

Ina CAMPBELL, age 2 months, cause of death: "found dead in bed", died: 11 Apr 1911, record (1908-1912) #: 6512.

Unnamed INFANT, female, born: 9 Apr 1911, cause of death: "not borned at time", died: 12 Apr 1911, record (1908-1912) #: 6513.

Jane WHITE, age 58 years, born in Johnson Co., TN, married, cause of death: "consumption", died: 11 Mar 1911, record (1908-1912) #: 6514.

Althia WILLIAMS, age 68 years, born in Washington Co., TN, married, cause of death: "heart disease", died: 16 Jul 1910, record (1908-1912) #: 6515.

Glen ESTEP, age 4 months and 20 days, cause of death: "measles", died: 7 Mar 1912, record (1908-1912) #: 6516.

Mandie GRINDSTAFF, age 12 years, born: Doeville, Johnson Co., TN, cause of death: "measles", died: 14 Jan 1912, record (1908-1912) #: 6517.

Grace WILLIAMS, age 1 month, cause of death: "croup", died: 8 Jun 1912, record (1908-1912) #: 6517(a).

Bertie CAMPBELL, age 11 months, cause of death: "measles", died: 1 Apr 1912, record (1908-1912) #: 6518.

Kate RICHARDSON, age 10 years, cause of death: "miningitus", died: 15 Feb 1912, record (1908-1912) #: 6519.

Unnamed INFANT, female, cause of death: not stated, born/died: 7 Jun 1912, record (1908-1912) #: 6520.

BURLIE, (only name stated), male, age 3 months, born in North Carolina, cause of death: not recorded, died: 27 Jun 1912, record (1908-1912) #: 6521.

Elsie HINKLE, age 12 years, cause of death: "burned", died: 12 Feb 1912, record (1908-1912) #: 6522.

Josie WILLIAMS, age 36 years, married, cause of death: "tuberculosis", died: 3 Apr 1912, record (1908-1912) #: 6523.

Dora SHARP, age 4 years, cause of death: "diptheria", died: 18 Nov 1911, record (1908-1912) #: 6524.

Infant RITCHIE, age 6 weeks, child of Mollie Ritchie, cause of death: "whooping cough", died: 12 May 1912, record (1908-1912) #: 6525.

Infant SNYDER, cause of death: "born dead", child of Noah Snyder, born/died: 14 Jan 1912, record (1908-1912) #: 6526.

Infant CRUMLEY, male, born: 6 Jan 1912, child of E.Y. Crumley, cause of death: not stated, died: 9 Jan 1912, record (1908-1912) #: 6527.

Infant OLIVER, female, age 1 week, child of Andy
Oliver, cause of death: not stated, died: 17 Dec 1911,
record (1908-1912) #: 6528.
Infant NIDIFFER, female, age 1 week, child of Mary
Nidiffer, cause of death: not stated, died: 23 May
1912, record (1908-1912) #: 6529.
Infant JENKINS, female, age 3 weeks, child of Frank
Jenkins, cause of death: not stated, died: 14 Feb
1912, record (1908-1912) #: 6530.
Infant RASH, age 2 days, child of L.R. Rash, cause of
death: "unknown", died: 19 Dec 1911, record (1908-
1912) #: 6531.
Infant COMBS, female, age 3 days, child of Ben Combs,
cause of death: not stated, died: 23 Dec 1911, record
(1908-1912) #: 6536.
Infant OLIVER, female, age 2 days, child of Charles
Oliver, cause of death: not stated, died: 29 Dec 1912,
record (1908-1912) #: 6533.
Maggie MORRELL, age 46 years, married, cause of death:
"tuberculosis", died: 23 May 1912, record (1908-1912)
#: 6534.
Hubert PIERCE, age 2 years, cause of death: "measles",
died: 17 Mar 1912, record (1908-1912) #: 6535.
Monroe BOWER, age 37 years, single, cause of death:
"appendicitis", died: 14 Apr 1912, record (1908-1912)
#: 6536.
Hunter CANON, age 9 months, cause of death: "whooping
cough", died: 19 May 1912, record (1908-1912) #: 6537.
Virgil WILLIAMS, age 2 years, cause of death:
"measles", died: 17 Mar 1912, record (1908-1912) #:
6538.
Infant RICHARDSON, age 1 month, child of Dan
Richardson, cause of death: not stated, died: 10 Jan
1912, record (1908-1912) #: 6539.
Shelby NAVE, male, age 9 years, cause of death:
"measles", died: 5 Mar 1912, record (1908-1912) #:
6540.
Haynes NAVE, age 4 years, cause of death: "measles",
died: 7 Mar 1912, record (1908-1912) #: 6541.
S.H. HENDRIX, age 68 years, married, cause of death:
"rhumatism", died: 1 Feb 1909, record (1908-1912) #:
6542.
Callie ROBERTSON, age 40 years, born in Washington
County, cause of death: "locotmxa toxia", died: 13 May
1909, record (1908-1912) #: 6543.
Ethel STEWARD, age 3 years, born in Sullivan Co., TN,
cause of death: "stomach trouble", died: 4 Jun 1909,
record (1908-1912) #: 6544.

Catherine SMITH, age 45 years, married, cause of death: "consumption", died: 9 Jun 1909, record (1908-1912) #: 6545.
James RANGE, age 31 years, married, cause of death: "consumption", died: 1 Feb 1909, record (1908-1912) #: 6546.
Martin CROW, black, age 83 years, married, cause of death: "general decline", died: 11 Jun 1908, record (1908-1912) #: 6547.
Emily CROW, black, age 2 years, cause of death: "asthma", died: 9 May 1909, record (1908-1912) #: 6548.
R.W. SMALLING, age 85 years, born in Sullivan Co., TN, married, cause of death: "paralysis", died: 28 Mar 1909, record (1908-1912) #: 6549.
Wanaeta LITTLE, age 3 years, cause of death: "croup", died: 3 Oct 1908, record (1908-1912) #: 6550.
W.M. BISHOP, age 78 years, married, cause of death: "pneumonia", died: 4 Jun 1909, record (1908-1912) #: 6551.
Lottie WEBSTER, age 23 years, born in Knox Co., TN, married, cause of death: "pneumonia", died: 17 Nov 1908, record (1908-1912) #: 6552.
Grover HOUSTON, age 24 years, married, cause of death: "pneumonia", died: 17 Dec 1908, record (1908-1912) #: 6553.
William C. FAIR, age 83 years, married, cause of death: "general decline", died: 19 Jan 1909, record (1908-1912) #: 6554.
Julia COLE, age 22 years, married, cause of death: "consumption", died: 6 Apr 1909, record (1908-1912) #: 6555.
Nettie LEWIS, age 9 months, cause of death: "stomach trouble", died: 8 Jul 1909, record (1908-1912) #: 6556.
Samuel MOTTERN, age 3 years, cause of death: "accidental", died: 22 Sep 1908, record (1908-1912) #: 6557.
Infant HUGHES, age 1 day, cause of death: not stated, died: 20 Dec 1908, record (1908-1912) #: 6558.
Ellen HUGHES, age 43 years, married, cause of death: "consumption", died: 30 Aug 1908, record (1908-1912) #: 6559.
Luther HODGE, age 4 years, cause of death: "whooping cough", died: 28 Jul 1908, record (1908-1912) #: 6560.
Edgar ROBERTS, age 12 years and 6 months, cause of death: "flux", died: 12 Jun 1909, record (1908-1912) #: 6561.

Joseph WILSON, age 1 month, cause of death: "croup', died: 23 Sep 1908, record (1908-1912) #: 6562.

C.G. COLE, age 5 years, born in North Carolina, cause of death: "spinal trouble", died: 4 Jan 1909, record (1908-1912) #: 6563.

Virda ESTEP, age 11 months and 17 days, cause of death: "colrie in phantum", died: 19 Aug 1908, record (1908-1912) #: 6564.

Leolia STOUT, age 1 year and 3 months, cause of death: "whooping cough", died: 4 Aug 1908, record (1908-1912) #: 6565.

Unnamed INFANT, male, age 10 days, cause of death: "hives", died: 20 Jun 1909, record (1908-1912) #: 6566.

Dudley CAMPBELL, age 1 year and 9 days, cause of death: "hooping cought", died: 5 Oct 1908, record (1908-1912) #: 6567.

Martha GARLAND, age 26 years, married, cause of death: "child bed fever", died: 19 Dec 1908, record (1908-1912) #: 6568.

Unnamed INFANT, male, age 3 hours, cause of death: not stated, died: 12 Dec 1908, record (1908-1912) #: 6569.

Hannah ARNOLD, age 51 years, single, cause of death: "consumption", died: 29 Sep 1908, record (1908-1912) #: 6570.

Unnamed INFANT, male, age 1 hour, cause of death: "hives", died: 31 May 1909, record (1908-1912) #: 6571.

Infant BLEVINS, male, age 5 days, cause of death: "hives", died: 12 Dec 1908, record (1908-1912) #: 6572.

Ethel LOWE, age 16 years, cause of death: "consumption", died: 17 Mar 1909, record (1908-1912) #: 6573.

Sherman TAYLOR, age 45 years, married, cause of death: not recorded, died: (day not stated) Aug 1908, record (1908-1912) #: 6574.

Roby M. LIPPS, age 6 years, cause of death: illegible, died: 20 Sep 1908, record (1908-1912) #: 6575.

Alven TAYLOR, age 69 years, married, cause of death: "failure of the (illegible)", died: 21 Feb 1909, record (1908-1912) #: 6576.

Susie GWIN, age 19 years, married, cause of death: "taken by pain in head", died: 2 Feb 1909, record (1908-1912) #: 6577.

Henry BAKER, age 7 weeks, cause of death: "hooping cough", died: 8 Oct 1908, record (1908-1912) #: 6578.

Infant TICKLES, female, cause of death: "not known", died: 1 Feb 1909, record (1908-1912) #: 6579.
Tina ROBERTS, age 2 years, cause of death: "bold hives", died: 10 Feb 1909, record (1908-1912) #: 6580.
Infant ROBERTS, age 4 hours, child of Mrs. Coon Roberts, cause of death: "not known", died: 6 Dec 1908, record (1908-1912) #: 6581.
Infant TOWNSEND, male, child of Isaac Townsend, born dead, born/died: 10 May 1909, record (1908-1912) #: 6582. (additional child death below)
Infant TOWNSEND, male, child of Isaac Townsend, born dead, born/died: 10 May 1909, record (1908-1912) #: 6583.
John MOORE, age 72 years, married, cause of death: "not known", died: 28 Sep 1908, record (1908-1912) #: 6584.
J.M. TOLLY, age 45 years, married, cause of death: "killed by tree", died: 19 Jul 1908, record (1908-1912) #: 6585.
Arthur WHISENHUT, age 6 months, cause of death: "not known", died: 17 Jun 1908, record (1908-1912) #: 6586.
Tempa ODOM, female, age 5 years, cause of death: "croup", died: 12 Mar 1909, record (1908-1912) #: 6587.
James LEONARD, age 73 years, married, cause of death: "fever", died: 9 Jun 1909, record (1908-1912) #: 6588.
Ida HYDER, age 6 months, cause of death: "not known", died: 14 Jun 1909, record (1908-1912) #: 6589.
Pearl HYDER, age 8 months, cause of death: "hooping cough", died: 2 Jun 1909, record (1908-1912) #: 6590.
Rose HAZLEWOOD, age 56 years, married, cause of death: "consumption", died: 20 Jun 1909, record (1908-1912) #: 6591.
Unnamed INFANT, female, died at birth, born/died: 25 Mar 1909, record (1908-1912) #: 6592.
Walter CAMPBELL, age 7 years, 9 months and 8 days, cause of death: "pneumonia fever", died: 3 Feb 1909, record (1908-1912) #: 6593.
Essie BYERS, age 28 years, born at Neva, Johnson Co., TN, married, cause of death: "la grip", died: 28 Apr 1909, record (1908-1912) #: 6594.
Albert BLEVINS, age 1 year and 3 months, cause of death: "pneumonia fever" died: (day not stated) Mar 1909, record (1908-1912) #: 6595.
Frank EGGERS, age 6 years, cause of death: "scarlet fever", died: 31 Aug 1908, record (1908-1912) #: 6596.
Ray CRUMLEY, age 18 months, cause of death: "croup", died: 12 Sep 1908, record (1908-1912) #: 6598.

Unnamed INFANT, male, cause of death: not stated, died: 13 Sep 1908, record (1908-1912) #: 6599.

Unnamed INFANT, male, cause of death: not stated, died: 18 Apr 1909, record (1908-1912) #: 6600.

Amy OLIVER, age 18 months, cause of death: "croup", died: 14 Sep 1908, record (1908-1912) #: 6601.

Willie ANDERSON, male, age 3 years, cause of death: "croup", died: 14 Sep 1908, record (1908-1912) #: 6602.

B.D. BOWERS, age 88 years, married, cause of death: "paralysis", died: 17 Jul 1908, record (1908-1912) #: 6603.

Nanie LACY, age 30 years, married, cause of death: "failure of heart", died: 2 Jul 1908, record (1908-1912) #: 6604.

Flora SIMERLY, age 11 years, cause of death: "typhoid fever", died: 3 Dec 1908, record (1908-1912) #: 6605.

Benie SIMS, age 2 years, cause of death: "croup", died: 14 Oct 1908, record (1908-1912) #: 6606.

Unnamed INFANT, male, born dead, born/died: 15 Jul 1908, record (1908-1912) #: 6607.

Unnamed INFANT, female, born dead, born/died: 28 May 1909, record (1908-1912) #: 6608.

Harvie SIMS, age 16 days, cause of death: "croup", died: 2 Feb 1909, record (1908-1912) #: 6609.

Unnamed INFANT, male, born dead, born/died: 25 Oct 1908, record (1908-1912) #: 6610.

Dollie LEWIS, age not stated, single, cause of death: "whooping cough", died: 26 Apr 1912, record (1908-1912) #: 6611.

Harmon MORTON, age 4 years, cause of death: "measles", died: 29 Mar 1912, record (1908-1912) #: 6612.

N.W. VINES, age 32 years, married, cause of death: "consumption", died: 31 Jul 1912, record (1908-1912) #: 6613.

J. GENTRY, age 22 years, married, cause of death: "heart trouble and dropsy", died: 7 Mar 1912, record (1908-1912) #: 6614.

W.G.B. SMITH, age 60 years, 9 months and 10 days, married, cause of death: "peretonictis", died: 29 Oct 1911, record (1908-1912) #: 6615.

Dr. L.F. HYDER, age 64 years, single, cause of death: "heart failure" died: 9 Jul 1908, record (1908-1912) #: 6616.

T.L. EDMONSON, age 32 years, born at Millers Creek, NC, cause of death: "appendicitis", died: 18 Jul 1908 at Knoxville, TN, record (1908-1912) #: 6617.

Sarah MAYRNES, age 65 years, born at Red Hill, NC, married, cause of death: "heart disease", died: 12 Jun 1909, record (1908-1912) #: 6618.
Maggie BLEVINS, age 3 years, cause of death: "brain fever", died: 15 Nov 1908, record (1908-1912) #: 6619.
Bessie BLEVINS, age 28 years, married, cause of death: "consumption", died: 1 Dec 1908, record (1908-1912) #: 6620.
Edward VINES, age 6 months, cause of death: "fevor", died: 24 Jan 1911, record (1908-1912) #: 6621.
Rachel HIX, age 6 months, cause of death: "fever", died: 7 Apr 1911, record (1908-1912) #: 6622.
Virgo MILLER, age 3 years, female, cause of death: "fever", died: 22 Dec 1910, record (1908-1912) #: 6623.
Mary ALLEN, age 87 years, widow, cause of death: "lagrippe", died: 5 Sep 1909, record (1908-1912) #: 6624.
Infant NAVE, male, age not recorded, cause of death: "don't know", died: 9 Dec 1909, record (1908-1912) #: 6625.
Clarence ESTEP, age 18 months, cause of death: "croup", died: 9 Jun 1910, record (1908-1912) #: 6626.
Silas Hagy STEPP, age 2 months and 4 days, cause of death: "flux or similar cause", died: 10 Aug 1909, record (1908-1912) #: 6627.
Calie Mildred SHELL, age 4 years and 4 days, cause of death: "diptheria and croup", died: 4 Jun 1910, record (1908-1912) #: 6628.
Nancy J. CARAWAY, age 38 years, married, cause of death: "spinal trouble", died: 1 Feb 1910, record (1908-1912) #: 6629.
(Illegible) CALLOWAY, male, age 79 years, married, cause of death: "consumption", died: 9 Aug 1909, record (1908-1912) #: 6630.
Dorie JOHNSON, female, age 49 years, born in North Carolina, married, cause of death: "shot", died: 26 Dec 1909, record (1908-1912) #: 6631.
Oka JOHNSON, age 4 months and 5 days, cause of death: "bold hives, died: 1 Feb 1910, record (1908-1912) #: 6632.
Sussin FIELDS, age 7 years and 7 months, born in North Carolina, widow, cause of death: "old age", died: 18 Dec 1909, record (1908-1912) #: 6633.
Albert Oscar WAYCASTER, age 3 months, cause of death: "bold hives", died: 14 Jan 1911, record (1908-1912) #: 6634.

Dallas BRINKLEY, Jr., age 2 years and 2 months, cause of death: "pneumonia fever", died: 5 Mar 1910, record (1908-1912) #: 6635.
Bessie CORDELL, age 10 months, cause of death: "meningitis", died: 19 Aug 1908, record (1908-1912) #: 6636.
A.J. LUNSFORD, age 3 months, cause of death: not stated, died: 25 Mar 1909, record (1908-1912) #: 6637.
Allen BRUMIT, age 2 years, cause of death: "pneumonia fever", died: 7 Dec 1908, record (1908-1912) #: 6638.
Catherine HYDER, age 82 years, widow, cause of death: "paralysis and old age", died: 20 May 1909, record (1908-1912) #: 6639.
Lula JOHNSON, age 16 months, cause of death: "unknown", died: 19 Sep 1909, record (1908-1912) #: 6640.
Martha L. MARKLAND, age 70 years, widow, cause of death: "heart trouble and old age", died: 17 Oct 1908, record (1908-1912) #: 6641.
Edward PIERCE, age 7 years, cause of death: "erisypilas", died: 11 Nov 1908, record (1908-1912) #: 6642.
Monroe ARNETT, age 1 year, cause of death: "diarhoid", died: 18 Jun 1909, record (1908-1912) #: 6643.
Annie Austin WAGNER, age 11 months, cause of death: "pnuemonia", died: 28 May 1909, record (1908-1912) #: 6644.
Maggie NAVE, age 4 years, cause of death: "consumption", died: 29 May 1909, record (1908-1912) #: 6645.
Mary WILSON, age 20 years, married, cause of death: "smallpox", died: 18 May 1909, record (1908-1912) #: 6646.
Pansy Pearl WILSON, age 1 month, cause of death: "smallpox", died: 20 Jun 1909, record (1908-1912) #: 6647.
Ana Pearl RASAR, age 11 years, cause of death: "typhoid fever", died: 27 Jan 1909, record (1908-1912) #: 6648.
Georgia HARDIN, age 17 days, cause of death: "abscess of head", died: 1 Apr 1909, record (1908-1912) #: 6649.
G.J. LAWS, age 63 years, married, born at Johnson County, TN, cause of death: "consumption", died: 2 Sep 1908, record (1908-1912) #: 6650.
Eliza BLEVINS, age 9 months, cause of death: "not known", died: 5 Feb 1909, record (1908-1912) #: 6651.

Dworn M. GRINDSTAFF, female, age 15 months, cause of death: "whooping cough", died: 30 Jul 1908, record (1908-1912) #: 6652.
Lester RITCHIE, age 17 months, cause of death: not stated, died: 12 Jun 1909, record (1908-1912) #: 6653.
Ellen TAYLOR, age 30 years, married, death cause: "cancer", died: 5 May 1909, record (1908-1912) #: 6654.
Elizabeth SHEA, age 24 years, death cause: "child bed fever", died: 17 Oct 1980, record (1908-1912) #: 6655.
Infant SHEA, age 1 hour, child of George Shea, cause of death: not stated, died: 7 Oct 1908, record (1908-1912) #: 6656.
Amanda SHEA, age 6 years, cause of death: "croup", died at Mountain City, TN on 23 Jan 1909, record (1908-1912) #: 6657.
W.T. TAYLOR, age 60 years, married, cause of death: "heart trouble", died: 1 May 1909, record (1908-1912) #: 6658.
Elizabeth TAYLOR, age 16 years, cause of death: "dropsy", died: 16 Jun 1908, record (1908-1912) #: 6659.
Eliza COLE, age 60 years, widow, cause of death: "consumption", died: 9 May 1909, record (1908-1912) #: 6660.
Mamie RITCHIE, age 2 years, cause of death: "flux", died: 5 Jun 1909, record (1908-1912) #: 6661.
Elizabeth HINKLE, age 32 years, born in Alabama, married, cause of death: not recorded, died: 15 Mar 1909, record (1908-1912) #: 6662.
Daniel FORBES, age 5 years, cause of death: "scarlitina", died: 26 Oct 1908, record (1908-1912) #: 6663.
Rhodisa BROOKS, age 56 years, married, death cause: "consumption", died: 3 Jun 1909, record (1908-1912) #: 6664.
Nathaniel PIERCE, age 11 years, death cause: "diabelia", died: 20 Jul 1908, record (1908-1912) #: 6665.
Infant ESTEP, male, age 1 day, cause of death: "do not know", died: 23 Apr 1911, record (1908-1912) #: 6666.
Infant NAVE, male, age 1 day, cause of death: "do not know", died: 1 May 1911, record (1908-1912) #: 6667.
Robert HENRY, age 22 years, married, born at Gap Run, TN, cause of death: "fever pneumonia", died: 6 Mar 1911, record (1908-1912) #: 6668.

Alexander S. GRINDSTAFF, age 65 years, 2 months and 18 days, born at Pandora, Johnson County, TN, married, cause of death: "brights disease", died: 18 Mar 1911, record (1908-1912) #: 6669.
John W. HEATON, age 82 years, 7 months and 7 days, born at Pandora, Johnson County, TN, married, cause of death: "heart disease", died: 7 Aug 1910, record (1908-1912) #: 6670.
William H. LOVELESS, age 53 years, married, cause of death: "stomich disease", died: 20 Feb 1911, record (1908-1912) #: 6671.
Rosevelt HARDIN, age 12 days, cause of death: "do not know", died: 17 Mar 1911, record (1908-1912) #: 6672.
Sallie G. HARDIN, age 4 months, death cause: "do not know", died: 5 JUn 1911, record (1908-1912) #: 6673.
Infant HARDIN, age 7 days, cause of death: "do not know", died: 20 May 1911, record (1908-1912) #: 6674.
Harmon Sales KITE, age 6 months and 15 days, death cause: illegible, died: 1 Jul 1909, record (1908-1912) #: 6675.
Infant DAVIS, female, black, child of Link Davis, cause of death: not recorded, died: "date not known", death registered, 8 Aug 1911, record (1908-1912) #: 6676.
Andy STOVER, black, age 35 years, married, cause of death: "killed by train", died: 20 Oct 1910, record (1908-1912) #: 6677.
Infant MCRAFTS, male, black, child of Peter McRafts, cause of death: not stated, died: 1 Jun 1911, record (1908-1912) #: 6678.
James RITCHIE, age not stated, died: 7 Mar 1911, record (1908-1912) #: 6679.
Caroline TAYLOR, age 70 years and 12 days, married, cause of death: "kidney disease", died: 10 Aug 1910, record (1908-1912) #: 6689.
Willie WATSON, female, black, age 18 years, cause of death: "gave birth", died: 18 Mar 1911, record (1908-1912) #: 6681.
Infant WATSON, female, black, age 15 hours, child of Willie Watson, cause of death: not stated, died: 3 Mar 1911, record (1908-1912) #: 6682.
Hannah SIMS, age: "not known", married, cause of death: "general breakdown", died: 28 Jun 1911, record (1908-1912) #: 6683.
Francis LIVINGSTON, male, age 10 months, cause of death: "minnegitis", died: 26 Mar 1911, record (1908-1912) #: 6684.

Unnamed INFANT, female, age 1 day, cause of death: not stated, died: 29 Dec 1910, record (1908-1912) #: 6685.
George Dewey CATES, age 4 months, death cause: "bold hives", died: 15 Feb 1911, record (1908-1912) #: 6686.
Addie B. WILLIAMS, age 1 year, cause of death: "measles", place of birth: Oak Grove, died: 25 Jun 1911, record (1908-1912) #: 6687.
John L. TREADWAY, age 21 years, single, cause of death: "pneumonia fever, died: 10 Dec 1910, record (1908-1912) #: 6688.
Unnamed INFANT, male, age 3 months, death cause: not stated, died: 11 Aug 1910, record (1908-1912) #: 6689.
Bionett MORTON, age 2 years and 6 months, born at Johnson City, TN, cause of death: not recorded, died at Johnson City, TN, Route 6 on 3 Jul 1909, record (1908-1912) #: 6690.
A.M. MCKILHINE, age 39 years, married, cause of death: "pneumonia fever", died: date not stated, record (1908-1912) #: 6691.
Mrs. S.B. LIVINGSTON, age 47 years, married, born in Washington County, cause of death: "consumption", died: 23 May 1909, record (1908-1912) #: 6692.
Haskell LIVINGSTON, age 14 years, death cause: illegible, death date not stated, record (1908-1912) #: 6693.
Mrs. J.W. YOUNCE, age 62 years, married, death cause: "dropsy, died: 8 Dec 1909, record (1908-1912) #: 6694.
Infant PERSINGER, cause of death: "dead borned", born/died: 17 Aug 1908, record (1908-1912) #: 6695.
David CARRIGER, age 56 years, single, cause of death: "consumption", died: 16 Jul 1908, record (1908-1912) #: 6696.
A.J. RICHARDSON, age 54 years, married, cause of death: "cancer of stomach", died: 20 May 1909, record (1908-1912) #: 6697.
Bob HUGHES, age 2 days, cause of death: "bold hives", died: 15 May 1909, record (1908-1912) #: 6698.
Bunch GILLEY, female, age not recorded, born at Magnetic, NC, married, cause of death: "cancer of foot", died: 3 Sep 1908, record (1908-1912) #: 6699.
John JONES, age 4 hours, cause of death: "not known", died: 25 Dec 1908, record (1908-1912) #: 6700.
Clifford COX, age 4 months and 3 days, cause of death: "croup and bold hives", died: 27 Mar 1909, record (1908-1912) #: 6701.
Sallie MICHALS, age 6 days, cause of death: "bold hives", died: 3 May 1909, record (1908-1912) #: 6702.

Edward HUGHES, age 5 months and 12 days, cause of death: "mingechs", died: 2 May 1909, record (1908-1912) #: 6703.
Bessie JULIAN, age 1 day, cause of death: "not known", died: 7 May 1909, record (1908-1912) #: 6704.
Nat SIMERLY, age 85 years, single, born at Blount County, TN, cause of death: "old age and grip", died: 4 Apr 1909, record (1908-1912) #: 6705.
Zell HOPSON, female, age 40 years, married, born at Johnson City, TN, cause of death: "consumption", died: 2 Sep 1908, record (1908-1912) #: 6706.
Edmond PRICHARD, age 1 year and 6 months, cause of death: "diriar", died: 7 Sep 1908, record (1908-1912) #: 6707.
Clarence Clifford MILLER, age 1 month and one half, cause of death: "bold hives", died: 21 Nov 1908, record (1908-1912) #: 6708.
Charlie MILLER, age 13 days, cause of death: "bold hives", died: 29 Jun 1909, record (1908-1912) #: 6709.
Birtha BARNETT, age 16 years, 5 months and 10 days, married, cause of death: not stated, died: 27 May 1909, record (1908-1912) #: 6710.
Infant RASH, female, child of L.R. Rash, cause of death: not stated, died: 11 May 1911.
Johnie RASH, age 2 months, cause of death: "croup", died: 5 Jan 1911, record (1908-1912) #: 6712.
Ellie RICHARDSON, age 1 month, cause of death: "unknown", died: 18 Aug 1910, record (1908-1912) #: 6713.
Infant COMBS, male, age 4 months, child of Ben Combs, cause of death: "unknown", died: 27 May 1911, record (1908-1912) #: 6714.
Infant RICHARDSON, female, age 2 months, child of Delaney Richardson, cause of death: "unknown", died: 12 Mar 1911, record (1908-1912) #: 6715.
Walter KITE, age 2 months, cause of death: "hives", died: 12 Feb 1911, record (1908-1912) #: 6716.
Pearl MAY, age 2 years, born at Sugar Grove, North Carolina, cause of death: "choked", died: 21 Apr 1911, record (1908-1912) #: 6717.
Infants OLIVER, twin males, children of Oscar Oliver, cause of death: not stated, died: 15 Feb 1911, record (1908-1912) #: 6718.
Infant OLIVER, male, age 1 day, child of Grant Oliver, cause of death: "unknown", died: 17 Apr 1911, record (1908-1912) #: 6719.

Rosa OLIVER, age not stated, cause of death: "unknown", died: 8 Sep 1911, record (1908-1912) #: 6720.
Naoma HARDIN, age not stated, cause of death: not stated, died: 27 Jun 1910, record (1908-1912) #: 6721.
Alfred ANDERSON, age 14 months, cause of death: "croup", died: 31 Oct 1910, record (1908-1912) #: 6722.
Roy LACY, age not stated, cause of death: "unknown", died: 26 Mar 1911, record (1908-1912) #: 6723.
J.L. FRASIER, age 69 years, cause of death: "nea ralgia", married, died: 2 Apr 1911, record (1908-1912) #: 6724.
Ples DIALS, age not stated, single, cause of death: "gropsy", died: 1 Sep 1910, record (1908-1912) #: 6725.
Hannah MORTON, age: "unknown", cause of death: "epilepsy", died: 10 Sep 1910, record (1908-1912) #: 6726.
Martha LEWIS, age 14 years, cause of death: "unknown", died: 25 Jun 1911, record (1908-1912) #: 2727.
Infant OLIVER, male, age 1 month, child of Charles Oliver, cause of death: "croup", died: 15 May 1911, record (1908-1912) #: 6728.
Tressie GRINDSTAFF, age 1 year, cause of death: "cholera", died: 7 Jun 1911, record (1908-1912) #: 6729.
William COMBS, age 74 years, born in Sullivan County, TN, married, cause of death: "lagripp and heart failure", died: 7 Apr 1911, record (1908-1912) #: 6730.
Infant CRUMLEY, age 8 days, child of G.A. Crumley, cause of death: "unknown", died: 24 Feb 1911, record (1908-1912) #: 6731.
Luther H. CRUMLEY, age 5 years, cause of death: "croup", died: 19 Nov 1910, record (1908-1912) #: 6732.
Mirfie and Mary POTTER, (twins), age 2 years, cause of death: "croup", died: 15 Dec 1910, record (1908-1912) #: 6733.
William LUTHER, age 25 years, married, cause of death: "fever", died: 21 Jul 1910, record (1908-1912) #: 6734.
Flora BUNTON, age 2 months, cause of death: "hives", died: 28 Aug 1910, record (1908-1912) #: 6735.
Corley SHUFFIELD, age 23 years, single, cause of death: "overheat", died: 27 Mar 1911, record (1908-1912) #: 6736.

James SHUFFIELD, age 1 year, cause of death: not stated, died: 18 Jun 1911, record (1908-1912) #: 6737.
Edward LYONS, age 1 month, cause of death: "hives", died: 16 Apr 1910, record (1908-1912) #: 6738.
John DUGGER, age 24 years, married, cause of death: "perroles", died: 3 Sep 1910, record (1908-1912) #: 6739.
J.M. POTTER, age 80 years, married, cause of death: "fever", died: 24 May 1911, record (1908-1912) #: 6740.
Mary MONTGOMERY, age 80 years, married, cause of death: "peralisis", died: 15 Oct 1910, record (1908-1912) #: 6741.
Isabel POTTER, age 27 years, married, cause of death: "fevor", died: 15 Apr 1911, record (1908-1912) #: 6742.
Abraham Lincoln BOONE, age 9 years, 5 months and 27 days, cause of death: "acute farm brites", died: 16 Feb 1909, record (1908-1912) #: 6743.
James DELOACH, age 45 years, married, cause of death: "stomach and liver trouble", died: 26 May 1909, record (1908-1912) #: 6744.
Charles Preston TONCHAY, age 72 years, born at Abingdon, VA, married, cause of death: "apoplexy", died: 5 Mar 1909, record (1908-1912) #: 6745.
Mrs. Jennie BRADSHAW, age 28 years, married, cause of death: "consumption", died: 2 Dec 1908, record (1908-1912) #: 6746.
Samuel WILSON, black, age 37 years, born in North Carolina, died at Raleigh, W.VA, died: 13 Apr 1909.
Edgar GUESS, age 10 months, cause of death: "scarlet fever", died: 20 Sep 1908, record (1908-1912) #: 6748.
George Lee FOLSOM, age 42 years, single, cause of death: "cancer of the stomach", died: 1 Dec 1908, record (1908-1912) #: 6749.
Walter SHELL, age 1 day, cause of death: "died in child birth", died: 9 Jun 1909, record (1908-1912) #: 6750.
Lottie OLIVER, age 1 month and 15 days, cause of death: "bold hives", died: 20 Nov 1908, record (1908-1912) #: 6751.
Selma BRADSAHAW, female, age 26 years, single, cause of death: "bold hives", died: 17 Nov 1908, record (1908-1912) #: 6752.
Mattie E. MCCONNAHEAY, age 19 days, born at Johnson City, TN, cause of death: "summer sickness", died: 19 Jul 1908, record (1908-1912) #: 6753.

Pleasant PRESTON, black, age about 75 years, born in Lynchburg, VA, married, cause of death: "senility", died: 30 Jun 1909, record (1908-1912) #: 6754. (note this record was crossed out)
Minnie F. STONE, age 34 years, married, cause of death: "fever and liver trouble", died: 30 Aug 1908, record (1908-1912) #: 6755.
Infant THOMPSON, male, child of Charles Thompson, cause of death: "born dead", born/died: 20 May 1909, record (1908-1912) #: 6756.
Tessie CRUMLEY, age 4 months, cause of death: "bold hives", died: 13 Mar 1909, record (1908-1912) #: 6757.
R.M.A. LUNCEFORD, female, age 33 years, married, cause of death: "consumption", died: 14 May 1909, record (1908-1912) #: 6758.
Amos DAVENPORT, age 4 weeks, cause of death: "hives", died: 14 Dec 1908, record (1908-1912) #: 6759.
Dora SHUFFIELD, age 3 months, cause of death: "diorrha", died: 21 May 1909, record (1908-1912) #: 6760.
Jarvice GRINDSTAFF, age 8 months, born at Butler, TN, cause of death: "pneumonia", died: 8 Jan 1909, record (1908-1912) #: 6761.
Inen HICKS, age 9 months, cause of death: "cholera", died: 15 Jun 1909, record (1908-1912) #: 6762.
Ulyssis G. BUNTON, age 1 year and 6 months, cause of death: "croup", died: 24 Sep 1908, record (1908-1912) #: 6763.
Clide BURCHETT, age 2 months, born at Ashe County, NC, cause of death: "hives", died: 1 Mar 1909, record (1908-1912) #: 6764.
Vernia COOK, age 6 years, cause of death: "pneumonia fever", died: 4 Nov 1908, record (1908-1912) #: 6765.
E.B. POTTER, age 54 years, born at Johnson County, TN, married, died: 11 May 1909, record (1908-1912) #: 6766.
Young SHEETS, age 80 years, born at Ashe County, NC, cause of death: "old age", died: 24 Jul 1908, record (1908-1912) #: 6767.
Gracie POTTER, age 3 weeks, cause of death: "not known", died: 15 Jul 1908, record (1908-1912) #: 6768.
Sylvania POTTER, age 19 months, cause of death: "pneumonia and cattarah", died: 5 Jan 1909, record (1908-1912) #: 6769.
Infant VINES, age 1 month, cause of death: "whooping cough", died: 1 Mar 1909, record (1908-1912) #: 6770.

Junie MILLER, age 3 years, cause of death: "scarlet fever and lagrippe", died: 23 Apr 1909, record (1908-1912) #: 6771.

Infant HAYES, sex not stated, age 1 day, child of J.E. and Mary Hayes, cause of death: "not known", died: 22 Nov 1908, record (1908-1912) #: 6772.

Samuel A. HAYES, age 9 months, cause of death: "stomach and bowell trouble", died: 15 Jul 1908, record (1908-1912) #: 6773.

William R. HODGE, age 81 years, married, cause of death: "old age and kidney trouble", died: 19 Oct 1908, record (1908-1912) #: 6774.

Tommy BIRCHFIELD, age 3 days, cause of death: "not known", died: 20 Feb 1909, record (1908-1912) #: 6775.

Wriley JONES, age 96 years, born at Wilkes County, NC, married, cause of death: "old age", died: 28 Jan 1909, record (1908-1912) #: 6776.

Jake MILLER, age about 37 years, married, cause of death: "consumption", died: 12 Oct 1908, record (1908-1912) #: 6777.

Bonnie WRIGHT, age 3 months, cause of death: "not known", died: 11 Nov 1908, record (1908-1912) #: 6778.

Fred BLACKWELL, age 6 months, cause of death: "whooping cough", died: 11 Oct 1908, record (1908-1912) #: 6777.

Anderson HILL, age 1 month, cause of death: "bold hives", died: 28 Jul 1908, record (1908-1912) #: 6780.

Mary Alice OAKS, age 32 years, born at Watauga County, NC, married, cause of death: "white dropsy", died: 20 May 1909, record (1908-1912) #: 6781.

William CAMPBELL, age about 37 years, born at Alexander County, NC, married, cause of death: "consumption", died: 27 Oct 1908, record (1908-1912) #: 6782.

Luckey HUGHES, female, age 21 years, born at Valley, NC, single, cause of death: "mistreatment in child birth", died: 2 May 1909, record (1908-1912) #: 6783.

Abe FULKERSON, age 87 years, married, death cause: "old age", died: 7 Apr 1910, record #: 6784.

R.G. MINTON, age 71 years, born in North Carolina, married, cause of death: "fever", died: 28 Dec 1909, record (1908-1912) #: 6785.

Annie MINTON, age 65 years, born in North Carolina, married, cause of death: "fever", died: 12 Jan 1910, record (1908-1912) #: 6786.

Lottie MYHRS, age 20 years, married, cause of death: "consumption", died: 12 Apr 1910, record (1908-1912) #: 6787.

Julie E. MAY, age 3 months, death cause: "hives", died: 23 Jun 1910, record (1908-1912) #: 6788.
Infant BULLOCK, male, cause of death: "born dead", child of Sam Bullock, date not recorded, record (1908-1912) #: 6789.
Infant BULLOCK, male, age 9 weeks, child of Sam Bullock, cause of death: not stated, date not recorded, record (1908-1912) #: 6790.
Lettie DAVIS, age 1 year, cause of death: "teething", died: 2 Aug 1909, record (1908-1912) #: 6791.
Manna RANGE, age 3 years, cause of death: "paralysis", died: 31 Jan 1910, record (1908-1912) #: 6792.
Callie CLEMENS, age 2 years and 2 months, cause of death: "fever", died: 30 Jun 1910, record (1908-1912) #: 6793.
Infant CHAMBERS, female, child of A.L. Chambers, cause of death: "borned still", born/died: 22 Jan 1910, record (1908-1912) #: 6794.
Infant CLEMONS, female, child of John Clemens, cause of death: "fever", died: 7 Aug 1909, record (1908-1912) #: 6795.
Emma CLEMONS, age not stated, married, cause of death: "fever", died: 10 Aug 1909, record (1908-1912) #: 6796.
Mollie SLAGLE, age not stated, married, cause of death: not recorded, died: 16 Jul 1909, record (1908-1912) #: 6797.
James HOSS, age 66 years, married, cause of death: "parlaysis", died: 18 May 1911, record (1908-1912) #: 6798.
Crisley SIMERLY, male, age 72 years and 7 months, married, cause of death: "reumatism", died: 28 Oct 1910, record (1908-1912) #: 6799.
Lillie SIMERLY, age 31 years, married, cause of death: "stomach trouble", died: 1 Oct 1910, record (1908-1912) #: 6800.
Elie LEWIS, age 15 years, cause of death: "tuberculosis", died: 21 Sep 1910, record (1908-1912) #: 6801.
Sallie HOPSON, age 65 years, born in North Carolina, single, cause of death: "abscess", died: 25 Aug 1910, record (1908-1912) #: 6802.
Henry HOPSON, Jr., age 3 months, cause of death: "bold hives", died: 3 Feb 1911, record (1908-1912) #: 6803.
Homie PERRY, age 2 years, cause of death: "neumonious coope", died: 19 Dec 1910, record (1908-1912) #: 6804.

Hurmen Daton ELLIOTT, age 7 months, cause of death: "miningitus", died: 25 Jun 1911, record (1908-1912) #: 6805.
Abe DONSIL, age 53 years, born in North Carolina, married, cause of death: "marial .. (illegible)", died: 12 Jun 1911, record (1908-1912) #: 6806.
Hanck GREENLEE, age 70 years, single, cause of death: "paralysis", died: 10 Jun 1911, record (1908-1912) #: 6807.
Charles PERKINS, age 17 years, single, cause of death: "consumption", died: 29 Apr 1911.
Tilda GRAGG, age 51 years, born in North Carolina, single, cause of death: "paralysis", died: 8 Mar 1911, record (1908-1912) #: 6809.
George GOOD, age 27 years, born in North Carolina, married, cause of death: not recorded, died: 24 Aug 1910, record (1908-1912) #: 6810.
Pearl TEASTER, age 22 years, married, cause of death: "consumption", died: 28 Oct 1910, record (1908-1912) #: 6811.
Woodfin SHEPARD, age 3 months, cause of death: "miningitus", died: 30 Sep 1910, record (1908-1912) #: 6812.
J.P. JONES, male, age 69 years, single, cause of death: "brights disease", died: 30 Sep 1910, record (1908-1912) #: 6813.
Hardin JONES, age 73 years, married, cause of death: "brights disease", died: 22 Jul 1910, record (1908-1912) #: 6814.
Luna WATSON, age 55 years, born in Johnson County, TN, single, cause of death: "fever", died: 25 Nov 1910, record (1908-1912) #: 6815.
Robert Hobert ELLIOTT, age 10 days, cause of death: "bold hives", died: 7 Feb 1911, record (1908-1912) #: 6816.
Martha HUNTLEY, age 76 years, born in North Carolina, single, cause of death: "rheumatis", died: 4 Jun 1911, record (1908-1912) #: 6817.
S. WAYCASTER, age 63 years, born in North Carolina, single, cause of death: "cancer", died: 28 May 1911, record (1908-1912) #: 6818.
Winnie BORDEN, age 10 months, cause of death: "spinal trouble", died: 20 Jun 1911, record (1908-1912) #: 6819.
None ELLIOTT, age 3 weeks, cause of death: "bronchitious", died: 9 Nov 1910, record (1908-1912) #: 6820.

Sallie BUCK, age 31 years, born in Washington County, TN, married, cause of death: "consumption", died: 13 Sep 1910, record (1908-1912) #: 6821.
H.H. RANGE, age 74 years, single, cause of death: "heart trouble", died: 21 May 1912, record (1908-1912) #: 6822.
J.K. KELLY, female, age 42 years, married, cause of death: "pneumonia fever", died at Bristol, TN, 15 Dec 1911, record (1908-1912) #: 6823.
Ruce GRAYBEAL, age 17 years, born in North Carolina, single, cause of death: "fever", died: 8 Mar 1912, record (1908-1912) #: 6824.
Randal Jack HYDER, age 8 years, cause of death: "tuberculosis of the brain", died: 10 Jan 1912, record (1908-1912) #: 6825.
Hazel FAIR, cause of death: "born dead", born/died: 9 Oct 1911, record (1908-1912) #: 6826.
John S. TURNER, age 67 years, married, cause of death: "heart trouble", died: 11 Oct 1911, record (1908-1912) #: 6827.
Polly DOUGLAS, age 78 years, single, death cause: "dropsy", died: 17 Nov 1911, record (1908-1912) #: 6828.
Nancy ROBINSON, age 38 years, married, cause of death: "typhoid fever", died: 20 Nov 1911, record (1908-1912) #: 6829.
John TOLLY, age 42 years, married, death cause: "consumption", died: 4 Nov 1911, record (1908-1912) #: 6830.
Margaret WHITEHEAD, age 76 years, single, cause of death: "stomach trouble", died: 8 Dec 1911, record (1908-1912) #: 6831.
Edith HYDER, age 1 year and 6 months, death cause: "stomach trouble", died: 25 May 1912, record (1908-1912) #: 6832.
Emma INGRUM, age 35 years, married, cause of death: "dropsy", died: 20 Jul 1911, record #: 6833.
Hubert INGRUM, age 3 months, cause of death: "hives", died: 20 Aug 1911, record (1908-1912) #: 6834.
Winnie BARDER, female, age 1 year, cause of death: "spinal trouble", died: 7 Aug 1912, record (1908-1912) #: 6835.
Tine SHELL, female, age 65 years, born in North Carolina, single, cause of death: "dropsy", died: 18 Jun 1912, record (1908-1912) #: 6836.
Walter CAMEL, age 7 months, cause of death: "diptheria", died: 23 Jan 1911, record (1908-1912) #: 6837.

Susan WILLSON, age 63 years, single, cause of death: "did not know", died: 28 Oct 1911, record (1908-1912) #: 6838.
Samuel M. ESTEP, age 74 years and 5 months, married, cause of death: "heart trouble", died: date not recorded, record (1908-1912) #: 6839.
Robert A. RANGE, age 16 months, cause of death: "stomach trouble", died: 1 Apr 1912, record (1908-1912) #: 6840.
James W. HENIGER, age 57 years, born in Smith County, VA, marrid, cause of death: "heart failure", died: 8 Mar 1912, record (1908-1912) #: 6841.
Gusta GRINDSTAFF, age 2 years, male, cause of death: "burned", died: 27 Dec 1911, record (1908-1912) #: 6842.
Flosa MCKINNEY, age 1 month, cause of death: "bold hives", died: 2 Feb 1912, record (1908-1912) #: 6843.
Hester BUTLER, age 20 years, born in North Carolina, cause of death: "pneumonia fever", died: 29 Dec 1911, record (1908-1912) #: 6844.
Winnie WILLIAMS, age 6 years, cause of death: "minegetisa", died: 9 Jun 1912, record (1908-1912) #: 6845.
Sallie R. WILLIAMS, age 1 year, cause of death: "measles", died: 3 Jul 1911, record (1908-1912) #: 6846.
Ernest MILLER, age 2 years, cause of death: "hooping cough", died: 2 Jan 1912, record (1908-1912) #: 6847.
Launza SNEYD, age 6 weeks, born in Virginia, cause of death: "hooping cough", died: 7 Apr 1912, record (1908-1912) #: 6848.
Elbert SNEYD, age 2 years, born in Unicoi County, TN, cause of death: "hooping cough", died: 15 May 1912, record (1908-1912) #: 6849.
Robert M. CHAMBERS, age 2 days, cause of death: "came before time", died: 1 Mar 1912, record (1908-1912) #: 6850.
Elisa HARRIS, age 24 years, born in Unicoi County, TN, married, cause of death: "consumption", died: 19 Feb 1912, record (1908-1912) #: 6851.
Nettie STOUT, age 17 months, cause of death: "fever", died: 5 Jul 1911, record (1908-1912) #: 6852.
Mrs. Iva SMITH, age 61 years, married, cause of death: not stated, died: 1 Aug 1912, record (1908-1912) #: 6853.
David HOLLY, age 72 years, married, cause of death: "hart trouble", died; 9 Sep 1911, record (1908-1912) #: 6854.

Fred M. HOLLY, age 15 years, cause of death: "abscess", died: 19 Mar 1912, record (1908-1912) #: 6855.

Hester WILSON, colored, age 67 years, born at Yancy County, NC, married, cause of death: "hart trouble", died: 5 May 1912, record (1908-1912) #: 6856.

Addie BLEVINS, age 34 years, married, cause of death: "consumption", died: 25 Aug 1911, record (1908-1912) #: 6857.

Wallace PERKINS, age 3 weeks, cause of death: "don't know", died: 11 Nov 1911, record (1908-1912) #: 6858.

A.A. PHILLIPS, male, age 28 years and 6 months, born in Johnson County, TN, married, cause of death: "fever", died: 24 Jul 1911, record (1908-1912) #: 6859.

Ambros JONES, age 83 years, married, cause of death: "neum fever", died: 13 Mar 1912, record (1908-1912) #: 6860.

Matilda PHILLIPS, age 80 years, born in Ashe County, NC, single, cause of death: "hart trouble", died: 23 Mar 1912, record (1908-1912) #: 6861.

Inma WINTERS, female, age 1 year, born in Avery County, NC, cause of death: illegible, died: 14 Feb 1912, record (1908-1912) #: 6862.

Bertie Lee BERRY, age 2 years and 8 months, cause of death: "bronchitis", died: 3 Apr 1909, record (1908-1912) #: 6863.

Nellie LACY, age 17 years, 6 months and 2 days, cause of death: "diseased liver", died: 6 Jun 1909, record (1908-1912) #: 6864.

Robert Randall BOWERS, age 2 months, cause of death: "croup", died: 14 Feb 1909, record (1908-1912) #: 6865.

Mandie ROSENBALM, age 1 year and 5 months, cause of death: "croup", died; 19 Mar 1909, record (1908-1912) #: 6866.

Addison ESTEP, age 21 years, cause of death: "railroad wreck at Stone, VA", died: 12 Sep 1909, record (1908-1912) #: 6867.

Helen MAUPIN, age 1 year and 7 months, cause of death: "menengitis", died: 2 Jul 1908, record (1908-1912) #: 6868.

Clarie BRUMIT, age 1 month, cause of death: "spinal menangitis", died: 11 Oct 1908, record (1908-1912) #: 6869.

Thomas Hart FUGATE, cause of death: "born dead", born/died: 22 Mar 1908, record (1908-1912) #: 6870.

Mary A. CHASE, age not stated, born in Sullivan County, TN, cause of death: illegible, died: 5 Jan 1912.
Darvin CARAWAY, age 5 hours, cause of death: "not known", died: 10 May 1912, record (1908-1912) #: 6872.
Ed WHITE, age 2 months and 3 days, cause of death: "yellow jaundice", died: 31 Mar 1912, record (1908-1912) #: 6873.
Gurney MCKINNEY, age 1 month, cause of death: not known, died: 19 May 1912, record (1908-1912) #: 6874.
Catherine BLAIR, age 33 years, born in Johnson County, TN, cause of death: "child birth and chronic dearrha", died: 22 Jun 1909, record (1908-1912) #: 6875.
Julia BLAIR, age 5 weeks, cause of death: "chronic diarrhoea", died: 24 Jun 1909, record (1908-1912) #: 6876.
I. BLAIR, age 36 or 37 years, born at Pikeville, KY, cause of death: "railroad accident", died: 27 Sep 1908 in West Virginia, record (1908-1912) #: 6877.
Infant TROXELL, male, cause of death: "born dead", born/died: 30 Jul 1908, record (1908-1912) #: 6878.
Elizabeth NIDIFFER, age 82 years, married, cause of death: "old age", died: 1 Apr 1909, record (1908-1912) #: 6879.
Ira MCCLOUD, female, age 4 years, cause of death: "croup", died: 30 Oct 1908, record (1908-1912) #: 6880.
Infant DUNLOP, male, age not stated, cause of death: unknown, died: 2 Oct 1908, record (1908-1912) #: 6881.
Harold JENKINS, age 2 years and 1 month, cause of death: "accidental burn", died: 2 Feb 1909, record (1908-1912) #: 6882.
Walter ROBERTS, age 1 year and 6 months, cause of death: "membraneous croup", died: 11 Oct 1908, record (1908-1912) #: 6883.
John W. TIPTON, age 61 years, married, attorney, cause of death: "not stated" died: 7 Nov 1908, record (1908-1912) #: 6884.
Dellia CHAMBERS, age 1 year, cause of death: "unknown", died: 30 May 1910, record (1908-1912) #: 6885.
Harriett MURPHEY, age 83 years, born in North Carolina, married, cause of death: "broken foot and old age", died: 4 Nov 1909, record (1908-1912) #: 6886.
Charles MURPHEY, age 81 years, born in North Carolina, married, cause of death: "old age", died: 1 Apr 1910, record (1908-1912) #: 6887.

Clyde SIMERLY, age 3 years, cause of death: "croup", died: 8 Jan 1910, record (1908-1912) #: 6888.

David MOORE, age 30 years, single, cause of death: "consumption", died: 18 May 1910, record (1908-1912) #: 6889.

Stephen M. CROWDER, age 1 month and 12 days, cause of death: "bold hives", died: 15 Feb 1910, record (1908-1912) #: 6890.

Infant WISENHUT, male, cause of death: "born dead", born/died: 30 Dec 1909, record (1908-1912) #: 6891.

Henry HYDER, age 17 years, cause of death: "consumption", died: 25 Dec 1909, record (1908-1912) #: 6892.

Cinda HYDER, age 13 years, cause of death: "consumption", died: 9 Mar 1910, record (1908-1912) #: 6893.

Steward F. COLEMAN, age 5 months, cause of death: "bold hives", died: 18 Nov 1909, record (1908-1912) #: 6894.

Robie GUINN, age 5 months, cause of death: "stomach trouble", died: 8 Jan 1910, record (1908-1912) #: 6895.

Unnamed INFANT, male, cause of death: "died same day born", born/died: 2 Apr 1910, record (1908-1912) #: 6896.

William R. COCHRAN, age 1 year, cause of death: "bronchitus", died: 20 Nov 1909, record (1908-1912) #: 6897.

Illegible WOODS, female, age 3 months, cause of death: "bold hives", died: 15 Mar 1910, record (1908-1912) #: 6898.

Thomas J. ELLISON, age 1 day, cause of death: "bold hives", died: 2 Feb 1910, record (1908-1912) #: 6899.

Tennesse GUINN, male, age 1 day, cause of death: "croup", died: 2 Jan 1910, record (1908-1912) #: 6900.

Martha TOLLEY, age 15 years, cause of death: "fever", died: 17 Jan 1910, record (1908-1912) #: 6901.

Bob MILLER, age 20 years, single, cause of death: "killed in a fight", died: (day not stated) Dec 1909, record (1908-1912) #: 6901.

John COOK, age 55 years, married, cause of death: "consumption", died: 1 Dec 1909, record (1908-1912) #: 6902.

Rod Butler B..., (illegible surname), age not stated, single, cause of death: "bold hives", died: 5 Oct 1909, record (1908-1912) #: 6903,

Myrtle ROBERTSON, age 13 months, cause of death: "croup", died: 2 Oct 1909, record (1908-1912) #: 6904.

Callie TOWNSEND, age 1 year, cause of death: "croup",
died: 13 Sep 1909, record (1908-1912) #: 6905.
Rhoda HUBARD, age 15 years, cause of death: "dropsy",
died: 26 Dec 1909, record (1908-1912) #: 6907.
Ester WILSON, age 1 year, cause of death: "grip",
died: 18 Nov 1910, record (1908-1912) #: 6908.
Calline SMART, ag 28 years, single, born in North
Carolina, cause of death: "consumption", died: 28 Feb
1911, record (1908-1912) #: 6909.
Andson WILSON, age 1 year, cause of death: not stated,
died: 19 Jul 1910, record (1908-1912) #: 6910.
Ethel HODGE, age 18 years, married, cause of death:
"consumption", died: 6 Sep 1910, record (1908-1912) #:
6911.
Unnamed INFANT, male, age not stated, cause of death:
not stated, died: 19 Jun 1911, record (1908-1912) #:
6912.
E.D. HOLDER, age 57 years, born in North Carolina,
married, cause of death: "heart failure", died: 22 Nov
1910, record (1908-1912) #: 6913.
Harley HOLDER, age 1 year, cause of death: "flux",
died: 27 May 1911, record (1908-1912) #: 6914.
Clarence ESTEP, age 1 day, cause of death: not stated,
died: 31 Jul 1910, record (1908-1912) #: 6915.
M.A. ESTEP, female, age 38 years, married, cause of
death: "consumption", died: 10 Mar 1911, record (1908-
1912) #: 6916.
Salina GARLAND, female, age 43 years, married, cause
of death: "pneumonia fever", died: 7 Feb 1911, record
(1908-1912) #: 6917.
Nancy DENZAMORE, age 78 years, single, cause of death:
"gripp", died: 17 Jan 1911, record (1908-1912) #:
6918.
Eller ARNOLD, age 6 months, cause of death: "bold
hives", died: 20 Nov 1911, record (1908-1912) #: 6919.
Sysay ESTEP, age 75 years, married, born in Johnson
County, TN, cause of death: "heart dropsy", died: 16
Apr 1911, record (1908-1912) #: 6920.
Infant ESTEP, male, age 5 hours, cause of death: not
stated, died: 15 May 1911, record (1908-1912) #: 6921.
Evvie ELLIOTT, age 17 years, married, born in North
Carolina, cause of death: "pnuemonia fever", died: 10
Apr 1911, record (1908-1912) #: 6922.
Willie GARLAND, age 1 day, cause of death: not stated,
died: 19 Apr 1911, record (1908-1912) #: 6923.
Earmon BLEVINS, male, age 7 months, cause of death:
"liver", died: 25 Aug 1911, record (1908-1912) #:
6924.

Infant BLEVINS, age 1 day, cause of death: not stated, died: 25 Jan 1911, record (1908-1912) #: 6925.

Henry MARKLAND, age 3 weeks, cause of death: not stated, died: 21 Jul 1910, record (1908-1912) #: 6925A.

James DAVIDSON, age 78 years, born in England, widower, cause of death: "stomach trouble", died: 20 Dec 1909, record (1908-1912) #: 6926.

Elisa BOWERS, age 68 years, widow, cause of death: "dropsy", died: 7 May 1910, record (1908-1912) #: 6927.

Thomas TAYLOR, age 53 years, married, cause of death: "laryngitis", died: 9 Nov 1909, record (1908-1912) #: 6928.

Nannie TAYLOR, age 20 years, single, cause of death: "consumption", died: 9 Aug 1909, record (1908-1912) #: 6929.

Sarah WILSON, age 55 years, married, cause of death: not recorded, died: 4 Jan 1910, record (1908-1912) #: 6930.

Lewis PIERCE, age 64 years, married, cause of death: "pneumonia", died: 11 Dec 1909, record (1908-1912) #: 6931.

Bertie GRINDSTAFF, age 16 years, cause of death: "consumption", died: 13 May 1910, record (1908-1912) #: 6931A.

(first name illegible) OLIVER, male, age not stated, cause of death: not stated, died: 18 Feb 1910, record (1908-1912) #: 6932.

Infants WILLIAMS, twins (male and female), children of Sarance and Ivel Williams, cause of death: not stated, born/died: 4 Jul 1910, record (1908-1912) #: 6933.

Sissy BLEVINS, age: illegible, cause of death: "rumtism", died: 8 May 1910, record (1908-1912) #: 6934.

William RITCHIE, age 37 years, single, cause of death: "consumption", died: 6 Sep 1910, record (1908-1912) #: 6935.

Kinnie Anyies MYERS, age 3 years, cause of death: "neumoney fiver", died: 24 Mar 1910, record (1908-1912) #: 6936.

William POTTER, age 1 day, cause of death: "strangulation", died: 15 Apr 1911, record (1908-1912) #: 6937.

Unnamed INFANT, male, age 1 day, cause of death: "strangulation", died: 12 Nov 1910, record (1908-1912) #: 6938.

Unnamed INFANT, female, age 1 day, cause of death: "strangulation", died: 12 Nov 1910, record (1908-1912) #: 6939.

Grocen MORRIS, male, age about 58 years, born in North Carolina, married, cause of death: "paralysis", died: 11 Aug 1910, record (1908-1912) #: 6940.

Hazel HILL, age 1 year, cause of death: "croup", died: 26 Jul 1910, record (1908-1912) #: 6941.

Liddie MURPHY, age about 80 years, born in McDowel County, NC, cause of death: "paralysis", died: 28 Nov 1910, record (1908-1912) #: 6942.

C.C. COLEMAN, age 61 years, single, born in Burk County, NC, cause of death: "hemorrage of bowels, died: 3 May 1911, record (1908-1912) #: 6943.

Unnamed INFANT, male, age 1 day, cause of death: "strangulation", died: 23 Mar 1911, record (1908-1912) #: 6944.

Unnamed INFANT, male, age 1 day, cause of death: "strangulation", died: 28 Apr 1911, record (1908-1912) #: 6945.

Unnamed INFANT, male, age 1 day, cause of death: "strangulation", died: 15 Sep 1910, record (1908-1912) #: 6946.

Tenie MCKINNEY, female, age 51 years, born in Johnson County, TN, married, cause of death: "rheumatism and neuralgia", died: 9 Jun 1911, record (1908-1912) #: 6947.

Edath CORNETT, age 4 months, cause of death: "bowel trouble", died: 14 Jun 1911, record (1908-1912) #: 6948.

Myrtle CORNETT, age 4 months, cause of death: "bowel trouble", died: 16 Jun 1911, record (1908-1912) #: 6949.

Dovie HILIMON, age 6 months, cause of death: "croup", died: 26 Dec 1910, record (1908-1912) #: 6950.

Bettie BLEVINS, age 3 years and 2 months, cause of death: illegible, died: 7 Jun 1911, record (1908-1912) #: 6951.

Kattie LITTLE, age 4 years, cause of death: "typhoid fever", died: 28 Dec 1910, record (1908-1912) #: 6952.

Martha HEAD, age 68 years and 8 months, married, born in McDowel County, NC, cause of death: "rhumatism nerve trouble", died: 4 Nov 1910, record (1908-1912) #: 6953.

John CHAMBERS, age 87 years, born in North Carolina, married, cause of death: "paralysis", died: 30 Sep 1910, record (1908-1912) #: 6954.

J.H. CARVER, age 34 years, married, cause of death: "railroad car ran over him", died: 15 Aug 1910 at Spruce Pine, NC, record (1908-1912) #: 6955.

Genia INGRAM, age 3 years, cause of death: "clothing caught fire and burned", died: 28 Mar 1911, record (1908-1912) #: 6956.

Unnamed INFANT, male, age 2 days, cause of death: "hives", died: 8 Apr 1911, record (1908-1912) #: 6957.

John ELLISON, age 72 years, born in Ashe County, NC, married, cause of death: "consumption", died: 16 Feb 1911, record (1908-1912) #: 6958.

Robert GRINDSTAFF, age 2 years, cause of death: "spinal trouble", died: 17 Nov 1910, record (1908-1912) #: 6959.

Vada PARDIN, female, age 4 years, cause of death: "spinal trouble", died: 2 Oct 1910, record (1908-1912) #: 6960.

Herman ELLIOTT, age 2 years, cause of death: "spinal trouble", died: 20 Jan 1911, record (1908-1912) #: 6961.

James S. NAVE, age 41 years, married, cause of death: "typhoid fever", died: 11 Feb 1911, record (1908-1912) #: 6962.

Lee LEWIS, age 4 months, cause of death: "croup", died: 12 Feb 1911, record (1908-1912) #: 6963.

Guy GRINDSTAFF, age 4 months, cause of death: "spinal trouble", died: 1 Nov 1910, record (1908-1912) #: 6964.

Clayton TAYLOR, age 8 days, cause of death: "croup", died: 24 Feb 1911, record (1908-1912) #: 6965.

Infant GRINDSTAFF, female, age 1 day, cause of death: "do not know", died: 10 Jul 1911, record (1908-1912) #: 6966.

George WHITE, age 62 years, married, cause of death: "brights disease", died: 20 Mar 1912, record (1908-1912) #: 6967.

Mary WILLIAMS, age 54 years, married, cause of death: "yellow jaundice", died: 20 Jul 1911, record (1908-1912) #: 6968.

Ruth BUCKLES, age 61 years, married, cause of death: "lagripp", died: (day not stated) Feb 1912, record (1908-1912) #: 6969.

Raman NAVE, age 11 months, cause of death: "spinal trouble", died: 1 Aug 1911, record (1908-1912) #: 6970.

Bessie HAMPTON, age 7 months, cause of death: "consumption", died: 11 Oct 1911, record (1908-1912) #: 6971.

D.M. GRINDSTAFF, age 39 years, married, cause of death: "typhoid", died: 11 May 1912, record (1908-1912) #: 6972.

Maggie PETERS, age 5 months, cause of death: "cholera", died: 12 Jun 1912, record (1908-1912) #: 6973.

L.C. SHUFFIELD, age 54 years, married, cause of death: "paralysis", died: 22 Nov 1910, record (1908-1912) #: 6974.

Roy MARKLAND, age 8 years, cause of death: "spinal meningitus", died: 1 Jun 1912, record (1908-1912) #: 6975.

Unnamed INFANT, female, age not stated, cause of death: not stated, died: 30 May 1912, record (1908-1912) #: 6976.

Cilie BLEVINS, female, age 1 month, cause of death: "catah of stomach", died: 28 Aug 1912, record (1908-1912) #: 6977.

Roy BRUMIT, age 5 days, Cause of Death: not stated, died: 23 Feb 1912, record (1908-1912) #: 6978.

Marcella NAVE, age 8 months, Cause of Death: "fever", died: 28 Feb 1909, record (1908-1912) #: 6979.

Christian C. HARDIN, age 1 year, Cause of Death: "flux", died: 14 Jul 1908, record (1908-1912) #: 6980.

Martha HARDIN, age 8 years, Cause of Death: "fever", died: 8 Oct 1908, record (1908-1912) #: 6981.

Ottie MORRELL, male, age 3 years, Cause of Death: "croup", died: 2 Nov 1908, record (1908-1912) #: 6982.

Bulah TREADWAY, age 1 year, Cause of Death: "croup", died: 28 Oct 1909, record (1908-1912) #: 6983.

Infant CARDIN, female, age not recorded, Cause of Death: "croup", died: 11 Jul 1909, record (1908-1912) #: 6984.

George NAVE, age 9 months, Cause of Death: "whooping cough", died: 2 Aug 1909, record (1908-1912) #: 6985.

Daisy NAVE, age not stated, Cause of Death: not stated, died: 16 Dec 1908, record (1908-1912) #: 6986.

Caroline HARDIN, age 70 years, widow, pensioner, Cause of Death: "dropsy", died: 11 Jan 1909, record (1908-1912) #: 6987.

R.R. WILLIAMS, age 62 years, born in Johnson County, TN, married, Cause of Death: "stomach trouble", died: 7 Dec 1911, record (1908-1912) #: 6988.

Canan SHELL, male, age 76 years, married, Cause of Death: "organic disease of heart", died: 23 Nov 1911, record (1908-1912) #: 6989.

Roady LARAMER, age 42 years, born in Johnson City, TN, single, Cause of Death: "appilet fits", died: 22 Feb 1912, record (1908-1912) #: 6990.

Sinda SHELL, female, age 75 years, married, Cause of Death: "senility", died: 7 Feb 1912, record (1908-1912) #: 6991.

Alfred EARVIN, colored, age 35 years, married, Cause of Death: "hurt on railroad", died: 15 Oct 1911, record (1908-1912) #: 6992.

Clarence POWLARD, age 3 years, Cause of Death: "nephritis", died: 8 Mar 1912, record (1908-1912) #: 6993.

Samuel M. LACY, age 61 years, married, Cause of Death: "diesase heart", died: 11 Mar 1912, record (1908-1912) #: 6994.

James A. SHELL, age 29 years, married, Cause of Death: "tuberculosis", died: 12 Feb 1912, record (1908-1912) #: 6995.

Rebeca ADAMS, age 75 years, married, Cause of Death: "hart trouble", died: 26 Apr 1912, record (1908-1912) #: 6996.

Ramon KINNES, colored, age 6 months, Cause of Death: "spanesm", died; 8 Jun 1912, record (1908-1912) #: 6997.

Illegible INFANT, female, age 11 months, Cause of Death: "measles", died: 7 Jan (year illegible), record (1908-1912) #: 6998.

Clarence PETERS, age 3 months, Cause of Death: not stated, died: 18 Dec 1911, record (1908-1912) #: 6999.

Neomah GRINDSTAFF, age 5 days, Cause of Death: not stated, died: 14 Apr 1912, record (1908-1912) #: 7000.

Lizzie RICHARDSON, age 30 years, born in North Carolina, married, Cause of Death: not stated, died: 18 Jun 1912, record (1908-1912) #: 7001.

Infant RICHARDSON, male, age 1 day, Cause of Death: not stated, died: 14 (month not stated), 1912, record (1908-1912) #: 7002.

Infant STOUT, male, age 1 day, Cause of Death: not stated, died: 1 Apr 1912, record (1908-1912) #: 7003.

Illegible TAYLOR, male, age 56 years, married, Cause of Death: "paralysis", died: 27 Sep 1911, record (1908-1912) #: 7004.

Narva GRINDSTAFF, female, age 32 years, married, Cause of Death: "consumption", died: 15 Dec 1911, record (1908-1912) #: 7005.

Jane RICHARDSON, age 50 years, single, Cause of Death: "measles", died: 4 Mar 1912, record (1908-1912) #: 7006.

W.M. BLEVINS, age 64 years, single, Cause of Death: "pneumonia fever", died: 8 Feb 1912, record (1908-1912) #: 7007.

Hardon HURLEY, age 6 years, Cause of Death: "scarlet fever", died: 3 Oct 1911, record (1908-1912) #: 7008.

Infant HURLEY, male, age 1 day, Cause of Death: not stated, died: 23 Jan 1912, record (1908-1912) #: 7009.

Sara C. TAYLOR, age 65 years, single, Cause of Death: "dropsy", died: 22 Sep 1911, record (1908-1912) #: 7010.

W.R. ESTEP, age 52 years, married, Cause of Death: "laryngitis", died: 17 Jun 1912, record (1908-1912) #: 7011.

Ellen HURLEY, age 70 years, married, Cause of Death: "old age", died: (day not stated) Jul 1911, record (1908-1912) #: 7012.

Sallie HARDIN, age 52 years, married, Cause of Death: "pneumonia", died: 20 Jul 1911, record (1908-1912) #: 7013.

R.L. HAYES, female, age 72 years, born in North Carolina, single, Cause of Death: "cattarrah of stomach", died: 14 Feb 1911, record (1908-1912) #: 7014.

Joseph B. KITE, age 18 months, Cause of Death: "kidney trouble", died: 7 Aug 1910, record (1908-1912) #: 7015.

Junie BOWMAN, age 9 years, Cause of Death: "typhoid fever", died: 16 Oct 1910, record (1908-1912) #: 7016.

Nathaniel C. SHELL, age 20 years, single, cause of death: "stomach trouble", died: 2 Feb 1911, record (1908-1912) #: 7017.

Elsie MCKAY, age 3 months, cause of death: "throat disorder", died: 5 Sep 1910, record (1908-1912) #: 7018.

Susan C. PATTON, age 61 years, married, cause of death: "stomach trouble", died: 27 Sep 1910, record (1908-1912) #: 7019.

Daisy L. DOUGLAS, age 3 weeks, cause of death: "measles", died: 19 Mar 1911, record (1908-1912) #: 7020.

John H. BLEVINS, age 37 years, born at Travelers Rest, KY, married, cause of death: "tuberculosis", died: 4 Nov 1910, record (1908-1912) #: 7021.

Mattie HARDIN, age 29 years, born in Sullivan County, TN, married, cause of death: "tuberculosis", died: 21 Feb 1911, record (1908-1912) #: 7022.

Ellen POTTER, age 50 years, married, cause of death: "cancer", died: 28 Mar 1911, record #: 7023.

Blannie HARDIN, female, age 9 months, cause of death: "tuberculosis", died: 20 Jun 1911, record (1908-1912) #: 7024.

Issack WILLIAMS, male, age 32 years, married, cause of death: "paralysis", died: 7 Feb 1911, record (1908-1912) #: 7024A.

Jennie CLEMONS, age 32 years, married, cause of death: "dropsy of heart", died: 29 Apr 1911, record (1908-1912) #: 7025.

Alice CARR, age 1 day, cause of death: not stated, died: 10 Apr 1911, record (1908-1912) #: 7026.

Frank HARRIS, age not stated, married, cause of death: not stated, died: (day not stated) Apr 1911, record (1908-1912) #: 7027.

Ella M. CARR, age 20 years, single, cause of death: not stated, died: 8 Feb 1911, record (1908-1912) #: 7028.

A.C. HAMER, age 30 years, male, born in Washington County, TN, cause of death: "heart trouble", died: 6 May 1911, record (1908-1912) #: 7029.

Mary E. TAYLOR, age 65 years, born in Washington County, TN, married, cause of death: "stomic trouble", died: 8 May 1911, record (1908-1912) #: 7030.

R.M. ELLIS, age 43 years, born in Alabama, married, cause of death: "killed by Negro", died 16 Nov 1911 at Peters B., VA, record (1908-1912) #: 7031.

Martha Jane COCHRAN, age 6 months and 2 days, cause of death: "flucks", died: 27 Jul 1910, record (1908-1912) #: 7032.

Nancy TOLLEY, age 35 years, born in North Carolina, married, cause of death: "consumption, died: 12 Dec 1910, record (1908-1912) #: 7033.

Fred TOLLEY, age 7 years, 3 months and 13 days, cause of death: "flux", died: 30 Sep 1910, record (1908-1912) #: 7034.

Vista TOLLEY, female, age 7 days, cause of death: "fits", died: 30 Apr 1910, record (1908-1912) #: 7035.

Elbert CLARK, age 1 year and 4 months, cause of death: "flux", died: 10 Sep 1910, record (1908-1912) #: 7036.

Mary BERY, age 8 years, cause of death: "flucks", died: 24 Jul 1910, record (1908-1912) #: 7037.

Addala BERY, age 31 years, married, cause of death: "confindment", died: 20 Jan 1911, record (1908-1912) #: 7038.

Maud MILLER, age 1 year and 7 months, cause of death: "measles and typhoid fever", died: 24 Mar 1911, record (1908-1912) #: 7039.

Unnamed INFANT, female, age not stated, cause of death: "strangulation", died: 3 Apr 1911, record (1908-1912) #: 7040.

Charley STREET, age 70 years, born in Mitchell County, NC, married, cause of death: "consumption", died: 12 Nov 1910 at Mitchell County, NC, record (1908-1912) #: 7041.

John Wesley PHILLIPS, age 3 months and 2 days, cause of death: "croup", died: 2 Dec 1910, record (1908-1912) #: 7042.

Unnamed INFANT, male, age 1 month and 3 days, cause of death: "hives", died: 25 Jan 1911, record (1908-1912) #: 7042A.

Sallie WILSON, age 28 years, married, cause of death: "typhoid", died: 10 Sep 1911, record (1908-1912) #: 7043.

Clarence (UNKNOWN), age 2 years and 11 days, cause of death: "mingetis", died: 5 Aug 1912, record (1908-1912) #: 7044.

Pearl OLIVER, age 5 years and 6 months, cause of death: "janders", died: 3 Nov 1911, record (1908-1912) #: 7045.

Neas GIBSON, black, age about 48 years, born in Alabama, married, cause of death: "kidney trouble", died: 14 May 1910, record (1908-1912) #: 7046.

Sam BURROW, age about 52 years, married, cause of death: "cancer", died: 24 Oct 1911, record (1908-1912) #: 7047.

John Paul MURKLIN, age 7 months, cause of death: "croup, died: 14 Oct 1910, record (1908-1912) #: 7048.

Harry MERRIT, age 5 months, cause of death: "broncho pneumonia", died: 16 Jun 1910, record (1908-1912) #: 7050.

Unnamed INFANT, female, age 1 day, born at Bristol, TN, died: 7 Aug 1909 at Bristol, TN, record (1908-1912) #: 7051.

Mrs. Nancy VANHOY, age 86 years, born at Henry County, VA, married, cause of death: "paralysis", died: 15 Apr 1910, record (1908-1912) #: 7052.

Infant LACY, male, age not stated, child of J.W. Lacy, cause of death: not stated, died: 17 Feb 1910, record (1908-1912) #: 7053.

Eddie Harmon LEDWELL, age 8 months and 4 days, cause of death: "unknown", died: 6 Jun 1910, record (1908-1912) #: 7054.

Bennie MCEWEN, male, age 17 years, 6 months and 1 day, cause of death: "drowning", died: 27 Jun 1910, record (1908-1912) #: 7055.

Henry MYERS, age 59 years, married, cause of death: "heart trouble", died: 27 Mar 1910, record (1908-1912) #: 7056.

Heck NIDIFFER, female, age about 55 years, single, cause of death: "consumption", died: 23 Mar 1910, record (1908-1912) #: 7057.

R.A. LONG, male, age 52 years, born in Blount County, TN, married, cause of death: "brights disease", died: 27 Jul 1909, record (1908-1912) #: 7058.

Hunter HOLMES, age 2 years, cause of death: "flux", died: 18 Jul 1909, record (1908-1912) #: 7059.

Bonnie Bell MAUPIN, age 10 months, cause of death: "colera", died: 5 Apr 1910, record (1908-1912) #: 7060.

Mrs. Mollie ANGEL, age about 50 years, widow, cause of death: not recorded, died: (day not stated) Jun 1910, record (1908-1912) #: 7061.

Evaline LACY, age about 65 years, married, cause of death: "paralysis", died: 20 Dec 1909, record (1908-1912) #: 7062.

Hubert EDENS, age 2 years and 5 months, cause of death: "diptheria", died: 9 Jan 1910, record (1908-1912) #: 7063.

Hazel TURNER, age 2 months, cause of death: "unknown", died: 10 May 1910, record (1908-1912) #: 7064.

Infant PERCY, male, child of C.O. Percy, cause of death: "died at birth", died: 2 Jun 1910, record (1908-1912) #: 7065.

Joe WHITE, age 1 day, cause of death: not stated, died: 1 Sep 1909, record (1908-1912) #: 7066.

C.R. HAWKINS, age 27 years, born in Johnson County, TN, single, cause of death: "paralysis", died: 22 Nov 1909, record (1908-1912) #: 7067.

J.F. NANCE, male, age 46 years, born in Virginia, married, cause of death: "fever", died: 19 Jan 1910, record (1908-1912) #: 7068.

Amy BRANCH, age 88 years, 10 months and 18 days, born at Burk County, NC, widow, death cause: not recorded, died: 4 Apr 1910, record (1908-1912) #: 7069.

Floid GRINDSTAFF, female, age 17 days, cause of death: "bold hives", died: 29 May 1910, record (1908-1912) #: 7070.

Emaline PRICE, age 86 years, widow, cause of death: "old age and lagripp", died: 31 Mar 1910, record (1908-1912) #: 7071.

W.F. BOWMAN, age 45 years, married, cause of death: "typhoid fever", died: 29 Jun 1910, record (1908-1912) #: 7072.

Foy YOUNG, age 1 month and 16 days, cause of death: "nurses thresh", died: 26 Aug 1909, record (1908-1912) #: 7072A.

Myrtle MYERS, age 2 weeks and 2 days, cause of death: "bold hives", died: 8 Mar 1912, record (1908-1912) #: 7073.

Charles VAUGHN, age 23 years, married, cause of death: "consumption", died: 25 Nov 1911, record (1908-1912) #: 7074.

Birtie CULBERT, age 10 years, cause of death: "consumption", died: 9 Mar 1912, record (1908-1912) #: 7075.

D.T. CHAMBERS, age 79 years, born in South Carolina, married, cause of death: not stated, died: 27 Jul 1911, record (1908-1912) #: 7076.

J.A. REYNOLDS, age 55 years, born at Craig County, VA, married, cause of death: "brights", died: 8 Jun 1911, record (1908-1912) #: 7077.

Florence LYON, age 40 years, born in Sullivan County, TN, married, cause of death: "consumption", died: (day not stated) Apr 1912, record (1908-1912) #: 7078.

India PERRY, age 11 years, cause of death: not stated, died: (day not stated) Mar 1912, record (1908-1912) #: 7079.

Gusta CARR, female, age 15 years, cause of death: "hart trouble", died: (day not stated) Oct 1912, record (1908-1912) #: 7080.

Elizabeth SLAGLE, age 73 years, married, cause of death: "paralysis", died: 22 Feb 1912, record (1908-1912) #: 7081.

James BROOKS, colored, age 35 years, single, cause of death: "consumption", died: 23 Sep 1909, record (1908-1912) #: 7082.

D. HUGHES, black, age 50 years, married, cause of death: "got hurt", died: 26 Dec 1909, record (1908-1912) #: 7083.

Rhoda STOVER, age 40 years, married, cause of death: "consumption", died: 24 Sep 1909, record (1908-1912) #: 7084.

Margie R. JOHNSON, colored, age 10 months and 2 weeks, cause of death: "colick", died: 16 Mar 1910, record (1908-1912) #: 7085.

Adda COCHRAN, age 30 years, born in North Carolina, married, cause of death: "womb trouble", died: 17 Dec 1910, record (1908-1912) #: 7086.

Gertie HOMBRICK, age 3 days, cause of death: "unknown", died: 28 Jun 1910, record (1908-1912) #: 7087.

Ernest HYDER, age 8 years, cause of death: "croup", died: 8 Oct 1909, record (1908-1912) #: 7088.

Unnamed INFANT, male, cause of death: "unknown", born/died: 18 Jun 1910, record (1908-1912) #: 7089.

Maggie GRINDSTAFF, age 74 years, married, cause of death: "paralysis", died: 9 Jun 1910, record (1908-1912) #: 7090.

Doak STREET, male, age 54 years, born in North Carolina, cause of death: "spinal disease", died: 4 Jun 1910 in Knox County, TN, record (1908-1912) #: 7091.

Jane STREET, age 48 years, born in North Carolina, cause of death: "insanity", died: 28 Jul 1909, record (1908-1912) #: 7092.

Fred PRICE, age 3 years, cause of death: "spinal miningitis", died: 25 Oct 1909, record (1908-1912) #: 7093.

Allen BLEVENS, age 87 years, born in Sullivan County, TN, married, cause of death: "rheumatism", died: 4 Mar 1910, record (1908-1912) #: 7094.

Nola GRINDSTAFF, age 1 year and 11 months, cause of death: "miningitis", died: 9 Dec 1909, record (1908-1912) #: 7095.

Mary A. BRITT, age 13 years, cause of death: "lung and heart trouble", died: 28 Nov 1909, record (1908-1912) #: 7096.

Mary BLEVINS, age 22 years and 6 months, born in North Carolina, married, cause of death: "consumption", died: 30 Sep 1909, record (1908-1912) #: 7097.

Grace BLEVINS, age 2 years, cause of death: "consumption", died: 17 Mar 1910, record (1908-1912) #: 7098.

James LAWSON, age 63 years, married, cause of death: "heart trouble", died: 10 Jan 1910, record (1908-1912) #: 7099.

James GLENN, age 50 years, born at Russell County, VA, married, cause of death: "pnuemonia fever", died: 15 Sep 1909 at Washington County, TN, record (1908-1912) #: 7100.

T.D. RUSSELL, age 57 years, born at Greene County, TN, married, cause of death: "cancer of stomach", died: 15 Aug 1909 at Greene Co, TN, record (1908-1912) #: 7101.

Clemmie BLEVINS, age 42 years, married, cause of death: "consumption", died: 1 Aug 1909, record (1908-1912) #: 7102.

William SMITH, age 43 years, married, cause of death: "consumption", died: 3 Jan 1910 at Sullivan County, TN, record (1908-1912) #: 7103.

Unnamed INFANT, male, age 3 hours, cause of death: "unknown", died: 9 May 1910, record (1908-1912) #: 7104.

Carl FREEMAN, age 22 years, born at Mitchell County, NC, single, cause of death: "consumption", died: 25 Mar 1910, record (1908-1912) #: 7105.

Desmond FREEMAN, age 11 months, cause of death: "phethisic", died: 15 Apr 1910, record (1908-1912) #: 7106.

Mattie MYERS, age 25 years, married, cause of death: "consumption", died: 25 Nov 1909, record (1908-1912) #: 7107.

Bruce MYERS, age 3 years and 6 months, cause of death: "consumption", died: 17 Oct 1909, record (1908-1912) #: 7108.

May MYERS, age 2 years and 3 months, cause of death: "spinal disease", died: 26 May 1910, record (1908-1912) #: 7109.

Unnamed INFANT, male, age 1 month, cause of death: "measles", died: 17 Jun 1910, record (1908-1912) #: 7110.

Unnamed INFANT, male, cause of death: "unknown", born/died: 30 Nov 1910, record (1908-1912) #: 7111.

Nell MUMPOWER, age 2 months, death cause: "unknown", died: 23 Jun 1910, record (1908-1912) #: 7112.

Alfred RUSLE, age 18 months, cause of death: "direr", died: 28 Jun 1910 at Washington County, TN, record (1908-1912) #: 7113.

Elizabeth ROWE, age 56 years, born in Virginia, widow, cause of death: "liver trouble", died: 7 Jan 1910, record (1908-1912) #: 7114.

M.N. TAYLOR, age 57 years, married, cause of death: illegible, died: 17 Jun 1910, record (1908-1912) #: 7115.

Margaret (ILLEGIBLE), black, age 62 years, born in North Carolina, cause of death: not recorded, married, died: date not recorded, record (1908-1912) #: 7116.

Walter LARKINS, age 16 years, cause of death: "hurt by a car", died: 25 Jan 1910, record (1908-1912) #: 7117.

M.C. MILLER, age 59 years, married, cause of death: "indigestion", died: 6 Apr 1910, record (1908-1912) #: 7118.

Elbert JONES, age 16 years, cause of death: "consumption", died: 5 Dec 1909, record (1908-1912) #: 7119.

Mattie HARDIN, age 29 years, married, cause of death: "tuberculosis", died: 15 Feb 1911, record (1908-1912) #: 7120.

Blannie HARDIN, female, age 10 months, cause of death: "complication of disease", died: 31 Dec 1910, record (1908-1912) #: 7121.
Isaac WILLIAMS, age 24 years, married, cause of death: "paralysis", died: 7 Feb 1911, record (1908-1912) #: 7122.
James B. SHELL, age 44 years, married, cause of death: "cancer", died: 10 Jul 1910, record (1908-1912) #: 7123.
Mrs. Blanch CRUMLEY, age 25 years, born at Roanoke, VA, cause of death: "child birth", died: 12 Jul 1910, record (1908-1912) #: 7124.
Mrs. Elizabeth FOLSOM, age 38 years, cause of death: "typhoid, pneumonia", died: 11 Feb 1911, record (1908-1912) #: 7125.
Mrs. Sallie FOLSOM, age 67 years, born in Washington County, VA, cause of death: "pnuemonia", died: 16 Feb 1911, record (1908-1912) #: 7126.
Thomas LARGE, age 44 years and 9 days, born in Hawkins County, TN, single, cause of death: "acute brights disease", died: 30 Jun 1911, record (1908-1912) #: 7127.
Mrs. Rachel LARGE, age 72 years and 2 months, born at Wythe County, VA, married, cause of death: "kidney and liver", died: 15 Dec 1910, record (1908-1912) #: 7128.
Hazel POWERS, cause of death: "dead born", born/died: 16 Jun 1911, record (1908-1912) #: 7129.
M.P. ROBINSON, age 63 years, married, cause of death: "heart and liver trouble", died: 20 Apr 1911, record (1908-1912) #: 7130.
Millard Alvin WALKER, age 19 years, born in Johnson County, TN, single, cause of death: "tuberculosis", died: 14 Jan 1911, record (1908-1912) #: 7131.
Infant BUROW, female, cause of death: "born dead", child of Oscar Burow, born/died: 11 Mar 1911, record (1908-1912) #: 7132.
Clarence LANE, age 24 years, born at Wytheville, VA, married, cause of death: "tuberculosis", died: 10 Nov 1910, record (1908-1912) #: 7133.
Samuel P. BRADSHAW, age 52 years, born in Hawkins County, TN, married, cause of death: "disease of liver and result of operation", died: 2 Jul 1911 at Rogersville, TN, record (1908-1912) #: 7134.
Bonnie MAUPIN, age 2 months, cause of death: "pneumonia", died: 9 Feb 1911, record (1908-1912) #: 7135.

Lamlon C. HARKLEROAD, age 48 years and 8 months, born in Sullivan County, TN, married, cause of death: "accident in mill", died: 28 Sep 1910, record (1908-1912) #: 7136.

Emmaline BOWERS, age 77 years, married, cause of death: "paralysis", died: 13 Mar 1911, record (1908-1912) #: 7137.

Bonnie MAUPIN, age 10 months, cause of death: "cholera", died: 5 Jul 1910, record (1908-1912) #: 7138.

Thomas CROW, age 34 years, married, cause of death: "congestion of brain", died: 31 Oct 1911 at Erwin, TN, record (1908-1912) #: 7139. (note: also recorded in Unicoi County)

Willie Dean CLEMONS, age not stated, cause of death: "crushed skull", died: 22 Sep 1911, record (1908-1912) #: 7140.

Raymond GOODWIN, age 11 months, born at Doeville, Johnson County, TN, died: 4 Jun 1911 at Doe, Johnson County, TN, record (1908-1912) #: 7141.

Elbert MCCLOUD, age 22 years, single, cause of death: "hemorrage of lungs", died: 26 May 1911, record (1908-1912) #: 7142.

Margaret TONCRAY, age 3 years, born in Hawkins County, TN, cause of death: "pneumonia", died: 17 Sep 1910, record (1908-1912) #: 7143.

William GRAYSON, age 27 years, born at Roanoke, VA, married, cause of death: "gun shot (accidental)", died: 24 Dec 1910, record (1908-1912) #: 7144.

Col John G. FIRLARS, age 96 years, born in Greene County, TN, married, cause of death: "senility", died: 22 Sep 1910, record (1908-1912) #: 7145.

Thomas J. WILLIAMS, age 49 years, married, cause of death: "typhoid", died: 24 Aug 1910, record (1908-1912) #: 7146.

Dilha ALLEN, age 40 years, married, cause of death: "cancer of stomach", died: 19 Aug 1911, record (1908-1912) #: 7147.

Andrew ALBERTSON, age 50 years, born in North Carolina, married, cause of death: "tuberculosis", died: (day not stated) Apr 1911, record (1908-1912) #: 7148.

Infant CRUMLEY, age 29 days, child of G.D. Crumley, cause of death: "heart", died: 29 Jul 1910, record (1908-1912) #: 7149.

Callie HART, age 16 years and 10 months, cause of death: "tuberculosis", died: 2 Apr 1911, record (1908-1912) #: 7150.

Beatrice ELLIS, age 24 years, married, cause of death: "consumption", died: 24 Jun 1911, record (1908-1912) #: 7151.
Vadie HODGE, age 20 years, born at Johnson County, TN, married, cause of death: "pneumonia" died: 20 Dec 1910, record (1908-1912) #: 7152.
Beatrice GREGG, age 1 day, cause of death: "infant troubles", died: 10 Aug 1910, record (1908-1912) #: 7153.
Mrs. Emma CRUMLEY, age 64 years, married, cause of death: "stomach and liver disease", died: 16 Oct 1910, record (1908-1912) #: 7154.
Mrs. Lottie WHITE, age 87 years, married, cause of death: "paralysis", died: 27 Dec 1910, record (1908-1912) #: 7155.
Ralph CURRY, age 13 months, born at Watauga County, NC, cause of death: "spinal meningitis", died: 30 Apr 1911, record (1908-1912) #: 7156.
Robert A. SMITH, age 64 years, married, chancery court clerk and master, cause of death: "heart trouble", died: 8 Dec 1910, record (1908-1912) #: 7157.
Caroline TONCRAY, age 60 years, married, cause of death: "tuberculosis", died: 21 Jan 1910, record (1908-1912) #: 7158.
Charly SWAIN, age 1 month, cause of death: "membrance croup", died: 3 Sep 1910, record (1908-1912) #: 7159.
Willie Claud HARR, age 4 years, cause of death: "membrance croup", died: 28 Oct 1910, record (1908-1912) #: 7160.
James L. HARR, age 68 years, born in Sullivan County, TN, single, cause of death: "heart failure", died: 28 Sep 1910, record (1908-1912) #: 7161.
Robert L. HUGHES, age 42 years, married, cause of death: "consumption of bouls", died: 31 Mar 1911, record (1908-1912) #: 7162.
Lizzie GLOVER, age 4 years, cause of death: illegible, died: 15 Sep 1910, record (1908-1912) #: 7163.
Willie GLOVER, age 15 months, cause of death: illegible, died: 22 Sep 1910, record (1908-1912) #: 7164.
Infant DEMPSEYS, male, age 3 days, child of Milton Dempseys, cause of death: not stated, died: 28 Jul 1910, record (1908-1912) #: 7165.
Jerry B. RANGE, age 73 years, married, cause of death: "feaver", died: 27 Jan 1911, record (1908-1912) #: 7166.

Julie BRADLEY, colored, age 34 years, married, cause of death: not recorded, died: 15 Aug 1910, record (1908-1912) #: 7167.

William SCOTT, age 63 years, married, cause of death: "kidney trouble", died: 12 May 1911, record (1908-1912) #: 7168.

Jasper DUNLAP, age 68 years, born at Jefferson County (state illegible), married, cause of death: "kidney trouble", died: 11 May 1911, record (1908-1912) #: 7169.

Preston KINES, colored, age 6 months, cause of death: "croupe", died: 16 Dec 1910, record (1908-1912) #: 7170.

Cecil R. MOTTERN, age 18 months, cause of death: "stumic trouble", died: 12 Dec 1910, record (1908-1912) #: 7171.

Oscar HIRDS, age 1 day, cause of death: illegible, died: 8 Jul 1910, record (1908-1912) #: 7172.

Hatey Edith HARDIN, age 1 year, cause of death: "dyrar", died: 6 Jul 1910, record (1908-1912) #: 7173.

Ostland HOPKINS, age 4 years, male, cause of death: "fever", died: 17 Nov 1910, record (1908-1912) #: 7174.

Thomas R. CAMPBELL, age 6 months, cause of death: not stated, died: 30 Mar 1911, record (1908-1912) #: 7175.

Emma WILLIAMS, age 28 years, single, cause of death: "consumption", died: 16 Jan 1909.

Hobert L. LOUDY, age 1 year and 2 months, cause of death: "flux", died: 22 May 1909, record (1908-1912) #: 7177.

W.J. HUMPHREYS, age 53 years and 9 months, married, cause of death: "injury", blacksmith, died: 24 Apr 1909, record (1908-1912) #: 7178.

George D. TAYLOR, age 80 years, single, cause of death: "heart and liver trouble", died: 29 Jun 1909, record (1908-1912) #: 7179.

Reuben HUGHES, age 45 years, married, cause of death: "consumption", died: 22 Mar 1909, record (1908-1912) #: 7180.

Hupert SAYLOR, age 14 days, cause of death: "unknown", died: 22 Jan 1909, record (1908-1912) #: 7181.

Noah SAYLOR, age 78 years, born in Washington County, TN, married, died: 19 Jun 1909, record (1908-1912) #: 7182.

Unnamed INFANT, female, age 1 hour, cause of death: "unknown", died: 8 Feb 1909, record (1908-1912) #: 7183.

Polly J. HAMBRICK, age 24 years, single, cause of death: "consumption", died: 22 Dec 1908, record (1908-1912) #: 7184.
Mary L. FAIR, age 39 years, born in Watauga County, NC, married, cause of death: "internal ulserations", died: 29 Sep 1908, record (1908-1912) #: 7185.
Louize P. CLARK, age 64 years, born in Johnson County, TN, married, cause of death: "dropsy", died: 9 Aug 1908, record (1908-1912) #: 7186.
Unnamed INFANT, male, lived one-half hour, cause of death: "unknown", died: 17 May 1909, record (1908-1912) #: 7187.
Sarah E. EDENS, age 83 years, married, cause of death: "paralysis", died: 14 Jun 1909, record (1908-1912) #: 7188.
Emmaline WALKER, age 85 years, born in Washington County, TN, married, cause of death: "rheumatism", died: 2 Apr 1909, record (1908-1912) #: 7189.
Unnamed INFANT, male, lived one hour, cause of death: "unknown", died: 14 Mar 1909, record (1908-1912) #: 7190.
Rhoda J. HYDER, age 59 years, married, cause of death: "consumption", died: 16 May 1909, record (1908-1912) #: 7191.
Drucilla MCKINNEY, age 2 months and 2 weeks, cause of death: "unknown", died: 8 Oct 1908, record (1908-1912) #: 7192.
Cecil L. BLEVINS, age 5 years and 3 months, cause of death: "minnegitis", died: 17 Jun 1909, record (1908-1912) #: 7193.
Bernon SHELL, male, age 2 years and 6 months, cause of death: "croup", died: 20 Nov 1909, record (1908-1912) #: 7194.
Margaret HEATON, age 4 years, cause of death: "croup", died: 4 Dec 1909, record (1908-1912) #: 7195.
Vadie BURCHFIELD, age 11 days, cause of death: "thought to be meningitis", died: 2 Apr 1910, record (1908-1912) #: 7196.
Merion BENFIELD, age 74 years, born in McDowell County, NC, married, cause of death: not recorded, died: 14 Mar 1910, record (1908-1912) #: 7197.
Walter HONEYCUT, age 3 years, cause of death: "croup", died: 1 Nov 1909, record (1908-1912) #: 7198.
Jessie ODOM, age 10 months, cause of death: "meningitis", died: 11 Mar 1910, record (1908-1912) #: 7199.

Rubin STOCTON, age 54 years, born at Flag Pond, TN, married, cause of death: "pneumonia fever", died: 3 Mar 1910, record (1908-1912) #: 7200.
Viola MILLER, age 3 years, cause of death: "bullius fever", died: 20 Sep 1910, record (1908-1912) #: 7201.
Caroline FORBES, age 70 years, born at Mitchell County, NC, married, cause of death: "by taking nerve out of face", died: 11 Jan 1910, record (1908-1912) #: 7202.
Susan SMITH, age 39 years, married, cause of death: "died 2 hours after birth of a child", died: 20 Apr 1910, record (1908-1912) #: 7203.
Martha HILL, age 20 days, cause of death: "bold hives", died: 2 Jan 1910, record (1908-1912) #: 7203.
George HUGHES, age 13 days, cause of death: "found dead in bed", died: 11 Apr 1910, record (1908-1912) #: 7204.
Earl MILLER, age 7 years, cause of death: "diptheria", died: 21 Aug 1910, record (1908-1912) #: 7205.
Floyd MILLER, age 4 years, cause of death: "diptheria", died: 27 Aug 1909, record (1908-1912) #: 7206.
Johnie POWELL, age 28 days, cause of death: "found dead in bed", died: 26 Feb 1910, record (1908-1912) #: 7207.
Spincor GREEN, age 6 months, cause of death: "don't know", died: 28 Apr 1910, record (1908-1912) #: 7208.
Charlie GRINDSTAFF, age 5 months, cause of death: "bold hives", died: 1 Jan 1910, record (1908-1912) #: 7209.
Charles E. CORDELL, age 7 months, cause of death: "minengitis", died: 23 Feb 1910, record (1908-1912) #: 7210.
Ethel HAYES, age 2 years and 10 months, cause of death: "supposed to be fever", died: 22 Nov 1909, record (1908-1912) #: 7211.
Albert LEWIS, age 3 days, cause of death: "hives", died: 19 May 1910, record (1908-1912) #: 7212.
James DUGGER, age 58 years, married, cause of death: "heart failure", died: 1 Jun 1910, record (1908-1912) #: 7213.
Cassie MCKINNER, age 1 day, cause of death: "hives", died: 1 Jul 1910, record (1908-1912) #: 7214.
Dorothy POTTER, age 3 years, cause of death: "diarhea", died: 20 Aug 1909, record (1908-1912) #: 7215.

Dillie May POTTER, age 2 weeks, cause of death: "bold hives", died: 12 Jul 1910, record (1908-1912) #: 7216.
Revel SHELL, male, age 22 days, cause of death: "hives", died: 2 Oct 1908, record (1908-1912) #: 7217.
Flora WATSON, age 3 months and 10 days, cause of death: "whooping cough", died: 20 Aug 1908, record (1908-1912) #: 7218.
Daniel YOUNG, colored, age 65 years, married, cause of death: "burnt", died: 24 Aug 1908, record #: 7219.
Kate YOUNG, colored, age 80 years, married, cause of death: "stomach trouble", died: 22 Feb 1909, record (1908-1912) #: 7220.
Alexander TINNER, colored, age 70 years, born in North Carolina, married, cause of death: "paralysis", died: 15 Oct 1908, record (1908-1912) #: 7222.
Paul DOLEN, age 4 months, cause of death: "hives", died: 28 Aug 1908, record (1908-1912) #: 7223.
Mary OAKS, age 55 years, born at Alexander County, NC, married, cause of death: "cancer of stomach", died: 7 Jan 1909, record (1908-1912) #: 7224.
Berry OAKS, age 21 years, married, cause of death: "consumption", died: 29 Nov 1908, record (1908-1912) #: 7225.
Birgin BREWER, age 5 years and 6 months, cause of death: "consumption", died: 15 Dec 1908, record (1908-1912) #: 7226.
Nola CAMPBELL, age 7 months, cause of death: "whooping cough", died: 9 Apr 1909, record (1908-1912) #: 7227.
Jane CAMPBELL, age 1 day, cause of death: not stated, died: 11 Sep 1908, record (1908-1912) #: 7228.
George COOPER, age 1 day, cause of death: not stated, died: 11 Apr 1909, record (1908-1912) #: 7229.
Fannie EDWARDS, age 2 years, cause of death: "consumption and brain", died: 17 Dec 1908, record (1908-1912) #: 7230.
H.H. KEMMICK, age 73 years, born in Washington County, TN, married, cause of death: "kidney disease", died: 24 Nov 1908, record (1908-1912) #: 7231.
Lora HOSS, age 3 months and 12 days, cause of death: "whooping cough", died: 10 Sep 1908, record (1908-1912) #: 7232.
D.F. BRINKLEY, age 32 years, born in Mitchell County, NC, married, cause of death: "operation for gall stone", died: 19 Sep 1908 at Knoxville, TN, record (1908-1912) #: 7233.
Alice OAKS, age 30 years, married, cause of death: "consumption", died: 20 May 1909, record (1908-1912) #: 7234.

Lester HARDIL, colored, age 1 year and 2 months, cause of death: "meningitis", died: 14 Feb 1909, record (1908-1912) #: 7235.
Willie HARDIL, colored, age 2 months, cause of death: "meningitis", died: 28 Feb 1909, record (1908-1912) #: 7236.
Clyde JONES, age 3 years and 6 months, cause of death: "enlargement of liver", died: 20 Sep 1908, record (1908-1912) #: 7239.
James Hall GARRISON, age 2 years and 1 day, cause of death: "bowell trouble", died: 2 Jun 1909, record (1908-1912) #: 7238.
Francis RHEA, age 1 year and 3 months, cause of death: "croup", died: 10 Sep 1908, record (1908-1912) #: 7239.
Allen GOUGE, age 76 years, born at Mitchell County, NC, cause of death: "bowel trouble", died: 24 Apr 1911, record (1908-1912) #: 7240.
Bertie HONEYCUT, age 2 months and 10 days, cause of death: "bold hives", died: 24 May 1911, record (1908-1912) #: 7241.
Clarence GREER, age 2 days, cause of death: "not known", died: 9 Apr 1911, record (1908-1912) #: 7242.
Hensley ODEM, age 45 years, married, cause of death: "consumption", died: 28 Nov 1911, record (1908-1912) #: 7243.
Carter BARNETT, age 24 years, born in Mitchell County, NC, cause of death: "brites disease", died: 11 Apr 1911, record (1908-1912) #: 7244.
George CROWDER, age 2 years and 11 months, cause of death: "measles", died: 5 Jun 1911, record (1908-1912) #: 7245.
Frank FREEMAN, age 2 years, cause of death: "measles", died: 25 Mar 1911, record (1908-1912) #: 7246.
Infant FREEMAN, male, age 2 days, cause of death: "unknown", died: (day not stated) Jan 1911, record (1908-1912) #: 7247.
Infant FREEMAN, female, age 2 days, cause of death: "unknown", died: (day not stated) Jan 1911, record (1908-1912) #: 7248.
Mabel Gladdice BREWER, age 4 months and 15 days, cause of death: "croup", died: 20 Sep 1910, record (1908-1912) #: 7249.
Irelene PERRY, age 1 year, cause of death: "croupous pneumonia", died: 1 Jan 1911, record (1908-1912) #: 7250.
Homer PERRY, age 25 months, cause of death: "croupous pneumonia", died: 19 Dec 1910, record #: 7251.

I.P. BOONE, age 40 years, born in Mitchell County, NC, married, cause of death: "consumption", died: 5 Feb 1911, record (1908-1912) #: 7252.
Mary BOONE, age 18 months, cause of death: "consumption", died: 17 May 1911, record (1908-1912) #: 7253.
Herman BOONE, age 2 years, 2 months and 6 days, cause of death: "measles", died: 24 Mar 1911, record (1908-1912) #: 7254.
Infant BARNETT, female, age 8 hours, cause of death: "unknown", died: 19 Jan 1911, record (1908-1912) #: 7255.
Dallas ASHLEY, age 1 year, cause of death: "measles", died: 25 Mar 1911, record (1908-1912) #: 7256.
Pearl CAMPBELL, age 17 months, cause of death: not stated, died: 18 Nov 1910, record (1908-1912) #: 7257.
Janice M. BEDEMYER, age 65 years, single, cause of death: "female disease", died: 28 Mar 1911, record (1908-1912) #: 7258.
Gertie HUGHES, age 3 weeks, cause of death: "unknown", died: 9 Mar 1910, record (1908-1912) #: 7259.
Ida CALDWELL, age 26 years, born in North Carolina, married, cause of death: "child bed fever", died: 10 Jan 1911, record (1908-1912) #: 7260.
Clarence COLDWELL, age 1 year, cause of death: "bright disease", died: 24 Mar 1911, record (1908-1912) #: 7261.
Nellie COLDWELL, age 6 weeks, cause of death: "unknown", died: 1 Feb 1911, record (1908-1912) #: 7262.
Ernest MILLER, age 2 weeks, cause of death: "bold hives", died: 30 Jan 1911, record (1908-1912) #: 7267.
Bruce COMBS, age 3 years, cause of death: "membrancous croup", died: 30 Oct 1910, record (1908-1912) #: 7264.
Unnamed INFANT, male, age 2 weeks, cause of death: "bold hives", died: (day not stated) Sep 1910, record (1908-1912) #: 7265.
Infant SIMERLY, male, age 1 day, death cause: "unknown", died: 15 Nov 1910, record #: 7266.
Carl SMITH, age 62 years, married, cause of death: "stomach trouble", died: 3 Jul 1910, record (1908-1912) #: 7267.
Manuel LEWIS, age 45 years, born in North Carolina, married, cause of death: "murdered", died: (day not stated) Sep 1910, record (1908-1912) #: 7268.
Clark HAMPTON, age 3 months and 15 days, cause of death: "unknown", died: 25 Jul 1910, record (1908-1912) #: 7269.

Orda ROARK, male, age 12 days, cause of death: "kidney and rupture", died: 9 May 1909, record (1908-1912) #: 7270.

Leuse RHYMER, age 8 years, cause of death: "cold", died: 20 Sep 1909, record (1908-1912) #: 7271.

Desky DAVENPORT, female, age 21 days, cause of death: "bold hives", died: 3 Jan 1910, record (1908-1912) #: 7272.

Vadie PIERCE, female, age 24 years, single, cause of death: "fever", died: 22 Feb 1910, record (1908-1912) #: 7273.

Lenard BARNETT, age 3 hours, cause of death: "bold hives", died: 24 Oct 1910, record (1908-1912) #: 7274.

George CAMPBELL, age 65 years, married, cause of death: "dierher", died: 27 Oct 1909, record (1908-1912) #: 7275.

Melve GOODWIN, male, age 56 years, married, cause of death: "unknown", died: 23 Jun 1909, record (1908-1912) #: 7276.

Vere CARVER, female, age 28 years, married, cause of death: "gave birth to child", died: 8 May 1910, record (1908-1912) #: 7277, record (1908-1912) #: 7277.

Jane OLIVER, age 74 years, married, cause of death: "old age", died: 15 Jan 1910, record (1908-1912) #: 7278.

Infant CARDEN, male, cause of death: "stillborn", born/died: 12 Jan 1910, record (1908-1912) #: 7279.

Mary WILLIAMS, age 70 years, married, cause of death: "consumption", died: 1 Apr 1910, record (1908-1912) #: 7280.

Hettie LYONS, age 28 years, married, cause of death: "diabetes", died: 4 Mar 1910, record #: 7281.

Rosie LYONS, age 3 hours, cause of death: not stated, died: 5 Oct 1910, record (1908-1912) #: 7282.

Howard JONES, age: illegible, cause of death: "bowel .. (illegible), died: 15 May 1910, record (1908-1912) #: 7283.

Mary WAGNER, age 63 years, born at Doeville, Johnson County, TN, married, cause of death: "fever", died: 30 Mar 1910, record (1908-1912) #: 7284.

Gertie TIMBS, age 5 years, cause of death: "croup", died: 3 Nov 1909, record (1908-1912) #: 7285.

Esq MCNEELY, age 90 years, born in North Carolina, married, cause of death: illegible, died: 14 Dec 1909, record (1908-1912) #: 7286.

Rachael WHALEY, age 76 years, single, cause of death: "heart failure", died: 5 Jul 1909, record (1908-1912) #: 7287.

Unknown CHILD, male, age not known, cause of death: "body found dead in Watauga River", died: date not stated, recorded: 28 Jul 1910, record (1908-1912) #: 7288.
W.C. MATHESON, age 79 years, married, cause of death: not stated, died: 15 Nov 1909, record (1908-1912) #: 7289.
Grace CAMPBELL, age 7 months and 8 days, cause of death: "unknown", died: 23 Sep 1909, record (1908-1912) #: 7290.
Clarence WILSON, age 4 months and 23 days, cause of death: not stated, died: 22 Oct 1911, record (1908-1912) #: 7291.
Unnamed INFANT, female, cause of death: "died at birth", born/died: 16 Mar 1912, record (1908-1912) #: 7292.
Jane JULIAN, age 37 years, born in Mitchell County, NC, married, cause of death: "consumption", died: 28 Jul 1911, record (1908-1912) #: 7293.
Rader JULIAN, female, age 3 years, cause of death: "hooping cough", died: 19 Oct 1911, record (1908-1912) #: 7294.
Peggy JULIAN, age 68 years, born in Mitchell County, NC, married, cause of death: "consumption", died: 9 May 1912, record (1908-1912) #: 7295.
Simon STREET, age 55 years, born in Mitchell County, NC, married, cause of death: "killed by a log, lived 3 days", died: 14 Sep 1911, record (1908-1912) #: 7296.
Nancy HICKS, age 80 years, born in Cocke County, TN, widow, cause of death: "enysipelis", died: 23 Oct 1911, record (1908-1912) #: 7297.
Finley TOUNSEL, age 12 months, cause of death: "worms", died: 12 Jul 1911, record (1908-1912) #: 7298.
Emry SCOGGINS, male, age 18 months, cause of death: "pneumonia fever", died: 28 Mar 1911, record (1908-1912) #: 7299.
Mary WARD, age 7 years and 11 months, cause of death: "measles", died: 1 Mar 1912, record (1908-1912) #: 7300.
Hannah MILLER, age 79 years and 4 months, married, cause of death: "muscular rheumatism", died: 10 May 1912, record (1908-1912) #: 7301.
Clifford YOUNG, age 1 year and 9 months, cause of death: "bold hives", died: 20 Jun 1912, record (1908-1912) #: 7302.
Susan JOHNSON, age 56 years, married, cause of death: "paralysis", died: 2 Jun 1912, record #: 7303.

Unnamed INFANT, female, age 1 year and 8 days, cause of death: not stated, died: 17 Apr 1912, record (1908-1912) #: 7304.

Grace WHITE, age 26 years, male, married, cause of death: "car of wood turned over on him", died: 9 Mar 1912 at Johnson City, TN, record (1908-1912) #: 7305.

W.P. STALLINGS, age 58 years, born at Rock Hill, SC, married, cause of death: "apoplxe", died: 9 Sep 1911, record (1908-1912) #: 7306.

Sabrie WHITE, age 94 years, female, single, cause of death: "old age", died: 23 Feb 1912, record (1908-1912) #: 7307.

.... (illegible) HOLLOWAY, male, age not stated, cause of death: not stated, died: 20 Nov 1911, record (1908-1912) #: 7308.

Billy ADAMS, age 1 year, cause of death: "whooping cough and pneumonia", died: 20 Mar 1912, record (1908-1912) #: 7309.

May ADAMS, age 2 years, cause of death: "whooping cough and hives", died: 7 Mar 1912, record (1908-1912) #: 7310.

Ella GRIFFITH, male, age 4 years and 17 days, cause of death: "membros croup", died: 15 Dec 1911, record (1908-1912) #: 7311.

A.L. WARD, age 49 years, 10 months and 9 days, born at Bakers Gap, Johnson County, TN, married, cause of death: "typhoid fever", died: 16 Nov 1911, record (1908-1912) #: 7312.

William A.D. PIERCE, age 82 years, married, cause of death: "brights disease", died: 24 Jan 1911, record (1908-1912) #: 7313.

James H. RUSSEL, age 12 days, cause of death: "don't know", died: 15 Feb 1912, record (1908-1912) #: 7314.

L.W. MESSINER, age not stated, born in Pennsylvania, married, cause of death: "infected bowels", died: 29 May 1909, record (1908-1912) #: 7315.

Hannah E. OSBORNE, age 29 years, married, cause of death: "consumption", died: 28 Feb 1912, record (1908-1912) #: 7316.

Mandy HEAD, age 7 months, cause of death: "hooping cough", died: 28 Mar 1912, record (1908-1912) #: 7317.

Mary JOHNSON, age 64 years, married, cause of death: "perales", died: 10 May 1912, record (1908-1912) #: 7318.

J.M. JOHNSON, age 76 years, married, cause of death: "peralss", died: 24 Aug 1912, record (1908-1912) #: 7319.

A.B. WHISENHUT, age 47 years, born in Washington County, TN, married, cause of death: "dibtus", died: 25 Dec 1911, record (1908-1912) #: 7320.

Infant TIPTON, female, age 3 years, cause of death: "hooping cough", died: 18 Apr 1912, record (1908-1912) #: 7321.

James HYDER, age about 63 years, single, cause of death: "heart failure", died: 16 Aug 1911, record (1908-1912) #: 7328.

Sam S. GOURLEY, age 2 years, cause of death: "scarlet fever", died: 2 Jun 1912, record (1908-1912) #: 7329.

Molly CROW, age 56 years, married, cause of death: "stomach trouble", died: 25 Nov 1911, record (1908-1912) #: 7330.

Gernie LYONS, age 2 years, cause of death: "scarlet fever", died: 15 Feb 1912, record (1908-1912) #: 7331.

Mary E. MARTON, age 73 years, widow, cause of death: illegible, died: 26 Feb 1912, record (1908-1912) #: 7332.

William R. GOURLEY, age 66 years, born at Leesburg, TN, married, cause of death: "plegra", died: 11 May 1912, record (1908-1912) #: 7333.

Haley GOURLEY, female, age 63 years, married, cause of death: "pneumonia fever", died: 15 Dec 1911, record (1908-1912) #: 7334.

Unnamed INFANT, female, age 4 hours, cause of death: "deformed", died: 17 Nov 1911, record (1908-1912) #: 7335.

Joseph HYDER, age 56 years, married, cause of death: "heart trouble", died: 21 Sep 1911, record (1908-1912) #: 7336.

James GOODWIN, age 72 years, married, cause of death: "pirralles of the hart", died: 7 Apr 1912, record (1908-1912) #: 7337.

Danlia AUDES, male, age 7 months, cause of death: "croup", died: 17 Dec 1911, record (1908-1912) #: 7338.

Anney MCKINNIES, age 2 years, cause of death: "croup", died: 22 Sep 1911, record (1908-1912) #: 7333.

Thomas DUGGER, age 1 month, cause of death: "measles", died: 25 Jun 1912, record (1908-1912) #: 7334.

M.W. MCKINNIES, age 65 years, married, cause of death: "fevor", died: 22 Jul 1911, record (1908-1912) #: 7335.

Noah POTTER, age 70 years, married, cause of death: "consumption", died: 25 Nov 1911, record (1908-1912) #: 7336.

Hubert WATSON, age 3 days, cause of death: "croupe", died: 22 May 1912, record (1908-1912) #: 7337.

Dannia TESTER, age 2 days, cause of death: "croupe", died: 7 Apr 1912, record (1908-1912) #: 7338.

Enoch LUNCEFORD, age 89 years, born in Wilkes County, NC, single, cause of death: "perralas", died: 12 Apr 1912, record (1908-1912) #: 7339.

Ida C. COOK, age 18 years, single, cause of death: "measles", died: 17 Mar 1912, record (1908-1912) #: 7340.

Hobbert LUNCEFORD, age 2 days, cause of death: illegible, died: 2 Jun 1912, record (1908-1912) #: 7341.

Unnamed INFANT, female, age 2 days, cause of death: "bowel trouble", died: 18 Apr 1912, record (1908-1912) #: 7342.

Sallie WHITEHEAD, age 29 years, married, cause of death: "pneumonia fever", died: 28 Aug 1911, record (1908-1912) #: 7343.

Unnamed INFANT, female, age 24 hours, cause of death: "bowl trouble", died: 17 Apr 1912, record (1908-1912) #: 7344.

William CHAMBERS, age 76 years, married, cause of death: "fever and heart trouble", died: 7 Dec 1911, record (1908-1912) #: 7345.

Mary MOORE, age about 75 years, single, cause of death: "dropsy", died: 20 Feb 1912, record (1908-1912) #: 7346.

Celia ELISON, age 24 years, married, cause of death: "consumption", died: 13 Apr 1912, record (1908-1912) #: 7347.

Josie POTTER, age 19 years, married, cause of death: "consumption", died: 15 Jul 1911, record (1908-1912) #: 7348.

R.P. GOUGE, age 64 years, 11 months and 11 days, born in Mitchell County, NC, married, cause of death: "parelysis", died: 11 May 1912, record (1908-1912) #: 7349.

Celia MOORE, age 6 years, cause of death: "whooping cough", died: 21 Jun 1912, record (1908-1912) #: 7350.

Nora COCHRAN, age 9 months, cause of death: "bowl trouble", died: 19 Jul 1911, record (1908-1912) #: 7351.

Martha TOLLEY, age about 8 years, cause of death: "flucks", died: 15 Jul 1911, record #: 7352.

David GRINDSTAFF, age about 50 years, married, cause of death: "stomach trouble", died: 1 Apr 1912, record (1908-1912) #: 7353.

Vista WINTERS, female, age 23 years, born in Mitchell County, NC, single, cause of death: "dropsy", died: 24 Jun 1912, record (1908-1912) #: 7354.
G.W. GARLAND, age 60 years, born in Mitchell County, NC, married, cause of death: "fell from barn loft, lived 3 hours", died: 30 Apr 1912, record (1908-1912) #: 7355.
Garfield PRESNELL, age 36 years, born at Watauga County, NC, married, cause of death: "gangreene", died: 12 Apr 1912, record (1908-1912) #: 7356.
Janie HOLSCLAW, age 14 months, cause of death: "cholera", died: 6 Jan 1912, record (1908-1912) #: 7357.
Elizabeth GLENN, age 17 years, single, cause of death: "tuberculosis", died: 3 Nov 1910, record (1908-1912) #: 7358.
Roy FREEMAN, age 3 days, cause of death: "caused from birth", died: 21 Jun 1911, record (1908-1912) #: 7359.
Denny LUNDY, age 17 months, cause of death: "stomach trouble", died: 7 Jul 1910, record (1908-1912) #: 7360.
Mary Belle HUGHES, age 4 years, cause of death: "buring by fire", died: 30 Nov 1910, record (1908-1912) #: 7361.
Susan M. HUGHES, age 61 years, born in Sullivan County, TN, married, cause of death: "complication of disease", died: 27 Aug 1910, record (1908-1912) #: 7362.
Minnie LAWSON, age 21 years, single, cause of death: "tuberculosis", died: 5 Mar 1910, record (1908-1912) #: 7363.
O.D. BUCK, age 75 years, married, cause of death: "chronic dysentary", died: 21 Jul 1910, record (1908-1912) #: 7364.
Bessie HYDER, age 2 days, cause of death: not stated, died: 19 Jul 1910, record (1908-1912) #: 7365.
Sexton HYDER, age 2 years, cause of death: "spinal trouble", died: 9 Oct 1910, record (1908-1912) #: 7366.
Arnold HYDER, age 9 years, cause of death: "caused by a fall", died: 11 Dec 1910, record (1908-1912) #: 7367.
Willie WOODLEY, age 3 months, cause of death: "bold hives", died: 19 Sep 1910, record (1908-1912) #: 7368.
Allace HYDER, age 19 years, single, cause of death: "tuberculosis", died: 19 Feb 1910, record (1908-1912) #: 7369.

Othello LOVELESS, age 9 months, cause of death: "stomach trouble", died: 20 Aug 1910, record (1908-1912) #: 7370.
Zena RANGE, age 7 months, cause of death: "pneumonia fever", died: 26 Nov 1910, record (1908-1912) #: 7371.
Bishop FAIR, age 7 months, cause of death: "brain fever", died: 30 Oct 1910, record (1908-1912) #: 7372.
Lee BAKER, age 18 months, cause of death: "measles", died: 11 Apr 1910, record (1908-1912) #: 7373.
Edith OAKS, age 23 months, cause of death: "burn", died: 10 Dec 1909, record (1908-1912) #: 7374.
David BAKER, age 30 years and 5 months, born in Unicoi County, TN, married, cause of death: "accident", died: 10 Sep 1909, record (1908-1912) #: 7375.
Unnamed INFANT, female, age 2 days, cause of death: "unknown", died: 11 Mar 1910, record (1908-1912) #: 7376.
Sterling P. SORRELL, age 83 years, born in South Carolina, widower, minister, cause of death: "natural cause, old age", died: 11 Oct 1910, record (1908-1912) #: 7377.
C. Edward DANIELSON, age 29 years, born in Sweden, married, cause of death: "fever", died: 11 Oct 1910, record (1908-1912) #: 7378.
Mary NAVE, age 60 years, single, cause of death: "unknown", died: 26 Aug 1909, record (1908-1912) #: 7379.
William D. HARDIN, age 13 days, cause of death: "do not know", died: 29 Dec 1911, record (1908-1912) #: 7380.
Jessie H. COLE, age 6 years and 22 days, cause of death: "consumption", died: 29 Mar 1912, record (1908-1912) #: 7381.
Sarah DOUGHERTY, age 87 years, 3 months and 19 days, born in Coldwell County, NC, widow, cause of death: not recorded, died: 6 Mar 1912, record (1908-1912) #: 7382.
George PHILLIPS, colored, age 4 months, cause of death: "whooping cough", died: 12 Feb 1912, record (1908-1912) #: 7383.
Howard DELOACH, age 19 months, death cause: "measles", died: 10 Apr 1912, record (1908-1912) #: 7384.
Evelyn LOVELACE, age 13 months, cause of death: "stomach trouble", died: 26 Oct 1912, record (1908-1912) #: 7385.
Sarafina JOBE, age 87 years, born at Flag Pond, TN, widow, cause of death: "old age", died: 14 Apr 1912, record (1908-1912) #: 7386.

Harold MCCLOUD, age: a few hours, cause of death: "unknown", died: 9 dec 1911, record (1908-1912) #: 7386A.

Lola M. BRADLEY, age 8 days, cause of death: "unknown", died: 6 Jun 1912, record (1908-1912) #: 7387.

John F. BURROW, age 87 years, born in Wilkes County, NC, single, cause of death: "old age", died: 8 Feb 1912, record (1908-1912) #: 7388.

Jack CROW, age 18 months, cause of death: "measles", died: 12 Feb 1912, record (1908-1912) #: 7389.

Maggie CROW, age 62 years, born in Johnson County, TN, married, cause of death: "dropsy of the heart", died: 23 May 1912, record (1908-1912) #: 7390.

Mary EDENS, age 58 years, married, cause of death: "rheumatism", died: 28 Jan 1912, record (1908-1912) #: 7391.

Milda LAWS, age 90 years, born in Yancy County, NC, widow, cause of death: "dropsy and old age", died: 7 Nov 1911, record (1908-1912) #: 7392.

James TURNER, age: a few hours, cause of death: "unknown", died: 22 Jan 1912, record (1908-1912) #: 7393.

Lawrence E. ESTEP, age 8 months, cause of death: "disentary", died: 30 Jun 1912, record (1908-1912) #: 7394.

Elizabeth NAVE, age 64 years, married, cause of death: "dropsy", died: 18 Mar 1912, record (1908-1912) #: 7395.

William H. VIALS, age 8 days, cause of death: "unknown", died: 23 Apr 1912, record (1908-1912) #: 7396, record (1908-1912) #: 7396.

James H. RUSSELL, age 19 months, cause of death: "measles", died: 11 Mar 1912, record (1908-1912) #: 7397.

Mary TAYLOR, age 82 years, single, cause of death: "old age", died: 4 Dec 1911, record (1908-1912) #: 7398.

Ray SIMERLY, age 8 years and 4 months, born in Fairbury, IL, cause of death: "measles and whooping cough", died: 29 Feb 1912, record (1908-1912) #: 7399.

Robert H. HART, age 13 months, cause of death: "measles", died: 18 Mar 1912, record (1908-1912) #: 7400.

Charles P. LONG, age 27 years, born in Maryville, TN, married, cause of death: "fractured skull from fall", died: 25 Jun 1912 at Nashville, TN, record (1908-1912) #: 7401.

William J. TONCRAY, age: a few minutes, cause of death: "unknown", died: 19 Dec 1912, record (1908-1912) #: 7402.

Thomas LARGE, age 44 years, born in Sullivan County, TN, single, cause of death: "heart trouble", died: 7 Jul 1911, record (1908-1912) #: 7403.

Mary ALLEN, age: a few minutes, cause of death: "unknown", died: 2 Jan 1912, record (1908-1912) #: 7404.

Margaret SMITH, age 50 years, born in Johnson County, TN, single, cause of death: "heart dropsy", died: 12 Aug 1911, record (1908-1912) #: 7404A.

Infant HONEYCUTT, female, born: 12 Oct 1913, parents: William Honeycutt (NC) and Hattie Ingram (NC), cause of death: "pneumonia", informant: William Ingram (Roan Mountain), died: 11 Jan 1914, record (1914) #: 1.

Anna WHITEHEAD, born: 1 May 1882, married, parents: J.P. Willis (NC) and Polly Tolley, cause of death: "hypertrophy liver", informant: J.P. Willis (Hampton), buried: Fair View Cemetery, died: 20 Jan 1914, record (1914) #: 2.

Clyde ROYAL, born: 7 Apr 1910, parents: Vance Royal (NC) and Gracie Wright (NC), death cause: "pneumonia fever", informant: Vance Royal (Roan Mountain), buried: Blevins Cem., died: 5 Jan 1914, record #: 3.

Mrs. Mollie HICKS, age 47 years, married, parents: Bill Clemons and Sarah (surname illegible), cause of death: "double pneumonia with plourecy", informant: H.T. Daniel (Elizabethton), buried: Lyons Cemetery, died: 23 Jan 1914, record (1914) #: 4.

Henry LYON, born: Jan 1841, widower, parents: Jackson Lyon and Polly Smith, cause of death: "euremic poisoning", informant: G.W. Emmert (Elizabethton), buried: Chenquapin, Sullivan County, TN, died: 16 Jan 1914, record (1914) #: 5.

Rhoda PERRY, born: 19 Aug 1869, married, parents: Jerry Peeks and Matilda Smith, cause of death: "carcinoma of lower lip and throat", informant: G.W. Emmert (Elizabethton), buried: Carr Cemetery, died: 11 Jan 1914, record (1914) #: 6.

Sam FREEMAN, age: "don't know", widower, parents: "don't know", cause of death: "thought to be brights disease", informant: Stoker Freeman (Roan Mountain), died: date not stated, buried: 11 Jan 1914, record (1914) #: 7.

Samuel OSBORN, age 35 years, married, parents: John Osborn and mother's name unknown, cause of death: "tuberculosis", died: 24 Jan 1914, record (1914) #: 8.

I..(illegible) Ester JOHNSON, born: May 1908, parents: Jacob Alford Johnson and Emelyn Butler (Magnetic, NC), cause of death: "pernicious heremia", informant: J.A. Johnson (Roan Mountain), buried: Crabtree, TN, died: 2 Jan 1914, record (1914) #: 9.

Elva CROW, born: 10 Apr 1821, age: 83 years, 9 months and 18 days, married, born in Johnson County, TN, parents: Mr. McQueen (Mountain City, TN) and mother's name unknown (Johnson County, TN), cause of death: "brights disease", informant: J.W. Pippin (Roan Mountain), died: 23 Jan 1914, record (1914) #: 10.

John W. YOUNG, born: 21 Apr 1833 in Washington County, TN, widower, parents: H.P. Young, and (first name not stated) Beard, cause of death: "cardiac dropsy", informant: James L. Persinger (Johnson City, TN), died: 19 Jan 1914, record (1914) #: 11.

Mary FUGATE, born: 6 Jun 1880, married, parents: George More (NC) and Liluriana Guin (NC), cause of death: "tuberculosis", informant: Calvin Fugate (Hampton), buried: Whitehead Cemetery, died: 1 Jan 1914, record (1914) #: 12.

Ida JACKSON, born: 15 Apr 1871, married, parents: John Morgan and Eliza Richardson, cause of death: "purperfral sefisis and infection by midwife", informant: David Jones (Shell Creek), died: 1 Jan 1914, record (1914) #: 13.

Infant WILLIAMS, male, born: 30 Jan 1914, parents: W.G. Williams and Maggie Crow, death cause: "premature birth", informant: G.E. Campbell (Eliz-abethton), buried: Hunter, TN, died: 31 Jan 1914, record #: 14.

Lula DAVIS, black, age 30 years, single, parents: Link Davis and mother's name not stated, cause of death: "child birth", buried: McGee Cemetery, died: 31 Dec 1913, record (1914) #: 15.

Lula DAVIS, black, born: 1874, single, parents: William L. Davis and Cheny Rednick (NC), cause of death: "childbirth", informant: Link Davis (Eliz-abethton), died: 31 Dec 1913, record (1914) #: 16.

Lawton CAMPBELL, born: 5 Oct 1901, parents: E.M. Campbell (Magnetic, NC) and Polly Honeycutt (Magnetic, NC), cause of death: "tuberculosis of lungs", informant: E.M. Campbell (Hampton), buried: Honeycutt Cemetery, died: 8 Jan 1914, record (1914) #: 17.

Daniel L. LUNCEFORD, born: 13 Mar 1882, retired soldier, single, parents: James E. Lunceford and Clementine M. Whitehead, death cause: "tuberculosis", informant: L.M. Lunceford (Shell Creek), buried: Stout Cemetery, died: 20 Feb 1914, record (1914) #: 18.

Infant BRYANT, parents: Lewis G. Bryant and Lizzie Hardin, cause of death: "stillborn, caused by a fall by mother", informant: Lewis G. Bryant, buried: Lacy Cemetery, born/died: 18 Feb 1914, record (1914) #: 19.
Infant MILLER, born: 20 Dec 1913, parents: father's name not stated and Nancy Miller, cause of death: "bold hives", informant: Samuel Wright (Roan Mountain), buried: Lacy Cemetery, died: 6 Feb 1414, record (1914) #: 20.
Sarah ELLIS, age 73 years, widow, parents: Phillip Davis and mother's name unknown, cause of death: "dysentary", informant: W.T. Nave (Elizabethton), buried: Keenburg, died: 10 Feb 1914, record (1914) #: 21.
Infant PATTERSON, male, parents: W.C. Patterson and Emma Ferguson, cause of death: "stillborn", buried: Highland Cemetery, born/died: 9 Feb 1914, record (1914) #: 22.
Mattie STOVER, born: 10 May 1879 at Bluff City, Sullivan County, TN, married, parents: W.J. Williams (Sullivan Co. TN) and Adeline Britt (Sullivan Co. TN), cause of death: "tuberculosis pulmonary", informant: W.J. Williams (Bluff City), buried: Bluff City, TN, died: 19 Feb 1914, record (1914) #: 23.
Daniel STARNES, born: May 1836 in Akron, Ohio, single, parents: not stated, cause of death: "rhumatism, diarhorra", died: 17 Feb 1914, record (1914) #: 24.
James M. SCALF, born: 5 Feb 1914, parents: David Scalf and Rhoda Mitchell (Sullivan Co. TN), cause of death: not stated, died: 16 Feb 1914, record (1914) #: 25. (note record 25 is duplicated)
Thomas Taylor PRICE, born: 23 Aug 1853, married, postmaster, parents: Mordci Price and Mary Ruble, cause of death: "paralysis", informant: Sam Price (Johnson City, TN), buried: Milligan, TN, died: 9 Jan 1914, record (1914) #: 25. (note record 25 is duplicated)
Josephine WILLIAMS, black, age 8 months and 4 days, parents: Cass Williams and Rhoda Thompson, cause of death: "acute poliomyilitis", buried: Williams Cemetery, died: 16 Feb 1914, record (1914) #: 26.
Ira Annie Elizabeth KINNIS, born: 19 Oct 1851 at McMinn County, TN, single, parents: John Kinnis (Edenburg, Scotland) and Sallie Rockholds (Sullivan Co, TN), cause of death: "pulmonary tuberculosis", informant: John Kinnis (Watauga), died: 19 Feb 1914, record (1914) #: 27.

Eva Kate WILLIAMS, born: 16 Mar 1913, parents: Charles Williams and Louisa Livingston, cause of death: "diptheria", informant: R.J. Williams (Elizabethton), buried: Williams Cemetery, died: 16 Feb 1914, record (1914) #: 28.

Eva May MORRIS, born: 12 Nov 1910, parents: Jefferson Morris and Mollie Troxell, cause of death: "broncho pneumonia", buried: Morris Cem., died: 28 Feb 1914, record (1914) #: 29.

Sarah MILLER, age: about 76 years, married, parents: Thomas Badgett and mother's name unknown, cause of death: "organic heart disease", informant: Eva Reynolds (Elizabethton), buried: Reynolds Cemetery, died: 3 Feb 1914, record (1914) #: 31. (note record 30 is missing)

L.H. ELLIS, born: 1842, married, parents: R. Ellis and Lorrie Peters, cause of death: "tuberculosis of lungs", informant: J.T. Ellis (Elizabethton), buried: Colbaugh Cemetery, died: 2 Feb 1914, record (1914) #: 32.

Joseph Hooker ELLIS, age 50 years, parents: Daniel Ellis and Martha May (Jonesboro, TN), cause of death: "paralysis", informant: Emma Ellis (Hampton), buried: Ellis Cemetery, died: 17 Feb 1914, record (1914) #: 33.

Jane CAMPBELL, age: "unknown", widow, parents: Loon Blevins and Martha Garland, cause of death: not stated, informant: S.R. Estep, buried: Garland Cemetery, died: 9 Feb 1914, record (1914) #: 34.

James Claude PIERCE, born: 29 Dec 1913, parents: James Pierce and Sallie Campbell, cause of death: not stated, informant: R.M. Pierce (Carter), buried: Pierce Cemetery, died: 23 Feb 1914, record (1914) #: 35.

Lottie WILLIAMSON, born: 8 Jan 1884, married, parents: Luckey Estep and Rebecca Roberts, cause of death: "pulmonary tuberculosis", informant: James Hampton, buried: Grindstaff Cemetery, died: 23 Feb 1914, record (1914) #: 36.

Flora ORR, age 12 years, parents: W.B. Orr and Mirah Ramsey (NC), cause of death: "pneumonia fever", died: 3 Mar 1911, record (1914) #: 37.

John P. MCKINNEY, age: near 86 years, born in North Carolina, married, parents: "don't know", cause of death: "dropsy", informant: W.F. Heaton (Roan Mountain), buried: Burbank, died: 1 Mar 1914, record (1914) #: 38.

William Rily PERKINS, born: 14 Mar 1839 in Washington County, TN, parents: William Jacob Perkins (Johnson Co. TN) and Nancy Powel (NC), cause of death: not stated, informant: S.A. Perkins (Shell Creek), buried: Perkins Cem., died: 2 Feb 1914, record (1914) #: 39.

Infant LOWE, born: 12 Nov 1914, parents: H.W. Lowe (Johnson Co. TN) and Katie Lewis, cause of death: "diarrhoea", informant: H.W. Lowe (Hampton), buried: Hall Cemetery, died: 7 Mar 1914, record (1914) #: 40.

Willie ROBERTS, born: 9 Jun, age 4 years, 8 months and 16 days, parents: Edd Roberts (VA) and Josie Marklin, cause of death: "tuberculosis", informant: Josie Roberts (Hampton), buried: Hall Cemetery, died: 6 Mar 1914, record (1914) #: 41.

Isaac PERRY, age 64 years, married, parents: not stated, cause of death: "chronic diarrhoea", buried: Lyon Cemetery, died: 31 Mar 1914, record (1914) #: 42.

Charles L. HATHAWAY, born: 18 Mar 1873, parents: "do not know father's name" and Amelia Hathaway, cause of death: "tuberculosis", buried: Smith Cemetery, died: 23 Mar 1914, record (1914) #: 43.

Mary SWEENEY, born: 4 Sep 1840, single, parents: Jim Sweeney and Tenie Oliver (Sullivan County, TN), cause of death: "general decay or age", informant: E.M. Thompson (Watauga), buried: Dempsey Cemetery, Watauga, died: 9 Mar 1914, record (1914) #: 44.

Sallie MOSLER, born: 7 Jul 1857, married, parents: John Fullwalers (VA) and mother's name not stated, cause of death: "tuberculosis", died: 19 Mar 1914, record (1914) #: 45.

Effie BIRCHFIELD, born: 28 Sep 1914, parents: Nathan Birchfield and Effie Shell, cause of death: "croup", died: 2 Mar 1914, record (1914) #: 46.

William D. WILSON, age: "don't know", married, pensioner, cause of death: "brights disease", buried: Shell Creek, died: 26 Mar 1914, record (1914) #: 47.

Lockey TIPTON, female, born: 20 Dec 1913, parents: Bud Tipton and Clara Julian, cause of death: not stated, informant: Bud Tipton (Burbank), buried: Heaton Creek, died: 30 Mar 1914, record (1914) #: 48.

Hewbert MINTON, born: 2 Mar 1914, parents: Roscoe Minton and Minnie Blevins, cause of death: "premature birth", informant: R.A. Range, buried: Taylors Cemetery, died: 3 Mar 1914, record (1914) #: 49.

Infant CHAMBERS, parents: Eligah Chambers and Hattie Whitehead, cause of death: "not borned at full term", informant: Henry Elison (Hampton), buried: Chambers Cemetery, born/died: 9 Mar 1914, record (1914) #: 50.

Sidney PRICHARD, born: 23 Jun 1834 in Watauga County, NC, married, parents: Tomas Prichard and mother's name not known, cause of death: "old age", informant: J.E. McCury (Butler), buried: Smith Cemetery, died: 25 Mar 1914, record (1914) #: 51.
David CHEEK, born: Apr 1841 in Johnson County, TN, married, parents: father's name unknown and Mary Cheek, cause of death: "bronchitis", informant: W.O. Phillips (Fish Springs), buried: Fish Springs, died: 20 Mar 1914, record (1914) #: 52.
Otis SMITH, born: 18 Jun 1904, parents: L.L. Smith and C.L. McNeily, cause of death: "accidental hanging", informant: L.L. Smith (Butler), buried: Smith Cemetery, died: 14 Mar 1914, record (1914) #: 53.
John Ruben BEARD, born: 27 Feb 1914, parents: William Beard and Nora McCloud (Watauga County, NC), cause of death: "unknown", informant: William Beard (Dark Ridge, NC), died: 15 Mar 1914, record (1914) #: 54.
Roy HAYES, born: 24 Mar 1914, parents: John Hayes and Pearl Edith Heaton, cause of death: "unknown", informant: John Hayes (Shell Creek), buried: Cables Cemetery, died: 26 Mar 1914, record (1914) #: 55.
Infant POWELL, born: 17 Mar 1914, parents: Steward Powell and Sarah Allen Oaks (NC), cause of death: "miscarriage at 8 months", informant: Nancy Richardson (Shell Creek), died: 19 Mar 1914, record (1914) #: 56.
May Mary JONES, born: 19 Jan 1914, parents: David Jones, Jr. and Minnie Hamby, cause of death: not stated, informant: David Jones, Jr. (Shell Cr.), died: 20 Mar 1914, record (1914) #: 57.
Elizabeth OAKS, age 77 years, born in Johnson County, TN, parents: George Sizemore (SC) and Beckey Sizemore, cause of death: "valvulor heart disease", informant: Davis Oaks (Shell Creek), died: 26 Feb 1914, record (1914) #: 58.
William Riley PERKINS, born: 14 Mar 1839 in Washington County, TN, widower, parents: Jacob Perkins (Johnson County, TN) and Nancy Powell (NC), cause of death: "acute pneumonia with bowel problems", informant: S.A. Perkins (Shell Creek), buried: Perkins Cemetery, died: 2 Feb 1914, record (1914) #: 59.
Donald CASS, born: 13 Mar 1914, parents: Edward C. Cass and Lucy Crow, cause of death: "premature, 5 or 6 month", died: 13 Mar 1914, record (1914) #: 60.
Mrs. Milfred PUGART, age not stated, parents: A.J. Perry and M.E. Poston (Sullivan County, TN), cause of death: "cancer of breast", died: 12 Mar 1914, record (1914) #: 61.

Mrs. Jane E. SHELL, born: 22 Jun 1845, widow, parents: Noth R. Taylor and (first name illegible) Rockhard, cause of death: "pneumonia", informant: Bob Shell (Eliz. TN), died: 20 Mar 1914, record (1914) #: 62.

George M. PERRY, born: 9 Sep 1846, married, parents: James Perry and Morah Smith, cause of death: "nephritis", informant: Nat T. Perry (Eliz., TN), buried: Highland Cem., died: 11 Mar 1914, record (1914) #: 63.

David C. COOK, born: Feb 1834 in Johnson County, TN, married, parents: father's name not known and Patsey Cook, cause of death: "unknown", buried: Colbaugh Cemetery, died: 24 Mar 1914, record (1914) #: 64.

Mont TAYLOR, black, male, born: 4 Apr 1901, parents: father's name unknown and Jane Taylor, cause of death: "pulmonary tuberculosis", informant: William Taylor (Elizabethton), died: 3 Mar 1914, record (1914) #: 65.

Lula HORTON, colored, born: 4 Mar 1914, parents: A.H. Horton (NC) and Annie Moore (NC), cause of death: "pnuemonia", died: 13 Mar 1914, record (1914) #: 66.

Margaret Lillie HART, born: 15 Nov 1913, parents: C.W. Hart and Maggie T. Hart, cause of death: "intestinal tuberculosis", informant: C.W. Hart (South Knoxville, TN), died: 8 Mar 1914, record (1914) #: 67.

Florence DEMPSEY, born: 14 Jan 1906 in Bluff City, TN, parents: H.A. Dempsey (Piney Flats) and S.C. Lacy, cause of death: "spinal meningitis", informant: J.R. Lacy (Watauga), buried: Little Cemetery, died: 7 Mar 1914, record (1914) #: 68.

Sarah Jane COOPER, born: 1 Oct 1843, single, former school teacher, parents: Joel Cooper and Annie Hendrix, cause of death: "senility", buried: G.W. Mottern Cem., died: 11 Apr 1914, record (1914) #: 69.

Infant HART, male, parents: father's name not stated and Stella Hart, cause of death: "stillborn", informant: F.S. Hart (Elizabethton), buried: Hart Cemetery, died: 22 Apr 1914, record (1914) #: 70.

Infant WILLIAMS, male, born: 17 Mar 1914, parents: Henry Williams and Linda Fair, cause of death: "kidney trouble". died: 20 Mar 1914, record (1914) #: 71.

James BERRY, age 1 year and 6 months, parents: C.R. Berry and Effie Fair, cause of death: "bronchaitis", buried: Blevins Cemetery, died: 22 Apr 1914, record (1914) #: 72.

Roy JUSTICE, parents: Samuel Justice and Rhoda Pierce, cause of death: "atilictosis", informant: W.C. Pierce (Butler), born/died: 21 Apr 1914, record (1914) #: 73.

William R. CAMPBELL, age about 70 years, widower, parents: Zachary Campbell and mother's name unknown, cause of death: "pneumonia fever", informant: George P. Campbell (Butler), died: 24 Apr 1914, record (1914) #: 74.

Infant GRIFFITH, male, parents: Pleasant Griffith and Jane Campbell, cause of death: "stillborn", informant: Pleasant Griffith (Fish Sp.), died: 21 Apr 1914, record (1914) #: 75.

Sallie WILLIAMS, age 22 years, married, parents: Tennessee Crow and (first name not stated) Bowers, cause of death: "peritourtis", buried: Buckles Cemetery, died: 20 Apr 1914, record (1914) #: 76.

Elizabeth DUGGER, born: 30 Oct 1900, parents: George Dugger and Jennie Nidiffer, cause of death: "acute appendicitis", informant: S.T. Nidiffer (Watauga Valley), buried: Ritchie Cemetery, died: 30 Apr 1914, record (1914) #: 77.

Luther BOWLING, born: 6 Apr 1914, parents: Melvin Bowling (VA) and Bessie Treadway, cause of death: "8 month child", informant: Melvin Bowling (Elizabethton), buried: Treadway Cemetery, died: 6 Apr 1914, record (1914) #: 78.

Debby M. CRESS, born: 22 Mar 1818 in Johnson County, TN, parents: John Hawkins (Wilkes County, NC) and mother's name unknown, cause of death: "senility", informant: Stanley Gregg (Elizabethton), buried: Maymead, TN, died: 22 Mar 1914, record (1914) #: 79.

Bruce ALBERTSON, born: 3 Sep 1902 at Afton, TN, parents: Andrew C. Albertson and Elizabeth Miller (South Watauga), cause of death: "meningitis", informant: R.L. Miller (Cranberry, NC, died: 21 Apr 1914, record (1914) #: 80.

Leo T. WILLEY, born: 2 Jan 1914, parents: J.T. Willey (NC) and Elizabeth Vanhuss (NC), cause of death: "infant strangulation", buried: Highland Cem., died: 4 Apr 1914, record (1914) #: 81.

Samuel Patterson COLLINS, born: 4 Jan 1859, married, parents: Tilson O. Collins (Washington County, VA) and mother's name illegible, cause of death: "valvular heart disease", informant: G.O. Collins (Elizabethton), buried: Highland Cemetery, died: 24 Apr 1914, record (1914) #: 82.

Agnes SUSONG, black, age about 60 or 63 years, born in Virginia, married, parents: "don't know", cause of death: "lobar pneumonia", buried: Cedar Grove Cemetery, died: 2 Apr 1914, record (1914) #: 83.

Ophelia GARDNER, born: 4 Mar 1912, parents: Julius Gardner and Lena Farney, cause of death: "pneumonia, croupous", informant: John Gardener (Elizabethton), buried: Highland Cemetery, died: 10 Apr 1914, record (1914) #: 84.

David BOWERS, colored, born: 1 Apr 1909, parents: father's name not stated and Lelia Bowers, cause of death: "pneumonia, lobar", informant: Charles Bowers (Eliz. TN), died: 14 Apr 1914, record (1914) #: 85.

Sallie ERWIN, black, born: Apr 1912, parents: father's name not stated and Sallie Erwin, cause of death: "pulmonary tuberculosis", informant: Julia Erwin (Elizabethton), buried: Cedar Grove Cemetery, died: 21 Apr 1914, record (1914) #: 86.

Margaret Elizabeth BAKER, born: 4 Dec 1913, parents: William Wilson Baker (Unicoi County, TN) and Bettie Campbell, cause of death: "indigestion", informant: William Baker (Hampton), buried: Hall Cemetery, died: 15 Apr 1914, record (1914) #: 87.

Ida May CASEY, age 20 days, parents: Ernest William Casey and Maggie Henry, cause of death: "croup", informant: Ernest Casey (Hampton), buried: Hall Cemetery, died: 4 Apr 1914, record (1914) #: 88.

Infant MATHERLY, parents: James Matherly and Nola McKInney, cause of death: "unknown", born/died: 27 Apr 1914, record (1914) #: 89.

David BLEVINS, age: "supposed to be 27", single, parents: Isaac Blevins and Nancy Fletcher, cause of death: "pneumonia fever", informant: Isaac Campbell (Carter), buried: Garland Cemetery, died: 16 Mar 1914, record (1914) #: 90.

Adiline HARDIN, age 72 years, married, parents: John Deloach and Susan Oliver, cause of death: "pneumonia fever", informant: G.W. Hardin (Elizabethton), buried: Siam, died: 1 Apr 1914, record (1914) #: 91.

Infant OLIVER, parents: James Thomas Oliver (Ashe County, NC) and Zella Garland, death cause: "born dead", informant: James Oliver (Carter), buried: Richardson Cem., born/died: 1 Mar 1914, record #: 92.

George WILSON, age 50 years, widower, parents: John Wilson and Mary Wilson, cause of death: "pneumonia fever", informant: W.E. Asher (Carter), died: 22 Apr 1914, record (1914) #: 93.

Moriah RICHARDSON, female, age: "supposed to be 90", widow, parents: Thomas A. Worley (Scott County, VA) and Mary Beeler (Scott County, VA), cause of death: "measles", informant: H.T. Richardson (Carter), died: 10 Apr 1914, record (1914) #: 94.

Infant OLIVER, parents: William Oliver and Lizzie Lewis, cause of death: "lack of vitality", informant: Levi Nidiffer (Carter), born/died: 9 Feb 1914, buried: Cress Cemetery, record (1914) #: 95.

Alice SIMS, age 32 years, single, parents: Jackson Sims and Rachel Glover, cause of death: not stated, informant: John Sims (Roan Mountain), died: 16 Apr 1914, record (1914) #: 96.

Dela RICHARDSON, born: 3 Apr 1904, parents: Noah Richardson and Pussie Garland, cause of death: "measles", informant: William E. Asher (Carter), died: 28 Mar 1914, record (1914) #: 97.

Isaac BLEVINS, born: 23 Feb 1900, parents: William Blevins (Blount County, TN) and Lucresia Campbell, cause of death: "measles", informant: U.G. Cole (Carter), buried: Garland Cemetery, died: 1 Mar 1914, record (1914) #: 98.

Ella May GRINDSTAFF, born: 14 Feb 1914, parents: Wilburn Grindstaff and Alice Richardson, cause of death: "lagrippe", informant: H.M. Arnold (Carter), buried: Estep Cemetery, died: 8 Mar 1914, record (1914) #: 99.

Eliza Ellen ARNOLD, born: 1 Nov 1914, parents: James Thomas Arnold (Ashe County, NC) and Zella Garland, cause of death: "measles", informant: W.E. Asher (Carter), buried: Richardson Cemetery, died: 28 Mar 1914, record (1914) #: 100.

Nancy Elizabeth ASHER, born: 31 Jan 1914, parents: father's name not stated and Pearl Asher, cause of death: "measles", informant: W.E. Asher (Carter), buried: Richardson Cemetery, died: 30 Mar 1914, record (1915) #: 101.

Bonnie May DAVIS, born: 17 Mar 1914, parents: S.C. Davis and Alice Malissa Jones, cause of death: "sudden, unknown", informant: H.T. Daniels (Elizabethton), buried: Lyons Cemetery, died: 25 Apr 1914, record (1915) #: 102.

W.M. HAMIT, male, age not stated, married, parents names not stated, cause of death: "tuberculosis", died: 21 Apr 1914, record (1915) #: 103.

Mat JENKINS, age 61 years, married, parents: William Jenkins and Fannie White, cause of death: "heart failure", buried: Buckles Cemetery, died: 3 Apr 1914, record (1915) #: 104.

Grant TAYLOR, age 22 days, parents: Grant Taylor and first name not stated, Nave, cause of death: "jaundice", died: 25 Apr 1914, record (1915) #: 105.

Infant WILLIAMS, born: 7 Apr 1914, parents: Tom Williams and mother's name not stated, cause of death: "peritonitis", buried: Buckles Cemetery, died: 14 Apr 1914, record (1915) #: 106.

Roy HAYES, born: 24 Mar 1914, parents: John Hayes and Pearl Edith Heaton, cause of death: not stated, informant: John Hayes (Shell Creek), buried: Stout Cemetery, died: 26 Mar 1914, record (1915) #: 107.

Rebecca J. MILLER, born: 21 Dec 1849 in Johnson County, TN, married, parents: Zebulon Payne and Charity Payne, cause of death: not stated, informant: E.M. Miller (Butler), died: 25 May 1914, record (1915) #: 108.

Ray Earl JONES, born: 13 Apr 1914, parents: Johnie Jones and Lizzie Campbell, cause of death: "unknown", informant: William Jones (Valley Forge), buried: Williams Cemetery, died: 4 May 1914, record (1915) #: 109.

Rhoda Ann Thompson WILLIAMS, colored, born: 5 Feb 1876, married, parents: William Thompson (NC) and Martha Williams (NC), cause of death: illegible, buried: Watauga, TN, died: 1 May 1914, record (1915) #: 110.

William Harrison GARLAND, born: 24 Apr 1914, parents: Joe Garland and Dora Elliott, cause of death: "sore throat", informant: David Elliott (Carter), buried: Elliott Cem., died: 11 May 1914, record (1915) #: 111.

Rena KITE, born: 20 May 1862, divorced, parents: William Pierce and Dicey Morley, cause of death: "cancer of the womb", buried: Pierce Cemetery, died: 20 May 1914, record (1915) #: 112.

Infant BRADSHAW, male, parents: John Bradshaw and Eve Hatcher, cause of death: "undeveloped child", buried: Smith Cemetery, born/died: 14 May 1914, record (1915) #: 113.

Clyde VANDIKE, born: 12 May 1914, parents: P.M. Vandike (NC) and Carrie Cole, cause of death: "spina bifida", informant: R.M. Vandike (Elizabethton), buried: Highland Cemetery, died: 16 May 1914, drc 114.

Ethel STOVER, black, born: 9 Jun 1913, parents: Alex Stover and Sarah Gardner (NC), cause of death: "measles and whooping cough", informant: Alex Stover (Elizabethton), buried: Drake Cemetery, died: 9 May 1914, record (1915) #: 115.

Nellie ERWIN, black, born: 20 Aug 1905 in Johnson City, TN, parents: Clint Erwin and Mollie Watson, death cause: "pulmonary tuberculosis", buried: Cedar Grove Cem., died: 28 May 1914, record (1915) #: 116.

Beatrice STOVER, black, born: 18 Dec 1910, parents: Alex Stover and Sarah Gardner (NC), cause of death: "measles", buried: Drake Cemetery, died: 12 May 1914, record (1915) #: 117.

Elizabeth LARGE, born: 15 Nov 1866, married, parents: James Tillison (VA) and Nancy Perry (VA), cause of death: "carcinoma of the body of ... (illegible)", informant: Jessie Large (Elizabethton), buried: Colbaugh Cem., died: 7 May 1914, record (1915) #: 118.

Elmer SIMERLY, born: 17 Apr 1914, parents: Samuel Simerly and Vicie Odom, cause of death: "not born at full term, bowel hives", informant: Sallie Hill (Roan Mountain), died: 17 May 1914, record (1915) #: 119.

Infant WRIGHT, male, parents: Plato Wright and Mary J. Garland (NC), cause of death: "stillborn", buried: Blevins Station, born/died: 13 May 1914, record (1915) #: 120.

Clera COLE, born: 22 Mar 1874, married, parents: J.C. Brooks and Dicie Pierce, cause of death: "consumption of the bowels", informant: A.J. Cole (Watauga Valley), buried: Buckles Cemetery, died: 13 May 1914, record (1915) #: 121.

Infant COLE, male, born: 11 May 1914, parents: Cony Cole and Rosa Peters, cause of death: "no medical attention", informant: Thomas White (Carter), buried: Blevins Cem., died: 15 May 1914, record (1915) #: 122.

Theodore WOOD, born: 1 Apr 1914, parents: Thomas Wood and Carrie Royal, cause of death: "indigestion", informant: Theodore Wood (Hampton), buried: Hyder Cemetery, died: 19 May 1914, record (1915) #: 123.

Mary TRIPLETT, born: 12 Apr 1914, parents: Ernest Triplett (Maple Springs, NC) and Martha (surname illegible), cause of death: "unknown", informant: Ernest Triplett (Hampton), buried: Hall Cemetery, died: 11 May 1914, record (1915) #: 124.

M.D.L. MILLER, age 86 years, married, parents: Bayless Miller and Elizabeth Glover, cause of death: "uremia", informant: R.A. Range (Elizabethton), buried: Reynolds Cemetery, died: 19 May 1914, record (1915) #: 125.

John Reubin BEARD, born: 24 Feb 1914, parents: William Beard and Nora McCloud (Watauga County, NC), cause of death: not stated, informant: Dave Closson (Dark Ridge, NC), died: 15 Mar 1914, record (1915) #: 126.

Nannie DUFFIELD, age 63 years, single, parents: Samuel L. Duffield and Eliza Ferguson, cause of death: "cancer of breast", informant: D.S. Renfro (Elizabethton), buried: Colbaugh Cemetery, died: 4 Jun 1914, record (1915) #: 127.

George MERRITT, born: 8 Aug 1912, parents: Wheeler H. Merritt and Josie Glover, cause of death: "cholera", informant: Wheeler Merritt (Elizabethton), buried: Valley Forge, died: 3 Jun 1914, record (1915) #: 128.
Lottie HICKS, age 24 years, married, parents: Bud Lifton and Clara Julian, cause of death: not stated, informant: L.W. Webb (Roan Mountain), died: 10 Jun 1914, record (1915) #: 129.
T.C. CROW, born: 25 Mar 1825, widower, parents: Campbell Crow and Mrs. Williams, cause of death: "brights", informant: D.S. Crow (Elizabethton), died: 15 Jun 1914, record (1915) #: 130.
Infant TURNER, female, parents: Ralph Turner (NC) and Julia (illegible), cause of death: not stated, informant: W.F. Heaton, died: 1 Jun 1914, record #: 131.
Samuel TROXELL, age 73 years, married, parents: David Troxell and Mary Scott, cause of death: "intestinal tuberculosis", buried: Mottern Cemetery, died: 20 Jun 1914, record (1914) #: 132.
Eveline HICKS, age 60 years, born in North Carolina, single, parents: Joe Hicks (NC) and Sarah Hicks (NC), cause of death: "rhumiatise", informant: John Fields (Shell Creek), buried: Hicks Cemetery, died: 30 May 1914, record (1914) #: 133.
Infant HONEYCUTT, male, parents: Samuel Honeycutt and Bertha Hampton, death cause: "stillborn", born/died: 19 Jun 1914, record (1914) #: 134.
Isaac ESTEP, born: 26 Jun 1825, widower, parents: Levi Estep and Edith Hodge, cause of death: "old age", informant: James Cress (Carter), buried: Cress Cemetery, died: 20 Jun 1914, record (1914) #: 135.
Nancy RICHARDSON, age 72 years ("supposed"), married, parents: David Garland and Betsy Wilson, cause of death: "cattrrah of stomach", informant: J.J. Richardson (Carter), buried: Richardson Cemetery, died: 27 Jun 1914, record (1914) #: 136.
Pauline NAVE, born: 3 Dec 1914, parents: Andy Nave and Lilly Fletcher, cause of death: "broncho pneumonia", informant: W.J. Nave (Elizabethton), died: 25 Jun 1914, record (1914) #: 137.
A. Lincoln SHOUN, born: 26 Apr 1883, single, parents: Fred Shoun (Johnson Co, TN) and Margaret Hardin, death cause: "intestinal obstruction", informant: F.N. Peters (Carter), buried: Shoun Cemetery, died: 19 Jun 1914, record (1914) #: 138.
Robert BLEVINS, age 54 years, married, parents: "unknown", cause of death: "intestinal obstruction", died: 15 Jun 1914, record (1914) #: 139.

Henry HICKS, born: 15 Jul 1904, parents: C.L. Hicks and Alice Henson, cause of death: "unknown", informant: Charley L. Hicks (Shell Creek), buried: Stout Cem., died: 12 Jul 1914, record (1914) #: 140.
James STOVER, black, age 35 years, single, parents: Bob Stover and Tessie Carter, cause of death: "acute nephritis", buried: Drake Cemetery, died: 10 Jun 1914, record (1914) #: 141.
Infant ELLIOTT, male, parents: Charlie Elliott and Easter Dugger (Johnson Co., TN), "stillborn", informant: Charlie Dugger (Eliz., TN), buried: Drake Cem., born/died: 17 Jun 1914, record (1914) #: 142.
Mary HATCHER, born: 14 Jan 1914 in North Carolina, parents: father's name not stated and Mary Hatcher, cause of death: "cholera", informant: Mrs. Lucy Lucas (Hampton), buried: Oak Grove, died: 6 Jun 1914, record (1914) #: 143.
John J. EDENS, born: 21 Aug 1831, married, parents: Nathaniel T. Edens and Lersnia Hyder, cause of death: "senility", informant: J.N. Edens (Elizabethton), buried: Highland Cemetery, died: 9 Jun 1914, record (1914) #: 144.
Infant EPPERSON, male, parents: J.B. Epperson (Sullivan County, TN) and M. Dougherty (Washington County, TN), cause of death: "strangulation cord", informant: J.B. Epperson (Elizabethton), buried: Highland Cemetery, born/died: 8 Jun 1914, record (1914) #: 145.
Maggie TRUSLER, age 26 years, born in Sullivan County, TN, single, parents: George Trusler (Sullivan County, TN) and Mollie Widner, cause of death: "tuberculosis lungs", informant: W.M. Trusler (Elizabethton), buried: Sullivan County, died: 16 Jun 1914, record (1914) #: 146.
James Cecil TRENT, black, born: 1 Jun 1914, parents: Andrew Trent (Lee County, VA) and Sara Crawford, cause of death: "cholera", informant: Mrs. L.L. Minton (Johnson City, TN), died: 11 Jul 1914, record #: 147.
Nancy Anne SWEENEY, born: 25 Jan 1858 in Sullivan County, TN, married, parents: John T. Vandeventer and Adline Barr (Sullivan County, TN), cause of death: "intestinal tuberculosis", died: 11 Jul 1914, record (1914) #: 148.
Herbert HOBSON, born: 16 Jul 1914, parents: George Hobson and Rosa Shepperd (Burk County, NC), cause of death: not stated, informant: George Hobson (Shell Creek), buried: Harris Cemetery, died: 19 Jul 1914, record (1914) #: 149.

George Hardin SNIDER, born: 15 Jun 1857 in North Carolina, married, parents: G.W. Snider (NC) and Sallie Hardin (NC), cause of death: "cirrosis of liver, alcoholic", informant: Mrs. J.H. Snider (Shell Creek), died: 21 Jul 1914, record (1914) #: 150.

Robert Thomas CARRIER, born: 26 Sep 1913, parents: Alex Carrier and Bessie Birchfield, cause of death: "cholera infantum", informant: Alex Carrier (Elizabethton), buried: Lyons Cemetery, died: 12 Jun 1914, record (1914) #: 151.

Flora J. COLE, born: 1 Mar 1867, married, parents: Riley Daniels and Abigale Morrell (Sullivan County, TN), cause of death: "apoplexy or organic heart disease", informant: H.T. Daniels (Elizabethton), buried: Cole Cemetery, died: 14 Jul 1914, record (1914) #: 152.

William G. WHIPPLE, born: 4 Aug 1834 in Connecticut, married, parents: William Whipple (Conn.) and (first name not stated) Woodward (Conn.), cause of death: "heart failure", informant: James A. Meeker (Roan Mountain), buried: Little Rock, AR, died: 17 Jul 1914, record (1914) #: 153.

Nellie HEATON, age not stated, born in North Carolina, married, parents: John (surname illegible) and mother's name "not known", cause of death: "tuberculosis", informant: Stephen Street (Roan Mountain), buried: Heaton Creek, died: 20 Jul 1914, record (1914) #: 154.

Clara A. TIPTON, born: 11 Apr 1869, married, parents: James N. Julian and Eliza Heaton, cause of death: "tuberculosis", informant: Andy Jones (Roan Mountain), buried: Heaton Creek, died: 7 Jul 1914, record #: 155.

Infant WOOD, male, parents: R.F. Wood and Ollie Shell, cause of death: not stated, informant: R.F. Wood (Roan Mountain), died: 9 Jul 1914, record (1914) #: 156.

Delia VANOVER, born: 6 Oct 1912, parents: Roby Vanover and Eulia Endy (VA), cause of death: "not known", informant: John Edny (Roan Mountain), died: 16 Jul 1914, record (1914) #: 157.

Infant JENKINS, male, born: 3 Jul 1914, parents: James Edward Jenkins and Ollie Pearce, cause of death: "infantile debility", informant: C.R. Jenkins (Hampton), buried: Hall Cemetery, died: 15 Jul 1914, record (1914) #: 158.

Infant TRIVETT, female, parents: Kelly Trivett (NC) and Nannie Maine, cause of death: "stillborn", informant: Kelly Trivett (Hampton), buried: Morton Cem., born/died: 17 Jul 1914, record (1914) #: 159.

Minnie Bell MCINTOSH, born: 29 Apr 1913, parents: Thomas McIntosh and Lidia Hazlewood, cause of death: "cholera infantum", informant: Thomas McIntosh (Hampton), died: 21 Jul 1914, record (1914) #: 160.

Mrs. Caroline HOLLY, born: 1838, widow, parents: father's name not known and Caroline Lacy, cause of death: "paralysis", informant: I.P. Brumitt (Hampton), buried: Hyder Cemetery, died: 28 Jul 1914, record (1914) #: 161.

Jessie Loyd MCKINNEY, age 5 months and 29 days, parents: David M. McKinney and Ellen Harrold (NC), cause of death: "dysentary", informant: David McKinney (Hampton), buried: Simerly Cemetery, died: 28 Jul 1914, record (1914) #: 162.

James W. RENFRO, born: 27 Feb 1857, married, parents: Joseph C. Renfro (KY) and Mary A. O'Brien, cause of death: "valvulor heart disease", informant: C.C. Hacker (Elizabethton), buried: Watauga Valley, died: 2 Jul 1914, record (1914) #: 163.

Frank L. LACY, born: 24 Jul 1914, parents: L.C. Lacy and Hattie Morrell, cause of death: "heart lieson", informant: J.F. Williams (Johnson City, TN), buried: Hopson, TN, died: 6 Aug 1914, record (1914) #: 164.

John BOWERS, born: 10 Apr 1870, married, parents: Murray Bowers and Matilda Campbell, cause of death: "pulmonary tuberculosis", informant: Mrs. Hunter Allen (Elizabethton), buried: Highland Cemetery, died: 31 Jul 1914, record (1914) #: 165.

Alice STOVER, born: 27 Sep 1912, parents: John Stover and Mollie Trusler (Sullivan County, TN), cause of death: "cholera infantum", informant: John Stover (Elizabethton), buried: Bluff City, TN, died: 14 Jul 1914, record (1914) #: 166.

Ina DAVIS, colored, born: 27 Aug 1907, parents: Lincoln Davis (NC) and Titia Brown (NC) cause of death: "typhoid fever", informant: Lincoln Davis (Elizabethton), buried: Cedar Grove Cemetery, died: 5 Jul 1914, record (1914) #: 167.

Jack Mariah HOWARD, black, born: 2 Oct 1912, parents: father's name not stated and Laura Howard, cause of death: "cholera infantum", informant: Mariah Howard (Elizabethton), buried: Odd Fellows Cemetery, died: 4 Jul 1914, record (1914) #: 168.

Miller DAVIS, colored, born: 21 Dec 1897, single, parents: L.K. Davis (NC) and Tissie Brown (NC), cause of death: "tuberculosis", informant: L.K. Davis (Elizabethton), buried: Cedar Grove Cemetery, died: 27 Jul 1914, record (1914) #: 169.

James Edward MARKLAND, born: 8 Feb 1913, parents: Will Markland and Lula White, cause of death: "cholera infantum", informant: Will Markland (Elizabethton), buried: Hyder Cemetery, died: 29 Jul 1914, record (1914) #: 170.

Paul A. MCQUEEN, born: 14 Sep 1913 in Johnson County, TN, parents: David L. McQueen (Johnson County, TN) and Kate Bowers, cause of death: "acute diarrhoa or dysentary", informant: David L. McQueen (Eliz. TN), died: 7 Jul 1914, record (1914) #: 171.

Hellen Kate BURROW, born: 11 Jul 1912, parents: Oscar Burrow and Nannie Jerdin, cause of death: "cholera infantum", informant: Oscar Burrow (Elizabethton), buried: Highland Cemetery, died: 4 Jul 1914, record (1914) #: 172.

Jane BARNETT, age 58 years, born in North Carolina, married, parents: Bill Hughes and Cresie Prichet (NC), cause of death: "pulmonary tuberculosis", informant: S.B. Barnett (Roan Mountain), died: 13 Jul 1914, record (1914) #: 173.

Lee BUCKLES, born: 1837, married, parents: William Buckles and Kate Jones, cause of death: "dropsy", informant: J. Buckles (Watauga Valley), died: (day not stated) Mar 1914, record (1914) #: 174.

John W. HAMILTON, born: 3 Mar 1871, single, parents: J.C. Hamilton (Sullivan County, TN) and Belle Love (VA), cause of death: "..(illegible) of the heart", informant: F.D. Nave (Watauga Valley), buried: Boyd Cemetery, died: 2 Jul 1914, record (1914) #: 175.

Infant RITCHIE, male, parents: Will Ritchie and Bessie Davis, cause of death: "probably atelectosis", informant: Will Davis (Watauga Valley), born/died: 29 Jul 1914, record (1914) #: 176.

Infant RITCHIE, male, parents: Will Ritchie and Bessie Davis, cause of death: "stillborn", informant: Will Davis, died: 29 Jul 1914, record (1914) #: 177.

William T. TAYLOR, born: 13 Jul 1899, parents: James Taylor and Maggie Colbaugh, death cause: "hemorrhagia measles", died: 30 Mar 1914, record (1914) #: 178.

Anderson HINKLE, born: 12 Sep 1895, single, parents: Franklin Hinkle and Mary Blevins, cause of death: "tuberculosis", buried: Ritchie Cemetery, died: 16 Mar 1914, record (1914) #: 179.

Andy HAMITT, age 45 years, married, parents: father's name unknown and Fannie Hamitt, death cause: "pellegra", informant: F.M. Hodges (Johnson City, TN), buried: Lyons Cemetery, died: 25 Jul 1914, record (1914) #: 180.

Infant STOUT, male, parents: David Stout and Catherine Estep, cause of death: "stillborn", informant: Mose Estep (Carter), buried: Estep Cemetery, died: 4 Jul 1914, record (1914) #: 181.

Earvan GARLAND, male, born: 11 Sep 1913, parents: David Garland and Nancy Hurley, cause of death: "diarhoea", informant: David Garland (Carter), buried: Garland Cem., died: 21 Jul 1914, record (1914) #: 182.

Infant TAYLOR, female, parents: Joe Taylor and Grace Taylor, cause of death: "asphyia", informant: Samuel Taylor (Carter), buried: Pierce Cemetery, died: 24 Jul 1914, record (1914) #: 183.

Charles ESTEP, born: 10 Mar 1895, single, parents: Andrew Estep and Eliza Campbell, cause of death: "cerebral hemorrhage", informant: Andrew Estep (Carter), buried: Garland Cemetery, died: 11 Jul 1914, record (1914) #: 184.

Mary E. FLETCHER, born: Dec 1875 in Sullivan County, TN, married, parents: J.R. Hendrix and Mary C. Fletcher (Sullivan County, TN), cause of death: illegible, informant: J.R. Hendrix (Elizabethton), buried: Highland Cemetery, died: 7 Jul 1914, record (1914) #: 185.

Washington Franklin NORRIS, born: 15 Jul 1837 in Unicoi County, TN, parents: Joshua Norris (Unicoi County, TN) and Eva Elizabeth Swingle (Unicoi County, TN), cause of death: "heart disease", informant: M.A. Anderson (Johnson City, TN), buried: Anderson Cemetery, Johnson City, died: 28 Aug 1914, record (1914) #: 186.

Infant CAMPBELL, female, born: 21 Aug 1914, parents: Dayton Campbell and Mollie Myers, death cause: "bold hives", informant: J.G. Pierce (Watauga Valley), buried: Buckles Cem, died: 23 Aug 1914, record #: 187.

Herman NAVE, born: May 1914, parents: William Nave and Laura Bowers, cause of death: "spinal disease", informant: Grant Pierce (Watauga Valley), died: 23 Aug 1914, record (1914) #: 188.

Hutchins ROBERTS, born: 22 Mar 1852 in Wilkes County, NC, married, parents: John Roberts (Wilkes County, NC) and Nancy Roberts (Wilkes County, NC), cause of death: "carcinoma of neck", informant: Nancy Roberts (Hampton), buried: Roberts Cemetery, died: 18 Aug 1914, record (1914) #: 189.

Mary Jane HYDER, born: 1871, married, parents: Richard Hazlewood and Bettie Campbell, cause of death: "pellagra", informant: J.N. Hyder (Elizabethton), died: 4 Sep 1914, record (1914) #: 190.

Infant LANDY, male, parents: George Landy and Kate Garland, cause of death: "died during birth", born/died: 9 Aug 1914, record (1914) #: 191.

Thomas C. MCKINNEY, age about 63 years, married, parents: Joseph McKinney and mother's name unknown, death cause: "hemiplegia", informant: N.N. McKinney (Elizabethton, TN), died: 24 Aug 1914, record (1914) #: 192.

Lutishia RICHARDSON, age 10 months, parents: Loss Richardson and Ellen Garland, cause of death: "croup", informant: Sam Richardson, buried: Richardson Cemetery, died: 31 Jul 1914, record (1914) #: 193.

Alvin TAYLOR, born: 11 Jul 1914, parents: General Taylor and Laura Campbell, cause of death: "measles", buried: Garland Cemetery, died: 13 Aug 1914, record (1914) #: 194.

Laura TAYLOR, born: 28 Mar 1844, married, parents: John Campbell and Delila Estep, cause of death: "measles", informant: General Taylor (Carter), buried: Garland Cem., died: 7 Aug 1914, record (1914) #: 195.

Mrs. Charles SLAGLE, born: 16 Jul 1893 in Sullivan County, TN, married, parents: George Trusler and Mollie Nidiffer, cause of death: "childbirth, heart failure", informant: C.C. Hacker (Elizabethton), buried: Sullivan County, TN, died: 19 Aug 1914, record (1914) #: 196.

Earl FORBES, parents: John Forbes and Liddie Arwood (NC), cause of death: "croup", born/died: 19 Aug 1914, record (1914) #: 197.

Infant CAMPBELL, female, parents: Lawson Campbell and Elsie Goodwin, cause of death: "injury during birth", informant: Lawson Campbell (Hampton), buried: Goodwin Cemetery, born/died: 9 Sep 1914, record (1914) #: 198.

Infant HART, female, parents: Walter Hart and Bessie Morrell, death cause: "unknown", informant: F.S. Hart (Eliz. TN), died: 21 Aug 1914, record (1914) #: 199.

Will LEDWELL, born: 1 Mar 1869 in Unicoi County, TN, married, parents: Robert Leadwell (Randolph County, NC) and Rebecca Canter (Washington County, TN), cause of death: "cancer of the thyroid gland", informant: Nat Honeycutt (Elizabethton), died: 7 Aug 1914, record (1914) #: 200.

George W. BREEDLOVE, black, born: 23 Dec 1846 in South Carolina, widower, parents: Robert S. Breedlove (SC) and mother's name unknown, cause of death: "acute nephritis", buried: Morristown, TN, died: 9 Aug 1914, record (1914) #: 201.

Racr. GARVIN, male, born: 15 Aug 1914, parents: Robert Johnson, Jr., and Flora Garvin, cause of death: "convulsions", informant: Mrs. J.A. Garvin (Elizabethton), buried: Highland Cemetery, died: 15 Aug 1914, record (1914) #: 202.

Lela BOWERS, born: 1 Apr 1914, parents: S.M. Bowers and Myrtle Berry, death cause: "pneumonia and infantile paralysis", informant: I.N. Bowers, buried: Carriger Cemetery, died: 26 Sep 1914, record #: 203.

Infant GIBBS, colored, female, born: 21 Sep 1914, parents: Fain Gibbs and Dora Wilburn, cause of death: "premature birth", informant: Fain Gibbs (Elizabethton), buried: Odd Fellows Cemetery, died: 22 Sep 1914, record (1914) #: 204.

Infant ESTEP, male, born: 24 Sep 1914, parents: Henry Estep and Bert Scalf, cause of death: "congenital heart trouble", informant: R.B. Hyder, buried: Hyder Cemetery, died: 25 Sep 1914, record (1914) #: 205.

Henry Clay BEASLEY, born: 5 May 1832 in Patrick County, VA, widower, parents: Shadrack Beasley (Patrick County, VA) and Patsy Harris (Patrick County, VA), cause of death: "supposition, heart failure", informant: C.G. Beasley (Elizabethton), buried: Highland Cem., died: 1 Aug 1914, record (1914) #: 206.

Mable B. HINKLE, born: 27 Apr 1914, parents: Edward C. Hinkle and Emerly B. Collins, cause of death: "cholera infantum", informant: E.C. Hinkle (Elizabethton), buried: Collins Cem., died: 3 Aug 1914, record #: 207.

S.B. BRASWELL, age 66 years, born: May (day and year not stated) in Caldwell County, NC, married, parents: William Braswell and (first name not stated) Shell, cause of death: "typhoid, pneumonia", informant: W.M. Braswell (NC), buried: Highland Cemetery, died: 2 Aug 1914, record (1914) #: 208.

William ARWOOD, born: 4 Mar 1863 in North Carolina, married, parents: Sam Arwood (NC) and Ellen Winters, cause of death: "typhoid fever, heart failure", informant: Nina Arrowood (Johnson City, TN), buried: Ensor Cem., died: 15 Sep 1914, record (1914) #: 209.

Hubert HINKLE, born: 7 Aug 1911, parents: John B. Hinkle and Hannah Miller, cause of death: "diabetes melitus", informant: John B. Hinkle (Carter), died: 15 Sep 1914, record (1914) #: 210.

Samuel STREET, age 59 years, born in North Carolina, married, parents: Peter Street (NC) and Elizabeth Garland (NC), cause of death: "tuberculosis", informant: C.T. Miller (Roan Mountain), buried: Burbank, died: 23 Sep 1914, record (1914) #: 211.

Celia Dunn CURD, born: 5 Mar 1872 in Johnson County, TN, married, parents: Wesley Dunn (Johnson County, TN) and Mary Jennings (Johnson County, TN), cause of death: "purpura hemorrhagica", died: 22 Sep 1914, record (1914) #: 212.

Infant PERRY, parents: George Perry, Sr. and Lizzie Hampton, cause of death: "stillborn", informant: R.A. Range (Eliazbethton), buried: Webb Cemetery, born/died: 21 Sep 1914, record (1914) #: 213.

Bessie GRINDSTAFF, born: 18 May 1883, married, parents: Richard Glover and Mary Lewis, cause of death: "gangreen of hand", informant: L.L. Grindstaff (Elizabethton), buried: Glover Cemetery, died: 20 Sep 1914, record (1914) #: 214.

John GLOVER, born: 12 Sep 1897, single, parents: William A. Glover and Lucy Williams, cause of death: "acute rhumatism and disease of heart", informant: W.A. Glover (Elizabethton), buried: Glover Cemetery, died: 24 Sep 1914, record (1914) #: 215.

Infant BOWERS, born: 1 Sep 1914, parents: George Bowers (VA) and Ella Gallaher (VA), cause of death: "stillborn", died: 1 Sep 1914, record (1914) #: 216.

Sarah F. RANGE, born: 20 Dec 1839, widow, parents: Thomas Gourley (NC) and Susan Simerly, cause of death: "chronic diarrhoea", informant: Robert Range (Eliz., TN), died: 15 Sep 1914, record (1914) #: 217.

Lela BOWERS, born: 1 Apr 1914, parents: S.M. Bowers and Clo Berry, cause of death: "pneumonia and infantile paralysis", informant: S.M. Berry (Elizabethton), buried: Carriger Cemetery, died: 26 Sep 1914, record (1914) #: 218.

James B. ARRANTS, born: 20 Sep 1873 in Sullivan County, TN, parents: N.M. Arrants (Sullivan County, TN) and N.C. Booker (Sullivan County, TN), cause of death: "intermitten fever", buried: Bluff City, TN, died: 3 Sep 1914, record (1914) #: 219.

Earnest MCCURRY, born: 27 Dec 1906, parents: Clyde Curry (NC) and Julia May (NC), cause of death: "obstruction of bowels", informant: Clyde Curry (Elizabethton), buried: Bradley Cemetery, died: 7 Sep 1914, record (1914) #: 220.

Edwin Vernon EDENS, born: 10 Jun 1898, single, parents: E.L. Edens and Maggie Shell, cause of death: "killed by freight train", informant: E.L. Edens (Elizabethton), buried: Highland Cemetery, died: 8 Sep 1914, record (1914) #: 221.

Eugene LOGAN, colored, born: 26 Sep 1898 in Hendersonville, NC, single, parents: Albert Logan (Hendersonville, NC) and Lucinda Fletcher (NC), cause of death: "pulmonary tuberculosis", buried: Cedar Grove Cem., died: 15 Sep 1914, record (1914) #: 222.

William GILBERT, born: 19 Jul 1913, parents: Ed. Gilbert and Lizzie Campbell, cause of death: "pneumonia:, informant: Will Turner (Elizabethton), buried: Turner Cemetery, died: 9 Sep 1914, record (1914) #: 223.

Cal CHESTER, age unknown, county asylum inmate, cause of death: "cardiac dropsy", buried: County Cemetery, died: 1 Oct 1914, record (1914) #: 224.

Herman Zachariah HOLLY, born: 5 Oct 1914, parents: Fred Holly and Bessie Croy, cause of death: "unknown", buried: Mottern Cemetery, died: 31 Oct 1914, record (1914) #: 225.

Mrs. Lizzie HALL, born: 1 Jan 1831, widow, parents: Michael Grindstaff and Sallie Chambers, cause of death: "paralysis", informant: Mikl Hall (Hampton), buried: Hall Cemetery, died: 9 Oct 1914, record (1914) #: 226.

Liddie Ellen ARROWOOD, age not stated, single, parents: William Arrowood (NC) and Nina Griffin (NC), cause of death: "typhoid fever", informant: Nina Arwood (Johnson City, TN), died: 10 Oct 1914, record (1914) #: 227.

Hamp GRINDSTAFF, born: 20 Aug 1914, parents: D.L. Grindstaff and Bessie Glover, cause of death: "cholera infantum", informant: D.L. Grindstaff, buried: Valley Forge, died: 24 Oct 1914, record #: 228.

Bate GRINDSTAFF, born: 20 Aug 1914, parents: D.L. Grindstaff and Bessie Glover, cause of death: "cholera infantum", informant: D.L. Grindstaff, buried: Valley Forge, died: 28 Oct 1914, record (1914) #: 229.

Sarah A. HART, born: 2 Dec 1836 in Bluff City, TN, widow, parents: James Newton (Sullivan County, TN) and Katie Emmert (Sullivan County, TN), cause of death: illegible, informant: E.M. Hart (Elizabethton), buried: Highland Cemetery, died: 22 Oct 1914, record (1914) #: 230.

E.J. POTTER, female, age about 85 years, born in Johnson County, TN, widow, parents: Robert Closson (Johnson County, TN) and Sarah (surname illegible) (Johnson County, TN), cause of death: "unknown", informant: J.C. Morgan (Dark Ridge, NC), died: 29 May 1914, record (1914) #: 231.

Charlotie LINEBACK, age about 70 years, parents: John Wilson (Johnson County, TN) and (first name not stated) Heaton, cause of death: "dropsy", informant: H. Lineback (Butler), buried: Lineback Cemetery, died: 19 Jun 1914, record (1914) #: 232.

S.J. PERKINS, female, age about 85 years, born in Ohio, married, parents: Peter Slimp (Johnson County, TN) and Elizabeth Slimp (Johnson County, TN), cause of death: "unknown", informant: James Perkins (Butler), buried: Whitehead Cemetery, died: 21 Oct 1914, record (1914) #: 233.

Floyd ELLIOTT, born: 7 Nov 1914, parents: John Elliott and Ruth Nave, cause of death: "pneumonia", informant: Bill Elliott (Watauga Valley), buried: Buckles Cemetery, died: 7 Nov 1914, record (1914) #: 234.

Infant GRINDSTAFF, male, parents: Nicholas Grindstaff (Johnson County, TN) and A. Greenwell (Butler), cause of death:: "stillborn", buried: Cable Cemetery, born/died: 6 Nov 1914, record (1914) #: 235.

Infant MCKHIN, female, parents: Frank McKhin and Annie Gourley. cause of death: "lack of vitality, premature delivery", informant: R.N. Gourley (Johnson City, TN), died: 23 Nov 1914, record (1914) #: 236.

Alexander WILSON, age about 36 years, parents: "unknown", cause of death: "paralysis due to blood clot", informant: W.J. Nave (Elizabethton), buried: County Cem., died: 26 Nov 1914, record (1914) #: 237.

Lottie HARDIN, born: 23 Mar 1913, parents: Dayton Hardin and Kate VanDeventer, cause of death: "croup", informant: Robert Hardin (Watauga Valley), buried: Buckles Cem., died: 10 Nov 1914, record (1914) #: 238.

James CURD, born: 25 Oct 1892, widower, parents: Ezekiel Curd and mother's name not recorded, cause of death: "typhoid fever", informant: Wesley Curd (Watauga), died: 8 Nov 1914, record (1914) #: 239.

William Henry Harrison DEMPSY, born: 14 May 1845, parents: Nathan Dempsy and Melvina Thompson, cause of death: "croupous pneumonia", buried: Dempsy Cemetery, died: 6 Nov 1914.

Alfred Boyd SMALLING, born: 24 May 1850, married, parents: Robert Washington Smalling (Sullivan Co., TN) and Harrett Elizabeth Shell (Sullivan Co., TN), cause of death: "organic disease of the heart", buried: Smalling Cem, died: 23 Nov 1914, record (1914) #: 241.

William Sutton WILLIAMS, born: 23 Mar 1913, parents: Robert Williams and Caroline Emert (Pueblo, CO), death cause: "dysentery", informant: Robert Williams (Hampton), died: 18 Nov 1914, record #: 242.

Charles JOHNSON, born: 3 Mar 1899, parents: W.C. Johnson and Alice Gray. cause of death: "shot and died 5 minutes later", informant: W.C. Johnson (Hampton), buried: Campbell Cemetery, died: 1 Nov 1914, record (1914) #: 243.

Mrs. Lillie POTTER, born: 2 Feb 1844 in Johnson County, TN, widow, parents: Daniel Potter (Johnson County, TN) and mother's name not stated, cause of death: "senility", informant: Dick Potter (Elizabethton). buried: Cole Cemetery, died: 15 Nov 1914, record (1914) #: 244.

Maggie RUSSELL, born: 26 Aug 1914, parents: Jim Russell and Caroline Williams, cause of death: "unknown", buried: Hyder Cemetery, died: 10 Nov 1914, record (1914) #: 245.

Barney SWANER, born: 9 Oct 1914, parents: Taylor Swaner and Lula Ward, cause of death: "convulsions", informant: Thomas T. Ward (Fish Springs), died: 19 Nov 1914, record (1914) #: 246.

Edkar ODOM, born: 24 Oct 1914, parents: Father's name illegible and Serhie Odom (NC) cause of death: not stated, died: 5 Non 1914, record (1914) #: 247.

Dishmonia LACY, born in NC, date not stated, parents: Milt Young (NC) and Hannah Hughes (NC), death cause: "typhoid", informant: A.S. Lacy (Hampton), buried: Burbank, died: 10 Nov 1914, record (1914) #: 248.

Benson Herman WAYCASTER, born: 10 Aug 1913, parents: Isaac Waycaster (NC) and mother's name illegible, cause of death: "croup", informant: Sarah Cordelia Waycaster (Roan Mountain), buried: Crabtree, died: 4 Nov 1914, record (1914) #: 249.

Infant PIPPIN, female, parents: Frank Pippin and Okie Hayes, cause of death: "capillory bronchitis", informant: John McKinney (Roan Mountain), died: 20 Nov 1914, record (1914) #: 250.

Jackson WHITEHEAD, age 55 years, married, parents: Larkin L. Whitehead and (first name not stated) Hill (Mitchell County, NC), cause of death: "found dead, was drinking, lay under a fence in the rain and chilled to death", informant: J.G. Barnett (Roan Mountain), buried: Hollys Cemetery, died: 24 Dec 1914, record (1914) #: 251.

William HONEYCUTT, born: 25 Sep 1862 in North Carolina, married, parents: Nathan Honeycutt (NC) and Salley Garland (NC), cause of death: "tuberculosis", informant: M.R. Honeycutt (Hamton), died: 21 Dec 1914, record (1914) #: 252.

James Madison WOODS, born: 24 Aug 1914, parents: Ruben Woods and Mollie Ward, cause of death: "boul hives", informant: Ruben Woods (Roan Mountain), buried: Blevins Cem., died: 24 Dec 1914, record (1914) #: 253.
William H. TESTER, age about 69 years, born in Watauga County, NC, married, parents: John Tester (Watauga County, NC) and Nelly Estep (Watauga County, NC), cause of death: "dropsy of the heart", informant: B.G. Tester (Shell Creek), buried: Stouts Cemetery, died: 24 Dec 1914, record (1914) #: 254.
William Pinkney TESTER, born: 9 Dec 1914, parents: B.G. Tester (Watauga County, NC) and B.J. Odom, cause of death: "unknown", died: 10 Dec 1914, record #: 255.
James Madison BOROGUS, born: 3 Sep 1914 in Washington County, TN, parents: W.M. Borogus and Lindy Grindstaff, death cause: "supposed to be bold hives", informant: W.F. Kipping (Johnson City), buried: Milligan, died: 22 Dec 1914, record (1914) #: 256.
William Henry ADKINS, born: 20 Jun 1855 in Yancy County, NC, married, parents: father's name not stated and Isabelle Whitson (NC), cause of death: "anurysm of abdominal aorta", informant: W.I. Williams (Johnson City), died: 2 Jan 1915, record (1914) #: 257.
Charlotte PETERS, born: 17 Nov 1836, married, parents: William and Rebecca Creed, death cause: "rhematism", informant: H.C. Lewis (Watauga Valley) buried: Wilson Cem., died: 4 Dec 1914, record (1914) #: 258.
Infant MARKLAND, female, parents: James Markland and Mollie Bartie, cause of death: "stillborn", informant: General Taylor (Carter), buried: Ensor Cemetery, died: 31 Dec 1913, record (1914) #: 259.
Blanche HOLDER, born: 18 Nov 1914, parents: Nick Holder and Dora Estep, cause of death: "dropsy", informant: James Holder (Carter), buried: Richardson Cemetery, died: 5 Dec 1914, record (1914) #: 260.
Delcinia BARTIE, age 66 years, single, parents: Joseph Bartie and Anna Blevins, cause of death: "pulmonary tuberculosis", informant: General Taylor, buried: Ensor Cem, died: 31 Dec 1914, record (1914) #: 261.
William J. CARTER, born: 23 Sep 1849, married, parents: Landon Carter and Debbie Ellis, cause of death: "chronic brights disease", buried: Newton Cemetery, died: 3 Dec 1914, record (1914) #: 262.
Harmon Tipton MILLER, born: 25 Mar 1896, single, parents: Lee F. Miller (St. Louis, MO) and Flora K. Tipton, cause of death: "accidental discharge of pistol", buried: Highland Cemetery, died: 1 Dec 1914, record (1914) #: 263.

Will W. ROBERTS, born: 7 Mar 1845 in Washington Count, VA, married, parents: George Roberts (VA) and Patsy Pippin (VA), cause of death: "bronchrea pneumonia", informant: George Roberts, Jr. (Elizabethton), buried: Colbaugh Cemetery, died: 18 Dec 1914, record (1914) #: 264.

Hubert EDRUS, born: 14 Feb 1893, single, parents: Dave Edrus (Cocke County, TN) and Mary Miller, cause of death: "pulmonary tuberculosis", informant: D.F. Edan, buried: Highland Cemetery, died: 10 Dec 1914, record (1914) #: 265.

David Alexander BISHOP, born: 27 Apr 1868 in Washington County, TN, married, parents: W.M. Bishop and Mary Newton (Sullivan County, TN), cause of death: "acute heart trouble, informant: W.E. Bishop (Elizabethton), buried: Smith Cemetery, died: 29 Dec 1914, record (1914) #: 266.

Mary Etta Jane HOBSON, born: 22 Oct 1894, single, parents: William Hobson and Hannah Hendricks (Carrol Co, VA), cause of death: "tuberculosis of lungs", informant: William Hobson (Shell Creek), buried: Richardson Cemetery, died: 20 Dec 1914, record (1914) #: 267.

Infant GASTIGER, male, born: 14 Dec 1914, parents: L.D. Gastiger (PA) and Margaret (last name illegible), informant: L.D. Gastiger (Hampton), buried: Hall Cemetery, died: 21 Dec 1914, record (1914) #: 268.

Frankie Juanita GOURLEY, born: 5 Oct 1914, parents: Cad Gourley and Ida May Forbs, cause of death: "gastro intestinal disorder", informant: R.N. Gourley (Johnson City. TN), buried: Payne Cemetery, died: 29 Dec 1914, record (1914) #: 269.

Infant STREET, male, parents: Daunt Street and Mintie Carden, death cause: "stillborn", informant: Daunt Street (Hampton), died: 12 Dec 1914, record (1914) #: 270.

Robert ENSOR, born: 5 Aug 1834, single, parents: John K. Ensor and Trephoria Williams, death cause:: "uremia", buried: Ensor Cemetery, died: 30 Jan 1915, record (1915) #: 1.

Infant SIMERLY, male, parents: Sam Simerly and Vicy Odem, death cause: "stillborn", born/died: 20 Jan 1915, record (1915) #: 2.

Willie MCCLELLAN, age 19 years, parents: Frank McClellan (Unicoi, Co., TN) and Low Hicks, death cause: "pneumonia", informant: John McClellan (Roan Mountain), buried: Wilson Cemetery, died: 22 Jan 1915, record (1915) #: 3.

Thomas CROWE, born: 9 Jul 1912, parents: George Crowe and Rebecca Alfred, death cause: "spinal minengitis", informant: John Alfred (Watauga Valley), buried: Ritchie Cemetery, died: 10 Jan 1915, record (1915) #: 4.

John GRINDSTAFF, born: 19 Jun 1844, married, parents: John Grindstaff and mother's name unknown, death cause: "valvulor heart disease", informant: W.G. Collins (Carter), buried: Grindstaff Cemetery, died: 19 Jan 1915, record (1915) #: 5.

Infant PIERCE, male, parents: R.M. Pierce and Matilda Ensor, death cause: "stillborn", informant: E.D. Ensor (Carter), buried: Ensor Cemetery, died: 10 Jan 1915, record (1915) #: 6.

Taft HYDER, born: 7 Jan 1915, parents: Nat T. Hyder and Mae Livingston, death cause: "atalectosia", informant: Nat T. Hyder (Elizabethton), died: 10 Jan 1915, record (1915) #: 7.

David LOWE, born: 19 Jan 1915, parents: Henry Lowe (VA) and Gloria Alen, death cause: "unknown", informant: Henry Lowe (Elizabethton), died: 28 Jan 1915, record (1915) #: 8.

Eric Garton FAIR, born: 27 Feb 1912, parents: George W. Fair (NC) and Lucy V. Humphrieys, death cause: "typhoid fever", informant: George W. Fair (Johnson City), died: 4 Jan 1915, record (1915) #: 9.

Ulie MILLER, born: Apr 1911, parents: Nat Miller and Sallie Boling, death cause: "pneumonia fever", informant: Henry Boling (Roan Mountain), died: 14 Jan 1915, record (1915) #: 10.

Leon CALDWELL, born: Dec 1913, parents; John Caldwell and Nannie Hoss, death cause: "pneumonia fever", informant: Bryan Caldwell (Roan Mountain), died: 11 Jan 1915, record (1915) #: 11.

Infant HEATON, male, parents: Elijah Frank Heaton and Sarah Prichard, death cause: "stillborn", informant: Elijah Heaton (Roan Mountain), born/died: 17 Jan 1915, record (1915) #: 12.

William Harrison GILES, born: 20 Jul 1840 married, parents: Dunbar Giles (VA) and Mary Hayse, death cause: "mal-nutrition due to old age", informant: Mrs. W.H. Giles (Milligan), buried: Milligan Cemetery, died: 11 Jan 1915, record (1915) #: 13.

Alfred A. BUCKNER, age about 75 years, born in North Carolina, married, parents: not stated, death cause: "cerebral hemorrhage, paralysis", informant: S.N. Hawkins (Johnson City), buried: Taylor's Chapel, died: 19 Jan 1915, record (1915) #: 14.

Nannie STEVENS, age near 33 years, born in North Carolina, married, parents: Calvin Reagan (Watauga Co., NC) and Sallie Bryant (Watauga Co., NC), death cause: "delivered triplets, did well until 5th day", informant: J.F. Williams (Johnson City), buried: Williams Cemetery, died: 22 Jan 1915, record (1915) #: 15.

Infant WILLIAMS, female, parents: Henry Williams and Nannie Nidiffer, death cause: "stillborn", informant: Grant Pierce (Watauga Valley), buried: Buckles Cemetery, died: 23 Jan 1915, record (1915) #: 16.

Mrs. Harriett ELLIS, born: Oct 1859 in Sullivan County, TN, parents: George Cole (Sullivan Co) and Joanna Cole (VA), death cause: "organic heart disease", informant: William Cole (Elizabethton), buried: Cole Cemetery, died: 23 Jan 1915, record (1915) #: 17.

Frank TAYLOR, born: 15 Mar 1897, single, parents: Elijah Taylor (Sullivan Co) and Nannie Jane Robinson (NC), death cause: "pulmonary tuberculosis", informant: Lillie Clemons (Elizabethton), buried: Sullivan Co, died: 9 Jan 1915, record (1915) #: 18.

Mrs. Carrie CLEMONS, born: 25 Jun 1876, married, parents: James Hayes and Rebecca Lyon, death cause: "pulmonary tuberculosis", informant: James Hayes (Elizabethton), buried: Crow Cemetery, died: 13 Jan 1915, record (1915) #: 19.

T.A. BALIFF, born: 13 Feb 1831 in Virginia, married, parents: Daniel Baliff and mother's name unknown, death cause: "heart disease", informant: Mrs. J.F. Eggers (Elizabethton), buried: Elk Park, NC, died: 28 Jan 1915, record (1915) #: 20.

David BRITT, age 88 years, parents: David Britt and Annie Britt, death cause: "endo carditis", informant: F.S. Patton (Johnson City), died: 15 Jan 1915, record (1915) #: 21.

Mary Martha BRUMMITT, born: 31 Oct 1858 in North Carolina, married, parents: Sidney Branch (NC) and Amy Benfield (NC), death cause: "cancer of left breast", informant: J.W. Brummitt (Johnson City), buried: Simmons Cemetery, died: 31 Jan 1915, record (1915) #: 22.

Campbell BRADLEY, born: 17 Jan 1905, parents: Nat T. Bradley and Gengie Higgins (Knox Co), death cause: "hemplegia", informant: S.T. Bradley (Carter), buried: Bradley Cemetery, died: 5 Jan 1915, record (1915) #: 23.

Magnolia ALEXANDER, black, born: 15 Sep 1905 at Knoxville, TN, parents: Julian Alexander and Eva Taylor, death cause: "pulmonary tuberculosis", informant: Will Taylor, buried: Cedar Grove, died: 12 Jan 1915, record (1915) #: 24.

Infant LONG, male, black, parents: William Long and Carrie Gardner, death cause: "born dead", born/died: 16 Jan 1915, record (1915) #: 25.

George Albert CURRY, age 54 years, born in Cocke County, TN, married, parents: Thomas Curry and mother's name unknown, death cause: "intestinal nephritis", informant: Jennie Curry (Elizabethton), buried: Bradley Cemetery, died: 22 Jan 1915, record (1915) #: 26.

Infant ODOM, male, parents: Waits Odom (NC), and Oullie Hill, death cause: "stillborn", informant: Waits Odom (Roan Mountain), buried: Odom Cemetery, born/died: 25 Jun 1915, record (1915) #: 27.

W.M. PENLAND, black, age 59 years, single, parents: Monthia Penland (NC) and Louise Penland, death cause: "pneumonia", informant: Melvin Young (Roan Mountain), buried: Chambers Cemetery, died: 29 Jan 1915, record (1915) #: 28.

Conley STEVENS, born: 5 Sep 1913, parents: Taylor Stephens and Harriett Stephens, death cause: "bronchitis", informant: Taylor Stephens (Hampton), died: 8 Jan 1915, record (1915) #: 29.

Minie BYRD, born: 31 Mar 1913, parents: Hutson Byrd (NC) and Martha Woodley (Unicoi, Co), death cause: "parlysis", informant: Huston Byrd (Hampton), buried: Fairview Cemetery, died: 25 Jan 1915, record (1915) #: 30.

Infant MATHERLY, male, born: 6 Feb 1915, parents: James Matherly and Nolie McKinney, death cause: "untimely birth", buried: Sims Cemetery, died: 7 Feb 1915, record (1915) #: 31.

Evaline LEWIS, age 68 years, widow, parents: George Oliver and Nancy Oliver, death cause: "tuberculosis", informant: Charles Oliver (Watauga Valley), buried: Wilson Cem., died: 27 Feb 1915, record (1915) #: 32.

George W. BLEVINS, age 74 years, born in North Carolina, married, parents: not stated, death cause: "bladder trouble", informant: I.S. Blevins, buried: Watauga Cem., died: 1 Feb 1915, record (1915) #: 33.

Louisa DAVIS, born: 17 Dec 1846, widow, parents: John Morrell and Elizabeth Mottern, death cause: "paralysis", informant: B.T.F. Morrell (Watauga), buried: Mottern Cem., died: 6 Feb 1915, record #: 34.

Arther Winfield HARRISON, born: 19 Sep 1914, parents: Anderson Harrison and Sallie Townsend (Watauga Co. NC), death cause: "unknown", informant: George Harrison (Shell Creek), buried: Harrison Cemetery, died: 22 Feb 1915, record (1915) #: 35.
Howard DAVENPORT, born: 9 Sep 1913, parents: M.A. Davenport and Margie Treadway, death cause: "broncho pneumonia", informant: M.A. Davenport (Elizabethton), died: 6 Feb 1915, record (1915) #: 36.
Infant MATHERLY, male, born: 6 Feb 1915, parents: James Matherly and Mollie McKinney, death cause: "untimely birth", buried: Sims Cemetery, died: 7 Feb 1915, record (1915) #: 37.
Willie Mae PIERCE, born: 4 Jan 1915, parents: Henry Pierce and Minnie Brookshire, death cause: "bold hives", informant: S.J. Brookshire (Carter), buried: Ensor Cemetery, died: 4 Feb 1915, record (1915) #: 38.
Robert A. ESTES, born: 18 Mar 1848, widower, parents: Millaoy Estes (NC) and Sallie Crisp (NC), death cause: "acute gastritis", buried: Ensor Cemetery, died: 21 Feb 1915, record (1915) #: 39.
Infant HICKS, male, born: 4 Feb 1915, parents: Jordan Hicks (Mitchell Co. NC) and Love Scott (Pennsylvania Co. VA), death cause: "over work of mother", informant: Jordan Hicks (Butler), died: day "unknown" 1915, record (1915) #: 40.
Ruby CANTER, born: 8 May 1910, parents: Will Canter (Washington Co. VA) and Nannie Ledford (Hawkins Co. TN), death cause: "acute meningitis", informant: R.B. Hyder (Elizabethton), buried: Hyder Cemetery, died: 23 Feb 1915, record (1915) #: 41.
Thedore MOORE, black, age 56 years, married, born in North Carolina, parents: Isaac Moore (NC) and Harriett Connelly (NC), death cause: "acute indigestion", buried: Cedar Grove, died: 12 Feb 1915, record #: 42.
Hildred LAWS, born: 25 Mar 1915 (1914 ?), parents: K.W. Laws and Bessie Clarke (Claiborn Co. TN), death cause: "lobar pneumonia", buried: Colbaugh Cemetery, died: 2 Feb 1915, record (1915) #: 43.
Caline Donald MILLER, born: 24 Aug 1914, parents: E. Dudley Miller (Washington Co. VA) and Pauline Walforn (Illinois), death cause: "acute indigestion", buried: Highland Cemetery, informant: J.T. Miller (Elizabethton), died: 20 Feb 1915, record (1915) #: 44.
John WHITEHEAD, born: 16 Mar 1828, widower, parents: James Whitehead (NC) and Jennie Garland, death cause: "dilalation of heart", informant: K.M. Hill, buried: Whitehead Cem., died: 4 Feb 1915, record (1915) #: 45.

Marion Allen LARGER, born: 30 Aug 1913, parents: John Larger and Lydia Roberts, death cause: "croup", buried: Nelson Cemetery, died: 15 Feb 1915, record (1915) #: 46.

Infant CARVER, born: 16 Feb 1915, parents: John Carver and Bettie Moore, death cause: illegible, informant: Henry Moore (Hampton), buried: Whitehead Cemetery, died: 18 Feb 1915, record (1915) #: 47.

Nellie HAYES, age 7 years, parents: J.S. Hayes and Mollie Taylor, death cause: "nephritis", informant: S.C. Tayor (Johnson City), buried: Williams Cemetery, died: 18 Feb 1915, record (1915) #: 48.

Rosie SIMS, born: 27 Dec 1915, parents: Andy Sims and Hattie Guinn, death cause: "not known", informant: Andy Sims (Roan Mountain), buried: Ripshin, died: 8 Feb 1915, record (1915) #: 49.

Dealie GARLAND, female, age 66 years, widow, parents: Charlie Hughes (Magnetic, NC) and Betty Honeycutt (NC), death cause: "pneumonia fever", informant: David Garland (Roan Mountain", died: 13 Feb 1915, record (1915) #: 50.

Elbert RITCHIE, age 64 years, married, parents: Anderw Ritchie and Jennie Jenkins, death cause: "pneumonia", buried: Ritchie Cemetery, Watauga Valley, died: 28 Feb 1815, record (1915) #: 51.

R. Bennick HYDER, Jr., born: 6 Sep 1912, parents: R. Bennick Hyder and Annie L. Gourley (Washington Co. TN), cause of death: "ptomaine poison", informant: R. Bennick Hyder (Milligan), died: 5 Feb 1915, record (1915) #: 52.

Neiley WILSON, male, colored, born: 22 Apr 1817 in North Carolina, married, parents: "don't know", cause of death: "lobar pneumonia", informant: Gilbert Wilson, buried: Smith Cemetery, died: 17 Mar 1915, record (1915) #: 53.

Dorothy Lanice CARDIN, born: 5 Jan 1915, parents: Alfred Carden and mother's name not stated, cause of death: illegible, informant: Alfred Carden, buried: Horse Shoe, died: 8 Mar 1915, record (1915) #: 54.

Mrs. Rhody WARD, age 38 years, born in North Carolina, married, parents: not stated, cause of death: "anemia", buried: Hampton, died: 11 May 1915, record (1915) #: 55.

Clary SHUFFIELD, born: 10 Sep 1843, married, parents: John L. Stout and first name not stated Shuffield, cause of death: "bronchial asthma", informant: Coose Shuffield (Butler), buried: Elk Church Cemetery, died: 13 Mar 1915, record (1915) #: 56.

William CLARK, born: 20 Dec 1914, parents: Frank Clark and Maggie Treadway, cause of death: illegible, buried: McEwen Cemetery, died: 3 Mar 1915, record (1915) #: 57.

Mary CRESS, born: 11 Dec 1833 in North Carolina, widow, parents: James Brown (NC) and mother's name not known, cause of death: "lagrippe", informant: James Cress (Carter), died: 20 Mar 1915, record (1915) #: 58.

Sallie ENSOR, born: 24 Apr 1949, married, parents: Robinson Cole and Mollie Lowe, cause of death: "pulmonary tuberculosis", informant: G.W. Ensor (Carter), buried: Ensor Cemetery, died: 11 Mar 1915, record (1915) #: 59.

Foster CAMPBELL, born: 1 Sep 1913, parents: Jack Campbell and Mary South, cause of death: "diabetes", informant: Ike Campbell (Carter), buried: Cole Cemetery, died: 18 Mar 1915, record (1915) #: 60.

Alice ADKINS, age 40 years, married, parents: "don't know", cause of death: "post pasture hemmorhage", informant: John Adkins (Johnson City), buried: Buck Cemetery, died: 14 Mar 1915, record (1915) #: 61.

Joshua C. HAMILTON, born: 21 Apr 1838 in Sullivan County, married, parents: Joshua Hamilton and first name not stated Holbough, cause of death: "cancer of stomach", buried: Boyd Cemetery, died: 26 Mar 1915, record (1915) #: 62.

C.N. GRIFFITH, male, parents: Frank Griffith and Susan Oliver, cause of death: "heart failure", informant: W.C. Ellis (Watauga Valley), born/died: 23 Mar 1915, record (1915) #: 63.

Joseph DELOACH, born: 4 Mar 1915, parents: Robert Deloach and mother's name illegible, cause of death: "stillborn", buried: Hyder Cemetery, died: 4 Mar 1915, record (1915) #: 64.

Cardie HARDIN, born: 8 Jan 1914, parents: Ham Hardin and Sarah J. Hardin, cause of death: "acute indigestion", died: 15 Mar 1915, record (1915) #: 65.

Andrew J. PERRY, born: 28 May 1850, married, parents: father's name unknown and Mary Anne Perry, cause of death: "cirrosis of liver", informant: J.T. Perry, buried: Highland Cemetery, died: 16 Mar 1915, record (1915) #: 66.

Charles MARTIN, age 53 years, 9 months and 28 days, born in Grasey (Grayson ?) County, VA, married, parents: Hamp Martin and mother's name unknown, cause of death: "brights disease", buried: Bradley Cemetery, died: 4 Mar 1915, record (1915) #: 67.

Calloway ROBERTS, born: 20 Mar 1824, retired old soldier, married, parents: John Roberts and mother's name unknown, cause of death: "pneumonia", informant: Mrs. Calloway Roberts, buried: Green Hill Cemetery, died: 13 Mar 1915, record (1915) #: 68.

Milford HENDERLITER, born: 24 May 1901 in Pennsylvania, parents: D.C. Henderliter and Rosetta Goodman (PA), cause of death: "typhoid fever", buried: Colbaugh Cemetery, died: 13 Mar 1915, record (1915) #: 69.

Infant COLBAUGH, male, parents: George Colbaugh, Jr., and Bestie Hensley (Washington Co, VA), cause of death: "stillborn", informant: Mrs. Mary Hensley, buried: Colbaugh Cemetery, died: 18 Mar 1915, record (1915) #: 70.

Hartie TOLLEY, male, born: 18 Mar 1915, parents: Brownlow Tolley and Dovie Stephens, cause of death: "disformed", informant: Dock Tolley (Hampton), died: 24 Mar 1915, record (1915) #: 71.

Luther DAVIS, born: 17 Jan 1915, parents: Willima Davis and Nalie Clark, cause of death: "don't know", died: 7 Mar 1915, record (1915) #: 72.

Infant CORNETT, male, parents: Frank Cornett and Myrtle Stevens, death cause: "not born at full term", buried: Cornett Cem., died: 17 Mar 1915, record #: 73.

Infant SIMERLY, female, parents: John Hande Simerly and Susan Chambers, cause of death: "stillborn", informant: Susan Simerly (Roan Mountain), buried: Chambers Cem., died: 21 Mar 1915, record (1915) #: 74.

Warner Guy BENFIELD, born: 19 Feb 1915, parents: Matthew Benfield (NC) and mother's name not stated, cause of death: not stated, buried: Lost Cove, died: 24 Mar 1915, record (1915) #: 75.

Eva C. GOUGE, born: 11 Oct 1897, married, parents: J.M. Moffate (Watauga Co. NC) and N.J. Ingram, death cause: "falling in fire and burned to death", informant: J.R. Kite (Elizabethton), buried: Simmons Cemetery, died: 17 Mar 1915, record (1915) #: 76.

Evaline PAYNE, age 67 years, 1 month and 11 days, parents: Joseph surname illegible and first name not stated Young, death cause: tuberculosis of lungs and bowels, informant: E.H. Taylor (Johnson City), buried: Payne Cem., died: 27 Mar 1915, record (1915) #: 77.

Dallas Earl PERKINS, born: 17 Nov 1914, parents: Oscar Perkins and Lillie Ingram (Magnetic City, NC), death cause: "pnuemonia", informant: J.C. Perkins (Shell Creek(, buried: Perkins Cemetery, died: 4 Mar 1915, record (1915) #: 78.

Lucy ELLIOTT, born: 7 Mar 1915, parents: father's name not stated and Nora Elliott, death cause: "no doctor attended", informant: William Elliott (Shell Creek), buried: Isaacs Cemetery, died: 23 Mar 1915, record (1915) #: 79.

Lester JONES, born: 24 Mar 1915, parents: J.H. Jones and Alice Morgan, death cause: "paremature birth", died: 25 Mar 1915, record (1915) #: 80.

David C. BUCK, age 52 years, married, parents: George W. Buck and Susan Wilson, death cause: "atrophy of liver", informant: Mrs. D.E. Buck (Shell Creek), died: 26 Mar 1915, record (1915) #: 81.

William Garman OAKS, born: 10 Jul 1896, single, parents: Julus Oaks (Mitchell Co. NC) and Lissie Kite (Johnson County), death cause: "fracture of skill, homicide", informant: Julus Oaks (Shell Creek), buried: Oaks Cemetery, died: 30 Mar 1915, record (1915) #: 82.

Infant BRYANT, female, parents: Louis Bryant (NC) and Elizabeth Hardin (NC), death cause: "premature", informant: James Oxendine (Hampton), died: 19 Mar 1915, record (1915) #: 83.

Albert STAFFORD, born: 29 May 1914, parents: Thomas Stafford (Green County) and Gracie Waycaster, death cause: "fits and the blood ran to its head", died: 22 Mar 1915, record (1915) #: 84.

Infant SHELL, male, parents: John Shell and Pearl Taylor, death cause: "premature birth", informant: John Shell (Hampton), born/died: 6 Mar 1915, record (1915) #: 85 (twin below).

Emily C. CARDIN, born: 30 Apr 1838, widow, parents: Melvin Goodwin and Nancy Bradley, death cause: "chronic bronchitis and dilulation of the heart", informant: N.J. Cardin (Hampton), died: 31 Mar 1915, record (1915) #: 86.

Infant SHELL, male, parents: John Shell and Pearl Taylor, death cause: "premature birth", informant: John Shell (Hampton), born/died: 6 Mar 1915, record (1915) #: 87.

Benjamin Baker WHALEY, born: 14 Apr 1860, married, parents: Harrison Whaley (NC) and Liddy M. Clemons, death cause: "struck by locomotive engine", informant: Patsy Pritchard (Butler), died: 14 Apr 1915. record (1915) #: 88.

Alford J. BERRY, age 68 years, married, parents: James Berry and Polly Berry, death cause: "pilegary", informant: J.F.M. Berry (Watauga Valley), buried: Buckles Cem., died: 17 Apr 1915, record (1915) #: 89.

Infant STOUT, female, parents: father's name not stated and Fanny L. Stout (NC), death cause: not stated, informant: J.A. Stout (Fish Springs), born/died: 29 Jan 1915, record (1915) #: 90.

Herman MCQUEEN, born: 14 Mar 1915, parents: Ed McQueen and Nancy Deloach, death cause: not stated, informant: Ed McQueen (Fish Springs) date of death not stated, record (1915) #: 91.

Mrs. Hannah GOUGE, born: 25 Aug 1846, widow, parents: Jacob Simerly and Mary D. Morton, death cause: "pulmonary tuberculosis and lagrippe", buried: Simerly Cemetery, died: 27 Apr 1915, record (1915) #: 92.

Henry MCKINNEY, born: Nov 1833, married, parents: Cam McKinney and Lila Adkinson, death cause: "pneumonia", informant: D.M. McKinney (Hampton), buried: McKinney Cemetery, died: 27 Apr 1915, record (1915) #: 93.

Ellen HARDIN, age 32 years, born: Apr 2nd, married, parents: father's first name illegible Potter and Ellen Heaton, death cause: "nephritis", buried: Siam, TN, died: 30 Apr 1915, record (1915) #: 94.

Infant HARDIN, male, parents: James T. Hardin and Ellen Potter, death cause: illegible, born/died: 29 Apr 1915, record (1915) #: 95. (note: mother's record # 94, above)

Edward CAMPBELL, age 4 years, parents: William C. Campbell and Nola Manning, death cause: "spinal menengitis", buried: Hampton, TN, died: 8 Apr 1915, record (1915) #: 96.

Vadie GRINDSTAFF, born: 4 Mar 1914, parents: Elbert Grindstaff and Lyddia Peters, death cause: "said to be hives", informant: Emma Peters, buried: Grindstaff Cemetery, died: 17 Apr 1915, record (1915) #: 97.

Elizabeth TAYLOR, born: 17 Mar 1915, parents: J.J. Taylor, Jr. and Nancy Garland, death cause: not stated, informant: Ike Garland (Carter), buried: Blevins Cemetery, died: 23 Apr 1915, record (1915) #: 98.

Onie SIMERLY, female, born: 16 Dec 1884, married, parents: R.A. Ellis and Amelia Hathaway, death cause: "pneumonia", informant: C.E. Ellis (Elizabethton), buried: Smith Cemetery, died: 5 Apr 1915, record (1915) #: 99.

Sarah Ann GRINDSTAFF, born: 11 Dec 1845 in Jonesborough, TN, widow, parents: William McCathern (SC) and Maria Hill (VA), death cause: "cancer of face", informant: W.J. Grindstaff (Elizabethton), buried: Grindstaff Cemetery, died: 7 Apr 1915, record (1915) #: 100.

Lucy GLOVER, born: 20 Jan 1866, married, parents: A.J. Williams and Diza Ann Garrison (NC), death cause: "ovarian cyst", informant: W.A. Glover (Elizabethton), buried: Glover Cemetery, died: 28 Apr 1915, record (1915) #: 101.

Laura EDENS, age 7 years, parents: Will Edens and mother's name illegible, death cause: "scarlet fever", informant: W.R. McInturff (Elizabethton), buried: Jones Cem., died: 18 Apr 1915, record (1915) #: 102.

Hascal RANGE, born: 26 Apr 1912, parents: W.A. Range and Ettie Range, death cause: "diarrhea and tuberculosis", informant: W.A. Range (Elizabethton), died: 22 Apr 1915, record (1915) #: 103.

Infant ESTEP, male, parents: Samuel Estep and Eliza Richardson, death cause: "unknown", informant: Samuel Estep (Carter), buried: Estep Cemetery, born/died: 1 Apr 1915, record (1915) #: 104.

Infant WINTERS, male, parents: William Winters and Bessie Winters, death cause: "stillborn", informant: William Winters (Shell Creek), buried in North Carolina, born/died: 6 Apr 1915, record (1915) #: 105.

Infant SHELL, male, born: 2 Apr 1915, parents: Hubert Shell and mother's illegible, death cause: not stated, informant: Hubert Shell (Shell Creek), buried: Richardson Cemetery, died: 5 Apr 1915, record #: 106.

Tom DELOACH, age 16 years, parents: Ike Deloach and D. Deloach, death cause: illegible, informant: Dave Scalf, buried: Hyder Cemetery, died: 23 Apr 1915, record (1915) #: 107.

Joe ELLIOTT, born: 23 Jan 1828, widower, parents: Thom Elliott (NC) and first name not stated Bullard, death cause: not stated, informant: Dan Elliott (Elizabethton), died: 23 Apr 1915, record (1915) #: 108.

George D. ROBERTS, born: 18 Sep 1842, widower, parents: Henderson Roberts (Kingsport, TN) and Nancy Keen (Kingsport, TN), death cause: "acute regingitation", informant: W.C. Roberts, buried: Highland Cemetery, died: 9 Apr 1915, record (1915) #: 109.

John WILSON, colored, age about 50 years, born in North Carolina, single, parents: Robert Wilson (NC) and mother's name unknown, death cause: "aortic regurgitation, paralysis", buried: Smith Cemetery, died: 5 Apr 1915, record (1915) #: 110.

Calvin HICKS, born: 22 Oct 1845 in Washington County, TN, married, parents: John Hicks (NC) and Marian Jones (Washington Co. TN), death cause: "parlaysis", informant: Elizabeth J. Jones (Elizabethton), buried: Colbaugh Cem., died: 6 Apr 1915, record (1915) #: 111.

Rachel T. BOATHR, born: 30 Jan 1835 in South Carolina, widow, parents: William Riley and Cassie Finiher, death cause: "lagrippe and old age", informant: W.H. Boather (Knox County), buried: Erwin, TN, died: 17 Apr 1915, record (1915) #: 112.

Henry BOWMAN, age 73 years, 11 months and 15 days, born in Washington County, TN, widower, parents: Joseph Bowman (Washington Co, TN) and Mahala Carr (Washington Co, TN), death cause: "senility", died: 5 Apr 1915, record (1915) #: 113.

Lillie MATHERSON, born: 24 Nov 1876, married, parents: Esq McNeely (Watauga Co. NC) and Nancy Carver (Watauga Co. NC), death cause: "pellagra", informant: G.W. Matherson (Butler), died: 23 May 1915, record #: 114.

Dolly BARNETT, age 93 years, born in North Carolina, widow, parents: John Garland (NC) and mother's name not stated, death cause: "not known", informant: Elisha Garland (Roan Mountain), buried: Burbank, died: 25 May 1915, record (1915) #: 115.

Nancy A. HILEMAN, born: 10 May 1915, parents: Thomas Hileman (Mitchell Co. NC) and Rhoda Roberts, death cause: "not born at full term and thrash", informant: John H. Roberts (Roan Mountain), buried: Nelson Cemetery, died: 18 May 1915, record (1915) #: 116.

Burtie DAVIS, born: 12 Apr 1915, parents: Arthur Davis and Ettie Childers, death cause: "premature birth", informant: Arthur Davis (Roan Mountain), buried: Blevins Cem., died: 27 May 1915, record (1915) #: 117.

Emmie HILMAN, born: 10 May 1915, parents: Thomas Hilman (Mitchell Co. NC) and Rhoda Roberts, death cause: " not born at full term", died: 10 May 1915, record (1915) #: 118.

Arzella Jane BOREN, age 74 years, parents: A. Julian Williams and first name illegible McFarland, death cause: "heart failure", buried: Boren Cemetery, died: 22 May 1915, record (1915) #: 119.

Infant BRADSHAW, female, parents: John Bradshaw (Hawkins Co. TN) and Eva Hatcher, death cause: "undeveloped child", died: 31 May 1915, record #: 120.

Mrs. L.J. VANHOY, born: Apr 1840 in North Carolina, parents: father's name unknown and first name not stated Marshall (NC), death cause: "carcinoma of lympth glands", informant: Lee Smith, buried: Foust Cemetery, died: 6 May 1915, record (1915) #: 121.

Leo DENNY, born: 27 Jun 1914 in Kentucky, parents: John H. Deny (NC) and Lydie Bradshaw, death cause: "acute diarrhoea", buried: Colbaugh Cemetery, died: 29 May 1915, record (1915) #: 122.

Eliza E. DELOACH, born: 7 Feb 1915, parents: Henry Deloach and M. Russell, death cause: illegible, buried: Deloach Cemetery, died: 3 May 1915, record (1915) #: 123.

Lewis WHITE, age 19 years, single, parents: Alexander White and Julia Pierce, death cause: "brights disease", buried: Grindstaff Cemetery, died: 8 May 1915, record (1915) #: 124.

Lizzie GARLAND, age 40 years, married, parents: George Garland and Rebecca Arnett (NC), death cause: "tuberculosis", informant: Davie Garland (Carter), buried: Estep Cemetery, died: 17 May 1915, record (1915) #: 125.

Rose Lee GARLAND, born: 8 Apr 1915, parents: Joe Garland and Dora Elliott, death cause: "croup", informant: Joe Taylor (Carter), buried: Elliott Cemetery, died: 17 May 1915, record (1915) #: 126.

Mrs. Mollie SHELL, born: 15 Jun 1877, married, parents: Joseph Richardson and Lottie Smith, death cause: "pulmonary tuberculosis", informant: James Shell (Elizabethton), buried: Shell Cemetery, died: 4 May 1915, record (1915) #: 127.

Pleasant JAMES, age not stated, parents: William James and Rosa Williams, death cause: "typhoid fever", informant: William James (Elizabethton), buried: Williams Cem., died: 4 May 1915, record (1915) #: 128.

Infant STOUT, female, parents: G.W. Stout (Johnson Co. TN) and Maud Adams (Washington Co) death cause: "born dead", buried: Highland Cemetery, born/died: 8 May 1915, record (1915) #: 129.

Tesh WINTERS, female, born: 17 Jan 1876 in Ashe County, NC, married, parents: Alexander Latham (Ashe Co. NC) and Sarah Parsons (Alleghany Co. NC), death cause: "sudden death", buried: Caraway Cemetery, died: 12 May 1915, record (1915) #: 130.

Mary Rebechea PALMER, born: 11 May 1914, parents: Joseph Felix Palmer (NC) and Berthia A. Oaks, death cause: "pneumonia", died: 11 May 1915, record #: 131.

Flora Ossie CLARK, born: 27 Jan 1892, married, parents: David F. McKeehan and Dora Kite, death cause: "tuberculosis", informant: David McKeehan, buried: McKeehan Cem., died: 6 May 1915, record (1915) #: 132.

George Allen HOLOWAY, born: 6 Jun 1915, parents: George A. Holloway and Eloise Holden (NC), death cause: "asphyxia caused by pheglm in lungs", informant: G.A. Holoway (Butler), died: 7 Jun 1915, record (1915) #: 133.

Bula D. WHALEY, born: 19 May 1915, parents: Nathan W. Whaley and Nancy C. Smith, death cause: not stated, informant: L.L. Smith (Butler), date of death not stated, record (1915) #: 134.
Infant HUGHES, male, parents: father's name not given and Ellen Hughes (NC), death cause: "stillborn", informant: E.W. Sizemore (Roan Mountain), born/died: 30 June 1915, record (1915) #: 135.
Dautan SIMERLY, born: 29 May 1914, parents: W.H. Simerly and Mary Banks (Unicoi Co. TN), death cause: "edema of lungs", informant: W.H. Simerly (Hampton), buried: Gouge Cem., died: 2 Jun 1915, record #: 136.
Infant CATES, male, parents: Millard Cates and Nola Little, death cause: "stillborn", informant: Ellis Lacy (Hopson), buried: Holley Cemetery, born/died: 7 Jun 1915, record (1915) #: 137.
Jefferson TAYLOR, born: 1 Sep 1856, married, parents: Michael Taylor and Sallie Lewis, death cause: "renal colerts hydronsphrosis", died: 21 Jun 1915, record (1915) #: 138.
Nancy PETERS, born: 16 Jul 1836, widow, parents: George Morton and Adaline Campbell, death cause: "brights disease", informant: Ben Peters (Hampton), died: 8 Jun 1915, record (1915) #: 139.
Belle BLEVINS, born: 13 Mar 1896, single, parents: Allen Blevins and Sarah Garland, death cause: "pulmonary tuberculosis", informant: Allen Blevins (Carter), buried: Estep Cemetery, died: 30 Jun 1915, record (1915) #: 140.
Infant BLEVINS, female, parents: William Allen Blevins and Lee Ann Garland, death cause: "still birth", buried: Piney Flats, born/died: 26 Jun 1915, record (1915) #: 141.
George W. BULLOCK, born: 7 Mar 1841, parents: John H. Bullock and mother's name not stated, death cause: "organic heart disease", informant: S.T. Bullock (Watauga), buried: Malone Cemetery, died: 30 Jun 1915, record (1915) #: 142.
John BECK, age about 73 years, born in Ashe County, NC, widower, parents: Joel Beck (Ashe Co. NC) and first name not stated Foster (Ashe Co. NC), death cause: "pellagra", buried: Brooks Cemetery, died: 20 Jun 1915, record (1915) #: 143.
Infant CAMPBELL, female, parents: John Campbell and Annie Prichet (Elk Park, NC), death cause: "still born", informant: John Campbell (Elizabethton), born/died: 11 Jun 1915, record (1915) #: 144.

Infant CRUMLEY, male, born: 17 Jun 1915, parents: Robert Crumley and Ida Campbell, death cause: "cholera", died: 12 Jun 1915, record (1915) #: 145.

Mary Sue GIESLER, born: 4 Oct 1864, married, parents: Dowel Scott and (first name not stated) Simerly, death cause: "anemia with cardiac failure", informant: E.E. McKinney (Hampton), died: 4 Jul 1915, record #: 146.

James M. BLACK, born: 1 Jun 1849 in Ashe County, NC, married, parents: John J. Black (NC) and Elenor Parsons (NC), death cause: "progressive paralysis", informant: William H. Black (Butler), died: 6 Jul 1915, record (1915) #: 147.

William ADAMS, age 60 years, born in Johnson County, TN, married, parents: father's name unknown and Pollie Adams (Johnson Co. TN), death cause: "dropsy", inforamant: James A. Messimer (Butler), died: 4 Jul 1915, record (1915) #: 148.

Vara CAMPBELL, born: 2 Jul 1915, parents: father's name not given and Mamie Campbell, death cause: "premature delivery", informant: Clyde Ramsey (Butler), died: 7 Jul 1915, record (1915) #: 149.

Polly LONG, black, born: 14 Jan 1849 in North Carolina, parents: Morton Hampton and mother's name illegible, death cause: not stated, buried: Shell Creek, died: 19 Jul 1915, record (1915) #: 150.

Ellen HUGHES, age about 17 years, single, parents: not stated, death cause: not stated, informant: Lish Garland (Roan Mountain), died: 3 Jul 1915, record (1915) #: 151.

Bell BLEVINS, born: 12 Aug 1898, parents: John Blevins and Erma Gilland, death cause: "tuberculosis pulmonary", informant: Bill Milams (Roan Mountain), died: 4 Jul 1915, record (1915) #: 152.

Paul MILAMS, born: 6 Jun 1915, parents: George Milams and Ethel Garland (Unicoi Co. TN), death cause: "bold hives", informant: John Garland (Roan Mountain), buried: Blevins Cem, died: 6 Jul 1915, record #: 153.

Infant MOOR, male, parents: Henry Moor and Carrie Cates, death cause: "malformation", informant: A.L. Cates (Hampton), buried: Whitehead Cemetery, died: 21 Jul 1915, record (1915) #: 154.

Sarah WALSH, age 85 years, born in Johnson County, TN, widow, parents: Jerry Lowe (Johnson Co. TN) and mother's name illegible, death cause: "old age", informant: W.R. Walsh (Butler), buried: Johnson County, died: 23 Jul 1915, record (1915) #: 155.

Emily HIGGINS, black, age 85 years, born in South Carolina, widow, parents: "unknown", death cause: "senile decay", informant: Isaac Higgins (Johnson City), buried: Horton Cemetery, died: 21 Jul 1915, record (1915) #: 156.

Infant COLE, male, parents: James Cole (Sullivan Co. TN) and Ellie surname illegible (Washington Co.), death cause: "stillborn", born/died: 14 Jul 1915, record (1915) #: 157.

Elizabeth RYAN, born: 14 Jun 1837, widow, parents: John Singletary (NC) and Nancy A. Johnson, death cause: "kidney, heart and old age", informant: George W. Ryan (Elizabethton), buried: Green Hill, died: 7 Jul 1915, record (1915) #: 158.

Edward E. HATHAWAY, born: 11 Jul 1915, parents: Harry Hathaway and Alice D. Lacy, death cause: "heart failure", informant: J.M. Lacy, buried: Highland Cemetery, died: 13 Jul 1915, record (1915) #: 159.

Beulah Evely REYNOLDS, born: 10 Feb 1906, parents: James Reynolds and Anna Mottern, death cause: "chronic mitral stenosis", informant: H.T. Daniel (Elizabethton), buried: Reynolds Cemetery, died: 11 Jul 1915, record (1915) #: 160.

Infant WILLIAMS, male, parents: H.C. Williams and Alice Morrell, death cause: "stillborn", informant: A.C. Williams (Watauga Valley), born/died: 3 Jul 1915, record (1915) #: 161. (note: twin record below)

Infant WILLIAMS, female, parents: H.C. Williams and Alice Morrell, death cause: "stillborn", informant: A.C. Williams (Watauga Valley), born/died: 3 Jul 1915, record (1915) #: 162.

Ula BOWERS, female, born: 28 Nov 1914, parents: Sal Bowers and Mary Bowers, death cause: "cholera", informant: D.S. Buckles (Watauga Valley), buried: Bowers Cem., died: 18 Jul 1915, record (1915) #: 163.

Earl BERRY, born: 8 Apr 1915, parents: Alvin Berry and Josie Bowers, death cause: "spinal meningitis", buried: Buckles Cemetery, died: 1 Jul 1915, record (1915) #: 164.

Harvey WILLIAMS, born: Feb 1856, age 59 years and 5 months, married, parents: Pleasant Williams and Vica Pierce, death cause: "carcinoma of stomach", informant: Sam Williams (Watauga Valley), buried: Buckles Cem., died: 15 Jul 1915, record (1915) #: 165.

Bula PETERS, born: 26 Apr 1914, parents: Powell Peters and Julia Vance (VA), death cause: "pneumonia", informant: C.C. Peters (Carter), buried: Blevins Cemetery, died: 6 Jul 1915, record (1915) #: 166.

Caroline LAWSON, born: 12 May 1837, widow, parents: "unknown", death cause: "dropsy", informant: Smith Hinkle (Carter), buried: Garland Cemetery, died: 12 Jul 1915, record (1915) #: 167.
Jane WILSON, age 50 years, married, parents: Mordica Wilson and Hannah Wilson, death cause: "dementia paralytica", informant: David Wilson (Carter), buried: Garland Cem., died: 12 Jul 1915, record (1915) #: 168.
Lona SLAGE, born: 23 Jun 1908, parents: Noah Slagle and Bessie Webb, death cause: "dropsy", died: 7 Jul 1915, record (1915) #: 169.
Alice Della SIMPSON, born: 9 Feb 1914, parents: James Simpson (Hawkins Co. TN) and Julia Blevins, death cause: "acute menningitis", died: 27 Jul 1915, record (1915) #: 170.
Worley S. GRINDSTAFF, born: 29 Jan 1905, parents: D.L. Grindstaff and Bessie Glover, death cause: "tuberculosis of glands", buried: Glover Cemetery, died: 10 Jul 1915, record (1915) #: 171.
Robert MCRATH, black, born: 28 Jun 1915, parents: Pete McRath (NC) and Lizzie Taylor, death cause: "premature birth", buried: Cedar Grove, died: 4 Jul 1915, record (1915) #: 172.
Henry W. ALBERTSON, born: 9 Sep 1867 in North Carolina, married, parents: E.S. Albertson (NC) and mother's name not stated, death cause: "pulmonary tuberculosis", informant: Mrs. H.W. Albertson (Elizabethton), buried: Highland Cemetery, died: 10 Jul 1915, record (1915) #: 173.
Frank Edward MORGAN, born: 11 Jun 1915, parents: James Morgan and Alice Phillips, death cause: not stated, informant: James Morgan (Shell Creek), buried: Richardson Cem., died: 29 Jul 1915, record #: 174.
James Henry HOSS, born: 8 Sep 1909, parents: Clifton Hoss and Matilda Lewis, death cause: "typhoid fever", buried: Perry Cem., died: 17 Jul 1915, record #: 175.
Annie Lee HINKLE, born: 27 Feb 1915, parents: Bob Richardson and Josie Hinkle, death cause: "intestinal intoxication", informant: Josie Hinkle (Watauga Valley), died: 25 Jul 1915, record (1915) #: 176.
Rebecca PIERCE, born: 24 May 1888, single, parents: Armstead Pierce and Minnie Pierce, death cause: "typhoid fever", informant: W.C. Pierce (Butler), buried: Pierce Cem., died: 24 Aug 1915, record #: 177.
Sidney HODGE, age 3 years, parents: Abe Hodge and Ester Cole, death cause: "croup", informant: Rebecca Cole (Carter), buried: Cole Cemetery, died: 19 Apr 1915, record (1915) #: 178.

David ARNOLD, age about 65 years, parents: Daniel Arnold (Johnson Co. TN) and Susan surname unknown, death cause: "unknown", informant: James Cable (Butler), buried: Cable Cemetery, died: 15 Aug 1915, record (1915) #: 179.
Nicholas Decatur BLEVINS, born: 3 Jul 1914, parents: Loone Blevins and Mollie Campbell, death cause: "acute nephritis", informant: J.L. Pierce (Carter), buried: Garland Cem., died: 4 Aug 1915, record (1915) #: 180.
J.A. ALFORD, born: 9 Mar 1915, parents: John Alford and Dora Ritchie, death cause: "cerebral meningitis", buried: Ritchie Cem., died: 3 Aug 1915, record #: 181.
Joseph A. GLOVER, born: 11 Nov 1869, married, parents: Daniel Glover and Joana Carrier, death cause: "suppurative pluracy", informant: Mrs. J.A. Glover (Elizabethton), died: 24 Aug 1915, record #: 182.
Samuel J. PLEASANT, born: 23 Aug 1873, married, parents: Joseph Pleasant and Mary Lowe, death cause: "tuberculosis", informant: W.M. Colbaugh, buried: Grindstaff Cem., died: 29 Aug 1915, record #: 183.
Pherba HARDIN, age 64 years, 9 months and 8 days, widow, parents: Allen Robert and Mary McYea, death cause: "cancer", buried: Grindstaff Cemetery, died: 7 Aug 1915, record (1915) #: 184.
Arvy CAMPBELL, female, born: 20 Jun 1915, parents: father's first name illegible Campbell and Sarah E. Campbell, death cause: "hives", informant: E.A. Potter (Shell Creek), died: 26 Aug 1915, record #: 185.
Luisia BRYANT, born: 22 Jun 1853 in Watauga County, NC, married, parents: Jessy Harvsin (Watauga Co. NC) and Martha Hodge (Watauga Co. NC), death cause: "paralysis", died: 30 Aug 1915, record (1915) #: 186.
Infant CAMPBELL, male, parents: D.C. Campbell and Mollie Myers, death cause: "premature birth", buried: Buckles Cem., died: 7 Aug 1915, record (1915) #: 187.
Harrison SHELL, born: 13 Oct 1879 in North Carolina, widower, Parents: James S. Shell and Mary Johnson (NC), death cause: "opticemia, injury to the knee", buried: Shell Creek, died: 13 Aug 1915, record #: 188.
Ellen LOVELESS, born: 16 Aug 1895, single, parents: Elijah Loveless and Mary Wilson, death cause: "tuberculosis", informant: Tom Loveless (Elizabethton), buried: Loveless Cemetery, died: 14 Aug 1915, record (1915) #: 189.
Hazel Marie SIMERLY, born: 29 Jul 1913, parents: Walter Simerly and Pearl Jenkins, death cause: illegible, buried: Valley Forge, died: 18 Aug 1915, record (1915) #: 190.

Franklin D. GREER, born: 14 Apr 1901, parents: Thomas Greer (Watauga Co. NC) and Sarah A. Lunceford, death cause: "inflamatory rhumatism", informant: Thomas Greer (Shell Creek), died: 7 Aug 1915, record #: 191.

Illegible INFANT, black, parents: Clarence, surname illegible and first name illegible, Wilson, death cause: "born dead", died: 31 Aug 1915, record #: 192.

Kennith WITHERSPOON, born: 14 Mar 1915, parents: Sam Witherspoon and Linda Smith, death cause: not stated, informant: Heague Brown (Roan Mountain), died: 27 Aug 1915, record (1915) #: 193.

May RICH, born: 11 Mar 1914 in Virginia, parents: Boon Rich (VA) and Sarah Townsend, death cause: "unknown", informant: James Townsend (Banner Elk, NC), died: 11 Aug 1915, record (1915) #: 194.

Infant WATSON, colored, parents: Will Watson (NC) and Hattie Mitchell (NC), death cause: "born dead", buried: Cedar Grove Cemetery, died: 16 Aug 1915, record (1915) #: 195.

John W. KEEN, born: 27 Apr 1848, married, parents: Enoch Keen (NC) and Polly Orr (VA), death cause: "acute indigestion". buried: Price Cemetery, died: 7 Aug 1915, record (1915) #: 196.

Infant TAYLOR, male, parents: George Taylor and Mary Roberts, death cause: "unknown", born/died: 25 Sep 1915, record (1915) #: 197.

Infant RICHARDSON, male, parents: Cass Richardson and Mary Garland, death cause: "stillborn", born/died: 25 Sep 1915, record (1915) #: 198.

Mary BUCKLES, born: 8 Oct 1874, married, parents: Thomas Buckles and Celia Williams, death cause: "pellagra", buried: Buckles Cemetery, died: 7 Sep 1915, record (1915) #: 199.

Infant CATES, female, born: 9 Sep 1916, parents: Robert Cates and Rhoda Simerly, death cause: illegible, buried: Simerly Cemetery, died: 10 Sep 1915, record (1915) #: 200.

Infant SMITH, male, parents: Burl W. Smith and Emina Hall, death cause: "unknown", informant: Burl Smith (Hampton), buried: Smith Cemetery, born/died: 6 Sep 1915, record (1915) #: 201.

William DOUGLAS, age about 82 years, married, parents: James Douglas (NC) and mother's name not known, death cause: "cancer of stomach and intestines", informant: Walter Douglas (Elizabethton), buried: McKeehan Cemetery, died: 12 Sep 1915, record (1915) #: 202.

Infant PILKERTON, born: 9 Sep 1915, parents: father's name not given and Dora Pilkerton, death cause: not stated, informant: W.S. Hatley (Butler), died: 25 Sep 1915, record (1915) #: 203.

Flosy Ann HICKS, born: 3 May 1915, parents: Alfonso Hicks and Nancy R. Guin, death cause: illegible, died: 20 Sep 1915, record (1915) #: 204.

Nancy Jane CLOSSON, born: Jan 1910, parents: Lafayett Clausson and Elizabeth Hollifield, death cause: "clothes caught fire and burned to death", informant: W.M. Closson (Dark Ridge, NC), died: 13 Sep 1915, record (1915) #: 205.

Susanna MOTTERN, born: 16 Mar 1822 in Sullivan County, TN, married, parents: John Smith (Sullivan Co) and Mary Smith (Sullivan Co), death cause: "senility", buried: Mottern Cemetery, died: 20 Sep 1915, record (1915) #: 206.

Flora Annice PIERCE, born: 17 Jan 1915, parents: Robert H. Pierce and Annie Rains, death cause: "intestinal intoxication", died: 12 Sep 1915, record (1915) #: 207.

Infant HYDER, male, parents: Cecil Hyder and Amanda Nidiffer, death cause: "asphixia, stillborn", informant: James Hyder (Watauga Valley), buried: Hyder Cemetery, died: 4 Sep 1915, record (1915) #: 208.

France R. TOLLEY, age 82 years, born in North Carolina, widower, parents: France Tolley (NC) and Larkie Emaline Tolley, death cause: "dropsy and old age", informant: Charlie Willis (Hampton), buried: Tolley Cemetery, died: 11 Sep 1915, record #: 209.

Clarsey HILL, age 79 years, born in North Carolina, widow, parents: John Gouge (NC) and Susie Spraks (NC), death cause: "uremia", informant: Lee Moore (Hampton), buried: Whitehead Cemetery, died: 8 Sep 1915, record (1915) #: 210.

Julia ROBERTS, born: 24 Feb 1893, single, parents: W.C. Roberts and Rebecca McNess (Green Co), death cause: "gastro entemic catomah", informant: W.C. Roberts (Elizabethton), buried: Highland Cemetery, died: 9 Sep 1915, record (1915) #: 211.

Infant GOUGE, female, parents: James Gouge (NC) and Bettie Smith, death cause: "stillborn", informant: J.N. Gouge (Elizabethton), buried: Highland Cemetery, died: 18 Sep 1915, record (1915) #: 212.

Clyde Owens CROW, born: 21 Jun 1893, single, parents: D.B. Crow and Mollie Gourley, death cause: "pulmonary tuberculosis", informant: F.D. Crow (Johnson City), buried: Milligan, died: 21 Sep 1915, record #: 213.

Dorcia HODGE, age about 65 years, widow, parents: John Campbell (Johnson County) and Eliza Stout, death cause: "diarrhoea", informant: Tishie Estep (Carter), buried: Richardson Cemetery, died: 25 Oct 1915, record (1915) #: 214.

Walter GRINDSTAFF, born: 21 Sep 1915, parents: William H. Grindstaff and Sarah J. Grindstaff, death cause: "croup", informant: M. Garland (Carter), buried: Garland Cemetery, died: 31 Oct 1915, record #: 215.

Ray INGRAM, born: 15 Jun 1915, parents: Charles Ingram and Emma Miller, death cause: "marasmus", informant: Emma Ingram (Hampton), died: 30 Oct 1915, record (1915) #: 216.

John BURCHETT, age about 50 years, born in Wilkes Co., NC, married, parents: father's name unknown and Cora Birchett (Butler), buried: Whitehead Cemetery, died: 12 Oct 1915, record (1915) #: 217.

Mary CASEY, born: 18 Mar 1915, parents: George Casey and Jennie Gourley, death cause: "croup", informant: George Casey (Hampton), died: 19 Oct 1915, record (1915) #: 218.

Geneva STOUT, born: 29 Jul 1914, parents: George Stout and Nancy Howel, death cause: "croup", informant: George Stout (Braemer), buried: Hampton, died: 5 Oct 1915, record (1915) #: 219.

Anna B. WILLIAMS, born: 19 Oct 1915, parents: E.J. Williams and Sallie Hopson, death cause: "not known", informant: E.B. Weaver (Watauga Valley), buried: Buckles Cemetery, died: 24 Oct 1915, record #: 220.

Nora ANGEL, born: 14 Oct 1887, married, parents: Joe Grindstaff and Catherine Peters, death cause: "tuberculosis", informant: Folsome Angel (Carter), buried: Grindstaff Cemetery, died: 20 Oct 1915, record (1915) #: 221.

William BUCKLES, age 18 months, parents: Toy Buckles and Grace Bullock, death cause: "stomach trouble", died: 26 Oct 1915, record (1915) #: 222.

Margaret BULLOCK, age 8 years, born in Virginia, parents: Will Bullock (Sullivan County) and Ida Millhorn (Sullivan County), death cause: "diptheria", informant: S.T. Bullock (Watauga), died: 20 Oct 1915, record (1915) #: 223.

Thelma BULLOCK, born: 8 Feb 1905, parents: W.M. Bullock and Ida Millhorn, death cause: "diptheria", informant: S.T. Bullock (Watauga), died: 12 Oct 1915, record (1915) #: 224.

Nellie Gertrude MASINGILL, born: 7 Jan 1912 in Sullivan County, parents: C.D. Masingill (Sullivan County) and Mary Elizabeth Smith (Sullivan County), death cause: "diptheria", died: 9 Oct 1915, record (1915) #: 225.

Elise CARSON, negro, born: Jun 1914, parents: father's name not stated and Willy Carson, death cause: "typhoid", informant: mother (Shell Creek), died: 17 Oct 1915, record (1915) #: 226.

Nancy WOODRUFF, age 80 years, 1 month and 24 days, born in Ashe County, NC, single, parents: William Phillips (NC) and Gemima Yates (NC), death cause: "gastr enterilis", informant: E.M. Woodruff (Shell Creek), buried: Woodruff Cemetery, died: 13 Oct 1915, record (1915) #: 227.

Leslie G. CARDIN, born: 12 Aug 1890, single, parents: Grant Cardin and Isabell Goodwin, death cause: "typhoid fever", informant: Loyd Cardin (Hampton), buried: Cardin Cemetery, died: 12 Oct 1915, record (1915) #: 228.

Lucy HODGE, born: 13 Sep 1914, parents: H.. (illegible) Hodge and Minnie Williams, death cause: "consumption of bowels", buried: Jenkins Cemetery, died: 1 Oct 1915, record (1915) #: 229.

Sarah USARY, age 78 years, widow, parents: Yansal Walker and mother's name unknown, death cause: "endo carditis", informant: David Usary (Johnson City), buried: Milligan, died: 24 Oct 1915, record #: 230.

Arvel Scott SIMERLY, born: 6 Feb 1915 in West Virginia, parents: Martin Simerly and Lizzie Carver, death cause: "pneumonia fever", informant: Rossie Simerly (Hampton), buried: Fair View Cemetery, died: 21 Oct 1915, record (1915) #: 231.

Manda A. GOURLEY, born: 14 Sep 1837 in Johnson County, widow, parents: P.M. Williams and Sarah Smithpeters (Johnson County), death cause: "chronic cattarrh of stomach", informant: P.G. Range (Elizabethton), buried: Jones Cem., died: 13 Oct 1915, record #: 232.

John HARRIS, colored, age 85 years, born in Florida, parents: "don't know", death cause: "paralysis", informant: George Susong, died: 14 Oct 1915, record (1915) #: 233.

Infant MCQUEEN, female, parents: Ransom McQueen and Sinda Williams, death cause: "stillborn", died: 28 Oct 1915, record (1915) #: 234.

Elizabeth LACY, born: 21 Sep 1911, parents: W.B. Lacy and Lisey Collins, death cause: "diptheria", buried" Highland Cem., died: 27 Oct 1915, record #: 235.

Hal GEISLER, born: 20 Oct 1915, parents: D.E. Geisler (Sullivan County) and Nanie Band (Sullivan County), death cause: "partial paralysis, convulsions", buried: Highland Cem., died: 21 Oct 1915, record #: 236.

Dave HIX, born: 28 Nov 1894, married, parents: J.J. Hix and Kate Hix, death cause: "typhoid and malaria fever", buried: Green Hill Cemetery, died: 30 Oct 1915, record (1915) #: 237.

Edna USARY, age 46 years, married, parents: father's name not known and Cinda McIntire, death cause: "apoplexy", informant: Samuel Usary (Milligan), buried: Milligan, died: 27 Nov 1915, record #: 238.

Infant TAYLOR, black, parents: John Taylor and Adda Davis, death cause: "born dead", died: 25 Nov 1915, record (1915) #: 239.

Lesley C. GOUGE, born: 4 Nov 1915, parents: R.H. Gouge (NC) and Ettie Kelley, death cause: "heart disease", buried: Kelley Cem., died: 24 Nov 1915, record #: 240.

William Dainey CHASE, MD, born: 2 Aug 1875 in Sullivan County, married, parents: Thomas R. Chase (Sullivan County) and Mary Ann Yokley (Sullivan County), death cause: "cerebral hemorrhage", informant: W.S. Taylor, MD, (Milligan), buried: Burnsville, NC, died: 20 Nov 1915, record (1915) #: 241.

Edwin Ellis MILLER, age 65 years and 2 months, dentist, widower, parents: Robert MIller and Elizabeth Ellis, death cause: "gun shot by accident", died: 10 Nov 1915, record (1915) #: 242.

Addie Bell LOVELESS, born: 26 Jul 1915, parents: W.P. Loveless and Debbie Douglas, death cause: "indigestion", buried: Gap Creek, died: 22 Nov 1915, record (1915) #: 243.

Harrison MCKINNEY, born: 3 Oct 1915, parents: G.A. McKinney and Lucy McKinney, death cause: "infantile paralysis", died: 6 Nov 1915, record (1915) #: 244.

Mollie CAMPBELL, born: 18 Apr 1890, married, parents: first name illegible Myers and Rina Pierce, death cause: "tuberculosis of lungs", informant: D.C. Campbell, buried: Buckles Cemetery, died: 15 Nov 1915, record (1915) #: 245.

Infant LIVINGSTON, male, parents: G.A. Livingston and Kate Headrick, death cause: "born dead", informant: J.S. Simerly, buried: Simerly Cemetery, died: 21 Nov 1915, record (1915) #: 246.

Freddie JONES, born: 25 Sep 1915, parents: Johnie Jones and Lizzie Campbell, death cause: "larangitis and cold", informant: William Jones, buried: Williams Cemetery, died: 25 Nov 1915, record (1915) #: 247.

Infant LINKES, female, parents: Hiram Linkes (Hawkins County) and S.J. Beard, death cause: "mother was hurt in fall 3 months before delivery", buried: Elk Church Cemetery, born/died: 1 Nov 1915, record (1915) #: 248.

Jessie HINKLE, born: Jun 1893, single, parents: William Hinkle and Lizzie Hurley, death cause: "pulmonary tuberculosis", informant: Eliza Oliver (Watauga Valley), buried: Ritchie Cemetery, died: 13 Nov 1915, record (1915) #: 249.

Eliza C. WILSON, age not stated, married, parents: John Collins, and Lusie Collins, death cause: "no positive diagnosis", informant: A.R. Collins (Watauga Valley), buried: Wilson Cemetery, died: 10 Nov 1915, record (1915) #: 250.

Infant TUCKER, female, parents: A.J. Tucker and Lucy Greer, death cause: "stillborn", buried: Roan Mountain, died: 1 Nov 1915, record (1915) #: 251.

Rosia JERRITT, born: 5 Jul 1837 in North Carolina, widow, parents: "unknown", death cause: "old age", died: 30 Nov 1915, record (1915) #: 252.

T.J. MCADAMS, colored, born: 1 Jul 1915, parents: Thomas McAdams (NC) and Mary Irvin, death cause: not stated, informant: Henry McAdams (Shell Creek), died: 30 Nov 1915, record (1915) #: 253.

Mary E. THOMPSON, born: 11 Mar (year illegible) age: 66 years, 8 months and 5 days, married, parents: Henry Range and Elizabeth Taylor, death cause: "diabetes", buried: Range Cem., died: 16 Nov 1915, record #: 254.

Dorothy May HART, born: 8 Jul 1913, parents: Edgar Hart and Ida Mottern, death cause: "diptheria", buried: Mottern Cemetery, died: 9 Nov 1915, record (1915) #: 255.

Infant HART, male, parents: Edgar Hart and Ida Mottern, death cause: "prolapsed cord", buried: Mottern Cem., died: 10 Nov 1915, record (1915) #: 256.

M.C. HONEYCUTT, female, born: 15 Jun 1900, parents: William Honeycutt (NC) and Bettie Street (NC), death cause: "pulmonary tuberculosis", informant: Mrs. Bettie Honeycutt (Hampton), buried: Honeycutt Cemetery, died: 18 Nov 1915, record (1915) #: 257.

Infant MERRITT, female, parents: John Merritt and Minnie Fair, death cause: "stillborn", informant: John Merritt (Elizabethton), died: 12 Nov 1915, record (1915) #: 258.

Edith BOLING, born: 9 Nov 1913, parents: Abe Boling (Sullivan County) and Laura Boling, death cause: "tonsilitis, croup", informant: S.D. Scalf, buried: Range Cem., died: 9 Nov 1915, record (1915) #: 259.

Frankie HATCHER, born: 26 Jun 1912, parents: Will Hatcher and Emma Nave, death cause: "obstructed bowel", buried: Highland Cemetery, died: 9 Nov 1915, record (1915) #: 260.

James Peter SLAGLE, born: 12 Jan 1861, married, parents: Peter Slagle and June Claymon, death cause: "lobar pneumonia", informant: Roy A. Slagle (Knoxville, TN), buried: Slagle Cemetery, died: 12 Nov 1915, record (1915) #: 261.

Willie BAYS, female, age 66 years, born in Virginia, parents: Richmond Sheppard (VA) and Betty Sadler (VA), death cause: "general breakdown", informant: C.B. Rosenbaum, buried: Green Hill, died: 14 Nov 1915, record (1915) #: 262.

Anthony M. FERGUSON, born: 12 Nov 1836 in Russell County, VA, minister, parents: Andrew Ferguson and Margaret Kelly (VA), death cause: "dilitation of heart", informant: A.A. Ferguson, buried: Johnson City, died: 21 Nov 1915, record (1915) #: 263.

Infant LONG, black, parents: Will Long and Corrie Gardner, death cause: "stillborn, strangulation", born/died: 23 Nov 1915, record (1915) #: 264.

Sidney G. WILLIAMS, born: 4 Apr 1915 in North Carolina, parents: L.C. Williams (NC) and Dara O. Miller (Bluff City), death cause: "unknown, sudden death", buried: Jones Cemetery, died: 9 Nov 1915, record (1915) #: 265.

Loyd Monroe PARLIER, born: 12 Sep 1896 in Watauga County, NC, single, parents: Anthony Parlier (Wilkes County, NC) and Amanda Ashley (Watauga County, NC), death cause: "dropsy", informant: Arthur Parlier (Whaley, NC), buried: Fall Creek, NC, died: 10 Dec 1915, record (1915) #: 266.

Arlie M. MORGAN, female, born: 6 Jun 1910, parents: James Morgan and Alice Morgan (NC), death cause: not stated, informant: James Morgan (Shell Creek), buried: Richardson Cem., died: 3 Dec 1015, record #: 267.

Lassie GRINDSTAFF, born: 20 Aug 1914, parents: D.J. Grindstaff and Catherine Osborne, death cause: "gastro enteretis", informant: John Grindstaff (Valley Forge), died: 12 Dec 1915, record (1915) #: 260.

Adline KITE, born: 2 Apr 1847 in North Carolina, Parents: Isham Doby (NC) and Nancy Griff (NC), death cause: "apoplexy", informant: J.H. Starnes (Shell Creek), buried: Doby Cemetery, died: 3 Dec 1915, record (1915) #: 269.

Mark Maynard HYDER, born: 14 Nov 1915, parents: Robert D. Hyder and Mattie Brummit, death cause: "pertussus", buried: Highland Cemetery, died: 16 Dec 1915, record (1915) #: 270.
Josephine Emile JOHNSON, born: 11 Jul 1866, married, parents: J.H. Hyder and Elizabeth Fletcher Hyder, death cause: "heart failure", informant: C.E. Smith (Elizabethton), buried: Highland Cemetery, died: 13 Dec 1915, record (1915) #: 271.
Lee DIXON, age 24 years, parents: James Dixon (NC) and Mandy Thomas (NC), death cause: "tuberculosis of hip", buried: McRath Cemetery, died: 14 Dec 1915, record (1915) #: 272.
Cleo MORRIS, born: 28 Mar 1913, parents: Walter Morris and mother's name illegible, death cause: "croup, diptheria", buried: Keenburg, died: 15 Dec 1915, record (1915) #: 273.
Infant VINES, female, born: 13 Dec 1915, parents: William Vines and Tina Pierce, death cause: "atelectusis", informant: William Vines (Fish Springs), died: 14 Dec 1915, record (1915) #: 274.
Infant BUCKLES, male, parents: F.D. Buckles and Lizzie Smith, death cause: "stillborn", informant: F.D. Buckles (Watauga Valley), born/died: 20 Dec 1915, record (1915) #: 275.
Caroline SHULL, born: 22 Apr 1862, married, parents: George F. Morton and first name not stated Campbell, death cause: "tuberculosis", informant: John Shull (Hampton), died: 23 Dec 1915, record (1915) #: 276.
John Edward GLOVER, born: 17 Nov 1915, parents: John A. Glover and Anna F. Campbell, death cause: "pneumonia fever", informant: Edward Glover (Hampton), died: 17 Dec 1915, record (1915) #: 277.
A.N.D. KITE, born: 15 Aug 1841, married, parents: Anderson Kite and Peggy Landown, death cause: "dysentary", died: 12 Dec 1915, record (1915) #: 278.
Samuel B. LYON, age 2 years, 4 months and 14 days, parents; John Lyon and Jane Glover, death cause: "pneumonia", informant: J.R. Kite, buried: McKeehan Cemetery, died: 16 Dec 1915, record (1915) #: 279.
Lydia HART, age 26 years, parents: Riley Hart and Ellen Shell, death cause: "tuberculosis of lungs", buried: Shell Cemetery, died: 11 Dec 1915, record (1915) #: 280.
Gay SHUPE, born: 23 Jan 1915, parents: Isaac Shupe and Mary Belle Dickson (VA), death cause: "indigestion", buried: Milligan, died: 14 Dec 1915, record #: 281.

Isaac BOWMAN, age 65 years, born in Sullivan County, married, parents: Peter Bowman (Sullivan) and Mary Griffith (NC), death cause: "dropsy", informant: John Peeples (Johnson City), buried: Buck Cemetery, died: 28 Dec 1915, record (1915) #: 282.

Mary Virginia DICKSON, age 19 years, single, born in Sullivan County, parents: Henry Dickson and Nancy N. Smalling, death cause: "tuberculosis", buried: Milligan, died: 30 Dec 1915, record (1915) #: 283.

Alberta GILLIM, black, parents: James M. Gillim (SC) and Ella Hawkins (SC), death cause: not recorded, born/died: 3 Dec 1915, record (1915) #: 284.

Alford MICHAELS, age about 70 years, parents: "don't know", death cause: not stated, buried: Heaton Creek, died: 12 Dec 1915, record (1915) #: 285.

Joe CALHOUN, age about 75 years, parents: "don't know", death cause: not stated, buried: Heaton Creek, died: 16 Dec 1915, record (1915) #: 286.

Fred WINTERS, age about 33 years, parents: Carrirk Winters and mother's name unknown, death cause: not stated, buried: Roan Mountain, died: 24 Dec 1915, record (1915) #: 287.

Pearl ELLISON, born: 29 Aug 1915, parents: Samuel Ellison and Biddie Odom (Mitchell Co., NC), death cause: "pneumonia", informant: Samuel Ellison (Roan Mountain), buried: Lacy Cemetery, died: 20 Jan 1916, record (1916) #: 1.

Smith H. COFFEE, born: 15 May 1821 in North Carolina, married, parents: S. Coffee (NC) and Mary E. Moore (NC), death cause: "paralysis of heart", informant: Mrs. Ada Coffee (Watauga Valley), died: 11 Jan 1916, record (1916) #: 2.

H. Taylor BOWERS, born: 24 Jul 1896, single, parents: C.B. Bowers and Susan (surname illegible), death cause: "lagrippe", died: 23 Jan 1916, record #: 3.

Johnnie LEWIS, parents: W.D. Lewis and Rettie Campbell, death cause: "weak heart", buried: Wilson Cemetery, born/died: 25 Jan 1916, record (1916) #: 4.

Laura RAMSEY, born: 20 Jul 1870, single, parents: H.R. Ramsey and mother's name not known, death cause: "tuberculosis", buried: Roan Mountain, died: 1 Jan 1916, record (1916) #: 5.

Harry CARDIN, born: 27 Jan 1912, parents: Dan Cardin and Naome Moody (NC), death cause: "dropsy", informant: Dan Cardin (Hampton), died: 29 Jan 1916, record (1916) #: 6.

Infant BOWGUS, male, parents: Marshall Bowgus and Linda Grindstaff (Unicoi County), death cause: "congestion of brain", born/died: 30 Jan 1916, record (1916) #: 7.
Walter BLEVINS, age 10 years, parents: Loone Blevins and Mollie Campbell, death cause: "cardiac dropsy", informant: R.M. Pierce (Carter), buried: Garland Cemetery, died: 31 Jan 1916, record (1916) #: 8.
Jaunita Grace GRANT, born: 6 Apr 1915 in Washington Co., VA, parents: Robert E. Grant (Washington Co., VA) and Miner Miller (Washington Co., VA), death cause: "indigestion and atropsy liver", buried: Abingdon, VA, died: 20 Jan 1916, record (1916) #: 9.
Kittie MANNING, female, born: 23 Jul 1871 at Elk Park, NC, parents: D.C. Manning and Rhoda Ellis (Elk Park, NC), death cause: "tuberculosis of lungs", buried: Elk Park, NC, died: 20 Jan 1916, record (1916) #: 10.
Mariah TAYLOR, colored, born: 1844, married, parents: David Stover and Patsey Stover, death cause: "hemorrhage of brain", informant: William Taylor, buried: Cedar Grove, died: 23 Jan 1916, record (1916) #: 11.
Minnie HODGE, age not stated, married, parents: John Williams and Susannah Matherly, death cause: "pulmonary tuberculosis", buried: Jenkins Cemetery, died: 2 Jan 1916, record (1916) #: 12.
Violet WIDENER, age 2 years, parents: Joe Widener (NC) and Addie McClure, death cause: "diptheria", buried: A.J. Little Cemetery, died: 5 Jan 1916, record #: 14.
Monta E. SHELL, born: 11 Oct 1894 in North Carolina, parents: Joe E. Shell and Polly Johnson (NC), death cause: "tuberculosis", informant: Alvin Shell (Platt, NC), buried: Shell Creek, died: 4 Jan 1916, record (1916) #: 13.
Clarence CARTER, age about 2 years, parents: Landon Carter and Nannie Carr, death cause: "acute dysentary", informant: Frank Carter (Elizabethton), buried: Carr Cemetery, died: 6 Jan 1916, record #: 15.
Mrs. Susie Ann STEPHENS, age 87 years, born in Mitchell County, NC, widow, parents: John Gouge (NC) and Susan Sparks (NC), death cause: "chronic apendicitis", informant: W.T. Stephens (Hampton), buried: Stephens Cemetery, died: 9 Jan 1916, record (1916) #: 16.
Infant ODOM, male, born: 1 Jan 1916, parents: Waits Odom (NC) and Sallie Hill, death cause: "unknown", informant: Waits Odom (Hampton), buried: Odom Cemetery, died: 11 Jan 1916, record (1916) #: 17.

Landon C. PERRY, born: 12 Jun 1831, married, parents: Thomas Perry and Nancey Ellis, death cause: "uremia poisoning", informant: R.L. Bowling (Shell Creek), buried: Perry Cem., died: 11 Jan 1916, record #: 18.
Melvina DUGGER, age about 45 years, single, parents: James Dugger (Johnson County) and Nancy Slimp (Johnson County), death cause: "dropsy", buried: Hurley Cemetery, Carter, died: 14 Feb 1916, record (1916) #: 19.
Nancy P. LAWS, born: 30 Mar 1822 in North Carolina, widow, parents: Samuel Montgomery (NC) and (first name not stated) Swanson (NC), death cause: "unknown", informant: D.E. Montgomery (Shell Creek), buried: Cable Cem., died: 21 Feb 1916, record (1916) #: 20.
Russell WEAVER, born: 2 Dec 1856, widower, parents: Henry Weaver and Polly Booker, death cause: probably acute dilitation of heart", informant: William Griffith (Watauga Valley), buried: Wilson Cemetery, died: 18 Feb 1916, record (1916) #: 21.
Lonnie R. HARDIN, born: 8 Sep 1915, parents: R.H. Hardin and Jennie Fletcher, death cause: "pneumonia", informant: W.H. Hardin (Carter), buried: Blevins Cemetery, died: 28 Feb 1916, record (1916) #: 22.
Eave HARRISON, age 94 years, born in Virginia, widow, parents: Enoch Green (VA) and mother's name not given, death cause: "think, old age", informant: George Harrison (Shell Creek), buried: Harrison Cemetery, died: 24 Feb 1916, record (1916) #: 23.
Myrtle MARKLAND, born: 9 Feb 1916, parents: A.C. Markland and Mildred Brown (NC), death cause: not stated, died: 13 Feb 1916, record (1916) #: 24.
Stella SHEAR, Negro, born: 16 Mar 1889 in Boone, NC, married, parents: Helley Horton (Wilkes Co, NC) and Fanny Little (Boone, NC), death cause: "shock in child birth, the child was never delivered", informant: John Shear (Shell Creek), died: 18 Feb 1916, record #: 25.
Decova BROOKS, colored, male, age 9 years and 2 months, parents: father's name "unknown" and Stella Brooks, death cause: "alcoholic poison", informant: Dave Brooks, buried: Cedar Grove, died: 14 Feb 1916, record (1916) #: 26.
Infant WILSON, black, male, parents: Gilbert Wilson (NC) and Minnie Brady, death cause: "stillborn", died: 6 Feb 1916, record (1916) #: 27.
Sarah Bula UNDERWOOD, born: 27 Sep 1910 in Johnson County, parents: John Underwood (NC) and Lillie Vaught (Johnson County), death cause: illegible, informant: John Underwood (Elizabethton), died: 27 Feb 1916, record (1916) #: 28.

Dora GIBBS, colored, age 43 years, married, parents: Sam Wilburn (NC) and Maggie Smith, death cause: "valvulor heart disease", informant: Fain Gibbs (Elizabethton), buried: Odd Fellows Cemetery, died: 25 Feb 1916, record (1916) #: 29.

Calvin HURLEY, age 63 years, widower, parents: Harden Hurley and Nancy Hodge, death cause: "dropsy", informant: James Hurley (Carter), buried: Estep Cemetery, died: 8 Feb 1916, record (1916) #: 30.

Mollie MARKLAND, age 63 years, married, parents: Joseph Robinson (Johnson County) and Delcenia Burty, death cause: "paralysis", informant: W.H. Lowe (Carter), buried: Ensor Cemetery, died: 20 Feb 1916, record (1916) #: 31.

Franklin M. PIERCE, born: 12 Jan 1833, married, parents: George M. Pierce (NC) and Vina Campbell, death cause: "bronchial pneumonia", informant: W.O. Phillips (Fish Springs), buried: Pierce Cemetery, died: 21 Feb 1916, record (1916) #: 32.

George W. LYLE, born: 28 Dec 1845, married, parents: Allen Lyle and mother's name unknown, death cause: "tuberculosis", buried: Sinking Creek, died: 17 Feb 1916, record (1916) #: 33.

Mary Eva JOBE, born: 28 Mar 1850, widow, parents: Nathaniel Taylor and (illegible) Haynes, death cause: "anemia", informant: Rhoda E. Reeves (Johnson City), buried: Happy Valley, died: 2 Feb 1916, record #: 34.

Floid SWANNER, born: 7 May 1899, parents: R.F. Swanner and Sarah Price, death cause: "tuberculosis", died: 28 Feb 1916, record (1916) #: 35.

Infant MATHERLY, female, parents: James Matherly and (illegible) McKInney, death cause: not stated, informant: Frank Glover (Elizabethton), died: 15 Feb 1916, record (1916) #: 36.

Odis WILLIAMS, born: 20 Feb 1914, parents: George Williams and Laura Oliver, death cause: "spinal miningitis", informant: Pat Oliver (Watauga Valley), buried: Bowers Cemetery, died: 25 Feb 1916, record (1916) #: 38.

Infant TESTER, male, parents: L.A. Tester (Watauga Co., NC) and (first name not stated) Dyson (Watauga Co., NC), death cause: "unknown", buried: Elk Mills, born/died: 26 Feb 1916, record (1916) #: 39.

William Harrison RICHARDSON, born: 13 Dec 1916, parents; Ernest Richardson (Watauga Co., NC) and (first name illegible) Cook, death cause: "unknown", informant: Thomas Cook (Shell Creek), buried: Cable Cemetery, died: 21 Feb 1916, record (1916) #: 40.

Infant HOLOWAY, female, born: 27 Feb 1916, parents: father's name not stated and Oda Holoway, death cause: "unknown", informant: Daniel McGee (Fish Springs), buried: Smith Cemetery, died: 28 Feb 1916, record (1916) #: 40.

Hazel HEAD, born: 17 Jan 1915, parents: T.H. Head and Janie Smith, death cause: "croup", informant: T.H. Head (Roan Mountain), buried: Lacy Cemetery, died: 5 Feb 1916, record (1916) #: 41.

Grace CARVER, born: 10 Feb 1916, parents: Elijah Carver and Hulda Moore, death cause: "difficult birth", informant: Henry Moore (Hampton), buried: Whitehead Cemetery, died: 12 Feb 1916, record #: 42.

Daniel TOLLEY, age 86 years, born in North Carolina, parents: Frances Tolley (NC) and Darkei Bennett (NC), death cause: "old age, heart failure, tuberculosis", informant: John Tolley (Hampton), buried: Tolley Cemetery, died: 19 Feb 1916, record (1916) #: 43.

Clarence CLARK, born: 30 Oct 1915, parents: N.H. Clark (Watauga Co., NC) and Sarah Berry, death cause: "boul hives", informant: G.A. Franklin (Hampton), died: 27 Feb 1916, record (1916) #: 45.

Martha YOUNG, born: 20 Oct 1858 in North Carolina, married, parents: Jonas Hughes (NC) and Bettie Honeycutt (NC), death cause: "nervous breakdown", informant: S.S. Young (Roan Mountain), died: 18 Mar 1916, record (1916) #: 46.

Hazel MALONE, black, born: 6 Mar 1916 in Johnson County, parents: A.L. Malone (Johnson County) and Mollie Louerson (Watauga Co., NC), death cause: "tumor of bowels", informant: Alf Maleon (Johnson City), buried: Horton Cemetery, died: 6 Mar 1916, record (1916) #: 47.

Mary Elizabeth JOHNSON, parents: W.C. Johnson and Eliza Cox, death cause: "pneumonia with other complications", buried: Taylor Chapel, born/died: 14 Mar 1916, record (1916) #: 48.

Frankie SHEPHERD, age 3 years, parents: J.A. Shepherd (NC) and (first name illegible) Jarrett (NC), death cause: "broncho pneumonia", buried: Peeples Cemetery, died: 6 Mar 1916, record (1916) #: 49.

Nathaniel Epheaim David BUCK, born: 31 Oct 1883, married, parents: N.T. Buck and Clementine Taylor, death cause: "pulmonary tuberculosis", informant: D.M. Buck (Johnson City), died: 6 Mar 1916, record (1916) #: 50.

William A. HYDER, born in 1869, married, parents: Jesse Hyder and Susan Richard (Sullivan County), death cause: "heart failure from pallegra", informant: Lula Hyder, buried: Hyder Cemetery, died: 7 Mar 1916, record (1916) #: 51.

Eunice SHANKLE, age 4 years, parents: Frank Shankel (VA) and Maggie Shipley, death cause: "whooping cough". buried: Weaver Cemetery, died: 30 Mar 1916, record (1916) #: 52.

Charley HODGE, age 4 months and 9 days, parents: George Hodge and Sarah Jane Garland, death cause: "hives", informant: W.E. Asher (Carter), buried: Estep Cemetery, died: 9 Mar 1916, record (1916) #: 53.

W.A. ORR, born: 18 Nov __, age 52 years, married, parents: James Orr and Annis Perkins, death cause: "heart failure", informant: Robert Orr (Raon Mountain), died: 6 Mar 1916, record (1916) #: 54.

Infant PETERS, male, parents: Powell Peters and Julia Vance, death cause: "pneumonia", buried: Blevins Cemetery, born/died: 11 Mar 1916, record (1916) #: 56.

Bonnie K. GRIFFITH, born: 15 Feb 1916, parents: Frank Griffith and Susie Oliver, death cause: "heart failure", informant: Joe Buckles (Watauga Valley), buried: Buckles Cemetery, died: 28 Mar 1916, record (1916) #: 55.

Leonard H. HARDIN, born: 22 Jul 1915, parents: Alvin Hardin and Bessie Bowers, death cause: "probably congestion of lungs", informant: Bob Hardin (Watauga Valley), buried: Bowers Cemetery, died: 9 Mar 1916, record (1916) #: 57.

Hampton HODGE, age not given, parents: not stated, death cause: "paralysis", informant: W.T. Nave, buried: County Cemetery, died: 21 Mar 1916, record (1916) #: 58.

Earl NAVE, born: 28 Jun 1915, parents: Judson Nave and Euna Treadway, death cause: "broncho pneumonia", buried: Academy Cemetery, died: 25 Mar 1916, record (1916) #: 59.

Andy J. PLEASANT, born: 10 Feb 1852, married, parents: not stated, death cause: "chronic diarrhoea", informant: George Nave (Watauga Valley), buried: Bowers Cem., died: 28 Mar 1916, record (1916) #: 60.

Hickey Rosevelt DAVIS, born: 7 Jun 1907, parents: Link Davis (NC) and Lutice Brown, death cause: "diptheria", buried: Green Hill Cemetery, died: 9 Mar 1916, record (1916) #: 61.

John H. TIPTON, born: 20 Dec 1875, married, parents: J.W. Tiptin and Mary G. Hubble (VA), death cause: "heart failure", informant: James D. Jenkins, buried: Highland Cem., died: 16 Mar 1916, record (1916) #: 62.

Florence Ettie SHELL, born: 1 Mar 1874 in Kentucky, married, parents: W.B. Baker (KY) and Mary Jackson (KY), death cause: "heart failure", buried: Highland Cemetery, died: 18 Mar 1916, record (1916) #: 63.

Hariett HARDIN (or HORTON), colored, age 60 years, parents: Jim Brewer and Rachel Brown Tipton, death cause: "murder", informant: Andy Horton, buried: Cedar Grove, died: 29 Mar 1916, record (1916) #: 64.

F. Devey CABLE, born: 13 Jul 1899, parents: Lafayette Cable and Julia Goodwin, death cause: "pneumonia", informant: S.L. Goodwin (Butler), buried: Goodwin Cemetery, died: 6 Mar 1916, record (1916) #: 65.

Infant SHELL, female, parents: Noah T. Shell and Dora Morrell (Bluff City), death cause: "born dead", buried: Mottern Cemetery, died: 20 Apr 1916, record (1916) #: 66.

Hazel WILLIAMS, born: 23 Apr 1916, parents: S.W. Williams and Lorena Vandeventer, death cause: "unknown", informant: J.P. Vandeventer (Watauga Valley), buried: Buckles Cemetery, died: 23 Apr 1916, record (1916) #: 67.

Infant TAYLOR, male, parents: J.W. Taylor and Ollie Bowman, death cause: "premature birth", buried: Hampton, died: 6 Apr 1916, record (1916) #: 68.

Nannie TRIVETT, born: 28 May 1886, single, parents: J.M. M..(illegible)(Johnson County) and E.J. Wagner (Johnson County), death cause: "pulmonary tuberculosis", buried: Elk Mills, died: 17 Apr 1916, record (1916) #: 69.

Clementine M. LUNCEFORD, born: 18 May 1849, married, parents: Daniel Whitehead and Clementine M. Step, death cause: "tuberculosis", informant: E.M. Lunceford (Hampton), buried: Shell Creek, died: 22 Apr 1916, record (1916) #: 70.

Mary LYONS, born: 12 Nov 1863 in Indiana, married, parents: William Roberts (Indiana) and L. Roberts (Indiana), death cause: "intestinal tuberculosis", informant: William Lyons (Hampton), died: 1 Apr 1916, record (1916) #: 71.

James Franklin LIVINGSTON, born: 21 Nov 1915, parents: George Livingston and Katie Headrick, death cause: "whooping cough", died: 7 Apr 1915, buried: Valley Forge, record (1916) #: 72.

Valentine B. BOWERS, age 68 years, married, parents: William Bowers and Rebecca Waldren, death cause: "heart trouble, hemiphlegia", informant: Martha Ellis (Elizabethton), buried: Bowers Cemetery, died: 12 Apr 1916, record (1916) #: 73.

Wilburn PIERCE, born: 9 Mar 1872, married, parents: William Pierce and Celia Ann Lewis, death cause: "articular rhumatism", informant: Henry Nave (Elizabethton), buried: Pierce Cemetery, died: 19 Apr 1916, record (1916) #: 74.

Henry R. HYDER, born: 16 Dec 1861, married, parents: Samuel W. Hyder and Visa Edens, death cause: "valvulor heart disease", informant: Frank M. Hyder, buried: Oak Grove Cemetery, died: 16 Apr 1916, record (1916) #: 75.

Tina LEWIS, age 82 years, single, parents: Hampton Lewis and mother's name unknown, death cause: "some kind of heart lesion", buried: Sims Cemetery, died: 16 Apr 1916, record (1916) #: 76.

James Herbert LOVELESS, born: 23 Jan 1895, single, parents: W.P. Loveless and Debbie Douglas, death cause: "acute rhumatism", died: 30 Apr 1916, record (1916) #: 77.

C.M. EMMERT, born: 19 Jan 1840, physician, married, parents: Jacob B. Emmert and Catherine Morrell, death cause: "organic heart disease", informant: W.N. Thompson, buried: Highland Cemetery, died: 25 Apr 1916, record (1916) #: 78.

Bettie GILLIAM, colored, age 91 years, born in Virginia, parents: "don't know", death cause: "senility", informant: Walter Gilliam, buried: Drake Cemetery, died: 3 Apr 1916, record (1916) #: 79.

Grace WALKER, born: 11 Feb 1916, parents: Carr Walker and Nancy Lyons, death cause: "bronchitis", informant: C. Walker, buried: Jones Cemetery, died: 27 Apr 1916, record (1916) #: 80.

Edward Scalf GREGG, born: 22 Apr 1916, parents: James L. Gregg and Nannie Scalf, death cause: "premature birth", died: 23 Apr 1916, record (1916) #: 81.

Infant SPEER, male, parents: Edwin Speer and Daisy Smith, death cause: "weakness of mother", informant: Daisy Smith (Carter), buried: Smith Cemetery, died: 8 Apr 1916, record (1916) #: 82.

Nancy JONES, age 76 years, married, parents: Eli (surname illegible) and Nancy (surname illegible), death cause: "bronchitis with kidney affection", died: 13 Apr 1916, record (1916) #: 83.

Infant CAMPBELL, male, parents: Robert Campbell and Lizzie Bowers, death cause: "stillborn", informant: C.B. Williams (Watauga Valley), buried: Academy Cemetery, born/died: 15 Apr 1916, record (1916) #: 84.

Elizabeth S. HAMPTON, age 68 years, born in Telford, TN, married, parents: John Salts (Sullivan County) and Susan Salts, death cause: "epilepsy", informant: David Bowman (Milligan), buried: Payne Cemetery, died: 4 Apr 1916, record (1916) #: 85.

E.A. DOTSON, age 75 years, born in North Carolina, widower, parents: James A. Dotson (NC) and Susie Dawson (NC), death cause: "burned to death in his house", informant: J.G. Barnett (Roan Mountain), buried: Dotson Cemetery, died: 27 Apr 1916, record (1916) #: 86.

Infant WISENHUNT, female, parents: Willy Wisenhunt and Mary McClellan, death cause: "stillborn", buried: Blevins Cemetery, died: 10 Apr 1916, record (1916) #: 87.

Daniel HYDER, born: 10 Oct 1914, parents: D.S. Hyder and Julia Gilbert, death cause: "broncho pneumonia", informant: D.S. Hyder (Hampton), buried: Hyder Cemetery, died: 6 Apr 1916, record (1916) #: 87 (duplicate).

Sallie SAMS, born: 9 Dec 1880, married, parents: Jesse N. Hyder and Susan Richard (Sullivan County), death cause: "lobar pneumonia", informant: W.P. Loveless (Elizabethton), buried: Hyder Cemetery, died: 6 Apr 1916, record (1916) #: 88.

Mrs. Lillie HENRY, born: 5 Apr 1875, married, parents: Jacob Treadway and Katherine Collins, death cause: "pulmonary tuberculosis", informant: S.G. Nave, buried: Charity Hill, died: 4 Apr 1916, record (1916) #: 89.

Mary Ainner PIERCE, born: 31 Mar 1835, widow, parents: Bonua Blevins and Kattie McQueen, death cause: "pneumonia fever", informant: H.S. Pierce (Fish Springs), died: 28 Apr 1916, record (1916) #: 90.

Ray Blain HATLEY, age 2 days, parents: Skiles Hatley and Fannie Davenport, death cause: "supposed to be hives", informant: Skiles Hatley (Butler), died: 20 May 1916, record (1916) #: 91.

Fred SHULER, parents: Hank Shuler and Emma Lenear (Knoxville), death cause: "atalectosis", informant: Houk Shuler (Johnson City), buried: Hughes Cemetery, born/died: 24 May 1916, record (1916) #: 92.

A.B. FAIR, age 47 years, married, parents: Shird Fair and Marthie Fair, death cause: "congested lungs", informant: A.B. Fair (Elizabethton), buried: Jones Cemetery, died: 14 May 1916, record (1916) #: 93.

Worlie WILSON, born; 4 Nov 1898, parents: Smith Wilson and Eliza Garland, death cause: "heart failure", informant: Bate McKinney, buried: McKinney Cemetery, died: 6 May 1916, record (1916) #: 94.

Esther RITCHIE, born: 12 Oct 1886 in Virginia, married, parents: J.L. Johnston (VA) and M.T. Miller (VA), death cause: "dysentary", informant: N.B. Creed (Watauga Valley), buried: Ritchie Cemetery, died: 22 May 1916, record (1916) #: 95.

Infant RITCHIE, parents: Thomas Ritchie and Esther Johnson (VA), death cause: "stillborn", buried: Ritchie Cemetery, born/died: 11 May 1916, record (1916) #: 96 (twin below).

Infant RITCHIE, parents: Thomas Ritchie and Esther Johnson (VA), death cause: "stillborn", buried: Ritchie Cemetery, born/died: 11 May 1916, record (1916) #: 97.

James O. SAYLOR, born: 12 Oct 1893 in Scott County, VA, parents: Flanders Saylor (VA) and Margaret Sdipery (VA), death cause: "murder by gunshot, homicide", buried: Johnson City, died: 8 May 1916, record (1916) #: 98.

Infant PERRY, male, born: 20 May 1916, parents: George Perry and Lizzie Hampton, death cause: "premature birth", informant: R.A. Range, buried: Sullivan County, died: 21 May 1916, record #: 99 (twin below).

Infant PERRY, male, born: 20 May 1916, parents: George Perry and Lizzie Hampton, death cause: "premature birth", informant: R.A. Range, buried: Sullivan County, died: 21 May 1916, record (1916) #: 100.

Hazel ARNOLD, born: 3 May 1915, parents: Claud Arnold and Eliza Pierce, death cause: "whooping cough", informant: Richard Pierce (Carter), buried: Ensor Cemetery, died: 14 May 1916, record (1916) #: 101.

John Henry ANDERSON, born: 17 Jun 1847 in North Carolina, married, parents: C.M. Anderson (NC) and Margaret (surname illegible), death cause: "chronic heart trouble", informant: F.A. Anderson (Johnson City), buried: Highland Cemetery, died: 20 May 1916, record (1916) #: 102.

Mike TAYLOR, born: 28 Feb 1873, single, parents: L.D. Taylor and Elizabeth Ritchie, death cause: "pellagra", buried: Ritchie Cem., died: 18 May 1916, record #:103.

Malinda HARDIE, colored, age 72 years, widow, death cause: "don't know", death cause: "aortic insufficiency", informant: George W. Tinner, died: 6 May 1916, record (1916) #: 106.

William TAYLOR, colored, age 76 years, widower, parents: Reyfus Taylor and Moriah Stover, death cause: "aortic insufficiency", informant: Will Taylor, Jr., buried: Cedar Grove, died: 3 May 1916, record #: 105.

Z.J. CROY, born: 19 Nov 1832 in Montgomery County, VA, parents: Udem Croy (VA) and Elizabeth Smith (VA), death cause: "chronic diarrhoea", buried: G.W. Mottern Cemetery, died: 20 May 1916, record (1916) #: 106.

Gustava MCKINNEY, parents; Walter McKinney and Maude Stevens, death cause: "stillborn", informant: E. Howell (Unicoi County), buried: Lewis Cemetery, born/died: 4 May 1916, record (1916) #: 107.

John Wesley PIPPIN, age 63 years, born in Virginia, married, parents: Henry Pippin and mother's name unknown, death cause: "tuberculosis", informant: S.B. Pippin (Roan Mountain), died: 28 May 1916, record (1916) #: 108.

Sarah Netie FREEMAN, born: 14 Oct 1915, parents: Henry Freeman and Dollie Arnett, death cause: "unknown", informant: Bill Miller (Roan Mountain), died: 30 May 1916, record (1916) #: 109.

Thomas MORGAN, born: 19 May 1856 in South Carolina, parents: Charlie Morgan and mother's name unknown, death cause: "pneumonia fever", informant: Lasson Morgan (Roan Mountain), died: 19 May 1916, record (1916) #: 110.

Essie Mable SHELL, born: 28 Apr 1916, parents: Hurbert Shell (NC) and mother's name illegible, death cause: "found dead in bed", informant: Hubert Shell (Shell Creek), buried: Richardson Cemetery, died: 11 May 1916, record (1916) #: 111.

Lillie BLEVINS, born: 6 Jan 1901, parents: Charlie Blevins (VA) and Clemie Blevins, death cause: "dysentary", informant: W.A. Rice (Johnson City), died: 18 Jun 1916, record (1916) #: 112.

Pearl RICHARDS, age 22 years, married, parents: Griff Minton (NC) and Cinda Richards, death cause: "probably tuberculosis of intestines", informant: Will Collins (Watauga Valley), died: 21 Jun 1916, record #: 113.

Mollie J. BILLINGS, born: 6 Jan 1858 in North Carolina, married, parents: Enoch McNeil (NC) and Elizabeth Miller (NC), death cause: "chronic gastritis and nervous indigestion", informant: R.C. Billings (Watauga Valley), died: 7 Jun 1916, record #: 114.

Lillie E. SIGLER, born: 17 Sep 1887, married, parents: Jim Brck and Mary Nave, death cause: "cancer of uterus", informant: D.F. Nave, buried: Nave Cemetery, died: 7 Jun 1916, record (1916) #: 115.

Darsie HARDIN, born: 20 Jan 1915, age 1 year, 4 months and 20 days, parents: Harrison Hardin and first name illegible, Holoway, death cause: "teething and diarrhoea", informant: James Hardin, buried: Hardin Cemetery, died: 18 Jun 1916, record (1916) #: 116.

Vera RADFORD, born: 30 Dec 1910, parents: Austin Radford and Clircie Waycaster, death cause: "broncho pneumonia", died: 10 Jun 1916, record (1916) #: 117.

George W. GARLAND, age 67 years, widower, parents: Monte Garland and Hannah Wilson (VA), death cause: "think stock of paralysis", informant: Dave Garland (Shell Creek), buried: Markland Cemetery, died: 12 Jun 1916, record (1916) #: 118.

Ruth BUCK, born: 8 Dec 1915, parents: Charles Buck and Callie Barker, death cause: "hives", informant: Charlie Buck (Shell Creek), buried: Buck Cemetery, died: 10 Jun 1916, record (1916) #: 119.

Lillie BLEVINS, born: 15 Jun 1901, parents: Charlie Blevins (VA) and (first name illegible) Blevins, death cause: "flux, measles", informant: James Prichard (Johnson City), buried: Hughes Cemetery, died: 15 Jun 1916, record (1916) #: 120.

Fred Carr DEMPSY, born: 27 Apr 1896 in Sullivan County, single, parents: John A. Dempsy (SC) and Martha Ann Carr (Sullivan County), death cause: illegible, buried: Piney Flats, died: 5 Jun 1916, record (1916) #: 121.

Fred BURROW, born: 10 Feb 1914, parents: R.B. Burrow and Mattie Jennings (NC), death cause: "diptheria", informant: R.B. Burrow (Hampton), died: 10 Jun 1916, record (1916) #: 122.

Amanda STOUT, born: 5 Apr 1870 in Johnson County, married, parents: Daniel Ward (Johnson County) and Nancy Moreland (Johnson County), death cause: "tuberculosis of lungs", informant: A.G. Stout (Elizabethton), buried: Neva, TN., died: 20 Jun 1916, record (1916) #: 123.

Emana GOODE, colored, born: 24 Mar 1880 in Burke County, GA, married, parents: Handy Griffin (GA) and Mary Griffin (GA), death cause: "pulmonary tuberculosis", informant: D. Goode, buried: Cedar Grove Cemetery, died: 11 Jun 1916, record (1916) #: 124.

Infant TINNER, black, parents: James A. Tinner and Lula Baker, death cause: "born dead", buried: McRath Cemetery, born/died: 1 Jun 1916, record (1916) #: 125.
Adam WAGNER, born: 19 Apr 1915 in North Carolina, parents: Elis Wagner (NC) and Rachel (surname illegible), death cause: "cholera", died: 11 Jun 1916, record (1916) #: 126.
Mary GUESS, parents: Charles Guess (Sullivan County) and Lieda Floyd (Sullivan County), death cause: "premature birth", buried: Hyder Cemetery, born/died: 14 Jun 1916, record (1916) #: 127 (twin's record below).
Marie Catherine SHAW, born: 15 Apr 1915 in Johnson County, parents: John Shaw (Johnson County) and Ellie Stevens, death cause: "diarrhoea", buried: Hyder Cemetery, died: 25 Jun 1916, record (1916) #: 128.
Sarah TAYLOR, born: 8 Dec 1865 in Hardin County, KY, married, parents: Robert Hunt (VA) and M.A. Blevins (Johnson County), death cause: "pellagra", informant: Mrs. M.A. Hunt (Elizabethton), buried: Highland Cemetery, died: 21 Jun 1916, record (1916) #: 129.
Henry GUESS, parents: Charles Guess (Sullivan County) and Lieda Floyd (Sullivan County), death cause: "premature birth", buried: Hyder Cemetery, born/died: 14 Jun 1916, record (1916) #: 130.
Wiley J. MARLEY, born: 7 Apr 1868, married, parents: father not stated, father born in North Carolina, and Dicy Copley (NC), death cause: "injury by fall of tree", informant: Charles Pierce (Watauga Valley), buried: Pierce Cemetery, died: 9 Jun 1916, record (1916) #: 131.
Howard Kenneth WILSON, born: 13 Jun 1916, parents: James Wilson and Jane Oliver, death cause: not stated, informant: James Wilson (Hampton), buried: Wilson Cemetery, died: 14 Jun 1916, record (1916) #: 132.
Dortha CAMPBELL, born: 13 Mar 1916, parents: Charles Campbell and Sallie McIntosh, death cause: "congenital heart disease", informant: Paul Campbell (Hampton), died: 2 Jul 1916, record (1916) #: 133.
Thomas Wilson PETERS, born: 8 Feb 1891, married, parents: Bill Peters and Angie Markland, death cause: "pulmonary tuberculosis", informant: Angie Peters (Hampton), died: 3 Jul 1916, record (1916) #: 134.
Ruley JONES, female, born: 9 Jul 1916, parents: Austin Jones (NC) and Rosa Osborn, death cause: "delivery", informant: Austin Jones (Hampton), died: 11 Jul 1916, record (1916) #: 135.

Infant FREEMAN, female, parents: Elik Freeman and Becky McKinney, death cause: "stillborn", informant: Sarah Freeman (Roan Mountain), born/died: 24 Jul 1916, record (1916) #: 136.

J.R. ANDERSON, age 69 years, married, parents: Richard Anderson (GA) and (first name not stated) Oliver, death cause: "locomotor ataxie", buried: Watauga Valley, died: 24 Jul 1916, record (1916) #: 137.

Infant HURLEY, male, age about 6 weeks, parents: Tennessee Hurley and Sarah Wilson, death cause: "tonsilitis", informant: Levi Nidiffer (Carter), buried: Estep Cemetery, died: 4 Jul 1916, record (1916) #: 138.

Ray HUGHES, born: 13 Jul 1913, parents: D.W. Hughes and Fannie Fair (NC), death cause: "dysentary", buried: Hughes Cemetery, died: 4 Jul 1916, record (1916) #: 139.

Rebecca Jane DOTSON, born: 18 Sep 1886 in Sullivan County, married, parents: William Henry Dickison and Ann Smalling, death cause: "pulmonary tuberculosis", buried: Kingsport, TN, died: 1 Jul 1916, record (1916) #: 140.

Infant SHUPE, female, born: 7 Jul 1917, parents: Isaac Shupe (Johnson County) and May B. Dickison (Sullivan County), death cause: "premature", buried: Milligan, died: 9 Jul 1916, record (1916) #: 141.

Mrs. Maggie Elizabeth GILES, born: 11 Sep 1840 in Sullivan County, parents: Randolph McAllister (Ireland) and Rebecca Hayes (Sullivan County), death cause: "acute indigestion", buried: Milligan Cemetery, died: 28 Jul 1916, record (1916) #: 142.

Lizzie Bell LIVINGSTON, born: 3 May 1916, parents: John Livingston adn Eliza Humphrey, death cause: "cholera", died: 12 Jul 1916, record (1916) #: 143.

Infant STOUT, male, born: 21 Apr 1916, parents: Will Stout and Nannie Feathers, death cause: not stated, buried: Turkeytown, died: 20 Jul 1916, record (1916) #: 144.

May BLACKBURN, born: 5 Jul 1916, parents: Walter Blackburn (NC) and Mary Wagner (NC), death cause: "pneumonia", died: 15 Jul 1916, record (1916) #: 145.

Infant TURBYFIELD, male, born: Aug (day not stated) 1915 in Sullivan County, parents: John Turbyfield (NC) and Ellen Roberts (VA), death cause: "ilio colitis", buried: Colbaugh Cemetery, died: 27 Jul 1916, record (1916) #: 146.

Alva NEALY, born: 19 Oct 1836 in North Carolina, widow, parents: Haynes Kilog (NC) and Franie Adams, death cause: "senility", informant: Mrs. J.C. Laws (Elizabethton), buried: Colbaugh Cemetery, died: 20 Jul 1916, record (1916) #: 147.

Infant FAIR, male, parents: John H. Fair and Una Bell Blackburn, death cause: "born dead", informant: James H. Fair (Elizabethton), buried: Hyder Cemetery, born/died: 17 Jul 1916, record (1916) #: 148.

Clyde RAINS, born: 13 Feb 1905, parents: D.K. Rains and Lizzie Markland, death cause: "acute dysentary", informant: M.L. Holly (Elizabethton), buried: Green Hill Cem., died: 21 Jul 1916, record (1916) #: 149.

Pauline FAIR, born: 15 Feb 1916, parents: Jerry Fair and Victoria Nave, death cause: "acute indigestion", informant: Jerry Fair, buried: Highland Cemetery, died: 28 Jul 1916, record (1916) #: 150.

Hosa TOLLEY, male, parents: Samson Tolley and Laura Willis (NC), death cause: "stillborn", informant: Samson Tolley (Roan Mountain), born/died: 2 Jul 1916, record (1916) #: 151.

Emma SIMERLY, born: 24 Jun 1915, parents: John B. Simerly and Ida Hyder, death cause: "cholera", informant: W.M. Simerly (Hampton), died: 20 Jul 1916, record (1916) #: 152.

Gomer STREET, born: 28 Jul 1916, parents: Bud Street and Nancy Jones (NC), death cause: not stated, informant: Jessie Triplett (Roan Mountain), died: 30 Jul 1916, record (1916) #: 153.

B. Caroline STEER, age 87 years, parents: first name not stated, Greer (Watauga County, NC) and Mickey Greer (Watauga County, NC), death cause: "pneumonia fever", died: 9 Jul 1916, record (1916) #: 154.

Fred SHIPLEY, born: 29 Oct 1910 in Sullivan County, parents: J.M. Shipley and M.L. Shipley, death cause: "acute dysentery", informant: John Vandeventer (Watauga), buried: Webb Cemetery, died: 5 Jul 1916, record (1916) #: 155.

Mary C. WINTERS, born: 10 Mar 1851 in Caldwell County, NC, married, parents: Henry Webb (NC) and Nancy Meramer (NC), death cause: illegible, informant: Henry T. Norman (Elk Park, NC), buried in North Carolina, died: 13 Aug 1916, record (1916) #: 156.

Mollie POTTER, born: 7 May 1865 in North Carolina, married, parents: Allen Hamby (NC) and Nancy Hamby (NC), death cause: "cancer of uterus", informant: Sam Potter (Shell Creek), buried: Potter Cemetery, died: 26 Aug 1916, record (1916) #: 157.

Richard GLOVER, born: 16 Aug 1837 in Virginia, married, parents: Steven Glover (VA) and Susan Thomas (VA), death cause: "nephritis", informant: Mary Glover (Elizabethton), died: 1 Aug 1916, record #: 158.

Nat HONEYCUTT, born: 25 Dec 1871, married, parents: Robert Honeycutt and Nancy Miller, death cause: "hemorage of lungs", informant: M.S. Cannon (Johnson City), died: 1 Aug 1916, record (1916) #: 159.

Mrs. Malissa DAVIS, age 30 years, married, parents: W.H. Jones (Sullivan County) and Cordie Collins, death cause: "nervous frustration", buried: Lyons Cemetery, died: 3 Aug 1916, record (1916) #: 160.

Maggie Maud GRACE, born: 20 May 1916, parents: John Grace and Catherine Salts (VA), death cause: "bold hives or hooping cough", buried: Valley Forge, died: 8 Aug 1916, record (1916) #: 161.

Archie HOPSON, age 11 years, parents: Marian Hopson and Mary Whitson, death cause: "dysentary (flux)", informant: J.S.E. Range (Elizabethton), died: 8 Aug 1916, record (1916) #: 162.

Eugin NAVE, born: 22 Sep 1915, parents: D.E. Nave and Ethel Berry, death cause: "dysentary", died: 9 Aug 1916, record (1916) #: 163.

Mary E. ELLIOTT, born: 5 Jan 1845, widow, parents: Eli Fletcher and Vina Nave, death cause: "tuberculosis and age", informant: J.C. Campbell (Hampton), buried: Siam Community, died: 9 Aug 1916, record (1916) #: 164.

Carolina WARD, born: 15 Sep 1841 in North Carolina, widow, parents: Charles Holder (NC) and Peggie Green (NC), death cause: not stated, informant: Jessie Triplett (Roan Mtn), died: 9 Aug 1916, record #: 165.

Zora HODGE, male, born: 26 Mar 1916, parents: Will Hodge and Catherine Taylor, death cause: "bronchitis", informant: Roy Asher (Carter), buried: Richardson Cemetery, died: 9 Aug 1916, record (1916) #: 166.

Henry DELOACH, born: 10 May 1916, parents: Robert Deloach and (first name illegible) Crumley (Scott County, VA), death cause: "infantile diarrhoea", died: 10 Aug 1916, record (1916) #: 167.

Mary C. HENDRIX, born: 13 Sep 1844, married, parents: William Feathers (Sullivan County) and Elizabeth Myers (Sullivan County), death cause: "pneumonia", informant: C.T. Hendrix, buried: Highland Cemetery, died: 13 Aug 1916, record (1916) #: 168.

Charles Ray CLARKE, born: 10 Jun 1916, parents: O.W. Clarke (Johnson County) and Rossie Alice Dickens (Johnson County), death cause: "dysentary", buried: Colbaugh Cem, died: 13 Aug 1916, record (1916) #: 169.

Wiley Stacy SMITH, born: 18 Nov 1896, student, parents: J.A. Smith and Minnie Goodwin (Johnson County), death cause: "pellagra", buried: Highland Cemetery, died: 15 Aug 1916, record (1916) #: 170.
Alex PIERSON, black, born: 1 Dec 1842 in North Carolina, parents: "unknown", death cause: "pulmonary tuberculosis", informant: Walter Pierson (Johnson City), buried: Buffalo Cemetery, died: 15 Aug 1916, record (1916) #: 171.
Hazel ESTEP, born: 29 Sep 1915, parents: Jacob Estep and (first name illegible), Holder, death cause: "cholera", informant: Jack Campbell (Carter), buried: Richardson Cemetery, died: 16 Aug 1916, record #: 172.
Mrs. Susie COLE, age 55 years, born in Sullivan County, married, parents: Anderson Carr (Sullivan County) and Mary Trusler (Sullivan County), death cause: "broncho pneumonia", buried: Buck Cemetery, died: 16 Aug 1916, record (1916) #: 173.
Lucy ARCHER, born: 27 Jul 1845, married, parents: Henry Dickson and Annie Smalling, death cause: "pulmonary tuberculosis", died: 18 Aug 1916, record (1916) #: 174.
Maggie HONEYCUTT, age 1 year and 28 days, parents: Sam Honeycutt and Berthie Hampton, death cause: "dysentery", died: 18 Aug 1916, record (1916) #: 175.
Robert CARROLL, born: 9 Nov 1915, parents: Robert Carroll and Alice Daniels, death cause: illegible, buried: Taylors Chapel, died: 20 Aug 1916, record (1916) #: 176.
John Manley GOUGE, born: 18 Aug 1916, parents: Ruby Gouge and Addie Birchfield (Unicoi County), death cause: "convulsions", informant: Elisah Collins (Hampton), buried: Simerly Cemetery, died: 20 Aug 1916, record (1916) #: 177.
Nelson CANON, age 86 years, parents: "unknown", informant: Landon Wilson (Watauga Valley), died: 20 Aug 1916, record (1916) #: 178.
Manuel TAYLOR, colored, female, born: 2 May 1911, parents: Will Taylor and Manda Crawford (Washington County, TN), death cause: "pellagra", buried: Cedar Grove, died: 21 Aug 1916, record (1916) #: 179.
Everett MORTON, age 3 years and 1 month, parents: E.E. Morton and Dollie Gouge, death cause: "intestinal tuberculosis", died: 23 Aug 1916, record #: 180.
Mary Elizabeth HAMPTON, age 1 year and 3 months, parents: Steward Hampton (Washington County, TN) and Florence Johnson (Green County), death cause: "dysentary", died: 23 Aug 1916, record (1916) #: 181.

Miss Margaret Matilda WRIGHT, age 31 years and 11 months, born in Washington County, VA, parents: Samuel Smitherman Wright and Rebecca Mangle Hughes (Washington Co., VA), death cause: "pellagra", informant: W.S. Taylor, buried: Milligan, died: 23 Aug 1916, record (1916) #: 182.

Pollie MCKINNEY, age 89 years, born in North Carolina, widow, parents: Thomas Gouge (NC) and Sallie Gouge (NC), death cause: "paralysis", informant: David McKinney (Hampton), buried: McKinney Cemetery, died: 24 Aug 1916, record (1916) #: 183.

R.R. ALFRED, born: 18 Aug 1916, parents: John H. Alford and Dora Ritchie, death cause: "hurt at birth", informant: John Alford (Carter), buried: Ritchie Cemetery, died: 26 Aug 1916, record (1916) #: 184.

John H. PERSINGER, born: 1 Jul 1841 in Virginia, married, parents: George Persinger (VA) and Julia Ann Carper (VA), death cause: "carcinoma of rectum", informant: G.H. Persinger (Johnson City), buried: Patton Cem., died: 27 Aug 1916, record (1916) #: 185.

Floyd OLIVER, age 4 years, parents: Pat Oliver and (first name not given), Bowers, death cause: "cholera", buried: Teter Bowers Cemetery, died: 28 Aug 1916, record (1916) #: 186.

Anna TAYLOR, parents: James Taylor and Maggie Colbaugh, death cause: "pertussis", informant: Frank Markland (Carter), buried: Taylor Cemetery, born/died: 5 Aug 1916, record (1916) #: 187.

James BUCHANAN, age about 53 years, born in North Carolina married, parents: father not stated and Elizabeth Buchanan, death cause: "fel dead at work", informant: E.M. Woodruff (Shell Creek), buried: Richardson Cemetery, died: 5 Aug 1916, record #: 188.

W.E. HUNTER, born: 20 Jul 1873, married, parents: D.E.E. Hunter and Mollie Jobe, death cause: "auguia pectoris", buried: Highland Cemetery, died: 28 Aug 1916, record (1916) #: 189.

Infant WILLIAMS, male, parents: Bryan Williams and (first name illegible), Williams, death cause: "stillborn", buried: Highland Cemetery, died: 26 Aug 1916, record (1916) #: 190.

Infant STOUT, female, parents: George W. Stout (Johnson County) and Maud Adams (Washington County), death cause: "born dead", buried: Highland Cemetery, born/died: 13 Aug 1916, record (1916) #: 191.

Infant SIMERLY, male, parents: Dan Simerly and Biddie Carrier, death cause: "stillborn", informant: W.M. Simerly, died: 17 Aug 1916, record (1916) #: 192.

Martha AVERY, black, born: 6 Sep 1901, parents: Tom Avery (NC) and Susa Shade (NC), death cause: "peritoniter", buried: Shell Creek, died: 6 Sep 1916, record (1916) #: 193.
Daniel Henry HAMPTON, born: 4 Mar 1844, married, parents: Losson Hampton and Polly Vance, death cause: "valvulor heart disease, nephritis", informant: W.L. Hampton, buried: Highland Cemetery, died: 1 Sep 1916, record (1916) #: 194.
Annie Jean WILLIAMS, born: 15 Sep 1849, married, parents: Charles Headrick and Rose Anah Chambers, death cause: "osto mo locia and epilepsy", informant: W.L. Williams, buried: Williams Cemetery, died: 3 Sep 1916, record (1916) #: 195.
Mattie Cox DENTON, age 65 years, parents: Jim Cox and Rachel Douglas, death cause: "tuberculosis of bowels", informant: Joe Sampson (Milligan), buried: Milligan Cemetery, died: 6 Sep 1916, record (1916) #: 196.
James WILSON, born: 7 Nov 1868 in Yancey County, NC, married, parents: Jordan Wilson (Yancey County) and Harriett Wilson (Yancey County), death cause: "dysentary", informant: Andy Wilson (Johnson City), buried: Taylor Cem., died: 8 Sep 1916, record #: 197.
Augusta A. WINTER, female, single, born: 8 Nov 1878 in Atlanta, GA, parents: Henry Winter (Indiana), and Mary B. Winter (GA), death cause: "suicide by firearm (pistol)", buried: Atlanta Georgia, died: 11 Sep 1916, record (1916) #: 198.
James GILBERT, Jr., born: 1856, married, parents: James Gilbert, Sr. and Matilda Williams, death cause: "pneumonia", informant: Frank Markland, buried: Grindstaff Cem, died: 11 Sep 1916, record #: 199.
Gourley SWANER, born: 16 Jul 1916, parents: Luther Swaner and Julia Clark, death cause: "broncho pneumonia", informant: N.H. Clark (Hampton), buried: Berry Cem., died: 13 Sep 1916, record (1916) #: 200.
Bryan FRENCH, age 76 years, 7 months and 15 days, married, inmate at soldier's home, parents: "don't know", death cause: "rhumatic fever", informant: Jane French (Milligan), buried: Milligan Cemetery, died: 20 Sep 1916, record (1916) #: 201.
Charlie DELOACH, born: 13 Jul 1916 in Knoxville, parents: Henry Deloach and M. Russell, death cause: "cholera", died: 20 Sep 1916, record (1916) #: 202.
Selma OLIVER, female, age about 4 years, parents: Walter Oliver and Decia Feathers (Sullivan County), death cause: "tuberculosis, dysentary", died: 21 Sep 1916, record (1916) #: 203.

Clyde CREEDE, age 5 months, parents: G.W. Creede and Delie Pain, death cause: "dysentary (flux)", buried: Pain Cem., died: 22 Sep 1916, record (1916) #: 204.

Louisa HOSS, born: 4 Feb 1915, parents: Clifton Hoss and Matilda Lewis, death cause: "broncho pneumonia", informant: George Hoss (Shell Creek), buried: Perry Cemetery, died: 24 Sep 1916, record (1916) #: 205.

Minnie Elizabeth DALTON, black, age 1 year, 5 months and 28 days, parents: Willie Dalton (Johnson City) and Ethel Gills (NC), death cause: "dysentary", informant: Wheeler Connelly (Milligan), buried: Taylor Cemetery, died: 25 Sep 1916, record (1916) #: 206.

Chrisly CHANCE, age 73 years, poor house inmate, parents: "unknown", death cause: "paralysis", died: 28 Sep 1916, record (1916) #: 207.

Paul Raymon ARNOLD, born: 15 Oct 1913, parents: John Arnold and Ida Lunceford, death cause: not stated, inormant: John Arnold (Hampton), buried: Butler, died: 30 Sep 1916, record (1916) #: 208.

Infant LITTLE, male, parents: Walter Little (Unicoi County) and Abby Norris (Unicoi County), death cause: "stillborn due to twisted cord", buried: Little Cem., born/died: 26 Sep 1916, record (1916) #: 209.

Infant FAIR, male, parents: S.S. Fair and Mattie Bradshaw (Hawkins County), death cause: "born dead", buried: Highland Cemetery, died: 28 Sep 1916, record (1916) #: 210.

Winfield OLIVER, age 55 years, parents: James Oliver and (first name not stated) Pain, death cause: "blood poison", died: 3 Oct 1916, record (1916) #: 211.

Etta STREET, age 27 years, born in North Carolina, married, parents: W.M. Honeycutt (NC) and Bettie Street (NC), death cause: "pulmonary tuberculosis", informant: H.M. Street (Hampton), buried: Honeycutt Cemetery, died: 1 Oct 1916, record (1916) #: 212.

Houston MYERS, born: 11 Mar 1847, married, parents: Marian Myers (Bristol) and Annie (surname illegible, possibly Hoss ?)(Bristol), death cause: "motral regugatitis", informant: Byon Myers, buried: Green Hill Cemetery, died: 2 Oct 1916, record (1916) #: 213.

Nat T. BRADLEY, age 63 years, married, parents: James Bradley and Polly Moor, death cause: "tuberculosis of bowels", informant: S.T. Bradley, buried: Bradley Cemetery, died: 10 Oct 1916, record (1916) #: 214.

Jennie TAYLOR, colored, female, age 30 years, widow, parents: father's name unknown and Julia Erwin (NC), death cause:: "tuberculosis", buried: Cedar Grove, died: 8 Oct 1916, record (1916) #: 215.

Caroline CONSTABLE, born: 11 Dec 1836, married, parents: Jim McKeehan (NC) and Caroline McKeehan, death cause: "cancer", informant: J.H. Constable (Elizabethton), buried: Hyder Cemetery, died: 26 Oct 1916, record (1916) #: 216.

Anna Grace MORRELL, born: 3 Jul 1890, married, parents: John F. Ryan and Mollie Bowers, death cause: "..illegible, carcinoma", informant: L.T. Morrell (Elizabethton), buried: Highland Cemetery, died: 28 Oct 1916, record (1916) #: 217.

Othie Mae GOODE, colored, born: 22 Mar 1915, parents: D. Goode and C.J. Goode (GA), death cause: "tuberculosis", informant: George Goode, buried: Cedar Grove, died: 22 Oct 1916, record (1916) #: 218.

Bonnie Dell BARNES, born: 19 Feb 1916, parents: Avery Barnes and N..(illegible) Grindstaff, death cause: "whooping cough", informant: J.E. Davis, buried: Slagle Cem., died: 11 Oct 1916, record (1916) #: 219.

John Gilbert PETERS, born: 12 Aug 1914, parents: Alf Peters and Belle Loveless, death cause: "hooping cough", informant: Harrison Hardin, buried: Peters Cemetery, died: 26 Oct 1916, record (1916) #: 220.

Luther Blane NAVE, born: 25 Jan 1912, parents: R.W. Nave and Julia Goodwin, death cause: "diptheria", informant: R.W. Nave (Hampton), died: 20 Oct 1916, record (1916) #: 221.

Herman JORDAN, born: 23 Oct 1916, parents: John Jordan and Ader Pierce, death cause: "not known", buried: Blevins Cem., died: 26 Oct 1916, record (1916) #: 222.

George Washington HOBSON, born: 20 Sep 1896, single, parents: Jackson Hobson (Mitchell Co., NC) and Catherine Potter (Mitchell Co., NC), death cause: "typhoid fever", buried: Shell Creek, died: 31 Oct 1916, record (1916) #: 223.

Ned Leon SORRELL, born: 19 May 1915, parents: M.E. Sorrell and Myrtle Lambert, death cause: "diptheria", informant: W.A. Sorrell (Hampton), died: 19 Oct 1916, record (1916) #: 224.

Willie BOWMAN, born: 3 Jul 1895, married, parents: S.M. Bowman and Mary E. McKinney, death cause: "typhoid", informant: S.M. Bowman (Hampton), died: 14 Oct 1916, record (1916) #: 225.

Thomas FONDERANT, born: 2 Jul 1853, married, parents: William Fondren and Crochia (left blank), death cause: "Brights disease", informant: S.A. Fondren (Elizabethton), buried: Hampton, died: 2 Oct 1916 (death date must be an error), buried: 30 Oct 1916, record (1916) #: 226.

Richard H. SANDERS, born: 19 Feb 1848 in North Carolina, married, parents: "don't know", death cause: "perincious enemia", informant: Floyd Sanders (Johnson City), buried: Taylors Chapel, died: 2 Oct 1916, record (1916) #: 227.

Infant JOHNSON, male, parents: Stuart Johnson and Bertha Heaton, death cause: "stillborn", buried: Roan Mountain, born/died: 28 Oct 1916, record #: 228.

Infant JORDAN, mele, parents: John Jordan and Adas Pierce, death cause: "stillborn", informant: W.B. Pierce (Carter), buried: Blevins Cemetery, died: 23 Oct 1916, record (1916) #: 229.

Elen CLOSSON, age about 45 years, married, parents: Peter Potter and Patty Guin, death cause: "lagripp", informant: William Vines (Dark Ridge, NC), buried: Closson Cem., died: 8 Nov 1916, record (1916) #: 230.

Assa PHILLIPS, born: 26 Jul 1855 in North Carolina, widow, parents: John Nilson and Nancy Wilson (NC), death cause: "heart disease", informant: Isaac Phillips (NC), buried: Honeycutt Cemetery, died: 21 Nov 1916, record (1916) #: 231.

Tom HOPSON, age 28 years, single, born in North Carolina, parents: Marian Hopson and Mary (surname illegible), death cause: "acute toxemia, myocarditis", informant: J.S.E. Range (Johnson City), buried: Taylor Cemetery, died: 6 Nov 1916, record (1916) #: 232.

Griff H. MINTON, age 70 years, married, parents: "unknown", death cause: "apoplixy", died: 21 Nov 1916, record (1916) #: 233.

Granville COLLINS, born: 19 Sep 1916, parents: Dock Collins and Sallie Williams, death cause: "whooping cough", informant: Grant Collins (Elizabethton), buried: Bowers Cemetery, died: 8 Nov 1916, record (1916) #: 234.

Nora ANDERSON, born: 12 Oct 1916, parents: Grant Anderson and Lula J. Foster, death cause: "unknown", informant: Grant Anderson (Siam), died: 28 Nov 1916, record (1916) #: 235.

Annie STOUT, born: 27 Sep 1915, born: Watdon Arkansas, parents: James Stuart (Edgefield, SC) and Lela Deffenbough (Arkansas), death cause: "meningitis", buried: Colbaugh Cemetery, died: 29 Nov 1916, record (1916) #: 236.

Frank BRADLEY, born: 5 Oct 1910, parents: W.T. Bradley and Georgia M. Hagan, death cause: "tuberculosis", informant: Georgia Bradley, buried: Bradley Cemetery, died: 13 Nov 1916, record (1916) #: 237.

Infant ROBERSON, male, parents: C.S. Roberson and Stella Taylor, death cause: "born dead", buried: Highland Cem., died: 2 Nov 1916, record (1916) #: 238.
Annie Evley SIMERLY, born: 12 Jul 1913, parents: Charlie Simerly and Burtha Shell, death cause: "broncho pneumonia", informant: Charlie Simerly (Shell Creek), buried: Wilson Cemetery, died: 13 Nov 1916, record (1916) #: 239.
Howard, CURTIS, parents: William Curtis and Helen Kidwell, death cause: "whooping cough", buried: Mottern Cem., died: 6 Mar 1916, record (1916) #: 240.
Ina Vaneda HINKLE, age 7 years, parents: not stated, death cause: "whooping cough", buried: Garland Cemetery, died: 19 Nov 1916, record (1916) #: 241.
Henry GARLAND, born: 15 Jul 1914 in Sullivan County, parents: J.C. Garland and Lizzie Richardson (Sullivan County), death cause: "worms", buried: Stoney Creek, died: 12 Nov 1916, record (1916) #: 242.
Peter ANDES, parents: Joseph W. Andes and (first name illegible) Potter, death cause: "unknown", died: 4 Dec 1916, record (1916) #: 243.
Bulah HEATON, born: 5 Oct 1916, parents: Gaston Heaton and Ida Cable, death cause: "unknown", informant: Clarence Miller (Shell Creek), buried: Cable Cemetery, died: 24 Dec 1916, record (1916) #: 244.
Wright HURLEY, born: 8 Jun 1853, married, parents: William Hurley and Sarah Moreland, death cause: "billious colic", informant: James Cress (Carter), buried: Hurley Cemetery, died: 16 Dec 1916, record (1916) #: 245.
Call BRUER, age 65 years, parents: not stated, death cause: illegible, buried: Limestone Cove, died: 18 Dec 1916, record (1916) #: 246.
Viola ESTEP, born: 30 May 1916, parents: Bruce Estep and Eliza Carden, death cause: "croup", buried: Carden Cemetery, died: 4 Dec 1916, record (1916) #: 247.
David PERRY, age 70 years, married, parents: William Perry and mother not stated, death cause: "chronic diarrhoea", informant: J.E. Perry, buried: Sullivan County, died: 26 Dec 1916, record (1916) #: 248.
Mrs. Sallie LYONS, born: 22 May 1862, parents: D.J. Chambers (SC) and Mrs. Mary Smith, death cause: "carcinoma of breast", informant: W.A. Lyons (Huntington, W.VA), buried: Ellis Cemetery, died: 1 Dec 1916, record (1916) #: 249.
Ossa May MCKEEHAN, born: 26 Nov 1916, parents: Frank McKeehan and Pearl Pate (Unicoi County), death cause: illegible, died: 17 Dec 1916, record (1916) #: 250.

Mr. Joe MORRELL, born: 2 Sep 1849, married, parents: John S. Morrell and (first name not stated) Mottern [editorial note: her name was Elizabeth, daughter of John Mottern], death cause: "pneumonia", informant: Mrs. J.P. Morrell, buried: Morrell Cemetery, died: 20 Dec 1916, record (1916) #: 251.
Camron HODGE, born: 29 Aug 1913, parents: F.M. Hodge and Virgie Smith, death cause: "diptheria", buried: Colbaugh Cemetery, died: 11 Dec 1916, record #: 252.
Helen Margaret EDENS, born: 29 Nov 1916, parents: A.W. Edens and Maude Vilis (NC), death cause: "bronchitis", buried: Highland Cemetery, died: 8 Dec 1916, record (1916) #: 253.
Mary K. DEMPSY, age 49 years, married, parents: J.J. Lilley and Mattie Cole, death cause: "organic heart disease", buried: Thompson Cemetery, died: 11 Dec 1916, record (1916) #: 254.
Lawrence MASSINGILL, born: 7 Nov 1916, parents: John Massingill and Hattie Slagle, death cause: "broncho pneumonia", buried: Sullivan County, died: 28 Dec 1916, record (1916) #: 255.
Noah Taylor HOLLEY, born: 20 Oct 1916, parents: Walter Holley and Feby Hart, death cause: "hypertrophy of liver", died: 10 Dec 1916, record (1916) #: 256.
Dora ALFORD, born: 21 Dec 1884, married, parents: W.C. Ritchie and Rebecca Buckles, death cause: "tuberculosis", informant: D.E. Ritchie (Watauga Valley), buried: Ritchie Cemetery, died: 21 Dec 1916, record (1916) #: 257.
Loos (illegible) WHITEHEAD, male, born: 16 Mar 1894, parents: George Whitehead and Mollie Carver, death cause: "pulmonary tuberculosis", buried: Whitehead Cem., Roan Mountain, 9 Dec 1916, record (1916) #: 258.
Jesse COOPER, age: "unknown", married, parents: "not known", death cause: "killed instantly by falling timber", informant: J.M. Hall (Hampton), buried: Bluff City, died: 12 Jan 1917, record (1917) #: 1.
Allen WAYCASTER, born: 1 Aug 1869 at Newport, Cocke County, married, parents: E.B. Waycaster (NC) and S.M. Biddix (NC), death cause: "cardiac failure", informant: O.C. Waycaster (Braemar), buried: Crabtree Cemetery, died: 28 Jan 1917, record (1917) #: 2.
L.L. MAPLES, born: 2 May 1835 in Sevier County, married, parents: Dempsy Maples (Sevier County) and Rahcel McMan (Sevier County), death cause: "ulcer of stomach", informant: M.B. Reece (Butler), died: 13 Jan 1917, record (1917) #: 3.

Logan MORGAN, age 30 years, married, parents: J.G. Morgan (Watauga Co., NC) and Rosilee Potter, death cause: "lagripp", informant: Jake Trivett (Dark Ridge, NC), died: 31 Jan 1917, record (1917) #: 4.

Emeline SIMERLY, age: "unknown", married, parents: Daniel Oaks and Ruth Moreland, death cause: "dropsy", informant: Will Potter (Roan Mountain), died: 23 Jan 1917, record (1917) #: 6.

Titia GARLAND, age about 1 year, parents: Daniel Garland and Nancy Hurley, death cause: "diarrhoea", informant: Smith Garland (Carter), buried: Garland Cemetery, died: 15 Jan 1917, record (1917) #: 6.

Bill LOUDY, born: 1 Jun 1899, married, parents: Nat Snodgrass and (first name illegible) Gourley, death cause: illegible, informant: Bob Loudy (Johnson City), died: 26 Jan 1917, record (1917) #: 7.

Sallie BRYANT, age 95 years, single, born in North Carolina, parents: Barney Bryant (NC) and Susan Turner (NC), death cause: "pulmonary arthima", informant: J.A. Bryant, buried: Lyons Cemetery, died: 27 Jan 1917, record (1917) #: 8.

Susan Bell BLACK, born: 7 Sep 1915, parents: father not stated and Lula Janne Black (Ashé Co., NC), death cause: "supposed to be croup", informant: Charlie Cook (Shell Creek), died: 24 Jan 1917, record (1917) #: 9.

Joe YOUNG, age 84 years, born in North Carolina, married, parents: Joe Young (NC) and Sarah Young (NC), death cause: "rhumatism and old age", informant: Sukie Young (Roan Mountain), buried: Chambers Cemetery, died: 23 Jan 1917, record (1917) #: 10.

F. Ross JUSTICE, age 1 year and 2 months, parents: William Justice and Bell Bowers, death cause: "bold hives", died: 25 Jan 1917, record (1917) #: 11.

Shelby ANDERSON, male, born: 7 Jun 1915, parents: Sam Anderson and Cordia Bowers, death cause: "lagripp and cold", died: 28 Jan 1917, record (1917) #: 12.

Mrs. Adellia SHARP, born: 3 Mar 1844, married, parents: Henry Nave and Margaret Erwin, death cause: "lagripp and heart and kidney disease", informant: W.H. Sharp (Bluff City), buried: Kitte-Miller Cemetery, died: 30 Jan 1917, record (1917) #: 13.

Susan CABLE, age 82 years, married, parents: William Buckles and mother's name not stated, death cause: "paralysis", died: 31 Jan 1917, drec 14.

Nancy HINKLE, age 84 years, parents: Nicholas Miller and Kittie Blevins, death cause: "cancer of throat and old age", informant: J.N. Colbaugh, Sr., buried: Ritchie Cem., died: 9 Jan 1917, record (1917) #: 15

Eliza LEWIS, age 55 years, single, parents: Lewis D. Lewis and Fannie Peters, death cause: "cancer of cervix", informant: N.R. Lewis (Carter), buried: Grindstaff Cemetery, died: 30 Jan 1917, record #: 16.
Infant BLEVINS, female, parents: Dan Blevins and Rebecca Estep, death cause: "weakness of mother", informant: Clara Ensor (Carter), buried: Ensor Cemetery, born/died: 8 Jan 1917, record (1917) #: 17.
Infant EST, male, parents: Isaac Est and Eva Taylor, death cause: "weakness of mother", informant: Murray Lewis (Carter), buried: Garland Cemetery, born/died: 4 Jan 1917, record (1917) #: 18.
Maggie NAVE, born: 8 Jan 1917, parents: Coy E. Nave and Nannie Hyder, death cause: "not known", informant: Daniel Chambers, died: 18 Jan 1917, record #: 19.
Elizabeth HARDIN, born: 27 Jan 1853, single, parents: Isaac Hardin and (first name illegible) Oliver, death cause: "lagrippe", informant: John Hardin, buried: Hardin Cem., died: 22 Jan 1917, record (1917) #: 20.
Caroline DOLAN, born: 5 May 1858, parents: John Irick and Sarah Jones (Washington County), death cause: "lagrippe and pneumonia", informant: Sam Dolan (Shell Creek), died: 20 Jan 1917, record (1917) #: 21.
Infant SCALF, male, parents: James Scalf and Carrie Salts, death cause: "stillborn", born/died: 7 Jan 1917, record (1917) #: 22.
Minnie MITCHELL, colored, born: 21 Apr 1892 in North Carolina, single, parents: Robert Mitchell (NC) and (first name illegible) Bowers (NC), death cause: "tuberculosis", buried: Cedar Grove Cemetery, died: 31 Jan 1917, record (1917) #: 23.
Edna G. CARRIGER, born: 9 Apr 1838, widow, parents: Samuel Dugger and Hannah Potter, death cause: "chronic nephritis", informant: W.M. Vaught, buried: Highland Cemetery, died: 28 Jan 1917, record (1917) #: 24.
Hattie WATSON, black, born: 10 Nov 1892, married, parents: Robert Mitchell (NC) and Maggie Bowers (NC), death cause: "chronic nephritis", informant: Tom Mitchell, buried: Cedar Grove Cemetery, died: 9 Jan 1917, record (1917) #: 25.
Georgia MCRATH, black, born: 14 Feb 1899, parents: Henry McRath (NC) and Mary Ervin (NC), death cause: "pulmonary tuberculosis", informant: Pete McRath, buried: Cedar Grove, died: 2 Jan 1917, record #: 26.
R.W. ROWE, born: 9 Apr 1857 in Unicoi County, married, parents: Robert R. Rowe and mother's name illegible, death cause: "lobar pneumonia", buried: Rowe Cemetery, Unicoi County, died: 4 Jan 1917, record (1917) #: 27.

Massy HOPSON, female, born: 27 Aug 1862 in North Carolina, married, parents: Abe Whitson (NC) and Sally Whitson (NC), death cause: "pneumonia and heart failure", informant: J.S.E. Range (Johnson City), buried: Taylor Town Cemetery, died: 10 Feb 1917, record (1917) #: 28.

Willard MILLER, age 28 years, single, born in Watauga County, NC, parents: Richard Miller (Watauga Co., NC) and Hannah Rowton (Watauga Co., NC), death cause: "mealses and complications", informant: Clarence Miller, buried: Cable Cemetery, died: 19 Feb 1917, record (1917) #: 29.

Eldrith WILSON, born: 14 Feb 1914, parents: Jackson Wilson and Ruth Bowers, death cause: "hooping cough, pneumonia", informant: R.J. Campbell (Watauga Valley), buried: Bowers Cemetery, died: 3 Feb 1917, record (1917) #: 30.

James R. WILSON, age 79 years, married, parents: father's name "unknown" and Polly Wilson, death cause: "paralysis", informant: Isaac Lewis (Watauga Valley), buried: Wilson Cemetery, died: 11 Feb 1917, record (1917) #: 31.

Arthur NIDIFFER, born: 4 Feb 1917, parents: William Nidiffer and _____ Bowers, death cause: "whooping cough", informant: Henry Nidiffer (Watauga Valley), died: 20 Feb 1917, record (1917) #: 32.

Infant ESTEP, male, parents: George Estep and Julia Robinson (NC), death cause: "weakness of mother", informant: Will Asher (Carter), buried: Garland Cemetery, born/died: 12 Feb 1917, record (1917) #: 33.

Raymond ELLIOTT, born: 28 Mar 1916, parents: James Elliott and Hula Oliver, death cause: "spinal meningitis", informant: James Elliott (Carter), buried: Hurley Cemetery, died: 11 Feb 1917, record (1917) #: 34.

Wilburn Paul PIERCE, born: 14 Jun 1916, parents: Wilburn Pierce and Eliz Gourley, death cause: "bronchitis", informant: Eliz Pierce, buried: Pierce Cemetery, died: 6 Feb 1917, record (1917) #: 35.

Edie HILL, male, born: 20 Sep 1909, parents: John Hill and Bettie Johnson, death cause: "boul hives", informant: John Hill (Hampton), buried: Whitehead Cemetery, died: 28 Feb 1917, record (1917) #: 36.

Emily STREET, age 85 years, married, parents: Mike Grindstaff and Sallie _____, death cause: "tuberculosis and old age", informant: B.G. Hyder (Hampton), buried: McKinney Cemetery, died: 1 Feb 1917, record (1917) #: 37.

William E. SHUFFIELD, born: 8 Jan 1839, widower, parents: George Shuffield and Hiley Kimick, death cause: "pneumonia fever", informant: G.G. Shuffield (Butler), died: 18 Feb 1917, record (1917) #: 38.

Fantha Maud HART, born: 21 Dec 1916, parents: father not stated and Stella Hart, death cause: not stated, informant: J.D. Croy (Watauga), buried: Hart Cemetery, died: 14 Feb 1917, record (1917) #: 39.

Clarissa Hellen PEEBLES, born: 7 Feb 1841 in Yancey County, NC, married, parents: Henry Ray (Yancey Co., NC) and Elizabeth Wilson (Yancey Co., NC), death cause: "pulmonary tuberculosis", informant: J.W. Peoples (Johnson City), buried: Okalona Cemetery, died: 3 Feb 1917, record (1917) #: 40.

Basmath Emmaline ROWE, born: 17 Oct 1837, single, parents: John L. Rowe and Rachel Peoples (Washington Co., TN), death cause: "lobar pneumonia", informant: L.L. Rowe (Johnson City), buried: Rowe Cemetery, died: 25 Feb 1917, record (1917) #: 41.

Infant HURLEY, male, parents: James Hurley and Bessie Taylor, death cause: "hives", informant: R.M. Ensor, buried: Estep Cemetery, born/died: 7 Feb 1917, record (1917) #: 42.

Lidy DAVIS, male, age 7 years, parents: Rheuben Davis (West VA) and Lina Harvey (West VA), death cause: "accidentally shot", informant: Rhuben Davis (Carter), died: 4 Nov 1917, record (1917) #: 43.

Buell Stokes BUCK, born: 21 Jan 1916, parents: John E. Buck and Savannah Clark (NC), death cause: not stated, informant: John E. Buck (Shell Creek), died: 6 Feb 1917, record (1917) #: 44.

Thomas RANDOLF, born: 1 Dec 1841 in North Carolina, widower, parents: Thomas Randolf (NC) and _____ Brumit (NC), death cause: "refused medicine", informant: Thomas McCauley (Shell Creek), buried: McLane Cem., died: 6 Feb 1917, record #: 45.

Mrs. Annie CARDIN, born: 12 Feb 1832, widow, parents: John Estep and Nancy Sneed, death cause: "pneumonia", informant: A.G. Cardin (Hampton), buried: Cardin Cemetery, died: 15 Feb 1917, record (1917) #: 46.

Laura May BRADSHAW, born: 8 Sep 1916, parents: John F. Bradshaw and Eva Hatcher, death cause: "lagrippe and cold", buried: Highland Cemetery, died: 24 Feb 1917, record (1917) #: 47.

Sally UNDERWOOD, black, born: 12 Feb 1912, parents: John Underwood and Lillie Vaught, death cause: "pulmonary tuberculosis", buried: McGee Cemetery, died: 3 Feb 1917, record (1917) #: 48.

Elizabeth GRIFFITH, black, born: 18 Oct 1837, parents: not stated, death cause: "lagrippe", buried: Odd Fellows Cem., died: 7 Feb 1917, record (1917) #: 49.

Richell WAGNER, age 27 years, born in North Carolina, married, parents: Cleveland Lane (NC) and Mary Royal (NC), death cause: "seplilenia [editorial note: two babies are listed below]", informant: Wilson Wagner, buried: Hodge Cemetery, died: 20 Feb 1917, record (1917) #: 50.

Infant WAGNER, male, born 17 Feb 1917, parents: Wilson Wagner and Rechill Lane, death cause: "unknown", informant: Wilson Wagner, buried: Hodge Cemetery, died: 19 Feb 1917, record (1917) #: 51.

Infant WAGNER, female, born: parents: Wilson Wagner and Rechill Lane, death cause: "unknown", informant: Wilson Wagner, buried: Hodge Cemetery, born/died: 17 Feb 1917, record (1917) #: 52.

Rufus COULEY, black, age 70 years, born in McDowell County, NC, parents: "don't know", death cause: "lobar pneumonia", informant: W.M. Forbes (Milligan), buried: Taylor Cem., died: 16 Feb 1917, record (1917) #: 53.

Alice Loretta BOWERS, born: 11 Mar 1917, parents: Ernest Bowers and Rena Brown (NC), death cause: "pneumonia", informant: T.A. Hardin (Hampton), buried: Hall Cemetery, died: 19 Mar 1917, record (1917) #: 54.

Mrs. M.J. WHITE, born: 24 Mar 1858, married, parents: John G. Shuffield and _____ Shell (NC), death cause: "lagrippe", informant: M.C. Miller, died: 6 Mar 1917, record (1917) #: 55.

Infant TAYLOR, male, parents: Joe and Grace Taylor death cause: "unknown", died: 6 Mar 1917, record #: 56.

Infant FIPPS, female, born: 13 Mar 1917, parents: Daniel Fipps and Maggie Lewis, death cause: "hives", buried: Lewis Cem., died: 23 Mar 1917, record #: 57.

Ben RICHARDS, age about 72 years, married, parents: Ben Richards and Nancy Glover (Sullivan County), death cause: "organic heart disease", informant: Mary McReynolds, buried: Morris Cemetery, died: 10 Mar 1917, record (1917) #: 58.

Infant MCCLOUD, parents: John McCloud and Maggie Marsh, death cause: "born dead", buried: Colbaugh Cemetery, born/died: 1 Mar 1917, record (1917) #: 59.

Delsa Virginia SNEED, born: 20 Jan 1917, parents: A.J. Sneed and Sindy Hale, death cause: not stated, buried: Highland Cem., died: 13 Mar 1917, record (1917) #: 60.

Infant Grace BOWERS, parents: John N. Bowers and Mary McClain, death cause: "hydrocephalue", born/died: 18 Mar 1917, record (1917) #: 61.

Ruby Pearl COLE, born: 8 Mar 1890, married, parents: William Hicks and Martha Clemons, death cause: "vomiting, pergnancy", informant: Nannie Absher, buried: Lines Cemetery, died: 19 Mar 1917, record (1917) #: 62.

Elizabeth FAIR, born: 11 Mar 1847, widow, parents: John H. Fair and Elizabeth Fletcher, death cause: "pneumonia", informant: R.F. Fair (Elizabethton), buried: Jones Cemetery, died: 19 Mar 1917, record (1917) #: 63.

Mary Louise WAGNER, parents: A.R. Wagner (NC) and Sofia Wagner (NC) death cause: "born dead", born/died: 23 Mar 1917, record (1917) #: 64.

Mrs. Hattie ANDREWS, born: 10 Dec 1896 in North Carolina, married, parents: Andy Greer and Jane Turbyfield, death cause: "lukemia", informant: D.C. Andrews, buried: Colbaugh Cemetery, died: 28 Mar 1917, record (1917) #: 65.

Mrs. Margaret HUGHES, born: 14 Dec 1859, widow, parents: Will Hagan (NC) and mother not stated, death cause: "ulcer on ankle", informant: Mrs. G.M. Bradley, buried: Wilcox Cemetery, died: 23 Mar 1917, record (1917) #: 66.

Sarah Elizabeth HOLLY, born: 11 Mar 1871, married, parents: William Brownlow Davis and Louise Morrell (Sullivan County), death cause: illegible, buried: Wm Mottern Cem., died: 14 Mar 1917, record (1917) #: 67.

Selvia EDNY, age 4 years, parents: John Edny and (first name illegible) Johnson, death cause: "measles", informant: E.F. Heaton (Roan Mountain), died: 10 Mar 1917, record (1917) #: 68.

Mary Margaret WRIGHT, born: 10 Mar 1917, parents: Plato Wright and Mary Jane Garland, death cause: "not known", buried: Roan Mountain, died: 27 Mar 1917, record (1917) #: 69.

Evelyn CRUMLEY, born: Mar 1913, parents: Augustus Crumley and May Hampton, death cause: "pneumonia", informant: W.P. Hampton (Roan Mountain), died: 20 Mar 1917, record (1917) #: 70.

Elliot S. REED, age 72 years, born in Massachusetts, widower, parents: "not known", death cause: "heart failure", buried: Ritchie Cemetery, died: 20 Mar 1917, record (1917) #: 71.

Daniel R. FORBES, born: 10 Mar 1838, widower, parents: Simon Forbes (NC) and Rachel Richardson (NC), death cause: "pneumonia and old age", informant: M.S. Forbes (Watauga Valley), buried: Forbes Cemetery, died: 13 Mar 1917, record (1917) #: 72.

Infant RICHARDSON, female, parents: Thomas Richardson and Ellen Myers, death cause: "weakness of mother", informant: Jesse Richardson (Carter), born/died: 13 Mar 1917, record (1917) #: 73.

Infant FIPPS, female, born: 13 Mar 1917, parents: Daniel Fipps and Maggie Lewis, death cause: "hives", buried: Ensor Cem., died: 23 Mar 1917, record #: 74.

Buledene CAMPBELL, born: 16 Apr 1917, parents: N.R. Campbell and Lou Lewis, death cause: not stated, informant: Willis Lewis, died: 16 Mar 1917, record (1917) #: 75.

Shelby OLIVER, born: 13 Nov 1916, parents: Burgie Oliver and mother's name not stated, death cause: "whooping cough, minengitis", died: 13 Mar 1917, record (1917) #: 76.

Lena SHARP, age 30 years, married, parents: J.J. Morrell and Carrie Ellis, death cause: "cancer of liver", died: 7 Mar 1917, record (1917) #: 77.

Albert D. MAYS, age 4 years, born in North Carolina, parents: not stated, death cause: "larangitis", died: 27 Mar 1917, record (1917) #: 78.

Lizzie HODGE, age 46 years, born in North Carolina, married, parents: Marques Vandike and Luened McGee (NC), death cause: "pulmonary tuberculosis", informant: J.C. Hodge, buried: Simmons Cemetery, died: 10 Mar 1917, record (1917) #: 79.

John PRICHARD, born: 14 Aug 1844, married, parents: Thomas Prichard and Pollie Mody (NC), death cause: "kidney trouble", informant: M.F. Prichard (Shell Creek), buried: Perry Cemetery, died: 14 Mar 1917, record (1917) #: 80.

Arimility HARDIN, female, born about 1854. parents: John R. Stout and Elizabeth Bunton (Johnson County), death cause: "dropsy", informant: T.J. Stout (Butler), buried: Elk Mills, died: 11 Mar 1917, record #: 81.

Ernistine BERRY, born: 16 Nov 1857, married, parents: Moses Banks and (first name illegible) Davis, death cause: "cancer of uterus", informant: G.H. Franklin (Hampton), buried: Berry Cemetery, died: 10 Mar 1917, record (1917) #: 81.

John CARVER, age 61 years, married, parents: Aiden Carver and Nancy Banks, death cause: "lobar pneumonia", informant: Frank Carver (Hampton), buried: Fair View Cem., died: 7 Mar 1917, record (1917) #: 83.

Mat S. MURRAY, born: 11 Oct 1866, married, parents: William Murray and Catherine Miller, death cause: "tuberculosis of lungs", informant: Bill Clark (Elizabethton), died: 6 Mar 1917, record (1917) #: 84.

James ARNOLD, age 38 years, born in North Carolina, married, parents: George Arnold (NC) and Hannah Richardson, death cause: "heart dropsy", informant: James Garland (Carter), buried: Richardson Cemetery, died: 21 Mar 1917, record (1917) #: 85.
Mrs. Catherine WAGNER, age: "unknown", married, parents: Phillip F. Brumit and Sarah An _____, death cause: "peritonitis", informant: D.S. Wagner (Hampton), died: 16 Mar 1917, record #: 86.
Joseph Thomas RICHARDSON, born: 13 Feb 1917, parents: Ernest Richardson and Manila Cook, death cause: "unknown", informant: Thomas Cook (Shell Creek), buried: Walnut Mountain, died: 16 Mar 1917, record (1917) #: 87.
Beuna VINES, female, born: 20 Mar 1909, parents: father's name not given and Josie Vines, death cause: "measles", informant: Calvin Fugate, buried: Smith Cemetery, died: 24 Apr 1917, record (1917) #: 88.
Nancy Ann RUSSELL, age 38 years, married, parents: "unknown", death cause: "heart trouble, childbirth", informant: John Hardin, died: 16 Apr 1917, record (1917) #: 89. (note: babies death record below)
Infant RUSSELL, female, parents: William H. Russell and Nancy A. Holoway, death cause: "premature birth", buried: Hardin Cemetery, born/died: 12 Apr 1917, record (1917) #: 90.
W.B. TREADWAY, born: 10 Dec 1846, married, parents: J.H. Treadway and Jamima Hardin, death cause: "ruptured appendix", informant: A.J. Treadway, buried: Treadway Cem., died: 7 Apr 1917, record (1917) #: 91.
Theodore Roosevelt SIMERLY, born: 2 Nov 1912, parents: John F. Simerly and Alice Headrick, death cause: "measles", buried: Smith Cemetery, Valley Forge, died: 3 Apr 1917, record (1917) #: 92.
Jane STEPP, age about 76 years, widow, parents: Moses McFarland and Elizabeth McFarland, death cause: "cerebral hemorrhage", informant: Lidia McFarland (Piney Flats), buried: Simmons Cemetery, died: 28 Apr 1917, record (1917) #: 93.
Laura WHISENHUNT, born: 2 Feb 1917, parents: Isaac Whisenhunt and Lilly Royal, death cause: "bowl hives", informant: A.J. Miller (Roan Mountain), buried: Blevins Cem., died: 24 Apr 1917, record (1917) #: 94.
Bettie SIMERLY, age 26 years, married, parents: James Carver and (first name not stated) Brumit, death cause: "intestinal obstruction", informant: James Carver (Hampton), buried: Fair View Cemetery, died: 26 Apr 1917, record (1917) #: 95.

Birdie Alma VANCE, born: 11 Jan 1908, parents: John Vance and Bessie Johnson, death cause: "pneumonia", informant: John Vance (Shell Creek), buried: Richardson Cemetery, died: 17 Apr 1917, record (1917) #: 96.

Debbie SHELL, born: 20 Jan 1873, married, parents: William Gregg (NC) and Tilda Gregg (NC), death cause: "Brights disease", informant: Andy Shell (Shell Creek), buried: Richardson Cemetery, died: 23 Apr 1917, record (1917) #: 97.

Herment TEAGUE, born: 23 Feb 1916, parents: Thomas Teague (NC) and Alice Markland, death cause: "cholera", informant: A.C. Markland (Shell Creek), buried: Markland Cemetery, died: 26 Apr 1917, record (1917) #: 98.

Lila Hattie MAY, born: 5 May 1917, parents: David E. May (NC) and Euretha Guy (Idaho), death cause: "heart disease", informant: T.C. Murray (Watauga Valley), died: 1 Apr 1917, record (1917) #: 99.

Helen Louise MCKEEHAN, born: 8 Apr 1917, parents: Lee McKeehan and Mattie Smith, death cause: "broncho pneumonia", buried: McKeehan Cemetery, died: 17 Apr 1917, record (1917) #: 100.

Elizabeth SHOUN, parents: George Shoun and Maggie Lowe, death cause: "unknown, died 15 hours after birth", informant: S.J. Lowe, born/died: 16 Apr 1917, record (1917) #: 101 (twin below).

Harry SHOUN, born: 16 Apr 1917, parents: George Shoun and Maggie Lowe, death cause: not stated, informant: Powel Shoun, died: 22 Apr 1917, record (1917) #: 102.

Mintta HYDER, age 47 years, married, parents: John Hyder and Susan McNeese, death cause: "hart failure", informant: J.W. Hyder (Elizabethton), buried: Hyder Cemetery, died: 19 Apr 1917, record (1917) #: 103.

Elizabeth DAVENPORT, age 81 years, 5 months and 14 days, widow, parents: Thomas Gourley and mother's name not stated, death cause: "kidney disease and chronic indigestion", informant: Peter Range (Elizabethton), buried: Jones Cemetery, died: 11 apr 1917, record (1917) #: 104.

Samuel E. BLEVINS, born: 25 Aug 1869, married, parents: Dillard Blevins and Lorattie McQueen, death cause: "pneumonia", informant: N.P. Blevins, buried: Highland, died: 17 Apr 1917, record (1917) #: 105.

Ray Elmer TREADWAY, born: 30 Mar 1917, parents: G.H. Treadway and Nola Hammit, death cause: "not known", buried: Treadway Cemetery, died: 1 Apr 1917, record (1917) #: 106.

Mrs. Maggie BRADSHAW, born: 19 Mar 1885, married, parents: James Deloach and Maggie Williams, death cause: "pulmonary tuberculosis", informant: W.F. Bradshaw (Elizabethton), buried: Hyder Cemetery, died: 29 Apr 1917, record (1917) #: 107.

Barbara E. BOWERS, born: 27 Nov 1848, parents: Jacob Vandeventer and Barbara Vandeventer, death cause: illegible, informant: Nora Bowers (Elizabethton), died: 18 Apr 1917, record (1917) #: 108.

Nora Ethel WAGNER, age 3 years, 10 months and 27 days, parents: Ezekiel Nelson and Deliah Wagner, death cause: "injuries from fall", informant: I.G. Wagner, buried: Hyder Cemetery, died: 1 Apr 1917, record (1917) #: 109.

Christina Adeline FEATHERS, born: 12 Apr 1851, married, parents: Henry Little (Sullivan County) and Matilda Mottern, death cause: "apoplexy", buried: Wm Mottern Cem., died: 7 Apr 1917, record (1917) #: 110.

John W. SMITH, born: 30 May 1834, married, parents: not stated, death cause: "pleurisy", informant: John Smith (Butler), died: 24 Apr 1917, record (1917) #: 111.

Lilian DEMPSY, age about 30 years, married, parents: Franklin Scott and (first name illegible) Taylor, death cause: "typhoid and child birth", died: 30 Apr 1917, record (1917) #: 112.

Infant DEMPSY, male, parents: Jack Dempsy and Lilian Scott, death cause: "premature birth", born/died: 30 Apr 1917, record (1917) #: 113.

Catherine PRESNELL, age 38 years, married, born in Watauga County, NC, parents: Robert Tester (Watauga Co., NC) and Cata Beard (Watauga Co., NC), death cause: "parlaysis of 12 years", informant: Sincon Presnell (Butler), buried: Watauga Co., NC, died: 28 Apr 1917, record (1917) #: 114.

Infant DUGGER, female twins, parents: father not stated and Dora Dugger, death cause: "died 10 minutes after birth", born/died: 27 Apr 1917, record (1917) #: 115.

Coy BUNTON, born: 16 Oct 1882 in Johnson County, married, parents: Harrison Bunton and Eliza Dugger, death cause: "pneumonia", informant: G.L. Dugger (Butler), died: 2 May 1916 (note: 1916 record filed with 1917), record (1917) #: 116.

Goldie WAYCASTER, born: 27 May 1914, parents: William Waycaster (NC) and Addie Byrum, death cause: "gastro-colitis", buried: Crabtree, died: 31 May 1917, record (1917) #: 117.

James Spencer HALL, born: 8 Aug 1915, parents: Elijah S. Hall and Ruth Presnell, death cause: "measles, pneumonia", informant: Mike Hall (Hampton), buried: Hall Cemetery, died: 5 May 1917, record (1917) #: 118.
Eva LYONS, age about 74 years, widow, parents: "unknown", death cause: "cyalites (malignant)", informant: Frank Britt, buried: Oak Grove Cemetery, died: 1 May 1917, record (1917) #: 119.
William LYNN, born: 1 Oct 1885, married, parents: Robert C. Lynn and mother's name not known, death cause: "accidental kick in stomach by mule", informant: Hattie Lynn (wife), buried: Smith Cemetery, died: 20 May 1917, record (1917) #: 120.
Infant LIVINGSTON, female, parents: George Livingston and Kattie Headrick, death cause: "premature birth", informant: George Livingston (Valley Forge), born/died: 31 May 1917, record (1917) #: 121.
James A. NAVE, born: Jan 1853, married, parents: Joel Nave and Sarah McQueen, death cause: "colic, heart failure", informant" Porter Nave (Siam), buried: J.B. Nave Cem., died: 31 May 1917, record (1917) #: 122.
Fred Eugene WETZEL, Jr. born: 23 Aug 1915, parents: Fred L. Wetzel (Indin) and Anna J. Bontregie (Iowa), death cause: illegible, buried: Highland Cemetery, died: 8 May 1917, record (1917) #: 123.
Nancy HONEYCUTT, age not stated, widow, parents: not stated, informant: W.A. Norris, buried: Morris cemetery, died: 12 May 1917, record (1917) #: 124.
John TAYLOR, black, parents: John Taylor and Addie Davis, death cause: "born dead", buried: Cedar Grove, died: 17 May 1917, record (1917) #: 125.
Lela BOWERS, black, born: 8 Mar 1883, married, parents: Henry Bowers (NC) and Eliza Gordon (NC), death cause: "mitral stenosis", informant: Charlie Bowers (Elizabethton), buried: Bowers Cemetery, died: 25 May 1917, record (1917) #: 126.
Hubert Eugene LEDMIRE, parents: Joel Hardin and Liza Ledmire, death cause: "disease of heart", buried: Highland Cemetery, born/died: 25 May 1917, record (1917) #: 127.
Violet ELLIOTT, age 2 months, parents: David Elliott and (name not stated) Combs, death cause: "whooping cough", died: 31 May 1917, record (1917) #: 128.
Mrs. Franklin SHAW, age 44 years, born in North Carolina, married, parents: Eligah Greer (NC) and Sallie Greer (NC), death cause: "cerebral hemorrhage", died: 17 May 1917, record (1917) #: 129.

Susan DOUGLAS, age 96 years, single, parents: James Douglas and Elizabeth Simerly, death cause: "acute dilitation of heart", buried: Meriedith Cemetery, died: 28 May 1917, record (1917) #: 130.
Roy Dexter SCOTT, born: 11 Sep 1914, parents: William Scott and Livcy Daniels, death cause: "acute nephritis", died: 11 May 1917, record (1917) #: 131.
Stella HART, born: Jan 1897, parents: F.S. Hart and Tildy Ann Humphreys, death cause: "tuberculosis", died: 3 May 1917, record (1917) #: 132.
Easter MORTON, born: 29 Mar 1891, single, parents: M.Y. Morton, and R.C. McKinney, death cause: "operation for gall bladder infection", informant: D.S. Morton (Hampton), buried: Stevens Cemetery, died: 31 May 1917, record (1917) #: 133.
Katherine BYRD, age 60 years, born in North Carolina, parents: father's name not known and Liddy Henderlien, death cause: "pneumonia", informant: James Johnson (Hampton), buried: Whitehead Cemetery, died: 1 May 1917, record (1917) #: 134.
William J. CLARK, born: 4 Apr 1854, married, parents: John Clark and Elizabeth Bacon, death cause: "heart failure caused by anger", informant: Mrs. Julia Clark (Johnson City), buried: Old Buck Cemetery, died: 1 May 1917, record (1917) #: 135.
Alice TAYLOR, born: 13 May 1917, parents: John Taylor and Lillie Arwood (NC), death cause: "premature delivery", informant: R.T. Persinger (Johnson City), buried: Ensor Cemetery, died: 20 May 1917, record (1917) #: 136.
Infant HYDER, female, parents: Nat Hyder and May Livingston, death cause: "stillborn", died: 13 Jun 1917, record (1917) #: 137.
Birdie Lee STREET, born: 16 Mar 1917, parents: Harrison Street and Lilly Brown, death cause: "not known", informant: Lee Brown (Roan Mountain), died: 14 Jun 1917, record (1917) #: 138.
Oscar HAMBY, born: 6 Jun 1917, parents: Loss Hamby and Mary Basket, death cause: "child lived 3 hours", informant: Loss Hamby (Shell Creek), buried: Briggs Cemetery, died: 6 Jun 1917, record (1917) #: 139.
Delia BUCKLES, age 24 years, born in Virginia, married, parents: C.W. Noland (VA) and mother's name not known, death cause: "consumption of bowels", informant: Abe Buckles (Watauga Valley), buried: Buckles Cem., died: 29 Jun 1917, record (1917) #: 140.

Sallie WILLIAMS, age 24 years, married, parents: W.B. Hopson and _____ Orr, death cause: "typhoid fever", informant: E.J. Williams (Watauga Valley), buried: Buckles Cemetery, died: 30 Jun 1917, record (1917) #: 141.

David NAVE, age 59 years, married, parents: William Nave and _____ Lewis, death cause: "pelagra", died: 5 Jun 1917, record (1917) #: 142.

Lee GUY, age "unknown", born in Johnson County, married, parents: "unknown", death cause: "shot with pistol in public duel", died: 29 Jun 1917, record (1917) #: 143.

Pearl OLIVER, born: 5 Apr 1917, parents: Judson Oliver and Cordia Bowers, death cause: "stomach trouble", buried: Siam, died: 20 Jun 1917, record (1917) #: 144.

Elsie Pearl GARRISON, born: 1 Sep 1916, parents: W.C. Garrison and Bessie Headrick, death cause: "cholera", informant: W.C. Garrison (Valley Forge), buried: Smith Cemetery, died: 28 Jun 1917, record (1917) #: 145.

Bennie NAVE, born: 13 May 1917, parents: A.J. Nave and Lillie Fletcher, death cause: "premature birth", informant: A.J. Nave (Siam), died: 2 Jun 1917, record (1917) #: 146.

Samuel C. WHITE, born: 7 Nov 1895, parents: Ben White and Usral (surname illegible), death cause: "congestion of brain and measles", informant: Mrs. S.A. Williams, buried: Siam. died: 19 Jun 1917, record (1917) #: 147.

George W. HARKLEROAD, born: 7 Feb 1833 in Sullivan County, widower, parents: Jacob Harkleroad (Sullivan County) and Rosane Riley (Sullivan County), death cause: "non-malignant tumor in throat", informant: Katherine Little (Bluff City), buried: Bluff City, died: 2 Jun 1917, record (1917) #: 148.

Harmon Persinger HART, born: 3 Feb 1916, parents: Abe Hart and Julia Pearl Persinger, death cause: "dysentary", buried: Mottern Cemetery, died: 24 Jun 1917, record (1917) #: 149.

Lidia Ann RANGE, born: 11 Jun 1852 in Arkansas, widow, parents: _____ Clamon (Sullivan County) and Lydia Peters, death cause: "pulmonary tuberculosis", informant: Martha Hayes (Elizabethton), buried: Range Cemetery, died: 16 Jun 1917, record (1917) #: 150.

William PERRY, age 75 years, married, parents: William Perry and mother's name not known, death cause: "organic heart disease", informant: W. Perry, buried: Sullivan County, died: 3 Jun 1917, record #: 151.

Mrs. Maud EGGERS, age 40 years, born in Surry County, NC, married, parents: Abner Baliff and (first name not stated) Stockner (Carrel Co., VA), death cause: "carcinoma of uterus", informant: Mrs. John Eggers, buried: McCorkle Cemetery, died: 14 Jun 1917, record (1917) #: 152.

Mrs. Bettie HILL, age 45 years, married, parents: Bill Johnson and Biddie Gouge, death cause: "cancer of uterus", informant: Charlie Hill (Hampton), buried: Whitehead Cemetery, died: 15 Jun 1917, record #: 153.

Walter COLE, age 18 years, parents: A.J. Cole and Cora Parker, death cause: "tuberculosis of lateral sinus", informant: Henry Pierce (Watauga Valley), buried: Buckles Cem., died: 13 Jun 1917, record (1917) #: 154.

John H. GRINDSTAFF, age 62 years, married, parents: Walter Grindstaff and Sarah Lowe (Johnson County), death cause: "tuberculosis of lungs", informant: Thomas Grindstaff (Carter), buried: Grindstaff Cemetery, died: 11 Jun 1917, record (1917) #: 155.

Jody Burnet LUNCEFORD, born: 3 Nov 1908, parents: Carter Lunceford and Rachel Heaton, death cause: "drowned", informant: D.E. Lunceford (Shell Creek), buried: Stout Cemetery, died: 1 Jun 1917, record (1917) #: 156.

David OAKS, born: Mar 1829 in Mitchell County, NC, parents: David Oaks and (first name not stated) Davis, death cause: "Brights disease", informant: David Oaks, Jr. (Shell Creek), buried: Oaks Cemetery, died: 4 Jun 1917, record (1917) #: 157.

David M. WHITE, age 74 years, 4 months and 18 days, married, parents: Lawson W. White and Nerue McNeely, death cause: "concussion of brain, struck by piece of lumber", informant: D.M. Hamby (Butler), died: 8 Jun 1917, record (1917) #: 158.

John C. WILLIAMS, born: 1 Jun 1917, parents: Godfrey Williams and Eliza Jane Oliver, death cause: "pneumonia", informant: Andy Williams (Watauga Valley), buried: Buckles Cemetery, died: 1 Jul 1917, record (1917) #: 159.

Sarah RITCHIE, age 35 years, married, parents: William Grindstaff and Mahala Lowe, death cause: "pelegra", informant: Ham Roberts (Bristol), buried: Ritchie Cemetery, died: 1 Jul 1917, record (1917) #: 160.

Lorettie GRINDSTAFF, age 52 years, married, parents: James Dugger (Johnson County) and Nancy Slimp (Johnson County), death cause: "tuberculosis", informant: R.M. Ensor (Carter), buried: Hurley Cemetery, died: 4 Jul 1917, record (1917) #: 161.

Polly SHELL, age: "unknown", born in North Carolina, parents: John Birchfield (NC) and (first name not stated) Baker, death cause: "unknown", informant: W.D. Shell (Roan Mountain), died: 6 Jul 1917, record (1917) #: 162.
John LEWIS, age 68 years, married, parents: Ephrem Lewis and mother's name unknown, death cause: "cardiac dropsy", died: 9 Jul 1917, record (1917) #: 163.
Annis Pritchell CAMPBELL, born: 25 Dec 1898 in North Carolina, married, parents: Alf Pritchell (NC) and Sara Sims (NC), death cause: "tuberculosis of intestines", informant: Lorrie Pritchell (Elizabethton), buried: Highland Cemetery, died: 9 Jul 1917, record (1917) #: 164.
Uretha GUY, born: 14 Jun 1867, widow, parents: Powell Campbell and Rebecca Pierce, death cause: "measles", informant: O.C. Guy (Butler), died: 10 Jul 1917, record (1917) #: 165.
Delila BOWMAN, age 50 years, born in Sullivan County, married, parents: Thomas Bowman (Sullivan County) and Mary (surname not stated)(Sullivan County), death cause: "dropsy", informant: Harris Bowman (Johnson City), buried: Buck Cemetery, died: 10 Jul 1917, record (1917) #: 166.
David BOONE, age not stated, parents: James Boone and Ret Tipton, death cause: "accidental gun shot wound", informant: Steve Barnett (Roan Mountain), died: 10 Jul 1917, record (1917) #: 167.
Sarah Ann WHITEHEAD, age about 60 years, widow, parents: Larkin Whitehead and Bettie Hill, death cause: "dropsy", informant: Marvel Whitehead (Roan Mountain), buried: Whitehead Cemetery, died: 10 Jul 1917, record (1917) #: 168.
William R. TAYLOR, born: 16 Aug 1871, married, parents: W.T. Taylor and Elizabeth Culbert, death cause: "consumption of bowels", informant: Lee Taylor (Carter), buried: Taylor cemetery, died: 13 Jul 1917, record (1917) #: 169.
Christian James HARDIN, colored, born: 10 Mar 1916, parents: John Hardin and Minnie Shade, death cause: "cholera", buried: Shell Creek Cemetery, died: 14 Jul 1917, record (1917) #: 170.
Nancy L. PIERCE, born: 18 Dec 1862, married, parents: William C. Pierce and Sarah J. Dugger, death cause: "disease of heart", informant: W.C. Pierce (Butler), died: 14 Jul 1917, record (1917) #: 171.

Charlotte Ann WILLIAMS, born: 11 Oct 1844, married, parents: Thomas Hodges (NC) and Jennie Wilcox (NC), death cause: "cancer of liver", informant: J.T. Williams (Johnson City), buried: Williams Cemetery, died: 14 Jul 1917, record (1917) #: 172.

Susan CARDEN, born: 14 Feb 1893, married, parents: James Campbell and Malissa Glover, death cause: "pulmonary tuberculosis", informant: Crisley Campbell (Fish Springs), died: 15 Jul 1917, record (1917) #: 173.

Rachel ARNET, age 77 years, widow, parents: William H. Arnet (NC) and Sarah Townsend (NC), death cause: "chronic diorie", informant: William Arnet (Roan Mountain), buried: Nelson Cemetery, died: 15 Jul 1917, record (1917) #: 174.

John COLLINS, Jr., born: 28 Jul 1916, parents: John Collins and Ida Buck, death cause: "measles", buried: Shell Creek, died: 16 Jul 1917, record (1917) #: 175.

Taxana FREEMAN, age 4 years, parents: Will Freeman and Jane Ward (NC), death cause: "flux", informant: R.T. Persinger (Johnson City), buried: Ensor Cemetery, died: 17 Jul 1917, record (1917) #: 176.

Mary Ann CARVER, age 34 years, married, parents: H.K. Hyder and O.J. McKinney, death cause: "palegra", informant: Samuel Morton (Hampton), buried: Hyder Cemetery, died: 17 Jul 1917, record (1917) #: 177.

Annie F. WIDNER, born: 14 Oct 1916, parents: Willis Widner (Washington Co., VA) and Tennie Sweeney, death cause: "ilio colitis", residence: Watauga, died: 21 Jul 1917, record (1917) #: 178.

Eugene Taylor HUGHES, age not stated, parents: John Hughes and Nannie Gobble (VA), death cause: "unknown", informant: E.H. Little (Johnson City), buried: Taylor Town Cem., died: 23 Jul 1917, record (1917) #: 179.

Pearlie CAMPBELL, born: 10 Jul 1916, parents: John Campbell and Annie Prichett, death cause: "tuberculosis", informant: Joe Hampton (Elizabethton), buried: Highland Cemetery, died: 24 Jul 1917, record (1917) #: 180.

Lanna ROBERTS, age 2 years, parents: Russell Roberts and Celie McKinney, death cause: "boul hives", informant: T.C. McKinney (Hampton), buried: McKinney Cemetery, died: 25 Jul 1917, record (1917) #: 181.

Herman Alfred RICHARDSON, born: 24 Feb 1915 in Mingo County, W.VA), parents: Alf Richardson and Cretie Ward, death cause: "gastro enleritis", informant: Alf Richardson (Shaker Mines, W.VA), died: 31 Jul 1917, record (1917) #: 182.

Sarah J. GROGAN, born: 30 Oct 1849, married, parents: G.W. Stout and Mary A. Moreland (Johnson County), death cause: "acute diorhear", informant: A.C. Odom (Shell Creek), buried: Stout Cemetery, died: 31 Jul 1917, record (1917) #: 183.

Infant FLETCHER, male, parents: Ernest E. Fletcher and Minnie Horton (NC), death cause: "stillborn", informant: E.E. Fletcher (Hampton), died: 28 Jul 1917, record (1917) #: 184.

Infant TAYLOR, female, parents: John Taylor and Ollie Bowman, death cause: "stillborn", buried: Milligan Cemetery, died: 28 Jul 1917, record (1917) #: 185.

Harrison BRIGGS, born: 19 Feb 1898, single, parents: Rufus Briggs (NC) and Fannie McKinney (NC), death cause: "hurt in mines and took typhus fever", informant: James Briggs (Watauga Valley), died: 4 Aug 1917, record (1917) #: 186.

Cordie Eva WATSON, age 2 years, parents: Roy Watson and Rose Watson, death cause: "indigestion", informant: Roy Watson (Shell Creek), buried: Stout Cemetery, died: 5 Aug 1917, record (1917) #: 187.

Ella Burl CARTER, born: 17 Jun 1917, parents: C.C. Carter and Lillie Ellis, death cause: "indigestion", informant: C.C. Carter, buried: Emmert Cemetery, died: 6 Aug 1917, record (1917) #: 188.

Clay YOUNG, born: 13 Sep 1916, parents: Garrett Young (NC) and Lilly Hughes (NC), death cause: "not known", buried: Roan Mountain, died: 8 Aug 1917, record (1917) #: 189.

Johney SAMS, born: 20 Mar 1910, parents: Berry Sams and Maggie Scalf, death cause: "acute nephritis", informant: Berry Sams, buried: Carr Cemetery, died: 9 Aug 1917, record (1917) #: 190.

Elizabeth MCKINNEY, born: 8 May 1854, married, parents: George Morton and Adalade Campbell, death cause: "rhumatism and abscess of leg", informant: Elbert Smith (Hampton), died: 10 Aug 1917, record (1917) #: 191.

Eva LOWE, age 8 years, parents: Noah Lowe and Lillie Pierce, death cause: "spinal meningitis", informant: C.H. Hyder (Watauga Valley), buried: Pierce Cemetery, died: 12 Aug 1917, record (1917) #: 192.

Jessie HUGHES, born: 19 Nov 1916, parents: Ell Hughes (NC) and Ura Biddix (NC), death cause: "not known", informant: Jim Pritchard (Roan Mountain), died: 12 Aug 1917, record (1917) #: 193.

Allen COCHRAN, born: 15 Jul 1917, parents: James Cochran and Mary Carver, death cause: not recorded, informant: Nat Carver (Hampton), buried: Fairview Cemetery, died: 13 Aug 1917, record (1917) #: 194.

Julia C. DICKSON, born: 18 Apr 1877, single, parents: William H. Dickson (Washington County) and Nancy A. Smalling (Washington County), death cause: "pulmonary tuberculosis", buried: Milligan, died: 5 Aug 1917, record (1917) #: 195.

Herman BARNETT, born: 13 Aug 1917, parents: Erley Barnett and Ettie Johnson, death cause: "not known", informant: Erley Barnett (Roan Mountain), died: 16 Aug 1917, record (1917) #: 196.

Florence MORRIS, born: 5 Aug 1916, parents: E.E. Morris and (first name illegible) Bowers, death cause: "gastro (illegible)", buried: Colbaugh Cemetery, died: 18 Aug 1917, record (1917) #: 197.

Infant HEATON, male, parents: W.F. Heaton and Dollie (surname illegible), death cause: "not born at full term", residence: Roan Mountain, died; 19 Aug 1917, record (1917) #: 198.

Allen TAYLOR, born: 25 Dec 1891, married, parents: John Taylor and Lorettie Archer, death cause: "diabetes", informant: Allen Archer (Carter), buried: Ensor Cem., died: 21 Aug 1917, record (1917) #: 199.

Nellie Cleo Paline TURNER, born: 28 Jan 1917, parents: Sam Turner and Dora Bowling, death cause: "pnuemonia and congenital pellagra", informant: Sam Turner (Elizabethton), buried: Turner Cemetery, died: 21 Aug 1917, record (1917) #: 200.

Allen P. SHELL, born: 13 Jun 1838, married, parents: "unknown", death cause: "paralysis", resided at Watauga, died; 24 Aug 1917, record (1917) #: 201.

Mrs. Carline WILLIAMS, born: 8 Dec 1835, widow, parents: Mike Grindstaff and Sallie Chambers, death cause: "paralysis", informant: C.V. Whitehead (Hopson), buried: Hall Cemetery, died: 24 Aug 1917, record (1917) #: 202.

Wheeler HEAGAN, born: 3 Feb 1867 in Washington County, parents: William Heagan and Laura Lutrell, death cause: "nephritis", informant: D.P. Lacy (Elizabethton), buried: Highland Cemetery, died: 26 Aug 1917, record (1917) #: 203.

Kittie STOUT, age 26 years, married, Parents: Allen Blevins and Sarah Garland, death cause: "tuberculosis", informant: Charlie Blevins (Carter), buried: Garland Cemetery, died: 26 Aug 1917, record (1917) #: 204.

Bert BARNETT, born: 13 Aug 1917, parents: Erby Barnett and Ettie Johnson (NC), death cause: "not known", died: 28 Aug 1917, record (1917) #: 205.

Andy PRICE, age 29 years, born in Ashe County, NC, single, parents: William Price (Ashe Co., NC) and R.J.C. Hash (Ashe Co., NC), death cause: "pulmonary tuberculosis", informant: Cart Smith (Fish Springs), buried: Ashe County, NC, died: 29 Aug 1917, record (1917) #: 206.

Alice WARRICK, colored, age 55 years, married, parents: father's name not stated and Alice Hyder, death cause: "typhoid fever", informant: A.C. Jackson (Johnson City), buried: Milligan, died: 31 Aug 1917, record (1917) #: 207.

Ruby SPOON, born: 3 Dec 1918, parents: Charles Spoon and Ruthie Buck, death cause: "typhoid fever", buried: Milligan, died: 31 Aug 1917, record (1917) #: 208.

Lena Helen SIMERLY, born: 16 Aug 1916, parents: David H. Simerly and Mary J. Headrick, death cause: "colitis", informant: D.H. Simerly (Valley Forge), died: 31 Aug 1917, record (1917) #: 209.

Abraham JENKINS, born: Mar 1853, married, parents: William Jenkins and Sarah Margaret Carver, death cause: "gall stones", resided at Valley Forge, buried: Hodge Cem., died: 31 Aug 1917, record (1917) #: 210

Infant JONES, male, parents: William Jones and Rosa Williams, death cause: "premature birth", born/died: 9 Aug 1917, record (1917) #: 211. (twin below)

Infant FRASIER, male, parents: W.O. Frasier and Flora Taylor, death cause: "stillborn", informant: W.O. Frasier (Carter), buried: Blevins Cemetery, died: 23 Aug 1917, record (1917) #: 212.

Infant JONES, male, parents: William Jones and Rosa Williams, death cause: "premature birth", born/died: 9 Aug 1917, record (1917) #: 213.

Willie PRITCHARD, born: 27 Apr 1917, parents: John Pritchard and Bessie Hurley, death cause: "hives", informant: Bessie Pritchard (Carter), buried: Garland Cemetery, died: 7 Sep 1917, record (1917) #: 214.

Worley Ernest WILSON, born: 22 Oct 1915, parents: Richard Wilson and Flora Oliver, death cause: "reported to be spinal trouble", buried: Bowers Cemetery, died: 2 Sep 1917, record (1917) #: 215.

James Harmon RIGGS, born: 15 Mar 1915, parents: Robert Riggs and Flora Crow, death cause: "diptheria", informant: Robert Riggs (Carter), buried: Colbaugh Cemetery, died: 5 Sep 1917, record (1917) #: 216.

Infant HARDIN, male, parents: John Hardin and May Lipford, death cause: "not known", informant: John Hardin (Siam), born/died: 5 Sep 1917, record #: 217.
Harry Lee BUCK, born: 28 Mar 1917, parents: Charlie Buck and Callie Baker, death cause: "cholera", informant: Charlie Buck (Shell Creek), buried: Buck Cemetery, died: 6 Sep 1917, record (1917) #: 218.
Ora BREWER, born: 17 Nov 1901, parents: Wesley Brewer and Bell Lathern (NC), death cause: "typhoid", informant: Wesley Brewer (Shell Creek), buried: Turbeyfield Cem., died: 14 Sep 1917, record #: 219.
Infant STOUT, female, parents: Nathan Stout and Lena Lewis, death cause: not stated, informant: Nathan Stout (Hampton), born/died: 15 Sep 1917, record (1917) #: 220.
Lannie REYNOLDS, female, age about 68, single, parents: Andrew Reynolds and Elizabeth (surname illegible), death cause: "apoplexy", informant: S.E. Reynolds, buried: Reynolds Cemetery, died: 15 Sep 1917, record (1917) #: 221.
Vana MCKINNEY, age about 82 years, widow, parents: Thomas Merritt and Rebecca Bowers, death cause: "blood poison", informant: D.C. Hampton, buried: McKinney Cemetery, died: 15 Sep 1917, record (1917) #: 222.
Samuel HODGE, born: 12 Aug 1843, married, parents: Thomas Hodge (NC) and Jennie Wilcox (NC), death cause: "paralysis", informant: Sarh Hodge (Shell Creek), buried: Potter Cemetery, died: 16 Sep 1917, record (1917) #: 223.
Elizabeth REYNOLDS, age 95 years, parents: not stated, death cause: "heart disease", informant: S.E. Reynolds, buried: Reynolds Cemetery, died: 19 Sep 1917, record (1917) #: 224.
Hellen CAMPBELL, born: 5 Mar 1917, parents: John S. Campbell and Callie Shaw, death cause: "cholera, informant: J.S. Campbell (Hampton), buried: Hall Cemetery, died: 21 Sep 1917, record (1917) #: 225.
Matilda CRUMLEY, age 46 years, married, parents: W.O. Frazier and Margaret Hinkle, death cause: not stated, buried: Watauga Academy Cemetery, died: 22 Sep 1917, record (1917) #: 226.
Joseph Herrell LOVELESS, born: 23 Aug 1917, parents: David K. Loveless and Emma Brumit, death cause: "cholera", informant: D.K. Loveless (Elizabethton), buried: Watauga Valley, died: 23 Sep 1917, record (1917) #: 227.

James Davis Burl ANDREWS, born: 22 Mar 1917, parents: D.C. Andrews and Hety Greer (NC), death cause: illegible, informant: J.W. Andrews (Butler), buried: Elk Mills, died: 25 Sep 1917, record (1917) #: 228.

Georgia JONES, age 1 year and 17 months, parents: Littleton Jones (NC) and (first name illegible) Campbell (NC), death cause: "marsinmus", buried: Campbell Cemetery, died: 28 Sep 1917, record #: 229.

John C. WILLIAMS, age 2 years, 6 months and 20 days, parents: Samuel Williams and _____ Bowers, death cause: "not stated", informant: Charles Bowers (Watauga Valley), died: 30 Sep 1917, record #: 230.

Infant HERMAN, female, parents: Condon Herman and Callie Buckles, death cause: "stillborn", informant: Condon Herman (Watauga Valley), buried: Buckles Cem., born/died: 17 Sep 1917, record (1917) #: 231.

Infant HAMPTON, male, parents; Leonard Hampton and Mary E. Nave, death cause: "born dead", informant: Grant Nave (Gap Creek), buried: Sims Cemetery, died: 19 Sep 1917, record (1917) #: 232.

Tilda MONTGOMERY, age 55 years, married, parents: William Whitehead and mother's name not stated, death cause: "typhoid fever", informant: Jeff Montgomery (Shell Creek), buried: Street Cemetery, died: 1 Oct 1917, record (1917) #: 233.

Infant SAMS, male, parents: R.M. Sams and Carrie Richards, death cause: "premature", informant: Lee Sams (Elizabethton), buried: Colbaugh Cemetery, died: 20 Oct 1917, record (1917) #: 234.

Mrs. Hannah KEEN, born: 24 Aug 1850, widow, parents: George W. Daniels and Susan Morris, death cause: "pulmonary tuberculosis", informant: Charles L. Price (Johnson City), buried: Price Cemetery, died: 2 Oct 1917, record (1917) #: 235.

Evelyn MILLER, born: 7 Aug 1917, parents: Elbert Miller and Addie Gregg, death cause: not stated, informant: Margaret Cox (Roan Mountain), died: 4 Oct 1917, record (1917) #: 236.

J.J. WHITE, born: 18 Jan 1846, widower, parents: Abraham White and Nancy Jennings (VA), death cause: "cardiac asthma", informant: George White (Milligan), buried: Milligan Cemetery, died: 5 Oct 1917, record (1917) #: 237.

Harvie Elmer MESSIMER, Jr., born: 23 Jul 1917 in Alabama, parents: H.E. Messimer (PA) and Ruby Hathaway, death cause: "pneumonia", informant: W.C. Hathaway (Hampton), died: 5 Oct 1917, record (1917) #: 238.

Estel LYON, age 7 years, 3 months and 7 days, parents: John Lyon and _____ Glover, death cause: "pneumonia", buried: McKeehan Cemetery, died: 6 Oct 1917, record (1917) #: 239.

Rosa Edith GLOVER, born: 19 Sep 1916, parents: W.A. Glover and Mary Chambers, death cause: "pneumonia fever", informant: D.M. Matherly (Valley Forge), died: 7 Oct 1917, record (1917) #: 240.

Frank L. BRADLEY, Jr., born: 18 Mar 1909, parents: Frank L. Bradley and Annis Slagle, death cause: "membraneous croup", informant: J.C. Bradley (Elizabethton), died: 7 Oct 1917, record #: 244.

Lillie CASEY, born: 29 Jul 1916, parents: George Casey and Jenie Gourley, death cause: "malnutrition", informant: George Casey (Hampton), buried: Hall Cemetery, died: 9 Oct 1917, record (1917) #: 245.

Alleen HYDER, born: 19 Apr 1915, parents: Daniel L. Hyder and Sallie Little (Johnson City), death cause: "diptheria", informant: R.B. Hyder, buried: Little Cemetery, died: 9 Oct 1917, record (1917) #: 246.

Nancy GRINDSTAFF, born: 1 Apr 1833, widow, parents: Wright Moreland and Mary Ann Grindstaff, death cause: "old age", informant: George Grindstaff (Carter), buried: Hurley Cem., died: 10 Oct 1917, record #: 247.

Crystal Jane MILLER, born: 21 Jan 1917, parents: Samuel Miller (Mitchell Co., NC) and Maggie Lipford, death cause: illegible, informant: Wesley Miller (Shell Creek), died: 12 Oct 1917, record #: 248.

Orris Willard WEBB, born: 12 Oct 1917, parents: Albert Webb and Ruth Brown, death cause: not stated, informant: Elbert Webb (Shell Creek), buried: Shell Creek Cem., died: 13 Oct 1917, record (1917) #: 249.

Howard FAIR, born: 5 Oct 1917, parents: Sam H. Fair and Lillie Umphris [Humphrey ?], death cause: "not known", informant: Sam H. Fair (Elizabethton), buried: Hyder Cem., died: 17 oct 1917, record (1917) #: 250.

Ruby SMITH, born: 9 Jul 1915, parents: C.C. Smith and Carry Ellis, death cause: "cholera", died: 18 Oct 1917, record (1917) #: 251.

Susan DUGGER, born: 31 May 1833, widow, parents: Daniel Campbell and mother's name unknown, death cause: "pneumonia", buried: Carden's Bluff Cemetery, died: 26 Oct 1917, record (1917) #: 252.

James GARDNER, black, born: 5 Mar 1891, married, parents: John Gardner (NC) and mother's name unknown, death cause: "hypertrophy of liver", informant: George Gardner, buried: Cedar Grove Cemetery, died: 28 Oct 1917, record (1917) #: 253.

Mary BOWERS, age 4 years, parents: Teter Bowers and _____ Marklin [Markland ?], death cause: "supposed to be bronchitis", died: 30 Oct 1917, record #: 251.

Arther JULIAN, parents: Cain Julian and Lener Ingram, death cause: "strangulation", informant: Hacker Julian, buried: Lacy Cem., born/died: 2 Oct 1917, record (1917) #: 252.

Haskell B. BOWERS, born: 16 Apr 1888, married, parents: Millard F. Bowers and Sallie Bowers, death cause: "lumbago, neuralgia, palpitation of the heart", buried: Crow Cem., died: 3 Nov 1917, record #: 253.

Lizzie Culbert TAYLOR, age 72 years, widow, parents: James Culbert and Matilda Williams, death cause: "dropsy", informant: Leevi Taylor (Carter), buried: Taylor Cem., died: 4 Nov 1917, record (1917) #: 254.

David MORRIS, age 61 years, married, parents: Henry Morris and Betty Scott, death cause: "supposed to be organic heart disease", informant: Mrs. Rhoda Perry, buried: Morris Cem., died: 8 Nov 1917, record #: 255.

Cassie HUMPHREY, born: 14 Nov 1888, married, parents: John Henry Johnson and Lavonia Morris, death cause: "nephritis", informant: Fred Johnson, buried: Valley Forge, died: 9 Nov 1917, record (1917) #: 256.

Nannie OLIVER, born: 21 Jun 1882, married, parents: father's name unknown and Sallie Campbell, death cause: "tuberculosis", informant: H.A. Oliver (Hampton), buried: Cardens Bluff, died: 12 Nov 1917, record (1917) #: 257.

Dewey ROBERTS, age 11 years, parents: Russell Roberts and _____ McKinney, death cause: "spinal meningitis", informant: Sincler McKinney (Hampton), buried: McKinney Cemetery, died: 13 Nov 1917, record #: 258.

Dora WILLIAMS, born: 17 Nov 1916, parents: E.J. Williams and Sallie Hopson, death cause: "dysentery", informant: J.C. Williams (Watauga Valley), buried: Buckles Cem., died: 16 Nov 1917, record (1917) #: 259.

Arthur Blaine DUNLOP, born: 21 Oct 1916, parents: Walter Dunlop and Mollie Riggs, death cause: "pneumonia", informant: Bob Riggs, buried: Colbaugh Cemetery, died: 17 Nov 1917, record (1917) #: 260.

Henry BOWLING, born: 28 Apr 1856, married, parents: Jake Bowling and mother's name not known, death cause: "tuberculosis", informant: Frank Bowling (Roan Mountain), died: 19 Nov 1917.

Julian NAVE, born: 28 Apr 1884, married, parents: David Nave and Mangla Mathison, death cause: "pulmonary tuberculosis", informant: Charles Morrell, buried: Hunter, died: 29 Nov 1917, record #: 262.

William MCKINNEY, age 33 years, married, parents: Thomas McKinney and Hester Stevens, death cause: "tuberculosis of lungs", buried: McKinney Cemetery, died: 21 Nov 1917, record (1917) #: 263.
Eliza GARLAND, age "unknown", married, parents: Poe Wilson and Nancy Garland, death cause: "old age", informant: Andy Wilson (Carter), buried: Garland Cemetery, died: 23 Nov 1917, record (1917) #: 264.
Sam HUGHES, born: 8 Jan 1897, single, parents: Brother Hughes (NC) and CArolina Barnett, death cause: not stated, informant: Luna Hughes (Roan Mountain), died: 25 Nov 1917, record (1917) #: 265.
Hila GRINDSTAFF, age 72 years, born in Johnson County, widow, parents: David Stout (Johnson County) and Salina (surname illegible)(Johnson County), death cause: "heart dropsy", informant: George Estep (Carter), buried: Grindstaff Cemetery, died: 27 Nov 1917, record (1917) #: 266.
Roy CLOSSON, born: 15 Sep 1900, single, parents: James Closson and Jane Vines (Johnson County), death cause: "paralysis from spinal injury", informant: George Closson (Dark Ridge, NC), died: 27 Nov 1917, record (1917) #: 267.
Infant GOUGE, male, parents: Frank Gouge and Bell Whitehead, death cause: "strangulation during birth", buried: Whitehead Cemetery, born/died: 4 Nov 1917, record (1917) #: 268.
Lagrand WHAILEY, born: 2 Jul 1864, married, parents: James Gregg (NC) and Jinie Singleton (NC), death cause: "rhumatisl and hsyseria", informant: C.C. Whailey (Butler), buried: Smith Cemetery, died: 17 Dec 1917, record (1917) #: 269.
James Lester CALHOUN, born: 29 Sep 1899, parents: David Calhoun (NC) and Margaret Graybeal (NC), death cause: "pneumonia fever", informant: David Calhoun (Roan Mountain), died: 2 Dec 1917, record #: 270.
Sam BIRCHFIELD, age 80 years, born in North Carolina, married, parents: Rheuben Birchfield (NC) and Celia Hughes (NC), death cause: "Brights disease", buried: Roan Mountain, died: 3 Dec 1917, record (1917) #: 271.
Joseph GLOVER, born: 21 Jul 1888, married, parents: James Glover and Mary E. Campbell, death cause: illegible, buried: Campbell Cemetery, died: 6 Dec 1917, record (1917) #: 272.
Cora B. MCCLEAN, born: 12 Aug 1880, born in New York, parents: Thomas Soules and mother's name not known, death cause: "childbirth", buried: Bramar, died: 7 Dec 1917, record (1917) #: 273.

George HINLY, age 57 years, born in North Carolina, married, parents: "not known", death cause: "ulcerated stump of leg from operation several years ago", buried: Bowers Cemetery, died: 7 Dec 1917, record (1917) #: 274.

Earl FULTON, born: 4 Nov 1915, parents: Sam Fulton (Washington Co., VA) and Fannie Cornett, death cause: "membraneous croup", informant: J.A. Cornett (Elizabethton), buried: Highland Cemetery, died: 7 Dec 1917, record (1917) #: 275.

Paul HOPSON, born: 29 Nov 1917, parents: J.P. Hopson and Nannie Arnett (NC), death cause: "boul hives", informant: Carl Simerly (Roan Mountain), died: 8 Dec 1917, record (1917) #: 276.

Cad SNODGRASS, born: 29 Jan 1882, married, parents: J.S. Snodgrass (Jonesoro) and T.S. Pridghead (Elaxender Co., NC), death cause: "pulmonary tuberculosis", informant: G.W. Snodgrass (Watauga), buried: Hughes Cemetery, died: 11 Dec 1917, record (1917) #: 277.

Iona GRINDSTAFF, born: 3 Nov 1917, parents: Claude Grindstaff and Daisy Williams, death cause: "hives", informant: Lonnie Williams (Watauga Valley), buried: Grindstaff Cem., died: 12 Dec 1917, record #: 278.

Margaret COLE, born: 13 Dec 1854, married, parents: Thomas Heatherly and Elizabeth Fair, death cause: "supposed to be heart failure", informant: A.J. Fletcher (Watauga Valley), buried: Ritchie Cemetery, died: 13 Dec 1917, record (1917) #: 279.

Floyd BOWMAN, age 9 years, parents: John P. Bowman and Emma Bowman, death cause: not stated, informant: John Bowman (Johnson City), buried: Buck Cemetery, died: 13 Dec 1917, record (1917) #: 280.

George HUMPHREYS, age 56 years, born in Sullivan County, widower, parents: Henry J. Humphreys and Perlina Lilley (Sullivan Co.), death cause: "pulmonary tuberculosis", died: 14 Dec 1917, record #: 281.

Arnold ELLIS, age 84 years, widower, parents: Radford Ellis and Louie Drake, death cause: "pneumonia", informant: D.G. Ellis (Elizabethton), buried: Ellis Cemetery, died: 18 Dec 1917, record (1917) #: 282.

Riley HART, age 60 years, married, parents: Leonard Hart and Lizie Jenkins, death cause: "blood poison:, died; 18 Dec 1917, record (1917) #: 283.

Hazel Bulah OLIVER, born: 3 Jun 1917, parents: James Oliver and Nannie Campbell, death cause: not stated, informant: Emmett Roark (Hampton), buried: Cardens Bluff, died: 20 Dec 1917, record (1917) #: 284.

Bennick FAIR, born: 26 Jul 1914, parents: C.D. Fair and Mary Livingston, death cause: "lobar pneumonia", informant: W.F. Fair (Johnson City), buried: Archer Cemetery, died: 20 Dec 1917, record (1917) #: 285.

Zeak GRINDSTAFF, age 44 years, married, parents: A.J. Grindstaff and Louise Prichet, death cause: "heart failure", died: 23 Dec 1917, record (1917) #: 286.

William M. SHELL, born: 24 Dec 1853, parents: William Shell and Mary Ann (surname illegible), death cause: "heart disease", informant: Andy Shell, buried: Highland Cem., died: 24 Dec 1917, record #: 287.

Gracie Belle CAMPBELL, born: 26 Sep 1913, parents: Ed Campbell and Rosa Garland, death cause: "broncho pneumonia", died: 26 Dec 1917, record (1917) #: 288.

Lula Cornelia SNIDER, born: 19 Apr 1859 in Watauga County, NC, widow, parents: Henry W. Hardin (Watauga Co., NC) and Lucinda Horton (Watauga Co., NC), death cause: "gall stones", informant: Walter F. Church (Shell Creek), died: 26 Dec 1917, record #: 289.

Easter ELLIOTT, born: 6 Apr 1880 in Johnson County, married, parents: J.P. Arnold (Johnson County) and mother's name unknown, death cause: "disease of kidney", informant: Charles Elliott (Elizabethton), died: 28 Dec 1917, record (1917) #: 290.

Georgie May LIVINGSTON, born: 14 Jan 1914, parents: Pettibone Livingston and Susan Estep, death cause: "pneumonia fever", informant: John Taylor (Carter), buried: Garland Cemetery, died: 28 Dec 1917, record (1917) #: 291.

Carter HODGE, age 31 years, single, parents: Siamon Hodge and Caroline Church, death cause: "measles", buried: Garland Cemetery, died: 28 Dec 1917, record (1917) #: 292.

Sarafina BUNTON, born: 15 Jul 1849, married, parents: Daniel Cable and Elizabeth Shuffield, death cause: "typhoid fever", informant: D.F. White (Butler), died: 28 Dec 1917, record (1917) #: 293.

Jennie HUGHES, born: 16 Dec 1917, parents: J.M. Hughes (VA) and Maggie Taylor, death cause: "unknown", informant: E.E. Taylor (Carter), buried: Grindstaff Cemetery, died: 30 Dec 1917, record (1917) #: 294.

James DELOACH, age 75 years, parents: Thomas Deloach and Paulina Oliver, death cause: "chronic diarrohea", informant: W.G. Campbell (Hampton), died: 31 Dec 1917, record (1917) #: 295.

Infant PARHAM, male, parents: Ezry Parham and Mollie Ingram, death cause: "stillborn", buried: Holly Hill Cemetery, died: 28 Dec 1917, record (1917) #: 296.

Infant MCCLAIN, female, parents: Alex McClain and Cora Soules (NY), death cause: "stillborn", informant: Alex McClain (Braimer), buried: Hall Cemetery, died: 2 Dec 1917, record (1917) #: 297.
Earl MORRELL, parents: E.A. Morrell and Blanche Bowers, death cause: "stillborn", buried: Ellis Cemetery, died: 27 Dec 1917, record (1917) #: 298.
Ollie HART, female, age 19 years, parents: C.W. Hart and Margaret Hart, death cause: "pulmonary tuberculosis", died: 1 Jan 1918, record (1918) #: 1.
Mrs. Rose M. ROBERTS, born: 1 Dec 1841 in Richmond, VA, parents: father's name unknown and Rosa M. Toler (Richmond, VA), death cause: "pneumonia", buried: Lynchburg, VA, died: 2 Jan 1918, record (1918) #: 2.
Lucy GARLAND, born: 28 Nov 1914, parents: David Garland and Hila Curtis Garland, death cause: "measles", informant: Jesse Heatherly (Carter), buried: Garland Cemetery, died: 2 Jan 1918, record (1918) #: 3.
Alfred LIVINGSTON, born: 17 Jun 1917, parents: Bat Livingston and Finer Taylor, death cause: "measles", informant: Bat Livingston (Carter), buried: Garland Cemetery, died: 4 Jan 1918, record (1918) #: 4.
W.M. WILSON, age 89 years, born in Mitchell County, NC, widower, parents: Jim Willson (Mitchell Co., NC) and Mitchel Wilson (Mitchell Co., NC), death cause: "old age", died: 8 Jan 1918, record (1918) #: 5.
Hobart Francis CHAMBERS, born: 1 Jun 1918, parents: W.A. Chambers and Lelia Whitehead, death cause: "heart trouble", informant: W.A. Chambers (Valley Forge), died: 9 Jan 1918, record (1918) #: 6.
Lefler WILSON, born: 17 Dec 1917, parents: Ray Wilson and Mae Pearce, death cause: "unknown", informant: Ray Wilson (Fish Springs), buried: Pearce Cemetery, died: 9 Jan 1918, record (1918) #: 7.
Bettie WHITE, born: 13 Jan 1895, married, parents: James Campbell and Sarah Hyder, death cause: "gastric ulcer", informant: James Campbell (Butler), buried: Stalling Cem., died: 12 Jan 1918, record (1918) #: 8.
Andrew Jackson PEEBLES, born: 16 Jan 1829, widower, parents: William Peebles and Elizabeth Sheetz (VA), death cause: "paralysis", informant: John W. Peoples (Johnson City), buried: Peebles Cemetery, died: 13 Jan 1918, record (1918) #: 9.
Verness SWANER, female, born: 31 Oct 1917, parents: Thomas Swaner and Mary Swaner, death cause: "bowl hives", informant: C.C. Street (Hampton), died: 13 Jan 1918, record (1918) #: 10.

William PETERS, age 81 years, married, parents: William Peters and _____ Brooks, death cause: "heart failure", informant: J.W. Carrier (Watauga Valley), died: 14 Jan 1918, record (1918) #: 11.

Bill HATCHER, age 66 years, married, parents: Lee Hatcher and Martha Tipton, death cause: illegible, buried: Smith Cemetery, died: 19 Jan 1918, record (1918) #: 12.

Robert Lee HENDRICKSON, born: 18 Nov, age 3 years, parents: Edward Hendrickson and Minnie Crumley, death cause: "diptheria", informant: W.L. Hampton, buried: Highland Cem., died: 20 Jan 1918, record (1918) #: 13.

Charles M. MCGEE, colored, born: 5 Apr 1895, parents: Daniel McGee (NC) and Sallie Fitzsimmons, death cause: "pneumonia", informant: W.R. Fitzsimmons (Elizabethton), died: 21 Jan 1918, record (1918) #: 14.

Lanier GUINN, born: 29 Jun 1911, female, parents: David Guinn and Julia Sims, death cause: "heart failure", informant: A.J. Arnett (Roan Mountain), buried: Nelson Cemetery, died: 21 Jan 1918, record (1918) #: 15.

R.C. BUCKLES, male, born: 20 May 1820, widower, parents: Cass Hughes (VA) and Mary Buckles (VA), death cause: "old age", informant: James Buckles (Watauga Valley), buried: Buckles Cemetery, died: 23 Jan 1918, record (1918) #: 16.

Jim WARDECK, black, age: "unknown", parents: "unknown", death cause: "polio", informant: A.C. Jackson (Johnson City), died: 25 Jan 1918, record (1918) #: 17.

Toy SIMERLY, born: 1 Apr 1815, parents: Robert L. Simerly and Vici Odom, death cause: "typhoid fever", informant: J.B. Shoun (Hampton), died: 25 Jan 1918, record (1918) #: 18.

Christopher BOWMAN, born: 11 Oct 1837, widower, parents: William Bowman and _____ Moreland, death cause: "mitral regurgitation", informant: D.A. Bowman (Johnson City), buried: Bowman Cemetery, died: 25 Jan 1918, record (1918) #: 19.

Isaac GUINN, age about 65 years, married, parents: Alex Guinn and Rebecca Guinn, death cause: "mitral regurgitation", informant: H.F. Pircy (Elizabethton), buried: Colbaugh Cemetert, died: 26 Jan 1918, record (1918) #: 20.

Thomas Dayton CARVER, born: 26 Dec 1917, parents: James Carver and Hettie Clark, death cause: "boul hives", informant: Henry Clark (Roan Mountain), buried: Carver Cem., died: 26 Jan 1918, record #: 21.

Peter Hamilton POTTER, age about 88 years, married, parents: Peter Potter and _____ Guin (Watauga Co., NC), death cause: "supposed to be rhumatism", informant: John Potter (Butler), buried: Elk Church Cemetery, died: 27 Jan 1918, record (1918) #: 22.

Butler ESTEP, born: 14 Feb 1865 in Virginia, married, parents: father's name unknown and Low Estep, death cause: "croupous pneumonia", informant: A.J. Blevins (Elizabethton), buried: Carter Cemetery, died: 28 Jan 1918, record (1918) #: 23.

Infant SMITH, male, parents: Bruce Smith and Celia Griffith, death cause: "stillborn", informant: Bruce Smith (Fish Springs), buried: Smith Cemetery, died: 21 Jan 1918, record (1918) #: 24.

Tine WINTERS, female, parents: William Winters and Bessie Winters (NC), death cause: "born dead", informant: William Winters (Shell Creek), died: 13 Jan 1918, record (1918) #: 25.

Infant ODOM, male, parents: Ancil Odom and Julia Ingram, death cause: "stillborn", informant; Ancil Odom (Shell Creek), buried: Stout Cemetery, died: 29 Jan 1918, record (1918) #: 26.

Infant WILLIAMS, male, born: 1 Feb 1918, parents: Samuel Williams and Callie Bowers, death cause: "deformity", informant: F.A. Williams (Watauga Valley), buried: Buckles Cemetery, died: 2 Feb 1918, record (1918) #: 27.

Goldy ELLIOTT, age 4 months, parents: Alexander Elliott and Connie Brookshire (Johnson County), death cause: "heart failure", informant: J.B. Crosswhite, died: 5 Feb 1918, record (1918) #: 28.

Infant LEWIS, male, parents: Lawson Lewis and Katy Morris (Johnson County), death cause: "abortion, mother had measles", informant: G.M. Lewis (Butler), died: 4 Feb 1918, record (1918) #: 29.

Lee MOODY, born: 29 Nov 1913, parents: Joseph H. Moody and Josey Vines, death cause: "pneumonia fever", informant: Edward Stout (Dark Ridge, NC), buried: Closson Cem., died: 5 Feb 1918, record (1918) #: 30.

Adalade BUNTON, age 68 years, married, parents: Thomas Perry and Nancy Ellis, death cause: "refused medicine", informant: Henry Shell (Shell Creek), buried: Perry Cemetery, died: 5 Feb 1918, record (1918) #: 31.

Infant TREADWAY, female, born: 1 Feb 1918, parents: John Treadway and Ina Nidiffer, death cause: "unknown", informant: John Treadway (Valley Forge), died: 5 Feb 1918, record (1918) #: 32.

Isaac M. HEATON, born: 25 Nov 1850, married, parents: John W. Heaton and Katie Vanhuss, death cause: "injury to chest by rolling log", informant: J.L. Heaton (Valley Forge), died: 7 Feb 1918, record (1918) #: 33.
Pearl PETERS, born: 29 Oct 1897, single, parents: William Peters and Angie Markland, death cause: "tuberculosis", informant: J.C. Baker (Hampton), buried: Morton Cemetery, died: 8 Feb 1918, record (1918) #: 34.
Closson WILSON, born: 13 Sep 1897, single, parents: David Wilson and Jane Wilson, death cause: "pneumonia fever", informant: David Wilson (Carter), buried: Highland Cem., died: 8 Feb 1918, record (1918) #: 35.
Thomas Samuel FAIR, born: 10 Apr 1917, parents: Thomas Fair and Nancy Bradshaw, death cause: "cerebral meningitis", informant: Sheriff Fair (Elizabethton), buried: Carter Cemetery, died: 8 Feb 1918, record (1918) #: 36.
Nancy HIX, age about 50 years, born in Watauga County, NC, married, parents: Morgan Steen (Grayson Co., NC) and Polly Greer (Ashe Co., NC), death cause: "acute paralysis", informant: Morgan Steen (Dark Ridge, NC), buried: Steen Cemetery, died: 9 Feb 1918, record (1918) #: 37.
Josie NAVE, born: 11 Nov 1880, married, parents: Isaac Morrell and Minnie Vanhuss, death cause: "disease heart", died: 11 Feb 1918, record (1918) #: 38.
Ina Mae HOLLY, age 2 years, 3 months and 29 days, parents: G.W. Holly and Kate Pierce, death cause: "acute intestinal catarrh), informant: T. Pierce (Morristown), buried: G.W. Mottern Cemetery, died: 12 Feb 1918, record (1918) #: 39.
Mrs. Rebecca HYDER, age 74 years, parents: Thomas Merritt and Rebecca Bowers, death cause: "pneumonia", informant: R.B. Whitamore (Johnson City), buried: Hyder Cem., died: 12 Feb 1918, record (1918) #: 40.
Martha Lucy WATERS, born: 6 Apr 1879 in Johnson County, parents: J.W. Rouse (Johnson County) and mother's name not stated, death cause: "cancer", buried: J.W. Mottern Cemetery, died: 13 Feb 1918, record (1918) #: 41.
Clarinda JENKINS, born: 17 Aug 1835, married, parents: David (surname illegible) and Annie (surname illegible), death cause: "lagrippe and old age", informant: Hugh Jenkins (Valley Forge), died: 13 Feb 1918, record (1918) #: 42.

E.M. PIERCE, female, born: 3 Aug 1866, married, parents: Alexander Eggers (NC) and Sarah (surname illegible), death cause: "measles settled in lungs", buried: Whitehead Cemetery, died: 16 Feb 1918, record (1918) #: 43.

Lucy Jane WILSON, born: 11 Jul 1833 in Lewisburg, VA, married, parents: James Luttrell and Nancy Arlington, death cause: "arterisclerosis, autoxemia", buried: Wilson Cem., died: 16 Feb 1918, record (1918) #: 44.

Lillie STOUT, age 21 years, 2 months and 12 days, born in Neva, Johnson County, parents: A.G. Stout (Neva) and Mandy Ward (Neva), death cause: "supposed to be tuberculosis", informant: James Stout (Elizabethton), buried: Neva, TN, died: 17 Feb 1918, record #: 45.

Partrive MCKINNEY, female, born: 2 May 1917, parents: Bruce McKinney and Polly (surname illegible), death cause: "meningitis", informant: T.C. McKinney (Elizabethton), died: 20 Feb 1918, record (1918) #: 46.

Margaret Hurley GARLAND, age 74 years, widow, parents: Hardin Hurley and Nancy Hodge, death cause: "tuberculosis", informant: W.G. Nidiffer (Carter), buried: Garland Cemetery, died: 21 Feb 1918, record (1918) #: 47.

Mrs. Rebecca Catherine MOTTERN, born: 29 Nov 1972 in Sullivan County, parents: David G. Weaver (Sullivan County) and Elizabeth Arants (Sullivan County), death cause: "carcinoma uteri", buried: W.J. Mottern Cemetery, died: 22 Feb 1918, record (1918) #: 48.

Mary A. CROSSWHITE, age 65 years, born in Johnson County, parents: Joseph Robertson (Johnson County) and Mary A. Robertson (Johnson County), death cause: "apoplexy", buried: Doe Valley, Johnson County, died: 23 Feb 1918, record (1918) #: 49.

Lena FAIR, born: 2 Aug 1900, parents: W.F. Fair and Lizzie Campbell, death cause: "tuberculosis", informant: W.F. Fair (Elizabethton), died: 23 Feb 1918, record (1918) #: 50.

Matilda Elizabeth FAIR, born: 20 Oct 1883, married, parents: Alexander Campbell and Nancy Taylor, death cause: "tuberculosis", informant: David A. Fair (Elizabethton), buried: Siam, died: 27 Aug 1918, record (1918) #: 51.

Infant SUONG, black, female, parents: James Susong and Lillie Smith (Johnson County), death cause: "stillborn", buried: Odd Fellows Cemetery, died: 15 Feb 1918, record (1918) #: 52.

Malcolm McCurry TUCKER, born: 29 Mar 1868 in North Carolina, married, parents: Joseph Tucker (Washington Co., TN) and Jane Burleson (NC), death cause: "chronic brights, liver disease", informant: Dolly Tucker (Shell Creek), buried: Cranberry, NC, died: 1 Mar 1918, record (1918) #: 53.

Infant BLEVINS, male, born: 26 Feb 1918, parents: David Blevins and Mary Garland, death cause: "supposed to be hives", informant: David Blevins (Carter), buried: Garland Cem, died: 3 Mar 1918, record #: 54.

George Washington ELLIOTT, born: 9 Feb 1918, parents: Will Elliott (NC) and Mary Jane Hopson, death cause: not stated, buried: Isaacs Cemetery, died: 4 Mar 1918, record (1918) #: 55.

Samuel CLARK, born: 6 Jan 1898, parents: James Clark and Jane Cochran, death cause: "peritonitis", informant: James Clark (Roan Mountain), buried: Fair View Cemetery, died: 4 Mar 1918, record (1918) #: 56.

Maggie HAWKINS, age 30 years, born at Rock Creek, NC, married, parents: Samuel Greer (Rock Creek, NC) and _____ Gibbs, death cause: "chronic gastritis", informant: Harrison Green (Elizabethton), buried: Heaton Creek, died: 6 Mar 1918, record (1918) #: 57.

Lucinda OAKS, born: 10 Feb 1829, widow, parents: Thomas Perry and Nancy Ellis, death cause: "old age", informant: J.S. Oaks (Shell Creek), buried: Oaks Cemetery, died: 6 Mar 1918, record (1918) #: 58.

Roy HEAD, age 11 months, parents: J.H. Head and mother's name not stated, death cause: "pneumonia", informant: J.V. Jordan (Hampton), died: 7 Mar 1918, record (1918) #: 59.

George HARDIN, born: 24 Dec 1844, widower, parents: Isaac Hardin and Sallie Oliver, death cause: "supposed to be heart failure", informant: Johnie Hardin (Valley Forge), buried: Hardin Cemetery, died: 7 Mar 1918, record (1918) #: 60.

Daniel STOUT, born: 10 Jun 1867, married, parents: G.W. Stout and Patsy Cable, death cause: "pneumonia", informant: Carter Lunceford (Shell Creek), buried: Shell Creek, died: 8 Mar 1918, record (1918) #: 61.

Claud BLEVINS, born: 26 Feb 1918, parents: David Blevins and Mary Blevins, death cause: "hives", informant; W.L. Nidiffer (Carter), buried: Garland Cemetery, died: 9 Mar 1918, record (1918) #: 62.

Amanda Markland RAINS, age 72 years, widow, parents: Parrot Markland and Joanah Basentine, death cause: "dropsy", informant: Sam Taylor (Carter), buried: Markland Cem., died: 9 Mar 1918, record (1918) #: 63.

Anner ISAACS, born: 20 Dec 1903, female, born in North Carolina, parents: Aaron Isaacs and Mattie Ashley (NC), death cause: "unknown", informant: Aaron Isaacs (Shell Creek), buried: Isaacs Cemetery, died: 9 Mar 1918, record (1918) #: 64.

Francis Norris BENNETT, born: 28 Oct 1917, parents: Claude D. Bennett and Josephine Jones, death cause: illegible, informant: Bob Jones, buried: Highland Cemetery, died: 11 Mar 1918, record (1918) #: 65.

Charles Raymond MCKEEHAN, born: 9 Mar 1918, parents: Frank McKeehan and Pearl Pate (Unicoi County), death cause: "asphixia caused at birth", informant: W.M. Loveless, buried: McKeehan Cemetery, died: 12 Mar 1918, record (1918) #: 66.

Infant JOHNSON, female, born: 4 Mar 1918, parents: Carrick Johnson and Laura Wilson, death cause: "yellow jaundice", informant: John Johnson (Roan Mountain), died: 14 Mar 1918, record (1918) #: 67.

Finley MCQUEEN, age 84 years, born in Johnson County, widower, parents: unknown, death cause: "unknown", informant: Will Oliver (Watauga Valley), buried: Buckles Cem., died: 16 Mar 1918, record (1918) #: 68.

Evert SAMS, born: 16 Mar 1918, parents: Lee Sams and Mattie Carr, death cause: "premature birth", informant: Lee Sams (Elizabethton), died: 17 Mar 1918, record (1918) #: 69.

Mary E. TURNER, born: 19 Apr 1846, widow, parents: Samuel Angel and Martha Burrow, death cause: "lagrippe and heart disease", informant: M.N. Folsom (Elizabethton), buried: Turner Cemetery, died: 18 Mar 1918, record (1918) #: 70.

William Arther KELLEY, born: 26 Jan 1917, parents: James Kelley and Lillie Estep, death cause: "membraneous croup", informant: Charles Elliott (Elizabethton), died: 19 Mar 1918, record (1918) #: 71.

David Powell WILCOX, age 87 years, 9 months and 23 days, wodower, born in Washington County, parents: John Wilcox and Letitia Tilson, death cause: "old age, organic heart disease", informant: O.A. Wilcox (Unicoi County), died: 23 Mar 1918, record (1918) #: 72.

Sallie NAVE, born: 24 Mar 1868, single, parents: William Nave and Margaret Lewis, death cause: "consumption of bowels", buried: Buckles Cemetery, died: 23 Mar 1918, record (1918) #: 73.

Eliza M. HART, born: 21 Jul 1844, widow, parents: James Newton and Katie Newton (Sullivan County), death cause: "aortic insufficiency", died: 23 Mar 1918, record (1918) #: 74.

Ethel E. HUGHES, age 27 years, married, parents: J.N. Hart and Julie Treadway, death cause: "pulmonary tuberculosis", buried: W.J. Mottern Cemetery, died: 24 Mar 1918, record (1918) #: 75.

Hampton CAMPBELL, age 61 years, parents: Johnie Campbell and Beckie Hyder, death cause: "lobar pneumonia", buried: McKeehan Cemetery, died: 27 Mar 1918, record (1918) #: 76.

Hasel Ruth GRINDSTAFF, born: 30 Jan 1918, parents: R.D. Grindstaff and Anna Peters, death cause: "croupous pneumonia", buried: Grindstaff Cemetery, died: 27 Mar 1918, record (1918) #: 77.

Infant STOUT, male, parents: Edward Stout and Margaret Vines, death cause: "unknown", informant: William Vines (Dark Ridge, NC), buried: Closson Cemetery, born/died: 2 Mar 1918, record (1918) # 78.

Infant ADKINS, male, parents: Sam Adkins and Emma Peters, death cause: "stillborn", born/died: 20 Mar 1918, record (1918) #: 79.

Infant DELANEY, negro, male, parents: Clarence Delaney and Matissie (surname illegible), death cause: "stillborn", died: 28 Mar 1918, record (1918) #: 80.

Carrie BERRY, born: 2 Jun 1892, married, parents: Jack Collins and Roder Heaton, death cause: "mitral stenosis", informant: John A. Elliott (Watauga Valley), buried: Buckles Cemetery, died: 19 Apr 1918, record (1918) #: 81.

Charles INGRAM, age 37 years, single, parents: Sam Ingram and Cinda Burchfield (NC), death cause: "nephritis", buried: Ingram Cemetery, died: 2 Apr 1918, record (1918) #: 82.

Roderick Brownlow GOUGE, born: 1 Jan 1917, parents: Marion Gouge and Nettie Street, death cause: "strangulated hernia", residence: Hampton, died: 3 Apr 1918, record (1918) #: 83.

Vena BUCKLES, born: 4 Apr 1913, parents: Alf Buckles and Abba Nave, death cause: "typhoid fever", informant: Mack Nave (Watauga Valley), buried: Buckles Cemetery, died: 4 Apr 1918, record (1918) #: 84.

Emma TOLLEY, age 32 years, married, parents: Blake Byrd (NC) and Hannah Davis, death cause: "acute nephritis", informant: Charlie Tolley (Hampton), buried: Tolley Cemetery, died: 4 Apr 1918, record (1918) #: 85.

Emma Francis HUGHES, born: 7 Apr 1851, widow parents: "not known", death cause: "heart disease and old age", died: 7 Apr 1918, record (1918) # 86.

Isaac LARGE, age 53 years, born in Sullivan County, married, parents: Wilson Large (Hawkins County), parents: "not given", death cause: "mitral stenosis", informant: Jess Large (Elizabethton), buried: Colbaugh Cemetery, died: 11 Apr 1918, record (1918) #: 87.

Sarah DOUGHERTY, born: 2 Apr 1843, widow, parents: "unknown", death cause: "organic heart disease", buried: Roan Mountain, died: 13 Apr 1918, record (1918) #: 88.

Cecil VANDEVENTER, born: 12 Oct 1901, parents: Marion Vandeventer and ____ McQueen (Johnson County), death cause: "relaps on measles", buried: Buckles Cemetery, died: 13 Apr 1918, record (1918) #: 89.

Creston FRAZIER, age 11 months and 5 days, parents: W.A. Frazier and Mattie V. Williams, death cause: "epeleptic fits", buried: Wilson Cemetery, died: 21 Apr 1918, record (1918) #: 90.

Lucinda Dempsy LACY, born: 14 May 1877 in Sullivan County, married, parents: John R. Dempsy (VA) and Martha Adams (Sullivan County), death cause: "pulmonary tuberculosis", died: 21 Apr 1918, record #: 91.

Mrs. Mary Ann COGSWELL, age 88 years, born in South Carolina, married, parents: John Eakin (SC) and Nancy Wallace (SC), death cause: "unknown, and old age", buried: Milligan Cemetery, died: 23 Apr 1918, record (1918) #: 92.

Tassie Lee SMITH, born: 28 May 1898, single, parents: Butler Smith and Nora Morgan, death cause: "tumor of stomach", informant: Butler Smith (Shell Creek), buried: Wilson Cemetery, died: 23 Apr 1918, record (1918) #: 93.

James Wesley HAYES, born: 19 Apr 1918, parents: J.W. Hayes and Pearlie Heaton, death cause: "abortion of unknown cause", informant: J.W. Hayes (Shell Creek), died: 24 Apr 1918, record (1918) #: 94.

Smith BRUMIT, born: 24 May 1912, parents: A.B. Brumit (Washington Co., TN) and Alice Smith, death cause: "convulsions", buried: Highland Cemetery, died: 24 Apr 1918, record (1918) #: 95.

Elizabeth KEMP, age 52 years, born in North Carolina, parents: (first name illegible) Burger and Cinda Roberts, death cause: "lobar pneumonia", informant: A.R. Roberts (Hampton), buried: Simerly Cemetery, died: 25 Apr 1918, record (1918) #: 96.

Merrian Arnold HALL, female, age 40 years, married, parents: not stated, death cause: illegible, informant: J.J. Richardson (Carter), buried: Richardson Cem, died: 26 Apr 1918, record (1918) #: 97.

John H. SHORT, born: 13 Feb 1846, married, parents: not stated, death cause: "paralysis", buried; Highland Cemetery, died: 26 Apr 1918, record (1918) #: 98.

E.C. CARR, male, age 83 years, widower, parents: Joseph Carr and Margaret Feathers, death cause: "acute nephritis", informant: Johnson Carr (Elizabethton), buried: Carr Cemetery, died: 28 Apr 1918, record (1918) #: 99.

Joseph PERKINS, born: 17 Mar 1837, married, parents: Jacob Perkins (Johnson County) and Nancy Powell (NC), death cause: "lagrippe", informant: R.T. Jones (Shell Creek), buried: Wilson Cemetery, died: 29 Apr 1918, record (1918) #: 100.

Patsy LYONS, born: 25 Dec 1816, age 102, 4 months and 4 days, widow, parents: James Glover and Katie Sams, death cause: "organic heart disease", informant: G.T.H. Lyons (Elizabethton), buried: Lyons Cemetery, died: 29 Apr 1918, record (1918) #: 101.

Charlie CARROLL, age 73 years, born in Illinois, married, parents: not stated, death cause: "dropsy", informant: Matilda Carroll, buried: Garland Cemetery, died: 30 Apr 1918, record (1918) #: 102.

Infant FRANKLIN, female, parents: Roby Franklin (NC) and Iva Pierce, death cause: "born dead", informant: A.E. Franklin (Elizabethton), buried: Valley Forge, died: 14 Apr 1918, record (1918) #: 103.

Infant MORELEY, parents: W.B. Moreley and Cassie Lowe, death cause: "stillborn", informant: E.S. Short (Watauga Valley), buried: Johnson County, died: 1 Apr 1918, record (1918) #: 104.

Tinka TAYLOR, female, born: 11 Apr 1916, parents: Jacob Taylor and Martha Lowe, death cause: "broncho pneumonia and measles" informant: H.D. Lowe (Carter), buried: Grindstaff Cemetery, died: 2 May 1918, record (1918) #: 105.

Vinney LEADFORD, born: 13 Mar 1878 in North Carolina, married, parents: Jim McFall (NC) and Caroline Waycaster (NC), death cause: "cancer of uterus", informant: David Ledford (Shell Creek), buried: Harris Cemetery, died: 2 May 1918, record (1918) #: 106.

Infant SIMERLY, male, parents: Sam E. Simerly and Millie Holly, death cause: "premature birth", informant: Sam Simerly (Valley Forge), died: 2 May 1918, record (1918) #: 107.

Millie Holly SIMERLY, born: 28 Sep 1885, married, parents: James Holly and Tempie Cates, death cause: "tuberculosis and pregnancy", buried: Blevins Cemetery, died: 2 May 1918, record (1918) #: 108.

Roy MCKINNEY, born: 11 Apr 1918, parents: William McKinney and Stella Shell, death cause: "broncho pneumonia", informant: Will McKinney (Shell Creek), buried: Richardson Cemetery, died: 11 May 1918, record (1918) #: 109.

Finley HATAHWAY, born: 3 Jun 1897, single, parents: Charles Hathaway and Rosa Smith, death cause: "tuberculosis of bowels", buried: Smith Cemetery, died: 11 May 1918, record (1918) #: 110.

Mrs. Mollie WHITEHEAD, age 48 years, married, parents: George Carver and Mattie Lewis, death cause: "cancer of stomach", informant: George Whitehead (Roan Mountain), buried: Whitehead Cemetery, died: 12 May 1918, record (1918) #: 111.

Fred Deforest MARTIN, born: 30 Dec 1914, parents: C.L. Martin (Grayson Co., VA) and Mandy Fair, death cause: "articulor rhumatism", informant: G.M. Dunn (Elizabethton), buried: Bradley Cemetery, died: 17 May 1918, record (1918) #: 112.

Howard GLOVER, age 9 months and 5 days, parents: Will Glover and Cordelia Peters, death cause: "auto intoxication", informant: Robert Stout (Hampton), died: 15 May 1918, record (1918) #: 113.

Carrie VANDEVENTER, age 14 years, 1 month and 5 days, parents: Marian Vandeventer and _____ McQueen (Johnson County), death cause: "relaps on measles and pneumonia", buried: Buckles Cemetery, died: 20 May 1918, record (1918) #: 114.

Infant LOWE, female, born: 20 May 1918, parents: Daniel Lowe and Sallie Davis, death cause: "not known", informant: R.B. Davis (Watauga Valley), buried: Lowe Cemetery, died: 23 May 1918, record (1918) #: 115.

W. Emery SNODGRASS, born: 18 Apr 1850, widower, parents: John C. Snodgrass and Sarah C. Williams, death cause: "pulmonary tuberculosis", informant: Laura C. Hughes (Johnson City), died: 23 May 1918, record (1918) #: 116.

William Grimston COLE, born: 17 Mar 1918, parents: Oscar Heaton and Nancy Cole, death cause: "lobar pneumonia", informant: Ethel Cole (Johnson City), buried: Cole Cemetery, died: 23 May 1918, record (1918) #: 117.

Sarah Jane Elizabeth ROBERTS, born: 9 Apr 1860 in North Carolina, widow, parents: Jackson Jones (NC) and mother's name unknown, death cause: "broken compensation of heart", informant: J.B. Shoun (Hampton), died: 23 May 1918, record (1918) #: 118.

Claud MOODY, born: 9 May 1918, parents: Joe H. Moody (Watauga Co., NC) and Jose Vines (Johnson County), death cause: "supposed to be diptheria", informant: Edward Stout (Dark Ridge, NC), buried: Closson Cemetery, died: 27 May 1918, record (1918) #: 119.
Paul WILLIAMS, born: 2 May 1918, parents: Allen Williams and Lucy Myers, death cause: "acute indigestion", informant: J.T. Miller (Elizabethton), buried: Highland Cemetery, died: 29 May 1918, record (1918) #: 120.
Infant TREADWAY, female, parents: C.E. Treadway and Hattie Garrison, death cause: "stillborn", informant: W.C. Williams (Valley Forge), died: 4 May 1918, record (1918) #: 121.
McDowell BREWER, born: 9 Aug 1896, single, parents: James Brewer and Josephine Justis (NC), death cause: "think, tuberculosis", informant: James Brewer (Shell Creek), buried: Richardson Cemetery, died: 3 Jun 1918, record (1918) #: 122.
Paul HURLEY, age 3 months, parents: Jessie Hurley and Lula Garland, death cause: "hives", informant: Robinson Garland (Carter), buried: Richardson Cemetery, died: 6 Jun 1918, record (1918) #: 123.
Martha C. HEATON, born: 20 Aug 1862 in Wilkes County, NC, married, parents: James C. Hayes (Wilkes Co., NC) and Elizabeth Estep (Wilkes Co., NC), death cause: "pulmonary tuberculosis", informant: G. Heaton (Shell Creek), buried: Cable Cemetery, died: 12 Jun 1918, record (1918) #: 124.
Jennie Ann MILLER, age about 54 years, married, parents: Ezekiel Hill and Biddie Whitehead, death cause: "dropsy", informant: Samuel Miller (Raon Mountain), buried: Miller Cemetery, died: 14 Jun 1918, record (1918) #: 125.
Rosy Kate WEST, born: 2 Apr 1918, parents: Johnson James West and Mary Osborn, death cause: "cleft palate, unable to take food", informant: J.V. Jordan (Hampton), died: 14 Jun 1918, record (1918) #: 126.
Ellen Coleman KEEN, age 87 years, widow, parents: "unknown", death cause: "old age", informant: James Pritchard (Johnson City), buried: Hughes Cemetery, died: 20 Jun 1918, record (1918) #: 127.
Eliza GRINDSTAFF, born: 22 Aug 1839 in Johnson County, widow, parents: John Slemp (Johnson County) and mother's name not stated, death cause: illegible, buried: Siam Cemetery, died: 22 Jun 1918, record (1918) #: 128.

Nancy Jane GLOVER, born: 26 Apr 1890, single, parents: James Glover and Mary Campbell, death cause: "pulmonary tuberculosis", informant: John Glover (Hampton), died: 22 Jun 1918, record (1918) #: 129.
Mary Jane RANGE, born: 23 Apr 1847, widow, parents: Jacob Range and mother's name not stated, death cause: "pneumonia", died: 24 Jun 1918, record (1918) #: 130.
Infant CROW, age 3 years, parents: Frank Crow and mother's name illegible, death cause: "brights disease", buried: Highland Cemetery, died: 25 Jun 1918, record (1918) #: 131.
Thomas J. ELLIOTT, born: 25 Dec 1867, married, parents: David Elliott (Johnson County) and Rachel Stout (Johnson County), death cause: "acute heart disease", informant: Dan Elliott (Elizabethton), buried: Highland Cemetery, died: 25 Jun 1918, record (1918) #: 132.
Charlie ASHLEY, born: 28 Mar 1918, parents: James Ashley (NC) and Harriett Grindstaff, death cause: "spinal fever", informant: James Ashley (Shell Creek), buried: Harris Cemetery, died: 26 Jun 1918, record (1918) #: 133.
Worley LINVILLE, born: 12 Jul 1827 in Virginia, widower, parents: Brocen Linville (VA) and Cinda Glover (VA), death cause: "carcinoma of liver", informant: Mrs. Hugh Cox (Johnson City), buried: Hughes Cem., died: 28 Jun 1918, record (1918) #: 134.
Vestley BUTLER, born: 25 May 1918, parents: John Butler (NC) and Vistie Campbell (NC), death cause: "bowl hives", informant: John Butler (Roan Mountain), buried in North Carolina, died: 30 Jun 1918, record (1918) #: 135.
Thomas DUGGER, age 29 years, 9 months and 17 days, single, parents: Tuck Dugger and Liza Fair, death cause: "pulmonary tuberculosis", informant: Joe Williams (Elizabethton), died: 1 Jul 1918, record (1918) #: 136.
Unice DAVIS, female, born: 23 Mar 1918, parents: William Davis and Nola Clark, death cause: "gastro enteritis", informant: N.B. Clark (Hampton), buried: Clark Cem., died: 4 Jul 1918, record (1918) #: 137.
Mrs. Lorena BRUMIT, born: 9 Apr 1872, married, parents: Haynes Ellis and Sarah Miller, death cause: "tuberculosis", informant: C.H. Brumit (Elizabethton), buried: Highland Cemetery, died: 7 Jul 1918, record (1918) #: 138.

Sarah Jane LAMBERT, age 56 years, born in Ashe County, NC, married, parents: George Pope (Ashe County, NC) and mother's name not stated, death cause: "tuberuclosis", informant: John Lambert (Butler), died: 7 Jul 1918, record (1918) #: 139.

Margaret PEOPLES, age 56 years, married, parents: Duke Smalling and Nancy Baker, death cause: "carcinoma of intestines", informant: R.W. Peoples (Johnson City), died: 8 Jul 1918, record (1918) #: 140.

Mrs. Mattie HART, born: 7 Nov 1896 in Sullivan County, married, parents: George Trusler and ____ Nidiffer, death cause: "pulmonary tuberculosis", informant: A.P. Slagle, died: 11 Jul 1918, record (1918) #: 141.

Nettie May CHAMBERS, born: 19 Aug 1916, parents: O.L. Chambers and Laura Messimer (NC), death cause: "brights disease", informant: J.T. Peaks, buried: Emmert Cemetery, died: 12 Jul 1918, record (1918) #: 142.

Roxil May LAWS, age 26 years, married, born in Fall Branch, TN, parents: Houston Grindstaff and mother's name unknown, death cause: "tuberculosis", informant: Mrs. J.E. Laws (Elizabethton), buried: Colbaugh Cemetery, died: 13 Jul 1918, record (1918) #: 143.

Junior Etta MASTON, female, born: 24 Apr 1899, parents: J.F. Maston and Emma Boyd, death cause: illegible, informant: J.F. Maston (Johnson City), buried: Payne Cemetery, died: 14 Jul 1918, record (1918) #: 144.

Paul KITE, born: 1 Jan 1899, parents: J.R. Kite and Maggie Simmons (Craig County, VA), death cause: "valvulor heart disease", informant; J.R. Kite (Elizabethton), buried: Simmons Cemetery, died: 14 Jul 1918, record (1918) #: 145.

Habakkuh HAYNES, colored, age 55 years, married, parents: George Haynes and mother's name not given, death cause: "lupus of skin and infection", buried: Williams Cemetery, died: 17 Jul 1918, record (1918) #: 146.

Will MURPHY, born: 4 May 1860 in North Carolina, widower, parents: Charley Murphey (NC) and mother's name not stated, death cause: "mitral regurgitation with broken compensation", informant: Andy Arnet (Roan Mountain), buried: Morgan Cemetery, died: 18 Jul 1918, record (1918) #: 147.

Bessie RAINS, age 2 years, parents: father not stated and Lucy Rains, death cause: "whooping cough", informant: Presley Rains (Carter), buried: Grindstaff Cemetery, died: 19 Jul 1918, record (1918) #: 148.

Clarence Butler FERGUSON, born: 4 Jun 1917, parents: Everett Ferguson and Linnie Roe (Rowe?), death cause: "acute dysentary", informant: Mrs, Everett Ferguson (Elizabethton), buried: Highland Cemetery, died: 21 Jul 1918, record (1918) #: 149.
Mrs. Biddie HILL, age about 75 years, parents: James Whitehead and Jennie Garland, death cause: "apoplexy", informant: Alexander Hill (Roan Mountain) buried: Hill Cemetery, died: 23 Jul 1918, record (1918) #: 150.
Neva COMBS, age 38 years, married, parents: A.J. Richardson and ____ Smith, death cause: "brights disease, fever", died: 24 Jul 1918, record #: 151.
Mrs. E.M. MADRON, age 44 years, born in North Carolina, married, parents: Dr. Bingham (NC) and mother's name unknown, death cause: "tuberculosis", buried: Kitsmiller Cemetery, died: 25 Jul 1918, record (1918) #: 152.
Dora HINKLE, age 49 years, married, born in Green County, parents: father's name not stated and Caroline (surname illegible), death cause: "dropsy", informant: L. Smith Hinkle (Carter), buried: Garland Cemetery, died: 25 Jul 1918, record (1918) #: 153.
Phebia CALHOUN, age 77 years, born in North Carolina, married, parents: ____ Graybeal and mother's name not stated, death cause: "cancer of stomach", buried: Roan Mountain, died: 28 Jul 1918, record (1918) #: 154.
Elijah CAMPBELL, born: 22 Jan 1914, parents: Wilburn Campbell and Leander Plott, death cause: "whooping cough", informant: W.H. Campbell (Hampton), buried: Campbell Cemetery, died: 28 Jul 1918, record #: 155.
Finley Winton SPARKS, born: 5 Aug 1917 in Vale, NC, parents: Sam Sparks (Mitchell Co., NC) amd Neiley Sluder (Mitchell Co., NC), death cause: "dysentary", informant: J.A. Sparks (Elizabethton), buried in North Carolina, died: 31 Jul 1918, record (1918) #: 156.
Roy M. CAMPBELL, born: 18 Oct 1917, parents: Wilburn G. Campbell and Nola Manning, death cause: "whooping cough", informant: Horace Campbell (Hampton), buried: Hall Cemetery, died: 1 Aug 1918, record (1918) #: 157.
Charlie HICKS, born: 30 Jul 1918, parents: Marsh Hicks and Cinda Winters (NC), death cause: "not born at full term", informant: A.J. Arnet (Roan Mountain), buried: Miller Cem., died: 2 Aug 1918, record (1918) #: 158.
Andrew Jackson TAYLOR, age 93 years, married, parents: Billy Taylor and Nancy Grindstaff, death cause: "paralysis", informant: George Hinkle (Carter), buried: Grindstaff Cemetery, died: 8 Aug 1918, record (1918) #: 159.

Arlon Clarence ARWOOD, born: 25 Feb 1918, parents: John W. Arwood (NC) and Stella Simerly, death cause: "indigestion", buried: Williams Cemetery, Valley Forge, died: 10 Aug 1918, record (1918) #: 160.
Kyle BEADLY, colored, age 14 years, parents: Wat Beadly and ____ Holly, death cause: "tuberculosis", resided: Watauga, died: 10 Aug 1918, record (1918) #: 161.
Isabell CAMPBELL, born: 23 Jul 1916, parents: Wilburn Campbell and Leander Platt, death cause: "whooping cough", informant: N.H. Campbell (Hampton), died: 11 Aug 1918, record (1918) #: 162.
Cordie INGLE, born: 7 May 1882, married, parents: Dolf McClain (Watauga Co., NC) and Rebecca Hoss (NC), death cause: illegible, informant: J.H. Bowers (Shell Creek), buried: McClain Cemetery, died: 11 Aug 1918, record (1918) #: 163.
Isabell HARDIE, black, born: 15 Apr 1918, parents: John Hardie and Minnie Shade (NC), death cause: "cholera", informant: John Hardie (Sehll Creek), died: 11 Aug 1918, record (1918) #: 164.
Lester Carmuel HAMBY, born: 29 Jan 1918, parents: Dennuel Hamby and Flora Brown, death cause: "think summer disease", informant: J.L. Hamby (Shell Creek), buried: Hamby Cemetery, died: 15 Aug 1918, record (1918) #: 165.
Golda BLEVINS, born: 21 Jul 1916, parents: Charles Blevins and Maudie Smith, death cause: "pneumonia", informant: J.V. Jordan (Hampton), buried: Smith Cemetery, died: 17 Aug 1918, record (1918) #: 166.
Mollie HAMBRICK, age 56 years, divorced, parents: Bill Moor and Mollie Moor, death cause: "pulmonary tuberculosis", informant: Lena Hambric (Elizabethton), died: 17 Aug 1918, record (1918) #: 167.
Dewey ARWOOD, born: 7 May 1918, parents: Manuel Arwood and Grace Estep (NC), death cause: "dysentery", informant: F.C. McLemore (Johnson City), buried: Williams Cem., died: 24 Aug 1918, record (1918): 168.
Eliza KINNICK, age about 73 years, widow, parents: Allen Hamby and Nancy Hamby, death cause: "pulmonary tuberculosis", informant: J.H. Simerly (Elizabethton), buried: Shell Creek, died: 24 Aug 1918, record (1918) #: 169.
Ruby SCALF, born: 25 Jun 1917, parents: (first name illegible) Scalf and Anna Turner, death cause: "cholera", informant: Anna Turner (Elizabethton), buried: Hyder Cemetery, died: 25 Aug 1918, record (1918): 170.

Lelia MARKLIN, age 9 months, parents: William Marklin and Lula Perkins, death cause: "whooping cough", informant: Thomas J. Proffitt (Elk Park, NC), buried: Perkins Cem., died: 26 Aug 1918, record (1918): 171.

M.E. STOUT, female, born: 18 May 1870 in Johnson County, married, parents: Wash Wilson and mother's name unknown, death cause: "tuberculosis pera tonitis", informant: James R. Stout (Butler), buried: Cable Cemetery, died: 28 Aug 1918, record (1918): 172.

Paul MILLER, born: 10 Feb 1918, parents: father not stated and Nancy Miller, death cause: "bowl hives", informant: Henry Ellison (Hampton), buried: Lacy Cemetery, died: 29 Aug 1918, record (1918): 173.

Henderson F. THOMAS, born: 9 Mar 1872, married, parents: W.S. Thomas (Sullivan County) and Jennie Fair, death cause: "nephritis", informant: Fred Lewis (Elizabethton), buried: Thomas Cemetery, died: 29 Aug 1918, record (1918): 174.

F.W. HUMPHREYS, age 1 year, 2 months and 23 days, parents: John Humphreys and Cora Keller (NC), death cause: "cholera and indigestion", informant: (illegible) Curd, buried: W.J. Mottern Cemetery, died: 30 Aug 1918, record (1918): 175.

Loura CARTER, black, born: 1 Aug 1858, married, parents: Rube Williams and Teener Taylor, death cause: "nephritis", informant: Will Taylor (Elizabethton), buried: Cedar Grove Cemetery, died: 31 Aug 1918, record (1918): 176.

Mary Jane BURLESON, born: 13 Aug 1861 at Red Hill, NC, married, parents: (illegible) Garland (NC) and Rebecca Garland (NC), death cause: "pellagra", informant: L.W. Burleson (Johnson City), buried: Milligan Cemetery, died: 31 Aug 1918, record (1918): 177.

Infant WINTERS, female, parents: Monroe Winters (NC) and Belle Deloach, death cause: "born dead", informant: Will Estep (Elizabethton), buried: Estep Cemetery, born/died: 21 Aug 1918, record (1918): 178.

Infant DUGGER, male, parents: T.A. Dugger and Ellen M. Syren (Sweden), death cause: "born dead", buried: Highland Cem., died: 25 Aug 1918, record (1918): 179.

Ester COLBAUGH, born: 1 Sep 1916, parents: James Colbaugh and Bessie Arnett, death cause: "dysentery", informant: E.F. Forbes (Carter), buried: Forbes Cemetery, died: 1 Sep 1918, record (1918): 180.

Angeline L. NORRIS, born: 25 Apr 1863, married, parents: Washington White and Silva Bunton, death cause: "tuberculosis", informant: G.H. Bunton (Butler), died: 3 Sep 1918, record (1918): 181.

Eula May MARLOW, born: 9 Nov 1915, parents: William Marlow (NC) and Lula Perkins, death cause: "bronchial pneumonia", buried: Perkins Cemetery, died: 7 Sep 1918, record (1918): 182.
Brownlow LEWIS, born: 8 Oct 1917, parents: U.R. Lewis and Tissie Lowe, death cause: "spinal meningitis", informant: Fender Peters (Carter), buried: Lowe Cemetery, died: 8 Sep 1918, record (1918): 183.
James RAINS, born: 25 Feb 1862, married, parents: Presley Rains and Sarah A. Hopkins, death cause: "interstinal nephritis", informant: Will Rains (Carter), buried: Grindstaff Cemetery, died: 8 Sep 1918, record (1918): 184.
Catherine WHITE, born: 14 Apr 1918, parents: Thomas White and Ethel Rainbolt, death cause: "diptheria", informant: Thomas White (Butler), died: 10 Sep 1918, record (1918): 185.
Presley PEEKS, born: 23 Aug 1915, parents: J.T. Peeks and Lola Ellis, death cause: "intestinal parasites", informant: David Chambers (Elizabethton), buried: Ellis Cemetery, died: 13 Sep 1918, record (1918): 186.
Jefferson Dale BLAIR, born: 4 Apr 1901 in Watauga County, NC, single, parents: Job Blair (Watauga Co., NC) and Tina Parker (Watauga Co., NC), death cause: "typhoid fever", buried: Highland Cemetery, died: 13 Sep 1918, record (1918): 187.
Carl A. BOWERS, born: 12 Apr 1901, single, parents: Joseph P. Bowers and Josie M. Fletcher, death cause: "congenital heart disease and typhoid fever", buried: Highland Cemetery, died: 14 Sep 1918, record (1918): 188.
Evelyn COLBAUGH, born: 11 Jan 1918, parents: Fred Colbaugh and Mary Smith, death cause: "acute indigestion", buried: Colbaugh Cemetery, died: 14 Sep 1918, record (1918): 189.
Lola CAMPBELL, age not stated, single, parents: Isaac Campbell and Nancy Estep, death cause: "infulenza", informant: Moses Estep (Carter), buried: Estep Cemetery, died: 15 Sep 1918, record (1918): 190.
Elizabeth MEREDITH, born: 24 Apr 1836, parents: (first name not stated) February and Sallie Williams, death cause: "tuberculosis", buried: Williams Cemetery, died: 19 Sep 1918, record (1918): 191.
Crosley TIMBS, born: 19 Dec 1910, parents: father's name illegible and Abbie Timbs, death cause: "diptheria", informant: Abbie Timbs (Butler), died: 20 Sep 1918, record (1918): 192.

Ocran CAMPBELL, male, born: 18 Mar 1918, parents: Melvin Campbell and Josie Louise Glover, death cause: "whooping cough", informant: Melvin Campbell (Hampton), buried: Campbell Cemetery, died: 21 Sep 1918, record (1918): 193.
Era Milling Mell PERKINS, born: 17 Dec, age 2 years, 7 months and 9 days, born in North Carolina, parents: Joseph Perkins (NC) and Dora Richardson, death cause: "whooping cough", informant: J.C. Perkins (Shell Creek), buried: Perkins Cemetery, died: 23 Sep 1918, record (1918): 194.
Zeb Theodore KELLER, born: 24 May 1917, parents: Loflin A. Keller (Avery County, NC) and Minnie E. Laws, death cause: "cholera", informant: Loflin A. Keller (Shell Creek), died: 23 Sep 1918, record (1918): 195.
Samuel RICHARDSON, age 34 years, married, parents: Sam Richardson and Sis Campbell, death cause: "typhoid fever", informant: R.M. Ensor (Carter), buried: Richardson Cemetery, died: 25 Sep 1918, record (1918): 196.
David DUGGER, age 24 years, single, parents: John Dugger and Clara Grindstaff, death cause: "tuberculosis", informant: Robert Grindstaff (Carter), buried: Hurley Cemetery, died: 26 Sep 1918, record (1918): 197.
Samuel STREET, age about 89 years, born in North Carolina, widower, parents: Henry Street (NC) and Bekie Street (NC), death cause: "chronic dirhea and old age", informant: Henry Street (Hampton), buried: McKinney Cemetery, died: 29 Sep 1918, record (1918): 198.
M.C. MORGAN, age about 32 years, married, parents: W.M. Closson and Charlotte Hicks, death cause: illegible, informant: W.M. Closson (Butler), buried: Hicks Cemetery, died: 30 Sep 1918, record (1918): 198a.
Mary SIMS, parents: Daniel Sims and Kate Forbs, death cause: "born at 5 months", informant: Daniel Sims (Roan Mountain), buried: Nelson Cemetery, born/died: 29 Sep 1918, record (1918): 199.
Jasper ROSENBAUM, born: 1 Jul 1917, parents: M.L. Rosenbaum and mother's name not stated, death cause: "dysentery", died: 1 Oct 1918, record (1918): 200.
Galle CAMPBELL, female, age 4 years, parents: Isaac Campbell and Nancy Estep, death cause: "diarrhoea", buried: Estep Cemetery, died: 2 Oct 1918, record (1918): 201.

Infant PIERCE, male, parents: John Pierce and Anna White, death cause: "pertussis", informant: John Pierce (Fish Springs), born/died: 4 Oct 1918, record (1918): 202.

James Frank ROBINSON, born: 23 Oct 1866 in Green County, married, parents: J.C. Robinson (Green County) and ____ Bayler (Green County), death cause: "paraphlegia", buried: King Cemetery, died: 6 Oct 1918, record (1918): 203.

Maree JOHNSON, born: 8 Oct 1917, parents: Stewart Johnson and Bertha Heaton, death cause: "flue", informant: Stewart Johnson (Roan Mountain), died: 8 Oct 1918, record (1918): 204.

Mary Virginia ROGERS, born: 3 Apr 1917, parents: William Rogers and Mary Gibson, death cause: "pneumonia", informant: Mrs. Mary Rogers (Braemer), buried: Hall Cemetery, died: 9 Oct 1918, record (1918): 205.

Cora ECHOLS, born: 22 Apr 1896, single, parents: John B. Echols and Rosa Hardin, death cause: "bronchial pneumonia", informant: W.M. Colbaugh (Carter), buried: Blevins Cemetery, died: 9 Oct 1918, record (1918): 206.

Dr. Edwin Eugene HUNTER, born: 10 Oct 1845 in Washington County, TN, married, parents: Joseph Hunter (Washington County) and Mollie Jobe Hunter, death cause: "run over by a locomotive engine in Elizabethton", informant: Nat T. Perry, buried: Highland Cemetery, died: 10 Oct 1918, record (1918): 207.

Sam Newton COLLINS, born: 27 Nov 1891, single, parents: Isaac Collins and Martha Treadway, death cause: "pneumonia and lagrippe", buried: Patton Cemetery, died: 11 Oct 1918, record (1918): 208.

Albert HARDIN, born: 19 May 1918, parents: John R. Hardin and Ettie Frazier, death cause: not stated, informant: W.O. Frazier (Carter), buried: Blevins Cemetery, died: 11 Oct 1918, record (1918): 209.

Harrold HEATON, age 4 years, parents: Jim Heaton and Abbigail Michaels (NC) death cause: "not known", informant: Jim Heaton (Roan Mountain), died: 12 Oct 1918, record (1918): 210.

Herman RICHARDS, born: 3 Feb 1917, parents: Jim Richards (Sullivan County) and Eliza Perry, death cause: "pertissis", informant: Berry Sams (Elizabethton), buried: Highland Cemetery, died: 12 Oct 1918, record (1918): 211.

Thomas H. JENKINS, born: 31 Jul 1881, single, parents: Will Jenkins and Eliza Cathern, death cause: "Spanish flu", informant: Fannie Jenkins, buried: Hyder Cemetery, died: 12 Oct 1918, record (1918): 212.

Hattie ROBERTS, age about 32 years, married, parents: Jasper Clark (NC) and Tlitha Butler (NC), death cause: "abortion", informant: John Roberts (Roan Mountain), buried: Clark Cem., died: 12 Oct 1918, record: 213.

Nancy Jane SHUFFIELD, born: 1 Nov 1838 in Washington County, TN, widow, parents: John Kinnick (NC) and Mary Shuffield, death cause: "bronchia.. (illegible)", informant: C.A. Voncanon (Butler), died: 12 Oct 1918, record (1918): 214.

Tribble GARLAND, male, born: 25 Dec 1913, parents: John Garland and Martha Campbell, death cause: "influenza", informant: John Garland (Carter), buried: Garland Cem., died: 12 Oct 1918, record (1918): 215.

Mary Jane LACY, born: 18 Nov 1837, widow, parents: William S. Lyon and Rebecca Stanfield, death cause: "paralysis", informant: J.M. Lacy (Elizabethton), buried: Highland Cemetery, died: 13 Oct 1918, record (1918): 216.

Annie OLIVER, born: 21 May 1856, married, parents: Milas Jolly and Jennie Morton (or Marton ?), death cause: "pulmonary tuberculosis", informant: J.M. Oliver (Hampton), buried: Marton Cemetery, died: 15 Oct 1918, record (1918): 217.

Herbert CHATMAN, born: 6 Nov 1916, parents: Arch Chatman and Ella Jones, death cause: "croupous pneumonia", informant: H.T. Daniels (Elizabethton), buried: Jones Cem., died: 16 Oct 1918, record #: 218.

Katie M. JORDAN, born: 22 Feb 1918, parents: John Jordan and Ada Pierce, death cause: "thought to be Spanish flu", informant: T.N. Peters (Carter), buried: Blevins Cem., died: 16 Oct 1918, record (1918): 219.

Robert CATES, age 29 years, married, parents: Robert Combs and ____ Cates, death cause: "influenza", informant: Tempie Holly (Valley Forge), died: 17 Oct 1918, record (1918): 220.

Gordy HURLEY, born: 22 Jan 1916 in Virginia, parents: Ham Hurley and Mary Cox Hurley, death cause: "broncho pneumonia", died: 17 Oct 1918, record (1918): 221.

Mrs. Martha A. LACY, born: 4 Oct 1842, married, parents: Isaac Crow and ____ Hart (editorial note: mother was Elizabeth "Betsy" Hart, daughter of Leonard Hart, Sr.), death cause: "stomach cancer", informant: R.S. Lacy (Hopson), buried: Lacy Cemetery, died: 17 Oct 1918, record (1918): 222.

John H. TAYLOR, age 1 year, 10 months and 2 days, parents: George Taylor and Mary Roberts, death cause: "influenza", informant: J.T. Taylor (Hampton), buried: Roberts Cem., died: 18 Oct 1918, record (1918) #: 225.
Pausy PETERS, female, born: 18 Sep 1911, parents: John Peters and Pheba Peters, death cause: "influenza", informant: W.M. Peters (Watauga Valley), buried: Peters Cem., died: 18 Oct 1918, record (1918) #: 224.
Alice A. BESS, age 42 years, married, parents: Sampson Robinson and Louisa Grindstaff, death cause: "influenza", informant: C.L. Grindstaff (Carter), buried: Grindstaff Cemetery, died: 18 Oct 1918, record (1918) #: 223.
Francis Raymond SIMERLY, male, born: 6 Jun 1916, parents: J.C. Simerly and Nellie Jenkins, death cause: "infleunza" informant: J.C. Simerly (Valley Forge), died: 19 Oct 1918, record (1918) #: 226.
Lucy HEATON, age 9 years, parents: Jim Heaton and Abbigail Michaels (NC), death cause: "not known", informant: Jim Heaton (Roan Mountain), died: 19 Oct 1918, record (1918) #: 227.
Rhoda CATES, born: 26 Dec 1891, widow, parents: George Simerly and Nancy Guinn, death cause: "influenza, pneumonia and abortion", residence: Valley Forge, died: 20 Oct 1918, record (1918) #: 228.
Arthur S. TAYLOR, born: 7 Dec 1916, parents: George Taylor and Mary Roberts, death cause: "influenza, whooping cough", informant: J.H. Taylor (Hampton), buried: Roberts Cemetery, died: 20 Oct 1918, record (1918) #: 229.
Hester PRICHARD, age 74 years, widow, parents: John Shell and Rebecca Wilcox (NC), death cause: "stroke of paralysis", informant: Cordie Prichard (Shell Creek), buried: Perry Cem., died: 20 Oct 1918, record #: 230.
Aubry DAVIS, age 1 years and 5 months, parents: Rheuben Davis (W.VA) and Lina Hany, death cause: "Spanish enfluenzy", informant: Linda Davis (Carter), buried: Davis Cem., died: 21 Oct 1918, record #: 231.
Helen CHESTER, age 4 years, 2 months and 6 days, parents: John Chester and Josie Jones, death cause: "croupous pneumonia", informant: H.T. Daniels (Elizabethton), buried: Jones Cemetery, died: 21 Oct 1918, record (1918) #: 232.
Tlitha CLARK, age 51 years, born in North Carolina, married, parents: John Butler (NC) and Jane Morgan, death cause: "Spanish flu", informant: John Roberts (Roan Mountain), buried: Clark Cemetery, died: 21 Oct 1918, record (1918) #: 233.

James Haskel BERRY, born: 19 Apr 1914, parents: James Berry and Vicey Combs, death cause: "diptheria", informant: Mrs. Jim Berry (Butler), died: 22 Oct 1918, record (1918) #: 234.

Roy CAMPBELL, born: 9 Aug 1917, parents: J.R. Campbell and Bessie Nave, death cause: "lobar pneumonia", buried: Hall Cemetery, died: 23 Oct 1918, record (1918) #: 235.

Hellen RAMSEY, born: Apr 1914 in Johnson County, parents: Joe E. Ramsey (Johnson County) and Parlie Campbell (Johnson County), death cause: "influenza", buried: Fish Springs, died: 23 Oct 1918, record (1918) #: 236.

Lyda CLARK, age about 18 years, parents: Jasper Clark (NC) and Tlitha Butler (NC), death cause: "Spanish flu, pneumonia", informant: Love Clark (Hampton), buried: Clark Cemetery, died: 23 Oct 1918, record (1918) #: 237.

Charles CARDEN, born: 7 Oct 1915, parents: Daniel Carden and Naome Moody, death cause: "pneumonia", informant: Daniel Carden (Hampton), died: 23 Oct 1918, record (1918) #: 238.

Biddie Jane COX, age 73 years, born in North Carolina, married, parents: (first name illegible) Gardiner (NC) and Sallie Stanley (NC), death cause: "flue", informant: S.M. Cox (Roan Mountain), died: 23 Oct 1918, record (1918) #: 239.

Vestal ROBERTS, male, born: 7 Dec 1916, parents: Arthur Roberts and Lizzie Clark, death cause: "pneumonia", informant: George Taylor (Hampton), buried: Roberts Cemetery, died: 24 Oct 1918, record (1918) #: 240.

Edna Christine CATES, age 2 years, parents: Robert Cates and Rhoda Simerly, death cause: "influenza, pneumonia", residence: Valley Forge, died: 24 Oct 1918, record (1918) #: 241.

Mary HILL, born: 2 Jul 1918, parents: James Hill, Jr. and Suda Whitehead, death cause: "Spanish flu", buried: Holly Cem., died: 25 Oct 1918, record #: 242.

Ismael FORBES, born: 13 Aug 1904, parents: E.F. Forbes and Minnie Hardin, death cause: "pneumonia", informant: Powel Shoun (Carter), buried: Blevins Cemetery, died: 26 Oct 1918, record (1918) #: 243.

Rosa CAMPBELL, born in 1896, married, parents: (first name illegible) Hodge and Catherine Taylor, death cause: "influenza, pneumonia, abortion", informant: Will Campbell (Carter), buried: Grindstaff Cemetery, died: 26 Oct 1918, record (1918) #: 244.

Ercle HARDIN, born: May 1910, parents: Dock Hardin and (first name illegible) Trivett, death cause: "influenza", informant: Will Closson (Dark Ridge, NC), died: 26 Oct 1918, record (1918) #: 245.

Adam GUINN, age about 54 years, born in North Carolina, parents: Isaac Guinn (NC) and Lizzie Hicks (NC), death cause: "enfluenzia and broncho penumonia", informant: Jake Guinn (Hampton), buried: Fair View Cemetery, died: 27 Oct 1918, record (1918) #: 246.

Hobart BEAVER, born: 16 Jan 1898, married, parents: Steven Beaver (NC) and Mary Howell (NC), death cause: "influenza", informant: Rosevelt Beaver (Elizabethton), buried: Simerly Cemetery, died: 27 Oct 1918, record (1918) #: 247.

L.W. BRUMIT, female, born: Aug 1876, married, parents: Robert Holly and Caroline Lacy, death cause: "dropsy", informant: J.A. Hardin (Hampton), buried: Halls Cemetery, died: 27 Oct 1918, record (1918) #: 248.

James J. HUGHES, age 35 years, married, parents: G.W. Hughes (NC) and mother not stated, death cause: "flu", buried: Roan Mountain, died: 28 Oct 1918, record: 249.

Earl ROBERTS, born: 10 Nov 1917, parents: Arther Roberts and Lizzie Clark, death cause: "influenza, pneumonia", buried: Roberts Cemetery (Hampton), died: 28 Oct 1918, record (1918) #: 250.

Hobart J. FAITLEY, born: 8 Feb 1918 in Virginia, parents: Clarence Faitley (Va) and Sallie Hennigar (VA), death cause: "influenza", informant: John Hennigar (Elizabethton), buried: Nave Cemetery, died: 28 Oct 1918, record (1918) #: 251.

Castine TOLLEY, age about 25 years, single, parents: Avery Tolley and Susan Tolley, death cause: "influenza, tuberculosis", informant: Sampson Tolley (Roan Mountain), buried: Tolley Cemetery, died: 28 Oct 1918, record (1918) #: 252.

Pearl PERRY, born: 24 Jun 1917, parents: O.E. Perry and Nora Glover, death cause: "influenza", informant: O.E. Perry (Elizabethton), buried: Childers Cemetery, died: 29 Oct 1918, record (1918) #: 253.

James HARDIN, born: 26 Sep 1898, parents: John Moreland and Jennie Hardin, death cause: "pneumonia", informant: W.R. Hardin (Carter), buried: Grindstaff Cem., died: 29 Oct 1918, record (1918) #: 254.

Mary GEISLER, born: 28 Apr 1907 in Bluff City, parents: Albert Geisler (Sullivan County) and Maggie Denton (Sullivan County), death cause: "influenza", informant: Hick Geisler (Elizabethton), buried: Highland Cem., died: 29 Oct 1918, record #: 255.

Troy WILSON, black, age 4 years, 4 months and 4 days, parents: Jim Wilson (NC) and Laura Wilson (NC), death cause: "bronchial pneumonia", buried: Taylor Cemetery, died: 29 Oct 1918, record (1918) #: 256.

Dovie TRIVETT, born: 10 Jun 1883 in Watauga County, NC, married, parents: William Hicks (Watauga Co., NC) and Lilly Closson, death cause: "influenza", died: 30 Oct 1918, record (1918) #: 257.

Bert CLARK, born: 1 Oct 1915, parents: Burt Roberts and Lyda Clark, death cause: "Spanish flu", informant: Isaac Roberts (Roan Mountain), buried: Clark Cemetery, died: 31 Oct 1918, record (1918) #: 258.

Ruby Ellen MATHESON, born: 23 Mar 1918, parents: John Mathis and Callie Lions (VA), death cause: "pertussis", informant: E.L. Lions (Fish Springs), buried: Highland Cemetery, died: 31 Oct 1918, record (1918) #: 259.

Millie HARDIN, age 6 years, parents: Dock Hardin and (first name illegible) Trivett, death cause: "influenza", died: 31 Oct 1918, record (1918) #: 260.

Infant TAYLOR, male, parents: William Taylor and Hattie Elliott, death cause: "stillborn", informant: George Lowe (Carter), buried: Elliott Cemetery, died: 19 Oct 1918, record (1918) #: 261.

Paul BERRY, age 1 year and 9 months, parents: Samuel Berry and (first name illegible) Burleson (NC), death cause: "influenza", informant: Jasper Clark (Roan Mountain), buried: Clark Cemetery, died: 1 Nov 1918, record (1918) #: 262.

Sester TOLLEY, female, age about 45 years, married, parents: John Ledford (NC) and mother's name illegible, death cause: "influenza", informant: Sampson Tolley (Roan Mountain), buried: Tolley Cemetry, died: 1 Nov 1918, record (1918) #: 263.

Sarah BRIDGES, black, parents: Mathew Bridges (NC) and Lillie (surname unknown)(VA), death cause: not stated, informant: Will Stover, buried: McGee Cemetery, died: 1 Nov 1918, record (1918) #: 264.

William Brownlow WILSON, born: 14 Mar 1879 in Johnson County, parents: William Nathaniel Wilson (NC) and Winnie Smith, death cause: "lung trouble and grip", informant: Ida Wilson, resided: Shell Creek, died: 1 Nov 1918, record (1918) #: 265.

Pauline LIVINGSTON, age 14 years, parents: George Pettibone Livingston and Susan Estep, death cause: "Spanish influenza", informant: Bat Livingston (Carter), buried: Garland Cemetery, died: 2 Nov 1918, record (1918) #: 266.

Lottie BRIGGS, colored, age 17 years, married, born in Virginia, parents: "don't know", death cause: "influenza and premature childbirth", informant: Will Stover, buried: Odd Fellows Cemetery, died: 2 Nov 1918, record (1918) #: 267. (editorial note: believe this is "Lillie Bridges" in record # 264, above)

A.K. LACY, age 73 years, widower, parents: not stated, death cause: "pulmonary tuberculosis", residence: Watauga, died: 2 Nov 1918, record (1918) #: 268.

Laura WATERS, born 18 May 1895, married, parents: Jim Smith and ____ Curtis, death cause: "tuberculosis", buried: Dempsy Cemetery, resided: Watauga, died: 4 Nov 1918, record (1918) #: 269.

Waits H....(illegible), age 49 years, parents: Spencer (last name illegible) and Mary Barnett (NC), death cause: "cerebral hemorrhage", died: 5 Nov 1918, record (1918) #: 270.

James Franklin ESTEP, born: 1 Sep 1917, parents: (first name illegible) Estep and Lillie Garland, death cause: "acute nephritis", informant: Autie Humphreys (Johnson City), died: 5 Nov 1918, record #: 271.

Stella LIPPS, age 3 years, parents: James Lipps and Ellen Nelson, death cause: "influenza", informant: D.W. Lipps (Carter), buried: Ensor Cemetery, died: 5 Nov 1918, record (1918) #: 272.

Hellen NIDIFFER, born: 12 Aug 1916, parents: Cephas Grant Nidiffer and Lizzie Myers, death cause: "hooping cough and pneumonia", buried: Ritchie Cemetery, died: 6 Nov 1918, record (1918) #: 273.

Birdie HINKLE, age 24 years, divorced, parents: Will Hinkle and Eva Myers, death cause: "Spanish influneza", informant: W.L. Nidiffer (Carter), buried: Garland Cem., died: 17 Nov 1918, record (1918) #: 274.

Frank Walford FINLEY, Jr., born: 6 Jan 1903 in Williamsburg, parents: Frank Finley, Sr. (Williamsburg, KY) and Annis M. Preston (VA), death cause: "pneumonia", informant: J.W. Preston, Md. (Roanoke, VA), buried: Williamsburg, VA, died: 7 Nov 1918, record (1918) #: 275.

Kinzie BIRCHFIELD, age 4 years, parents: Dave Birchfield and Delia Garland, death cause: "pneumonia", informant: David Birchfield (Roan Mountain), died: 7 Nov 1918, record (1918) #: 276.

Anna STOUT, born: 13 May 1902, parents: Samuel Stout and mother's name not stated, death cause: "influenza, broncho pneumonia", informant: Jim Ellis (Elizabethton), buried: Stout Cemetery, died: 9 Nov 1918, record (1918) #: 277.

Sarah Emaline CABLE, born: 13 Jun 1855 in Watauga County, NC, parents: David Hicks (Watauga Co., NC) and Elizabeth Hicks (Watauga Co., NC), death cause: "chronic nephritis", informant: J.J. Cable (Butler), buried: Cable Cemetery, died: 9 Nov 1918, record (1918) #: 278.

Infant MATHERLY, male, parents: James Matherly and Nola McKinney, death cause: "premature birth", informant: James Matherly (Valley Forge), born/died: 11 Nov 1918, record (1918) #: 279.

Ellen Myers RICHARDSON, age 39 years, married, parents: Hiram Myers and Mary Pierce, death cause: "influenza", informant: W.E. Asher (Carter), buried: Richardson Cemetery, died: 11 Nov 1918, record (1918) #: 280.

Nannie BURROW, born: 23 May 1892, married, parents: C.H. Jordan and Mattie Fair, death cause: "influenza, childbirth and heart failure", buried: Highland Cemetery, died: 11 Nov 1918, record (1918) #: 281.

Clint BUTLER, born: 11 Jul 1906, parents: E.S. Butler (Scott Co., VA), and Suda Shell, death cause: "influenza and pneumonia", informant: R.B. Sluder (Milligan), buried: Potter Cemetery, died: 11 Nov 1918, record (1918) #: 282.

Zella TAYLOR, born: 10 Jun 1914, parents: I.C. Taylor and Nelia Johnson, death cause: "Spanish influenza", informant: John J. Taylor (Johnson City), buried: Taylors Chapel, died: 12 Nov 1918, record (1918) #: 283.

Virginia BOWERS, black, born: 14 Jun 1914, parents: John Henry Bowers and Maggie Taylor, death cause: "influenza", informant: John Carter, buried: Cedar Grove Cem., died: 13 Nov 1918, record (1918) #: 284.

George POTTER, age 41 years, married, parents: Dave Potter and Mollie Hamby, death cause: "pneumonia, tuberculosis", informant: Murphy Potter (Shell Creek), buried: Potter Cemetery, died: 14 Nov 1918, record (1918) #: 285.

Rosa Etta STREET, born: 23 Jun 1910, parents: (first name illegible) Steet (NC), and Sindie Philips (NC), death cause: "pneumonia", informant: David McKinney (Hampton), buried: Simerly Cemetery, died: 15 Nov 1918, record (1918) #: 286.

Arthur GUINN, born: 12 Jun 1918, parents: Jake Guinn and Sallie Whitehead, death cause: "influenza, broncho pneumonia", informant: Robert Byrd (Hampton), buried: Fair View Cemetery, died: 16 Nov 1918, record (1918) #: 287.

John TOLLEY, age 17 years, parents: Wilburn Tolley, and Sester Ledford, death cause: "influenza and pneumonia", informant: Sampson Tolley (Roan Mountain), buried: Tollys Cemetery, died: 16 Nov 1918, record (1918) #: 288.

Mary Lewis ELLIOTT, age 28 years, married, parents: Murray Lewis and Evaline Heatherly, death cause: "Spanish influenzy, pneumonia", informant: W.M. Lewis (Carter), buried: Grindstaff Cemetery, died: 17 Nov 1918, record (1918) #: 289.

John GARLAND, age about 64 years, married, parents: Isaac Garland and Annie Estep, death cause: "tuberculosis", informant: J.M. Lewis, buried: Carter Cemetery, died: 20 Nov 1918, record (1918) #: 290.

Frankie MCKEEHAN, born: 25 May 1917, parents: Frank McKeehan and Annie Gourley, death cause: "influenza and pneumonia", informant: J.R. Kite (Powder Branch), died: 20 Nov 1918, record (1918) #: 291.

Clarence BANGE, age 3 years, parents: Dan Bange and mother's name not known, death cause: "pneumonia", informant: O.L. McLean (Johnson City), buried: Roan Mountain, died: 21 Nov 1918, record (1918) #: 292.

Carrie L. HENRY, age 19 years, parents: James Henry and Lettie Treadway, death cause: "pulmonary tuberculosis", informant: Monroe Treadway (Gap Creek), buried: Charity Hill, died: 23 Nov 1918, record (1918) #: 293.

Yetta ROGERS, born: 20 May 1918, parents: W.W. Rogers and Mary Gibson, death cause: "influenza and pneumonia", informant: Mary Rogers (Bramer), buried: Hall Cemetery, died: 24 Nov 1918, record (1918) #: 294.

D.M. SHAW, born: 24 Aug 1835 in Salem, NC, married, parents: Thomas Shaw (NC) and Elizabeth Cave, death cause: "influenza", informant: Albert Shaw (Elizabethton), died: 24 Nov 1918, record (1918) #: 295.

Annie SMITH, age 11 years, parents: father's name not known and Luster Smith, death cause: "flue", informant: Ed Smith (Roan Mountain), died: 25 Nov 1918, record (1918) #: 296.

Cathaline BURROW, born: 8 Jun 1917, parents: John Burrow and Minnie Campbell, death cause: "pneumonia", informant: Jake Burrow (Hampton), buried: Hall Cemetery, died: 25 Nov 1918, record (1918) #: 297.

Micael TAYLOR, age 42 years, married, parents: Andrew Taylor and Harrette Combs, death cause: "dropsy", informant: Joe Taylor, buried: Taylor Cemetery, died: 25 Nov 1918, record (1918) #: 298.

Catherine Marie MORRELL, born: 29 Jan 1915, parents: Lee Morrell and Annie Grace Ryan, death cause: "flue and croup", informant: L.T. Morrell (Elizabethton), buried: Highland Cemetery, died: 26 Nov 1918, record (1918) #: 299.

Charles Urban THOMAS, born: 15 Apr 1911 in Sherman, Texas, parents: John V. Thomas (NC) and Sarah E. Wilburn (VA), death cause: "whooping cough, measles, broncho pneumonia", informant: John V. Thomas (Milligan), buried: Milligan Cemetery, died: 26 Nov 1918, record (1918) #: 300.

Dovie Leota ARNOLD, born: 22 Jul 1916, parents: John Arnold and Ida Lunceford, death cause: "whooping cough", informant: John Arnold (Hampton), buried: Stallings Cemetery, died: 26 Nov 1918, record (1918) #: 301.

Mary SMITH, age: "not known", married, parents: father's name not known and Linda Shell, death cause: "flue", informant: Ed Smith (Roan Mountain), died: 28 Nov 1918, record (1918) #: 302.

Mary HART, born: 1 Nov 1886, married, parents: Rufus Story (NC) and Eliza Hodge (NC), death cause: "influenza, tuberculosis", informant: John Webb (Elizabethton), buried: Mottern Cemetery, died: 28 Nov 1918, record (1918) #: 303.

Wilbur Toney NAVE, born: 8 Sep 1918, parents: Joel Nave and Hattie Campbell, death cause: "bronchial pneumonia", informant: Joel Nave (Hampton), buried: Hall Cem., died: 28 Nov 1918, record (1918) #: 304.

Julie NORIS, born: 12 Jun 1891, married, parents: Enick Pilkerson (Watauga Co., NC) and Clementine Noris (Watauga Co., NC), death cause: "influenza and pneumonia", informant: Enick Pilkerson (Butler), died: 29 Nov 1918, record (1918) #: 305.

Infant GUY, male, born: 17 Nov 1918, parents: Lowery Guy (Watauga Co., NC) and Rebecca Starling (Watauga Co., NC), death cause: "overstrain of mother by lifting loads", informant: Mary A. Trivett (Dark Ridge, NC), died: 18 Nov 1918, record (1918) #: 306.

Infant BURROW, male, parents: Oscar Burrow and Nannie Burrow, death cause: "stillborn", informant: Oscar Burrow (Elizabethton), buried: Highland Cemetery, died: 11 Nov 1918, record (1918) #: 307.

Conley Phill FAIR, born: 26 May 1916, parents: David Fair and Annie Hampton, death cause: "influenza", informant: David Fair (Valley Forge), died: 1 Dec 1918, record (1918) #: 308.

Amanda HATLEY, born: 16 Nov 1918, parents: Alvin Hatley and Minnie Arnold, death cause: "whooping cough", informant: Alvin Hatley (Butler), buried: Staling Cem., died: 1 Dec 1918, record (1918) #: 309.
George LIVINGSTON, age 80 years, married, parents: "unknown", death cause: "pneumonia fever", informant: Bat Livingston (Carter), buried: Garland Cemetery, died: 3 Dec 1918, record (1918) #: 310.
Alice B. BLEVINS, born: 16 Sep 1917, parents: Sherman Blevins (Johnson County) and Callie Little, death cause: "influenza", informant: Sherman Blevins (Elizabethton), buried: Little Cemetery, died: 3 Dec 1918, record (1918) #: 311.
Eva Margaret RYAN, born: 6 Apr 1909, parents: John Ryan and Mollie Bowers, death cause: "influenza", informant: Ora Jenkins (Elizabethton), buried: Highland Cem., died: 4 Dec 1918, record (1918) #: 312.
Annie WOODBY, born: 21 Apr 1917, parents: (first name illegible) Woodby and Florence Morton, death cause: "pneumonia fever", buried: Lyons Cemetery, died: 5 Dec 1918, record (1918) #: 313.
Lottie Ann LEE, born: 30 Aug 1879, married, parents: Lee (surname illegible) and Lottie Crow, death cause: "influenza and pneumonia", buried: Highland Cemetery, died: 6 Dec 1918, record (1918) #: 314.
Julia BUCKLES, born: Dec 1881, married, parents: T.J. Buckles and Celia Williams, death cause: "influenza", informant: Abe Buckles (Watauga Valley), buried: Buckles Cem., died: 7 Dec 1918, record (1918) #: 315.
Cornelia Taylor ESTEP, age 26 years, married, parents: Losson Taylor and Sarah Campbell, death cause: "tuberculosis", informant: Will Estep (Carter), buried: Taylor Cemetery, died: 7 Dec 1918, record (1918) #: 316.
Walter D. DUNLOP, born: 27 Nov 1864, married, parents: not stated, death cause: "influenza", informant: Bob Riggs (Elizabethton), buried: Colbaugh Cemetery, died: 10 Dec 1918, record (1918) #: 317.
Daniel RICHARDSON, age 4 years, parents: Thomas Richardson and Elen Myers, death cause: "diarrhoea", informant: W.E. Asher, buried: Richardson Cemetery, died: 8 Dec 1918, record (1918) #: 316a.
Manda LORD, age 71 years, born in North Carolina, widow, parents: Jessie South (NC) and Lizzie Hodge (NC), death cause: "tuberculosis of bowels", informant: W.P. Loveless (Elizabethton), buried: Lyons Cemetery, died: 16 Dec 1918, record (1918) #: 318.

Clytie HOLDER, female, age 2 years, parents: Curtis Holder and Alice Wilson, death cause: "pneumonia fever", informant: N.R. Holder (Carter), buried: Richardson Cemetery, died: 11 Dec 1918, record (1918) #: 319.

May Malissie BOWERS, born: 12 Jan 1854, parents: Calven Cable (NC) and ____ Buckles, death cause: "pneumonia", died: 12 Dec 1918, record (1918) #: 320.

Infant (name illegible) BRUMIT, female, born: 24 Jan 1917, parents: Jacob Brumit and Fannie Carrier (Bluff City), death cause: "paralysis of intestines and obstruction", informant: J.D. Brumit (Elizabethton), buried: Highland Cemetery, died: 12 Dec 1918, record (1918) #: 321.

Carrie RICHARDSON, age 64 years, married, parents: James Smith and ____ Foister, death cause: "dropsy", died: 12 Dec 1918, record (1918) #: 322.

Frankie WAGNER, female, black, born: 22 Dec 1902, parents: (illegible) Wagner and Mollie Watson (NC), cod "pulmonary tuberculosis", buried: Cedar Grove Cemetery, died: 13 Dec 1918, drec 323.

James DUNLOP, born: 8 Nov 1914, parents: W.D. Dunlop and Mollie Riggs, death cause: "influenza", informant: Bob Riggs (Eliazbethton), buried: Colbaugh Cemetery, died: 13 Dec 1918, record (1918) #: 224.

Nancy Taylor LEWIS, born: 1 Feb 1863, married, parents: Alvin Taylor and Sarah Markland, death cause: "tuberculosis, informant: Alvin Fipps (Carter), buried: Markland Cemetery, died: 13 Dec 1918, record (1918) #: 225.

John MORRIS Sr., age 72 years, married, parents: "not known", death cause: "influenza", informant: William Perry (Elizabethton), buried: Morris Cemetery, died: 14 Dec 1918, record (1918) #: 226.

Infant NEAL, female, born: 7 Dec 1918, parents: Roy A. Neal (Green County) and (illegible) Bell Smith, death cause: "malnutrition", informant: Roy A. Neal (Elizabethton), buried: Hyder Cemetery, died: 15 Dec 1918, record (1918) #: 227.

Selina PIERCE, born: Dec 1828, widow, parents: Stephen Lewis and Dicy Heatherly, death cause: "old age", informant: Armstead Pierce (Watauga Valley), buried: Buckles Cem., died: 17 Dec 1918, record (1918) #: 228.

Nathaniel TREADWAY, born: 18 Feb 1901, parents: James S. Treadway and Bert Hednick, death cause: "double pneumonia", informant: Monroe Treadway (Elizabethton), buried: Charity Hill Cemetery, died: 18 Dec 1918, record (1918) #: 229.

Webster CROSSWHITE, born: 17 Apr 1889 in Johnson County, parents: Lonzo Crosswhite (Unicoi County) and Mary Robinson (Johnson County), death cause: "lobar pneumonia", informant: Mrs. J.B. Crosswhite (Elizabethton), buried: Johnson County, died: 18 Dec 1918, record (1918) #: 230.

Willy ROYAL, born: 20 Jul 1838, married, parents: ___ Royal (Scotland) and Jennie Fairclaw (NY), death cause: "influenza, heart trouble, old age", informant: Vance Royal (Roan Mountain), died: 19 Dec 1918, record (1918) #: 331.

George W. EMMERT, born: 8 Jan 1829, widower, parents: George W. Emmert and Mary Hendrix, death cause: "fracture of neck and right femur from fall", informant: Mrs. R.A. Range (Elizabethton), buried: Emmert Cem., died: 19 Dec 1918, record (1918) #: 332.

Roy Hill PRESNELL, born: 17 May 1917, parents: Sam Presnell (Watauga Co., NC) and Florence (illegible) (Watauga Co., NC), death cause: "broncho pneumonia", buried: Norris Cem., died: 20 Dec 1918, record #: 333.

James H. GOUGE, born: 20 Nov 1865 in North Carolina, married, parents: Edmon Gouge (NC) and Sarah Wilson (NC), death cause: "influenza, tuberculosis", informant: H. Gouge (Shell Creek), buried: Elizabethton, died: 21 Dec 1918, record (1918) #: 334.

Mrs. Eliza E. SLAGLE, born: 4 Mar 1844 in Sullivan County, widow, parents: "not known", death cause: "supposed apoplexy", informant: Alvin Lyon (Elizabethton), buried: Slagle Cem., died: 21 Dec 1918, record (1918) #: 335.

Frank BURROW, born: 26 Oct 1918, parents: Frank Burrow and May Fair, death cause: "not known", buried: Carter Cemetery, died: 23 Dec 1918, record (1918) #: 336.

Annie WEST, born: 5 Aug 1914, parents: Johnson James West and May Osborn, death cause: "diptheria", informant: Joseph B. West (Hampton), buried: Hall Cemetery, died: 25 Dec 1918, record (1918) #: 337.

Mrs. Mollie SANDERS, age 63 years, married, parents: G.W. Swanner and Mandy Keen, death cause: "cancer of uterus", buried: Taylors Chapel, died: 25 Dec 1918, record (1918) #: 338.

Mrs. Hettie BAKER, born: 17 Oct 1875, married, parents: John T. Campbell and Mary Smith, death cause: "heart disease", informant: William G. Campbell (Hampton), buried: Hall Cemetery, died: 28 Dec 1918, record (1918) #: 339.

Blannie Edith CARTER, born: 3 Jun 1916, parents: Walter Deloach and Ruth Turner, death cause: "influenza", informant: Ruth Turner, died: 30 Dec 1918, record (1918) #: 340.

Infant NIDIFFER, female, parents: Will Nidiffer and Carolina Bowers, death cause: "stillborn", buried: Treadway Cem., died: 13 Dec 1918, record #: 341.

Infant SEABOCK, male, parents: Roy Seabock (NC) and Rhoda Russell, death cause: "stillborn", died: 6 Dec 1918, record (1918) #: 342.

Lawrence Edward CURTIS, born 21 Mar 1918, parents: William T. Curtis and Lue Hellen Kidwell, death cause: "supposed to be measles, died: 5 Jan 1919, record (1919) #: 1.

Rosa PRICE, born: 6 Apr 1915 in North Carolina, parents: father not stated and Rosanna Price (NC), death cause: "pertussis", informant: Albert Price (Fish Springs), buried: Smith Cemetery, died: 6 Jan 1919, record (1919) #: 2.

Grace HEATON, born: 4 Jan 1919, parents: Rhudy Heaton and Rosa Deloach, death cause: "not known", informant: Tom Heaton (Siam), died: 6 Jan 1919, death record not numbered.

Mary Blevins ESTEP, age 55 years, married, parents: Loone Blevins and Patsy Garland, death cause: "cancer of breast", informant: S.R. Estep (Carter), buried: Garland Cem., died: 6 Jan 1919, record (1919) #: 3.

Earl CAMPBELL, born: 29 Jan 1917, parents: James G. Campbell and Ethel Pierce, death cause: "pneumonia and spinal menningitis", informant: W.C. Pierce (Butler), buried: Smith Cemetery, died: 9 Jan 1919, record (1919) #: 4.

Arthur MERRITT, born: 26 Nov 1918, parents: Charles Merritt and Venie Jenkins, death cause: "pneumonia", informant: W.H. Merritt (Valley Forge), died: 12 Jan 1919, record (1919) #: 5.

Elizabeth WILLIAMS, born: 12 Aug 1832, parents: Griffin Pierce and Pollie Crowlie, death cause: "lobar pneumonia and influenza", informant: J.G. Williams (Watauga Valley), buried: Buckles Cemetery, died: 12 Jan 1919, record (1919) #: 6.

Ida SCOTT, age 18 years, born in Washington County, TN, parents: K.A.B. Scott and Mary France, death cause: "influenza and penumonia", died: 13 Jan 1919, record (1919) #: 7.

William D. RUTLIDGE, age 86 years, born in Sullivan County, married, parents: "unknown", death cause: not stated, died: 14 Jan 1919, record (1919) #: 8.

James CARVER, age about 63 years, married, parents: Adin Carver and Nancy Banks (Haywood Co., NC), death cause: "mitral murmer", informant: John Carver (Hampton), buried: Fair View Cemetery, died: 14 Jan 1919, record (1919) #: 9.

Charlie CHAMBERS, age 23 years, parents: Dan Chambers and Eliza Simes, death cause: "lobar pneumonia and influenza", informant: Grant Nave, buried: Simes Cemetery, died: 15 Jan 1919, record (1919) #: 10.

Wes JONES, age 70 years, born in North Carolina, parents: Sam Jones (NC) and mother's name unknown, death cause: "lobar pneumonia", informant: George Morse, buried: Jones Cemetery, died: 15 Jan 1919, record (1919) #: 11.

John RAINBOLT, age near 60 years, parents: T. Dugger and Caroline Rainbolt, death cause: "unknown", informant: Smith Dugger (Butler), buried: Cobbs Creek, died: 17 Jan 1919, record (1919) #: 12.

Roy B. CAMPBELL, born: 12 Apr 1904, parents: George P. Campbell and Leeaner White, death cause: "influenza and pneumonia", informant: George P. Campbell (Butler), died: 18 Jan 1919, record (1919) #: 13.

Evelyn Inez SMITH, born: 24 Sep 1918, parents: Bruce A. Smith and Della Absher, death cause: "Spanish influenza", buried: Highland Cemetery, died: 18 Jan 1919, record (1919) #: 14.

Dewey BUCHANAN, age 3 months, parents: Duer Buchanan (NC) and Dalie Dials, death cause: not stated, informant: Jim Buchanan, buried: Jones Cemetery, died: 18 Jan 1919, record (1919) #: 15.

Mollie DELOACH, age 54 years, married, parents: Joel Beck (NC) and Emeline Calton (NC0, death cause: "organic heart trouble", informant; Sam Deloach (Valley Forge), buried: Williams Cemetery, died: 18 Jan 1919, record (1919) #: 16.

Lon CARVER, age 6 years, parents: ____ Carver and ____ Hall, death cause: "measles and pneumonia", informant: Joe Carver (Johnson City), buried; Blevins Cemetery, died: 19 Jan 1919, record (1919) #: 17.

Henry BOWMAN, age 2 years and 8 months, parents: Roy Bowman and Vicy Trivett, death cause: "influenza and pneumonia", informant: Vicy Trivett, buried: Minton Cemetery, died: 19 Jan 1919, record (1919) #: 18.

Nellie SWANNER, age 18 years, parents: J.P. Swanner and Sarah Price, death cause: "pulmonary tuberculosis and influenza", buried: Taylor's Chapel, died: 19 Jan 1919, record (1919) #: 19.

Clyde STOVER, born: 27 Dec 1897, single, parents: John Stover and Rody Shell, death cause: "influenza", informant: John Stover (Elizabethton), buried: Shell Cem., Watauga, died: 19 Jan 1919, record (1919) #: 20.

Carl Haynes CLEMONS, born: 5 Jan 1916, parents: David Clemons and Lillie Taylor, death cause: "influenza and pneumonia", informant: H.T. Daniels (Elizabethton), buried: Lyons Cemetery, died: 20 Jan 1919, record (1919) #: 21.

Henry MARKLAND, born: 21 Apr 1898, married, parents: Wilburn Markland and Mary Hardin, death cause: "influenza, lobar pneumonia", informant: Frank Markland (Carter), buried: Blevins Cemetery, died: 21 Jan 1919, record (1919) #: 22.

Lottie WALLIS, age 17 years, born in Johnson County, parents: Sherman Wallis (Johnson County) and Elizabeth Johnson (Johnson County), death cause: "influenza", informant: Sherman Wallis (Elizabethton), buried: Stevens Cem., died: 22 Jan 1919, record (1919) #: 23.

Helen Orbell MARKLAND, born: 11 Sep 1918, parents: Will Markland and Lou White, death cause: "measles", buried: Hyder Cemetery, died: 22 Jan 1919, record (1919) #: 24.

William Washington ROGERS, born: 10 apr 1870 in Pennsylvania, married, parents: "not known", death cause: "organic heart disease", informant: Mrs. Mary Rogers (Braemar), died: 22 Jan 1919, record (1919) #: 25.

Carmen Robert MILLER, born: 15 Aug 1919, parents: Robert Miller and Sarah Head, death cause: "influenza", informant: J.D. Miller (Siam), died: 22 Jan 1919, record (1919) #: 26.

Laura CARION, age 49 years, married, parents: father's name not stated and Eliza Hinkle, death cause: "flu, pneumonia", died: 23 Jan 1919, record (1919) #: 27.

C.T. ESTEP, born: 23 Apr 1849, married, parents: Shaderic Estep and Nellie Tester (NC), death cause: "heart trouble", buried: Estep Cemetery, died: 23 Jan 1919, record (1919) #: 28.

Mrs. Maggie WILLIAMS, born: 30 Jun 1880 in Watauga County, NC, married, parents: James Culver (NC) and Ella Shoemaker (NC), death cause: "influenza", informant: Allie Eggers (Elizabethton), buried: Eggers Cemetery, died: 23 Jan 1919, record (1919) #: 29.

Henry BOWERS, colored, born: 24 Jun 1839 in Ashe County, NC, parents: "unknown", death cause: "influenza", buried: Cedar Grove Cemetery, died: 21 Jan 1919, record (1919) #: 30.

Harry William FAIR, born: 21 Dec 1918, parents: Thomas Fair and Mary Bradshaw, death cause: illegible, informant: Thomas Fair (Elizabethton), buried: Carter Cemetery, died: 24 Jan 1919, record (1919) #: 31.
Mrs. Margaret WHITEHEAD, age about 77 years, parents: Larkin Whitehead and Bettie Hill, death cause: "pneumonia", informant: Herbert Whitehead (Roan Mountain), died: 25 Jan 1919, record (1919) #: 32.
Virginia Adelaide SHUPE, born: 23 Jun 1915, parents: Isaac Shupe and Marabelle Dickerson, death cause: "broncho pneumonia", informant: Isaac Shupe (Milligan), died: 26 Jan 1919, record (1919) #: 33.
Glenn BLEVINS, born: 12 May 1916, parents: John Blevins and Belle Lilly, death cause: "influenza", informant: Charlie Blevins (Elizabethton), buried: Slagle Cem., died: 26 Jan 1919, record (1919) #: 34.
Susan GRINDSTAFF, born: 22 Feb 1863, widow, parents: Noah Potter and Ann Dugger, death cause: "mitralstenosis", informant: Claud Grindstaff (Valley Forge), died: 26 Jan 1919, record (1919) #: 35.
Henry DAUGHERTY, born: 31 Mar 1839 in Ohio, married, parents: "unknown", death cause: "chronic diarohea", informant: Donna Daugherty, buried: Highland Cemetery, died: 27 Jan 1919, record (1919) #: 36.
Thomas LARGEN, age about 64 years, born in Denver Colorado, married, parents: "unknown", death cause: "articulor rhumatism", informant: Land Largen (Roan Mountain), buried: Whitehead Cemetery, died: 28 Jan 1919, record (1919) #: 37.
Infant MILLER, born: 13 Jan 1919, parents: Orville Miller and Maude Stout (Johnson County), death cause: "measles", informant: Grant Stout (Elizabethton), buried: Highland Cemetery, died: 28 Jan 1919, record (1919) #: 38.
Rollie Allen Edward DAVIS, born: 18 Apr 1917 in Knoxville, TN, parents: J.H. Davis and Annie Bowline, death cause: "relapse of measles", informant: Annie Davis, buried: Highhand Cemetery, died: 29 Jan 1919, record (1919) #: 39.
Anna Lee KITE, born: 10 Nov 1900, single, parents: J.R. Kite and Maggie Mae Simmons (VA), death cause: "influenza", buried: Simmons Cemetery, died: 29 Jan 1919, record (1919) #: 40.
Alice Lee KENT, born: 29 Jan 1855 in Maryland, spinster, parents: James Kent (MD) and Mary S. Kent (MD), death cause: "broncho pneumonia", informant: R.S. Fife (Elizabethton), buried: Johnson City, died: 29 Jan 1919, record (1919) #: 41.

Mrs. Ella LAMBERT, born: 9 Oct 1860 in Washington County, TN, widow, parents: William May (Washington County) and Eliza H. King (VA), death cause: "mitral murmur", informant: D.D. Campbell (Hampton), buried: Sorrell Cem., died: 30 Jan 1919, record (1919) #: 42.
Ruth COLEMAN, parents: Nat Coleman and Linda Brummitt (Unicoi), death cause: "stillborn", informant: Nat Coleman (Hampton), born/died: 23 Jan 1919, record (1919) #: 43.
Infant MILLER, male, parents: Orville Miller and Maude Stout, death cause: "stillborn", informant: S.A. Miller (Elizabethton), buried: Highland Cemetery, died: 13 Jan 1919, record (1919) #: 44.
Charles Kennith MATHERSON, born: 16 Aug 1915, parents: William Taylor Matherson (Johnson County) and Lillie Neatherly (Johnson County), death cause: "measles, lobar pneumonia", informant: Mrs. N.D. Matherson (Elizabethton), buried: Highland Cemetery, died: 1 Feb 1919, record (1919) #: 45.
James P. WILSON, born: 27 Nov 1908, parents: John A. Wilson and Sallie (surname illegible), death cause: "edema of lungs", informant: John A. Wilson (Fish Springs), died: 1 Feb 1919, record (1919) #: 46.
Ina Dorris CARENDER, born: 2 Aug 1901 in Watauga County, NC, single, parents: Jospeh L. Carender (Wilkes Co., NC) and Hessie Rominger (Watauga Co., NC), death cause: "influenza", informant: Joseph L. Carender (Butler), buried in North Carolina, died: 2 Feb 1919, record (1919) #: 47.
Lola TAYLOR, born: 9 Nov 1902, parents: Nat Taylor and Maggie Jones, death cause: "pneumonia and influenza", buried: Jones Cem., died: 4 Feb 1919, record #: 48.
Sallie MCGEE, colored, age about 65 years, parents: "unknown", death cause: "tuberculosis", informant: C.H. Fitzsimmons, buried: Fitzsimmons Cemetery, died: 4 Feb 1919, record (1919) #: 49.
Mary Elizabeth BOWLING, born: 1 Jul 1917, parents: Charles Bowling and Emma Martin, death cause: "measles and pneumonia", buried: Highland, died: 5 Feb 1919, record (1919) #: 50.
Estal GOSS, age 75 years, born in Ashe County, NC, widower, parents: Andy Goss (Ashe Co., NC) and Rachel Perkins (Ashe Co., NC), death cause: "old age", informant: L.H. Goodwin (Butler), died: 6 Feb 1919, record (1919) #: 51.
Robert E. REED, born: 25 Dec 1918, parents: Wesley Reed and _____ Humphreys, death cause: "broncho pneumonia", died: 6 Feb 1919, record (1919) #: 52.

Edith C. SMITH, born: 14 Sep 1917, parents: G.C. Smith and Tilla Bell Large, death cause: "lobar pneumonia", informant: D.J. Smith (Elizabethton), buried: Colbaugh Cemetery, died: 6 Feb 1919, record (1919) #: 53.

Johnie ROBERTS, born: 17 Aug 1914, parents: Will Roberts (NC) and mother's name not stated, death cause: "influenza and pneumonia", informant: Willis Widner (Watauga), buried: Stoney Creek, died: 6 Feb 1919, record (1919) #: 54.

Rexter SHEPARD, age 17 years, born in North Carolina, parents: Jacob Shepard (NC) and Rhoeba Jarredd (NC), death cause: "grippe and pneumonia", buried: Mableton, TN, died: 6 Feb 1919, record (1919) #: 55.

Benjamin Butler FRAZIER, born: 24 Oct 1863, married, parents: U.O. Frazier and Margaret Hankal (Hinkle ?), death cause: "heart failure (dropped dead)", died: 7 Feb 1919, record (1919) #: 56.

Daisy LOVELESS, born: 8 Nov 1914, parents: Allen F. Loveless and Rebecca Heaton, death cause: "enfluenza and pneumonia", informant: Elijah Hardin (Valley Forge), buried: Bowers Cemetery, died: 8 Feb 1919, record (1919) #: 57.

Waita LOVELESS, female, born: 2 Oct 1918, parents: Thomas Loveless and Cassie Russell, death cause: "broncho pneumonia", informant: Elijah Hardin (Valley Forge), buried: Williams Cemetery, died: 8 Feb 1919, record (1919) #: 58.

Hester CARDIN, born: 18 Oct 1884, married, parents: Harry Cardin and Rena Morley, death cause: "influenza and pneumonia", informant: Harry Cardin (Siam), buried: Horse Shoe, died: 9 Feb 1919, record (1919) #: 59.

Infant FIPPS, born: 9 Feb 1919, parents: Daniel Fipps and Maggie Lewis, death cause: "weakness of mother", informant: Hastin Lewis (Carter), buried: Lewis Cemetery, died: 10 Feb 1919, record (1919) #: 60.

W.R. MCNEESE, born: 22 Jan 1853 in Green County, married, parents: William McNeese and Pharaba Hawkins, death cause: "pulmonary tuberculosis", informant: Mrs. Alice McNeese (Watauga), buried: Range Cemetery, died: 11 Feb 1919, record (1919) #: 61.

Pearl OLIVER, born: 5 Apr 1917, parents: Judson Oliver and Cordie Bowers, death cause: "influenza", resided: Siam, died: 11 Feb 1919, record (1919) #: 62.

Otta C___ (Illegible), age 37 years, married, parents: father not stated and Mat Jenkins, death cause: "flu, pneumonia", died: 11 Feb 1919, record (1919) #: 63.

Laura LOVELESS, born: 20 Sep 1916, parents: Allen Loveless and Rebecca Heaton, death cause: "influenza and pneumonia", buried: Bowers Cemetery, died: 12 Feb 1919, record (1919) #: 64.

Emma ADKINS, born: 12 Jul 1898, married, parents: William Peters and Anga Markland, death cause: "pulmonary tuberculosis", informant: Samuel Adkins (Hampton), buried: Morton Cemetery, died: 13 Feb 1919, record (1919) #: 65.

Jane WEST, born: 1840, widow, parents: Isaac Nave and J.V. B___ (illegible), death cause: "tuberculosis of bowels", informant: J.G. Nave (Butler), buried: Hall Cemetery, died: 14 Feb 1919, record (1919) #: 66.

Bessie MITCHELL, black, born: 25 Nov 1889 in North Carolina, single, parents: Bob Mitchell (NC) and Mahalie Bowers (NC), death cause: "influenza and tuberculosis", informant: W.W. Watson, buried: Cedar Grove Cemetery, died: 14 Feb 1919, record (1919) #: 67.

Christian C. BOWERS, male, born: 18 May 1850, married, parents: Teter N. Bowers and Polina Bowers, death cause: "intestinal nephritis", informant: J.H. Bowers (Eliazbethton), buried: Bowers Cemetery, died: 11 Feb 1919, record (1919) #: 68.

Homer Rosevelt CLOSSON, born: 23 Mar 1918, parents: T.C. Closson and Mary E. Cable, death cause: "influenza", informant: J.J. Cable (Butler), buried: Closson Cemetery, died: 17 Feb 1919, record (1919) #: 69.

Infant GRINDSTAFF, male, born: 8 Feb 1919, parents: R.D. Grindstaff and Anna Peters, death cause: "jaundice", buried: Grindstaff Cemetery, died: 18 Feb 1919, record (1919) #: 70.

William C. WARD, born: 15 Dec 1837 in Johnson County, married, parents: John Ward and ____ Wilson (editorial note: Nancy Wilson daughter of Tapley Wilson), death cause: "heart disease", buried: Dugger Cemetery (Butler), died: 18 Feb 1919, record (1919) #: 71.

Daniel FIPPS, born: 15 May 1877, married, parents: Peter Fipps (VA) and Betty Blevins, death cause: "influenza", informant: R.M. Ensor (Carter), buried: Lewis Cemetery, died: 19 Feb 1919, record (1919) #: 72.

Hildred Pauline BOWLING, born: 11 Feb 1919, parents: Robert Bowling and Bessie Scalf, death cause: "sposmatic croup", informant: Bill Bowling (Elizabethton), buried: Highland Cemetery, died: 19 Feb 1919, record (1919) #: 73.

James TOWNSEND, born: Apr 1888, married, parents: J__ (illegible) Townsend and Emma Hill, death cause: "lobar pneumonia", informant: Taylor Townsend (Hampton), buried: Whitehead Cemetery, died: 20 Feb 1919, record (1919) #: 74.

Lonia Charlotie CLOSSON, born: 27 May 1909, parents: T.C. Closson and Mary E. Cable, death cause: "influenza", informant: J.J. Cable (Butler), buried: Closson Cem., died: 20 Feb 1919, record (1919) #: 75.

James Elmore CLOSSON, born: 18 Mar 1912, parents: T.C. Closson and Mary E. Cable, death cause: "influenza", informant: J.J. Cable (Butler), buried: Closson Cemetery, died: 21 Feb 1919, record (1919) #: 76.

Francis Marion HYDER, male, born: 18 Mar 1838, married, parents: Joseph D. Hyder and Eliza A. Nelson, death cause: "intestinal nephritis", informant: Mrs. Martha Hyder (Elizabethton), died: 21 Feb 1919, record (1919) #: 77.

Roy B. SMITH, born: 21 Mar 1902, parents: James C. Smith and Mollie Pierce, death cause: "influenza", informant: James C. Smith (Butler), buried: Smith Cemetery, died: 21 Feb 1919, record (1919) #: 78.

Grace SHELL, born: 8 Mar 1914, parents: George H. Shell and Maggie Coleman (Watauga Co., NC), death cause: "pneumonia", informant: George H. Shell (Shell Creek), buried: Richardson Cemetery, died: 22 Feb 1919, record (1919) #: 79.

Pearlie M. BLACK, born: 25 Apr 1893, married, parents: John F. Hatley (Watauga Co., NC) and Martha L. McNeely (Coldwell Co., NC), death cause: "influenza", informant: Martha L. Hatley (Butler), buried: Hatley Cemetery, died: 24 Feb 1919, record (1919) #: 80.

Mae TIMBS, born: 29 Mar 1916, parents: Dock Timbs and Callie Clemons, death cause: "influenza", informant: James Whaley (Butler), buried: Smith Cemetery, died: 23 Feb 1919, record (1919) #: 81.

Betsy WEST, born: 7 Oct 1918, parents: William West and Kate Whitemore, death cause: illegible, informant: William West (Hampton), buried: Hall Cemetery, died: 23 Feb 1919, record (1919) #: 82.

William Varney CLOSSON, born: 13 Jan 1916, parents: T.C. Closson and Mary E. Cable, death cause: "influenza", informant: J.J. Cable (Butler), buried: Closson Cem., died: 24 Feb 1919, record (1919) #: 83.

Sarah Adney CLOSSON, born: 6 Mar 1911, parents: T.C. Closson and Mary E. Cable, death cause: "influenza", informant: J.J. Cable (Butler), buried: Closson Cemetery, died: 25 Feb 1919, record (1919) #: 84.

Walter FLETCHER, born: 7 Sep 1917, parents: A.J. Fletcher and Mollie Nave, death cause: "influenza and miningitis", buried: Buckles Cemetery, died: 25 Feb 1919, record (1919) #: 85.

Mandie SMITH, born: 16 Feb 1905, parents: James C. Smith and Mollie Pierce, death cause: "influenza and pneumonia", informant: James C. Smith (Butler), died: 25 Feb 1919, record (1919) #: 86.

Virginia STOUT, age 6 months, parents: Millard Stout and Anna Vaun, death cause: "pneumonia", buried: A.J. Little Cem., died: 26 Feb 1919, record (1919) #: 87.

Nellie Elizabeth HART, born: 14 Jan 1917, parents: F.S. Hart and B.M. Elliott, death cause: "meningitis", informant: F.S. Hart, buried: Mottern Cemetery, died: 27 Feb 1917, record (1919) #: 80.

Samuel J. CARRIGER, born: 14 Sep 1860, parents: John Carriger and mother unknown, death cause: "influenza and bladder disease", died: 28 Feb 1919, record # 89.

William Quintin TREADWAY, born: 28 Dec 1918, parents: Roderick Randolph Treadway and Grace Van Hook (Campbell Co., KY), death cause: "whooping cough and pneumonia", informant: W.R. Treadway (Johnson City), died: 28 Feb 1919, record (1919) #: 90.

Edith SCOGGINS, born: 9 Feb 1919, parents: Charlie Scoggins and Bessie Minton, death cause: "stillborn", informant: Luta Daniels (Elizabethton), buried: Minton Cemetery, died: 9 Feb 1919, record (1919) #: 91.

Paris GOUGE, born: 19 Feb 1919, parents: Marion Gouge and Nettie Street, death cause: "bowl hives", informant: Marion Gouge (Hampton), buried: McKinney Cemetery, died: 1 Mar 1919, record (1919) #: 92.

Rosie WATSON, age 27 years, married, parents: Alex Bunton (Sullivan County) and Elizie Watson (Johnson County), death cause: "influenza", informant: Roy Watson (Shell Creek), buried: Stout Cemetery, died: 2 Mar 1919, record (1919) #: 93.

Infant SHELL, female, born: 29 Oct 1918, parents: Henry Shell and Etta Bunton, death cause: "pneumonia", informant: Mrs. Bud Tucker (Shell Creek), buried: Perry Cemetery, died: 3 Mar 1919, record (1919) #: 94.

Orval HAYES, born: 5 Mar 1919, parents: John Hayes and Peallie Heaton, death cause: "measles caused abortion and death", informant: Frank Hayes (Shell Creek), died: 5 Mar 1919, record (1919) #: 95.

J.C. HUGHES, born: 1 Aug 1859, widower, parents: Jim Hughes and Margaret Persinger, death cause: "pelagra", informant: Roscoe Hughes (Johnson City), buried: Mottern Cem., died: 10 Mar 1919, record (1919) #: 96.

G.W. SNODGRASS, born: 31 May 1918, parents: G.W. Snodgrass and Hettie Range, death cause: "abscess", informant: Kate Range, died: 10 Mar 1919, record # 97.
Glenn LOVELESS, born: 6 Oct 1913, parents: Tom Loveless and Ellen Holloway, death cause: "lobar pneumonia", informant: Ellen Holloway (Butler), died: 10 Mar 1919, record (1919) #: 98.
Nicie BOWMAN, born: 12 Mar 1887 in Watauga County, NC, death cause: "measles", informant: Roy Bowman (Elizabethton), buried: Minton Cemetery, died: 13 Mar 1919, record (1919) #: 99.
Katie SHAW, age 78 years, married, parents: William Oliver and mother's name unknown, death cause: "organic heart disease", informant: John W. Arnett (Hampton), died: 14 Mar 1919, record (1919) #: 100.
Rhoda MOORE, age 54 years, married, parents: John Hill and Clarrie Gouge (NC), death cause: "uremia", buried: Whitehead Cem., died: 14 Mar 1919, record #: 101.
Georgia GREENWAY, born: 3 Oct 1918, parents: T.H. Greenway and Nellie Slagle, death cause: "broncho pneumonia", buried: Slagle Cemetery, died: 14 Mar 1919, record (1919) #: 102.
James Howard CATES, born: 24 May 1916, parents: Willard Cates and Nola Lee Little, death cause: "pneumonia", informant: Willard Cates (Hopson), buried: Holley Cem., died: 14 Mar 1919, record #: 103.
Oscar Howard CORNETT, born: 19 May 1917, parents: Daniel Cornett and Sula Jordan, death cause: "measles", informant: Dan Cornett (Elizabethton) buried: Highland Cemetery, died: 15 May 1919, record (1919) #: 104.
Laura Belle CATES, born: 14 Apr 1918, parents: Willard Cates and Nola Lee Little, death cause: "pneumonia", buried: Holley Cemetery, died: 15 Mar 1919, record (1919) #: 105.
Gladys HOSS, born: 13 Mar 1911, parents: Clifton Hoss and Matilda Lewis, death cause: "not stated", informant: Clifton Hoss (Shell Creek), buried: Perry Cemetery, died: 17 Mar 1919, record (1919) #: 106.
George M. MARKLAND, born: 12 Mar 1919, parents: Allen Markland and Eliza Grindstaff, death cause: "not known", informant: J.M. Pardue (Carter), buried: Grindstaff Cemetery, died: 19 Mar 1919, record #: 107.
(Illegible) BERRY, female, age 13 years, parents: J.M. Berry and May Boures (Bowers ?), death cause: "lobar pneumonia", buried: Blevins Cemetery, died: 20 Mar 1919, record (1919) #: 108.

W.S. HATLEY, age about 78 years, born in Watauga County, NC, widower, parents: William Hatley (Watauga Co., NC) and Ana Ford (Watauga Co., NC), death cause: "influenza and paralysis", informant: Monroe Davenport (Butler), buried: Whitehead Cemetery, died: 20 Mar 1919, record (1919) #: 109.

W.M. CARVER, age 71 years, married, parents: Aderi Carver and Nancy Banks, death cause: "asterio selorosis", informant: Will Carver (Hampton), buried: Carver Cem., died: 26 Mar 1919, record (1919) #: 110.

Mary Ruth HOLLEY, born: 12 Feb 1919, parents: Walter Holley and Feba Hart, death cause: "supposed to be liver trouble", buried: G.W. Mottern Cemetery, died: 27 Mar 1919, record (1919) #: 111.

Dasie LYONS, age 20 years, born in Watauga County, NC, parents: J.A. Stout (VA) and Rebecca Guy (Watauga Co., NC), death cause: "influenza, heart disease", informant: Dock Lyons (Butler), buried: Hamby Cemetery, died: 28 Mar 1919, record (1919) #: 112.

(Illegible) TAYLOR, male, age 62 years, parents: General J. Taylor and Harrett Combs, death cause: "dropsy", informant: J.V. Taylor (Carter), buried: Grindstaff Cem., died: 18 Mar 1919, record #: 113.

Nathaniel TAYLOR, born: 21 Feb 1919, parents: George Taylor and Mary Roberts, death cause: "unknown", informant: J.T. Taylor (Hampton), buried: Grindstaff Cemetery, died: 30 Mar 1919, record (1919) #: 114.

Eva OLIVER, age 10 years, parents: William Oliver and Lizzie Lewis, death cause: "measles", informant: R.M. Ensor (Carter), buried: Chappel Cemetery, died: 31 Mar 1919, record (1919) #: 115.

Verlean STREET, female, parents: William Street (NC) and Juda Garland (NC), death cause: "stillborn", informant: William Street (Hampton), buried: Simerly Cemetery, died: 23 Mar 1919, record (1919) #: 116.

Infant HONEYCUTT, female, parents: Samuel Honeycutt and Bertha Hampton, death cause: "born dead", buried: Sim Cemetery, died: 30 Mar 1919, record (1919) #: 117.

James HATCHER, born: 14 Oct 1848, married, parents: Lea Hatcher and Martha C. Tipton, death cause: "pulmonary tuberculosis", informant: Alf Hatcher (Kingsport), buried: Hyder Cemetery, died: 5 Apr 1919, record (1919) #: 118.

Mary E. LINDY, born: 8 Jun 1830 in Sullivan County, parents: _____ Little and mother's name unknown, death cause: "nephritis, broncho pneumonia", informant: W.M. Londy (Johnson City), buried: Taylor Cemetery, died: 6 Apr 1919, record (1919) #: 120.

Mandy Catie BRADSHAW, born: 28 Nov 1909, parents: John Bradshaw (Hawkins County) and Eva Hatcher, death cause: "spinal disease and disease of brain", informant: Sam Hatcher (Elizabethton), buried: Highland Cem., died: 5 Apr 1919, record (1919) #: 119.
Virginia STOUT, born: 1 Jun 1918, parents: Millard Stout and Anna Vaughn, death cause: "broncho pneumonia", buried: A.J. Little Cemetery, died: 6 Apr 1919, record (1919) #: 121.
Daniel OLIVER, age 1 year, parents: William Oliver and Lizzie Lewis, death cause: "measles", died: 1 Apr 1919, record (1919) #: 122.
Maxel LIVINGSTON, born: 4 Apr 1918, parents: J.B. Livingston and Victoria McKeehan, death cause: "measles, broncho pneumonia", informant: W.B. Loveless (Elizabethton), buried: McKeehan Cemetery, died: 7 Apr 1919, record (1919) #: 123.
Earl Haskel LAWS, born: 17 Feb 1919, parents: Henry Laws and Maggie Keller (NC), death cause: "influenza and pneumonia", informant: Henry Laws (Shell Creek), buried: Laws Cem., died: 7 Apr 1919, record #: 124.
Christine PILKERSON, born: 1 Apr 1919, parents: Filmore Pilkerson and Auston Baily, death cause: not stated, buried: Harrison Cemetery, Shell Creek, died: 10 Apr 1919, record (1919) #: 125.
Jemima J. LOWE, born: 2 Feb 1848, widow, parents: Henry Colbaugh and Vicy Nave, death cause: "tuberculosis of lungs", informant: Roy B. Lowe (Watauga Valley), buried: Grindstaff Cemetery, died: 13 Apr 1919, record (1919) #: 126.
John TOWNSEND, born: 15 Apr 1919, parents: Taylor Townsend and Bertha Glover, death cause: "lack of vitality", informant: John Townsend (Elizabethton), buried: Hyder Cem., died: 15 Apr 1919, record #: 127.
Mrs. Martha CASTEEL, age 34 years, married, parents: Martin J. Taylor and Mary C. Stepp, death cause: "measles, broncho pneumonia", informant: John Taylor (Johnson City), buried: Frank Anderson Cemetery, died: 22 Apr 1919, record (1919) #: 129.
Rosa Belle LOVELESS, born: 3 Aug 1917, parents: Frank Loveless and Frankie P. Livingston, death cause: "pneumonia", buried: Bowers Cemetery, died: 17 Apr 1919, record (1919) #: 128.
Clarie HILL, born: 16 Dec 1902, parents: John Hill and Bettie Johnson, death cause: "accidentally burned to death from a cooking stove", informant: Bill Hill (Hampton), buried: Whitehead Cemetery, died: 23 Apr 1919, record (1919) #: 130.

Arnold JOHNSON, born: 10 Apr 1919, parents; John Johnson and Maggie Little, death cause: "measles", death cause: "broncho pneumonia", informant: John Johnson (Johnson City), buried: Taylor Cemetery, died: 28 Apr 1919, record (1919) #: 131.

Mrs. (name illegible) NEAL, born: 27 Sep 1892, married, parents: T. Shell and Margaret Smith, death cause: "influenza", informant: R.A. Neal, died: 28 Apr 1919, record (1919) #: 132.

Lena Mae ARNETT, born: 21 Feb 1917, parents: John Wilson Arnett and Sarah Ann McKinney, death cause: "meningitis", informant: John Wilson Arnett (Hampton), buried: McKinney Cemetery, died: 28 Apr 1919, record (1919) #: 133.

Infant HART, male, parents: M.E. Hart and Mary E. Holly, death cause: "born dead", informant: M.E. Hart (Elizabethton), buried: Hart Cemetery, died: 6 Apr 1919, record (1919) #: 134.

George TOWNSEND, parents: Taylor Townsend and Bertha Glover, death cause: "stillborn", informant: John Townsend (Elizabethton), buried: Hyder Cemetery, died: 14 Apr 1919, record (1919) #: 135.

Infant MOORE, black, male, parents: Ed Moore and Ossie Bridges (Banner Elk, NC), death cause: "stillborn", buried: McGee Cemetery, died: 17 Apr 1919, record (1919) #: 136. (twin below)

Infant MOORE, black, male, parents: Ed Moore and Ossie Bridges (Banner Elk, NC), death cause: "stillborn", buried: McGee Cemetery, died: 17 Apr 1919, record (1919) #: 137. (twin above)

Frank GRIFFIN, age about 86 years, married, was a soldier, parents: "unknown", death cause: "pneumonia", informant: Sam Morton (Hampton), buried: Tolley Cemetery, died: 1 May 1919, record (1919) #: 138.

Hester POTTER, born: 10 Apr 1919, parents: Daniel Potter and Julia Stout, death cause: "pneumonia", informant: Nathaniel Bryon (Hampton), died: 3 May 1919, record (1919) #: 139.

Edgar DICKENS, Jr., born: 17 Apr 1919, parents: Edgar Dickson (or Dikens)(Mountain City) and Lena Robertson, death cause: "congestion of liver", buried: McKinney Cem., died: 4 May 1919, record (1919) #: 140.

Marie Jane RITCHIE, age 74 years, widow, parents: William C. Creed (NC) and Rebecca Heatherly, death cause: "pulmonary tuberculosis", informant: S.H. Williams (Watauga Valley), buried: Ritchie Cemetery, died: 6 May 1919, record (1919) #: 141.

Clingmon C. STREET, age about 54 years, born in Mitchell County, NC, married, parents: Capt. Steven Street (NC) and Nancy Street (NC) death cause: "broncho pneumonia", informant: C. Barnett (Unicoi), buried: Simerly Cemetery, died: 6 May 1919, record (1919) #: 142.

Jake MILLER, age 63 years, parents: James Miller (NC) and Deliah Hampton, death cause: "acute rhumatism", informant: Sam Miller (Elizabethton), died: 11 May 1919, record (1919) #: 143.

Lunna GARLAND, age 69 years, married, parents: Richard Anderson and mother's name not stated, death cause: "chronic nephritis", died: 14 May 1919, record #: 144.

James Hamilton GRAYSON, born: 15 Sep 1851 in Virginia, married, parents: Crocket Grayson (VA) and Tobetha Ward (VA), death cause: "apoplexy", informant: Harry Grayson (Elizabethton), buried: East Radford, VA, died: 15 May 1919, record (1919) #: 145.

Barsha SCOTT, born: 6 May 1856, parents: John M. Taylor and Charity Taylor, death cause: "tuberculosis", buried: Lacy Cemetery, died: 16 May 1919, record (1919) #: 146.

Ailace NORRIS, born: 20 Nov 1917, parents: Will Norris and Julia Pilks, death cause: "bowl hives", informant: Ed. Townsend (Hopson), buried: Holly Cemetery, died: 16 May 1919, record (1919) #: 147.

Rebecca WAGNER, age not stated, married, parents: Benjamin Treadway and mother not stated, death cause: "organic heart disease", informant: G.E. Wagner (Hampton), died: 17 May 1919, record (1919) #: 148.

John W. TAYLOR, Jr., born: 21 Apr 1919, parents: John Taylor and Ollie Bowman, death cause: "jaundice, bornchitis", informant: G.H. Persinger (Johnson City), buried: Taylor Cem., died: 19 May 1919, record #: 149.

Oscar GOUGE, born: 18 May 1903, parents: L.T. Gouge and Dollie Honeycutt (NC), death cause: "supposed influenza", informant: L.T. Gouge (Roan Mountain), died: 20 May 1919, record (1919) #: 150.

Mrs. Martha HYDER, age 78 years, married, parents: James Gourley and Susan Simerly, death cause: "broncho pneumonia, high blood pressure", informant: R.O. Hyder (Elizabethton), buried: Hyder Cemetery, died: 24 May 1919, record (1919) #: 151.

Charles M. GOURLEY, born: 5 Apr 1835, married, parents: Charles Gourley (Ireland) and _____ Morgan, death cause: "cancer of face and head", informant: H.H. Manning (Elizabethton), buried: Edens Cemetery, died: 26 May 1919, record (1919) #: 152.

Annie JOHNSON, born: 5 Jun 1905, single, parents: John B. Johnson and Sallie Hampton, death cause: "acute dysentary", informant: W.C. Johnson (Hampton), died: 29 May 1919, record (1919) #: 153.

Manda Adams HOPSON, born: 7 Jun 1862, widow, parents: George Hopson (NC) and Lila Stanly (NC), death cause: illegible, died: 29 May 1919, record (1919) #: 154.

Joseph Thadius KIRKPATRICK, age 69 years, born in Haywood County, NC, parents: Jasper Kirkpatrick (NC) and Mary Justice (NC), death cause: "blood poison from gun shot wound", informant: Tailor Kirkpatrick (Shell Creek), buried: White Oak Cemetery, died: 31 May 1919, record (1919) #: 155.

David Porter BISHOP, born: 6 Jan 1912, parents: Walter Bishop and Mary A. Cole, death cause: "poison from eating apple butter from can", informant: Mary Cole, buried: Dempsy Cemetery, died: 1 Jun 1919, record (1919) #: 156.

Amanda TAYLOR, born: 11 Nov 1856, married, parents: Henry Pierce and Phebe Crwe (illegible), death cause: "valvulor insufficiency", informant: Joe Taylor (Carter), buried: Taylor Cemetery, died: 1 Jun 1919, record (1919) #: 157.

William Hamilton LEWIS, age 51 years, married, parents: J.F.M. Lewis and Mary Jenkins, death cause: "apoplexy", died: 3 Jun 1919, record (1919) #: 158.

Carle Thomas SHELL, born: 7 Mar 1919, parents: Hubert Shell and Farthey Shell, death cause: "unknown", informant: Fathie Shell (Shell Creek), buried: Richardson Cemetery, died: 3 Jun 1919, record (1919) #: 159.

William OLIVER, age 70 years, born in North Carolina, married, parents: "unknown", death cause: "apoplexy", buried: Humphries Cemetery, died: 4 Jun 1919, record (1919) #: 160.

Lucindy WILLIAMS, black, born: 28 Feb 1877 at Watauga, married, parents: William Thompson and Martha Williams, death cause: "carcinoma uteri", buried: Williams Cem., died: 5 Jun 1919, record (1919) #: 161.

Loreta BLEVINS, born: 15 Nov 1845 in Johnson County, widow, parents: Elias McQueen and Loretta ____, death cause: "broncho pneumonia", informant: John Blevins (Elizabethton), buried: Highland Cemetery, died: 6 Jun 1919, record (1919) #: 162.

Rosco BOWERS, born: 22 Oct 1918, parents: Arnold Bowers and Hattie Nidiffer, death cause: "cholera", died: 6 Jun 1919, record (1919) #: 163.

Emma E. CARROLL, age 76 years, widow, parents: Sam Peoples and Polly Overholser (Washington Co., TN), death cause: "old age, senile decay", buried: Hawkins Cemetery, died: 14 Jun 1919, record (1919) #: 164.

Dora M. BLACK, born: 12 Feb 1919, parents: Henry Black (Ashe Co NC) and Pearl Hatley, death cause: "cholera", buried: Hatley Cem, died: 18 Jun 1919, record #: 165.

Mrs. Eliza SLAGLE, born: 13 Jun 1876, married, parents: Henry Morris and Percilla Carr, death cause: "cancer of stomach", buried: Morris Cemetery, died: 18 Jun 1919, record (1919) #: 166.

Sarah Elizabeth TREADWAY, born: 18 Apr 1841 at Okalona, parents: William Pugh and _____ Moreland, death cause: "acute indigestion", informant: William Treadway (Johnson City), buried: Patton Cemetery, died: 19 Jun 1919, record (1919) #: 167.

Jennie ROBERTS, age 3 years, parents: W.M. Roberts (NC) and Lila Birchfield, death cause: "worms and fits", informant: W.C. McKinney (Hampton), buried: Simerly Cem., died: 19 Jun 1919, record (1919) #: 168.

Howard HURLEY, born: 27 Oct 1919, parents: John Hurley and Catherine Hardin, death cause: "diarrhoea", informant: John Hurley (Carter), buried: Hurley Cemetery, died: 23 Jun 1919, record (1919) #: 169.

Infant HILL, male, parents: David Hill and Ollie Hamit, death cause: "stillborn", informant: Mandy Hill (Hopson), died: 4 Jun 1919, record (1919) #: 170.

Mary LYONS, parents: Thomas Lyons and Bessie Grindstaff death cause: "born dead", buried: Lyons Cemetery, died: 5 Jun 1919, record (1919) #: 171.

May HENNIGER, born: 18 Mar 1918, parents: John Henniger (VA) and Eliza Gourley, death cause: "cholera", informant: David Gourley (Valley Forge), died: 3 Jul 1919, record (1919) #: 172.

Dollie GOUGE, born: 5 Nov 1885 in North Carolina, married, parents: W.W. Honeycutt (NC) and Sarah Whitson (NC), death cause: "sepi carmia", informant: L.T. gouge (Roan Mountain), buried: Heaton Creek, died: 6 Jul 1919, record (1919) #: 173.

David Anderson BUCHANAN, age 14 months, parents: (name illegible) Buchanan and D.. (illegible) Sizemore, death cause: "cholera", informant: Dave Buchanan (Elizabethton), buried: Jones Cemetery, died: 6 Jul 1919, record (1919) #: 174.

Mrs. John R. PIERCE, born: Oct 1845, married, parents: Phillip Younce and Margaret Musgrove, death cause: "cancer of eyes", informant: J.A. Pierce, buried: Highland Cem., died: 8 Jul 1919, record (1919) #: 175.

Annie CAMPBELL, born: 15 Apr 1915, parents: James Campbell and Sarah Hyder, death cause: "typhoid", informant: John D. Campbell (Hampton), buried: Butler, died: 9 Jul 1919, record (1919) #: 176.

Frank CLARK, age 7 months and 24 days, parents: David Clark and Jane Berry, death cause: "gastro enteritis", informant: W.M. Clark (Hampton), buried: Berry Cemetery, died: 9 Jul 1919, record (1919) #: 177.

David NAVE, born: 2 Sep 1836, married, parents: Teter Nave and mother's name unknown, death cause: "bronchial pneumonia", informant: C.P. Holland (Elizabethton), buried: Nave Cemetery, died: 10 Jul 1919, record (1919) #: 178.

Mrs. Walter SHELL, born: 11 Apr 1901, parents: Charlie Rains and Jims Wilkens, death cause: "murdered by husband W.D. Shell", informant: Mrs. R.H. Pierce (Elizabethton), buried: Highland Cemetery, died: 10 Jul 1919, record (1919) #: 119.

W.D. SHELL, born: 14 Jan 1893, married, parents: James Shell and Julia Frazier, death cause: "self inflicted with pistol", informant: A.J. Shell (Elizabethton), buried: Highland Cemetery, died: 10 Jul 1919, record (1919) #: 180.

Eula Elizabeth JOHNSON, born: 31 May 1919, parents: Charlie J. Johnson and Hattie Arwood (NC), death cause: "premature, malnutrition", informant: Frank Johnson (Johnson City), buried: Taylor Chapel, died: 10 Jul 1919, record (1919) #: 181.

Hurd MORTON, female, born: 5 Jul 1919, parents: R.D. Morton and Maude Range, death cause: not stated, buried: Simes Cemetery, died: 10 Jul 1919, record (1919) #: 182.

Miss Anna ALLEN, born: 5 Jan 1898, single, parents: W.R. Allen and Sallie Smith, death cause: "drowned in Watauga River", informant: W.R. Allen (Elizabethton), buried: Highland Cemetery, died: 10 Jul 1919, record (1919) #: 183.

William Marion JULIAN, born: 23 Mar 1838 in Knox County, widower, parents: James Julian, Sr. (Knox County) and (illegible) Hampton, death cause: "cancer of mouth", informant: C.M. Julian (Roan Mountain), buried: Heaton Creek, died: 14 Jul 1919, record (1919) #: 184.

William FRANCIS, born: 28 Jun 1842 in North Carolina, widower, parents: J.C. Francis and Elizabeth Morrow (NC), death cause: "gastritis, dysentery", informant: E.M. Brumitt (Hampton), died: 14 Jul 1919, record (1919) #: 185.

William H. MILLER, born: 19 Oct 1844, married, parents: Absolom Miller and Bettie Johnson, death cause: "cardiac diletarium", informant: James Miller (Shell Creek), buried: McKinney Cemetery, died: 20 Jul 1919, record (1919) #: 186.

Rebecca ESTEP, born: 9 Jul 1837, widow, parents: Allen Roberts and Mary McElyea, death cause: "unknown", informant: Julia Campbell (Carter), buried: Estep Cemetery, died: 24 Jul 1919, record (1919) #: 187.

James W. HURDT, age 64 years, born in North Carolina, married, parents: James Hurdt (NC) and mother's name not recorded, death cause: "carditis", informant: Frank McKinney (Hampton), buried: McKinney Cemetery, died: 24 Jul 1919, record (1919) #: 188.

May SHUFFIELD, born: 22 Apr 1903, parents: L.C. Shuffield and Martha Shoun, death cause: "tuberculosis, influenza", informant: S.S. Cole (Carter), buried: Blevins Cemetery, died: 25 Jul 1919, record (1919) #: 189.

Richard COX, born: 10 Jun 1880 in Mitchell County, NC, married, parents: S.M. Cox (Mitchell Co., NC) and Jane Gardner (Mitchell Co., NC), death cause: "tuberculosis of lungs", informant: S.M. Cox (Roan Mountain), died: 25 Jul 1919, record (1919) #: 190.

Frank DISON, born: 6 Feb 1897 in Marion Virginia, single, parents: George W. Dison (NC) and Louil Sanders (NC), death cause: "injury to liver", informant: E.E. Estep (Elizabethton), buried in Virginia, died: 26 Jul 1919, record (1919) #: 191.

Mrs. Sarah Elizabeth GUFFIE, born: 7 Mar 1846 in McDowell County, NC, married, parents: Sam Lawhorn (NC) and Cinda Webb (NC), death cause: "lobar pneumonia", informant: Floyd McLemore (Johnson City), buried: Williams Cemetery, died: 27 Jul 1919, record (1919) #: 192.

Alice D. HATHAWAY, born: 15 Jun 1896, married, parents: Joseph M. Lacy and Lillie McAllister (Sullivan County), death cause: "obstruction of stomach", informant: Mrs. J.M. Lacy, buried: Highland Cem., died: 29 Jul 1919, record (1919) #: 193.

Francis JULIAN, born: 7 Apr 1919, parents: father not stated and Etta Julian, death cause: not stated, informant: U.S.G. Arnett (Roan Mountain), buried: Crabtree, died: 30 Jul 1919, record (1919) #: 194.

Mary HURT, age 84 years, born in North Carolina, widow, parents: George and Betsy Murphy (NC), death cause: "paralysis", informant: Mast Hurdt (Hampton), buried: McKinney Cem., died: 4 Aug 1919, record: 195.

Butler WARD, age 12 years, parents: A.S. Ward (Johnson County) and Alice Shuffield, death cause: "tuberculosis of lungs", informant: A.S. Ward (Butler), buried: Cable Cem., died: 6 Aug 1919, record #: 196.

Joshua Morgan PATTON, born: 5 Feb 1838, widower, parents: not stated, mother born in Wilkes Co., NC, death cause: "heart failure", informant: T.Y. Patton (Johnson City), buried: Patton Cemetery, died: 7 Aug 1919, record (1919) #: 197.

William Thomas WOODS, born: 22 Dec 1918, parents: R..(illegible) Woods and Mattie Ward, death cause: "pneumonia", informant: Wesley Street (Roan Mountain), buried: Blevins Cem., died: 9 Aug 1919, record #: 198.

Sarah Ann CAMPBELL, born: 11 Aug 1849, married, parents: _____ Weeks (or Weaks) and mother not stated, death cause: illegible, informant: J.R. Campbell (Hampton), buried: Hall Cemetery, died: Aug 1919, record (1919) #: 199.

S.. (illegible) MILLER, born: 4 Apr 1849, widower, parents: John Miller and Rhoda Krouse, death cause: "carcinoma of rectum", informant: John Britt (Johnson City), buried: Patton Cemetery, died: 15 Aug 1919, record (1919) #: 200.

Margaret BISHOP, born in 1832, widow, parents: Jessey Jenkins and Eliza Nave, death cause: "organic heart disease", informant: J.B. Fletcher (Hampton), buried: Hess Cem., died: 17 Aug 1919, record (1919) #: 201.

Robert JACKSON, colored, born: 18 Aug 1918, parents: Robert Jackson (NC) and Kattie Watson, death cause: "dysentery", buried: Jackson Cemetery, died: 21 Aug 1918, record (1919) #: 202.

Thomas Milton WRIGHT, born: 22 Apr 1859, married, parents: Thomas Wright and Margaret H. Swingle, death cause: "mitral lesion", buried: Oak Hill Cemetery, died: 25 Aug 1919, record (1919) #: 203.

Eliza ELLIS, born: Apr 1865, married, parents: Wat Collins (VA) and Eveline Williams, death cause: "organic heart disease", informant: Daniel Ellis (Elizabethton), buried: Ellis Cemetery, died: 26 Aug 1919, record (1919) #: 204.

Eva ELLIOTT, born: 9 Jul 1918, parents: M.D. Elliott and Rosa Herrill, death cause: "menengitis (spinal)", informant: N.D. Robinson (Carter), buried: Buckles Cemetery, died: 26 Aug 1919, record (1919) #: 205.

Rebecca PETERS, born: 27 Nov 1916, parents: Daniel Peters and Frona Ritchie, death cause: "croup, asthma", informant: Ike Peters (Carter), buried: Peters Cem., died: 30 Aug 1919, record (1919) #: 206.

Jacob R. LOWE, age 48 years, single, parents: John A. Lowe and Martha W. Lipps, death cause: "thought to be epeleptic fits", informant: H.D. Lowe (Carter), buried: Grindstaff Cemetery, died: 2 Sep 1919, record (1919) #: 207.

Hazel Viola SCOTT, born: 29 Mar 1919, parents: Tom Scott (VA) and Ruth Nave, death cause: "acute gastritis", informant: Thomas J. Proffitt (Elk Park, NC), died: 3 Sep 1919, record (1919) #: 208.

William R.C. JORDAN, born: 31 Mar 1919, parents: William D. Jordan, Jr., and Flora Perry, death cause: "cholera", informant: C.H. Jordan, buried: Highland cemetery, died: 9 Sep 1919, record (1919) #: 210.

Ora Ruth TIMBS, born: 26 Feb 1919, parents: Dock Timbs and Callie Clemons, death cause: "unknown", informant: Cynthia Clemons (Butler), died: 5 Sep 1919, record (1919) #: 209.

James M. PEARCE, born: 4 Jun 1918, parents: W.L. Pearce and Mattie Rainbolt, death cause: illegible, informant: W.L. Pearce (Butler), buried: Rainbolt Cemetery, died: 10 Sep 1919, record (1919) #: 211.

Katie MCKINNEY, born: 14 Apr 1835, widow, parents: Joseph McKinney and B. Adkins (NC), death cause: "old age", informant: Mrs. J.B. McKinney (Elizabethton), buried: Treadway Cem., died: 10 Sep 1919, record (1919) #: 212.

William Washington GUENLIE, born: 13 Feb 1842 in Green County, parents: father's name not stated and Hilda Davenport (Green County), death cause: "chronic nephritis", died: 10 Sep 1919, record (1919) #: 213.

Mary GLOVER, born: 8 Jul 1841, widow, parents: Tobias Lewis (NC) and Tobitha Hyder, death cause: "tuberculosis, pneumonia", buried: Valley Forge, died: 10 Sep 1919, record (1919) #: 214.

Eugene BOWERS, born: 2 Jul 1919, parents: A.J. Bowers and Eliza Deloach, death cause: "whooping cough", buried: Bowers Cem., died: 11 Sep 1919, record #: 215.

James GARLAND, born: 24 Nov 1846, married, parents: Frank Garland and Nancy Campbell, death cause: "lock bowels", informant: Camel Garland (Carter), buried: Garland Cem., died: 11 Sep 1919, record (1919) #: 216.

Clyde LEADFORD, born: 9 Jul 1915, parents: C.K. Leadford and Ida Townsend, death cause: "cholera", informant: Charles Ellison (Hampton), died: 11 Sep 1919, record (1919) #: 217.

Jessimine HAWKINS, born: 17 Jul 1919, parents: S.H. Hawkins (NC) and Julia Carroll, death cause: "dysentary, Carroll Cem., died: 13 Sep 1919, record #: 218.

Mary Elizabeth SHEETS, age 66 years, born in Ashe County, NC, single, parents: Young Sheets (Ashe Co., NC) and Peggy Black (Ashe Co., NC), death cause: "supposed to be pilegry", informant: Eliza Potter (Butler), buried: Elk Mills, died: 14 Sep 1919, record (1919) #: 219.

Samuel Burnett WOOD, age 58 years, married, parents: W.B. Wood (NC) and Evelyn McGee (NC) death cause: "nephritis", informant: J.A. Heaton (Roan Mountain), died: 17 Sep 1919, record (1919) #: 220.

Smith GARLAND, born: 20 Aug 1871, parents: Can Garland and Lizzie Wilson, death cause: "dropsy", informant: John Garland (Carter), buried: Garland Cemetery, died: 18 Sep 1919, record (1919) #: 221.

Ruby EDMONSON, born: 6 Jul 1919, parents: Willard Edmonson (NC) and Nannie Bowling, death cause: "acute indigestion", buried: Hyder Cemetery, died: 19 Sep 1919, record (1919) #: 222.

Minerve BRITT, born: 23 Sep 1919, parents: John Britt and Amanda Whisenhunt, death cause: "pneumonia fever", informant: Jerry Woodby (Elizabethton), buried: Lyons Cemetery, died: 25 Sep 1919, record (1919) #: 223.

Maggie ECHOLS, born: 14 Apr 1905, parents: John B. Echols and Rosa Hardin, death cause: "typhoid fever", informant: Pearl Echols (carter), buried: Blevins Cemetery, died: 28 Sep 1919, record (1919) #: 224.

James COLBAUGH, born: Jun 1886, married, parents: William Colbaugh and Lovina Hardin, death cause: "tuberculosis", informant: William Colbaugh (Carter), buried: Colbaugh Cemetery, died: 28 Sep 1919, record (1919) #: 225.

Ida GRINDSTAFF, born: Jan 1885, single, parents: Alexander Grindstaff and S. (illegible) Dugger, death cause: "cancer of stomach and liver", informant: Mrs. W.E. Nave, buried: Siam, died: 29 Sep 1919, record (1919) #: 226.

D.M. BLEVINS, born: 11 Apr 1856. married, parents: John B. Blevins and Lidia Dugger, death cause: "bronchitis", buried: Carter, died: 29 Sep 1919, record (1919) #: 227.

Infant SMITH, female, parents: Bruce Smith and Celia Griffith, death cause: "stillborn", informant: Bruce Smith (Fish Springs), buried: Smith Cemetery, died: 8 May 1919, record (1919) #: 228.

Infant BUCK, female, parents: Isaac Buck and ____ Jenkins, death cause: "stillborn", informant: Isaac Buck (Johnson City), died: 9 Sep 1919, record (1919) #: 229.

Infant WINTERS, sex not stated, parents: William Winters and Bessie Winters, death cause: "stillborn", informant: James Winters (Shell Creek), died: 13 Sep 1919, record (1919) #: 230.

Infant FISHER, male, parents: John Fisher (VA) and Clara Bradshaw, death cause: "born dead", buried: Colbaugh Cem, died: 17 Sep 1919, record (1919) #: 231.

Infant STOUT, sex not stated, parents: George Stout and Nancy Howell, death cause: "stillborn", buried: Hall Cem., died: 25 Sep 1919, record (1919) #: 232.

Pollie BIRCHFIELD, born: 1844 in North Carolina, parents: Ruben Birchfield (NC) and Celie Hughes (NC), death cause: "broncho pneumonia, mitral regurgitation", informant: W.L. Birchfield (Roan Mountain), died: 2 Oct 1919, record (1919) #: 233.

Luvenia PAYNE, born: May 1863, married, parents: Samuel Williams and Edne Miller (Sullivan County), death cause: "acute indigestion", informant: Mrs. W.S. Taylor (Milligan), buried: Milligan Cemetery, died: 4 Oct 1919, record (1919) #: 234.

Martha WHITE, born: 27 Apr 1847, single, parents: J.W. White and Sabra Bunton, death cause: "supposed, old age", buried: White Cemetery, Butler, died: 5 Oct 1919, record (1919) #: 235.

Julia A. HAWKINS, age 34 years, married, parents: Will Carroll and Ervena Peoples, death cause: "child birth", buried: Carroll Cemetery, Milligan, died: 8 Oct 1919, record (1919) #: 236.

Martha ODOM, born: 13 Oct 1919, parents: Gerrett Odom (NC) and Sallie Hughes, death cause: "unknown", informant: R.J. Gouge (Roan Mountain), died: 14 Oct 1919, record (1919) #: 237.

Wilma WIDENER, born: 6 Oct 1919, parents: Willis Widener (VA) and Tena Sweeney, death cause: illegible, buried: Dempsey Cemetery, died: 16 Oct 1919, record (1919) #: 238.

Bowman HENRY, born: 9 Mar 1908, parents: James Henry and Lillie Treadway, death cause: "appendicitis", informant: Monroe Treadway (Valley Forge), buried: Treadway Cem, died: 20 Oct 1919, record (1919) #: 239.

Benie EDENS, age 1 year and 8 months, parents: Nat Edens and Grace Dugger, death cause: "unknown", informant: Sam Edens (Elizabethton), died: 20 Oct 1919, record (1919) #: 240.

Hazel BARNETT, parents: Herby Barnett and Bessie Honeycutt, death cause: "premature birth", informant: Herby Barnett (Roan Mountain), born/died: 23 Oct 1919, record (1919) #: 242.

Lowisie PRICE, age 84 years, born in North Carolina, parents: Peter Townsend (NC) and Betsy Mitchell (NC), death cause: "paralysed and old age", informant: Thomas Price (Hampton), buried: Honeycutt Cemetery, died: 20 Oct 1919, record (1919) #: 241.

Abbigail DEVALT, age 68 years, born in Coldwell County, NC, parents: Johny Bean and Catherine Parmer (NC), death cause: "gangreen from finger bone infection", informant: N.C. Parmer (Shell Creek), buried: Richardson Cemetery, died: 23 Oct 1919, record (1919) #: 243.

Allen HARDIN, born: 11 Dec 1901, parents: Thomas Hardin and Ella Hardin, death cause: "typhoid fever", buried: Hall Cemetery, Hampton, died: 23 Oct 1919, record (1919) #: 244.

Bula SHELL, born: 3 Dec 1917, parents: John A. Shell and Annie McLain, death cause: "croupus pneumonia", informant: John A. Shell (Shell Creek), buried: Richardson Cem., died: 25 Oct 1919, record (1919) #: 245.

William A. DAVIS, born: 10 Oct 1849 in North Carolina, married, parents: Mark Allen Davis and Sarah Cameron (NC), death cause: "chronic nephritis", buried: Mottern Cem., died: 28 Oct 1919, record (1919) #: 246.

Virginia ROBERTSON, born: 25 Oct 1919, parents: George W. Robertson and Bessie Rumley, death cause: "icterus neonotorum", died: 28 Oct 1919, record (1919) #: 247.

Nancy CAMPBELL, born: 11 Nov 1837 in North Carolina, widow, parents: Henry Glen (NC) and mother's name unknown, death cause: "nephritis", informant: W.M. Campbell (Elizabethton), buried: Roan Mountain, died: 29 Oct 1919, record (1919) #: 248.

Anna Blanch BOLING, born: 30 Oct 1919, parents: James L. Boling and Ida Francis Mahaffey, death cause: "premature", informant: James L. Boling (Butler), died: 30 Oct 1919, record (1919) #: 249.

C.G. JOHNSON, age 71 years, 9 months and 27 days, born in Unicoi County, married, minister, parents: James Johnson (Mitchell Co., NC) and Alice Salts (Washington Co., TN), death cause: "paralysis", buried: Taylor Chapel, died: 30 Oct 1919, record (1919) #: 250.

James R. LITTLE, born: 31 Oct 1919, parents: H. Clay Little and Florence Miller, death cause: "premature birth", informant: J.D. Miller (Valley Forge), buried: Miller Cem., died: 1 Nov 1919, record (1919) #: 251.

Carry Stella ROGERS, born: 15 Aug 1890, married, parents: Charlie Leonard (NC) and Catherine Clark, death cause: "typhoid fever", informant: W.G. Rogers, buried; Leonard Cem., died: 3 Nov 1919, record #: 252.

Earl D. BERRY, born: 9 Sep 1916, parents: Alfred Berry and Lottie Oliver, death cause: "Brights disease", informant: Alfred Berry (Valley Forge), buried: Blue Springs, died: 4 Nov 1919, record (1919) #: 253.
Bertha L. OLIVER, born: 24 Oct 1906, parents: John Oliver and Martha Hilliard, death cause: "typhoid", died: 5 Nov 1919, record (1919) #: 254.
Evline ESTEP, age about 30 years, married, parents: Buck Taler (Taylor ?) and Elizabeth Culbert, death cause: "dropsy, informant: husband (Carter), buried: Garland Cem., died: 5 Nov 1919, record (1919) #: 255.
Reta PERRY, born: 16 Aug 1918, parents: Thomas Perry and Lou Holden, death cause: "influenza", informant: Harrison Perry (Shell Creek), buried: Perry Cemetery, died: 6 Nov 1919, record (1919) #: 256.
Infant BOMAN, male, parents: father not stated and Linea Boman (Coldwell Co., NC), death cause: "abortion", informant: Soloman Odom (Shell Creek), buried: Walnut Mountain, died: 6 Nov 1919, record (1919) #: 257.
Viola WILLIAMS, born: 13 Aug 1917, parents: L.T. Williams and May Jenkins, death cause: "spinal meningitis", informant: Elihu Williams (Watauga Valley), buried: Ritchie Cemetery, died: 7 Nov 1919, record (1919) #: 258.
William HUGHES, born: 14 Oct 1856 in North Carolina, married, parents: Charles Hughes (NC) and Bettie Garland (NC), death cause: "influenza", informant: R. Gouge (Roan Mtn), died: 13 Nov 1919, record #: 259.
John Robertson ESTEP, born: 12 Jun 1919, parents: Isaac Estep and Eva Taylor, death cause: "croup", informant: Isaac Estep (Carter), buried: Garland cemetery, died: 13 Nov 1919, record (1919) #: 260.
Charlie ERWIN, colored, age 76 years, born in North Carolina, parents: Charlie Erwin (NC) and mother not stated, death cause: "mitral insufficiency", informant: George Erwin, buried: Drake Cemetery, died: 15 Nov 1919, record (1919) #: 261.
William Howard ORR, born: 10 Dec 1909, parents: P.S. Orr (Washington Co., TN) and Elizabeth (illegible)(Mitchell Co., NC), death cause: "Hodgkins diesase", informant: P.S. Orr (Roan Mountain), buried: Peters Cemetery, died: 15 Nov 1919, record (1919) #: 262.
Hattie FAIR, born: Mar 1898, single, parents: W.F. Fair (Johnson County) and Eliza Campbell, death cause: "pulmonary tuberculisis", informant: W.F. Fair (Elizabethton), buried: Vanhuss Cemetery, died: 15 Nov 1919, record (1919) #: 263.

Fender PETERS, born: 19 Apr 1902, parents: Wiley Peters and Docia Richardson, death cause: "double pneumonia", informant: J.W. Peters (Carter), buried: Peters Cem., died: 17 Nov 1919, record (1919) #: 264.

Adalade FORD, born: 28 Nov 1848, widow, parents: A.S. Ford and mother not stated, death cause: "acute nephritis", buried: Highland Cemetery, died; 17 Nov 1919, record (1919) #: 265.

Sallie L. HYDER, born: 2 May 1859, widow, parents: Caswell Hyder and Ulara Huston, death cause: "uremic poison", informant: Myrtle Hyder (Johnson City), buried: Hyder Cemetery, died: 19 Nov 1919, record (1919) #: 266.

(illegible) Ann SHELL, age 78 years, 10 months and 3 days, widow, parents: Henry Range and Elizabeth Taylor, death cause: illegible, buried: A.P. Shell Cemetery, died: 19 Nov 1919, record (1919) #: 267.

Andy WILSON, age about 45 years, parents: father not stated and Mara Wilson, death cause: "supposed, heart failure", informant: P.W. Stout (Carter), buried: Richardson Cemetery, died: 20 Nov 1919, record (1919) #: 268.

Nathanial BIRCHFIELD, age 27 years, born in North Carolina, married, parents: John Birchfield (NC) and Cinda Blevins (NC), death cause: "tuberculosis and heart disease", informant: Zeb Honeycutt (Hampton), buried: Ingram Cemetery, died: 23 Nov 1919, record (1919) #: 269.

Julia HENSON, born: 19 Aug 1865 in North Carolina, married, parents: Reuben Honeycutt (NC) and Polly Green (NC), death cause: "catarrah", informant: R.F. Gouge (Roan Mtn), died: 23 Nov 1919, record #: 270.

Ruth May CROW, born: 26 Nov 1919, parents: F.D. Crow and Lottie P. Morton, death cause: "very small twins", informant: W.C. Campbell (Hampton), buried: Old Campbell Cem., died: 5 Dec 1919, record (1919) #: 271.

Effie Campbell JULIAN, born: 16 Nov 1888, married, parents: L.W. Campbell and Alice Shull, death cause: "dilitation of heart", informant: James J. Julian (Roan Mtn), died: 26 Nov 1919, record (1919) #: 272.

Pearl UNDERWOOD, black, age 29 years, 1 month and 10 days, parents: Dan McGee (VA) and Marian Morgan, death cause: "tuberculosis", informant: John Underwood, buried: Cedar Grove, died: 27 Nov 1919, record #: 273.

David CLEMONS, age 52 years, married, parents: Benjamin Clemons and Sarah Lewis, death cause: "lobar pneumonia", informant: William Clemons, buried: Lyons Cemetery, died: 27 Nov 1919, record (1919) #: 274.

Martha E. SMITH, born: 2 Jul 1873, married, parents: Carter Campbell and Saral Smith, death cause: "pulmonary tuberculosis", informant: J.R.E. Smith (Hampton), buried: Smith Cemetery, died: 28 Nov 1919, record (1919) #: 275.

Jennettie CORNETT, born: 6 Oct 1836 in Wilkes County, NC, married, parents: Daniel Rash and Ollie Fair (Wilkes Co., NC), death cause: "fell from a horse", informant: A.W. Heaton (Shell Creek), buried: Walnut Mountain, died: 29 Nov 1919, record (1919) #: 276.

Infant ELLIS, female, parents: Frank Ellis and Rena Johnson, death cause: "stillborn", informant: W.V. Johnson (Elizabethton), died: 2 Nov 1919, record (1919) #: 277.

Infant RITCHIE, sex not stated, parents: A.P. Ritchie and Cresie Alford, death cause: "stillborn", informant: A.P. Ritchie (Watauga Valley), died: 10 Nov 1919, record (1919) #: 278.

Alice SWANNER, born: 1 Dec 1864, parents: Amon Swanner and Katie Banks, death cause: "organic heart disease", informant: S.S. McKinney (Hampton), buried: Berry Cemetery, died: 1 Dec 1919, record (1919) #: 279.

Ruby Roy CROW, born: 26 Nov 1919, parents: Fervis D. Crow and Lottie Morton, death cause: "unknown", informant: W.G. Campbell (Hampton), died: 4 Dec 1919, record (1919) #: 280. (note: twin's record above)

Robert LEWIS, age 6 months, parents: Neal Lewis and Eliza Richardson, death cause: not stated, died: 6 Dec 1919, record (1919) #: 281.

Galilie TOWNSEND, female, married, parents: James Hill and Texie Stephens, death cause: "hypostatic pneumonia", informant: James Hill (Hampton), died: 7 Dec 1919, record (1919) #: 282.

Golda JONES, born: 9 Dec 1919, parents: Russell N. Jones and ____ Oaks, death cause: "unknown", informant: Russell Jones (Shell Creek), buried: Isaac Cemetery, died: 9 Dec 1919, record (1919) #: 283. (note: twin below)

Belva JONES, born: 9 Dec 1919, parents: Russell N. Jones and ____ Oaks, death cause: "unknown", informant: Russell Jones (Shell Creek), buried: Isaac Cemetery, died: 9 Dec 1919, record (1919) #: 284.

Barnet HARMON, age 6 years, parents: Mearing Harmon (Watauga Co., NC) and Ellen Trivett, death cause: "supposed to be croup or diptery", informant: Mearing Harmon (Dark Ridge, NC, buried: Harmon Cemetery, died: 10 Dec 1919, record (1919) #: 285.

Anniebell TEAGUE, born: 5 Feb 1918, parents: Thomas Teague (NC) and Alice Markland, death cause: "pneumonia", buried: Markland Cemetery, Shell Creek, died: 11 Dec 1919, record (1919) #: 286.

Elizabeth PHIPPS, age: "past middle age", married, parents: John Blevins and Elizabeth Blevins, death cause: "dropsy and heart failure", informant: Logan Phipps (Carter), buried: Blevins Cemetery, died: 17 Dec 1919, record (1919) #: 287.

John K. SMITH, born: 3 Oct 1830, parents: Alfred Smith and mother not stated, death cause: "septicemia, infected hand", informant: John P. Bradley, buried: Bradley Cem., died: 21 Dec 1919, record (1919) #: 288.

Sarah E. PIERCE, age 73 years, married, parents: Jacob Vandeventer and _____ Lewis, death cause: illegible, died: 22 Dec 1919, record (1919) #: 289.

Caloway HEARTLEY, age 69 years, married, parents: Calvin Heartley (Watauga Co., NC) and Susan Maze (Watauga Co., NC), death cause: "supposed, heart failure", informant: Albert Heartley (Dark Ridge, NC), buried: Clauson Cem., died: 24 Dec 1919, record # 290.

William D. NIDIFFER, age 75 years, married, old soldier, parents: John Nidiffer and _____ Ritchie, death cause: "paralysis", buried: Wilson Cemetery, died: 25 Dec 1919, record (1919) #: 291.

Noah LUNCEFORD, age 69 years, widower, born in Yancey County, NC, parents: Robert Lunceford (Yancey Co., NC) and Nancy May (Yancey Co., NC), death cause: "supposed, heart failure", informant: Andy Lunceford (Butler), buried: Elk Mills, died: 26 Dec 1919, record (1919) #: 292.

John A. HODGE, born: 20 Sep 1919, parents: John Finley Hodge and Hattie White, death cause: not stated, informant: John Finley Hodge (Butler), buried: White Cemetery, died: 26 Dec 1919, record (1919) #: 293.

Green PETERS, born: 10 May 1906, parents: W.C. Peters and Docia Richardson, death cause: "killed by falling tree", informant: J.W. Peters (Carter), buried: Peters Cemetery, died: 27 Dec 1919, record (1919) #: 294.

Alonzo SWANNER, born: 4 Jul 1919, parents: Thomas Swanner and Mary Swanner, death cause: "bowl hives", informant: John Grindstaff (Hampton), buried: Swanner Cemetery, died: 27 Dec 1919, record (1919) #: 295.

Mrs. Hannah C. MONTGOMERY, born: 7 May 1869, married, parents: James Lunceford and (first name illegible) Stepp, death cause: "(illegible) rhumatism", buried: Walnut Mtn, died: 29 Dec 1919, record (1919) #: 296.

Infant ANDES, male, age 1 year and 5 months, parents: father not stated and Nicie Andes, death cause: "supposed, dipthey", buried: Triplett Cemetery, died: 30 Dec 1919, record (1919) #: 297.

Eliza BOWERS, age 70 years, married, parents: James Berry and ____ Myers, death cause: "paralysis", died: 30 Dec 1919, record (1919) #: 298.

Infant PETERS, male, parents: James Peters and Nan Shoun, death cause: "stillborn", informant: Nan Colbaugh, buried: Peters Cemetery, died: 3 Dec 1919, record (1919) #: 299.

D.C. HARDIN, age 46 years, married, parents: Eliga Hardin and Merry Heaton, death cause: "supposed, heart failure", informant: Columbus Austin (Dark Ridge, NC), buried: Triplett Cemetery, died: 5 Jan 1920, record (1920) #: 1.

Charles Jessie RHEA, colored, age 53 years, 11 months and 9 days, born in Bristol, TN, parents: William Rhea (Washington Co., VA) and Nellie Netherlen (Kingsport), death cause: "tuberculosis", buried: Williams Cemetery, Watauga, died: 6 Jan 1920, record (1920) #: 2.

Littleton HODGE, age 94 years, married, parents: Isaac Garland and Nancy Hodge, death cause: "not known", informant: Nathan Hodge (Elizabethton), buried: Gouge Cemetery, died: 6 Jan 1920, record (1920) #: 3.

Essie Ellen MORRIS, born: 31 Dec 1862 in Sullivan County, widow, parents: James Riley (Sullivan Co.) and Sarah Ann Morrell (Sullivan Co.), death cause: "lobar pneumonia", informant: C.C. Carter (Elizabethton), buried: Morris Cemetery, died: 7 Jan 1920, record (1920) #: 4.

Lafayette LEWIS, born: 17 Mar 1910, parents: Lawson Lewis and Nannie Blevins, death cause: "hemorrhagia (illegible)", informant: Lawson Lewis (Hampton), buried: Lewis Cemetery, died: 8 Jan 1920, record (1920) #: 5.

Roy Edward ROBERTSON, age 2 years and 8 months, parents: J.T. Robertson and Mattie Deloach, death cause: "bronchitis and intero colitis", informant: J.T. Robertson, buried: Highland Cemetery, died: 8 Jan 1920, record (1920) #: 6.

Caloway HARTLEY, age 69 years, born in Watauga County, NC, married, parents: Calvin Hartley (Watauga Co., NC) and Alice Maze (Watauga Co., NC), death cause: "supposed, heart failure", informant: Albert Hartley (Dark Ridge, NC) died: ? Jan 1920, record (1920) #: 7.

William G. BLEVINS, age 49 years, married, parents: J.H. Williams and Margaret Buckles, death cause: "pneumonia and heart trouble", buried: Watauga Academy Cemetery, died: 10 Jan 1920, record (1920) #: 8.
Mattie LEWIS, age 48 years, married, parents: William Combs and ____ Morrell, death cause: not stated, died: 10 Jan 1920, record (1920) #: 9.
Gurney POTTER, born: 2 Feb 1917, parents: George Potter and Sallie Church (NC), death cause: "caught on fire at 11 o'clock", buried: Shell Creek, died: 10 Jan 1920, record (1920) #: 10.
Julie TAYLOR, age 3 days (?), parents: H.(illegible) Taylor and Cathern Hardin, death cause: "septicemia, abortion", died: 12 Jan 1920, record (1920) #: 11.
Bonnie Lyde BRINKLEY, born: 30 Nov 1888, married, parents: William F. Church (NC) and Cornelia Hardin (NC), death cause: "diabetic comma", informant: J.W. Brinkley (Shell Creek), buried: Ray Cemetery, died: 11 Jan 1920, record (1920) #: 12.
Clemmie Jane BUCK, born: 14 Oct 1848, widow, parents: James C. Taylor and May A. Saylor, death cause: "pulmonary tuberculosis", buried: Buck Cemetery, died: 13 Jan 1920, record (1920) #: 13.
Reuben HONEYCUTT, born: 8 Dec 1830 in North Carolina, married, parents: Nathan Honeycutt (NC) and (first name illegible) Bowman (NC), death cause: "old age", informant: Ezekel Barnett (Roan Mountain), died: 14 Jan 1920, record (1920) #: 14.
Myrtle BUCKLES, born: Jan 1897, married, parents: Tom Vanhuss and Effie ____, death cause: "lobar pneumonia", informant: J.H. Pierce (Watauga Valley), buried: Buckles Cem., died: 15 Jan 1920, record #: 15.
Clarence HATHAWAY, born: 30 Nov 1917, parents: father not stated and Jennie McKinney, death cause: "lobar pneumonia", informant: Jennie Hathaway (Valley Forge), died: 17 Jan 1920, record (1920) #: 16.
John STEVENS, age 83 years, married, parents: Joshua Stevens (NC) and Margaret Hill (NC), death cause: "cordio nephritis", informant: W.T. Stevens (Hampton), buried: Stevens Cem., died: 17 Jan 1920, record #: 17.
George MORRIS, born: 26 Mar 1870, parents: Jefa Morris and Catherine South, death cause: "Spanish influenza", informant: Will Morris, buried: Jones Cemetery, died: 18 Jan 1920, record (1920) #: 18.
Georgia TOWNSEND, age 3 years, parents: James Townsend and Bertie Simerly, death cause: "tape worm", informant: John Townsend (Elizabethton), buried: Whitehead Cem, died: 19 Jan 1920, record (1920) #: 19.

Gemmima MCNEAL, age 45 years, married, parents: J.W. Smith and Delia Laws (Johnson County), death cause: "tuberculosis of lungs", informant: Robert McNeal, buried: Smith Cemetery, died: 20 Jan 1920, record (1920) #: 20.

James HOWELL, age: about 64 years, born in South Carolina, parents: Thomas Howell (SC) and Nancy Riggins (SC), death cause: "nephritis", informant: Roda Howell (Butler), buried: Whitehead Cemetery, died: 20 Jan 1920, record (1920) #: 21.

Millard F. BOWERS, age 62 years, married, parents: David B. Bowers and ____ Brown, death cause: "abscess in stomach and bowels", died: 21 Jan 1920, record (1920) #: 22.

Delphia JOHNSON, born: 13 May 1829 in Watauga County, NC, widow, parents: Benjamin Hartley (NC) and Elizabeth Church (NC), death cause: "nephritis", informant: E.B. Maynard (Kingsport), buried: Hall Cemetery, died: 21 Jan 1920, record (1920) #: 23.

J.P. RITCHIE, born: 4 Jul 1842, married, parents: Alvin Ritchie and Jennie Jenkins, death cause: "apoplexy", buried: Ritchie Cemetery, died: 21 Jan 1920, record (1920) #: 24.

Addie E. VINES, born: 17 Jan 1917, parents: Harry Vines (NC) and Sallie Taylor, death cause: "pneumonia", informant: Harry Vines (Valley Forge), died: 25 Jan 1920, record (1920) #: 25.

Maud MILLER, born: 15 Mar 1891 in Johnson County, married, parents: A.G. Stout (Johnson County) and Mandy Ward (Johnson County), death cause: "tuberculosis", informant: A.G. Stout (Elizabethton), buried: Highland Cemetery, died: 28 Jan 1920, record (1920) #: 26.

U.B. CREED, born: 25 Apr 1853, widower, parents: William Creed and Rebecca Heatherly, death cause: "influenza", informant: A.S. Rithcie (Watauga Valley), buried: Ritchie Cemetery, died: 29 Jan 1920, record (1920) #: 27.

Belle JENKINS, born: 25 Dec 1887, married, parents: John Williams and Susanah Matherly, death cause: "falling in fire with fit, epilepsy", informant: John Williams (Valley Forge), died: 31 Jan 1920, record (1920) #: 28.

Infant MORGAN, female, parents: James Morgan (NC) and Sallie Johnson, death cause: "stillborn", informant: James Morgan (Hampton), buried: Dennis Cove, died: 1 Jan 1920, record (1920) #: 29.

Infant NAVE, male, parents: Dan Nave and Ethel Berry, death cause: "stillborn", informant: Edd Berry (Elizabethton), died: 1 Jan 1920, record (1920) #: 30.

Infant DAVIDSON, male, parents: C.E. Davidson and Lottie (surname illegible), death cause: "born dead", informant: W.C. Peters, died: 2 Jan 1920, record (1920) #: 31.

Infant BUCKLES, sex not stated, parents: Dave Buckles and Myrtle Vanhuss, death cause: "stillborn", informant: J.H. Pierce (Watauga Valley), buried: Buckles Cem., died: 5 Jan 1920, record (1920) #: 32.

Infant FAIR, male, parents: S.S. Fair and Mattie Bradshaw, death cause: "born dead", informant: S.S. Fair (Elizabethton), buried: Highland Cemetery, died: 14 Jan 1920, record (1920) #: 33.

Infant HICKS, sex not recorded, parents: Morris Hicks (Elk Park, NC) and Lucinda Winters (Elk Park, NC), death cause: "stillborn", died: 30 Jan 1920, record (1920) #: 34.

James MERITT, born: 26 Apr 1868, married, parents: John Meritt and Susan Hays, death cause: "tuberculosis", informant: John Meritt, buried: Glover Cemetery, died: 1 Feb 1920, record (1920) #: 35.

Nancy MCELLEN, age 88 years, widow, born in North Carolina, parents: Peter Nick Loury and Nancy Ann ____, death cause: "dropsy and rhumatism", informant: Frank McEllen (Roan Mountain), buried: Nelson Cemetery, died: 1 Feb 1920, record (1920) #: 36.

Joe PRICE, age 45 years, single, parents: Thomas Price (NC) and Louise Townsend (NC), death cause: "pulmonary tuberculosis", informant: Thomas Price (Hampton), buried: Honeycutt Cemetery, died: 2 Feb 1920, record (1920) #: 37.

Peggie MCKINNEY, born: 18 Feb 1841 in North Carolina, parents: John McKinney (NC) and Bettie McKinney (NC), death cause: "old age", informant: James McKinney (Roan Mountain), buried: Heaton Creek, died: 2 Feb 1920, record (1920) #: 38.

Aurge Burl BLEVINS, born: 5 Nov 1914, parents: Dave Blevins and Mary Garland, death cause: "unknown", informant: Charley Blevins, buried: Garland Cemetery, died: 6 Feb 1920, record (1920) #: 39.

Robert Kennith DAVIS, born: 10 Dec 1919, parents: Hicks Davis and Alice Morris, death cause: "broncho pneumonia", informant: J.C. Carter (Elizabethton), buried: Emmert Cemetery, died: 6 Feb 1920, record (1920) #: 40.

Bertha LAWS, born: 17 May 1910, parents: Robert E. Laws and Roxie Grmsley (Sullivan County), death cause: "lobar pneumonia", buried: Colbaugh Cemetery, died: 7 Feb 1920, record (1920) #: 41.

Creesie MORGAN, female, born: 9 Oct 1919, parents: father not stated and Malinda Morgan, death cause: "suppose influenza", informant: D.H. Potter (Dark Ridge, NC), buried: Potter Cemetery, died: 7 Feb 1920, record (1920) #: 42.

Mrs. Nancy HICKS, born: 8 Feb 1882, married, parents: Isaac Guinn (NC) and Elizabeth Hicks (NC), death cause: "purpural fever", informant: J.B. Shoun (Hampton), buried: Norris Cemetery, died: 8 Feb 1920, record (1920) #: 43.

Miss Cale Emmert NEWTON, born: 8 May 1875, single, parents: David Newton and Ella Miller, death cause: "tuberculosis", buried: Newton Cemetery, died: 8 Feb 1920, record (1920) #: 44.

Elizabeth C. ANDERSON, age 73 years, married, parents: A.C. Williams and Rebecca Berry, death cause: "supposed age and senility", informant: A.B. Bowers, Jr., died: 8 Feb 1920, record (1920) #: 45.

Henry CHESSER, born: 17 Sep 1875 in Missouri, married, parents: Frank Chesser and mother's name illegible, death cause: "accidental death in sawmill", informant: L.W. Brown (Bramer), buried: Lyon Cemetery, died: 10 Feb 1920, record (1920) #: 46.

Alfred Tailor POTTER, born: 30 Aug 1890, married, parents: E.A. Potter and Deliah Messer, death cause: "influenza, pneumonia", informant: E.A. Potter (Shell Creek), died: 10 Feb 1920, record (1920) #: 47.

Georgia Marion SCOTT, born: 12 Oct 1914, parents: Howard B. Scott (Indiana) and Mary Cox, death cause: "typhoid", informant: W.F. Scott (Elizabethton), buried: John Smith Farm, died: 10 Feb 1920, record (1920) #: 48.

Sam EADENS, age 60 years, married, parents: Sam Davenport and Elizabeth Berry, death cause: "influenza, pneumonia", informant: Charlie Brumit, buried: Jones Cem., died: 11 Feb 1920, record #: 49.

Ruby MILLER, age 19 years and 9 months, single, parents: David Miller and Elizabeth Vest, death cause: "sarcoma of left shoulder and side", buried: Little Cemetery, died: 11 Feb 1920, record (1920) #: 50.

Madge HOBSON, born: 7 Dec 1919, parents: Charlie Hobson and Ellen Arnett, death cause: "whooping cough", informant: Caney Hobson (Shell Creek), buried: Isaacs Cem., died: 12 Feb 1920, record (1920) #: 51.

Oliver Ritchie FIELDS, born: 15 Jan 1920, parents: Jeff Fields and Idas Morgan, death cause: "flue", informant: John Fields (Shell Creek), buried: Isaacs Cemetery, died: 16 Feb 1920, record (1920) #: 52.

John RUTLEDGE, age 38 years, parents: William Rutledge (Sullivan County) and Evelyn Nave, death cause: "influenza, heart lieson", informant: D.L. Grindstaff (Watauga Valley), buried: Watauga Valley Cemetery, died: 16 Feb 1920, record (1920) #: 53.

Dewey ANDERSON, age 8 years and 2 months, parents: Samuel Anderson and Cardia Bowers, death cause: "unknown", informant: Alfred Anderson (Watauga Valley), died: 16 Feb 1920, record (1920) #: 54.

Infant MONTGOMERY, male, born: 15 Feb 1920, parents: Samuel Montgomery and Minnie Hays, death cause: "premature birth", buried: Walnut Mountain, died: 17 Feb 1920, record (1920) #: 55.

Mollie HEATON, born: 12 Dec 1919, parents: Cain Heaton and Birdie Buchan (Buchanan ?), death cause: "not known", informant: Cain Heaton (Shell Creek), died: 18 Feb 1920, record (1920) #: 56.

Nancy TOLLEY, age 84 years, born in North Carolina, widow, parents: James Willis (NC) and M. Howell (NC), death cause: "enfluenza and pneumonia", informant: Dan Tolley (Hampton), buried: Tolley Cemetery, died: 18 Feb 1920, record (1920) #: 57.

Infant ORR, female, parents: Robert Orr and Cordia Radford, death cause: illegible, informant: Robert Orr (Roan Mountain), died: 19 Feb 1920, record #: 58.

Clinton Ervin TOLIVER, born: 1 Dec 1888 in Ashe County, NC, married, parents: D.C. Tolliver (Ashe Co., NC) and Sarrina Lewis (Ashe Co., NC), death cause: "Spanish influenza", informant: Montie Shell (Johnson City), buried: Simmons Cemetery, died: 20 Feb 1920, record (1920) #: 59.

Delia B. Payne CREED, born: 20 Feb 1888, married, parents: James D. Payne and Elva Grindstaff, death cause: "flu and bronchial pneumonia", informant: George Creed, died: 20 Feb 1920, record (1920) #: 60.

Mrs. Lutie B. DANIELS, born: 13 Mar 1887, married, parents: Capt. Landon Carter and Rebecca Garland, death cause: "pulmonary tuberculosis", informant: H.T. Daniel (Elizabethton), buried: Carter Cemetery, died: 20 Feb 1920, record (1920) #: 61.

Steward Thomas BLEVINS, born: 23 Mar 1916, parents: Nat Blevins and Pollie Oliver, death cause: "deptheria", informant: Nat Blevins (Roan Mountain), buried: Blevins Cem., died: 24 Feb 1920, record #: 62.

Anthony FARRANCE, age 78 years, (illegible) soldier, parents: unknown, death cause: "must be flue", informant: G.W. Keller (Shell Creek), buried: McLain Cemetery, died: 22 Feb 1920, record (1920) #: 63.
Ruby Kate BERRY, born: 10 Oct 1915, parents: Jim Berry and Mary Bowers, death cause: "influenza", informant: Jim Berry (Eliz), died: 22 Feb 1920, record #: 64.
Sarah Anna ARNETT, age 24 years, married, parents: Henry McKinney and Ellen Woodley, death cause: "influenza and pneumonia", informant: John Arnett (Hampton), buried: McKinney Cemetery, died: 22 Feb 1920, record (1920) #: 65.
Mrs. Minnie SMITH, born: 4 Jul 1881, married, parents: Alfred Peaks and Celia Smith, death cause: "pleurisy", informant: R.T. Ellis (Elizabethton), buried: Emmert Cemetery, died: 24 Feb 1920, record (1920) #: 66.
William R. STOUT, born: 20 May 1850 in Johnson County, parents: (illegible) Stout and mother unknown, death cause: "influenza and lobar pneumonia", informant: W.O. Philips (Fish Springs), buried: Judson, Indiana, died: 24 Feb 1920, record (1920) #: 67.
Maney M. SIMERLY, born: 25 Mar 1900, single, parents: David A. Simerly and Debby Perry, death cause: "tuberculosis and peneumonia", buried: Highland Cemetery, died: 25 Feb 1920, record (1920) #: 68.
Callie Pierce CAMPBELL, born: 28 Apr 1894, married, parents: Henry Pierce and Sarah Morley, death cause: "broncho pneumonia and abortion", informant: Dan Pierce (Butler), buried: Pierce Cemetery, died: 26 Feb 1920, record (1920) #: 69.
Elbert C. BERRY, born: 16 Oct 1860, married, parents: Samuel P. (Berry) and _____ Hethely (Heatherly ?), death cause: "flu, pneumonia", informant: B.S. Berry (Seattle, WA), died: 24 Feb 1920, record (1920) #: 70.
Don MILLER, born: 14 Feb, age 25 years, born in Mitchell County, NC, married, parents: "unknown", death cause: "influenza and penumonia", informant: William D. Tolley (Roan Mountain), buried: Tolley Cemetery, died: 27 Feb 1920, record (1920) #: 71.
F.F. YOUNCE, born: 16 Sep 1892 in Zionville, NC, married, parents: S.S. Younce (Zionville) and Mary Roten (Ashe Co., NC), death cause: "flu and pneumonia", informant: Ettie Younce (Butler), buried: Zionville, NC, died: 28 Feb 1920, record (1920) #: 72.
Hanah M. DUGGER, parents: George Dugger and Eliza Rotler (Unicoi County), death cause: "abortion", informant: J.W. Dugger (Butler), born/died: 29 Feb 1920, record (1920) #: 73.

William MILLER, born: 29 Aug 1919, parents: Floyd Miller and Nora Elliott, death cause: "influenza and pneumonia", informant: Floyd Miller (Roan Mountain), buried: Lacy Cemetery, died: 29 Feb 1920, record (1920) #: 74.

Infant HATLEY, male, parents: Gath Hatley and Lizzie Pilketon, death cause: "stillborn", informant: E.P. Pilketon (Hopson), buried: Holly Cemetery, died: 18 Feb 1920, record (1920) #: 75.

Infant RITCHIE, female, parents: David E. Ritchie and Belle Murry (Murray ?), death cause: "stillborn", buried: Stoney Creek, died: 23 Feb 1920, record (1920) #: 76.

Infant GRIFFITH, male, parents: Frank Griffith and Susan Oliver, death cause: "stillborn", informant: Huston Weaver (Watauga Valley), buried: Buckles Cemetery, died: 29 Feb 1920, record (1920) #: 77.

Eliza DUGGER, age about 25 years, born in Unicoi County, married, parents: father's name not known and _____ Ratler, death cause: "acute diorhear and abortion", informant: G.W. Dugger (Butler), buried: Whitehead Cem., died: 1 Mar 1920, record (1920) #: 78.

Marry GRINDSTAFF, born: 12 Dec 1831, single, parents: Michael Grindstaff and Mary Chambers, death cause: "paralysis", informant: G.W. Casey (Hampton), buried: Hall Cemetery, died: 2 Mar 1920, record (1920) #: 79.

Haven BRADSHAW, female, born: 3 Nov 1919, parents: John Bradshaw and Eva Hatcher, death cause: "influenza", buried: Highland Cemetery, died: 2 Mar 1920, record (1920) #: 80.

Hazel THOMAS, age 1 year and 6 months, born in North Carolina, parents: Henry Thomas (NC) and Deney Buchanan (NC), death cause: "influenza and pneumonia", informant: Henry Thomas (Shell Creek), buried: Brinkley Cem., died: 2 Mar 1920, record (1920) #: 81.

Geneva MORRIS, born: 5 Sep 1908, parents: W.A. Morris and Luby B. Glover, death cause: "pneumonia", informant: W.A. Morris (Elizabethton), died: 3 Mar 1920, record (1920) #: 82.

Lowrence NIDIFFER, born: 17 Dec 1918, parents: J.C. Nidiffer and Ruby Williams, death cause: "lobar pneumonia", informant: A.B. Williams (Watauga Valley), died: 5 Mar 1920, record (1920) #: 83.

Julia STEPHENS, born: 15 Sep 1886 in Unicoi County, married, parents: J.H. Davis and Jane Gouge, death cause: "tuberculosis", informant: C.S. Stevens (Hampton), died: 3 Mar 1920, record (1920) #: 84.

William Daniel BILLINGS, born: 14 Nov 1919, parents: J.A. Billings (NC) and Mary Ann Church (NC), death cause: "abscess of brain", buried in North Carolina, died: 5 Mar 1920, record (1920) #: 85.

Infant ESTEP, male, parents: Wiley Estep and Calrey Arnold (Johnson County), death cause: not stated, informant: Wiley Estep (Carter), buried: Hurley cemetery, born/died: 5 Mar 1920, record (1920) #: 86.

Lidia MURRAY, age 16 years, parents: Joseph Murray and Martha Ingram, death cause: "due to child birth", informant: E.E. Morton (Elizabethton), buried: Lyons Cemetery, died: 5 Mar 1920, record (1920) #: 87.

Mollie SLAGLE, born: 29 Aug 1855, single, parents: Levi Slagle and Margaret Holley, death cause: not stated, buried: Slagle Cemetery, died: 6 Mar 1920, record (1920) #: 88.

Jake TAYLOR, born in 1866, widower, parents: William Taylor and Susan Taylor, death cause: "influenza, tuberculosis", informant: W.F. Culbert (Carter), buried: Taylor Cem., died: 7 Mar 1920, record #: 89.

Henry WILSON, born: 5 Mar 1918, parents: J. Richard Wilson and Flora Oliver, death cause: "Spanish influenza", informant: J.R. Wilson (Eliz), buried: Bowers Cem., died: 7 Mar 1920, record (1920) #: 90.

Arther MCGEE, black, born: 22 Aug 1902, parents: John Taylor and Bettie Ervin, death cause: "pulmonary tuberculosis", informant: Will Taylor, buried: Cedar Grove Cemetery, died: 9 Mar 1920, record (1920) #: 91.

Eliza PETERS, born: 13 Oct 1846, married, parents: Jack Ellis and Liddie Lewis, death cause: "influenza", buried: Treadway Cem, died: 9 Mar 1920, record #: 92.

Lorina PETERS, age 43 years, married, parents: William Pierce and Betsie Williams, death cause: "tuberculosis", died: 9 Mar 1920, record (1920) #: 93.

Earl BOWERS, age 21 years, married, parents: A.B. Bowers, Jr., and ____ Morrell, death cause: "typhus, pneumonia", died: 10 Mar 1920, record (1920) #: 94.

Clause B. BENNETT, born: 18 Dec 1890 in Falls City, Alabama, married, parents: James A. Bennett (Falls City, AL) and Jona Kidd (Falls City, AL), death cause: "lobar pneumonia", informant: Mrs. C.D. Bennett (Elizabethton), buried: Highland Cemetery, died: 10 Mar 1920, record (1920) #: 95.

Mary Ellen PIERCE, born: 8 Nov 1916, parents: J.C. Pierce and mother's name illegible, death cause: "bronchial penumonia", informant: J.C. Pierce (Elizabethton), buried: Highland Cemetery, died: 11 Mar 1920, record (1920) #: 96.

Gilbert Sylvester McPherson MAST, born: 27 Mar 1919, parents: J.D. Mast and Deberah Sharp, death cause: "lobar pneumonia", informant: Mrs. D.P. Mast (Elizabethton), buried: Shouns, TN, died: 12 Mar 1920, record (1920) #: 97.

George W. CRETSINGER, age 67 years, born in Virginia, married, parents not stated, death cause: "pulmonary tuberculosis", buried: A.J. Little Cemetery, Watauga, died: 13 Mar 1920, record (1920) #: 98.

Frank STEVENS, age 16 years, 6 months and 10 days, parents: E.S. Stevens and Bettie Gouge, death cause: "pneumonia and influenza", informant: W.M. Gouge (Hampton), buried: Simerly Cemetery, died: 13 Mar 1920, record (1920) #: 99.

Luther TAYLOR, born: 2 Aug 1917, parents: Henry Taylor and Sarah Campbell, death cause: "spinal meningitis", informant: W.F. Culbert (Carter), buried: Taylor Cemetery, died: 14 Mar 1920, record (1920) #: 100.

Jane E. RICHARDS, born: 5 Mar 1841 in Cowell County, NC, married, parents: Caleb Bowman (NC) and _____ Conelly (NC), death cause: "lobar penumonia", informant: Mrs. F.W. Richards (Eliz.), buried in North Carolina, died: 15 Mar 1920, record (1920) #: 101.

Blanch ELLIS, born: 11 Mar 1920, parents: David Ellis and Della Perkins, death cause: "think, influenza", informant: David Ellis (Shell Creek), buried: Perkins Cemetery, died: 15 Mar 1920, record (1920) #: 102.

Albert HUGHES, age 50 years, single, parents: James Hughes and Jane Lindvill, death cause: "influenza, pneumonia", resided at Sinking Creek, died: 16 Mar 1920, record (1920) #: 103.

Darriel RICHARDSON, age 57 years, married, parents: not stated, death cause: not stated, informant: Landon Wilson (Roan Mountain), died: 14 Mar 1920, record (1920) #: 104.

Ruth TOLLEY, born: 9 Mar 1920, parents: David Tolley and Julia Hillman, death cause: "boul hives", informant: David Tolley (Hampton), buried: Tolley Cemetery, died: 17 Mar 1920, record (1920) #: 105.

William MASSINGILL, born: 11 Feb 1919, parents: William Massingill and Olie Shipley, death cause: "rupture of hypertrophied neavus", resided: Watauga, died: 20 Mar 1920, record (1920) #: 106.

Julia C. PIERCE, born: 3 May 1863, parents: L.D. Rowe and Sarah Hale, death cause: "lobar pneumonia", informant: D.T. Pierce (Fish Springs), buried: Smith Cemetery, died: 22 Mar 1920, record (1920) #: 107.

James L. HAYS, born: 27 Oct 1834, married, parents: George Hays (NC) and Honor Snow (NC), death cause: "lobar pneumonia", informant: H.T. Daniels (Elizabethton), died: 23 Mar 1920, record (1920) #: 108.

Myrtle HYDER, age 23 years, married, parents: J.H. Hyder and Bettie Achen, death cause: "Brights disease", informant: Samuel Hyder (Hampton), buried: Hyder Cem., died: 25 Mar 1920, record (1920) #: 109.

Alzenia MORRELL, born: 20 May 1844, widow, parents: Roy Carriger and Sarah Wagner, death cause: "apoplexy", informant: J.C. Bowers (Watauga Valley), died: 27 Mar 1920, record (1920) #: 110.

Callie WILLIAMS, age 39 years, married, parents: C.B. Bowers and _____ Oliver, death cause: "lobar pneumonia", informant: F.L. Hardin, died: 28 Mar 1920, record (1920) #: 111.

Infant NORIS, male, parents: Hobart Noris (or Norris ?) and Eva Stout, death cause: "stillborn", born/died: 8 Mar 1920, record (1920) #: 112.

Infant BRUMMIT, female, parents: Charles H. Brummit and Alice Tildon Adams, death cause: "born dead", buried: Highland, died: 30 Mar 1920, record #: 113.

John BISHOP, born: 25 Nov 1871, single, parents: William Mitchell Bishop and Mary Newton, death cause: "tumor of liver", informant: W. Edward Bishop (Elizabethton), buried: Newton Cemetery, died: 1 Apr 1920, record (1920) #: 114.

Emma WHITEHEAD, born: 26 Mar 1879, single, parents: L.L. Whitehead and Nanie Faigen, death cause: "broncho pneumonia", informant: T.H. Whitehead (Roan Mountain), buried: Holly Cemetery, died: 3 Apr 1920.

Mrs. Martha C. HAYS, age about 68 years, widow, parents: "unknown", death cause: "lobar pneumonia", died: 6 Apr 1920, record (1920) #: 116.

Mrs. Katie GRINDSTAFF, age 25 years, 7 months and 27 days, married, parents: A.J. Miller and Delia Chambers, death cause: "influenza, pulmonary tuberculosis", informant: A.J. Miller (Roan Mountain), buried: Chambers Cem., died: 6 Apr 1920, record: 117.

Rebecca PETERS, born: 31 Mar 1865 in Washington County, TN, widow, parents: Jackson Orr (Washington Co., TN) and Rebecca Sparks (Washington Co., TN), death cause: "apoplexy", informant: P.D. Orr (Roan Mountain), died: 6 Apr 1920, record (1920) #: 118.

John GARLAND, born: 4 Mar 1845, married, parents: John Garland and Hiley Hurts (? illegible), death cause: "heart failure", buried: Garland Cemetery, died: 7 Apr 1920, record (1920) #: 119.

Thomas Leonard LUNDY, born: 14 Oct 1844 in Virginia, parents: "unknown", death cause: "influenza and pneumonia", informant: Mrs. F.C. Campbell (Elizabethton), buried: Drake Cemetery, died: 13 Apr 1920, record (1920) #: 120.

Mary DOUGLAS, age 65 years, born in Sullivan County, widow, parents: Jeff Russell and mother's name illegible, death cause: "pneumonia", informant: J.H. Grindstaff (Johnson City), buried: Oak Grove Cemetery, died: 13 Apr 1920, record (1920) #: 121.

Aubre Geneva OAKS, born: 24 Mar 1894, married, parents: C.F. Frinklin (NC) and Alzy Laws, death cause: "influenza", informant: Ham Oaks (Shell Creek), buried: Taylor Cem, died: 13 Apr 1920, record #: 122.

Neah JINKINS, age 58 years, parents: Elijah Jenkins and _____ Crow, death cause: "bladder and kidney", died: 17 Apr 1920, record (1920) #: 123.

Andrew Allen SHELL, born: 13 Apr 1920, parents: Hubert Shell (NC) and Faitha Shell, death cause: "thought to be hives", buried: Richardson Cemetery, died: 19 Apr 1920, record (1920) #: 124.

Lorance INGRAM, born: 23 Mar 1920, parents: Charlie Oaks (NC) and Hattie Ingram, death cause: "premature and boul hives", informant: George Ingram (Roan Mountain), buried: Ingram Cemetery, died: 19 Apr 1920, record (1920) #: 125.

Mrs. Emily WILSON, born: 14 Aug 1848, widow, parents: John Smith and Mary Simerly, death cause: "uterine cancer", informant: G.A. Wilson (Hampton), buried: Smith Cem., died: 18 Apr 1920, record (1920) #: 126.

Sarah Ruby BROWN, black, born: 20 Feb 1920, parents: Benson Brown (Burke Co., NC) and Ida Young (Johnson City), death cause: "unknown", informant: Benson Brown (Shell Creek), died: 19 Apr 1920, record (1920)#: 127.

Susan TESTER, age 74 years, born in Watauga County, NC, widow, parents: Samuel D__(illegible) and Urret Dier (Watauga Co., NC), death cause: "paralysis of heart", informant: L.A. Tester (Shell Creek), buried: Walnut Mountain, died: 20 Apr 1920, record #: 128.

John W. FLETCHER, born: 14 Jul 1852, married, parents: Loss Fletcher and _____ Hathaway, death cause: "double lobar penumonia", informant: Mark Fletcher (Elizabethton), buried: Buckles Cemetery, died: 21 Apr 1920, record (1920) #: 129.

George M. MALONE, born: 15 Jan 1844, married, parents: Jake Malone and Sallie Webb, death cause: "cerebral hemorhage", informant: Jane Malone (Elizabethton), buried: Colbaugh Cem, died: 21 Apr 1920, record: 130.

Steve LOWE, Jr., born: 15 Oct 1900, single, parents: Noah Lowe and Lettie Pierce, death cause: "cancer of left lung", informant: C.H. Hyder (Watauga Valley), buried: Lowe Cemetery, died: 22 Apr 1920, record (1920) #: 131.

J.M. SELLARS, age 95 years, 4 months and 17 days, widower, parents: "unknown", death cause: "disease of heart", resided: Watauga, died: 22 Apr 1920, record (1920) #: 132.

Wid HYDER, age 54 years, married, parents: John Hyder and Susan McArver, death cause: "dilitation of heart", informant: Charlie Brumit (Elizabethton), buried: Hyder Cem., died: 22 Apr 1920, record (1920) #: 133.

Hettie L. MOFFETT, born: 10 Mar 1920, parents: James Moffett and Florie Tate (VA), death cause:: "unknown", informant: James Moffett (Hampton), buried: Campbell Cemetery, died: 23 Apr 1920, record (1920) #: 134.

James B. LITTLE, born: 1 Oct 1849 in Sullivan County, married, parents: Martin Little (Sullivan County) and Sallie Lewis (Sullivan County), death cause: "influenza and broncho pneumonia", informant: Mrs. Mollie B. Little (Hopson), buried: Blevins Cemetery, died: 24 Apr 1920, record (1920) #: 135.

Ruby NIDIFFER, age 24 years, 8 months and 24 days, married, parents: A.G. Williams and Rettie Frasier, death cause: "flu and tuberculosis", buried: Wilson Cemetery, died: 24 Apr 1920, record (1920) #: 136.

Infant LYONS, female, parents: Alf Lyons and Edith Gregg, death cause: "premature birth", informant: C.T. Young (Elizabethton), buried: Douglas Town, born/died: 25 Apr 1920, record (1920) #: 137.

Hugh E. GEISLER, born: 21 Sep 1851, married, parents: Henry Geisler and _____ Hicks, death cause: "nephritis", informant: Hubert Geisler (Elizabethton), buried: Bluff City, died: 25 Apr 1920, record (1920) #: 138.

Franklin Eugene FAIR, born: 5 Mar 1920, parents: Charles S. Fair and Katherine McCloud, death cause: "convulsions", buried: Highland Cemetery, died: 25 Apr 1920, record (1920) #: 139.

Infant STREET, male, parents: Harrison Street and Lillie Brown, death cause: "stillborn", informant: Harrison Street (Roan Mountain), born/died: 19 Apr 1920, record (1920) #: 140.

Infant BROWN, colored, female, parents: James Brown (Elk Park, NC) and Laura Lee McNeal, death cause: "stillborn", informant: Larua Lee McNeal (Shell Creek), died: 22 Apr 1920, record (1920) #: 141.

Infant JOHNSON, female, born in Johnson City, parents: Charles Carter Johnson (Johnson City) and Hattie Bell Arrowood (NC), death cause: "stillborn", buried: Taylor Cem., died: 29 Apr 1920, record (1920) #: 142.

Ruby Ray LINKESS, born: 17 Apr 1920, parents: J.H. Linkess (Johnson County) and Sarah Jane Beard, death cause: "unknown", buried: Elk Mills, died: 1 May 1920, record (1920) #: 143.

James Naithen BIRCHFIELD, born: 1 May 1841 in North Carolina, divorced, parents: Rubin Birchfield and Celia Hughes (NC), death cause: "uremia", informant: W.L. Birchfield (Roan Mountain), died: 5 May 1920, record (1920) #: 144.

Bessie WHITEHEAD, born: 7 Mar 1920, parents: Earl Whitehead and Ruth McIntosh, death cause: "pneumonia", buried: Morton cemetery, died: 2 May 1920, record (1920) #: 145.

Mrs. Bessie CULBERT, born: 12 Jun 1902, married, parents: George Blevins and Phinia Hays, death cause: "organic heart disease", died: 6 May 1920, record (1920) #: 146.

Samuel Phelix NICHOLS, born: 7 Jun 1857 in Wilkes County, NC, married, parents: John Nichols (Wilkes Co., NC) and Harlow Bishop (Wilkes Co., NC), death cause: "progressive paralysis", buried: Newton Cemetery, died: 13 May 1920, record (1920) #: 147.

Z.C. CAMPBELL, born: 11 Feb 1842, married, parents: Wilbern G. Campbell and Elizabeth B. Minton, death cause: "heart failure", informant: James S. Campbell (Hampton), buried: Hall Cemetery, died: 16 May 1920, record (1920) #: 148.

Sue Pauline MANNING, age 1 year, 3 months and 15 days, parents: Sam Manning (NC) and Nola Colbaugh, death cause: "lobar pneumonia", buried: Colbaugh Cemetery, died: 22 May 1920, record (1920) #: 149.

Crawford COMBS, born: 18 Apr 1906, parents: Kel Combs and Ottie Jenkins, death cause: "mitral regurgitation", informant: Kel Combs, buried: Stoney Creek, died: 22 May 1920, record (1920) #: 150.

Esteline TAYLOR, female, born: 19 May 1920, parents: J.L. Taylor and Martha Lowe, death cause: "unknown", informant: Allen Markland (Carter), buried: Grindstaff Cemetery, died: 23 May 1920, record (1920) #: 151.

Frank PAYNE, age 32 years, born at Milligan, married, parents: Nathaniel G. Payne and ____ McKeehan, death cause: "tuberculosis", buried: Payne Cemetery, died: 26 May 1920, record (1920) #: 152.

Wailey Ray BLEVINS, male, born: 6 Feb 1920, parents: H.A. Blevins and Lillie Feathers, death cause: "bronchitis and malnutrition", buried: Mottern Cemetery, died: 26 May 1920, record (1920) #: 153.

Mack TOLLEY, age 54 years, born in Boonford, NC, married, parents: Swin Tolley (NC) and mother's name illegible, death cause: "loaded wagon turned over on him", informant: W.M. Tolley (Hampton), buried: Tolley Cemetery, died: 28 May 1920, record (1920) #: 154.

Margaret A. HOLLEY, born: 11 Oct 1840, widow, parents: George A. Persinger (VA) and Julia _____, death cause: "chronic nephritis", informant: Dave Holly, died: 29 May 1920, record (1920) #: 155.

Fuson LEWIS, age 37 years, single, parents: J.S. Lewis and _____ Frasser, death cause: "stomach trouble and dropsy", informant: Landon Wilburn, buried: Academy Cemetery, died: 30 May 1920, record (1920) #: 156.

Infant TAYLOR, male, parents: H.L. Taylor and Martha Cowe, death cause: "stillborn", informant: Allen Markland (Carter), buried: Grindstaff Cemetery, died: 19 May 1920, record (1920) #: 157.

Infant WOODS, female, parents: Emanuel Woods and Rebecca Royal, death cause: "stillborn", informant: Emanuel Woods (Roan Mountain), buried: Blevins Cemetery, died: 23 May 1920, record (1920) #: 158.

Murey LUIS, age 43 years, married, parents: Milbon Luis (Lewis ?) and Aney Garland, death cause: "influenza and bran fever", informant: D. Luis (brother)(Carter), buried: Garland Cemetery, died: 2 Jun 1920, record (1920) #: 159.

Ephraim LUNCEFORD, born: 16 Jun 1884, married, parents: A.E. Lunceford and C.M. Stephens, death cause: "pulmonary tuberculosis", informant: L.S. Williams (Hampton), buried: Walnut Mountain, died: 2 Jun 1920, record (1920) #: 160.

Rebecca CAMPBELL, born: 1 Jul 1846 in Johnson County, married, parents: George M. Pierce (Johnson County) and Lavina Campbell, death cause: "mitral stenosis of heart", informant: James D. Robinson (Butler), died: 3 Jun 1920, record (1920) #: 161.

Bedie JACKSON, black, born: 8 Dec 1919, parents: Robert Jackson (NC) and Kate Watson, death cause: "meinigitis", died: 3 Jun 1920, record (1920) #: 162.

David CARVER, born: 29 Apr 1910, parents: Arthur Carver and Ellen Carver, death cause: "steptococus infection caused by door of stove falling on foot", informant: Arthur Carver (Hampton), buried: Fair View Cemetery, died: 9 Jun 1920, record (1920) #: 163.

Roxie WILBIRD, age 15 years, parents: A.S. Wilbrd (Johnson County) and Alice Shuffield, death cause: "consumption of lungs", buried: Dry Hill Cemetery, died: 22 Jun 1920, record (1920) #: 164.

Jamie SIMS, age not stated, parents: Andrew Sims and Hattie (illegible), death cause: "dysentery", died: 24 Jun 1920, record (1920) #: 165.

Charles F. CARRIER, born: 3 Jul 1862 in Pennsylvania, married, parents: Isaac Carrier (PA) and Ellen Harris (PA), death cause: "apoplexy", buried: Johnson City, died: 25 Jun 1920, record (1920) #: 166.

Ethel Kate HARDIN, born: 20 Apr 1913, parents: J.N. Hardin and Sallie Hinkle, death cause: "meningitis", informant: L.S. Hinkle (Carter), buried: Hardin Cemetery, died: 25 Jun 1920, record (1920) #: 167.

Crumley TIMBS, age 6 years, 2 months and 23 days, parents: father not stated and Offie Timbs, death cause: "accidental shot in head with shot gun", informant: James D. Robinson (Butler), died: 26 Jun 1920, record (1920) #: 168.

Rachel SIMS, born: 8 Jul 1837, widow, parents: Stephen Glover (?) and mother's name unknown, death cause: "mitral insufficiency, acute indigestion", buried: Roan Mountain, died: 30 Jun 1920, record #: 169.

Dewey CANNON, born: 6 May 1898, single, parents: D.C. Cannon and Reba Bowers, death cause: "double lobar pneumonia", died: 30 Jun 1920, record (1920) #: 170.

William S. WARD, parents: Eugene Ward and Mandy Gregg, death cause: "stillborn", informant: Eugene Ward (Butler), buried: Crosswhite Cemetery, died: 8 Jun 1920, record (1920) #: 171.

Infant DELOACH, male, parents: William M. Deloach and Ida Blackburn (NC), death cause: "born dead", buried: Hyder Cem., died: 25 Jun 1920, record (1920) #: 172.

Charlotte HYDER, born: 8 Jul 1832 in North Carolina, widow, parents: Ambrose Carlton (NC) and Lucy Foster (NC) death cause: "apoplexy", informant: Samuel Hyder (Hampton), buried: Hyder Cemetery, died: 1 Jul 1920, record (1920) #: 173.

John V. WHITE, age 76 years, married, parents: Lawson White and Elizabeth Clark, death cause: "cancer of prostrate gland", informant: Robert White (Butler), buried: White Cem., died: 5 Jul 1920, record #: 174.

Sarah Frazier PETERS, age 72 years, widow, parents: William Frazier and Barbara Elliott, death cause: "nephritis and mitral regurgitation", informant: J.D. Morrell (Watauga Valley), buried: Highland Cemetery, died: 5 Jul 1920, record (1920) #: 175.

Harold MOTTERN, born: 6 Jul 1920, parents: Robert Mottern and Pearl Hodge, death cause: "cerebral hemorrhage", buried: Turkey Town, died: 7 Jul 1920, record (1920) #: 176.

Frank SCOTT, Jr., born: 7 Oct 1901, parents: Franklin Scott and Barah Taylor, death cause: "mitral regurgitation of heart", informant: Ross R. Scott (Watauga), buried: Lacy Cem., died: 10 Jul 1920, record #: 177.

Jesse Lorence BOLEN, born: 10 Mar 1920, parents: Frank Bolen and Hattie Smith, death cause: "cholera", informant: John Mackley (Roan Mountain), died: 12 Jul 1920, record (1920) #: 178.

Eliza J. LINDY, born: 9 Apr 1848 in Virginia, widow, parents: John Baker (Surrey County, NC) and Matilda Thatney (Stokes County, NC), death cause: "bronchial pneumonia", informant: Mrs. F.C. Campbell, buried: Drake Cem., died: 13 Jul 1920, record (1920) #: 179.

William H. PETERS, born: 10 Jun 1920, parents: John W. Peters and Vena Colbaugh, death cause: "not known", informant: R.H. Peters (Carter), buried: Peters Cemetery, died: 15 Jul 1920, record (1920) #: 180.

Emsley ISAACS, Jr., born: 5 May 1848 in Watauga County, NC, married, parents: Emsley Isaacs (NC) and Jane Aldredge (NC), death cause: "old age", informant: J.B. Isaacs (Shell Creek), buried: Isaacs Cemetery, died: 16 Jul 1920, record #: 181.

Samuel POTTER, born: 5 Sep 1882, married, parents: David Potter and Molle Hamby, death cause: "influenza, tuberculosis", informant: Murphey Potter (Shell Creek), died: 18 Jul 1920, record (1920) #: 182.

Mary GUINN, age 43 years, born: 14 Sep in North Carolina, married, parents: Bill Roberts (NC) and Lizzie Swift (NC), death cause: "typhoid", informant: D.H. Guinn (Hampton), buried: Elk Park, NC, died: 19 Jul 1920, record (1920) #: 183.

Mrs. Lillie Brown STREET, born: 10 Jul 1895, married, parents: Lee Brown (NC) and Mary Johnson, death cause: "typhoid", informant: Thomas Brown (Roan Mountain), died: 19 Jul 1920, record (1920) #: 184.

Ray DENNIS, born: 19 May 1918, parents: Frank Dennis (NC) and Rosanna Price (NC), death cause: "spinal meningitis", informant: Amos Price (Fish Springs), died: 20 Jul 1920, record (1920) #: 185.

Sarah J. OXENDINE, born: 15 Oct 1851 in Virginia, married, parents: Robert Houges (Va) and mother's name not stated, death cause: "influenza, cardiac regurgitation", informant: Edward Oxendine (Roan Mountain), died: 22 Jul 1920, record (1920) #: 186.

Christopher C. PETERS, born: 9 Oct 1846, widower, parents: Alfred Peters and Nancy Berry, death cause: "intestinal nephritis", informant: Mort Peters, buried: Siam, died: 22 Jul 1920, record (1920) #: 187.
Henry HYDER, born: 3 Jan 1854, married, parents: Ed Hyder and Annie Davenport, death cause: "mitral regurgitation", informant: Charles Collins (Elizabethton), buried: Hyder Cemetery, died: 25 Jul 1920, record (1920) #: 188.
Infant RASOR, born: 12 Jul 1920, parents: Snyder Rasor and Lela Hyder, death cause: "unknown", informant: C.H. Hyder (Watauga Valley), buried: Hyder Cemetery, died: 27 Jul 1920, record (1920) #: 189.
Charles RANGE, born: 14 Aug 1905, parents: G.M. Range and Mollie Shell, death cause: "drowned in Watauga River", informant: Thomas Davis (Elizabethton), died: 29 Jul 1920, record (1920) #: 190.
Infant PIPPIN, female, parents: Franklin Pippin and Okie (surname illegible)(NC), death cause: "stillborn", informant: Franklin Pippin (Roan Mountain), died: 8 Jul 1920, record (1920) #: 191.
Cora Belle HAMPTON, born: 21 Feb 1920 in Virginia, parents: Henry Hampton and Florence McClain (VA), death cause: "masmarus", informant: Florence McClain (Bramar), buried: Hall Cemetery, died: 2 Aug 1920, record (1920) #: 192.
Paul S. MORGAN, parents: David M. Morgan and Lilian Oaks, death cause: "asphixia at birth", informant: David M. Morgan (Hampton), buried: Hall Cemetery, died: 2 Aug 1920, record (1920) #: 193.
Thomas HYDER, born: 23 Oct 1862, widower, parents: Carvil Hyder and Clara Houston, death cause: "paralysis of right side", informant: R.C. Collins, buried: Powder Branch, died: 2 Aug 1920, record (1920) #: 194.
William LYONS, Jr., born: 7 Apr 1920, parents: William Lyons and Blanche Honeycutt, death cause: illegible, informant: William Lyons (Hampton), buried: Lyons Cemetery, died: 4 Aug 1920, record (1920) #: 195.
H.A. BRYANT, born: 31 May 1866, married, parents: Franklin Britt (Bryant ?) and Emma Carter, death cause: "cancer of liver", informant: W.R. Bryant, buried: Highland Cemetery, died: 6 Aug 1920, record (1920) #: 196.
Mary EDENS, age 38 years, married, parents: _____ Profit and _____ South, death cause: "typhoid fever", informant: Dave Edens (Elizabethton), buried: Highland Cemetery, died: 7 Aug 1920, record (1920) #: 197.

Milburn CAMPBELL, age 75 years, married, parents: Naten Campbell and Lizzie Jones (NC), death cause: not stated, informant: Jane Campbell (Fish Springs), died: 8 Aug 1920, record (1920) #: 198.

Joseph Kint BLEVINS, born: 11 May 1918, parents: Arthur Blevins and Virgie Adams, death cause: "acute dysentery", informant: Arthur Blevins (Elizabethton), buried: Mountain City, died: 8 Aug 1920, record (1920) #: 199.

Grace LYONS, born: 8 May 1920, parents: J.T. Lyons and Eliza Millhorn (Sullivan County), death cause: "supposed to be malnutrition", died: 9 Aug 1920, record (1920) #: 200.

Florence JONES, born: 15 Apr 1916 in North Carolina, parents: Robert J. Jones and Rosa Gregg, death cause: "croup", informant: Robert J. Jones (Hampton), buried: Isaac Cem., died: 10 Aug 1920, record (1920) #: 210.

Clarence E. LOVELESS, born: 19 Jun 1920, parents: David K. Loveless and Emma Brumit, death cause: "cholera", informant: D.K. Loveless (Eliazbethton), buried: Hunter, died: 10 Aug 1920, record (1920) #: 202.

Carrie Jane TAYLOR, born: 13 Jul 1871, married, parents: Levi Slagle and Margaret Holly, death cause: "dysentery", buried: Milligan Cemetery, died: 13 Aug 1920, record (1920) #: 203.

Widlow BLEVINS, age 2 years, 4 months and 2 days, parents: ____ Blevins and ____ Estep, death cause: illegible, informant: Widlow Estep (Carter), buried: Ensor Cem., died: 17 Aug 1920, record (1920) #: 204.

Henry C. GOODWIN, born: 9 Jan 1896, single, parents: R.E. Goodwin and Sallie Wilson, death cause: "cattarah of stomach and bowels", informant: Sallie Goodwin (Butler), died: 19 Aug 1920, record (1920) #: 206.

Mary E. BOWERS, age 78 years, married, parents: Richard Anderson (NC) and Susan Oliver, death cause: "heart trouble", died: 22 Aug 1920, record #: 207.

Tessie DAVIS, colored, born: 23 Apr 1875 in North Carolina, married, parents: Hickman Brown (NC) and Harriet Hayes (NC), death cause: "child birth", informant: Lincoln Davis, buried: Cedar Grove, died: 23 Aug 1920, record (1920) #: 208.

Emma GREEN, age 52 years, born in North Carolina, married, parents: Ruben Randolph (NC) and Jermima Young (NC), death cause: "basillary dysentary", buried: North Carolina, died: 29 Aug 1920, record (1920) #: 210.

Danil SHELL, born: 23 Mar 1919, parents: Fletcher Shell and Vernie Curd, death cause: "acute dysentery", buried: A.J. Little Cemetery, died: 26 Aug 1920, record (1920) #: 209.

Mary Jane HURLEY, born: 20 Aug 1920, parents: John Hurley and Kathern Harels (Johnson City), death cause: illegible, informant: John Hurley (Carter), died: 30 Aug 1920, record (1920) #: 211.

Mrs. Mollie JULIAN, born: 18 Feb 1846 in Mitchell County, NC, parents: John Hughes (Mitchell Co., NC) and Mary Short (Mitchell Co., NC), death cause: "chronic uraemia", informant: Pierce Julian (Roan Mountain), died: 31 Aug 1920, record (1920) #: 212.

Infant LYONS, female, parents: father not stated and Kate Lyons, death cause: "asphixiation", informant: R.B. Hyder (Johnson City), buried: McKeehan Cemetery, born/died: 6 Aug 1920, record (1920) #: 213.

Sarah Fletcher ROBERTS, born: June 1852, widow, parents: Eli Fletcher and mother not stated, death cause: "old age and disease of lungs and heart", buried: Highland Cemetery, died: 2 Sep 1920, record (1920) #: 214.

W.T. ARCHER, age 53 years, born in Sullivan County, married, parents: William Archer and mother not stated, death cause: "pulmonary tuberculosis", buried: Archer Cem., died: 4 Sep 1920, record (1920) #: 215.

Illegible WHITEHEAD, female, born: 11 May 1919, parents: Albert Whitehead and Sara Barnett (Mithcell Co., NC), death cause: "cholera", informant: J.S. Arnett (Hampton), died: 6 Sep 1920, record #: 216.

Joe L. SUSONG, black, born: 14 May 1919, parents: George Susong and Rosa Harris, death cause: "accidentally drowned", buried: Toncray Cemetery, died: 9 Sep 1920, record (1920) #: 217.

Nervie MILLER, female, age about 72 years, born in North Carolina, parents: John Gouge (NC) and Suckie Sparks (NC), death cause: "hemorrhagie dysentery", informant: S.A. Perkins (Shell Creek), buried: Richardson Cemetery, died: 13 Sep 1920, record (1920) #: 218.

Gerald DEAN, born: 3 Aug 1919, parents: Archer Dean (NC) and Elsie Garland, death cause: "acute infection", informant: C.H. Garland (Elizabethton), buried: Crandell, died: 13 Sep 1920, record (1920) #: 219.

Mrs. Julia WEBB, age 55 years, married, parents: Calvin Campbell and Pheba Hart, death cause: "apoplexy", informant: Charles Webb (Elizabethton), buried: Colbaugh Cem., died: 15 Sep 1920, record: 220.

James Fred COLDWELL, born: 20 Dec 1919, parents: Walter H. Coldwell and Georgia Goodson, death cause: "spinal meningitis", informant: W.J. Goodson (Roan Mountain), died: 16 Sep 1920, record (1920) #: 221.

Sam CROW, colored, age 59 years, parents: Martin Crow and Thursday Stover, death cause: "tuberculosis", informant: John Taylor (Elizabethton), died: 19 Sep 1920, record (1920) #: 222.

Ida BLEVINS, born: 6 Mar 1889, married, parents: Wesley Jones and ____ Edens, death cause: illegible, informant: James Blevins (Johnson City), died: 19 Sep 1920, record (1920) #: 223.

Luther JULIAN, born: 3 Sep 1920, parents: J.F. Julian and Lydia Knight (Valley, NC), death cause: "yellow jaundice", informant: J.F. Julian (Roan Mountain), died: 19 Sep 1920, record (1920) #: 224.

Margaret CALHOUN, born: 17 Dec 1852 in Ashe County, NC, widow, parents: David Graybeal and ____ Ashley, death cause: "hemorrhagic dysentery", informant: Florence Graybeal (Roan Mountain), died: 27 Sep 1920, record (1920) #: 225.

Infant LIPPS, male, parents: Raymond Lipps (Bristol, VA) and Mary Barnett, death cause: "stillborn", informant: Raymond Lipps (Roan Mountain), died: 14 Sep 1920, record (1920) #: 226.

Charles W. GOUGE, age 56 years, born in Yancey County, NC, divorced, parents: John W. Gouge (NC) and Rachel Forbes (NC), death cause: "unknown, found dead on farm of T.E. Williams, court inquiry made", informant: Robert C. Gouge (Unicoi), buried: Unicoi, died: probably Oct 1920, record (1920) #: 227.

Minnie C. FRANKLIN, born: 8 Feb 1899, single, parents: Columbus Franklin and A.C. Franklin, death cause: "tuberculosis", informant: Phil Sheppard (Shell Creek), buried: Taylor Cemetery, died: 4 Oct 1920, record (1920) #: 228.

Bert Stewart BERRY, born: 20 Aug 1907, parents: Will Berry and Ladie Carden, death cause: "pneumonia", buried: Hyder Cemetery, died: 5 Oct 1920, record: 229.

Dawson WHITEHEAD, born: Aug 1856 in Blount County, parents: G.W. Whitehead and Martha J. Davis, death cause: "hernia, chronic gastritis", informant: T.S. Wagner (Shell Creek), buried: Whitehead Cemetery, died: 6 Oct 1920, record (1920) #: 230.

Clad CABLE, female, parents: Thomas Cable and (illegible) Toler, death cause: not stated, informant: Will Grindstaff (Carter), buried: Garland Cemetery, born/died: 1 Oct 1920, record (1920) #: 231.

Riley ROBERTS, female, born: 17 Aug 1920, parents: J.H. Roberts and Julia Sanders (Macon Co., NC), death cause: "pneumonia", buried: Nelson Cemetery, died: 8 Oct 1920, record (1920) #: 232.

Glenn COLBAUGH, age 6 years, 8 months and 4 days, parents: Fred Colbaugh and Mary Smith, death cause: "diptheria", informant: George Colbaugh, buried: Colbaugh Cem., died: 9 Oct 1920, record (1920) #: 233.

Mary Alice SEIGLER, born: 8 Oct 1920, parents: John M. Seigler (Illinois) and mother not stated, death cause: "pneumonia", buried: Highland Cemetery, died: 14 Oct 1920, record (1920) #: 234.

Armstead P. PEARCE, born: 4 Sep 1851, parents: father's name unknown and Minnie Jenkins, death cause: "Bright disease", informant: C.C. Pearce (Butler), buried: Pearce Cemetery, died: 14 Oct 1920, record (1920) #: 235.

Sarah Louise BENFIELD, born: 1 Oct 1920, parents: Amos Benfield (NC) and Mary Culbertson (NC), death cause: not stated, informant: J.C. Benfield (Elizabethton), buried: Valley Forge, died: 14 Oct 1920, record (1920) #: 236.

Leslie B. CROW, born: 24 Jul 1906, parents: J.B. Crow and Mary L. Crow, death cause: "fell from bicycle and fractured skull", buried: Colbaugh Cemetery, died: 11 Oct 1920, record (1920) #: 237.

Milton RICHARDSON, age about 58 years, parents: Thomas Richardson and mother's name illegible, death cause: "intestinal obstruction", died: 19 Oct 1920, record (1920) #: 238.

Jennie LEWIS, age 24 years, 4 months and 17 days, married, parents: ____ Briggs (NC) and ____ McKinney, death cause: "tuberculosis", died: 19 Oct 1920, record (1920) #: 239.

Nellie PRICHARD, born: 1 Aug 1898, married, parents: Littleton Hodge and mother's name illegible, death cause: "typhoid fever", informant: Jerry Prichard (Butler), buried: Gouge Cemetery, died: 25 Oct 1920, record (1920) #: 240.

Samuel THOMPSON, born: 12 Nov 1836, parents: father's name not stated and ____ Garland (SC), death cause: "pulmonary tuberculosis", resided: Watauga, died: 20 Oct 1920, record (1920) #: 241.

Findly HODGE, age 28 years, married, parents: Littleton Hodge and C. Lunceford (NC), death cause: "typhoid fever and tuberculosis", informant: William Hodge (Butler), died: 21 Oct 1920, record #: 242.

Agnes Hays CALOWAY, age 14 years and 2 months, born in North Carolina, parents: Dock Caloway (NC) and ____ Hays (NC), death cause: "pneumonia", died: 22 Oct 1920, record (1920) #: 243.

Charles Ben MURRAY, born: 20 Sep 1920, parents: Frank Murray and Bessie Hinkle, death cause: "hooping cough", informant: C.E. Murray, buried: Ritchie Cemetery, died: 25 Oct 1920, record (1920) #: 244.

Nancy Ann CAMPBELL, born: 25 Nov 1845, widow, parents: father's name illegible and Patsy Garland, death cause: not stated, informant: Dayton Campbell, died: 26 Oct 1920, record (1920) #: 245.

Mrs. Minnie JONES, age 25 years, married, parents: D.C. Blevins and ____ Taylor, death cause: "tuberculosis", informant: D.C. Blevins (Johnson City), buried: Blevins Cemetery, died: 20 Oct 1920, record (1920) #: 246.

Malisey ESTEP, age 60 years, parents: Robert Nidiffer and Mlisey Nidiffer, death cause: "dropsy", buried: Garland Cem., died: 30 Oct 1920, record (1920) #: 247.

James L. BLACKWELL, born: 4 Aug 1862, married, parents: William P. Blackwell (NC) and Emily Miller, death cause: "unknown", informant: George W. Blackwell (Greenville), died: 4 Nov 1920, record (1920) #: 248.

Infant ERWIN, female, born: 1 Nov 1920, parents: Cain Erwin and Marry Chambers, death cause: "boul hives", informant: Cain Erwin (Hampton), buried: Chambers Cemetery, died: 5 Nov 1920, record (1920) #: 249.

Jack BRADSHAW, parents: John Bradshaw and Elvie Hatcher, death cause: "premature birth", buried: Highland Cemetery, born/died: 8 Nov 1920, record (1920) #: 250.

Stephen BARNETT, born: 13 Dec 1887, parents: Criss Barnett (NC) and Edith Street (NC), death cause: "nephritis and tuberculosis", informant: Robert Crowder (Roan Mountain), died: 9 Nov 1920, record (1920) #: 251.

Paul GOODSON, born: 4 Oct 1904, parents: W.J. Goodson and Ida Calhoun, death cause: "homicidal gun shot wound", informant: W.J. Goodson (Roan Mountain), died: 11 Nov 1920, record (1920) #: 252.

Martha Carr DONNELL, born: 26 Sep 1873 in Middlesex, NY, married, parents: Edward Carr (NY) and Martha Case (NY) death cause: "uremic poisoning", informant: W.H. Donnell, buried: Highland Cemetery, died: 17 Nov 1920, record (1920) #: 253.

Sarah H. BOWERS, born: 3 May 1880, married, parents: John W. Headrick and Cordelia Fletcher, death cause: "Brights disease", informant: J.W. Headrick (Valley Forge), buried: Bowers Cemetery, died: 18 Nov 1920, record (1920) #: 254.

Mary A. ADAMS, born: 19 Sep 1866, married, parents: Isaac Gragin (Johnson County) and Sarah Jane Gragan, death cause: "supposed to be heart failure", informant: Blaine Heaton (Shell Creek), died: 19 Nov 1920, record (1920) #: 255.

Dave OLIVER, age 75 years, married, parents: James Oliver and mother not stated, death cause: "Brights disease", informant: Pat Oliver (Elizabethton), buried: Bowers Cemetery, died: 20 Nov 1920, record (1920) #: 256.

Robert Lafayette NIDIFFER, born: 24 Jul 1915, parents: William Nidiffer and Josephine Lewis, death cause: "diptheria", informant: L.G. Lewis (Hampton), buried: Lewis Cem., died: 26 Nov 1920, record (1920) #: 257.

John L. SHELL, born: 29 Nov 1847, married, parents: John Shell (Hickory, NC) and Rebecca Wilcox (Jefferson, NC), death cause: "hemorrhage dysentery", informant: W.D. Shell (Roan Mountain), died: 28 Nov 1920, record (1920) #: 256.

Edna HYDER, born: 29 Apr 1919, parents: Martin Hyder and Vida Young (Avery Co., NC), death cause: "whooping cough", informant: Cad Hyder (Hampton), buried: Hyder Cemetery, died: 28 Nov 1920, record (1920) #: 257.

Martha CANON, age 62 years, born in Johnson County, married, parents: John Heaton (Johnson County) and Martha Heaton (Johnson County), death cause: "cardiac dropsy", informant: Ham Fox (Carter), buried: Ensor Cemetery, died: 13 Nov 1920, record (1920) #: 260.

Infant ELLIS, female, parents: James Ellis and Cenia Stout, death cause: "stillborn", born/died: 30 Nov 1920, record (1920) #: 261.

Eliza Lucinda SORRELL, born: 25 Mar 1855 in Johnson County, married, parents: Alfred S. McQueen (Johnson County) and Rebecca Smith, death cause: "pulmonary tuberculosis", informant: W.A. Sorrell (Hampton), buried: Sorrell Cemetery, died: 1 Dec 1920, record (1920) #: 262.

Joe MILAM, age 26 years, single, parents: T.L. Milam (NC) and Louise Ellis, death cause: "pulmonary tuberculosis", buried: Milligan, died: 2 Dec 1920, record (1920) #: 263.

Martha Preston VANOY, born: 9 Jul 1853 in Marion, Smith County, VA, married, parents: William P. Dugan (Smith Co. VA) and Marhta E. Jones (Smith Co., VA), death cause: "cataral gastritis and Brights disease", buried: Highland Cemetery, died: 5 Dec 1920, record (1920) #: 264.

James Vounum HAGIE, born: 18 May 1852 in Wytheville, VA, married, parents: Daniel Hagie (Winston Salem) and Martha Taylor (Winston Salen), death cause: "acute indigestion", informant: Mrs. J. Hagie (Hampton), buried: Dark Ridge, NC, died: 9 Dec 1920, record (1920) #: 265.

Smith DUGGER, born: 4 Oct 1878 in Johnson County, married, parents: John E. Dugger (Johnson County) and Martha Greenwell (Johnson County), death cause: "influenza, pneumonia and paralysis", buried: Butler, died: 9 Dec 1920, record (1920) #: 266.

Ruth A. JOHNSON, born: 17 Jul 1919, parents: C.G. Johnson and Ethel Little, death cause: "pneumonia and bronchitis", informant: C.G. Johnson (Valley Forge), died: 13 Dec 1920, record (1920) #: 267.

Rosie Estel ODOM, parents: Soloman Odom and Linnie Boman (Coldwell Co., NC) death cause: "abortion", informant: Soloman Odom (Shell Creek), buried: Daniel Stout Cem., died: 13 Dec 1920, record (1920) #: 268.

George Washington BYRD, born: 22 Mar 1862 in Wilkes County, NC, married, parents: Gibe Smatt (Wilkes Co., NC) and Delphia Byrd (Wilkes Co., NC), death cause: "pulmonary tuberculosis", informant: J.B. Walker (Braimar), buried: Whitehead Cemetery, died: 20 Dec 1920, record (1920) #: 269.

Mary Jane FAIR, born: 18 Apr 1865, married, parents: John Deloach and Susie Oliver, death cause: "lobar pneumonia", informant: James H. Fair (Elizabethton), buried: Hyder Cemetery, died: 20 Dec 1920, record (1920) #: 270.

John HARDIN, born: 21 Jul 1876, married, parents: Elijah D. Hardin and Clara Heaton (Johnson County), death cause: "tuberculosis", informant: Charles P. Hardin (Elizabethton), buried: Treadway Cemetery, died: 20 Dec 1920, record (1920) #: 271.

Finly OAKS, born: 20 Nov 1878, single, been in Army 3 years, parents: John Oaks (KY) and Delie Gregg, death cause: "pneumonia and been gassed (WWI war gas ?), informant: John Oaks (Shell Creek), died: 24 Dec 1920, record (1920) #: 272.

Thomas Leonard PRITCHARD, born: 17 Sep 1853, married, parents: father's name illegible (erased) and Annie Pritchard (NC), death cause: "apoplexy", informant: J.W. Wagner (Roan Mountain), died: 25 Dec 1920, record (1920) #: 273.

Thelma MARKLAND, born: 15 May 1914, parents: Charlie Markland and Bertha Jordan, death cause: "clothing caught fire, burned", buried: Highland Cemetery, died: 26 Dec 1920, record (1920) #: 274.

Clinton Ellis SMITH, born: 12 Aug 1874, married, parents: Robert A. Smith and Rosa Ellis, death cause: "cerebral hemorrhage", informant: W.T. Johnson (Elizabethton), buried: Highland Cemetery, died: 27 Dec 1920, record (1920) #: 275.

Lucinda Jane MORELAND, born: 20 Jul 1844, married, parents: Mark Hyder and Nancy Nelson (SC), death cause: "lobar pneumonia", informant: R.B. Moreland (Elizabethton), buried: Highland Cemetery, died: 29 Dec 1920, record (1920) #: 276.

Sallie HARTLEY, born: 13 Dec 1865 in North Carolina, married, parents: ____ Cole and mother's name unknown, death cause: "tuberculor systicis of bladder", informant: Nat Simerly (Elizabethton), buried: Valley Forge, died: 30 Dec 1920, record (1920) #: 277.

William Claud MCKINNEY, born: 10 Nov 1920, parents: J.B. McKinney and Letta Cambell, death cause: "boul hives", buried: McKinney Cemetery, died: 30 Dec 1920, record (1920) #: 278.

Michael STEPHENS, born: 16 Jun 1845, married, parents: Joshua Stephens (NC) and Margaret Hill (NC), death cause: "nephritis", informant: J.K. Stephens (Hampton), buried: Stephens Cemetery, died: 30 Dec 1920, record (1920) #: 279.

Infant WINTERS, female, parents: Mack Winters (NC) and Anna Wilson, death cause: "stillborn", informant: Mack Winters (Elizabethton), buried: North Carolina, born/died: 11 Dec 1920, record (1920) #: 280.

Infant GOURLEY, male, parents: R.H. Gourley and Blanch Ferguson (Washington County), buried: Simmons Cemetery, died: 15 Dec 1920, record (1920) #: 281.

Infant LAWS, female, parents: Robert Laws and mother not stated, death cause: "stillborn", buried: Colbaugh Cemetery, died: 18 Dec 1920, record (1920) #: 282.

Infant HYDER, male, parents: R. Brooks Hyder and Annie Toncray, death cause: "stillborn", buried: Highland Cemetery, died: 18 Dec 1920, record (1920) #: 283.

Infant SHELL, female, parents names not stated, death cause: "stillborn", informant: Charles Shell (Elizabethton), buried: Highland Cemetery, died: 24 Dec 1920, record (1920) #: 284.

Howard WARD, age 1 year, parents: A.S. Ward (Johnson County) and Alice Sheffield, death cause: "consumption of lungs", informant: A.S. Ward (Butler), buried: Dry Hill Cemetery, died: 1 Jan 1921, record (1921) #: 1.

Mary Bell HYDER, born: 5 Jul 1851, married, parents: Jack Williams and Elizabeth Haun (?), death cause: "apoplexy", informant: Ora Hyder, buried: Oak Grove, died: 2 Jan 1921, record (1921) #: 2.

Martha JOHNSON, age 93 years, born in Wilkes County, NC, parents: father's name not known and Bertha Edwards (Wilkes Co., NC), death cause: "old age and complications", informant: Will Townsend (Roan Mountain), died: 3 Jan 1921, record (1921) #: 3.

Clerie HICKS, born: 16 Sep 1916, parents: J.P. Hicks and Nancy Steen (Johnson County), death cause: "clothing caught fire and burned to death", informant: Joseph Hicks (Dark Ridge, NC) died: 9 Jan 1921, record (1921) #: 4.

Joseph Mark LACY, born: 24 Sep 1857, married, parents: William S. Lacy and Jane Lyons, death cause: "mitral regurgitation of heart and nephritis", informant: Lillie Lacy (Elizabethton), buried: Highland Cemetery, died: 10 Jan 1921, record (1921) #: 5.

Nancy Taylor HORTON, black, born: 12 Jul 1891, married, parents: John Taylor and Annie Taylor, death cause: "pulmonary tuberculosis", informant: John Taylor (Elizabethton), died: 11 Jan 1921, record (1921) #: 6.

Gladys Marie CROW, born: 18 Jun 1919, parents: Overtte (?) Crow and Bessie Smith, death cause: "abscess of brain", buried: Highland Cemetery, died: 12 Jan 1921, record (1921) #: 7.

Bruce Edward HART, born: 4 Jan 1921, parents: Frank Hart and Ida Jones, death cause: "lobar pneumonia", informant: Alex Jones (Elizabethton), died: 14 Jan 1921, record (1921) #: 8.

Arch J. VEST, born: 7 Oct 1844, widower, parents: John Vest and Susan Mottern, death cause: "paralysis", informant: Lottie Vest, buried: Will Mottern Cemetery, died: 15 Jan 1921, record (1921) #: 9.

Ida Bell WHITE, born: 2 Apr 1895, married, parents: James Richard Smith and Martha Campbell, death cause: "child birth", informant: Burl Smith (Bramar), buried: Williams Cem., died: 17 Jan 1921, record (1921) #: 10.

Nancy Jane CAMPBELL, born: 1 Jun 1832, widow, parents: Henry Simerly and mother's name not known, death cause: "hemiplegia", informant: Davis Campbell (Hampton), buried: Campbell Cemetery, died: 18 Jan 1921, record (1921) #: 11.

Cinda MONDA, born: 17 Aug 1870 in North Carolina, single, parents: Robert Monda (NC) and Sarah _____ (NC), death cause: "peligra", informant: Grant Stout (Elizabethton), buried: Highland Cemetery, died: 19 Jan 1921, record (1921) #: 12.

Charles GRINDSTAFF, Jr., parents: Charles M. Grindstaff and Hattie Hill, death cause: "7 months, not known", infomant: J.B. Grindstaff (Carter), buried: Grindstaff Cemetery, born/died: 21 Jan 1921, record (1921) #: 13.

Rosie Adeline Potter BRYANT, born: 29 Jun 1884, married, parents: William Potter and Hester McIntosh, death cause: "pulmonary tuberculosis", buried: Hampton, died: 21 Jan 1921, record (1921) #: 14.

Infant HOWARD, black, male, parents: father not stated and Florence Howard, death cause: illegible, informant: G.W. Phillips, buried: Odd Fellows Cemetery, died: 23 Jan 1921, record (1921) #: 15.

Charles Thomas BROWN, black, born: 15 Jan 1921, parents: Benson Brown (NC) and Ida Young (Johnson City), death cause: not stated, buried: Shell Creek, died: 23 Jan 1921, record (1921) #: 16.

Cloyd MCKINNEY, born: 15 Mar 1920, parents: father not stated and Bessie McKinney, death cause: "whooping cough", informant: James McKinney (Valley Forge), died: 24 Jan 1921, record (1921) #: 17.

Dora TAYLOR, negro, born: 7 Sep 1888, married, parents: Joe Mills (NC) and Mollie Love (?), death cause: "pulmonary tuberculosis", informant: John Taylor, buried: Cedar Grove Cemetery, died: 24 Jan 1921, record (1921) #: 18.

Walter Alexander MOREFIELD, born: 3 Jan 1882 in Johnson County, married, parents: Jefferson Morefield (Johnson County) and Lou Simerly, death cause: "intestinal adenoma", informant: Mrs. H.R. Parrott (Johnson City), buried: Simerly Cemetery, died: 25 Jan 1921, record (1921) #: 19.

C.C. PETERS, age 53 years, married, parents: Reubin Peters and Nancy Oliver, death cause: "typhoid fever", informant: R.H. Peters (Carter), buried: Blevins Cemetery, died: 26 Jan 1921, record (1921) #: 20.

T.J. RITCHIE, age 55 years, married, parents: David C. Ritchie and Jane Creed, death cause: "bronchial pneumonia", informant: W.B. Ritchie (Watauga Valley), buried: Ritchie Cemetery, died: 27 Jan 1921, record (1921) #: 21.

James Walter FREEMAN, born: 24 Jan 1921, parents: Fred Freeman and Delia Wood, death cause: "unknown", informant: Fred Freeman (Roan Mountain), died: 27 Jan 1921, record (1921) #: 22.

Catherine LEWIS, age 45 years, married, parents: John Wilson and Eveline Hetherly, death cause: "pneumonia", buried: Garland Cemetery, died: 28 Jan 1921, record (1921) #: 23.

Infant JENKINS, male, parents: Ed Jenkins and Maud Simerly, death cause: "stillborn", informant: Ed Jenkins (Valley Forge), born/died: 9 Jan 1921, record (1921) #: 24.

Infant BROWN, black, female, parents: Benson Brown (NC) and Ida Young, death cause: "born dead", buried: Shell Creek, died: 15 Jan 1921, record (1921) #: 25.

Infant EDENS, female, parents: Nat Edens and Grace Dugger, death cause: illegible, informant: R.B. Hyder (Johnson City), born/died: 21 Jan 1921, record #: 26.

Ben HARDIN, born: 16 Oct 1902, parents: Dock Hardin and (illegible) Trivett, death cause: "accidental gun shot", informant: Abe Trivett (Dark Ridge, NC) buried: Austin Cem., died: 2 Feb 1921, record (1921) #: 27.

Mary HOPSON, born: 3 Feb 1921, parents: Jason Hopson (Magnetic, NC) and Bessie McLaughlin (Unicoi County), death cause: illegible, buried: Hampton, died: 6 Feb 1921, record (1921) #: 28.

Lula HARRIS, born: 18 May 1873 in Virginia, married, parents: Calvin Eaton (VA) and Lucinda Gilbert (Patrick, VA), death cause: "sarconi of lungs", informant: Lucinda Bowers (Roan Mountain), buried in North Carolina, died: 7 Feb 1921, record (1921) #: 29.

Maud WILSON, age 19 years and 3 months, married, parents: father not stated and Mag Lewis, death cause: "sleeping sickness", died: 9 Feb 1921, record #: 30.

James BIRCHFIELD, born: 1 Jun 1899, single, parents: Dave Birchfield (NC) and Annie Miller, death cause: "nephritis", informant: David Birchfield (Roan Mountain), buried: Crabtree, died: 9 Feb 1921, record (1921) #: 31.

Martha HOPSON, born: 3 Feb 1921, parents: Jason Hopson (Magnetic, NC) and Bessie McLaughlin (Unicoi), death cause: illegible, buried: Hall Cemetery, died: 10 Feb 1921, record (1921) #: 32.

Elmer PUGH, born: 31 Jul 1874, divorced, parents: Zachari Pugh and Caroline Keen, death cause: "cancer of testicle", informant: W.T. Pugh (Fordstown), buried: Pugh Cemetery, died: 11 Feb 1921, record (1921) #: 33.

James Patterson MAST, born: Jun 1876 in Watauga County, NC, married, parents: Andrew J. Mast (Watauga Co., NC) and Joanna King (Missouri), death cause: "gun shot wound in bowels, homicidal", buried in North Carolina, died: 12 Feb 1921, record (1921) #: 34.

Charles Franklin ANGEL, born: 2 Oct 1901, single, parents: George Angel and Sarah Bowling, death cause: "chronic diabetes", buried: Highland Cemetery, died: 12 Feb 1921, record (1921) #: 35.

Joseph WAGNER, born: 13 May 1845, widower, parents: Joseph W. Wagner (Johnson County) and Nancy Wagner (Johnson County), death cause: "nephritis", informant: G.E. Wagner (Hampton), died: 17 Feb 1921, record (1921) #: 36.

Sarah MCRATH, black, age 75 years, born in North Carolina, parents: father's name not known and Sarah Gardner (NC), death cause: "cerebral hemorrhage", informant: Pete McRath (Elizabethton), died: 19 Feb 1921, record (1921) #: 37.

Joseph BREWER, born: 10 Jun 1851 in North Carolina, married, parents: James Brewer (NC) and Nancy Terry, death cause: "cirrhosis of liver", informant: Hampton Brewer, son (Shell Creek), buried: Hampton Creek Cemetery, died: 19 Feb 1921, record (1921) #: 38.

Callie HOUSTON, age 24 years, married, parents: A.S. Buckner (NC) and Denie Swanner, death cause: "pulmonary tuberculosis", buried: Taylor Chapel Cemetery, died: 20 Feb 1921, record (1921) #: 39.

Thomas Newton MCKINNIS, age 75 years, born in Catauba County, NC, parents: John McKinnis (Catawba Co., NC) and (illegible) Grifine (NC), death cause: illegible, informant: George McKinnis (Shell Creek), died: 21 Feb 1921, record (1921) #: 40.

Nannie A.E. Lacy ALLEN, born: 19 Jun 1846, married, parents: John W. Lacy and Nancy Hyder, death cause: "arteroselosis", informant: John F. Allen (Elizabethton), buried: Highland Cemetery, died: 22 Feb 1921, record (1921) #: 41.

James T. RAINBOLT, born: 10 May 1855, married, parents: Dugger Rainbolt and Lucinda Veniable (Mountain City), death cause: "mitral stenosis of heart", informant: S.B. Dugger (Butler), buried: Rainbolt Cem., died: 23 Feb 1921, record (1921) #: 42.

Charles Richard JONES, born: 20 Feb 1921, parents: Charles Haddon Jones and Clara Jenette Clark (RI), death cause: "premature birth", informant: Charles Jones (Eliz.), died: 23 Feb 1921, record (1921) #: 43.
J.W. BERRY, age 69 years, widower, parents: John Berry and Margaret McKinney death cause: "mitral lesion of heart", informant: John Berry (Hampton), buried: Berry Cemetery, died: 24 Feb 1921, record (1921) #: 44.
Sylva Alice MANNING, age 2 years, parents: Emmert Manning and Josie Lady, death cause: "weak valve in heart", informant: Emmert Manning (Elizabethton), died: 28 Feb 1921, record (1921) #: 45.
Delphia EDMONDSON, born: 6 Oct 1853 in North Carolina, married, parents: Hary Foster (NC) and Lorina Eller (NC), death cause: "disorder of bowels and liver", informant: Millard Edmonson (Elizabethton), buried: Hyder Cem., died: 28 Feb 1921, record (1921) #: 46.
Infant JONES, male, parents: John Jones and Lizzie Campbell, death cause: "stillborn", informant: John Jones (Valley Forge), died: 11 Feb 1921, record (1921) #: 47.
Mary Jane WHITEHEAD, born: 10 Feb 1921, parents: C.V. Whitehead and Judie Stevens, death cause: "boul hives", informant: Henry Stevens (Roan Mountain), buried: Whitehead Cemetery, died: 1 Mar 1921, record (1921) #: 48.
Elisha HENDRICKSON, born: 18 Apr 1843 in Taswell County, VA, married, parents: George Hendrickson (VA) and Annie McPherson (VA), death cause: "mitral lesion of heart", inforant: D.S. Stout (Hampton), buried: Roan Mountain, died: 5 Mar 1921, record (1921) #: 49.
Joseph GLOVER, born: 26 Jan 1918, parents: Joseph Glover and Madge Justice, death cause: "caught fire at heating stove, burned sevierly", buried: Campbell Cem., Hampton, died: 6 Mar 1921, record (1921) #: 50.
Edith HICKS, born: 23 Feb 1921, parents: Hahnie Hicks and Lillie Birchett (Ashe County, NC), death cause: "unknown", informant: Charlie Hicks (Butler), buried: Perkins Cem., died: 7 Mar 1921, record (1921) #: 51.
Mave PRICHET, age 2 years, female, informant: John Prichet and Betsy Hurley, death cause: "masel", buried: Garland Cemetery, died: 10 Mar 1921, record (1921) #: 52.
Martha CARVER, age 73 years, widow, parents: ___ Davis and mother's name not stated, death cause: "functional heart disease and paralysis, informant: James Carver (Raon Mountain), buried: Carver Cemetery, died: 12 Mar 1921, record (1921) #: 53.

Joseph C. PERKINS, born: 13 Oct 1868, married, parents: Wrily R. Perkins and Altha Caraway, death cause: "influenza and pneumonia", informant: Sam Perkins (Shell Creek), buried: Perkins Cemetery, died: 13 Mar 1921, record (1921) #: 54.

Larkin OXENDINE, born: 1814 in South Carolina (age 107 years), parents: "unknown", death cause: "old age", informant: T.A. Arnett (Roan Mountain), died: 13 Mar 1921, record (1921) #: 55.

Mary Ann LEDFORD, born: 4 Oct 1857, divorced, parents: Thomas Hopson and (first name illegible) Shortt, death cause: "lobar pneumonia fever", informant: H.H. Ledford (Cranberry, NC), buried: Roan Mountain, died: 15 Mar 1921, record (1921) #: 56.

Sara BLEVINS, age 58 years, married, parents: Voltin Garland and ___ Carter, death cause: "rumtis fer yrs", informant: husband, buried: Garland Cemetery, died: 15 Mar 1921, record (1921) #: 57.

David WHITEHEAD, age 88 years, parents: James Whitehead (NC) and Jennie Garland, death cause: "gangrene and paralysis", informant: W.C. Hill (Roan Mountain), buried: Whitehead Cemetery, died: 15 Mar 1921, record (1921) #: 58.

David Thomas NEWTON, born: 27 May 1899, single, parents: (illegible) Newton and Ella Miller, death cause: "hemorrhage of lungs, tuberculosis", informant: C.M. Newton (Elizabethton), buried: Newton Cemetery, died: 16 Mar 1921, record (1921) #: 59.

Martha PENIX, born: 20 Aug 1846, widow, parents: "unknown", death cause: "mitral insufficiency", informant: John Penix, buried: Colbaugh Cemetery, died: 19 Mar 1921, record (1921) #: 60.

John Andrew CREASMAN, born: 9 Jun 1875, married, parents: Dave Creasman (NC) and mother's name illegible, death cause: "explosion from .. (illegible)", informant: Mrs. J.A. Creasman (Elizabethton), buried: Highland Cemetery, died: 23 Mar 1921, record (1921) #: 61.

Paul Alfred WILLIAMS, born: 31 Dec 1899, single, parents: Dr. Mike C. Williams and Mollie (surname illegible), death cause: "World war, tuberculosis", informant: B.C. Ledford (Elizabethton), buried: Highland Cem., died: 25 Mar 1921, record (1921) #: 62.

Elizabeth ROTON, age 88 years, born in Watauga County, NC, parents: "not known", death cause: "old age", informant: Mose Eller (Butler), buried: Zionville, NC, died: 26 Mar 1921, record (1921) #: 63.

Preston Eugene KELLEY, born: 28 Nov 1920, parents: James A. Kelley and Lillie Elliott, death cause: "croup", informant: James A. Keller (Elizabethton), died: 28 Mar 1921, record (1921) #: 64.

Infant ARNET, female, born: 24 Mar 1921, parents: Dan Arnet (Johnson County) and Nora Nidiffer, death cause: "bol hives", buried: Estep Cemetery, died: 29 Mar 1921, record (1921) #: 65.

Infant TAYLOR, male, parents: M.C. Taylor and Lizzie Taylor, death cause: "stillborn", informant: M.C. Taylor (Carter), buried: Grindstaff Cemetery, died: 15 Mar 1921, record (1921) #: 66.

Infant ROBERSON, female, parents: Clyde Roberson and Gades Wheeler (Oklahoma), death cause: "stillborn", informant: T.H. Roberson (Elizabethton), buried: Highland Cem., died: 27 Mar 1921, record (1921) #: 67.

Robert David MORGAN, born: 14 Mar 1921, parents: ____ Morgan and Roxie Potter, death cause: not stated, informant: Frank Morgan (Hampton), buried: Hall Cemetery, died: 3 Apr 1921, record (1921) #: 68.

Elijah D. OLIVER, age 73 years, married, parents: James Oliver and Mary Payne, death cause: not stated, informant: J.L. Carriger (Watauga Valley), died: 5 Apr 1921, record (1921) #: 69.

Nancy Lillian COLE, born: 2 Apr 1871, married, parents: Hamilton Berry and Mary Price, death cause: "measles and pneumonia", informant: G.W. Cole (Johnson City), buried: Sinking Creek, died: 5 Apr 1921, record (1921) #: 70.

Lucinda FRANCIS, born: 16 Oct 1836 in Washington County, married, parents: Daniel Huffine and Oxie Delanie, death cause: "senility", buried: G.W. Mottern Cemetery, died: 5 Apr 1921, record (1921) #: 71.

Mary E. ROYSTON, born: 21 Jun 1844, widow, parents: Isaac Royston and Polly Royston, death cause: "mitral .. (illegible)" informant: J.M. Royston (Bluff City), buried: Sullivan County, died: 5 Apr 1921, record (1921) #: 72.

Harry BLEVINS, born: 20 Aug 1919, parents: John Blevins and Belle Lilley, death cause: "accidental poisoning with concentrated lye", informant: A.C. Slagle (Eliz), died: 6 Apr 1921, record (1921) #: 73.

W.D. JULIAN, age 32 years, married, parents: father not stated and Ellen Julian, death cause: "heart failure", informant: James Blevins (Roan Mountain), buried: Nelson Cemetery, died: 6 Apr 1921, record (1921) #: 74.

E.H. HARDIN, born: 7 Aug 1866, divorced, parents: Elija Hardin and Lydia Forbes, death cause: "by drawing falling fits", informant: Emily Peters (Carter), buried: Blevins Cemetery, died: 7 Apr 1921, record (1921) #: 75.

Bruce HUTSON, born: 5 Sep 1862, married, parents: Sam Hutson (KY) and ____ Cretsinger, death cause: "dropsy", informant: E. Hyett, buried: A.J. Little Cemetery, died: 7 Apr 1921, record (1921) #: 76.

Lowell MORGAN, born: 12 Mar 1919, parents: James Morgan and Alice Phillips, death cause: "influenza and pneumonia", informant: James Morgan (Shell Creek), buried: Richardson Cemetery, died: 8 Apr 1921, record (1921) #: 77.

Infant HILL, male, born: 21 Mar 1921, parents: Eligah Hill and Vina (surname illegible), death cause: "boul hives, informant: Eligah Hill (Roan Mountain), buried: Carver Cem., died: 10 Apr 1921, record (1921) #: 78.

Fran M. GLOVER, born: Oct 1852, married, preacher, parents: Harrison Glover and mother's name unknown, death cause: "chronic nephritis and cyrossis of liver", informant: G.V. Blevins (Elizabethton), buried: Sullivan County, died: 11 Apr 1921, record (1921) #: 79.

Jack FREEMAN, Jr., born: 31 Mar 1921, parents: Monroe Freeman and Hattie Brown (Ashe County, NC), death cause: "enlargement of lungs, asthema of heart", informant: Monroe Freeman (Roan Mountain), died: 13 Apr 1921, record (1921) #: 80.

William Lawson MORGAN, born: 1 Jun 1870, married, parents: Thomas Morgan and Eva Glover, death cause: "pentonitis, intestinal obstruction", informant: S.J. Caldwell (Roan Mountain), buried: Carter Cemetery, died: 14 Apr 1921, record (1921) #: 81.

William SMITH, born: 8 Jan 1874 in Sullivan County, married, parents: William Smith and Sallie Micals, death cause: "influenza and (illegible)", informant: Mrs. William Smith (Watauga), buried: Piney Flats, died: 18 Apr 1921, record (1921) #: 82.

Louis HUGHES, born: 11 Apr 1921, parents: Walter Hughes and Jane Hughes, death cause: "bold hives", informant: Custer Odom (Roan Mountain), died: 21 Apr 1921, record (1921) #: 83.

Ethel Bill CROW, colored, age 17 years, parents: Samuel Crow and Elizabeth Bowers, death cause: "accidentally drowned in Watauga River", informant: John H. Bowers (Elizabethton), buried: Watauga Point, died: 21 Apr 1921, record (1921) #: 84.

Lafayette LEWIS, born: 21 Oct 1840 in North Carolina, married, parents: Gidwon Lewis (NC) and Polly Goodwin, death cause: "valvulor heart lesion", informant: L.G. Lewis (Hampton), buried: Cardins Bluff, died: 21 Apr 1921, record (1921) #: 85.

Myrtle Jeanella BERRY, born: 3 Feb 1921, parents: Griffin Berry and Dana Rainbolt, death cause: "bold hives", informant: Griffin Berry (Butler), buried: Pearce Cem., died: 23 Apr 1921, record (1921) #: 86.

D.B. CROW, age 67 years, married, parents: Isaac Crow and Mary Crow, death cause: "heart disease", informant: H.T. Crow (Johnson City), buried: Milligan Cemetery, died: 27 Apr 1921, record (1921) #: 87.

Infant TOLLEY, female, parents: Robert T. Tolley and L___ Morrell, death cause: "valvulor heart lesion", informant: J.M. Morrell (Elizabethton), buried: Highland Cemetery, born/died: 27 Apr 1921, record (1921) #: 88.

Martha BOWERS, age 82 years, widow, parents: Godfrey Crow and ____ Crow, death cause: "apoplexy", born: 29 Apr 1921, record (1921) #: 89.

Novella RAINBOLT, born: 13 Mar 1918, parents: William B. Rainbolt and Anna McNeely, death cause: "caught fire by striking matches", informant: William B. Rainbolt (Butler), buried: Smith Cemetery, died: 30 Apr 1921, record (1921) #: 90.

Infant CLARK, female, parents: William C. Clark and Mollie Tolley, death cause: "premature birth", informant: William C. Clark (Hampton), buried: Tolley Cemetery, died: 16 Apr 1921, record (1921) #: 91.

Mrs. M..(illegible) BEAVERS, born: 7 Oct 1875, parents: N.T. Williams and Martha Daniel, death cause: "cerebral hemorrhage", informant: Chase M. Beavers (Milligan), buried: Milligan Cemetery, died: 2 May 1921, record (1921) #: 92.

William BRADLEY, Jr., parents: William Bradley and Mary McLeod, death cause: "premature birth", informant: Clyde McEwen (Elizabethton), buried: Bradley Cem., died: 4 May 1921, record (1921) #: 93.

Sarah WELSH, negro, born: 2 May 1833 in Virginia, married, parents: "unknown", death cause: "pulmonary tuberculosis", informant: Joe Welsh (Elizabethton), buried: Cedar Grove Cemetery, died: 5 May 1921, record (1921) #: 94.

Ollie Belle HILL, born: 23 Jan 1907, parents: Ezekiel Hill and Mollie Head, death cause: "diptheria", informant: Mauuel Honeycutt (Hopson), buried: Hill Cemetery, died: 5 May 1921, record (1921) #: 95.

Eik PRICHARD, born: 9 May 1921, parents: John Prichard and Bess Hurley, death cause: not stated, died: 9 May 1921, record (1921) #: 96.

Eidy GRINDSTAFF, age 22 years, married, parents: Sam Cass and Edia Estep, death cause: "tubloks", buried: Cass Cemetery, died: 11 May 1921, record (1921) #: 97.

Finly CAROWAY, born: 5 Oct 1870, married, parents: William Caroway and Martha Stout, death cause: "he was shot to death", informant: N.G. Ingram (Shell Creek), buried: Caraway Cemetery, died: 12 May 1921, record (1921) #: 98.

Infant OLIVER, female, parents: Roy Oliver and Annie Richardson, death cause: "premature delivery", informant: Roy Oliver (Hampton), buried: Hall Cemetery, born/died: 12 May 1921, record (1921) #: 99.

Samuel L. ELLIOTT, born: 9 Jul 1869, married, parents: Michael Elliott and Martha Anderson, death cause: "organic heart disease", informant: Martha Elliott Harvy (Johnson City), buried: A.J. Little Cemetery, died: 12 May 1921, record (1921) #: 100.

George A. BREEDLOVE, black, born: 6 Oct 1906, parents: W.A.C. Breedlove and Joanna Welch, death cause: "pulmonary tuberculosis", buried: Odd Fellows Cemetery, died: 16 May 1921, record (1921) #: 101.

Harvey Elmer BYRD, born: 17 Jun 1919, parents: George Byrd and Mary Woods, death cause: "accidental mercury poisoning", informant: John Byrd (Braemar), buried: Whitehead Cemetery, died: 20 May 1921, record (1921) #: 102.

Bill FAIR, born: 9 Apr 1902, parents: W.F. Fair and Elizabeth Campbell, death cause: "tuberculosis pulmonary", informant W.F. Fair (Elizabethton), died: 23 May 1921, record (1921) #: 103.

Mary Ann JONES, born: 17 Jun 1840, widow, parents: Daniel Snyder and Polly Foster, death cause: "sarcoma of breast", informant: Joe Wagner (Elizabethton), buried: Highland Cemetery, died: 23 May 1921, record (1921) #: 104.

Benjamin CARVER, age 70 years and 7 months, married, parents: Aden Carver and Nancy Banks, death cause: "mitral heart lesion", informant: Frank Carver (Hampton), buried: Fair View Cemetry, died: 23 May 1921, record (1921) #: 105.

Mary Ellen WIDNER, parents: Willis M. Widner (Washington County) and Mary E. Swiney, death cause: "bale hives and jaundice", buried: Dempsey Cemetery, born/died: 24 May 1921, record (1921) #: 106.

Mrs. Emma B. MILLER, born: 26 Nov 1851, widow, parents: John Coleman and Annie Smith, death cause: "old age", informant: Joe Miller (Johnson City), buried: Williams Cemetery, died: 26 May 1921, record (1921) #: 107.
Nannie Nave FLETCHER, born: 24 May 1852, parents: William Nave and Margaret Lewis, death cause: "fracture of hip joint", informant: M.N. Fletcher, buried: Buckles Cemetery, died: 27 May 1921, record (1921) #: 108.
Gail BOWERS, age 8 months, parents: Rob Bowers and ___ Jenkins, died: 29 May 1921, record (1921) #: 109.
John Alexander HAMPTON, born: 17 Apr 1921, parents: David Hampton and Annie Richardson, death cause: "unknown", died: 31 May 1921, record (1921) #: 110.
Infant BLEVINS, female, parents: father not stated and Josa Blevins, death cause: "born dead", inforant: John Blevins (Carter), buried: Garland Cemetery, born/died: 21 May 1921, record (1921) #: 111.
Mary MILLER, born: 16 Oct 1862, married, parents: Henry Pierce and Phoba J. Pierce, death cause: "aortic regurgitation", informant: Allen Pierce (Carter), buried: Pierce Cem., died: 3 Jun 1921, record #: 112.
Mary OLIVER, age 73 years, single, parents: father's name illegible and Mary Oliver, death cause: illegible, informant: Tom Grindstaff (Carter), buried: Cress Cem., died: 5 Jun 1921, record (1921) #: 113.
Plato WRIGHT, born: 16 Dec 1877 in North Carolina, widower, parents: Wesley Wright (NC) and Polly Hopson (NC), death cause: not stated, informant: Lourence Wright (Hopson), buried: Blevins Cemetery, died: 6 Jun 1921, record (1921) #: 114.
Leon WILLIAMS, born: 3 Sep 1919, parents: W.R. Johnson and Emma Williams, death cause: "bronchial pneumonia", informant: E.B. Williams (Hampton), buried: Hall Cemetery, died: 7 Jun 1921, record (1921) #: 115.
Samuel TAYLOR, age 72 years, single, parents: Thomas Taylor and Nancy Grindstaff, death cause: not stated, buried: Markland Cemetery, died: 7 Jun 1921.
Wheeler MCQUEEN, born: 9 Apr 1878, married, parents: William L. McQueen (Mountain City) and Elizabeth White, death cause: "unknown, found dead in bed", informant: Roy White (Fish Springs), buried: Gouge Cemetery, died: 7 Jun 1921, record (1921) #: 117.
Ralph Reece WHITEHEAD, born: 8 Aug 1920, parents: Lass Whitehead and Ella Morris, death cause: "gastro entero colitis", informant: W.P. Loveless (Elizabethton), buried: Tolley Cem., died: 12 Jun 1921, record #: 118.

George W. WAGNER, born: 2 Dec 1857, widower, parents: Joe Wagner and Mary Vaught, death cause: "mitral regurgitation, brights disease", informant: Mrs. J.N. Razor (Elizabethton), buried: Maymead, TN, died: 13 Jun 1921, record (1921) #: 119.

Delia Stout LOFTON, born: Oct 1881, parents: Lum Stout and Eliza Jane Powell, death cause: "heart (illegible)", informant: Lum Stout (Elizabethton), buried: Doe, TN, died: 15 Jun 1921, record (1921) #: 120.

Illegible CORDELL, female, born: 5 Oct 1900, married, parents: David C. Smith and Dellis Morgan, death cause: "killed by lightening", informant: B.J. Bumgardner (Shell Creek), died: 17 Jun 1921, record (1921) #: 121.

Sallie M. COLE, born: 14 Feb 1885, married, parents: J.F.M. Lewis and Mary A. Jenkins, death cause: "carconoma of breast", informant: W.J. Cole (Carter), buried: Ritchie Cemetery, died: 18 Jun 1921, record (1921) #: 122.

Mary Florence SIMERLY, born: 8 Feb 1911, parents: Walter Simerly and Pearl Jenkins, death cause: "typhoid fever", informant: Walter Simerly (Valley Forge), died: 20 Jun 1921, record (1921) #: 123.

Rachel CARVER, age 72 years, widow, parents: not stated, death cause: "broncho pneumonia", buried: Carver Cem., died: 21 Jun 1921, record (1921) #: 124.

Ethel Goss CREGER, born: 29 Sep 1890 in North Carolina, married, parents: Marion Goss (NC) and Elizabeth Jones (NC), death cause: "tuberculosis, abortion about 2 months and abscess of lung", informant: Mrs. Emma Lineback (Elizabethton), buried: Goss Cem., died: 21 Jun 1921, record (1921) #: 125.

Carrie Dungur RHUDY, born: 24 Mar 1847 in Marion, VA, married, parents: William Dingar (Va) and Elizabeth Jones (VA), death cause: "paralysis", informant: L.H. Rhudy, buried: Highland Cemetery, died: 21 Jun 1921, record (1921) #: 126.

Eveline ESTEP, age 70 years, married, parents: Tom Heatherly and Betsy Estep, death cause: "gastro enteritis", informant: James Nidiffer (Carter), buried: Heatherly Cemetery, died: 22 Jun 1921, record (1921) #: 127.

Martha J. HYDER, born: 22 Sep 1833, single, parents: John W. Hyder and Lavina Williams, death cause: "functional heart disease", informant: Mrs. William Simerly (Hampton), buried: Hyder Cemetery, died: 24 Jun 1921, record (1921) #: 128.

John F. DUGGER, age 65 years, married, parents: David A. Dugger and Betty Bunton, death cause: "pneumonia", buried: Meredith Cemetery, died: 27 Jun 1921, record (1921) #: 129.

Loon BLEVINS, age 80 years, married, parents: Clark Blevins and Polly Stout, death cause: "brite disease", buried: Garland Cemetery, died: 27 Jun 1921, record (1921) #: 130.

Ricklas FORBES, born: 2 Mar 1838 in North Carolina, married, parents: John Forbes (NC) and Stacie Stanley (NC), death cause: "dysentery", informant: William Forbes (Milligan), buried: Campbell Cemetery, died: 20 Jun 1921, record (1921) #: 131.

Infant RITCHIE, female, born: 30 Jun 1921, parents: Alvin Ritchie and Lucresia Alford, death cause: "not known", buried: Ritchie Cemetery, died: 3 Jul 1921, record (1921) #: 132.

Blanch BANNER, born: 28 Jun 1919, parents: C.E. Banner (NC) and M.L. Grimsley (NC), death cause: "typhoid", informant; J.a. McNeal (Shell Creek), buried: Laurel Fork, died: 4 Jul 1921, record (1921) #: 133.

Mary Jane MARKLING, age 68 years, born in Johnson County, married, parents: Thomas Cable (Johnson County) and Jan Campbell, death cause: "suppose heart failure", informant: Hanry Markling (Carter), buried: Garland Cem., died: 9 Jul 1921, record (1921) #: 134.

Infant MERRITT, male, parents: Dan Merritt and Dottie Ward, death cause: "not known", informant: Charlie Merritt (Valley Forge), died: 10 Jul 1921, record (1921) #: 135.

Rhoda STREET, age 38 years, born in Mitchell County, NC, married, parents: Kirk Wright (NC) and mother not stated, death cause: "tuberculosis", informant: Byrd Honeycutt (Roan Mountain), buried: Mitchell County, NC, died: 11 Jul 1921, record (1921) #: 136.

Chester FREEMAN, born: 25 Aug 1914, parents: J.F. Freeman and Ida Johnson, death cause: "colitis", informant: James Johnson (Roan Mountain), died: 12 Jul 1921, record (1921) #: 137.

James D. NAVE, born: 18 Nov 1890, married, parents: J.B. Nave and Mary Allen, death cause: "Brights disease and blood pressure", buried: Siam, died: 16 Jul 1921, record (1921) #: 138.

Gladys Pauline GEISLER, born: 6 May 1919, parents: S.G. Geisler and Anna Mae Combs, death cause: "flux", informant: S.G. Geisler (Elizabethton), buried: Bluff City, died: 18 Jul 1921, record (1921) #: 139.

John OLIVER, age 10 years, parents: Roy Oliver and Abagail Williams, death cause: not stated, died: 21 Jul 1921, record (1921) #: 140.

Lena HYDER, age 39 years, born in Unicoi County, married, parents: David Sneed and Eveline Davis, death cause: "cerebral hemorrhage", informant: Harrison Hyder (Hampton), buried: Hyder Cemetery, died: 21 Jul 1921, record (1921) #: 141.

Emma H. MAIN, born: 4 Oct 1859 in Johnson County, widow, parents: A.C. Wagner (Johnson Co.) and Helen Baker (Johnson Co.), death cause: "apoplexy", informant: W.K. Main, died; 22 Jul 1921, record #: 142.

Hattie Mottern LEWIS, born: 19 Dec 1888, parents: Fate (Lafayette) Mottern and Alpha Merritt, death cause: illegible, informant: Houston Lewis, buried: Geo Mottern Cem., died: 23 Jul 1921, record (1921) #: 143.

Paul Edgar GLOVER, born: 5 Mar 1921, parents: W.A. Glover and Mary Chambers, death cause: "cholera", informant: W.A. Glover (Valley Forge), died: 25 Jul 1921, record (1921) #: 144.

Francis M. BOWERS, male, age 61 years, married, parents: W.A. Bowers and Mary Bowers, death cause: "a load of wood turned over on him", died: 29 Jul 1921, record (1921) #: 145.

Dewey William FORNEY, colored, born: 31 Aug 1921, parents: William Forney and Mammie Davis, death cause: "dysentery", buried: Cedar Grove, died: 31 Jul 1921, record (1921) #: 146.

John CROW, age 86 years, married, parents: Campbell Crow and ____ Williams, death cause: "kidney trouble", died: 31 Jul 1921, record (1921) #: 147.

Infant SIMS, male, parents: Thomas Sims and Ethel Cook, death cause: "stillborn", informant: Thomas Cook (Butler), buried: Whitehead Cemetery, died: 7 Jul 1921, record (1921) #: 148.

A.C. BAILEY, age 72 years, born in Mitchell County, NC, married, parents: Harm Bailey (NC) and Sarah Deaton (NC), death cause: "organic heart disease", died: 5 Aug 1921, record (1921) #: 149.

Tulva Grace ESTEP, born: 24 Mar 1903, single, parents: C.T. Estep and Eliza Ellis, death cause: "typhoid fever", informant: C.M. Newton (Elizabethton), buried: Estep Cem., died: 7 Aug 1921, record (1921) #: 150.

Cora Dickens ELLIOTT, age 27 years, married, parents: Clark Dickens (NC) and Elizabeth Norman (NC), death cause: "pulmonary tuberculosis", informant: J.J. Elliott (Johnson City), buried: A.J. Little Cemetery, died: 8 Aug 1921, record (1921) # 151.

Glenn Jobe ESTEP, born: 9 Dec 1912, parents: L.T. Estep and Eliza Ellis, death cause: "congestion of lungs", informant: C.M. Newton, buried: Estep Cemetery, died: 9 Aug 1921, record (1921) #: 152.

Harmon HICKS, born: 17 Aug 1851 in North Carolina, single, parents: Andrew Hicks (NC) and Cynthia Winters (NC), death cause: "kidney and liver disease", informant: Ruben Bumgardner (Shell Creek), died: 12 Aug 1921, record (1921) #: 153.

Clyde Williams BAILEY, born: 10 Jun 1921, parents: Floyd Cornelius Bailey and Bessie Rosa Lee Bailey (Neva, TN), death cause: not stated, informant: Floyd Bailey (Hampton), buried: Hill Cemetery, died: 14 Aug 1921, record (1921) #: 154.

William C. ROBERTS, born: 16 Jul 1853, married, parents: Dick Roberts and Nancy Keen, death cause: "paralysis", informant: William Carriger, buried: Highland Cemetery, died: 15 Aug 1921, record #: 155.

Bert FORBES, age 1 year, 6 months and 28 days, parents: Frank Forbes and Jennie Roberts, death cause: "gastro enteritis", informant: Dave Clark (Roan Mountain), buried: Nelson Cemetery, died: 15 Aug 1921, record (1921) #: 156.

Frankie WILSON, female, born: 8 Aug 1917, parents: William R. Wilson and Cora Winters (Elk Park, NC), death cause: "cholera", informant: William R. Wilson (Shell Creek), died: 15 Aug 1921, record #: 157.

Infant VANHUSS, female, parents: D.B. Vanhuss and Eliza Garrison, death cause: "congestion of lungs", informant: J.F. Vanhuss (Elizabethton), buried: Charity Hill, died: 21 Aug 1921, record (1921) #: 158.

Pierce TIPTON, born: 5 Feb 1898, single, parents: Sydney Tipton (NC) and Lou Julian, death cause: "gun shot wound in abdomen, homocide", informant: Aught Tipton (Hampton), buried: Roan Mountain, died: 23 Aug 1921, record (1921) #: 159.

Lola WALKER, born: Jul 1920, parents: Chester Walker and Bessie Nidiffer, death cause: "dysentery", informant: Shapp A. Williams, buried: Jones Cemetery, died: 24 Aug 1921, record (1921) #: 160.

Lourie WILLIAMS, born: 11 Feb 1921, parents: J.C. Williams and Rena Fletcher, death cause: "dysentery", informant: J.C. Williams (Watauga Valley), buried: Buckles Cem., died: 27 Aug 1921, record (1921) #: 161.

Susan GRIFFITH, born: 21 Aug 1884, married, parents: Lee Oliver and Adalin Campbell, death cause: "unknown", informant: F.M. Griffith (Watauga Valley), buried: Buckles Cem., died: 29 Aug 1921, record: 162.

Infant ROBERSON, male, parents: Clarence Roberson and Maud Guinn, death cause: "stillborn", informant: J.B. Guinn (Hopson), buried: Ingram Cemetery, died: 21 Aug 1921, record (1921) #: 163.

Mary H. BROOKS, born in Mountain City, parents: R. Kemp Brooks (Mountain City) and Callie Rash, death cause: "meningitis", parents reside at Watauga, born/died: 2 Sep 1921, record (1921) #: 164.

Hildred NAVE, born: 2 Sep 1921, parents: Isaac S. Nave and Cora White, death cause: "unknown", informant: Isaac S. Nave (Butler), buried: Gouge Cemetery, died: 9 Sep 1921, record (1921) #: 165.

Eliza RUSSELL, age 57 years, married, parents: Eliga Hardin and Caroline Montgomery, death cause: "typhoid fever", informant: Walter Russell (Elizabethton), buried: Siam, died: 11 Sep 1921, record (1921) #: 166.

Mattie E. DAVIS, colored, born: 24 Dec 1900, single, parents: Link K. Davis (NC) and Leutitia Brown (NC), death cause: "tuberculosis", buried: Cedar Grove Cemetery, died: 11 Sep 1921, record (1921) #: 167.

Mrs. Laura A. WHITAKER, born: 10 Jun 1845 in Washington County, TN, married, parents: Soloman Sellars and Mary Guinn, death cause: "pulmonary tuberculosis", informant: I.N. Whitaker (Watauga), died: 16 Sep 1921, record (1921) #: 168.

George LEONARD, born: 1 Nov 1919, parents: John Leonard and Myrtle Faidley (VA), death cause: "typhoid fever", informant: John Leonard (Hopson), buried: Holley Cem., died: 20 Sep 1921, record (1921) #: 169.

Lester PERRY, born: 21 Jul 1916, parents: Thomas Perry and Lula Holden, death cause: "ordema of the larynx, scarlet fever", informant: Thomas Perry (Shell Creek), buried: Perry Cemetery, died: 25 Sep 1921, record (1921) #: 170.

Mary MCKINNEY, born: 12 Mar 1921, parents: Puckney McKinney and Maud Matherly, death cause: "teething and meningitis", informant: James McKinney (Valley Forge), died: 26 Sep 1921, record (1921) #: 171.

Nannie TRIPLETT, born: 14 Nov 1877, married, parents: James Goodwin and Alice Johnson, death cause: "pulmonary tuberculosis", informant: Ruth Triplett (Hampton), buried: Cardens Bluff, died: 26 Sep 1921, record (1921) #: 172.

Mirah TOLLEY, age 23 years, 4 months and 11 days, single, parents: J.H. Tolley and Susan Whitehead, death cause: "pulmonary tuberculosis", informant: J.H. Tolley (Roan Mountain), buried: Tolley Cemetery, died: 27 Sep 1921, record (1921) #: 173.

Mrs. Francis DANIELS, age 67 years, 11 months and 5 days, married, parents: Enoch Keen (Kingsport) and Mary Orr (VA), death cause: "mitral insufficiency and possibly carcinoma of liver", informant: Charles L. Price (Johnson City), buried: Taylor Chappel, died: 28 Sep 1921, record (1921) #: 174.

Sherman HILL, born: 17 Sep 1921, parents: James Hill and Suda Whitehead, death cause: "boul hives", informant: James Hill (Hopson), buried: Holly Cemetery, died: 29 Sep 1921, record (1921) #: 175.

Eligia Arthur LOVELESS, born: 10 Mar 1921, parents: Ross Loveless and Mary Hardin, death cause: "cholera", informant: Ross Loveless (Siam), died: 2 Oct 1921, record (1921) #: 176.

June WILLIAMS, age 1 year and 3 months, parents: M.C. Williams and Lillie Bowers, death cause: "disentery", died: 2 Oct 1921, record (1921) #: 177.

Mandy MARTIN, born: 15 Jul 1872, married, parents: George Fair and Eliza Jane Loveless, death cause: "pulmonary tuberculosis", informant: George Fair (Elizabethton), buried: Bradley Cemetery, died: 5 Oct 1921, record (1921) #: 178.

Joseph E. MORRELL, age 59 years, born in Sullivan County, married, parents: Caleb Morrell (Sullivan County) and Levisa Crow, death cause: "heart failure, fell dead", died: 6 Oct 1921, record (1921) #: 179.

Albert HAMBRICK, age 3 years, parents: George Hambrick and Lena Glover, death cause: "lorengene dip", died: 8 Oct 1921, record (1921) #: 180.

Infant MORRIS, male, parents: Ernest Morris and Bessie Bowers, death cause: "wrapped cord", informant: Ernest Morris (Eliazbethton), buried: Colbaugh Cemetery, born/died: 9 Oct 1921, record (1921) #: 181.

Mary BOWMAN, age 59 years, born in Watauga County, NC, parents: Isaac Valentine Reece (NC) and Juritta Proffitt (NC), death cause: "acute appendicitis", informant: Christopher M. Bowman, buried: Thomas Cemetery, died: 10 Oct 1921, record (1921) #: 182.

Daniel Melvin MEREDITH, born: 12 Oct 1921, parents: (name illegible) Meredith and Geneva Snyder, death cause: "asphixiation", buried: Meredith Cemetery, died: 13 Oct 1921, record (1921) #: 183.

Walter HEATON, born: 7 Sep 1921, parents: A.R. Heaton and Ina Hicks, death cause: "unknown", informant: A.R. Heaton (Shell Creek), buried: Walnut Mountain, died: 14 Oct 1921, record (1921) #: 184.

Letha LOWE, born: 17 Sep 1921, parents: Roy B. Lowe and Sallie Pierce, death cause: "dyptheria", informant: Roy Lowe (Watauga Valley), buried: Buckles Cemetery, died: 17 Oct 1921, record (1921) #: 185.
Carrie Victoria CAMPBELL, born: 5 Sep 1921, parents: Thomas G. Campbell and Myrtle Etryl Mae Scalf, death cause: "erysipelse", resided: Watauga, died: 19 Oct 1921, record (1921) #: 186.
Ida PETERS, age 34 years, married, parents: N.C. Buckles and Eliza Taylor, death cause: "Spanish influenza", informant: Mike Peters (Carter), died: 20 Oct 1921, record (1921) #: 187.
William BOWERS, born: 18 Dec 1846 in North Carolina, married, parents: William Bowers (NC) and mother's name unknown, death cause: "chronic intestinal nephritis", informant: George F. Bowers (Minneopalis, NC), buried: Roan Mountain, died: 21 Oct 1921, record: 188.
Elaurau HARMON, female, born: 3 Mar 1921, parents: Virgle Harmon and Minnie Stout (Avery County, NC), death cause: "unknown", informant: Minnie Stout (Dark Ridge), buried: Harmon Cemetery, died: 22 Oct 1921, record (1921) #: 189.
Bessie TAYLOR, age 37 years, single, parents: A.B. Taylor and Elizabeth Richardson, death cause: "cancer", informant: R.C. Taylor (Carter), buried: Taylor Cem., died: 29 Oct 1921, record (1921) #: 190.
Sheeley LIVINGSTON, male, born: Oct 1914, parents: Ben Livingston and Violet McKeehan, death cause: "congestion of lungs", informant: W.P. Loveless (Johnson City), buried: McKeehan Cemetery, died: 24 Oct 1921, record (1921) #: 191.
Nelson DUFFIELD, colored, born: 16 Mar 1853, married, parents: father's name not known and Harriett Scott, death cause: "acute gastro enteritis", informant: Ollie Hoge, buried: Watauga, died: 24 Oct 1921, record (1921) #: 192.
Mariah JOHNSON, born: 1 Jan 1857, married, parents: Jacob Bowling and Jane Miller, death cause: "mitral regurgitation", informant: Sam Johnson (Roan Mountain), died: 28 Oct 1921, record (1921) #: 193.
Edna PIERCE, born: 30 Jul 1920, parents: Henry Pierce and Minnie Nave, death cause: "spinal meningitis, dysentery", buried: Buckles Cemetery, died: 30 Oct 1921, record (1921) #: 194.
Infant JULIAN, male, parents: J. Julian and Lydia Knight (NC), death cause: "stillborn", informant: J.F. Julian (Roan Mountain), died: 9 Oct 1921, record (1921) #: 195.

Warren OLIVER, born: 20 Jun 1920, parents: Hooker Oliver and Bonnie Morley, death cause: "unknown", informant: R.W. Smith (Cardens Bluff), buried: Morton Cemetery, died: 3 Nov 1921, record (1921) #: 196.

Henry E. WHITEHEAD, born: 18 Jul 1877, married, parents: John Whitehead and Nancy Schnider, death cause: "uraemia", informant: John L. Whitehead (Hampton), buried: Whitehead Cemetery, died: 5 Nov 1921, record (1921) #: 197.

Elizabeth JOHNSON, born: 11 Jan 1848, widow, parents: James Grant and Willim Mina Bowman, death cause: "pulmonary tuberculosis, mitral regurgitation", informant: John W. Johnson (Johnson City), buried: Taylor Chapel, died: 8 Nov 1921, record (1921) #: 198.

Nancie Margaret HAMILTON, born: 26 Mar 1850, parents: J.A. King (VA) and ____ McHaney, death cause: "broncho pneumonia", informant: J.W. King (Bluff City), buried: Bluff City, died: 7 Nov 1921, record (1921) #: 199.

Josephine Myter COLLINS, born: 7 Mar 1891, married, parents: A.F. Gourley and Cora Smalling, death cause: "tuberculosis", buried: Payne Cemetery, died: 10 Nov 1921, record (1921) #: 200.

Loftus WILSON, born: 1 Nov 1921, parents: Gilbert Wilson (NC) and Minnie Bradley, death cause: "bronchial pneumonia", informant: Dock Bradley (Elizabethton), buried: Smith Cemetery, died: 11 Nov 1921, record (1921) #: 201.

James Robert CARVER, born: 23 Oct 1921, parents: George Carver and Nancy Miller, death cause: "boul hives", informant: Charlie Ellison (Hampton), buried: Carver Cem., died: 14 Nov 1921, record (1921) #: 202.

James Edward SEIGLA, born: 14 Sep 1921, parents: John M. Sigla (Illinois) and Ruth M. Oaks (VA), death cause: "accidental gun shot wound", informant: John M. Sigla (Elizabethton), buried: Highland Cemetery, died: 14 Nov 1921, record (1921) #: 203.

Lusely GRINDSTAFF, born: 26 Oct 1921, parents: David Grindstaff and Ellen Grindstaff, death cause: "hives", informant: W.D. Loveless, buried: Grindstaff Cemetery, died: 16 Nov 1921, record (1921) #: 204.

Charles CAMPBELL, born: 4 Oct 1917, parents: William Campbell and Sarah E. Potter, death cause: not stated, informant: Jackson Potter (Shell Creek), died: 19 Nov 1921, record (1921) #: 205.

Cora PETERS, born: 20 Mar 1902, married, parents: Nathan Branch and Josie Blevins, death cause: "accidentally by gun shot", buried: Peters Cemetery, died: 20 Nov 1921, record (1921) #: 206.

Lonnie COLE, female, born: Jun 1914, parents: John S. Cole and Pearl Anderson, death cause: "supposed appendix", informant: John S. Cole (Watauga Valley), buried: Ritchie Cemetery, died: 20 Nov 1921, record (1921) #: 207.

Margaret RASOR, born: 2 Aug 1895, single, parents: I.W. Rasor and Lizzie Ellis, death cause: "pulmonary tuberculosis", informant: Dan Grindstaff (Carter), buried: Blevins Cemetery, died: 21 Nov 1921, record (1921) #: 208.

Martin CROW, colored, born: 16 Sep 1886, single, parents: Soloman A. Crow and Anna Folsom, death cause: "syphlis, gastritis", informant: Soloman A. Crow (Elizabethton), buried: Crow Cemetery, died: 26 Nov 1921, record (1921) #: 209.

Walter Ray OSBORNE, age 11 years and 7 months, born in North Carolina, parents: John Alvin Osborne (NC) and Martha Eggers (NC), death cause: "shock from operation for cyst on face", informant: John A. Osborne (Minneaopolis, NC), buried: North Carolina, died: 27 Nov 1921, record (1921) #: 210.

Infant MCKEEHAN, female, parents: Walter McKeehan and Sina Hayes, death cause: "premature", informant: Nat Payne (Milligan), buried: Payne Cemetery, born/died: 28 Nov 1921, record (1921) #: 211, (twin below).

Infant MCKEEHAN, female, parents: Walter McKeehan and Sina Hayes, death cause: "premature", informant: Nat Payne (Milligan), buried: Payne Cemetery, born/died: 28 Nov 1921, record (1921) #: 212, (twin above).

Lewis HUGHES, born: 3 Feb 1848 in North Carolina, married, parents: Charlie Hughes (NC) and Elizabeth Garland (NC(, death cause: "old age", informant: H. Hughes (Roan Mountain), died: 29 Nov 1921, record (1921) #: 213.

Infant BUTLER, female, parents: Lewis Butler and Gertrude Moffett, death cause: "stillborn", informant: W.P. Loveless (Elizabethton), born/died: 23 Nov 1921, record (1921) #: 214.

Infant MASSENGILL, male, parents: William Massengill and Ollie Shipley (Sullivan County), death cause: "stillborn", residence: Watauga, died: 27 Nov 1921, record (1921) #: 215.

Infant BUTLER, female, parents: Lewis Butler and Gertrude Moffett, death cause: "stillborn", informant: Sharpp Williams, buried: Smith Cemetery, born/died: 23 Nov 1921, record (1921) #: 216 (record appears to be duplicate of 214).

Infant COLE, female, parents: Floyd Cole (Watauga County, NC) and S. Miller, death cause: "abortion", informant: J.W. Miller (Butler), died: 3 Dec 1921, record (1921) #: 217.

Martha Adalade JOHNSON, born: 20 May 1874 in Sullivan County, married, parents: David Wilcox (Ashe County, NC) and Martha Hodge (Sullivan County), death cause: "dysentery and inflamation of gall bladder", informant: Mrs. Joshua Swanner (Johnson City), buried; Taylor Cem., died: 6 Dec 1921, record (1921) #: 218.

Evalyn L. SMALLING, born: 26 Apr 1871, parents: Samuel Jenkins and Kate Campbell, death cause: "bronchial asthma", informant: George Smalling (Hampton), buried: Hall Cemetery, died: 8 Dec 1921, record (1921) #: 219.

Samuel Paxton DOLEN, born: May 1837 at Fall Branch, TN, widower, parents: Nels Dolen and mother unknown, death cause: "pneumonia fever", informant: J.H. Dolen (Shell Creek), died: 10 Dec 1921, record #: 220.

Winnie VANCE, born: 22 Jan 1910, parents: John Vance and Bessie Johnson, death cause: "influenza", informant: J.P. Vance (Shell Creek), buried: Richardson Cemetery, died: 12 Dec 1921, record (1921) #: 221.

Mary LAWS, age 3 years, parents: R.D. Laws and Myrtle Webb, death cause: "diptheria", buried: Colbaugh Cemetery, died: 13 Dec 1921, record (1921) #: 222.

Ina PIERCE, born: 30 Oct 1921, parents: A.C. Pierce and Catherine Buckles, death cause: "acute indigestion", informant: A.C. Pierce (Watauga Valley), buried: Buckles Cemetery, died: 15 Dec 1921, record (1921) #: 223.

Mary Rose HATHAWAY, born: 14 Jun 1902, single, parents: C.L. Hathaway and Ida Smith, death cause: "tuberculosis of chest", buried: Smith Cemetery, died: 21 Dec 1921, record (1921) #: 224.

Hary Butler HART, born: 21 Dec 1921, parents: George L. Hart and Retta M. Morley, death cause: "premature birth", died: 21 Dec 1921, record (1921) #: 225. (twin ? below)

Thomas Andrew O'DONNELL, born: 9 Jun 1865 in Ireland, parents: "unknown", death cause: "dropsy", informant: John J. O'Donnell (Elizabethton), buried: Johnson City, died: 22 Dec 1921, record (1921) #: 226.

George LYONS, born: 14 Nov 1843 in Mississippi, married, parents: "not known", death cause: "influenza, mitral regurgitation", informant: Cash Ingram (Hopson), buried: Lacy Cemetery, died: 29 Dec 1921, record (1921) #: 227.

Nat C. NAVE, Jr., born: 10 Dec 1921 in South Carolina, parents: N.C. Nave and Mildred Sudwick (SC), death cause: illegible, informant: J.C. Harmon (SC), buried: Siam, died: 31 Dec 1921, record (1921) #: 228.

Infant ARNET, male, parents: father not given and Nell Arnet, death cause: "stillborn", informant: N.D. Robson (Carter), buried: Arnet Cemetery, born/died: 2 Dec 1921, record (1921) #: 229.

Thomas Allen HART, parents: George L. Hart and Letta M. Morley, death cause: "born dead", buried: Highland Cemetery, born/died: 19 Dec 1921, record (1921) #: 230. (twin above)

Claud WHITEHEAD, born: 30 Dec 1921, parents: Dan Whitehead and Bertha Ward, death cause: not stated, informant: G.L. Whitehead (Hampton), buried: Whitehead Cemetery, died: 2 Jan 1922, record (1922) #: 1.

Robert Earl SHOUN, age 1 month, parents: George Shoun and mother not stated, death cause: "pneumonia", died: 2 Jan 1922, record (1922) #: 2.

Willie Alford MALONE, black, born: 2 Jan 1922 in Johnson City, parents: Willie Malone and Edith Ethel Eloise Malone, death cause: not stated, informant: Alfred Malone (Johnson City), died: 6 Jan 1922, record (1922) #: 3.

Miss Jane HARDIN, born: 8 Jan 1844, single, parents: Ben Treadway and Phebe Hardin, death cause: "asthma, mitral regurgitation", died: 10 Jan 1922, record (1922) #: 4.

Raleigh Ruth FREEMAN, female, born Jan 1919, parents: F.N. Freeman (NC) and Bulah Lines (NC), death cause: "diptheria", informant: Jeter Freeman, buried: Blevins Cemetery, died: 16 Jan 1922, record (1922) #: 5.

Rosa JONES, born: 18 Aug 1885, married, parents: David Wilson and Mary Gragg, death cause: "yellow atrophy", informant: R.J. Jones (Shell Creek), buried: Isaacs Cemetery, died: 16 Jan 1922, record (1922) #: 6.

Moses ESTEP, age 75 years, married, parents: John Estep and Betsy Oliver, death cause: "mitral stenosis", informant: E.K. Campbell (Carter), buried: Estep Cemetery, died: 17 Jan 1922, record (1922) #: 7.

Nancey MCKINNEY, age 90 years, born in Mitchell County, NC, widow, parents: John McKinney (NC) and Nancy Freeman, death cause: not stated, informant: General McKinney (Roan Mountain), died: 18 Jan 1922, record (1922) #: 8.

Dale HAYS, born: 18 Dec 1921, parents: (first name illegible) Hayes and Myrtle Bingham (Vilas, NC), death cause: "unknown", died: 18 Jan 1922, record #: 9.

Rod D. GRINDSTAFF, born: 31 Dec 1921, parents: H.R. Grindstaff and Zillie Greenwell, death cause: not given, informant: Ottis Grindstaff (Carter), buried: Grindstaff Cemetery, died: 20 Jan 1922, record (1922) #: 10. (twin below)

Grace WHITEHEAD, born: 6 Oct 1921, parents: John Whitehead and Oma Johnson (Rigeon Roost, NC), death cause: "found dead in bed", informant: Dan Whitehead (Hampton), buried: Whitehead Cemetery, died: 20 Jan 1922, record (1922) #: 11.

Brownlow Claburn NAVE, born: 12 Dec 1894, married, parents: Joe Nave and Sallie White, death cause: "spinal meningitis", informant: Joe Nave (Elizabethton), buried: Siam, died: 24 Jan 1922, record (1922) #: 12.

Forrest NAVE, age 9 months, parents: Claud Nave and Laura Frasier, death cause: "astro myelitis", buried: Watauga Valley, died: 24 Jan 1922, record #: 13.

Mary Jane SIMERLY, age 62, widow, parents: William Stevens and Mary McKinney, death cause: "hurt from fall, septicocmia", informant: W.A. Simerly (Hampton), buried: Simerly Cemetery, died: 25 Jan 1922, record (1922) #: 14.

Pat D. GRINDSTAFF, born: 31 Dec 1921, parents: U.R. Grindstaff and Zillie Greenwell, death cause: not stated, informant: Ottis Grindstaff (Carter), died: 25 Jan 1922, record (1922) #: 15.

Landon JOHNSON, black, born: 12 Nov 1880, single, parents: Sandy Johnson and Martha Cannon, death cause: "pulmonary tuberculosis", died: 25 Jan 1922, record (1922) #: 16.

Nora C. PETERS, born: 2 Jan 1922, parents: J.W. Peters and Vena Colbaugh, death cause: "spinal meningitis, influenza", buried: Peters Cemetery, died: 27 Jan 1922, record (1922) #: 17.

George Frederick DUGGER, Jr., born: 22 May 1920, parents: T.A. Dugger and Ellen M. Syren (Sweden), death cause: "diptheria", informant: George Dugger (Elizabethton), buried: Highland Cemetery, died: 28 Jan 1922, record (1922) #: 18.

Charles ROBISON, age 50 years, born in Johnson County, married, parents: "unknown", death cause: "gun shot", died: 28 Jan 1922, record (1922) #: 19.

Elizabeth SCALF, born: 24 Feb 1837, married, parents: _____ Foust and Polly Foust, death cause: "mitral insufficiency", informant: William Scalf, died: 28 Jan 1922, record (1922) #: 20.

Ellman ANDREWS, born: 28 Sep 1921, parents: Cliff Andrews and Bell Goodwin, death cause: "unknown", informant: Cliff Andrews (Butler), buried: Cable Cemetery, died: 28 Jan 1922, record (1922) #: 21.
Jennie TESTER, born: 28 Jan 1922, parents: Carl Tester (Watauga Co., NC) and Jennie Ward (Watauga Co., NC), death cause: "premature birth", informant: Carl Tester (Elizabethton), died: 29 Jan 1922, record #: 22.
Annie DAVIS, black, born: 21 Jun 1904, single, parents: Lincoln Davis (NC) and Titia Brown (NC), death cause: "tuberculosis", informant: Link Davis, died: 29 Jan 1922, record (1922) #: 23.
Cruss SHELL, female, parents: George Henry Shell and Maggie Coleman (NC), death cause: "stillborn", informant: Ellen Guinn (midwife), buried: Richardson Cemetery, born/died: 4 Jan 1922, record (1922) #: 24.
Infant NIDIFFER, male, parents: Cecil Nidiffer and Grace Deloach, death cause: "stillborn", buried: Hyder Cemetery, died: 5 Jan 1922, record (1922) #: 25.
Infant CABLE, female, parents: Dayton Cable and Hattie Franklin, death cause: "stillborn", informant: J.S. Cable (Roan Mountain), buried: Stephens Cemetery, died: 6 Jan 1922, record (1922) #: 26.
Infant SHELL, female, parents: Sam Shell and Jane Taylor, death cause: "stillborn", died: 17 Jan 1922, record (1922) #: 27.
David William GREEN, born: 30 Sep 1921, parents: W.H. Green (NC) and Julie Fry, death cause: not stated, informant: W.H. Green (Johnson City), died: 1 Feb 1922, record (1922) #: 28.
Alfred LEWIS, born: 16 Mar 1863, married, parents: Tobias Lewis and Edith Livingston, death cause: "influenza", informant: W.H.K. Humphreys (Valley Forge), buried: Smith Cemetery, died: 1 Feb 1922, record (1922) #: 29.
D. Porter LACY, born: 18 Oct 1875, parents: W.S. Lacy and Jennie Lyons, death cause: "streptococ infection", informant: George Lacy (Elizabethton), buried: Highland Cem., died: 5 Feb 1922, record (1922) #: 30.
Ida Lou GWYN, born: 29 Dec 1921, parents: Warney Gwyn (NC) and Zilla Williams, death cause: "influenza", buried: Valley Forge, died: 7 Feb 1922, record #: 31.
Margerie Angeline SCALF, born: 11 Feb 1922, parents: father not stated and Dunie Scalf, death cause: "unknown", informant: Mrs. Angeline Scalf (Elizabethton), buried: Highland Cemetery, died: 11 Feb 1922, record (1922) #: 32.

Margaret DELOACH, born: 7 Aug 1863, married, parents: John Williams and Vice Oliver, death cause: "flue and pneumonia fever", informant: James Deloach (Elizabethton), buried: Hyder Cemetery, died: 11 Feb 1922, record (1922) #: 33.
Sarah COMBS, age 81 years, married, parents: Caleb Morrell and ____ Crow, died: 11 Feb 1922, record (1922) #: 34.
Harry HATHAWAY, Jr., born: 26 Dec 1918, parents: Harry Hathaway and Alice Lacy, death cause: "dyptheria", died: 11 Feb 1922, record (1922) #: 35.
Bate EMMITT, age 29 years, parents: Bill Emmitt and Martha Dugger, death cause: "influenza, pneumonia", died: 16 Feb 1922, record (1922) #: 36.
Nancy GARLAND, age 39 years, married, parents: Mufer Hurley and Ruthey Estep, death cause: not stated, informant: W.L. Nidiffer (Carter), buried: Garland Cemetery, died: 16 Feb 1922, record (1922) #: 37.
Annie LEWIS, born: 10 Dec 1836, widow, parents: George M. Pierce and Jenne Campbell, death cause: "unknown", informant: Ben Butler (Butler), buried: Teaster Cemetery, died: 17 Feb 1922, record (1922) #: 38.
David BROOKS, black, age 78 years, born in North Carolina, married, parents: "unknown", death cause: "cerebral hemorrhage", died: 19 Feb 1922, record: 39.
Fred CAMPBELL, born: 27 Jan 1921, parents: Jim Campbell and Ethel Pierce, death cause: "influenza and pneumonia", informant: Robert Berry (Butler), buried: Pierce Cem., died: 22 Feb 1922, record (1922) #: 40.
William Walter LAMBERT, born: 8 Oct 1862 in Georgia, married, parents: William Lambert (GA) and Evelyn Henry (GA), death cause: "paraphegia", informant: Ruth J. Lambert (Hampton), died: 22 Feb 1922, record #: 41.
John F. SHELTON, age 71 years, born in Wythe County, VA, married, parents: "unknown", death cause: "organic heart disease", informant: R.S. Houston (Watauga), buried: Mottern Cem., died: 23 Feb 1922, record #: 42.
Infant HICKS, male, parents: Charlie Hicks and Alice Henson, death cause: "abortion", informant: Charlie Hicks (Butler), died: 18 Feb 1922, record #: 43.
Infant NUSH, black, male, parents: Carl Nush (Alabama) and Lillie Gardner, death cause: "born dead", born/died: 22 Feb 1922, record (1922) #: 44.
Francis LINDAWOOD, age 24 years, 5 months and 2 days, married, parents: E.C. Grant (NC) and mother's name illegible, death cause: "burns caused by falling in fire during epileptic seizure", informant: John Lindawood (Eliz.), died: 2 Mar 1922, record #: 45.

Dela ARWOOD, age 36 years, married, parents: James Clark (NC) and Jane Cochran, death cause: "pneumonia", informant: John Berry (Hampton), buried: Fair View Cemetery, died: 3 Mar 1922, record (1922) #: 46.

Rena RED, black, age 70 years, born in Ashe County, NC, parents: Joe Bowers (NC) and Malinda Harless (NC), death cause: "pellegra", informant: Walter Red (Johnson City), buried: Horton Cemetery, died: 4 Mar 1922, record (1922) #: 27.

Rosa K. STREET, born: 15 Jun 1899 in Mitchell County, NC, married, parents: A.K. Knight (Ashe Co., NC) and Susan Cox (Ashe Co., NC), death cause: "suicide act with shot gun, tetnas infection", informant: J.F. Julian (Roan Mountain), died: 4 Mar 1922, record (1922) #: 48.

Nellie HOPSON, born: 29 Nov 1920, parents: George Hopson and Rosa Sheppard (NC), death cause: "pneumonia fever", informant: George Hopson (Shell Creek), died: 7 Mar 1922, record (1922) #: 49.

Susanah WILLIAMS, born: 10 Nov 1864, widow, parents: Alex Matherly and Jane Sims, death cause: "stroke, blood poison and septic fever", buried: Sims Cemetery, died: 7 Mar 1922, record (1922) #: 50.

Lena COLLINS, age 27 years, married, parents: Richard Jenkins and ____ Oliver, death cause: "influenza and pneumonia", informant: A.R. Collins (Watauga Valley), died: 7 Mar 1922, record (1922) #: 51.

Robert L. COMBS, born: 10 Apr 1866 in Bluff City, married, parents: William Combs (Bluff City) and Phoebe Little (Bluff City), death cause: "influenza and heppititis", informant: John Mockley (Roan Mountain), died: 9 Mar 1922, record (1922) #: 52.

Glades M. VONCANAN, born: 8 Oct 1921, parents: A.F. Voncanan and S.J. Miller, death cause: "unknown", buried: Elk Mills, died: 9 Mar 1922, record #: 53.

Nellie BUCHANAN, born: 29 Apr 1908, parents: James Buchanan (NC) and Pheby Miller, death cause: "influenza", informant: Creet Perkins, buried: Richardson Cem., died: 10 Mar 1922, record #: 54.

Hobart VINES, born: 10 Jun 1900, married, parents: (illegible) Vines and Celia Griffith, death cause: "influenza and pulmonary tuberculosis", informant: Dan Potter (Hampton), buried: Johnson Cemetery, died: 10 Mar 1922, record (1922) #: 55.

Janita Litta ANDISE, born: 9 Mar 1922, parents: David Stout and Ida Andise, death cause: "unknown", informant: David Stout (Butler), buried: Poga, died: 14 Mar 1922, record (1922) #: 46.

Mrs. Jessie Brummitt BAKER, born: 26 Aug 1883, married, parents: A.B. Brummit and Jane Irick (Washington County), death cause: "flu and lobar pneumonia", informant: A.B. Brummit (Elizabethton), buried: Highland Cemetery, died: 17 Mar 1922, record (1922) #: 57.
John Hubid HOLOWAY, born: 6 Feb 1922, parents: Paul Holloway and Ola Rainbolt, death cause: "not known", informant: D.E. Holoway (Butler), buried: Stallings Cemetery, died: 19 Mar 1922, record (1922) #: 58. (twin below)
Ida GARLAND, born: 19 Mar 1916, parents: John Garland and Verdie Elliott, death cause: "scarlet fever and diptheria", informant: L.M. Vines (Valley Forge), buried: Smith Cem., died: 19 Mar 1922, record #: 59.
Erven Hubert HOLOWAY, born: 6 Feb 1922, parents: Paul Holloway and Ola Rainbolt, death cause: "not known", informant: D.E. Holoway (Butler), buried: Stallings Cemetery, died: 24 Mar 1922, record (1922) #: 60. (twin above)
Wiley PRICE, born: 20 Mar 1875 in North Carolina, married, parents: John Price (NC) and mother not known, death cause: "tuberculosis", informant: Amos Price (Fish Springs), died: 24 Mar 1922, record #: 61.
Caroline CAMPBELL, born: 15 Apr 1860, married, parents: Lawson Hamby and mother's name not known, death cause: "pulmonary tuberculosis", informant: Jerry Campbell (Fish Springs), died: 26 Mar 1922, record (1922) #: 62.
Ganus W. RENFRO, born: 11 Aug 1890, married, parents: James Renfro and Emma Brown, death cause: "disease of heart", informant: C.C. Hacker (Elizabethton), died: 26 Mar 1922, record (1922) #: 63.
Robert SNODGRASS, born: 10 Mar 1921, parents: Bob Taylor Snodgrass and Bernico Burnett, death cause: "acute disease of heart", informant: James Brumitt (Elizabethton), buried: Highland Cemetery, died: 26 Mar 1922, record (1922) #: 64.
Frank CAMPBELL, born: 4 Aug 1861 in "Elexander" County, married, parents: Bentley Campbell ("Elexander" Co.) and ____ Vestie ("Elexander" Co.), death cause: not stated, informant: C.W. Julian (Roan Mountain), died: 24 Mar 1922, record (1922) #: 65.
Henry BUTLER, born: 10 Oct 1939 in Mitchell County, NC, parents: (first name illegible(Dyer Butler (Mitchell Co., NC) and mother's name unknown, death cause: not stated, informant: H. Street (Roan Mountain), died: 28 Mar 1922, record (1922) #: 66.

Alvin P. HARDIN, born: 14 Oct 1840, married, parents: John N. Hardin and Mary Fletcher, death cause: "influenza and pneumonia". informant: Frank Hardin (Watauga Valley), buried: Colbaugh Cemetery, died: 30 Mar 1922, record (1922) #: 67.

Emmit OLIVER, born: 4 Nov 1899, single, parents: Lee Oliver and Adeline Campbell, death cause: "pulmonary tuberculosis", informant: Mary Ratterman (Elizabethton), buried: Blue Springs, died: 31 Mar 1922, record (1922) #: 68.

David HINKLE, born: 10 Mar 1845, married, parents: John Hinkle and mother's name not known, death cause: "pulmonary tuberculosis", informant: Stacy Hinkle (Roan Mtn), died: 31 Mar 1922, record (1922) #: 69.

Infant MCKINNEY, male, parents: Sam S. McKinney (NC) and Rebecca Knight (NC), death cause: "stillborn", buried: Heaton Creek, died: 21 Mar 1922, record (1922) #: 70.

Virginia Ray TIPTON, age 7 days, parents: Walter P. Tipton and Ollie Mae Kun, death cause: "bold hives, buried: Gap Creek, died: 1 Apr 1922, record #: 71.

James Lace WILLIS, born: 8 Sep 1920, parents: W.M.R. Willis (NC) and Nancy An Tolley, death cause: "bowl hives", informant: Daniel Tolley (Hampton), buried: Clark Cemetery, died: 4 Apr 1922, record (1922) #: 72.

Ellen STOVER, black, age 82 years and 3 months, married, parents: Bob Jobe (NC) and Jane (surname illegible), death cause: "gall stones", informant: Will Stover (Elizabethton), buried: Drake Cemetery, died: 10 Apr 1922, record (1922) #: 73.

Linda MORGAN, age 33 years, widow, parents: Noah Potter and Annie Maise (Wilkes County, NC), death cause: "birth bed fever", informant: D.H. Potter (Dark Ridge, NC), buried: Potter Cemetery, died: 12 Apr 1922, record (1922) #: 74.

Rebecca McNeese ROBERTS, age about 68 years, born in Washington County, married, parents: Eli McNeese and mother's name not known, death cause: "tuberculosis", died: 25 Apr 1922, record (1922) #: 75.

Nathaniel SMITH, born: 16 Feb 1846, widower, parents: Nick Smith (KY) and Sallie Smith (KY), death cause: "uremia and nephritis", informant: Ed Smith (Roan Moutain), died: 22 Apr 1922, record (1922) #: 76.

Derkis CAMPBELL, female, born: 18 Jul 1894, married, parents: father not stated and Cynthia Clemons, death cause: "tuberculosis", informant: J.I. Campbell (Hampton), buried: Campbell Cemetery, died: 23 Apr 1922, record (1922) #: 77.

Jim ROYAL, born: 8 Jan 1917, parents: Vance Royal (NC) and (illegible) Wright, death cause: "croup", informant: H. Street (Roan Mountain), died: 23 Apr 1922, record (1922) #: 78.

Elila LEWIS, born: 9 Mar 1919, parents: father not stated and Hildred Lewis, death cause: "pnuemonia", informant: Will Lewis (Butler), buried: Whitehead Cemetery, died: 24 Apr 1922, record (1922) #: 79.

Dodge VIALL, age 70 years, 2 months and 18 days, born in Pennsylvania, married, parents: Frank Viall (PA) and Sallie Dodge (PA), death cause: "mitral regurgitation of heart", informant: Mrs. Arthur N. Edens (Elizabethton), died: 24 Apr 1922, record (1922) #: 80.

Lizzie Pearl JENKINS, born: 1 Apr 1922, parents: Vanie Jenkins and Annie Canon, death cause: "bold hives", informant: Dick Jenkins (Watauga Valley), buried: Wilson Cem., died: 25 Apr 1922, record (1922) #: 81.

Wiley WATSON, colored, age 62 years, 4 months and 22 days, born in North Carolina, married, parents: Wiley Watson (NC) and Rhoda Owens (NC), death cause: "pulmonary tuberculosis", died: 27 Apr 1922, record (1922) #: 82.

William Lafayette HOLSCLAW, born: 9 May 1841 in Mitchell County, NC, widower, parents: William Holsclaw (Watauga Co., NC) and Susan Smith, death cause: "chronic cirosis of liver", informant: J.W. Holsclaw (Roan Mountain), buried: Elk Park, NC, died: 28 Apr 1922, record (1922) #: 83.

Myrtle PAYNE, age 9 years, parents: Frank Payne and Willie Forbes, death cause: "tuberculosis", informant: Willie Forbes Payne (Johnson City), buried: Payne Cemetery, died: 28 Apr 1922, record (1922) #: 84.

John Folsom NAVE, parents: John D. Nave and Kittie Folsom, death cause: "stillborn", born/died: 3 Apr 1922, record (1922) #: 85.

Infant WILLIAMS, male, parents: Jess Williams and Maggie Wilson, death cause: "stillborn", buried: Blue Springs, died: 16 Apr 1922, record (1922) #: 86.

Edward SMITH, parents: Bruce Smith and Celia Griffith, death cause: "stillborn", informant: Bruce Smith (Fish Springs), buried: Smith Cemetery, born/died: 27 Apr 1922, record (1922) #: 87.

Jossie STREET, age 30 years, married, parents: B.G. Hyder and Beckie Street, death cause: "tuberculosis", informant: Ike Street (Hampton), buried: Hyder Cemetery, died: 5 May 1922, record (1922) #: 88.

Wilford WINTERS, born: 26 Apr 1915, parents: John Winters and Tish Latham (NC), death cause: "tuberculosis and mastoid abscess", informant: John Miller (Shell Creek), died: 5 May 1922, record (1922) #: 89.

Lee [editorial remark: Levi] CROW, born: 27 Apr 1848, married, parents: Isaac Crow and Elizabeth [editorial remark: Hart] Crow, death cause: "nephritis, mitral regurgitation", informant: Ebb Manning, buried: Highland Cem., died: 7 May 1922, record (1922) #: 90.

Emmer HOPSON, female, born: 4 Feb 1867, married, parents: Wilby Morgan and Lessie Elliott, death cause: "carcinoma of woumb", informant: Harris Hopson (Shell Creek), buried: Harrison Cemetery, died; 8 May 1922, record (1922) #: 91.

Samuel M. SMALLING, age 65 years, born in Monroe County, TN, widower, parents: not stated, death cause: "apoplexy", died; 10 May 1922, record (1922) #: 92.

Nancy J. SHELL, born: 13 Oct 1842, married, parents: Mike Grindstaff and Sallie Chambers, death cause: "chronic nephritis", informant: C.A. Jackson (Hampton), buried: Hall Cemetery, died: 11 Apr 1922, record (1922) #: 93.

Lurly TOLLEY, age 1 year and 1 month, parents: Lace Tolley and Bell Stevens, death cause: "diarrhoea", informant: Jackson Tolley (Roan Mountain), buried: Tolley Cem., died: 15 May 1922, record (1922) #: 94.

William Smith LEWIS, born: 27 Sep 1860, married, parents: Lawson Lewis and Isabel Campbell, death cause: "pneumonia and hanging self with rope", informant: Sam J. Carden, buried: Cardens Bluff, died: 21 May 1922, record (1922) #: 95.

Fitzhue SHELL, age 3 months, parents: John Shell and Tessie Harvey, death cause: "cholera", buried: Little Cem., Watauga, died: 22 May 1922, record (1922) #: 96.

Samuel WHITEHEAD, age 22 years, married, parents: William Whitehead and Sarah Jane Hopson, death cause: "shot by shot gun, killed instantly", informant: Willie Morgan (Roan Mountain", buried: Nelson Cemetery, died: 25 May 1922, record (1922) #: 97.

Lester FAIR, parents: Non Fair and Etta Roe, death cause: "stillborn", informant: J.E. Campbell (Elizabethton), buried: Highland Cemetery, died: 21 May 1922, record (1922) #: 98. (twin below)

Bessie FAIR, parents: Non Fair and Etta Roe, death cause: "stillborn", informant: J.E. Campbell (Elizabethton), buried: Highland Cemetery, died: 21 May 1922, record (1922) #: 99. (twin above)

Simon HODGE, age 90 years, parents: father said to be Isaac Garland and Nancy Hodge, death cause: not stated, buried: Garland Cemetery, died: 3 Jun 1922, record (1922) #: 100.

E. GUINN, born: 20 May 1922, parents: Worley Guinn and Myrtle Julian, death cause: not stated, informant: Worley Guinn (Roan Mountain), buried: Crabtree, died: 4 Jun 1922, record (1922) #: 101.

Lizzie FAIR, age 22 years, single, parents: Bill Fair and Addie Greenway, death cause: "pulmonary tuberculosis", died: 4 Jun 1922, record (1922) #: 102.

Joseph FISHER, born: 12 May 1853 in North Carolina, married, parents: Thomas Fisher (NC) and Pollie Dockrey (NC), death cause: "girgous appendix", informant: Mrs. Joseph Fisher (Elizabethton), buried: Colbaugh Cem., died: 5 Jun 1922, record (1922) #: 103.

Clyde Henry JONES, born: 5 Jun 1922, parents: Walter Jones and Mamie Oaks, death cause: not stated, informant: Robert Jones, Jr. (Shell Creek), buried: Jones Cem., died: 7 Jun 1922, record (1922) #: 104.

Jane MICHAELS, born: 9 May 1844, widow, parents: John Icenhour (Baker Co., NC) and Margaret Icenhour (Coker Co., NC), death cause: "flue and perralies", informant: Guss Michals (Elizabethton), buried: Heaton Creek, died: 8 Jun 1922, record (1922) #: 105.

James WALSH, age about 59 years, said to be born in Georgia, married, parents: "unknown", death cause: "suicide by shooting", informant: Mr. Isaacs (Braemar), died: 9 Jun 1922, record (1922) #: 106.

Mollie HEATON, born: 10 Jul 1858, married, parents: Don Vance and Lucy Street (NC), death cause: "acute cardiac dilitation", informant; Mrs. M.F. Miller (Elizabethton), buried: Roan Mountain, died: 10 Jul 1922, record (1922) #: 107.

William CROW, born: 10 Jan 1881, married, parents: Tennessee Crow and Hester Bowers, death cause: "asthma", buried: Crow Cemetery, died: 11 Jun 1922, record (1922) #: 108.

H.F. SHELL, born: 10 Jun 1829, married, parents: David Shell (NC) and Pollie Miller (NC), death cause: "old age", informant: William H. Shell (Shell Creek), buried: Richardson Cemetery, died: 17 Jun 1922, record (1922) #: 109.

Gladys FAIR, parents: John H. Fair and Nina Bell Blackburn, death cause: "premature birth", informant: James H. Fair (Elizabethton), buried; Hyder Cemetery, born/died: 17 Jun 1922, record (1922) #: 110.

C.C. TAYLOR, age 77 years, widower, parents: C.C. Taylor and Nancy Duncan, death cause: "cerebral hemorrhage and paralysis", buried: Milligan Cemetery, died: 18 Jun 1922, record (1922) #: 111.

Larkin TOWNSEND, age about 89 years, born in Watauga County, NC, married, parents: Peter Townsend (NC) and Sallie Mitchell (NC), death cause: "cerebral hemorrhage", informant: R.L. Hodge (Elizabethton), buried: Banner Elk, NC, died: 21 Jun 1922, record (1922) #: 112.

Mary Jane PRICE, born: 17 Sep 1860, born in Virginia, widow, parents: G. Perkins (VA) and Rosan Prichard (VA), death cause: "angina pectoris", informant: John C. Price (Johnson City), died: 24 Jun 1922, record (1922) #: 113.

William W. TEAGUE, born: 16 Jul 1866 in Catawba County, NC, married, parents: Logan Teague (NC) and mother not stated, death cause: "apoplexy", informant: R.A. Teague (Hampton), buried: Hall Cemetery, died: 26 Jun 1922, record (1922) #: 114.

Infant HURT, female, parents: Will Hurt (NC) and Nora Edney, death cause: not stated, informant: John Edney (Shell Creek), buried: Richardson Cemetery, born/died: 27 Jun 1922, record (1922) #: 115.

Leona G. PRICE, born: 19 Feb 1919, parents: Allen Price and Victoria Taylor, death cause: "scalded by boiling water", informant: Victoria Pierce (Carter), buried: Blevins Cem., died: 29 Jun 1922, record: 116.

Robert MCCLOUD, born: 4 Mar 1886 in Johnson County, single, parents: James McCloud (Johnson County) and Mary Walker (Johnson County), death cause: "tuberculosis", buried: Cobbs Creek, died: 30 Jun 1922, record (1922) #: 117.

Infant KYTE, male, parents: William Kyte and Lina Treadway, death cause: "stillborn", born/died: 7 Jun 1922, record (1922) #: 118.

Bonnie BLEVINS, parents: Alfred Blevins and Mattie Shell, death cause: "stillborn", buried: Campbell Cem., born/died: 25 Jun 1922, record (1922) #: 119.

Mary BOWERS, age 81 years and 8 months, widow, parents: Daniel S. Bowers and ____ Brown, death cause: not stated, informant: Mike G. Williams (Watauga Valley), died: 2 Jul 1922, record (1922) #: 120.

R.G. PETERS, Jr., born: 22 Jun 1922, parents: Robert G. Peters and Florence Pardue, death cause: "jaundice", informant: Hattie Grindstaff (Carter), buried: Grindstaff Cemetery, died: 5 Jul 1922, record (1922) #: 121.

Susan STOVER, colored, born: 5 Oct 1845, married, parents: Mack Humphrey and Susan Taylor, death cause: "apoplexy", buried: Milligan, died: 6 Jul 1922, record (1922) #: 122.

Rebecca FAIR, age 60 years, widow, parents: David Ritchie and Jane Creed, death cause: "consumption", informant: A.B. Ritchie (Watauga Valley), buried: Ritchie Cem., died: 7 Jul 1922, record (1922) #: 123.

Ellen JOHNSON, born: 10 Feb 1922, parents: Carrier Johnson and Laura Wilson, death cause: "unknown", informant: John Johnson (Roan Mountain), died: 10 Jul 1922, record (1922) #: 124.

Rev. David F. SMITH, born: 14 Feb 1875, married, parents: W.T. Smith (VA) and Julia Moody, death cause: "intestinal tuberculosis", informant: Mrs. Anna Belle Jones (Unicoi), buried: Hemlock, TN, died: 10 Jul 1922, record (1922) #: 125.

Almetta Rosabeth HARTLEY, born: 1 Jul 1875 in North Carolina, married, parents: Valentine Reese (NC) and Allie Blair (NV), death cause: "acute pertonitis, cancerous condition", informant: Dr. Hartley, buried: Holston Valley, died: 10 Jul 1922, record #: 126.

Paul LYONS, born: 15 Oct 1921, parents: John Lyons and Jane Glover, death cause: "colra", informant: Sam Lyons (Elizabethton), buried: McKeehan Cemetery, died: 15 Jul 1922, record (1922) #: 127.

Emma Celeste COLE, parents: S.S. Cole (Johnson County) and Eva A. Cole, death cause: "premature birth", buried: Milligan Cemetery, born/died: 15 Jul 1922, record (1922) #: 128.

Mrs. Mary CANTER, age about 62 years, born in North Carolina, widow, death cause: "acute kidney disorder, valvulor leison of heart", informant: Jessie Canter, buried: Treadway Cemetery, died: 16 Jul 1922, record (1922) #: 129.

Nat WALKER, age 26 years, married, parents: Canada Walker and Nancie Lyons, death cause: "pulmonary tuberculosis", informant: Will Loveless (Elizabethton), buried: McKeehan Cemetery, died: 16 Jul 1922, record (1922) #: 130.

Infant MORGAN, male, born: 12 Apr 1922, parents: father not given and Linda Morgan, death cause: "disformitory", informant: Caric Potter (Dark Ridge, NC), buried: Poga, died: 17 Aug 1922, record #: 131.

Hugh JENKINS, born: Mar 1828, widower, parents: Jesse Jenkins and Eliza Nave, death cause: "cerebral hemorrhage", informant: J.W. Headrick (Valley Forge), died: 17 Jul 1922, record (1922) #: 132.

Evline CHAMBERS, age 72 years, born in North Carolina, parents: not stated, death cause: "paralysis", informant: Nat Blevins (Roan Mountain), buried: Blevins Cem., died: 23 Jul 1922, record (1922) #: 133.
Wanatie ESTEP, age 14 days, parents: Levi Estep and Miley Richardson, death cause: not stated, informant: Levi Estep (Carter), buried: Heatherly Cemetery, died: 24 Jul 1922, record (1922) #: 134.
Lottie Peters DAVIDSON, born: 28 Jan 1899, married, parents: Will Peters and Emma Ferguson, death cause: "pulmonary tuberculosis", informant: Carl Davidson (Elizabethton), died: 28 Jul 1922, record #: 135.
N.D. RAMBO, born: 10 Feb 1922, parents: J.W. Rambo and Zillie Robinson, death cause: "broncho pneumonia", buried: Blevins Cemetery, died: 31 Jul 1922, record (1922) #: 136.
Mable BLEVINS, born: 28 Apr 1905, married, parents: Joe Shull and Maggie Fair, death cause: "typhoid fever", informant: Joe Shull (Hampton), buried: Campbell Cem, died: 31 Jul 1922, record (1922) #: 137.
Infant HYDER, female, parents: Lon T. Hyder and Nannie A. Treadway, death cause: "stillborn", informant: Lon T. Hyder (Valley Forge), buried: Little Cemetery, born/died: 11 Jun 1922, record (1922) #: 138.
Martha Catherine GOURLEY, parents: R.N. Gourley and Blanch Ferguson, death cause: "stillborn", born/died: 27 Jul 1922, record (1922) #: 139.
George W. CLARK, born: 20 Dec 1863, married, parents: Thomas Clark and ____ Williams, death cause: "heart block", buried: Mcewen Cemetery, died: 2 Aug 1922, record (1922) #: 140.
Malinda MELIM, black, age about 85 years, widow, parents: Jasper Taylor and Lena Taylor (SC), death cause: not stated, buried: Cedar Grove Cemetery, died: 3 Aug 1922, record (1922) #: 141.
Bessie Ann LITTLE, born: 15 Jul 1888, married, parents: Lewis Persinger (VA) and Elizabeth Campbell, death cause: "acute apendicitis", buried: Mottern Cemetery, died: 3 Aug 1922, record (1922) #: 142.
Susan GARLAND, age 90 years, born in North Carolina, widow, parents: Aaron Wright (NC) and Polly Briggs (NC), death cause: "paralysis", informant: Tennessee Blevins (Roan Mountain), buried: Blevins Cemetery, died: 5 Aug 1922, record (1922) #: 143.
Cassie HARMON, born: 7 Aug 1921, parents: Galher Harmon and Ada Green (NC), death cause: "unknown", informant: Henry Clawson (Dark Ridge, NC), buried: Green Cem. died: 8 Aug 1922, record (1922) #: 144.

Cassie HARMON, born: 7 Aug 1921, parents: Gaither Harmon and Ada Green (Watauga Co., NC), death cause: "unknown", informant: Henry Clauson (Dark Ridge, NC), buried: Flat Springs, died: 8 Aug 1922, record (1922) #: 145. (this record appears to be a duplicate)

Wilford McTaylor SUMMERLAND, born: 25 May 1905, parents: M.F. Summerland and Dora Reece, death cause: "abscess appendix, peritonitis", buried: Highland Cemetery, died: 10 Aug 1922, record (1922) #: 146.

W.N. SIMERLY, born: 13 Dec 1883, married, parents: John Simerly and M.J. Stevens, death cause: "accident on wagon, dislocation of vertabrae column", informant: J.B. Simerly (Hampton), buried: Simerly Cemetery, died: 15 Aug 1922, record (1922) #: 147.

A.J. TAYLOR, born: 11 Nov 1855, widower, parents: William Taylor and Susis Taylor, death cause: "hernia", informant: J.E. Taylor (Carter), buried: Taylor Cem., died: 16 Aug 1922, record (1922) #: 148.

Thomas MCELYEA, born: 22 Dec 1908, parents: Roy McElyea and Elizabeth Holsclaw (NC), death cause: "typhoid fever", informant: Roy McElyea (Elizabethton), buried: Maymead, TN, died: 16 Aug 1922, record (1922) #: 149.

Mattie Mays CROW, born: 18 Mar 1880, married, parents: Frank Mays and mother not stated, death cause: "opticemia", informant: E.E. Morris, buried: Newton Cemetery, died: 17 Aug 1922, record (1922) #: 150.

Elizabeth DUGGER, age about 70 years, married, parents: Morgan Treadway and May Pugh, death cause: "apoplexy", informant: Tom Dugger (Elizabethton), buried: Hyder Cemetery, died: 19 Aug 1922, record (1922) #: 151.

Ellar GREENLEE, colored, female, born: 11 Apr 1869 in Georgia, parents: illegible, death cause: "tuberculosis", informant: John Greenlee (Shell Creek), buried: North Carolina, died: 21 Aug 1922, record (1922) #: 152.

Lillie DENNIS, born: 19 Oct 1921, parents: Frank Dennis (NC) and Rosa Price (NC), death cause: "unknown", buried: Fish Springs, died: 23 Aug 1922, record (1922) #: 153.

Eva Kate BLEVINS, born: 7 Mar 1921, parents: James F. Blevins and Sallie Massengill, death cause: "diptheria", informant: J.F. Blevins (Elizabethton), buried: Blevins Cemetery, died: 27 Aug 1922, record (1922) #: 154.

Jesse FORBES, born: May 1914, parents: John Forbes (Mitchell Co., NC) and Lydia Arrowood (Mitchell Co., NC), death cause: "diptheria", informant: Robert Forbes (Buladeen, NC), died: 24 Aug 1922, record (1922) #: 155.

Infant BRYANT, male, born: 10 Aug 1922, parents: Nat Bryant (VA) and Lydia Lyons, death cause: "stillborn", informant: Jim Lyons (Elizabethton), buried: Lyons Cemetery, born/died: 15 Aug 1922, record (1922) #: 156. (twin below)

Infant BRYANT, male, born: 10 Aug 1922, parents: Nat Bryant (VA) and Lydia Lyons, death cause: "stillborn", informant: Jim Lyons (Elizabethton), buried: Lyons Cemetery, born/died: 15 Aug 1922, record (1922) #: 157. (twin above)

Dana MOODY, Jr., Dana Moody and Ira Minton, death cause: "stillborn", born/died: 17 Aug 1922, record (1922) #: 158.

J.J. CABLE, born: 17 Dec 1862, married, parents: Peter B. Cable and Mary Dunkin (VA), death cause: "heart failure", informant: McKinley Cable (Butler), buried: Cable Cem., died: 5 Sep 1922, record (1922) #: 159.

Sarra Taylor RIGGS, born: 29 Aug 1855, widow, parents: Cas Taylor and Delciena Hendrix, death cause: "cardiac dropsy", informant: R.J. Riggs (Elizabethton), buried: Colbaugh Cem., died: 7 Sep 1922, record (1922) #: 160.

Rebecca VANHUSS, born: 2 Jan 1834 in Washington County, widow, parents: Mathias Nead and Barbara Rhodi, death cause: "dropsy and old age", informant: Mrs. W.H. Chambers (Elizabethton), buried: Siam, died: 11 Sep 1922, record (1922) #: 161.

Sarrah Edna HODGE, born: 8 May 1856 in Johnson County, widow, parents: John M. Stout and H. Ellen Wilson, death cause: "unknown", informant: C.C. Stalcup (Shell Creek), buried: Tolley Cemetery, died: 11 Sep 1922, record (1922) #: 162.

Mary E. GRINDSTAFF, born: 17 Sep 1870, married, parents: Thomas H. Wilson and Sarah Grindstaff, death cause: "typhoid fever", informant: H.H. Grindstaff (Watauga Valley), buried: Ritchie Cemetery, died: 12 Sep 1922, record (1922) #: 163.

Louise Hyder WILLIAMS, born: 7 Aug 1867, married, parents: Marion Hyder and Martha Gourley, death cause: "intestinal tuberculosis", informant: L.S. Williams (Hampton), buried: Sorrell Cemetery, died: 18 Sep 1922, record (1922) #: 164.

George Edward HAWKINS, born: 8 Sep 1914, parents: Thomas H. Hawkins (Johnson County) and Minnie Minton, death cause: "flux", informant: Thomas H. Hawkins (Elizabethton), buried: Colbaugh Cemetery, died: 21 Sep 1922, record (1922) #: 165.

Rev. J.J. COLE, born: 19 Jul 1843, married, parents: Benjamin Cole and Dillie Loyd, death cause: "mitral insufficiency and hydro sericarditis", informant: W.J. Cole (Carter), buried: Ritchie Cemetery, died: 21 Sep 1922, record (1922) #: 166.

Edna M. FRAZIER, age 64 years, 10 months and 29 days, born in Washington County, TN, widow, parents: "unknown", death cause: "consumption", died: 23 Sep 1922, record (1922) #: 167.

William E. MORRELL, born: 2 Sep 1852, married, parents: John Morrell and Elizabeth Mottern, death cause: "organic heart disease", resided at Watauga, died: 26 Sep 1922, record (1922) #: 168.

Thomas M. MORRELL, born: 1 May 1850 in Sullivan County, married, parents: Caleb Morrell and Vicey Crow, death cause: "asthma and broncho pneumonia", informant: R.S. Lacey (Hopson), buried: Lacey Cemetery, died: 27 Sep 1922, record (1922) #: 169.

Shelly Searcy JETT, born: 24 Jun 1873 in Kentucky, married, parents: Stephen Jett (KY) and Anna Searcy (KY), death cause: "apoplexy and kidney disease", informant: Anna Jett (Elizabethton), buried: Highland Cemetery, died: 30 Sep 1922, record (1922) #: 170.

Delia POTTER, parents: Lon Potter and Bertha Birchifeld, death cause: "stillborn", informant: T.A. Hardin (Hampton), buried: Chambers Cemetery, died: 3 Sep 1922, record (1922) #: 171.

Infant WHISTENHUNT, male, parents: Joe Whistenhunt and Eva Swanner, death cause: "stillborn", informant: Hanner McClean (Roan Mountain), buried: Blevins Cemetery, died: 15 Sep 1922, record (1922) #: 172.

Infant MOTTERN, female, parents: William J. Mottern and Carrie Mottern, death cause: "stillborn", born/died: 17 Sep 1922, record (1922) #: 173.

Floe SIMERLY, female, parents: R.S. Simerly and Celia Whitehead, death cause: "stillborn", informant: R.S. Simerly (Hampton), buried: Whitehead Cemetery, died: 26 Sep 1922, record (1922) #: 174.

Donnie WILSON, female, age 19 years, parents: Z.N. Wilson and Laura Hinkle, death cause: "possibly tuberculosis", buried: Wilson Cemetery, died: 2 Oct 1922, record (1922) #: 175.

Infant SMITH, female, born: 30 Sep 1922, parents: Houston Smith and Oka Gentry, death cause: "unknown", informant: Hobart Smith (Carden Bluff), died: 3 Oct 1922, record (1922) #: 176.

Lola Maud RICHARDS, born: 1 Mar 1896 in North Carolina, married, parents: Leonard C. Wilson (Tracy, NC) and Julia E. Farthing (Sweetwater, NC), death cause: "supticomia", buried in North Carolina, died: 7 Oct 1922, record (1922) #: 177.

Thurman M. LITTLE, born: 20 Dec 1920, parents: A.R. Little and Mag Hather, death cause: "influenza", informant: Thomas Little (Elizabethton), buried: Little Cem., died: 13 Oct 1922, record (1922) #: 178.

Warren WALLACE, age 2 years, parents: Luther Wallace and Lillie Stephens, death cause: "child burned by catching fire when striking match", informant: C.C. McKinney (Hampton), buried: Stephens Cemetery, died: 16 Oct 1922, record (1922) #: 179.

Thelma STEPHENS, born: Jun 1920 in Seward, Ohio, parents: Willie Stephens and Sallie McKinney, death cause: "dipheria", informant: Florida Stephens (Hampton), buried: Stevens Cemetery, died: 18 Oct 1922, record (1922) #: 180.

George GOUGE, born: 18 Oct 1922, parents: Fletcher Gouge and Ethel Stevens, death cause: "not borned at full term", informant: Leneer Willis (Roan Mountain), buried: Blevins Cemetery, died: 17 Oct 1922, record (1922) #: 181.

Ruth HALL, born: 8 May 1875, married, parents: Henry Presnell (NC) and Jane Smith, death cause: "pellegra and mitral regurgitation of heart", informant: E.S. Hall (Hampton), buried: Hall Cemetery, died: 19 Oct 1922, record (1922) #: 182.

Dora TOLLEY, born: 20 Jun 1922, parents: L.M. Tolley and Lodinia Tolley, death cause: "meningitis", informant: Charlie Tolley (Hampton), buried: Tolley Cemetery, died: 20 Oct 1922, record (1922) #: 183.

Elizabeth Clark ROWE, born: 14 May 1877 in Washington County, TN, parents: James L. Clark (Washington County) and Rebecca E. (surname illegible), informant: L.L. Rowe (Johnson City), buried: Rowe Cemetery, died: 21 Oct 1922, record (1922) #: 184.

David R. FINE, born: 7 May 1874 in Washington County, parents: Nina Fine (Washington County) and Mary E. Swanner (Washington County), death cause: "gangrene", informant: Mrs. David A. Fine (Watauga), died: 23 Oct 1922, record (1922) #: 185.

Loyd E. HAWKINS, age 20 years, single, parents: S.H. Hawkins (NC) and Julia Carroll, death cause: "tonsils abscess, chicken pox", informant: S.H. Hawkins (Johnson City), died: 24 Oct 1922, record #: 186.

Charles MCLANE, Jr., parents: Charles McLane and Mannia Banner, death cause: not stated, informant: Charles McLane (Shell Creek), born/died: 27 Oct 1922, record (1922) #: 187.

Nola WHISTENHUNT, born: 28 Dec 1918, parents: Joe Whistenhunt and Eva Swanner, death cause: "burned to death, accidentally caught fire", informant: Taylor Swanner (Roan Mountain), buried: Blevins Cemetery, died: 28 Oct 1922, record (1922) #: 188.

Tempie HOLLY, born: 3 May 1848, widow, parents: father not known and Savina Cates, death cause: "inter (illegibel) bowels", informant: Mollie Little (Hopson), buried: Hopson, died: 29 Oct 1922, record (1922) #: 189.

Herald TURNER, born: 7 Sep 1917, parents: John F. Turner and Lina Cole, death cause: "diptheria", informant: Dam Turner (Elizabethton), died: 30 Oct 1922, record (1922) #: 190.

Margaret C. MURRAY, born: 29 Oct 1922, parents: Elbert Murray and Carrie Sams, death cause: "forcips delivery", buried: Colbaugh Cemetery, died: 31 Oct 1922, record (1922) #: 191.

Infant MASSENGILL, female, parents: William Massengill and Ollie Shipley, death cause: "stillborn", buried: Webb Cemetery, 10 Oct 1922, record (1922) #: 192.

Infant WHITE, female, parents: Ottie White and Lona WArd, death cause: "stillborn", informant: Ottie White (Hampton), buried: Hall Cemetery, died: 21 Oct 1922, record (1922) #: 193.

Infant DUGGER, female, parents: C.B. Dugger and Ethel Mullens, death cause: "born dead", buried: Highland Cemetery, died: 22 Oct 1922, record (1922) #: 194.

Infant ASHLEY, parents: Nora Ashley and Harriett Grindstaff (NC), death cause: "stillborn", informant: Harriett Ashley (Shell Creek), died: 26 Oct 1922, record (1922) #: 195.

Infant DAVIS, female, parents: Arthur Davis and Ettie (illegible), death cause: "congenital disease", informant: Ettie Davis (Hampton), buried: Campbell Cemetery, died: 1 Nov 1922, record (1922) #: 196.

Elbert Edward FEATHERS, born: 18 Jun 1919, parents: William Feathers and Mary Vest, death cause: "intestinal carairh", informant: D.S. Mottern (Elizabethton), died: 8 Nov 1922, record (1922) #: 197.

James LYONS, age 36 years, married, parents: W.M. Lyons and Mary Roberts, death cause: "tuberculosis", informant: Manuel Honeycutt (Hampton), buried: Gap Creek, died: 9 Nov 1922, record (1922) #: 198.

Hattie INGRAM, age 26 years, born in North Carolina, widow, parents: Sam Ingram (NC) and Cinda Birchfield (NC), death cause: "tuberculosis", informant: C. Davis (Hopson), buried: Ingram Cemetery, died: 9 Nov 1922, record (1922) #: 199.

David Alexander NEWTON, born: 27 Feb 1851, widower, parents: James Matison Newton (Sullivan County) and Catherine Emmert (Sullivan County), death cause: "chronic indigestion, cerosis of liver and dysentery", informant: Clifton Newton, buried: Newton Cemetery, died: 15 Nov 1922, record (1922) #: 200.

Mrs. Eliza BUCKLES, born: 20 Mar 1848, parents: Alfred Williams and Eliza Williams, death cause: "(illegible) of heart", informant: D.C. Buckles (Watauga Valley), buried: Buckles Cemetery, died: 17 Nov 1922, record (1922) #: 201.

Ellen CAMPBELL, born: 16 Jun 1922, parents: Will Campbell and Maggie Taylor, death cause: "unbelical hernia and influenza", informant: Joe Taylor (Carter), buried: Taylor Cemetery, died: 18 Nov 1922, record (1922) #: 202.

Mrs. Hannah A. SHELL, born: 13 Sep 1830, widow, parents: Larkin Thompson (SC) and Mary Garland, death cause: "lobar pneumonia", informant: E.W. Larrimer (Watauga), buried: Thompson Cemetery, died: 23 Nov 1922, record (1922) #: 203.

Ruby KNIGHT, born: 12 Oct 1922, parents: Marion Knight (NC) and Lula Burleson (NC), death cause: not stated, died: 24 Nov 1922, record (1922) #: 204.

Blanch PETERS, born: 2 Apr 1921, parents: Dan Peters and Frona Ritchie, death cause: "croup", informant: Alf Peters (Carter), buried: Peters Cemetery, died: 26 Nov 1922, record (1922) #: 205.

Raymond CORDELL, born: 24 Sep 1922, parents: Darris Cordell and Fesodo Harmon (NC), death cause: illegible, informant: Nat Cordell (Shell Creek), buried: Cordell Cemetery, died: 27 Nov 1922, record (1922) #: 206.

Alen ESTEP, born: 15 Jun 1921, parents: Isaac Estep and mother's name illegible, death cause: not stated, informant Isaac Estep (Carter), buried: Richardson Cemetery, died: 28 Nov 1922, record (1922) #: 207.

Ina Pearl HILTON, born: 26 Jun 1902 in Bristol, TN, married, parents: Mike Campbell and Josie McKeehan, death cause: "pulmonary tuberculosis", informant: Mike Campbell (Elizabethton), buried: McKeehan Cemetery, died: 28 Nov 1922, record (1922) #: 208.

Callie BLEVINS, born: 29 Nov 1869, widow, parents: Hence Williams and Maggie Buckles, death cause: "flu", informant: Walter Blevins (Elizabethton), buried: Highland Cem, died: 29 Nov 1922, record (1922) #: 209.

Marion (SURNAME ILLEGIBLE), born: 22 May 1848, widower, parents: Acia (illegible) and Martha Laws (NC), death cause: "peralysis", buried: Payne Cemetery, died: 30 Nov 1922, record (1922) #: 210.

Martha HUMPHREY, age 60 years, 1 month and 15 days, married, parents: James Garrison and Hannah Culbert, death cause: "pulmonary tuberculosis", informant: F.W. Humphrey (Valley Forge), buried: Smith Cemetery, died: 30 Nov 1922, record (1922) #: 211.

Infant GOUGE, male, parents: Elijah Gouge and Corda McKinney, death cause: "stillborn", informant: E. Gouge (Roan Mountain), buried: Chambers Cemetery, died: 25 Nov 1922, record (1922) #: 212.

Albert Shields LUTTRELL, born: 4 Jul 1854 in Washington County, TN, married, parents: Richard Henry Luttrell (VA) and Mary Ann Treadway (Washington Co.), death cause: "cardiac dropsy", buried: Mountain City, TN, died: 2 Dec 1922, record (1922) #: 213.

Paul WOODS, born: 13 Oct 1922, parents: Ruben Woods and Mattie Ward, death cause: "meningitis", informant: Taylor Swanner (Roan Mountain), buried: Blevins Cemetery, died: 3 Dec 1922, record (1922) #: 214.

Carl ARNETT, born: 10 Oct 1922, parents: Phillip Arnett and Annie Banner (Banner Elk, NC), death cause: "unknown", informant: Phillip Arnett (Shell Creek), died: 5 Dec 1922, record (1922) #: 215.

J.S. MARTON, age 57 years, married, parents: David Marton and Lydia Roberts, death cause: "dropsy", informant: Jerry Woodby (Elizabethton), buried: Stevens Cem., died: 6 Dec 1922, record (1922) #: 216.

Melvin Carter CAMPBELL, born: 18 May 1920, parents: Lawson Campbell and Elsie Goodwin, death cause: "fell in fire, burned abdomen, leg and face", informant: M.D. Campbell (Hampton), buried: Cardens Bluff, died: 9 Dec 1922, record (1922) #: 217.

Tessie G. OAKS, born: 1 Apr 1895, married, parents: James S. Oaks (son of C.G.) and Celia Justus (NC), death cause: "heart failure", informant: J.S. Oaks, buried: Perry Cem., died: 18 Dec 1922, record #: 218.

Infant MEREDITH, female, parents: Claud Meredith and Geneva Hyder, death cause: "yellow joundice", buried: Meredith Cem., died: 14 Dec 1922, record #: 219.

Disey Ellen MAYS, born: 7 Apr 1919, parents: John Wesley Mays (NC) and Vena Pitts (NC), death cause: "caught fire and burned face and abdomen", informant: J.W. Mays, buried: Hunter, died: 14 Dec 1922, record (1922) #: 220.

Larance RICHARDSON, female, age 16 years, parents: Delany Richardson and ____ Gentry, death cause: "epoliptic fits", died: 15 Dec 1922, record (1922) #: 221.

Infant HODGE, male, born: 14 Dec 1922, parents: Abe Hodge and Haret Garland, death cause: "convulsions, cause unknown", buried: Cole Cemetery, died: 19 Dec 1921, record (1922) #: 222.

Joseph PIERCE, born: 11 Nov 1840 in Overton County, TN, married, parents: C. Arthur Pierce (NC) and Rebecca Myers, death cause: "paralysis", informant: E.S. Pierce (Hampton), buried: Gouge Cemetery, died: 19 Dec 1922, record (1922) #: 223.

Clemtine PILKTSON, age 62 years and 4 months in Watauga County, NC, married, parents: James Norris and Rutha Norris (Watauga Co., NC), death cause: "heart failure supposed", buried: Whitehead Cemetery, died: 20 Dec 1922, record (1922) #: 224.

John L. MARTON, born: 6 Sep 1922, parents: David Morton and Maude Range, death cause: "unknown", informant: Percy Range (Elizabethton), died: 22 Dec 1922, record (1922) #: 225.

Allie GUINN, age 5 months, parents: Blake Guinn and Lucy Potter, death cause: "croup", informant; Luther Guinn (Raon Mountain), buried: Fair View Cemetery, died: 22 Dec 1922, record (1922) #: 226.

Jane DUGGER, born: 1862, age 66 years, divorced, parents: John Potter and Hanner Stout, death cause: "cancer of stomach", informant: R.M. Dugger (Dark Ridge, NC), died: 24 Dec 1922, record (1922) #: 227.

Wesley GARLAND, born: 11 Oct 1919, parents: William Garland (Mitchell Co., NC) and Luster Smith, death cause: "croup", died: 25 Dec 1922, record (1922) #: 228.

Infant SHELL, male, born: 12 Dec 1922, parents: Willie Shell and Myrtle Range, death cause: "premature birth, died: 26 Dec 1922, record (1922) #: 229. (twin)

Infant SHELL, female, parents: Willie Shell and Myrtle Range, death cause: "premature birth, born/died: 12 Dec 1922, record (1922) #: 229a. (twin)

Martha M. HAMPTON, born: 20 Feb 1846, widow, parents: not state, death cause: "sarcoma of bladder", informant: W.L. Hampton (Elizabethton), died: 26 Dec 1922, record (1922) #: 230.

William H. LONG, born: 9 Sep 1922, parents: George Long and Sondia Johnson, death cause: "pneumonia", buried: Johnson Cemetery, died: 29 Dec 1922, record (1922) #: 231.

George LINDSEY, black, age about 90 years, born in North Carolina, married, parents: "unknown", death cause: "influenza and pneumonia", informant: John Lindsey (Johnson City), died: 30 Dec 1922, record (1922) #: 232.

Nora ARNETT, born: 11 Sep 1922, parents: John A. Arnett and Rebecca Orr, death cause: "unknown, found dead in bed", informant: Andy J. Arnett (Roan Mountain), died: 31 Dec 1922, record (1922) #: 233.

George LINDSEY, record (1922) #: 234. (dupl of 232)

Infant SHELL, female, parents: Willie Shell and Myrtle Range, death cause: "stillborn", born/died: 12 Dec 1922, record (1922) #: 235.

David C. SIMERLY, born: 25 Jan 1856, married, parents: John Simerly and Susan Chambers, death cause: "tuberculosis, influenza", informant: J.L. Simerly (Roan Mountain), buried: Simerly Cemetery, died: 1 Jan 1923, record (1923) #: 1.

Eliza Jane HYDER, born: 10 Oct 1839, born at sea, widow, parents: David Carriger (Ireland) and Margaret Patterson (Ireland), death cause: "tuberculosis, hemorrhage of lungs", informant: J.C. Hyder (Elizabethton), died: 2 Jan 1923, record (1923) #: 2.

Infant NIDIFFER, female, born: 10 Dec 1922, parents: Alf Nidiffer and Suberb Nidiffer, death cause: "unknown", buried: Ritchie Cemetery, died: 3 Jan 1923, record (1923) #: 3.

Diza Allen HENNIGER, female, age about 40 years, married, parents: John Williams and Susanah Matherly, death cause: "influenza, pneumonia and child birth", informant: D.M. Matherly (Valley Forge), died: 4 Jan 1923, record (1923) #: 4.

Wallas Roe HICKS, born: 8 May 1919, parents: Elfnza Hicks and Mancy Guinn, death cause: "scarlet fever", informant: Isac Lambert (Dark Ridge, NC), buried: Clauson Cem., died: 5 Jan 1923, record (1923) #: 5.

Omar STOUT, born: 19 Dec 1922, parents: C.E. Stout and Bettie Smith, death cause: "bold hives", informant: Fred Stout (Shell Creek), buried: Elizabethton, died: 8 Jan 1923, record (1923) #: 6.

Earnest CARVER, born: 12 Dec 1920, parents: John Carver and Bettie Moore, death cause: "enfluenza", informant: Henry Moore (Hampton), buried: Fair View Cemetery, died: 8 Jan 1923, record (1923) #: 7.

Lorrie BRIGGS, born: 20 Jan 1840 in North Carolina, married, parents: John Bailey (NC) and Lovey May (NC), death cause: "bronchial asthma", informant: A.W. Briggs, buried: Monte Vista Cemetery, died: 9 Jan 1923, record (1923) #: 8.

James RICHARDSON, age 73 years, minister, married, parents: Thomas Richardson and mother's name illegible (NC), death cause: not stated, buried: Richardson Cemetery, died: 9 Jan 1923, record (1923) #: 9.

Sarah HARDIN, age 73 years, widow, parents: Alec Wilson and Nancy Garland, death cause: "flue", informant: D.C. Cole (Carter), buried: Peters Cemetery, died: 10 Jan 1923, record (1923) #: 10.

J.G. FAIR, age 68 years, born in North Carolina, married, parents: J.G. Fair (NC) and mother's name not stated, death cause: "flu, bronchial pneumonia", informant: Oscar M. Fair (Johnson City), died: 10 Jan 1923, record (1923) #: 11.

Other RICHARDSON, female, born: 4 May 1883, married, parents: Jerdson Whitehead and Florence Perkins, death cause: "tuberculosis", informant: G.W. Richardson (Fish Springs), died: 15 Jan 1923, record #: 12.

Roy TREADWAY, Jr., born: 22 Dec 1922, parents: Charles Treadway and Gay Nave, death cause: "pneumonia", informant: C.E. Treadway (Valley Forge), buried: Treadway Cem., died: 12 Jan 1923, record (1923) #: 13.

John ELLIOTT, born: 21 Aug 1851, married, parents: Joseph Elliott and Margaret Hopkins, death cause: "mitral (illegible)", informant: Roby Elliott (Elizabethton), died: 12 Jan 1923, record (1923) #: 14.

W.K. MCINTURF, born: 24 Dec 1852, married, parents: Wilson McInturff adn Sarah Birchfield, death cause: "double lobar pneumonia", informant: W.K. Smith (Elizabethton), buried: Gap Creek, died: 12 Jan 1923, record (1923) #: 15.

Marsha Ellen MORGAN, born: Jul 1853, married, parents: John Potter and mother's name unknown, death cause: "tuberculosis", informant: Charles Morgan (Sullivan County), buried: Stout Cemetery, died: 13 Jan 1923, record (1923) #: 16.

Clide CAMPBELL, born: 7 Feb 1922, parents: Nat Campbell and Marrie Ward (NC), death cause: "cholera", informant: Nat Campbell (Hampton), buried: Campbell Cemetery, died: 13 Jan 1923, record (1923) #: 17.

Mrs. N.H. HODGE, born: 14 Jan 1861 in Johnson County, married, parents: Andy Fritts (Johnson County) and Susie Porch (NC), death cause: "mitral regurgitation", informant: N.H. Hodge (Elizabethton), buried: Neva, TN, died: 15 Jan 1922, record (1923) #: 18.

Ranigh Ruth FREEMAN, age 3 years, parents: Ralph Freeman (NC) and Bluah Liner (NC), death cause: "diptheria", informant: Jeter Freeman, died: 16 Jan 1923, record (1923) #: 19.

James Cuarley DICKEN, born: 28 May 1920 at Neva, Johnson County, TN, parents: Thomas Dicken and Cassie O'Neal, death cause: "tonsilitis", informant: Thomas Dicken (Butler), buried: Smith Cemetery, died: 16 Jan 1923, record (1923) #: 20.

Dora LEWIS, age 36 years, married, parents: John Smith and Ollie (illegible), death cause: "flu", buried: Garland Cem., died: 17 Jan 1923, record (1923) #: 21.

Verna VANCE, born: 6 Apr 1906 in Avery County, NC, parents: Walter Vance (Mitchell Co., NC) and Berdie Taylor (Avery Co., NC), death cause: "operation for apendix, perotuits followed", informant: Walter Vance (Newland, NC), died: 17 Jan 1923, record (1923) #: 22.

Ace WARD, age 48 years, born in Johnson County, married, parents: "unknown", death cause: not stated, died: 20 Jan 1923, record (1923) #: 23.

Infant DUGR (DUGGER ?), female, born: 1 Dec 1922, parents: John Dugr and Dori Hurley, death cause: not stated, informant: W.C. Blevins (Carter), buried: Garland Cem., died: 20 Jan 1923, record (1923) #: 24.

Emma TAYLOR, born: 20 Mar 1919, parents: George W. Taylor and Matilda Peters, death cause: "influenza, bronchitis", informant: J.E. Taylor (Carter), buried: Taylor Cem., died: 20 Jan 1923, record (1923) #: 25.

Eliza OLIVER, age 71 years, 10 months and 28 days, married, parents: father's name not known and ____ Hinkle, death cause: "influenza, pneumonia", died: 21 Jan 1923, record (1923) #: 26.

James Phillips LACY, born: 2 Mar 1845, widower, parents: J.W. Lacy and Jane Hyder, death cause: "bronchial penumonia", informant: R.L. Williams (Elizabethton), buried: Hopson, died: 22 Jan 1923, record (1923) #: 27.

James ALFORD, age 74 years, married, parents: father's name not known and Polly Alford, death cause: "aortic regurgitation", informant: Nancy Hardin (Carter), buried: Ritchie Cemetery, died: 23 Jan 1923, record (1923) #: 28.

Rana BOWMAN, born: 6 Feb 1884, married, parents: John Morgan and Martha Potter, death cause: "pneumonia", informant: Charles Morgan (Shell Creek), buried: Stout Cemetery, died: 24 Jan 1924, record (1923) #: 29.

Andrew J. STOVER, born: 6 Mar 1860, parents: Daniel Stover and Nancy Johnson (Green County), death cause: "influenza and pneumonia", buried: Greenville, died: 25 Jan 1923, record (1923) #: 30.

Martha CAMPBELL, age 65 years, married, parents: Presto Carden and mother' name not known, death cause: "carcinoma of colon", informant: F.W. Crow (Elizabethton), died: 25 Jan 1923, record (1923) #: 31.

Susan BOWERS, age 67 years, married, parents: James Oliver and Mary Payne, death cause: "influenza and pneumonia", died: 26 Jan 1923, record (1923) #: 32.

John W. RICHARDSON, age 71 years, married, minister, parents: Thomas Richardson and ____ Forbes (NC), death cause: "flu", buried: Richardson Cemetery, died: 26 Jan 1923, record (1923) #: 33.

James Allen OLIVER, born: 28 Jul 1909, parents: James H. Oliver and Mollie Oliver, death cause: "myocarditis", informant: Morrell Oliver, buried: Vaughn Cemetery, died: 26 Jan 1923, record (1923) #: 34.

Infant LYONS, female, parents: George W. Lyons and Moxie Barker (VA), death cause: "congenital heart disease", informant: P.L. Lyons (Elizabethton), died: 26 Jan 1923, record (1923) #: 35.

Ruth GOUGE, born: 11 May 1922, parents: Arthur Gouge and Nora Buchanan, death cause: "croupus pneumonia", informant: Arthur Gouge (Roan Mountain), buried: Buchanan Cem., died: 28 Jan 1923, record (1923) #: 36.

Katherine MILLER, parents: Sam Miller (NC) and Maggie Ledford, death cause: "stillborn", informant: W.M. Miller (Shell Creek), died: 30 Jan 1923, record (1923) #: 37.

Martha BOWERS, age 61 years, single, parents: Landon Bowers and Creta Ensor, death cause: "carcinoma of breast", informant: Lee Williams (Watauga Valley), buried: Rithcie Cemetery, died: 1 Feb 1923, record (1923) #: 38.

Margaret SHOUN, age 71 years, married, parents: Elija Hardin and Lydia Forbes, death cause: "influenza", informant: Powel Shoun (Carter), buried: Shouns, died: 1 Feb 1923, record (1923) #: 39.

Maggie MILLER, born: 14 May 1885, married, parents: Isaac Ledford and Pollie Hopson, death cause: "nephritis", informant: W.M. Miller (Shell Creek), died: 2 Feb 1923, record (1923) #: 40. (see # 37)

Barnabas EASTRIDGE, age 82 years, born in North Carolina, parents: Pleas Eastridge and ____ Graybill, death cause: not stated, informant: W.F. Swift (Johnson City), died: 3 Feb 1923, record (1923) #: 41.
Infant HURLEY, male, born: 23 Jan 1923, parents: Jessey Hurley and Bertha Garland, death cause: "flu", died: 6 Feb 1923, record (1923) #: 42.
Maggie DELOACH, born: 7 Feb 1895, married, parents: Robert Ledwell and Rebecca Canter, death cause: "operation, abdominal, both ovaries", buried: Estep Cemetery, died: 7 Feb 1923, record (1923) #: 43.
Sarah C. BLEVINS, born: 25 May 1827, widow, parents: Robert H. King and Susan Weaver, death cause: "old age", informant: R.L. Blevins (Carter), buried: Ritchie Cem., died: 7 Feb 1923, record (1923) #: 44.
T.R. BURGIE, born: 12 Aug 1847 in Montgomery County, TN, married, parents: Joseph Burgie (Davidson Co., TN) and Mary Ann Allen (Montgomery Co., TN), death cause: "flu, pneumonia", informant: Harry Burgie (Elizabethton), buried: Highland Cemetery, died: 9 Feb 1923, record (1923) #: 45.
Joel Carriger FERGUSON, born: 28 May 1882, married, parents: B.B. Ferguson and Julia Lewis, death cause: "tuberculosis of lungs", informant: William Ferguson, buried: Highland Cemetery, died: 9 Feb 1923, record (1923) #: 46.
James H. MESSIMER, born: 4 Apr 1840, married, parents: Abraham Messimer (White Top, NC) and mother's name not known, death cause: "tuberculosis of lungs", informant: Victoria Messimer (Butler), buried: Smith Cemetery, died: 10 Feb 1923, record (1923) #: 47.
William Patton DUNCAN, born: 4 Apr 1857 in Virginia, parents: not stated, death cause: illegible, informant: Sexton Duncan, buried: Highland Cemetery, died: 11 Feb 1923, record (1923) #: 48.
Heril ESTEP, age 64 years, married, parents: Isaac Estep and Edey Hodge, death cause: "pneumonia", buried: Heatherly Cemetery, died: 12 Feb 1923, record (1923) #: 49.
Mildred WHITE, born: 16 Apr 1920, parents: Ben White and Eliza Hardin, death cause: "yellow atrophy of liver", buried: Highland Cemetery, died: 13 Feb 1923, record (1923) #: 50.
Rita BOWERS, born: 3 Jan 1921, parents: Allen Bowers and Berna Lundy, death cause: not stated, informant: John Smith, buried: Bowers Cemetery, died: 15 Feb 1923, record (1923) #: 51.

James MCKINNEY, born: 30 May 1868 in Mitchell County, NC, married, parents: Clingman McKinney (NC) and Peggie McKinney (NC), death cause: "apoplexy", buried: Roan Mountain, died: 16 Feb 1923, record (1923) #: 52.

Clarence LYONS, born: 5 Sep 1922, parents: John Lyons and Deina Messimer, death cause: "bold hives", informant: John Lyons (Butler), died: 17 Feb 1923, record (1923) #: 53.

Sarah DUGGER, born: 8 Jan 1917, parents: Robert Dugger and Nancy Sheets, death cause: "burned to death by close catching fire", informant: W.S. Hatly (Butler), buried: Whitehead Cemetery, died: 18 Feb 1923, record (1923) #: 54.

Sarah E. DUGGER, born: 8 Jan 1917, parents: Robert Dugger and Nancy Sheets, death cause: "burned to death, clothes caught on fire", informant: W.S. Hatley (Butler), buried: Elk Church Cemetery, died: 18 Feb 1923, record (1923) #: 55.

Bob TAYLOR, age 73 years, widower, parents: Jack Taylor and Catherin Combs, death cause: "Brights disease", buried: Grindstaff Cemetery, died: 20 Feb 1923, record (1923) #: 56.

Mrs. Alice Emma HYDER, born: 22 Jun 1868, married, parents: James L. Whitlow (VA) and Debora Harrison, death cause: "encocarditis", informant: G.W. Hyder, buried: Hyder Cemetery, died: 21 Feb 1923, record (1923) #: 57.

Glenn CHAPPELL, born: 18 Jan 1923, parents: Walt Chappell (NC) and Gussie Webb, death cause: "bold hives", resided at Watauga, died: 21 Feb 1923, record (1923) #: 58.

Susan E. DEMPSY, born: 10 Sep 1847, widow, parents: Andy Shell and ____ Gourley, death cause: "apoplexy", resided at Watauga, died: 22 Feb 1923, record #: 59.

W.C. RITCHIE, age 66 years, married, parents: Andrew Ritchie and Jennie Jenkins, death cause: "pulmonary tuberculosis", informant: H.W. Renfro (Carter), buried: Ritchie Cem., died: 23 Feb 1923, record #: 60.

William Charles BURROUGH, born: 7 Jan 1923, parents: H.M. Burrough and Mamie Chambers, death cause: "congenital heart disease", informant: R.A. Range, buried: Keenburg, died: 24 Feb 1923, record (1923) #: 61.

Sarah BRANCH, age 59 years, single, born in North Carolina, parents: Stanley Branch (NC) and Clarissa Bennett (NC), death cause: "cardiac dropsy", informant: Joe Branch (Elizabethton), buried: Highland Cemetery, died: 24 Feb 1923, record (1923) #: 62.

Ernie COCHRAN, age 5 years, parents: Jame Cochran and Mary Carver, death cause: "dyptheria", informant: John Berry (Hampton), buried: Fair View Cemetery, died: 25 Feb 1923, record (1923) #: 63.

James Aston PLASTER, born: 29 Jan 1923, parents: Newton Plaster (Honaker, VA) and Marie Perry, death cause: "septicemia", informant: Worley Williams (Elizabethton), buried: Highland Cemetery, died: 28 Feb 1923, record (1923) #: 64.

Roxie CLARK, age 2 years, parents: Charlie Clark and Maggie Cable, death cause: "dyptheria", informant: Bernie Berry (Roan Mountain), buried: Clark Cemetery, died: 1 Mar 1923, record (1923) #: 65.

Leonard WILSON, age 2 months and 15 days, parents: George Wilson and Maud Bulock (Sullivan County), death cause: "flue", died: 1 Mar 1923, record (1923) #: 66.

Elizabeth R. BRUMIT, born: 28 Dec 1879, married, parents: H.C. Smith and Sarah A. McIntosh, death cause: "angina pectoris", informant: J.D. Brumit, buried: Highland Cem., died: 1 Mar 1923, record #: 67.

Mrs. Lousia ELLIS, born: 18 Aug 1882 in Knox County, married, parents: John Ellis (Knox County) and Sallie Sellars (Knox County), death cause: "carcinoma of uterus", informant: Dan Ellis (Elizabethton), buried: Ellis Cemetery, died: 3 Mar 1923, record (1923) #: 68.

Mrs. Virgie ESTEP, born: 24 Oct 1904 in Sullivan County, married, parents: Sam Jones (Sullivan County) and Nannie Carr, death cause: "influenza and abscess of lung", informant: Sam Jones (Elizabethton), buried: Colbaugh Cem., died: 4 Mar 1923, record (1923) #: 69.

Mrs. Nannie Leona SHELL, born: 7 Oct 1886, married, parents: Andy Gilbert Collins and Crocha Josephine Fondren, death cause: "child birth, hemorrhage", informant: Ed Shell (Elizabethton), buried: Thomas Cemetery, died: 5 Mar 1923, record (1923) #: 70.

Coy MARTON, born: 29 Mar 1908, parents: W.C. Marton and Rhoda Goodwin, death cause: "pneumonia", informant: Frank Peters (Cardins Bluff), buried: Goodwin Cem., died: 6 Mar 1923, record (1923) #: 71.

John WILLIAMS, age 65 years, married, parents: Feb Williams and Lizzie Garson, death cause: "disentery", informant: Tom Braswell (Elizabethton), buried: Sims Cemetery, died: 6 Mar 1923, record (1923) #: 72.

Julia May PERSINGER, born: 16 Aug 1905, parents: C.W. Persinger and Lydie E. Shell, death cause: "tuberculosis of lungs", informant: C.W. Persinger (Johnson City), buried: Simmons Cemetery, died: 6 Mar 1923, record (1923) #: 73.

Alfred BERRY, born: 13 Jul 1910, parents: Robert Garfield Berry and Evaline Holden (Johnson County), death cause: "gangrenous appendix", informant: R.G. Berry (Butler), buried: Pierce Cemetery, died: 8 Mar 1923, record (1923) #: 74.

Elbert DICKEN, born: 8 Mar 1923, parents: Thomas Dicken (Johnson County) and Cassie O'Neal (Johnson County), death cause: "premature birth", informant: Thomas Dicken (Butler), died: 9 Mar 1923, record (1923) #: 75.

Essie Mae GOODWIN, born: 11 May 1922, parents: Clarence A. Goodwin and Grace Mae Williams, death cause: "flue and pneumonia", buried: Highland Cemetery, died: 10 Mar 1923, record (1923) #: 76.

Ida May PIERCE, born: 5 Jun 1902, married, parents: George Nave and Mary Bowers, death cause: "septicomia", informant: J.F.M. Pierce (Watauga Valley), buried: Buckles Cemetery, died: 10 Mar 1923, record (1923) #: 77.

Hannah M. MCCLOUD, born: 26 May 1848, married, parents: Andrew J. Duncan and Barsheba Rasor (Johnson County), death cause: "bronchial pneumonia", informant: J.F. McCloud (Elizabethton), died: 11 Mar 1923, record (1923) #: 78.

Eveline LOWE, age 67 years, married, parents: Henry Colbaugh and Vicy Nave, death cause: "pulmonary tuberculosis", informant: Noah Lowe (Watauga Valley), buried: Lowe Cemetery, died: 12 Mar 1923, record (1923) #: 79.

Eliazbeth WAGNER, born: 7 Apr 1846 in Johnson County, widow, parents: Phillip Gentry (NC) and Hettie Cable (Johnson County), death cause: "influenza", informant: P.D. Gentry (Hampton), buried: Hall Cemetery, died: 12 Mar 1923, record (1923) #: 80.

A.D. ESTEP, born: 2 Sep 1918, parents: A.J. Estep and E.A. Campbell, death cause: "influenza", buried: Garland Cem., died: 16 Mar 1923, record (1923) #: 81.

(Illegible) BERRY, female, age 33 years, 1 month and 5 days, born in Crossner, NC, parents: Joe Burleson (NC) and Josie Franklin (NC), death cause: "septicomia", informant: Arthur Berry (Roan Mountain), buried: Berry Cemetery, died: 16 Mar 1923, record (1923) #: 82.

William Smith WILSON, age 60 years, born in Lee County, VA, married, parents: Andrew Wilson and Mary Garland, death cause: "brights disease", informant: Red Wilson (Elizabethton), died: 16 Mar 1923, record (1923) #: 83.

Nancy MCNEELY, born: 29 Jun 1840 in Coldwell County, NC, widow, parents: John Carver (NC) and Cassie Feer (Coldwell Co., NC), death cause: "cancer on face and eye", informant: R.F. McNeely (Butler), buried: Hatley Cemetery, died: 17 Mar 1923, record (1923) #: 84.

Walter Wallace WEST, born: 7 Feb 1923, parents: J..(illegible) West and Mae Osborn, death cause: "influenza", buried: Hall Cemetery, died: 22 Mar 1923, record (1923) #: 85.

Jessie WOODBY, parents: Charlie Woodby and Rhoda Woodby, death cause: not stated, buried: Lyons Cemetery, born/died: 24 Mar 1923, record (1923) #: 86.

Iva PIERCE, born: 6 Mar 1923, parents: A.C. Pierce and Katherine Buckles, death cause: "not known", informant: C.S. Bowers (Watauga Valley), buried: Buckles Cem., died: 25 Mar 1923, record (1923) #: 87.

Soloman LEE, born: 15 Jul 1838 in New York, parents: "unknown", death cause: not stated, informant: A. Harrison (Shell Creek), buried: Lee Farm, died: 25 Mar 1923, record (1923) #: 88.

Nola TOWNSEND, age 4 months, parents: Walter Townsend and Emma Townsend, death cause: "yellow jaundice", informant: Walter Townsend (Hopson), buried: Birchfield Cem., died: 27 Mar 1923, record (1923) #: 89.

Mary Grace TIPTON, born: 7 Mar 1850 in Virginia, widow, parents: Henry Hubble (VA) and Freelove Blessing (VA), death cause: "pneumonia and paralysis", informant: Mrs. Lee F. Miller (Johnson City), buried: Highland Cem., died: 29 Mar 1923, record (1923) #: 90.

Bulia Christine PATTON, born: 19 Oct 1908, parents: Hugh Patton and Ada Childs (NC), death cause: "gougenous appendix", buried: Patton Cemetery", died: 31 Mar 1923, record (1923) #: 91.

Infant SHELL, male, parents: Ed Shell and Nannie Collins, death cause: "stillborn", informant: Ed Shell (Elizabethton), died: 5 Mar 1923, record (1923) #: 92.

Arna S. CURTIS, born: 13 Mar 1923, parents: W.E. Curtis (Marion, VA) and Christine Kite, death cause: "infection of hand", informant: Will Curtis (Elizabethton), died: 1 Apr 1923, record (1923) #: 93.

Howard TOLLEY, born: 31 Mar 1903, parents: Hobart Tolley and Martha Miller, death cause: "boul hives", infomant: Hobart Tolley (Hampton), buried: Tolley Cemetery, died: 2 Apr 1923, record (1923) #: 94.

Hassie BERRY, born: 6 Apr 1922, parents: Arthur Berry and Lou Byrd, death cause: "meningitis", informant: John Berry (Hampton), buried: Berry Cemetery, died: 2 Apr 1923, record (1923) #: 95.

Losson MILLER, age about 65 years, widower, parents: Sanford Miller and Bettie Simerly, death cause: "influenza", informant: Bill Miller (Roan Mountain), died: 3 Apr 1923, record (1923) #: 96.

Sallie A. INSCOE, born: 2 Jun 1845 in North Carolina, widow, parents: John Archer (NC) and mother's name unknown, death cause: "flu", informant: Mrs. Delia Crisp (Bristol), buried: Johnson City, died: 3 Apr 1923, record (1923) #: 97.

Mollie MORRIS, born: 14 Oct 1871 in Sullivan County, married, parents: Jim Troxell (Sullivan County) and Sarah Spears (Sullivan County), death cause: "hemorrhage of brain", informant: Joe Troxell (Johnson City), buried: Morris Cemetery, died: 14 Apr 1923, record (1923) #: 98.

Lillian E. ROBERTS, parents: George D. Roberts and Emily Burrow, death cause: "hemorrhage of (illegible)" buried: Highland Cemetery, born/died: 17 Apr 1923, record (1923) #: 99.

E. Lorena EGGERS, born: 15 Oct 1911 in North Carolina, parents: Fahe Eggers (NC) and Lillie Triplett (NC), death cause: "blud poison", informant: M.C. Eggers (Beech Creek, NC), buried: Triplett Cemetery, died: 20 Apr 1923, record (1923) #: 100.

Adam MILLER, age 78 years, born in Michigan, married, parents: "unknown", death cause: "heart disease", informant: William Fipps (Carter), buried: Sadie, died: 20 Apr 1923, record (1923) #: 101.

Lottie Kate HAWKINS, born: 14 Apr 1923, parents: Charles Hawkins (VA) and Eliza Williams, death cause: not stated, buried: Highland Cemetery, died: 23 May 1923, record (1923) #: 102.

Mrs. Frank M. RYAN, born: 14 Jan 1895, married, parents: S.P. Bradshaw and ____ Donlson, death cause: illegible, informant: Mrs. W.H. Hampton (Elizabethton), died: 23 Apr 1923, record (1923) #: 103.

Lida JACKSON, negro, age 38 years, born in North Carolina, married, parents: Marrion Mathis (NC) and Judia Hemphill (NC), death cause: "flue and pneumonia", informant: James Jackson (Roan Mountain), buried: Jackson Cemetery, died: 24 Apr 1923, record (1923) #: 104.

Cloyd CARVER, born: 19 Apr 1923, parents: father not stated and Nancy Carver, death cause: "premature birth", informant: James Carver (Hopson), buried: Carver Cem., died: 24 Apr 1923, record (1923) #: 105.

Wilson YOUNG, born: 18 Aug 1845 in North Carolina, retired minister, married, parents: Patterson Young (NC) and Elizabeth Hughs (NC), death cause: "spinal disease", informant: Mrs. Wilson Young (Elizabethton), buried: Siam, died: 25 Apr 1923, record (1923) #: 106.

E.J. WILLIAMS, born: 31 Dec 1845, widower, parents: P.P. Williams and mother not stated, death cause: "tuberculosis", buried: Buckles Cemetery, died: 25 Apr 1923, record (1923) #: 107.

M.B. COOPER, born: 5 May 1855, married, parents: William Cooper and Hannah Fair, death cause: "flue and pneumonia", informant: Mrs. J.E. Rumbly (Johnson City), buried: Cooper Cemetery, died: 26 Apr 1923, record (1923) #: 108.

Oscar BRITT, age 18 years, married, parents: Henderson Britt and Nora Adkins, death cause: "gun shot wound through chest, suicide", informant: Henderson Britt (Johnson City), buried: Buena Vista Cemetery, died: 26 Apr 1923, record (1923) #: 109.

Infant JOBE, male, born: 13 Apr 1923, parents: G.C. Jobe (NC) and Alma Aldridge (Ohio), death cause: "malnutrition", buried: Thomas Cemetery, died: 28 Apr 1923, record (1923) #: 110.

Edna M. MINNICH, born: 12 May 1875, widow, parents: John Gregg and Susan E. Cain, death cause: "apoplexy and paralysis", informant: Roy Hyder (Valley Forge), buried: Blountville, died: 30 Apr 1923, record (1923) #: 111.

Sarah ARCHER, age 88 years, parents: (Illegible) Pierce and Sarah (Illegible), death cause: "old age", buried: Pierce Cemetery, died: 30 Apr 1923, record (1923) #: 112.

Infant POTTER, male, parents: D.D. Potter and Love Triplett, death cause: "stillborn", buried: Austin Cemetery, died: 4 Apr 1923, record (1923) #: 113.

Infant GRINDSTAFF, male, parents: Paul Grindstaff and Dora Combs, death cause: "stillborn", informant: A.R. Collins (Watauga Valley), died: 14 May 1923, record (1923) #: 114.

Infant LOVELESS, female, parents: Herman Loveless and Allie Ellis, death cause: "stillborn", died: 16 Apr 1923, record (1923) #: 115.

Infant CAMPBELL, female, parents: father not stated and Stella Campbell, death cause: "stillborn", buried: Glover Cem., died: 17 Apr 1923, record (1923) #: 116.

Infant CAMPBELL, female, parents: Ralph Campbell and (Illegible) Carden, death cause: "stillborn", buried: Hall Cem., died: 31 May 1923, record (1923) #: 117.

Nancy CARVER, age 35 years, single, parents: George Carver and Mattie Davis, death cause: "pulmonary tuberculosis", informant: Charlie Carver (Johnson City), buried: Carver Cemetery, died: 1 May 1923, record (1923) #: 118.

Christine KUHN, born: 7 Mar 1923, parents: Sam Kuhn and Bertha Riggs, death cause: "not known", informant: Sam Kuhn (Elizabethton), buried: Harmony Cemetery, died: 6 May 1923, record (1923) #: 119.

George S. LOWE, born: 23 Jun 1866, parents: John A. Lowe and Martha Lipps, death cause: "influenza and paralysis", informant: H.D. Lowe (Carter), buried: Grindstaff Cem., died: 9 May 1923, record #: 120.

George Washington WAYCASTER, born: 16 Aug 1854 in North Carolina, married, parents: Elija Waycaster (NC) and Sarah Biddie (NC), death cause: "tuberculosis of lungs", informant: I.G. Waycaster (Roan Mountain), died: 15 May 1923, record (1923) #: 121.

Dolly Mae MILLER, born: 7 May 1923, parents: J.O. Miller (Johnson County) and Marry Bentley (NC), death cause: "hives", buried: Highland Cemetery, died: 15 May 1923, record (1923) #: 122.

George E. HOSS, born: 7 Nov 1866, parents: James H. Hoss and Nancy Perry, death cause: "ate stale meat, toxic poisoning causing bowel obstruction", informant: Nancy Hoss (Shell Creek), died: 20 May 1923, record (1923) #: 123.

Sara MARKLAND, age 51 years, married, parents: Lige Harden and Sara Harden, death cause: "influenza and pneumonia, informant: husband, buried: Markland Cemetery, died: 20 May 1923, record (1923) #: 124.

George Elcany HOSS, born: 7 Nov 1866, parents: James H. Hoss and Nancy Perry, death cause: "gangrenous appendix, ruptured gall bladder", informant: J.G. Hoss (Shell Creek), died: 20 May 1923, record (1923) #: 125. (duplicate of record # 123)

Eliza ROBERTS, born: 26 Dec 1880, married, parents: Lee Crow and Maggie Dugger, death cause: "cancer of uterus, hysterectomy", informant: Alexander Crow, buried: Highland Cem., died: 23 May 1923, record: 126.

Infant CURD, male, parents: S.H. Curd (Johnson County), and Blonde [editorial note: Viola Blanche] Feathers, death cause: "premature birth", resided at Watauga, died: 24 May 1923, record (1923) #: 127.

Will BARNETT, age 35 years, born in North Carolina, married, parents: Swin Barnett (NC) and Jane Wright (NC), death cause: not stated, informant: Aaron Wright (Roan Mountain), died: 29 May 1923, record #: 128.

Sarah Orr PERKINS, born: 31 Jul 1861, widow, parents: James W. Orr (Washington County) and Nancy Perkins, death cause: not stated, informant: C.B. Perkins (Roan Mountain), buried: Hampton Cemetery, died: 29 May 1923, record (1923) #: 129.

Samuel WRIGHT, age 71 years, born in Mitchell County, NC, married, parents: Aaron Wright (Mitchell Co., NC) and Pollie Briggs (Yancey Co., NC), death cause: "old age", informant: M.B. Honeycutt (Roan Mtn.), buried: Hopson, died: 29 May 1923, record (1923) #: 130.

Ethel CAMPBELL, born: 15 Apr 1915, parents: James Campbell and Susie Hyder, death cause: "gangrenous ulcer of left cheek", informant: James Campbell (Hampton), died: 29 May 1923, record (1923) #: 131.

Mrs. Laura HUGHES, born: 7 Apr 1869, widow, parents: George Moody and Jane Fair, death cause: "influenza and pneumonia", informant: Mrs. J.G. Curtis (Johnson City), died: 31 May 1923, record (1923) #: 132.

William Franklin GOBBLE, born: 19 Dec 1920, parents: Roy Gobble (VA) and Cora Marton, death cause: "mitral regurgitation", buried: Colbaugh Cemeter, died: 31 May 1923, record (1923) #: 133.

Infant HAYES, male, parents: William Hayes and Della Crow, death cause: "stillborn", informant: J.S. Hayes (Elizabethton), buried: Payne Cemetery, died: 29 May 1923, record (1923) #: 134.

Ivan Eugene CASEY, born: 15 Apr 1923, parents: Fred Casey and mother's name illegible, death cause: "not known", informant: Fred Casey (Hampton), buried: Hall Cemetery, died: 1 Jun 1923, record (1923) #: 135.

William Robert CRAIG, black, born: 14 Apr 1874, married, parents: Harim Craig and Harriett Craig, death cause: "aortic and mitral inconsistancy", informant: George Craig, died: 3 Jun 1923, record: 136.

Paul POTTER, born: 18 Mar 1912, parents: Daniel Potter and Ida Greenwell, death cause: "pneumonia fever", informant: Charlie Andise (Dark Ridge, NC), buried: Greenwell Cemetery, died: 6 Jun 1923, record #: 137.

William ALEXANDER, born: 17 Mar 1842 in Ireland, retired soldier, married, parents: "unknown", death cause: "fell on chest and pneumonia", informant: Mrs. William Alexander (Elizabethton), buried: Mohawk, TN, died: 7 Jun 1923, record (1923) #: 138.

Susan CLARK, born: 28 Jun 1828 in "Catauga" County, NC, widow, parents: Sam Rush (NC) and ____ Townsend (NC), death cause: "old age", informant: Arthur Berry (Hampton), buried: Clark Cemetery, died: 8 Jun 1923, record (1923) #: 139.

M. LUIS (Lewis ?), age 67 years, 5 months and 7 days, married, parents: L.D. Luis and Fancy Pitts, death cause: "influenza and pneumonia", informant" Landon Luis (Carter), buried: Grindstaff Cemetery, died: 8 Jun 1923, record (1923) #: 140.

Henry PETERS, born: Mar 1904, single, parents: C.C. Peters and Emily Hardin, death cause: "double pneumonia", informant: J.T. Nave (Carter), buried: Blevins Cem., died: 9 Jun 1923, record (1923) #: 141.

Rex HOPSON, Jr., born: 17 Feb 1923, parents: Rex Hopson (NC) and Diana Adkins (NC), death cause: "flu", informant: Rex Hopson (Johnson City), buried: Hughes Cemetery, died: 9 Jun 1923, record (1923) #: 142.

John HOLLY, born: 7 Jan 1843, married, parents: James Holly and Mary Barry (VA), death cause: "infected gall bladder and valvulor heart disorder", informant: G.H. Holly (Elizabethton), buried: Green Hill Cemetery, died: 10 Jun 1923, record (1923) #: 143.

David BARNETT, age 62 years, born in Mitchell County, NC, married, parents: Spencer Barnett (Mitchell Co., NC) and Alice Barnett, death cause: "cancer of stomach", informant: Alice Barnett (Roan Mountain), buried: Miller Cem., died: 12 Jun 1923, record #: 144.

William Wheeler RICHARDSON, born: 18 Jun 1876, married, parents: H.P. Richardson and Freelove Estep, death cause: "valvulor heart lesion and pneumonia", died: 13 Jun 1913, record (1923) #: 145.

J. Alford RICHARDSON, born: 19 Jun 1888, married, parents: H.P. Richardson and Freelove Estep, death cause: "tuberculosis and lukemia", informant: G.W. Richardson, buried: Hamby Cemetery, died: 16 Jun 1923, record (1923) #: 146.

Infant GARLAND, female, parents: David Garland and Sindy Ferches, death cause: "unknown", informant: Ike Garland, buried: Blevins Cemetery, born/died: 18 Jun 1923, record (1923) #: 147.

Cori LOW (Lowe ?), born: 28 May 1919, parents: Steve Low and Martha Luis, death cause: "flucks", informant: Steve Low (Carter), buried: Grindstaff Cemetery, died: 20 Jun 1923, record (1923) #: 148.

Raymond LOVELESS, born: 30 Apr 1921, parents: A.F. Loveless and Rebecca Heaton, death cause: "measles and bronchitis", informant: Tom Loveless (Valley Forge), buried: Bowers Cem., died: 23 Jun 1923, record #: 149.

Oma Marton SMITH, age 36 years, married, parents: James Morton and Ellen Lewis, death cause: "placinta .. (illegible)", informant: J.A.B. Smith (Cardens Bluff), died: 24 Jun 1923, record (1923) #: 150.

G. TRIPLETT, female, born: Apr 1921, parents: Charlie Triplett and Dealie (illegible), death cause: illegible, died: 25 Jun 1923, record (1923) #: 151.

Henry HURLEY, born: 26 Apr 1923, parents: Sam Hurley and Betsy Taylor, death cause: not stated, buried: Garland Cem., died: 26 Jun 1923, record (1923) #: 152.

Clyde R. SHOUN, born: 4 Sep 1885, County Court Clerk, married, parents: Landon Shoun and Mary Smith, death cause: "pulmonary tuberculosis", informant: Pete Elliott (Elizabethton), buried: Highland Cemetery, died: 30 Jun 1923, record (1923) #: 153.

Infant FAIR, male, parents: S.S. Fair and Mattie B. Bradshaw (Hawkins County), death cause: "stillborn", buried: Highland Cemetery, died: 4 Jun 1923, record (1923) #: 154.

Infant SAMS, female, parents: Silas Sams (Sullivan County) and Grace Fair, death cause: "stillborn", buried: Highland Cemetery, died: 4 Jun 1923, record (1923) #: 155.

Infant BERRY, male, parents: Bert Berry (NC) and Ethel Oaks, death cause: "stillborn", buried: Perry Cemetery, died: 16 Jun 1923, record (1923) #: 156.

Infant NAVE, sex not stated, parents: Robert Nave and Bessie Fair, death cause: "stillborn", informant: Robert Nave (Elizabethton), died: 17 Jun 1923, record (1923) #: 157.

Infant SMITH, male, parents: Oscar Smith and Rina Marton, death cause: "stillborn", informant: J.A.B. Smith (Cardens Bluff), died: 24 Jun 1923, record (1923) #: 158.

Vila TAYLOR, male, age 11 years, parents: Mike Taylor and Pheba Taylor, death cause: "catarrhal dysentery", buried: Taylor Cemetery, died: 7 Jul 1923, record (1923) #: 159.

Kallie TAYLOR, age 11 years, parents: Mike Taylor and Pheba Taylor, death cause: "flux", buried: Taylor Cemetery, died: 7 Jul 1923, record (1923) #: 160.

Bethean ARNOLD, female, age 71 years, parents: Nick Campbell and Susan Campbell, death cause: "tuberculosis", informant: Jess Arnold (Carter), buried: Cole Cemetery, died: 8 Jul 1923, record (1923) #: 161.

F.D. KITE, born: 21 Jun 1922, parents: Alvin Kite and Nittie Smith, death cause: "cholera", died: 9 Jul 1923, record (1923) #: 162.

Dock TIMBS, age 26 years, single, parents: father's name not given and Danna Timbs, death cause: "gun shot wound, homicidal", informant: Wade McQueen (Butler), buried: Fish Springs, died: 11 Jul 1923, record: 163.

J.L. GRINDSTAFF, born: 28 Apr 1921, parents" W.F. Grindstaff and Jennie Hardin, death cause: "dysentery", buried: Grindstaff Cemetery, died: 14 Jul 1923, record (1923) #: 164.

Ford JONES, born: 29 Dec 1913, parents: Robert Jones and Rosa Gregg, death cause: "peritonitis", buried: Miller Cemetery, Valley Forge, died: 15 Jul 1923, record (1923) #: 165.

Ford JONES, record is duplicate of 165, record (1923) #: 166.

Bruce MCKINNEY, age 30 years, married, parents: T.C. McKinney and Hester Stevens, death cause: "pulmonary tuberculosis", informant: Wilson McKinney (Hampton), buried: McKinney Cemetery, died: 15 Jul 1923, record (1923) #: 167.

Infant HURLEY, male, born: 26 Apr 1923, parents: James Hurley and Betsy Taylor, death cause: not recorded, informant: James Hurley (Carter), buried: Garland Cemetery, died: 16 Jul 1923, record (1923) #: 168.

Jean GOODWIN, born: 4 May 1922, parents: Lafayette Goodwin and Mollie Wilson, death cause: "measles and cholera", informant: B.H. Peters (Hampton), buried: Cardens Bluff, died: 17 Jul 1923, record #: 169.

James Campbell PETERS, born: 11 Aug 1921, parents: James Campbell and Mary Ann Peters, death cause: "measles and pneumonia", informant: Dan Peters (Hampton), buried: Morton Cemetery, died: 18 Jul 1923, record (1923) #: 170.

Marion Leon KITE, born: 16 May 1923 in Florida, parents: Marion B. Kite and Laura Ward, death cause: "pneumonia", informant: G.R. Simerly (Johnson City), buried: Valley Forge, died: 18 Jul 1923, record (1923) #: 171.

Mary Grace CAMPBELL, born: 8 Jun 1904, single, parents: T.C. Campbell and Magie Shell, death cause: "pulmonary tuberculosis", informant: Nat Campbell (Braemar), buried: Campbell Cemetery, died: 19 Jul 1923, record (1923) #: 172.

Katherine VEST, born in 1850, age 73 years, parents: Jeramiah Emmert and Fannie Moody, death cause: "cancer", resided at Watauga, died: 20 Jul 1923, record (1923) #: 173.

Netty LUIS, age 3 years, 5 months and 11 days, parents; Landon Luis and Bunch Smith, death cause: "dysentery", informant: Landon Luis (Carter), buried: Grindstaff Cemetery, died: 20 Jul 1923, record (1923) #: 174.

Lizzie FONDREN, born: 24 May 1841, parents: William Fondren (NC) and Crosha McAlister, death cause: "cardiac delatation", informant: George Fondren (Elizabethton), died: 20 Jul 1923, record (1923) #: 175.

China SMITH, born: 20 Feb 1923, parents: Carl Smith and Urath Harmon, death cause: "bowell efection", informant: Grant Harmon (Dark Ridge, NC), buried: Walnut Mountain, died: 21 Jul 1923, record #: 176.

Doris Christine ESTEP, born: 20 Jun 1921, parents: Wesley Estep and Flossie White, death cause: "measles and pneumonia fever", informant: H.D. Estep (Cardens Bluff), died: 21 Jul 1923, record (1923) #: 177.

Nick GRINDSTAFF, age 72 years, born in Johnson County, parents: "not known", death cause: not stated, died: 21 Jul 1923, record (1923) #: 178.

Odell WINTERS, born: 17 Jul 1923, parents: William M. Winters (Avery County, NC), and Bessie Lee Winters, death cause: "hives", informant: W.M. Winters (Shell Creek), died: 23 Jul 1923, record (1923) #: 179.

Floyd CULBERT, age 11 years and 10 months, parents: Robert Culbert and Mary Shuffield, death cause: "measles and dysentery", informant: J.N. Peters (Carter), buried: Grindstaff Cemetery, died: 22 Jul 1923, record (1923) #: 180.

Barbara CULBERT, born: 19 Jul 1923, parents: Robert Culbert and Mary Shuffield, death cause: "measles and dysentery", informant: H.M. Renfro (Carter), buried: Grindstaff Cem, died: 23 Jul 1923, record #: 181.

Infant ESTEP, male, parents: Wiley Estep and Clara Dugger, death cause: "not stated, lived 2 hours", informant: Witey Estep (Carter), buried: Hurley Cemetery, died: 23 Jul 1923, record (1923) #: 182.

Harsin ELLIOTT, age 72 years, parents: first name illegible Elliott and Elsey Loy, death cause: "old age", informant: Jane Elliott (Carter), died: 22 Jul 1923, record (1923) #: 183.

Alvin Bertie CROW, born: 12 Jun 1894, single, parents: D. Crow and Sallie Blevins, death cause: "overdose of opiate", informant: D. Crow, buried: Highland Cemetery, died: 23 Jul 1923, record (1923) #: 184.

Sarah J. WILSON, born: 12 Dec 1846, parents: Steve Cole and Winnie Cole, death cause: "tuberculosis", informant: Alf Nidiffer (Watauga Valley), buried: Ritchie Cem., died: 24 Jul 1923, record (1923) #: 185.

Siley CAMBLL, age 70 years, parents: Dave Garland and Bettie Wilson, death cause: "flux", informant: Isaac Cambll, buried: Cole Cemetery, died: 27 Jul 1923, record (1923) #: 186.

Ann SNODGRASS, born: 11 Dec 1873, married, parents: Richard Glover and May Lewis, death cause: "pernicious annemia", informant: John Snodgrass (Valley Forge), buried: Glover Cemetery, died: 27 Jul 1923, record (1923) #: 187.

_____ GARLAND, female, age 13 years, parents: first name illegible Garland and Margaret Williams, death cause: "flux", buried: Garland Cemetery, died: 28 Jul 1923, record (1923) #: 188.

Lee MOORE, age 68 years, married, parents: ____ Moore and Polly Carver, death cause: "influenza and cardiac dilitation", informant: Henry Moore (Hopson), buried: Whitehead Cemetery, died: 29 Jul 1923, record (1923) #: 189.

Rena PIERCE, born: 22 Oct 1922, parents: Joe Pierce and Bertha Bowers, death cause: "dysentery", informant: Thomas Williams (Braemar), buried: Buckles Cemetery, died: 30 Jul 1923, record (1923) #: 190.

George Albert MYERS, parents: Thomas Myers and Delia Sneed, death cause: "stillborn", died: 1 Jul 1923, record (1923) #: 191.

Infant LOVELESS, female, parents: A.F. Loveless and Rebecca Heaton, death cause: "premature birth", informant: A.F. Loveless (Valley Forge), born/died: 9 Jul 1923, record (1923) #: 192.

Jesse WALKER, born: 1 Apr 1915, parents: Elbert Walker and Lizzie Nidiffer, death cause: "septicenica from infected (illegible)", informant: Sol Wilson (Carter), buried: Taylor Cemetery, died: 1 Aug 1923, record (1923) #: 193.

Robert CULBERT, Jr., born: 6 Jan 1922, parents: Robert Culbert and May Shuffield, death cause: "measles and dysentery", buried: Grindstaff Cemetery, died: 5 Aug 1923, record (1923) #: 194.

William D. DAVIS, age 42 years, divorced, parents: Sam Davis (VA) and Nannie Brooks, death cause: "abscess in side caused by slate falling on him", informant: Sanford Davis (Carter), died: 6 Aug 1923, record (1923) #: 195.

Larance FORBS, age 3 months and 8 days, parents: George Forbs and Hattie Campbell (NC), death cause: "stomach and bowel trouble", informant: Loftis Jackson (Roan Mountain), buried: Nelson Cemetery, died: 6 Aug 1923, record (1923) #: 196.

John COLE, born: 4 Jun 1923, parents: D.C. Cole and Rosa Peters, death cause: "dysentery", informant: D.C. Cole (Carter), buried: Peters Cemetery, died: 8 Aug 1923, record (1923) #: 197.

Thelma Marie GOUGE, born: 10 Dec 1922, parents: Robert Avery Gouge (NC) and Ella Grace Holly, death cause: "colitis", died: 9 Aug 1923, record (1923) #: 198.

George GUINN, born: 13 Jan 1923, parents: first name illegible Guinn (NC) and Zillie Williams, death cause: "cholera", informant: Warnie Guinn (Hampton), buried: Valley Forge, died: 9 Aug 1923, record (1923) #: 199.

Thomas GARLAND, age 11 years, parents: James Garland and ____ Cole, death cause: "measles", informant: Bob Hardin (Carter), died: 11 Aug 1923, record #: 200.

Minnie Lee MILTON, born: 10 Oct 1901 in Johnson County, married, parents: Isaac Ward (Bakers Gap, Johnson Co., TN) and Mollie Arnold (Bakers Gap), death cause: "tuberculosis of lungs", informant: J.A. Lunceford (Butler), buried: Smith Cemetery, died: 12 Aug 1923, record (1923) #: 201.

Vicy CARVER, age 16 years, parents: Dan Potter and Nancy Carver, death cause: "typhoid fever", informant: Joe Carver (Elizabethton), buried: Blevins Cemetery, died: 12 Aug 1923, record (1923) #: 202.

Virgil BIRCHFIELD, born: 15 Sep 1905, single, parents: Sam Birchfield and Olivia Brewer (NC), death cause: "wood alcohol poisoning", informant: Samuel Birchfield (Roan Mountain), died: 14 Aug 1923, record #: 203.

Charles T. LACEY, born: 7 Nov 1881, married, parents: John L. Lacey and Celia Crow, death cause: "measles and pneumonia", informant: R.S. Lacey (Hopson), died: 14 Aug 1923, record (1923) #: 204.

Snide TAYLOR, age 4 years, 8 months and 16 days, parents: Bob Taylor and Luthrin Grindstaff, death cause: "floks", informant: Bob Taylor (Carter), died: 15 Aug 1923, record (1923) #: 205.

Callie E. PETERS, born: 28 Dec 1922, parents: Robert H, Peters and Maggie Lipps, death cause: "measles and dysentery", informant: R.H. Peters (Carter), buried: Blevins Cem., died: 15 Aug 1923, record (1923) #: 206.

Addie MATHESON, born: 10 Nov 1921, parents: Will Matheson (Johnson County) and Lillie Netherly (Johnson County), death cause: "abscess of right side of neck, ilio colitis", informant: Will Matheson (Elizabethton), buried: Highland Cemetery, died: 16 Aug 1923, record (1923) #: 207.

Ellen ROBERTS, born: Apr 1878 in Virginia, divorced, parents: W.W. Roberts (VA) and Julia Hayton (VA), death cause: "stroke", informant: John Roberts (Elizabethton), buried: Highland Cemetery, died: 18 Aug 1923, record (1923) #: 208.

Warren G. WILLIAMS, age 1 year and 2 months, parents: M.C. Williams and Lillie Bowers, death cause: "disentery", died: 18 Aug 1923, record (1923) #: 209.

Francis Jane SIMERLY, born: 5 Feb 1922, parents: Clayton Simerly and Creta Campbell, death cause: "measles", informant: M.D. Campbell (Cardens Bluff), buried: Valley Forge, died: 19 Aug 1923, record: 210.

Daniel Landrine REECE, born: 25 May 1857, married, parents: James F. Reece and Annie Eggers (NC), death cause: "accidental death from explosion", informant: M.F. Sumerlin (Elizabethton), buried: Neva, TN, died: 19 Aug 1923, record (1923) #: 211.

Cora ESTEP, age 33 years, 4 months and 3 days, married, parents: Kitch (illegible) and Mara Elliott, death cause: not stated, informant: Bob Estep, husband, (Carter), buried: Grindstaff Cemetrery, died: 19 Aug 1923, record (1923) #: 212.

Mary MORRIS, born: 4 Aug 1904, single, parents: James Morris and Patsy Glover (Sullivan County), death cause: "tuberculosis", died: 20 Aug 1923, record (1923) #: 213.

Barbara MARKLING, age 1 year and 4 months, parents: Wilbon Markling and Sara Hardin, death cause: not stated, infomant: Wilbon Markling (Carter), died: 20 Aug 1923, record (1923) #: 214.

Julia Ann ESTEP, age 90 years, widow, parents: Isah Garland and Nancy Hodge, death cause: "disentery", informant: S.R. Estep (Carter), buried: Garland Cemetery, died: 21 Aug 1923, record (1923) #: 215.

Sabina WARREN, born: 31 Jan 1896 in Watauga County, NC, married, parents: Lemuel Wilson (Watauga Co., NC) and Cornelia Wilson (Watauga Co., NC), death cause: "chronic nephritis", informant: Roe Warren (Watauga), buried: Boone, NC, died: 25 Aug 1923, record #: 216.

William HOLLOWAY, born: 8 Jul 1849 in Wilkes County, NC, married, parents: Daniel Holloway (NC), and Sarah Bougus (NC), death cause: "acute nephritis", informant: George W. Holloway (Watauga), buried: Chilhowie, VA, died: 25 Aug 1923, record (1923) #: 217.

William Paul LYONS, born: 25 Aug 1922, parents: Will Lyons and Blanche Honeycutt, death cause: "mennigitis", informant: William Lyons (Hampton), buried: Lyons Cem., died: 26 Aug 1923, record #: 218.

James LARGE, Jr., born: 8 Sep 1922, parents: James Large (VA) and Julia Riggs, death cause: "enteritis, colitis", informant: James Large (Elizabethton), buried: Colbaugh Cemetery, died: 26 Aug 1923, record (1923) #: 219.

Hiram CALLOWAY, born: 11 Apr 1845 in North Carolina, married, parents: "unknown", death cause: not stated, informant: Peter Range (Elizabethton), died: 22 Aug 1923, record (1923) #: 220.

Martha Bell CAMPBELL, age 8 years, parents: Mike Campbell and Elizabeth Wilson, death cause: "typhoid fever", informant: J.W. Salor (Johnson City), buried: Blevins Cem., died: 29 Aug 1923, record (1923) #: 221.

Mrs. Cordelia Ann BANNER, born: 11 Sep 1848, widow, parents: Johathon W. Hyder and Elizabeth Fletcher, death cause: "unknown", informant: H.H. Banner (Powder Branch), buried: Highland Cemetery, died: 2 Sep 1923, record (1923) #: 222.

Ford BOWMAN, born: 5 Nov 1921, parents: Roy Bowman and Hassie Edmonson, death cause: "dysentery", informant: Matt Bowman (Elizabethton), buried: Hyder Cemetery, died: 5 Sep 1923, record (1923) #: 223.

Sarah F. GREENLYE, born: 5 Feb 1859, widow, parents: Samuel Vance and Sarah Miller, death cause: "pulmonary tuberculosis", informant: W.R. Grindstaff (Johnson City), died: 1 Sep 1923, record (1923) #: 224.

Samuel LIVINGSTON, age 78 years, married, parents: "unknown", death cause: "nuralgia of heart", informant: M.T. Campbell (Elizabethton), buried: Smith Cemetery, died: 8 Sep 1923, record (1923) #: 225.

Virginia CROW, colored, born: Jun 1923, parents: John Crow and Magnolia Brown, death cause: not stated, informant: John Crow (Elizabethton, Rt 2), died: 8 Sep 1923, record (1923) #: 226.

Bill BLEVINS, age 43 years, married, parents: Isaac Blevins and Nancy Miller, death cause: "flux", informant: Nancy Blevins (Carter), buried: Garland Cemetery, died: 9 Sep 1923, record (1923) #: 123.

Dayton MATHERLY, born: 15 Nov 1922, parents: W.M. Matherly and Della Sims, death cause: "measles and pneumonia", informant: Willie Meredith (Elizabethton), buried: Sims Cem., died: 9 Sep 1923, record #: 228.

Anis ELLIOTT, age 6 years, parents: illegible Elliott and May Luis, death cause: "croup", buried: Grindstaff Cemetery, died: 11 Sep 1923, record (1923) #: 229.

Mrs. Jane CLARK, born: 11 Jul 1875, parents: William Henson and Kathern Colts, death cause: "dropsy", informant: Nat Clark (Johnson City), buried: Clark Cemetery, died: 11 Sep 1923, record (1923) #: 230.

Pearl GUINN, born: 23 Jan 1922, parents: J.B. Guinn and Sallie Whitehead, death cause: "gastro entertis", informant: John Berry (Hampton), buried: Fair View Cemetery, died: 12 Sep 1923, record (1923) #: 231.

James Gibson CARTER, born: 10 May 1851, married, parents: Landon Carter and Debbie Ellis, death cause: "apoplexy, brain hemorrhage", informant: D.E. Carter (Elizabethton), buried: Highland Cemetery, died: 16 Sep 1923, record (1923) #: 232.

Hubert Ray DUGGER, born: 7 Mar 1892, married, parents: John F. Dugger and Eliza Williams, death cause: "colitis", informant: S.E. Dugger (Elizabethton), buried: Meredith Cemetery, died: 17 Sep 1923, record (1923) #: 233.

Jack PETERS, born: 25 Jun 1923, parents: Jim Peters and Cinda Johnson, death cause: not stated, informant: Jim Peters (Hampton), buried: Johnson Cemetery, died: 18 Sep 1923, record (1923) #: 234.

John Eddie Odel SCALF, born: 8 Mar 1923, parents: Joe Bowers and Tissue Scalf, death cause: not stated, buried: Colbaugh Cem., died: 18 Sep 1923, record: 235.

James Harry WHITE, born: 5 Jul 1923, parents: Ed White and Josie Burrow, death cause: "colitis", informant: Josie Bowers (Elizabethton), buried: Highland Cemetery, died: 22 Sep 1923, record (1923) #: 236.

Minie Catherine HOUSTON, born: 15 Apr 1881, married, parents: Andrew Jackson Feathers and Christine Adaline Little, death cause: "tuberculosis of lungs", informant: R.S. Houston (Watauga), buried: Houston Cemetery, died: 23 Sep 1923, record (1923) #: 237.

Martha Nave DAVIS, born: 5 Aug 1848, single, parents: Phillip Davis (Washington County) and Axie Roberson (NC), death cause: "tuberculosis of bowels", informant: Mrs Lonie Long (Elizabethton), died: 23 Sep 1923, record (1923) #: 238.

Barbara CULBERT, age 74 years, widow, parents: Mirida Dugger and Hannah Arnold, death cause: "not known", informant: Leta Culbert (Carter), buried: Grindstaff Cemetery, died: 23 Sep 1923, record (1923) #: 239.

Brown Lowe BOWERS, born: 29 Jul 1878, married, parents: Millard F. Bowers and Sallie Bowers, death cause: "unloading dynamite hole in quarry which exploded", informant: Dr. Joe Bowers, Carter, died: 24 Sep 1923, record (1923) #: 240.

Fred BUCHANAN, age 13 years, parents: James Buchanan (NC) and Pheba Miller (NC), death cause: "flux", informant: John Buchanan (Shell Creek), buried: Richardson Cem., died: 24 Sep 1923, record (1923) #: 241.

Jess W. JENKINS, born: 11 May 1923, parents: Harve Jenkins and Ethel Simerly, death cause: "flux", informant: Harve Jenkins (Valley Forge), died: 26 Sep 1923, record (1923) #: 242.

Margarette BLEVINS, age 1 year, 2 months and 3 days, parents: William Blevins and Minnie Ellis, death cause: "colitis", informant: Claude Ellis (Elizabethton), buried: Ellis Cemetery, died: 27 Sep 1923, record (1923) #: 243.

W.T. LEE, born: 6 Apr 1918, parents: John Lee (Va) and Lottie Crow, death cause: "measles and dysentery", informant: John Lee (Elizabethton), buried: Highland Cemetery, died: 27 Sep 1923, record (1923) #: 244.

James R. OAKS, born: 29 Jan 1922, parents: Julis Oaks and Sarah (illegible)(NC), death cause: "pneumonia", informant: Julis Oaks (Shell Creek), buried: Cable Cemetery, died: 28 Sep 1923, record (1923) #: 245.

David STOUT, age 69 years, single, parents: John R. Stout and Eliza Bunton, death cause: "supposed, heart failure", informant: Thomas Stout (Butler), buried: Elk Mills, died: 29 Sep 1923, record (1923) #: 246.

Clide COFFER, born: 13 Mar 1922, parents: illegible Coffer (NC) and Martha Grindstaff, death cause: "flux", informant: Grace Grindstaff (Carter), buried: Grindstaff Cemetery, died: 29 Sep 1923, record (1923) #: 247.

Eugene MYERS, born: 22 Oct 1922, parents: not stated, death cause: "measles", informant: Silas Myers (Elizabethton), buried: Highland Cemetery, died: 29 Sep 1923, record (1923) #: 248.

Infant PRESNELL, male, parents: R.J. Presnell (NC) and Lillie A. Blair (NC), death cause: "stillborn", died: 19 Sep 1923, record (1923) #: 249.

Infant RITCHIE, male, parents: Andrew Ritchie and Cordia Nidiffer, death cause: "not known", informant: Bill Elliott (Watauga Valley), buried: Ritchie Cem., born/died: 23 Sep 1923, record (1923) #: 250.

Ellen HARMON, born: 13 Jul 1878 in Dark Ridge, NC, married, parents: W.A. Clauson (NC) and Lottie Hicks (NC), death cause: "supposed, Brights disease", informant: Grant Harmon (Dark Ridge, NC), buried: Clauson Cem., died: 2 Oct 1923, record (1923) #: 251.

Ellen HARMON, age 46 years, married, parents: William Harmon and Lottie Hicks (Watauga Co., NC), death cause: "heart failure", informant: Maris Clauson (Butler), buried: Clauson Cemetery, died: 2 Oct 1922. (appears to be same person as record # 251)

Robert TEAGUE, born: 11 Aug 1847, married, parents: Logan Teague (NC) and Franie Teague (NC), death cause: "cardiac dropsy", informant: Disey Teague (Hampton), buried: Hall Cemetery, died: 6 Oct 1923, record (1923) #: 253.

Mary Elizabeth SCALF, born: 7 Oct, age 78 years, single, parents: David Scalf and Sison Smalling, death cause: "cardiac dropsy", buried: Highland Cemetery, died: 6 Oct 1923, record (1923) #: 254.

Erest SHULL, born: 13 May 1922, parents: S.H. Shull and Nora Holden, death cause: "cholera", informant: S.H. Shull (Hampton), buried: Morton Cemetery, died: 8 Oct 1923, record (1923) #: 255.

Susie RICHARDSON, age 63 years, born in Sullivan County, married, parents: Thomas Richardson (Sullivan County) and Susy Richards, death cause: "flux", informant: husband (Carter), buried: Richardson Cemetery, died: 9 Oct 1923, record (1923) #: 256.

Allen F. HARDIN, born: 11 Feb 1923, parents: Cleveland Hardin and Celia Loveless, death cause: "flux", informant: John Hardin (Valley Forge), buried: Loveless Cem., died: 9 Oct 1923, record (1923) #: 257.

Mrs. M.M. MILLER, born: 5 Jun 1890, married, parents: Jacob Leonard and Louisa Range, death cause: "pulmonary tuberculosis and myocarditis", informant: M.M. Miller (Johnson City), buried: Simmons Cemetery, died: 11 Oct 1923, record (1923) #: 258.

Floy Veina PATTON, born: 25 Feb 1890, married, parents: Arch Vest and Nona Jackson, death cause: "typhoid fever", informant: F.S. Patton, buried: Simmons Cem., died: 12 Oct 1923, record (1923) #: 259.

Martina Rebecca JOHNSON, born: 19 Jan 1861 in North Carolina, married, parents: Samuel Brown (NC) and Rebecca (illegible), death cause: "fractured skull, thrown from buggy", buried: Boone, NC, died: 13 Oct 1923, record (1923) #: 260.

Boyle ELLIOTT, born: 26 Jan 1916, parents: W.D. Elliott and Bell Campbell, death cause: "colitis", informant: P.H. Elliott, buried: Highland Cemetery, died: 14 Oct 1923, record (1923) #: 261.

J.H. HYDER, age 66 years, married, parents: Benjamin Hyder and Lottie Calton, death cause: "dropsy", informant: Bennie Hyder (Hampton), buried: Hyder Cemetery, died: 19 Oct 1923, record (1923) #: 262.

Mary L. RICHARDSON, born: 6 Aug 1922, parents: George Richardson and Other Perkins, death cause: "meningitis", informant: S.P. Huntley (Fish Springs), died: 20 Oct 1923, record (1923) #: 263.

Marjorie Lillian Leona BOWERS, Negro, born: 13 Feb 1923, parents: John Bowers and Maggie Taylor, death cause: "ilo colitis", informant: John Bowers (Elizabethton), buried: Cedar Grove Cemetery, died: 20 Oct 1923, record (1923) #: 264.

Gracey Mae NIDIFFER, born: 2 Jan 1901, married, parents: John Deloach and Ruth Turner, death cause: "pellegra", informant: William Estep, buried: Highland Cemetery, died: 23 Oct 1923, record (1923) #: 265.

Elakander KNIGHT, born: 14 Mar 1859 in North Carolina, married, parents: William Knight (NC) and Beckie Osborne (NC), death cause: "supposed, cerebral hemorrhage", informant: Susie Knight (Roan Mountain), buried: Hampton Creek, died: 26 Oct 1923, record: 266.

Infant STORNES, female, parents: Dewey Stornes and Dora Harrison, death cause: "stillborn", informant: Drewey Stornes (Shell Creek), buried: Buck Mountain, died: 5 Oct 1923, record (1923) #: 267.

Infant MURRAY, female, parents: Hobert Murray and Bonnie Elliott, death cause: "stillborn", buried: Highland Cem., died: 9 Oct 1923, record (1923) #: 268.

Infant JENKINS, male, parents: Vance Jenkins and Anna Carrou, death cause: "disformed", born/died: 23 Oct 1923, record (1923) #: 269.

Foyst Delmer LOWE, born: 13 Sep 1921, parents: Charles D. Lowe and Lula Penington (KY), death cause: "spinal meningitis", informant: Charles D. Lowe (Carter), died: 3 Nov 1923, record (1923) #: 270.

Robert Elmer ROBERTS, born: 23 Oct 1918, parents: W.C. Roberts (VA) and Janes Wilson (Johnson County), death cause: "measles", informant: W.C. Roberts (Elizabethton), buried: Highland Cemetery, died: 3 Nov 1923, record (1923) #: 271.

Hildred Juanetia ROBERTS, born: 26 Mar 1909, parents: William Ernest Roberts (VA) and Janes Elizabeth Wilson (Johnson Co.), death cause: "measles and pneumonia", buried: Highland, died: 4 Nov 1923, record #: 272.

Martin ESTEP, born: 25 May 1921, parents: James Estep (VA) and Nannie Kelley, death cause: "croup", informant: James Estep (Elizabethton), buried: Highland Cemetery, died: 5 Nov 1923, record (1923) #: 273.

Infant PRESNELL, male, parents: Link Presnell (NC) and Emily Heaton, death cause: "supposed, abortion", informant: Link Presnell (Butler), born/died: 6 Nov 1923, record (1923) #: 274.

Lena WHISENHUNT, age 4 years, parents: Isaac Whisenhunt and Lillie Royal, death cause: "croup", informant: James Chambers (Roan Mountain), buried: Blevins Cem., died: 7 Nov 1923, record (1923) #: 275.

Lee Etta TOWNSELL, born: 7 Jun 1902 in North Carolina, parents: Will Townsell and Vick Johnson (NC), death cause: "pneumonia, cepticemia", informant: Jake Guinn (Crabtree), died: 8 Nov 1923, record (1923) #: 276.

Mrs. L.C. ELLIS, born: 17 Mar 1845 in Abingdon Virginia, married, parents: Thomas Reed (VA) and Polly Sallings (VA), death cause: "mitral inconsistency", informant: Richard Ellis (Minneapolis, MN), buried: Ellis Cem., died: 9 Nov 1923, record (1923) #: 277.

Mrs. Lucy Irene COLE, born; 3 May 1893, married, parents: D.A. Newton and Ella Miller, death cause: not recorded, informant: C.M. Newton (Elizabethton), buried: Newton Cemetery, died: 15 Nov 1923, record (1923) #: 278.

Polina FLETCHER, age 1 year and 17 days, parents: Sesil Fletcher and Bertha Shuffield, death cause: not stated, buried: Carter, died: 16 Nov 1923, record (1923) #: 279.

Jaunita SMITH, age 2 years, 1 month and 29 days, parents: Dr. Lee Smith and Lesetta J. Vanhoy (VA), death cause: "spinal meningitis", informant: Dr. Lee Smith (Elizabethton), buried: W.J. Mottern Cemetery, died: 19 Nov 1923, record (1923) #: 280.

Annie E. SCOGGINS, age 63 years, born in North Carolina, widow, parents: not stated, death cause: "lagrippe and hemorrhage from lungs", informant: Arthor Scoggins (Elizabethton), buried: Crabtree, died: 20 Nov 1923, record (1923) #: 201.

Frank PETERS, born: 16 Mar 1855, married, parents: Thomas Peters and mother's name illegible, death cause: "Brights disease", informant: Mrs. E.H. Bowers (Hampton), buried: Morton Cemetery, died: 23 Nov 1923, record (1923) #: 202.

Ornie Sanford STOUT, born: 21 Nov 1910, parents: Robert Stout and Alice Heatherly, death cause: "peritonitis, appendix operation", informant: Robert Stout (Hampton), died: 23 Nov 1923, record (1923) #: 203.

G. Edward WAGNER, born: 28 Feb 1871 in Johnson County, parents: Joseph Wagner (Johnson County) and Louisa Smith, death cause: "asthma and myocarditis", informant: D.S. Wagner (Hampton), buried: Fish Springs, died: 23 Nov 1923, record (1923) #: 284.

Martha LEWIS, age 35 years, married, parents: Murry Lewis and Jude Heatherly, death cause: "flux", buried: Grindstaff Cemetery, died: 25 Nov 1923, record (1923) #: 285.

Marthy LOW, born: 18 Jul 1891, married, parents: Murry Luis and Evaline Hetherly, death cause: "mesale", informant: Steve Low (Carter), buried: Grindstaff Cemetery, died: 25 Nov 1925, record (1923) #: 286. (May be the same person in record # 285 above.)

Jamie Owen HARDIN, born: 9 Sep 1919, parents: Will Hardin and Ellen Colbaugh, death cause: "croup", buried: Blevins Cemetery, died: 26 Nov 1923, record (1923) #: 287.

Joyce E. PRESNELL, born: 19 Sep 1923, parents: R.J. Presnell (NC) and Lillie Blair (NC), death cause: "measles and pneumonia", informant: Mary Marshall (Elizabethton), buried: Emmert Cemetery, died: 27 Nov 1923, record (1923) #: 288.

Francis OXENDINE, born: 9 Apr 1922, parents: W.E. Oxendine (NC) and Emma Douglas, death cause: "measles and pneumonia", resided at Watauga, died: 29 Nov 1923, record (1923) #: 289.

Maggie HUGHES, age 67 years, born in Mitchell County, NC, widow, parents: Wash Troutman (NC) and mother's name not stated, death cause: "flu and pneumonia", informant: J.L. Gray (Roan Mountain), died: 29 Nov 1923, record (1923) #: 290.

Neita WILSON, born: 10 Sep 1918 in North Carolina, parents: Toke Wilson (NC) and Cinday Harrell (NC) death cause: "epilepsy and pneumonia", informant: Toke Wilson (Johnson City), died: 31 Nov 1923, record (1923) #: 291.

Infant LEONARD, male, parents: Bob Leonard and Lilian Hilton, death cause: "stillborn", buried: Highland Cemetery, died: 15 Nov 1923, record (1923) #: 292.

Infants GRINDSTAFF, twin girls (Bula and Elicate), parents: Ira Grindstaff and Nola Lewis, death cause: "premature", informant: Mrs. E.H. Minton, midwife (Elizabethton), born/died: 25 Nov 1923, record (1923) #: 293.

Infant LEWIS, male, parents: Rile Lewis and Myrtle Marton, death cause: "stillborn", informant: Rile Lewis (Fish Springs), died: 28 Nov 1923, record (1923) #: 294.

Ira WATSON, parents: Ralph Watson and Flora Biris, death cause: "abortion", informant: Roy Watson (Shell Creek), buried: Dave Stout Cemetery, died: 30 Nov 1923, record (1923) #: 295.

Bessie Mara INGRAM, born: 3 Jun 1923, parents: Cash Ingram and Pearl Whitehead, death cause: "broncho pneumonia", informant: John Leonard (Hopson), buried: Lacy Cemetery, died: 1 Dec 1923, record (1923) #: 296.

John M. LUTTRELL, born: 1 Jun 1912 in Johnson County, parents: father not stated and Laura Luttrell, death cause: "fractured skull", informant: Laura Luttrell (Elizabethton), buried: Mountain City, died: 3 Dec 1923, record (1923) #: 297.

General H. FRANKLIN, born: 5 Oct 1839 in North Carolina, married, pensioner, parents: Levi Franklin (NC) and Barbary Taylor (NC), death cause: "apoplexy", informant: R.E. Franklin (Valley Forge), died: 3 Dec 1923, record (1923) #: 298.

Sallie A. NAVE, born: 9 Feb 1880, married, parents: Elick Grindstaff and Susan Dugger, death cause: "brights and asthma", informant: W.E. Nave (Elizabethton), buried: Grindstaff Cemetery, died: 4 Dec 1923, record (1923) #: 199.

John DELOACH, born: 1 Oct 1871, married, parents: John Deloach and Lucy Williams, death cause: "lobar pneumonia", buried: Estep Cemetery, died: 5 Dec 1923, record (1923) #: 300.

William Crockett BIRCHFIELD, born: 9 Jun 1865 in Virginia, married, parents: Charles Birchfield and Lucinda Fletcher (VA), death cause: "diabetes and gangrene of foot", informant: Nat Birchfield (Elizabethton), died: 7 Dec 1923, record (1923) #: 301.

Albert BYRD, born: 28 Oct 1923, parents: William Byrd and Millie Grindstaff, death cause: "suppose, bowl hives", informant: Arther Berry (Hampton), buried: Berry Cem., died: 9 Dec 1923, record (1923) #: 302.

Ella May BUCKLES, born: 1 Sep 1922, parents: Alf Buckles and Abbie Nave, death cause: "broncho pneumonia", died: 10 Dec 1923, record (1923) #: 303.

Eliza HAWKINS, age 37 years, married, parents: Thomas Williams and Nancy Williams, death cause: "abdominal acites with penicoidites", informant: Charles Hawkins (Johnson City), buried: Taylor Chappel, died: 11 Dec 1923, record (1923) #: 304.

Mary Ellen CARVER, born: 15 Mar 1923, parents: George Carver and Nancy Miller, death cause: "spinal disease", buried: Carver Cemetery, died: 13 Dec 1923, record (1923) #: 305.

Roy COCHRAN, born: 24 Jul 1923, parents: Joe Cochran and Lillie Clark, death cause: "spinal myegitis", informant: Jim Berry, died: 18 Dec 1923, record: 306.

J.H. FIELDS, born: 4 Aug 1874, single, parents: W.H. Fields and Nancy Brewer (NC), death cause: "rhumatism and stomach trouble", informant: W.H. Fields (Shell Creek), buried: Taylor Cemetery, died: 19 Dec 1923, record (1923) #: 307.

Garal CHURCH, born: 18 Jun 1902, single, parents: Phillip Church (Watauga Co., NC) and Alice Morgan, death cause: "shot and killed", informant: Phillip Church (Dark Ridge, NC), buried: Christian Church Cemetery, died: 20 Dec 1923, record (1923) #: 308.

Joel TRIPLETT, age 83 years, born in North Carolina, married, parents: Samuel Triplett (NC) and Rebecca Triplett, death cause: "supposed, brights disease", informant: Abe Triplett (Butler), buried: Triplett Cemetery, died: 20 Dec 1923, record (1923) #: 309.

Dennis BROWN, born: 21 Dec 1923, parents: Tom Brown (NC) and Maggie McClenen (NC), death cause: "stillborn", informant: Tom Brown (Roan Mountain), died: 21 Dec 1923, record (1923) #: 310.

Thomas Young PATTON, born: 22 Jun 1842, widower, parents: S.E. Patton and Temperance Morgan, death cause: "apoplexy", informant: Dave Patton (Johnson City), buried: Patton Cemetery, died: 21 Dec 1923, record (1923) #: 311.

Sarah HOSS, age: 1 month and 25 days, parents: Ted Hoss and Bonnie Little, death cause: "bowl hives", informant: M. Butler (Hopson), buried: Holly Cemetery, died: 25 Dec 1923, record (1923) #: 312.

Elizabeth B. CARTER, born: 27 Aug 1923, parents: F.L. Carter and Lucy Estep, death cause: "congenital heart disease", informant: D. Chambers (Elizabethton), buried: Estep Cemetery, died: 25 Dec 1923, record (1923) #: 313.

A.P. SPIVIA, age 74 years, widower, parents: "unknown", death cause: "mitral regurgitation of heart", informant: Nat Hyder (Hampton), died: 25 Dec 1923, record (1923) #: 314.

Infant GLOVER, male, born: 22 Dec 1923, parents: Milton Glover (Sullivan County) and May McKeehan, death cause: "lobar pneumonia", informant: A.M. Glover (Elizabethton), died: 27 Dec 1923, record #: 315.

Edward GILBERT, age: 67 years, 6 months and 13 days, born in North Carolina, married, parents: James Gilbert (NC) and Matilda Mays (MO), death cause: illegible, informant: C.J. Sheffield (Butler), buried: Whitehead Cem., died: 29 Dec 1923, record #: 316.

Ludley RICHARDSON, male, age 6 years, parents: Loss Richardson and (illegible) Garland, death cause: "missel and pneumony fevr", informant: Will Cable (Carter), buried: Richardson Cemetery, died: 29 Dec 1923, record (1923) #: 317.

Daniel S. WATSON, parents: Ray Watson and Mary Stout, death cause: "abortion", informant: Ray Watson (Shell Creek), died: 1 Dec 1923, record (1923) #: 318.

Infant BYERS, male, parents: Harrison V. Byers (NC) and Susie Bierd, death cause: "stillborn", informant: Harrison Byers (Elizabethton), buried: North Carolina, died: 24 Dec 1923, record (1923) #: 319.

Charlie MILLER, parents: Taylor Miller and Carry Whitehead, death cause: "stillborn", informant: Oscar Whitehead, buried: Miller Cemetery, died: 25 Dec 1923, record (1923) #: 320.

Jennie CROW, born: 1 Feb 1881, single, parents: Lee Crow and Maragret Dugger, death cause: "lukemia and tuberculosis of liver", informant: Mrs. Belle Elliott (Elizabethton), buried: Highland Cemetery, died: 5 Jan 1924, record (1924) #: 1.

Emma Love SHUPE, born: 10 Aug 1877, married, parents: J.B. Fletcher and (illegible) Campbell, death cause: "tuberculosis", buried: Johnson County, died: 6 Jan 1924, record (1924) #: 2.

Gracey BAILEY, born: 22 Nov 1923, parents: Burney Bailey (NC) and Nancy Clark, death cause: "croup", buried: Clark Cemetery, died: 7 Jan 1924, record (1924) #: 3.

Hettie STOUT, born: 1 Oct 1898, married, parents: W.S. Manning and Mollie E. Fair, death cause: "palegra and disentery", informant: W.S. Sams (Elizabethton), died: 7 Jan 1924, record (1924) #: 4.

George HARDIE, black, age 72 years, parents: not stated, death cause: "lagrippe", informant: John Hardie (Shell Creek), buried: Negro Cemetery, died: 9 Jan 1924, record (1924) #: 5.

Ella BAKER, colored, age 50 years, born in North Carolina, married, parents: John Gardner (NC) and Sallie ___, death cause: "aortic insufficiency and enlarged liver", informant: Mrs Cora Redrick (Elizabethton), died: 13 Jan 1924, record (1924) #: 6.

Stant PETERS, born: 6 Dec 1922, parents: John W. Peters and Vena Colbaugh, death cause: "croup", buried: Peters Cemetery, Carter, died: 15 Jan 1924, record (1924) #: 7.

Mary WAYCASTER, age 75 years, born in North Carolina, widow, parents: Bentley Hollyfield (NC) and Hanna Jane Hollyfield, death cause: "dropsy", informant: George Harrison (Shell Creek), buried: Harrison Cemetery, died: 15 Jan 1924, record (1924) #: 8.

Sarah Ann SMITH, born: 24 Jan 1844 in Alexander County, NC, widow, parents: "unknown", death cause: "mitral regurgitation", informant: A.J. Pippin (Roan Mountain), died: 16 Jan 1924, record (1924) #: 9.

Ralph Hyder BLEVINS, born: 4 Jan 1924, parents: Romley Blevins and Pearl Hyder, death cause: "influenza and bronchitis", informant: Willie Meredith (Elizabethton), buried: Hyder Cemetery, died: 15 Jan 1924, record (1924) #: 10.

Ruth STREET, born: 18 Jan 1924, parents: Ed Street and Maxie Boone, death cause: "not known", buried: Roan Mountain, died: 19 Jan 1924, record (1924) #: 11.

John H. WINTERS, born: 15 Mar 1875, widower, parents: W.M. Winters and Catherine Strickland, death cause: "cardiac regurgitation", informant: David Holden (Shell Creek), buried: Caroway Cemetery, died: 19 Jan 1924, record (1924) #: 12.

Eva Sarah May DANNER, born: 8 Dec 1886 in North Carolina, married, parents: L.G. Hodge (NC) and Laura Monday (NC), death cause: "pulmonary tuberculosis", informant: C.L. Danner (Elizabethton), buried: Highland Cemetery, died: 19 Jan 1924, record (1924) #: 13.

Albert MCNEAL, age 4 months, parents: John McNeal and Myrtle Whaley, death cause: "measles and pneumonia", informant: A.C. Whaley (Butler), buried: McNealy Cemetery, died: 22 Jan 1924, record (1924) #: 14.

A.M. MILLER, age 75 years, born in Virginia, widower, parents: "unknown", death cause: "influenza, double pneumonia", informant: J.G. Miller (Johnson City), buried: Oak Grove Cemetery, died: 23 Jan 1924, record (1924) #: 15.

Mrs. Eliza J. HYDER, born: 15 Oct 1857, widow, parents: Morgan Treadway and Martha Hyder, death cause: "apoplexy", informant: Gretchen Hyder (Milligan), buried: Milligan Cemetery, died: 24 Jan 1924, record (1924) #: 16.

Fletcher Perry ROBERTS, born: 21 Mar 1876, widower, parents: John Roberts and Sarah Fletcher, death cause: "chronic nephritis", informant: Kate King Roberts (Elizabethton), buried: Highland Cemetery, died: 27 Jan 1924, record (1924) #: 17.

Evaline HARDIN, age 1 year and 4 months, parents: F.L. Hardin and Lottie Hardin, death cause: "measles and pneumonia", died: 28 Jan 1924, record (1924) #: 18.

Owen E. SAMS, born: 29 Jan 1825, married, parents: "unknown", death cause: not stated, informant: Lee Sams (Keenburg), buried: Carr Cemetery, died: 29 Jan 1924, record (1924) #: 19.

Roy Earl NAVE, born: 8 Mar 1922, parents: Red Nave and Bessie Williams, death cause: "rickets and anemia", informant: Ollie Collins (Valley Forge), buried: Nave Cemetery, died: 30 Jan 1924.

Infant JOHNSON, female, parents: Charlie Johnson and Hattie Arwood (NC), death cause: "stillborn", informant: Frank Johnson (Johnson City), buried: Taylor Cemetery, died: 23 Jan 1924, record (1924) #: 21.

Hazy E. COOPER, age 72 years, married, parents: Eligah Hollyfield and Katie Elkins, death cause: not stated, informant: Abe Cooper (Shell Creek), buried: Taylor Cemetery, died: 1 Feb 1924, record (1944) #: 22.
William R. FITZSIMMONS, born: 2 Jan 1854, single, parents: Robert Fitzsimmons and Eliza Lacy, death cause: "apoplexy", informant: Eugene Deloach (Elizabethton), died: 3 Feb 1924, record (1944) #: 23.
Eliza MCKINNEY, born: 14 Apr 1861, married, parents: William McKinney and Kate McKinney, death cause: "sarcoma", informant: Edgar McKinney (Elizabethton), died: 3 Feb 1924, record (1924) #: 24.
Catherine FEINNEY, age 80 years, widow, born in Wilkes County, North Carolina, parents: Wilson Greenway (NC) and Sallie Greenway (NC), death cause: "measles", informant: R.A. Finney (Butler), buried: Elk Cemetery, died: 3 Feb 1924, record (1924) #: 25.
Carley COOK, parents: Claten Cook and Cay Black, death cause: "abortion", inforant: L.E. Montgomery (Butler), buried: Whitehead Cemetery, born/died: 4 Feb 1924, record (1924) #: 26.
Annetha LEWIS, born: 31 Jan 1868, married, parents: G.W. Wilson and Mollie Mueter (NC), death cause: "Brights", informant: Charles Oliver (Watauga Valley), buried: Wilson Cemetery, died: 6 Feb 1924, record: 27.
Nona WHITE, born: 21 Jan 1924, parents: D.L. White and Ethel Smith, death cause: "atelictosis", informant: D.L. White (Butler), buried: Smith Cemetery, died: 7 Feb 1924, record (1924) #: 28.
Willie SCOTT, born: 25 Dec 1922, parents: Thurman Scott (Washington County) and Bessie Stepp, death cause: "measles and pneumonia", informant: Thurman Scott, buried: Mottern Cemetery, died: 8 Feb 1924, record (1924) #: 29.
Nerva BLEVINS, age 48 years, born in North Carolina, parents: John Hileman (NC) and Emmaline Gillen (NC), death cause: "measles and pneumonia", informant: James Blevins (Hampton), buried: Simerly Cemetery, died: 11 Feb 1924, record (1924) # 30.
Gertie WILLIAMS, born: 30 Aug 1875 in North Carolina, married, parents: father not stated and Edith Sanders (NC), death cause: "Brights diease", informant: Daniel Williams (Valley Forge), buried: Smith Cemetery, died: 12 Feb 1924, record (1924) #: unnumbered.
Rosa LEDFORD, age 10 years, parents: illegible, death cause: illegible, informant: Mrs. L.L. Minton (Johnson City), buried: Taylor Chappel, died: date illegible, buried: 14 Feb 1924, record (1924) #: 32.

Nancy HAWKINS, age not stated, parents: Charles Hawkins and mother not stated, death cause: illegible, buried: Taylor Chappel, died: date illegible, buried: 14 Feb 1924, record (1924) #: 33.

Martha Jane HATHAWAY, born: 4 Jul 1837, widow, parents: John Wesley and Nancy Dolan, death cause: "lobar pneumonia", informant: Mollie Jenkins (Valley Forge), buried: Smith Cemetery, died: 14 Feb 1924, record (1924) #: 34.

Carl MILTON, born: 18 Jan 1923, parents: A.M. Milton and Minnie Ward, death cause: "measles and pneumonia", informant: Clate Ward (Butler), died: 15 Feb 1924, record (1924) #: 35.

Lois SMITH, born: 2 Apr 1923, parents: Grant Smith and Velia Morton, death cause: "infection of throat and pneumonia", informant: Grant Smith (Hampton), buried: Cardens Bluff, died: 17 Feb 1924, record (1924) #: 36.

Mrs. Blaine PHILLIPS, age 36 years, born in Mitchell County, NC, married, parents: Will (illegible) and Sissie Stanley (NC), death cause: "pulmonary tuberculosis", informant: Isaac Phillips (Milligan), buried: NC, died: 18 Feb 1924, record (1924) #: 37.

Maggie SWEENEY, born: 7 Aug 1901, single, born in Virginia, parents: Baker Swenny and Mollie Lawson, death cause: "pregnancy and ecloupsia", informant: Alice Sammons (Mountain City), buried: Mountain City, died: 20 Feb 1924, record (1924) #: 38.

Nancy NIDIFFER, age 72 years, widow, parents: P. Williams and ____ Pierce, death cause: "flu and pneumonia", died: 20 Feb 1924, record (1924) #: 39.

Roy WHALEY, born: 4 Feb 1922, parents: William Whaley and Stella Timbs, death cause: "measles and pneumonia", informant: Grover Vines (Fish Springs), buried: Smith Cemetery, died: 20 Feb 1924, record (1924) #: 40.

Ora Bell WHITEHEAD, born: 22 Aug 1923, parents: Loss Whitehead and Ella Marsh, death cause: "spinal menngites", buried: Dugger Cemetery, died: 22 Feb 1924, record (1924) #: 41.

Mary J. GOUGE, age about 60 years, married, parents: John Simerly and Susie Chambers, death cause: "cancer of womb", informant: William Gouge (Hampton), buried: Simerly Cem., died: 21 Feb 1924, record (1924) #: 42.

Infant WHITEHEAD, female, born: 22 Aug 1923, parents: Loss Whitehead and Ella Marsh, death cause: "infantile paralysis", informant: Grant Range (Elizabethton), buried: Dugger Cemetery, died: 22 Feb 1924, record (1924) #: 43.

Jennie WILLS, born: 27 Mar 1902, married, parents: Sam Estep (VA) and Ella Teague (NC), death cause: "pulmonary tuberculosis", informant: Sam Estep (Elizabethton), buried: Colbaugh Cemetery, died: 22 Feb 1924, record (1924) #: 44.

Lona Estaline CAMPBELL, born: 7 Apr 1923, parents: Sam Campbell and Eliza Beckner (Hawkins County), death cause: "pneumonia", buried: Highland Cemetery, died: 23 Feb 1924, record (1924) #: 45.

Bernice JOHNSON, born: 11 Feb 1924, parents: father not stated and Joda Johnson (NC), death cause: "hives", informant: Goldman Johnson (Shell Creek), buried: Markland Cemetery, died: 23 Feb 1924, record (1924) #: 46.

James H.T. WILLIAMS, born: 3 Apr 1851, married, parents: John B. Williams and Caroline Clark, death cause: "heart trouble", informant: R.L. Williams (Fish Springs), buried: Williams Cemetery, died: 25 Feb 1924, record (1924) #: 47.

Maritia THOMPSON, Negro, age about 80 years, born in Burnsville, NC, parents: Redding Williams and Lucinda Woodfin (Ashville, NC), death cause: "brain hemorrhage", resided at Watauga, died: 27 Feb 1924, record (1924) #: 48.

Mary A. NAVE, age 65 years, widow, parents: Joel D. Nave and Sarah A. McQueen, death cause: illegible, informant: Henry L. Nave (Elizabethton), buried: Nave Cemetery, died: 29 Feb 1924, record (1924) #: 49.

Infant RANGE, male, parents: Arnold Range and Della Leonard (Washington County), death cause: "stillborn", informant: Jake Range (Watauga), died: 2 Feb 1924, record (1924) #: 50.

Infant CHAMBERS, male, parents: C.L. Chambers and Hattie Whitehead, death cause: "stillborn", informant: C.L. Chambers (Roan Mountain), buried: Chambers Cemetery, died: 6 Feb 1924, record (1924) #: 51.

Infant ANDERSON, female, parents: Charlie Anderson and Altia Moody, death cause: "stillborn", informant: Charles Anderson (Elizabethton), buried: Sugar Grove Cemetery, died: 7 Feb 1924, record (1924) #: 52.

Infant LENDWELL, male, parents: A. Lendwell (Johnson City) and Lola Campbell, death cause: "stillborn", informant: C.N. Campbell, buried: Highland Cemetery, died: 26 Feb 1924, record (1924) #: 53.

Infant GOODMAN, male, parents: Clarence Goodman and Grace Williams, death cause: "stillborn", buried: Highland Cem., died: 29 Feb 1924, record (1924) #: 54.

Infant WARD, male, born: 20 Feb 1914, parents: W.G. Ward and Carrie Greenway, death cause: "deformity", informant: R.A. Range (Elizabethton), buried: Keenburg, died: 1 Mar 1924, record (1924) #: 55.

John H. HOBSON, born: 27 Sep 1893, married, parents: Jackson Hobson and Catherine Potter, death cause: "cerebral hemorrhage", buried: Isaac Cemetery, died: 2 Mar 1924, record (1924) #: 56.

Willis Harding ROBERTS, born: 1 Aug 1920, parents: Dudley Roberts and Blanch Crow, death cause: "measles and colitis", buried: Highland Cemetery, died: 5 Mar 1924, record (1924) #: 57.

Thomas DELOACH, age 21 years, single, parents: James Deloach and Emeline Deloach, death cause: "heart failure", informant: E.D. McQueen (Fish Springs), buried: Williams Cemetery, died: 6 Mar 1924, record (1924) #: 58.

Lockie BORDERS, born: 22 Aug 1904, parents: Harison Borders and Liza Miller, death cause: "pneumonia", informant: Walter Borders (Shell Creek), buried: Markland Cem., died: 7 Mar 1924, record (1924) #: 59.

Dorothy SMITH, born: 23 Jul 1920, parents: Loss Smith and Mary McKinney, death cause: "pneumonia and measles", informant: Loss Smith (Elizabethton), buried: Siam, died: 8 Mar 1924, record (1924) #: 60.

Bethwin COLLINS, born: 12 Jun 1911, parents: Ollie Collins, Jr. and Dessie Nave, death cause: "measles and pneumonia", buried: Nave Cemetery, died: 10 Mar 1924, record (1924) #: 61.

Ethel GARLAND, age 8 months and 5 days, parents: Petibone Garland and Elizabeth Estep, death cause: not stated, buried: Garland Cemetery, Carter, died: 11 Mar 1924, record (1924) #: 62.

Bertha WAGNER, born: 28 Apr 1893, married, parents: James Rains and Eliza Archer, death cause: "tuberculosis", informant: Eliza Rains (Carter), buried: Grindstaff Cemetery, died: 11 Mar 1924, record (1924) #: 63.

Margarette WILSON, age 71 years, married, parents: Richard Anderson (NC) and ____ Oliver, death cause: "pneumonia", died: 11 Mar 1924, record (1924) #: 64.

Infant ELLIS, female, born: 8 Mar 1924, parents: Claud Ellis and Neta Blevins, death cause: "purfura hoemorrhagica", informant: Claud Ellis (Elizabethton), buried: Ellis Cemetery, died: 11 Mar 1924, record (1924) #: 65.

Franklin SCOTT, age 66 years, widower, parents: Marshall Scott and Sallie McKanny, death cause: "cirrhosis of liver", buried: Scott Cemetery, resided: Watauga, died: 18 Mar 1924, record (1924) #: 66.

Polley HURT, born: 11 Apr 1836, married, parents: John Blevins and Liddie Dugger, death cause: "cerebral hemorrhage", informant: Dayton Hurt (Elizabethton), buried: Highland, died: 12 Mar 1924, record #: 67.

William H. LOWE, born: 13 Jun 1875, married, parents: John Lowe and Martha Lipps, death cause: "pulmonary tuberculosis", informant: John Lowe (Carter), buried: Grindstaff Cemetery, died: 12 Mar 1924, record #: 68.

Malcolm Nevil FOLSOM, born: 9 Mar 1862, married, parents: Benjamin F. Folsom and Sallie Ryan, death cause: "influenza and pneumonia", informant: Ruth Folsom (Elizabethton), buried: Highland, died: 12 Mar 1924, record (1924) #: 69.

Raymond ESTEP, born: 4 Mar 1924, parents: Henry Estep and Eliza Hays, death cause: not stated, informant: Henry Estep (Elizabethton), buried: Hyder Cemetery, died: 14 Mar 1924, record (1924) #: 70.

John J. MORRELL, born: 10 May 1852, married, parents: Caleb Morrell and Levisa Crow, death cause: "organic heart disease", informant: Ellis Morrell (Elizabethton), buried: Ellis Cemetery, died: 15 Mar 1924, record (1924) #: 71.

J. SAMES, male, born: 2 Mar 1824, parents: father's name illegible and Grace Fair, death cause: "premature delivery", buried: Highland Cemetery, died: 15 Mar 1925, record (1924) #: 72.

Lloyd Quinten WILLIAMS, born: 2 Nov 1923, parents: Albert Williams and Bell Bowers, death cause: "unknown", buried: Wilson Cemetery, Watauga Valley, died: 17 Mar 1924, record (1924) #: 73.

Jack HOBSON, age 76 years, 5 months and 12 days, born in North Carolina, married, parents: (illegible) Hobson (NC) and Catherine Short (NC), death cause: "enlarged prostate", informant: Charlie Hobson (Shell Creek), buried: Isaacs Cemetery, died: 17 Mar 1924, record (1924) #: 74.

Nick PIERCE, born: 8 Feb 1924, parents: Hobert Pierce and Eva Williams, death cause: not stated, informant: R.B. Laws, buried: Williams Cemetery, Watauga Valley, died: 18 Mar 1924, record (1924) # 75.

Bessie DELOACH, born: 10 May 1923, parents: Dave Deloach and Maggie Collins, death cause: "influenza and pneumonia", buried: Deloach Cemetery, died: 19 Mar 1924, record (1924) #: 76.

David H. MILLER, born: 22 May 1851, married, parents: Apsy Miller and Nancy Forbes, death cause: "mitral regurgitation of heart", informant: A.J. Arnett (Roan Mountain), buried: Miller Cemetery, died: 20 Mar 1924, record (1924) #: 77.

John THOMPSON, colored, age about 80 years, born in North Carolina, parents: not stated, death cause: "Brights and heart leakage", informant: John Bowers, died: 20 Mar 1924, record (1924) #: 78.

Joyce ROBERTS, born: 4 May 1922, parents: D.J. Roberts and Blanch Crow, death cause: "measles and marasums", D.J. Roberts (Elizabethton), buried: Highland, died: 23 Mar 1924, record (1924) #: 79.

Harry Dwight ROBERTS, born: 7 Jul 1923, parents: Burt Roberts and Cordie Simerly, death cause: "whooping cough", informant: Dave Clark (Roan Mountain), buried: Nelson Cem., died: 27 Mar 1924, record (1924) #: 80.

Infant BOWERS, female, parents: Emmert Bowers and Rena Brown (NC), death cause: "undeveloped child", informant: Emmert Bowers (Braemar), buried: Hill Cemetery, born/died: 27 Mar 1924, record (1924) #: 81.

Clarence Frinklin DAUGHTERRY, born: 8 Mar 1924, parents: Roy Daughterry and Nell Bowling, death cause: "bronchial pneumonia", informant: Melvin Bowling, buried: Highland, died: 30 Mar 1924, record #: 82.

Andy ESTEP, age 58 years, married, parents: Johnson Estep and Julian Hagie, death cause: "sapos pralas", informant: S.R. Estep (Carter), buried: Garland Cemetery, died: 31 Mar 1924, record (1924) #: 83.

Granville V. GLOVER, born: 9 Oct 1879 in Sullivan County, married, parents: Marion Glover (Sullivan County) and Mary A. Lilly (Sullivan County), death cause: "bronchitis", informant: Mrs. Mary A. Lilly (Elizabethton), died: 31 Mar 1924, record #: 84.

Infant SAMS, male, parents: Silas Sams and Grace Fair, death cause: "stillborn", informant: Silas Sams (Elizabethton), buried: Highland Cemetery, died: 2 Mar 1924, record (1924) #: 85.

Infant COLE, female, parents: Clide Cole and Marthy Garland, death cause: "born dead", buried: Cole Cemetery, died: 13 Mar 1924, record (1924) #: 86.

Ray SCOTT, parents: E.E. Scott and ____ Dempsey, death cause: "stillborn", informant: E.E. Scott (Watauga), buried: Lacy Cem., died: 28 Mar 1924, record #: 87.

Calvin Lester MEREDITH, parents: C.E. Meredith and Geneva Hyder, death cause: "stillborn", informant: J.A. Meredith (Elizabethton), buried: Meredith Cem., Gap Creek, died: 30 Mar 1924, record (1924) #: 88.

Howard NIDIFFER, age 2 years, parents: Roy Nidiffer and Amelia Ensor, death cause: "ileo colitis", informant: Cecil Nidiffer (Elizabethton), buried: Highland Cem., died: 2 Apr 1924, record (1924) #: 89.

Thomas C. PRICE, Sr., born: 4 Dec 1836 in North Carolina, married, parents: R.R. Price (NC) and Katie Odum (NC), death cause: "dilatation of heart", informant: T.C. Price, Jr. (Elizabethton), buried: Simerly Creek Cemetery, died: 2 Apr 1924, record (1924) #: 90.

Rosa Lee ARWOOD, born: 15 Feb 1924, parents: John Arwood (NC) and Stella Simerly, death cause: "valvulor heart trouble", informant: John Arwood (Valley Forge), buried: Williams Cemetery, died: 3 Apr 1924, record (1924) #: 91.

Mary Alice CORNETT, born: 17 Mar 1924, parents: Dan Cornett and Sela Jordin, death cause: "lobar pneumonia", informant; Dan Cornett (Elizabethton), buried: Highland Cemetery, died: 5 Apr 1924, record (1924) #: 92.

Mary RICHARDSON, born: 28 Feb 1924, parents: Noa Richardson (NC) and Saley (illegible), death cause: not stated, informant: Noa Richardson (Carter), buried: Garland Cemetery, died: 5 Apr 1924, record (1924) #: 93.

Dora CROWELL, age 45 years, married, parents: father's name unknown and Rachel Pugh, death cause: "dropsy", informant: Will Crowell (Johnson City), buried: Taylors Chappell, died: 5 Apr 1924, record #: 94.

Eliza GUINN, born: 5 Apr 1904, married, parents: Bud Culbert and Venie Buckles, death cause: "mitral insufficiency", informant: Chris Robinson (Elizabethton), buried: Free Will Church Cemetery, died: 6 Apr 1924, record (1924) #: 95.

Mandie Bill HARRISON, born: 24 Jan 1924, parents: Anderson Harrison and Sallie (illegible), death cause: "bold hives", informant: Anderson Harrison (Shell Creek), buried: Harrison Cemetery, died: 6 Apr 1924, record (1924) #: 96.

Marthy RICHARDSON, age 3 months and 1 day, parents: Noa Richardson and mother's name illegible, death cause: not stated, informant: Noa Richardson (Carter), buried: Garland Cem., died: 8 Apr 1924, record #: 97.

Benjamin W. HARTLEY, born: Jan 1858 in North Carolina, widower, parents: Jessie Hartley (NC) and Nancy Dyer (NC), death cause: "paralysis", informant: Dora Simerly (Valley Forge), buried: Williams Cemetery, died: 8 Apr 1924, record (1924) #: 98.

Infant POTTER, male, born: 3 Apr 1924, parents: Ham Potter and Hessie Andrews, death cause: "hives", informant: Ham Potter (Butler), buried: Andrews Cemetery, died: 13 Apr 1924, record (1924) #: 99.

Eveline TREADWAY, born: 5 Mar 1853, widow, parents: not stated, death cause: "nephritis", informant: Hicks Treadway (Elizabethton), buried: Hunter Cemetery, died: 14 Apr 1924, record (1924) #: 100.

Frances GARLAND, born: 8 Apr 1921, parents: Will Garland (Mitchell Co., NC) and Ida Julian, death cause: "whooping cough", informant: Will Garland (Roan Mountain), buried: Heaton Creek Cemetery, died: 15 Apr 1924, record (1924) #: 101.

Rosa Nell LYONS, born: 4 Sep 1911, parents: G.W. Lyons and Katie Wilson, death cause: "mitral regurgitation", informant: C.V. Whitehead (Roan Mountain), buried: Hopson, died: 15 Apr 1924, record (1924) #: 102.

Mrs. Margaret PERRY, born: 17 Sep 1855 in Sullivan County, widow, parents: Johua and Mary Roiston (Sullivan County), death cause: "apoplexy", informant: T. Perry (Elizabethton), buried: Highland Cemetery, died: 15 Apr 1924, record (1924) #: 103.

Rosa SIMS, born: 3 Jan 1922, parents: Dan Sims and Kate Forbs, death cause: "measles and pneumonia", buried: Nelson Cemetery, died: 18 Apr 1924, record (1924) #: 104.

Dalice SHELL, male, born: 19 Apr 1924, parents: Harrison Shell (NC) and Cerie Shell, death cause: "supposed to be abortion", informant: Harrison Shell (Shell Creek), buried: Stout Cemetery, died: 20 Apr 1924, record (1924) #: 105.

Clyde Sexton BUCKLES, born: 27 Jun 1894, married, parents: Thomas Buckles and Celia Williams, death cause: "auto accident, crushed skull", informant: A.F. Buckles (Watauga Valley), buried: Stoney Creek, died: 20 Apr 1924, record (1924) #: 106.

Arlena HODGE, age 25 years, 10 months and 11 days, married, parents: Scott Hodge and Julie Vandyke (NC), death cause: "suicide", buried: Bradley Cemetery, died: 21 Apr 1924, record (1924) #: 107.

Elmer CLARK, born: 26 Aug 1919, parents: Nat Clark and Pollie Simerly, death cause: "lobar pneumonia", died: 21 Apr 1924, record (1924) #: 108.

Jane GIBBS, born: 24 Feb 1908, parents: James Gibbs (NC) and Rosa Brown (Ashe Co., NC), death cause: "pulmonary tuberculosis", informant: Rosa Gibbs (Roan Mountain), buried: Hampton Creek Cemetery, died: 22 Apr 1924, record (1924) #: 109.

Jane MARSHALL, born: 15 Dec 1864, married, parents: father's name unknown and ____ South, death cause: "organic heart disease", buried: Colbaugh Cemetery, resided at Watauga, died: 27 Apr 1924, record (1924) #: 110.

Eliza J. LOWE, born: 17 Jun 1876, single, parents: George J. Lowe and Jane Colbaugh, death cause: "tuberculosis", informant: Roy Lowe, buried: Grindstaff Cem., died: 27 Apr 1924, record (1924) #: 111.

Infant BUCKLES, male, parents: Alfred Buckles and Jane Berry, death cause: "stillborn", buried: Buckles Cemetery, died: 3 Apr 1924, record (1924) #: 112. (twin below)

Infant BUCKLES, male, parents: Alfred Buckles and Jane Berry, death cause: "stillborn", buried: Buckles Cemetery, died: 3 Apr 1924, record (1924) #: 113.

Angy RICHARDSON, born: 29 Apr 1867, married, parents: David Garland and Sara (illegible), death cause: "influenza", buried: Richardson Cemetery, died: 2 Apr 1924, record (1924) #: 114.

Lula VEST, born: 8 May 1888, widow, parents: Marion Humphreys and Martha Shell, death cause: "shock from hysterectomy", informant: John Humphreys (Watauga), buried: Mottern Cemetery, died: 5 May 1924, record (1924) #: 115.

Andrew W. CHESSER, born: 30 May 1844, married, parents: Wilson Chesser and mother's name not known, death cause: "intestinal nephritis", informant: Mary Smith (Hampton), buried: Campbell Cemetery, died: 9 May 1924, record (1924) #: 116.

Alma COOK, born: 5 May 1905, single, parents: W.M. Cook (NC) and Dillie Cook, death cause: "gangrenous appendix and clot in brain", informant: J.M. Cook (Milligan College), buried: Milligan Cemetery, died: 11 May 1924, record (1924) #: 117.

Katie TOWNSELL, born: 26 Jul 1922, parents: father not stated and (illegible) Townsell, death cause: "whooping cough", informant: Jacob Guinn (Roan Mountain), buried: Crabtree Cemetery, died: 15 May 1924, record (1924) #: 118.

Will MOORE, black, born: 16 Jun 1865 in North Carolina, married, parents: Ike Moore (NC) and Harritte Erwin (NC), death cause: "diabetes", informant: Wheeler Conley, buried: Odd Fellows Cemetery, died: 16 May 1924, record (1924) #: 119.

Mary WILSON, age 80 years, single, parents: Poe Wilson and Nancy Garland, death cause: "old age", buried: Garland Cem., died: 17 May 1924, record (1924) #: 120.

Nancy WILCOX, born: 17 Dec 1835 in North Carolina, widow, parents: "unknown", death cause: "mitral regurgitation of heart", informant: J.L. Byrd (Hampton), buried: Whitehead Cemetery, died: 17 May 1924, record (1924) #: 121.

Mrs. Jennie THOMAS, age 87 years, parents: father not stated and Tempie Estep, death cause: "appoplexy", informant: Mrs. Addie Lewis (Elizabethton), buried: Thomas Cem., died: 19 May 1924, record (1924) #: 122.

Joseph MCCLOUD, born: 10 Jul 1840 in North Carolina, married, parents: Isham McCloud and Mary Fair (NC), death cause: "stroke, paralysis", informant: Mrs. Mollie McCloud (Hampton), buried: Hall Cemetery, died: 21 May 1924, record (1924) #: 123.

Angeline TAYLOR, age 86 years, widow, parents: "unknown", death cause: "paralysis", died: 24 May 1924, record (1924) #: 124.

Thomas Clay MURRAY, born: 18 May 1848, married, parents: not stated, death cause: "paralysis", buried: Highland, died: 26 May 1924, record (1924) #: 125.

Infant MONTGOMERY, male, parents: McKinley Montgomery and Grace Peters, death cause: "atelectosis", informant: E.L. Peters (Cardens Bluff), born/died: 26 May 1924, record (1924) #: 126.

Jim COCHRAN, born: 12 Apr 1888, married, parents: John Cochran and Sarah Simerly, death cause: "double lobar pneumonia", infomant: John Cochran (Johnson City), buried: Williams Cemetery, died: 27 May 1924, record (1924) #: 127.

James D. NAVE, born: 6 Aug 1921, parents: James D. Nave and Rebecca Morrell, death cause: "gangrenous appendix", informant: Mrs. James D. Nave (Elizabethton), buried: Nave Cemetery, died: 27 May 1924, record (1924) #: 128.

Maggie STOVER, age 32 years, married, parents: Pete Elliott and Rena Archer, death cause: "pulmonary tuberculosis and childbirth", informant: John L. Stover (Elizabethton), buried: Colbaugh Cemetery, died: 30 May 1924, record (1924) #: 129.

Infant WAGNER, female, parents: Joe Wagner and Julia Crow, death cause: "stillborn", informant: Frank Crow (Elizabethton), buried: Highland, died: 8 May 1924, record (1924) #: 130.

Thelma ISAACS, parents: Clint Isaacs and Jula Main (VA), death cause: "abortion", informant: Clint Isaacs (Butler), died: 24 May 1924, record (1924) #: 131.

Benjamin Hawkins PETERS, born: 3 Aug 1899, married, parents: Frank Peters and Joan Archer, death cause: "influenza and pulmonary tuberculosis", informant: Joan Peters (Hampton), buried: Martin Cemetery, died: 1 Jun 1924, record (1924) #: 132.
Philmore Oakley MILLER, born: 13 Apr 1923, parents: Wesley Miller and Mandie Elliott, death cause: "rickets", informant: Wesley Miller (Shell Creek), buried: Richardson Cemetery, died: 2 Jun 1924, record (1924) #: 133.
Infant RAMSEY, female, born: 1 Jun 1924, parents: Joseph Ramsey (Banner Elk, NC) and Pearl Campbell, death cause: "hemorrhage from nose and mouth", informant: Joseph Ramsey (Hampton), buried: Hall Cemetery, died: 3 Jun 1924, record (1924) #: 134.
Thomas WHITE, age 55 years and 6 days, married, parents: George White and Mary Buckles, death cause: "gangrenous appendix", buried: Forbs Cemetery, died: 4 Jun 1924, record (1924) #: 135.
J.P. STOVER, born: 6 Jan 1924, parents: John L. Stover and Maggie Elliott, death cause: "pertussis", buried: Colbaugh Cem., died: 6 Jun 1924, record (1924) #: 136.
Elbert MONTGOMERY, Jr., born: 27 May 1924, parents: Elbert Montgomery and Vernia Lacy, death cause: "general infection", informant: Elbert Montgomery (Hampton), buried: Campbell Cemetery, died: 8 Jun 1924, record (1924) #: 137.
Hilda HYDER, born: 12 Nov 1923, parents: Frank Hyder and Julia Ann McKinney, death cause: "paralysis", informant: Nat Haynes (Hampton), buried: Hyder Cemetery, died: 11 Jun 1924, record (1924) #: 138.
Wilkie S. STOUT, born: 29 Aug 1879, married, parents: A.K. Stout and Julia Cassida, death cause: "suicide, shot himself through head", informant: Arthur Stout (Elizabethton), buried: Harmony Church Cemetery, died: 12 Jun 1924, record (1924) #: 139.
Mrs. Pearl LEWIS, age 33 years, married, parents: Marton Bunton (Johnson County) and Jane Pardue, death cause: "drowned by cloud burst", informant: C.L. Lewis (Cardens Bluff), died: 13 Jun 1924, record #: 140.
Willard SMITH, born: 26 Apr 1915, parents: Columbus Smith and Julia Smith, death cause: "drowned by cloud burst", informant: J.A.B. Smith (Cardens Bluff), died: 13 Jun 1924, record (1924) #: 141.
Rosa Christine LEWIS, born: 6 Jan 1924, parents: C.C. Lewis and Pearl Pardue, death cause: "drowned by cloud burst and water spouts", informant: Mrs. Nancy Jane Lewis (Cardens Bluff), died: 13 Jun 1924, record: 142.

Ruby LEWIS, born: 22 Nov 1918, parents: C.C. Lewis and Pearl Pardue, death cause: "drowned by cloud burst", informant: C.C. Lewis (Cardens Bluff), died: 13 Jun 1924, record (1924) #: 143.

Mrs. Julie SMITH, born: 13 Jun 1888, married, parents: Will Ward and Synthie Clemons, death cause: "drowned by cloud burst and water spouts", informant: J.A.B. Smith (Cardens Bluff), died: 13 Jun 1924, record (1924) #: 144.

Raymond LEWIS, born: 6 Jun 1922, parents: C.C. Lewis and Pearl Perdue, death cause: "drowned by cloud burst", informant: Mrs. Mary Jane Lewis (Cardens Bluff), died: 13 Jun 1924, record (1924) #: 145.

May LEWIS, age 6 years and 10 months, parents: Neal Lewis and Eliza Richardson, death cause: "drowned by cloud burst", died: 13 Jun 1924, record (1924) #: 146.

Mrs. Stella GRINDSTAFF, born: 5 Jan 1887, married, parents: Gwnley Campbell and Mattie Gambell, death cause: "tuberculosis", informant: D.H. Grindstaff (Elizabethton), buried: Grindstaff Cemetery, died: 16 Jun 1924, record (1924) #: 147.

Oney HODGE, female, age 14 years, parents: Abe Hodge and Estes Cole, death cause: "spos fluks", informant: Abe Hodge (Carter), buried: Cole Cemetery, died: 19 Jun 1924, record (1924) #: 148.

Infant TOWNSEND, born: 7 May 1924, parents: Walter Townsend (Linville, NC) and Emma Townsend, death cause: "whooping cough", informant: Walter Townsend (Hopson), buried: Crabtree, died: 18 Jun 1924, record (1924) #: 149.

Forda HODGE, female, age 6 months, parents: Abe Hodge and Estes Cole, death cause: not stated, buried: Cole Cemetery, died: 19 Jun 1924, record (1924) #: 150.

Hattie VINES, born: 19 Oct 1900, widow, parents: Sam Justis and Sallie Johnson, death cause: "pulmonary tuberculosis", informant: S.A. Johnson (Hampton), buried: Johnson Cemetery, died: 19 Jun 1924, record (1924) #: 151.

Ida Grace FAIR, born: 18 Mar 1922, parents: John Fair and Berte Bradley, death cause: "cholera", buried: Highland, died: 20 Jan 1924, record (1924) #: 152.

Cornelius G. SNODGRASS, born: 30 Jun 1852 in Washington County, married, parents: John Snodgrass and Sarah Williams, death cause: "nephritis", informant: Mrs. Lucy Brumit, buried: Oak Grove Cemetery, died: 22 Jun 1924, record (1924) #: 153.

Gus MICHALS, born: 21 Apr 1889, married, parents: Alford Michals (NC) and Jane Overland (NC), death cause: "typhoid fever", informant: Margaret Cox (Elizabethton), buried: Roan Mountain, died: 23 Jun 1924, record (1924) #: 154.

Ruth HINKLE, born: 3 Mar 1923, parents: T.S. Hinkle and Annis Grindstaff, death cause: "gastro colitis", informant: T.S. Hinkle (Carter), buried: Garland Cemetery, died: 25 Jun 1924, record (1924) #: 155.

Suda BUCKLES, age 19 years, married, parents: C.C. Myers and ____ Williams, death cause: "tuberculosis and heart trouble", died: 27 Jun 1924, record (1924) #: 156.

Edna BUCK, born: 17 May 1924, parents: Will Buck and Ray Hoss, death cause: "whooping cough", informant: Will Buck (Shell Creek), buried: Buck Cemetery, died: 29 Jun 1924, record (1924) #: 157.

Shepard Anderson FOLSOM, born: 1 Jul 1919, parents: W.N. Folsom and Lillie Henry, death cause: "brain tumor", informant: Lillie Henry (Elizabethton), buried: Highland Cemetery, died: 29 Jun 1924, record (1924) #: 158.

John GARDNER, colored, age 75 years, born in North Carolina, widower, parents: not stated, death cause: illegible, informant: George Gardner (Elizabethton), buried: Colored Cemetery, died: 4 Jul 1924, record (1924) #: 159.

George RIDDLE, born: 5 Oct 1891, in North Carolina, married, parents: J.A. Riddle (NC) and Margaret Bowman (NC), death cause: "acute tuberculosis", informant: M.D. Riddle (Elizabethton), buried: Highland Cemetery, died: 5 Jul 1924, record (1924) #: 160.

Infant MCKINNEY, parents: Roy McKinney and Dora Ruth Hart, death cause: "premature birth", informant: C.H. Hart (Elizabethton), buried: Highland Cemetery, born/died: 5 Jul 1924, record (1924) #: 161.

Rex STOUT, born: 11 Apr 1923, parents: Geroge Stout and Mande Adams, death cause: "cholera", buried: Highland, died: 11 Jul 1924, record (1924) #: 162.

Sarah GUINN, age 64 years, married, parents: Asley Morgan and Bettie Whitehead, death cause: "gastro enteritis", informant: A.J. Arnett (Roan Mountain), buried: Nelson Cemetery, died: 12 Jul 1924, record (1924) #: 163.

Edith PIERCE, born: 2 Feb 1904, married, parents: W.B. Ritchie and Bessie Davidson, death cause: "pulmonary tuberculosis", informant: Dan Pierce (Watauga Valley), buried: Ritchie Cem., died: 12 Jul 1924, record: 164.

John WEST, age 81 years, widower, parents: John West and Bettie Chambers, death cause: "chronic nephritis", informant: J.B. West (Hampton), buried: Hall Cemetery, died: 12 Jul 1924, record (1924) #: 165.

Levi Chandler EDWARDS, born: Feb 1864 in North Carolina, married, parents: Obe Edwards (NC) and Levina Masters (NC), death cause: "carcinoma of prostate gland", informant: Richard G. Edwards (Erwin), died: 13 Jul 1924, record (1924) #: 166.

Beckie BRUMMIT, age 58 years, born in Unicoi County, married, parents: Jack Grindstaff and mother's name unknown, death cause: "tuberculosis", informant: Andy Brummett (Johnson City), buried: Lyon Cemetery, died: 14 Jul 1924, record (1924) #: 167.

Ben ANDERSON, born: 14 Oct 1923, parents: William G. Anderson and Lula Foster, death cause: "cholera", informant: W.G. Anderson (Elizabethton), died: 14 Jul 1924, record (1924) #: 168.

Nat LARGENT, age 30 years, single, parents: Thomas Largent (VA) and Liza Whitehead, death cause: "suicide, gun shot by himself", informant: Frank Whitehead (Roan Mountain), buried: Whitehead Cemetery, died: 16 Jul 1924, record (1924) #: 169.

Beatrice Mae BREWER, born: 26 Jul 1922 in Wise County, VA, parents: Dan Brewer and Manda Steward (VA), death cause: "menengitis", informant: Dan Brewer (Shell Creek), died: 16 Jul 1924, record (1924) #: 170.

Shelby LEWIS, born: 24 Sep 1922, parents: (illegible) Lewis and Anna Lewis, death cause: "colitis", informant: P.P. Lewis (Cardens Bluff), died: 17 Jul 1924, record (1924) #: 171.

Elmer BURCHETT, born: 30 Dec 1923, parents: Edward Burchett (NC) and Carrie Bristol (NC), death cause: "typhoid fever", informant: Earnest Richardson (Butler), buried: Whitehead Cemetery, died: 18 Jul 1924, record (1924) #: 172.

Pearl TOWNSEND, born: 15 Jun 1923, parents: Ed Townsend and Carline Norris, death cause: "whooping cough", informant: J.A. Morrell (Hopson), buried: Holly Cem., died: 18 Jul 1924, record (1924) #: 173.

Dortha RAINS, born: 13 Jun 1923, parents: Jess Rains (NC) and Loura Eliza Luttrell, death cause: "gastro enteritis", informant: Eliza Luttrell, buried: Mountain City, died: 19 Jul 1924, record #: 174.

Bety FIPS, age 11 years, parents: Pete Fips and Manley Fips, death cause: not stated, informant: Logn Fips (Carter), buried: Ensor Cemetery, died: 20 Jul 1924, record (1924) #: 175.

Frank ROSENBAUM, born: 17 Mar 1924, parents: Sam Rosenbaum and M.J. Godsey, death cause: "supposed cholera", resided at Watauga, died: 22 Jul 1924, record (1924) #: 176.

Kattie BRYANT, age 80 years, single, born in Coldwell County, NC, parents: Barny Bryant (Coldwell Co., NC) and Susan Tenner (Coldwell Co., NC), death cause: "paralysis", buried: Lyons Cemetery, died: 22 Jul 1924, record (1924) #: 177.

Porter HILL, born: 29 Mar 1892, married, parents: (illegible) Hill and Mollie Head, death cause: "pulmonary abscess", informant: Zeak Hill (Hampton), buried: Whitehead Cemetery, died: 22 Jul 1924, record (1924) #: 178.

Bruit ESTEP, male, age 2 years, parents: Jak Estep and Silia Holder, death cause: not stated, informant: Zak Estep (Carter), buried: Richardson Cemetery, died: 23 Jul 1924, record (1924) #: 179.

Lena Ruth BOWERS, born: 3 Sep 1923, parents: William Bowers and Gertrude Hicks, death cause: "cholera", informant: C.F. Bowers (Elizabethton), buried: Highland Cem., died: 24 Jul 1924, record (1924) #: 180.

Pauline LIVINGSTON, born: 7 Jun 1924, parents: W.M. Livingston and Laura Merritt, death cause: "bold hives", buried: Jenkins Cemetery, Valley Forge, died: 24 Jul 1924, record (1924) #: 181.

James T. ELLIS, born: 12 Apr 1845, married, parents: Rad Ellis (SC) and Louisa Peters, death cause: "chronic nephritis", informant: R.J. Ellis (Elizabethton), died: 26 Jul 1924, record (1924) #: 182.

Carl Garrison MEREDITH, born: 14 Sep 1918, parents: W.R. Meredith and Minnie Meredith, death cause: "colitis", buried: Smith Cemetery, died: 28 Jul 1924, record (1924) #: 183.

Charles THOMPSON, black, born: 6 Jul 1924, parents: Isam G. Thompson and Virdie Lee Kinnie, death cause: "stillborn", died: 6 Jul 1924, record (1924) #: 184.

Infant LIVINGSTON, male, parents: (illegible) Livingston and Nelie Nidiffer, death cause: "born dead", informant: W.L. Nidiffer (Carter), buried: Garland Cem., died: 6 Jul 1924, record (1924) #: 185.

Mary Jane OLIVER, parents: Burgie Oliver and Ida Dugger, death cause: "stillborn", died: 27 Jul 1924, record (1924) #: 186.

Frank E. DUGGER, born: 23 Apr 1924, parents: Henry Dugger and Rosa Winters, death cause: "colitis", informant: John Buchanan (Shell Creek), buried: Richardson Cemetery, died: 2 Aug 1924, record #: 187.

Jaunita COX, born: 1 Apr 1923, parents: Riley Cox (Mitchell County, NC) and Matilda Goodson, death cause: "gastro enteritis", informant: W.t. Goodson (Roan Mountain), died: 3 Aug 1924, record #: 188.

Ganes Wesley RICHARDSON, age 1 year and 11 months, parents: Will Richardson and May Bell Baker, death cause: not stated, informant: Janie Baker (Watauga Valley), died: 4 Aug 1924, record (1924) #: 189.

Loyd ROBERTS, born: 25 Apr 1903, single, parents: Russell Roberts (NC) and Celia McKinney, death cause: "pulmonary tuberculosis", informant: Wilson McKinney (Hampton), buried: McKinney Cemetery, died: 4 Aug 1924, record (1924) #: 190.

Sam GARLAND, age 64 years, single, parents: Dave Garland and Nancy Garland, death cause: "sepos flks", informant: Butler Richardson (Carter), buried: Garland Cemetery, died: 5 Aug 1924, record (1924) #: 191.

John DANNER Jr., born: 13 Dec 1923, parents: C.S. Danner (NC) and Eva Hodge (NC), death cause: "acute gastritis", informant: C.L Danner (Watauga Valley), buried: Highland Cemetery, died: 5 Aug 1924, record (1924) #: 192.

Roy BIRCHFIELD, born: 12 Apr 1917, parents: William Losson Birchfield and Lida Briggs (Ashe County, NC), death cause: "smallpox", informant: James Gibbs (Roan Mountain), buried: Hampton Creek Cemetery, died: 8 Aug 1924, record (1924) #: 193.

S.L. LOWE, born: 8 Sep 1851, widower, parents: Jacob Lowe and Rebecca Jackson, death cause: "intestinal tuberculosis", informant: Dan Lowe (Watauga Valley), buried: Lowe Cemetery, died: 8 Aug 1924, record (1924) #: 194.

George W. SMITH, born: 10 Oct 1838, married, parents: Nicholas Smith and Sallie Smith, death cause: "old age", informant: James Smith (Roan Mountain), died: 12 Aug 1924, record (1924) #: 195.

Virgie MYERS, born: 10 Oct 1881 in Johnson County, married, parents: Thomas J. Cobly (Johnson County) and Anna C. Rainbolt (Johnson County), death cause: "acute dysentery", informant: Thomas J. Cobly (Butler), buried: Highland Cemetery, died: 12 Aug 1924, record (1924) #: 196.

Ella J. HART, born: 9 Jan 1868, married, parents: George D. Roberts and Emma Bulson, death cause: "apoplexy", informant: Fred Hart (Elizabethton), buried: Highland Cemetery, died: 14 Aug 1924, record (1924) #: 197.

Bob STOVER, colored, born: 12 Jul 1846, married, parents: Shannon Stover and mother's name unknown, death cause: "epelectic fits and leakage of heart", buried: Drake Cemetery, died: 14 Aug 1924, record (1924) #: 198.

Mrs. John GENTRY, age 75 years, born in North Carolina, married, parents: Timothy Roarks and Susan Roarks, death cause: "spinal tuberculosis", informant: Mrs. Noah Gentry (Elizabethton), buried: Fish Springs, died: 16 Aug 1924, record (1924) #: 199.

Robert BORDERS, born: 21 Dec 1923, parents: father not stated and Lockie Borders, death cause: "meningitis", informant: Walter Borders (Shell Creek), died: 20 Aug 1924, record (1924) #: 200.

Robert HARDIN, age 40 years, married, parents: Eli Hardin and ____ Forbes, death cause: "pelegry", died: 23 Aug 1924, record (1924) #: 201.

Ruth PERKINS, born: 9 May 1924 in McClure, VA, parents: Crede Perkins and Claracy Hoss, death cause: "unknown", informant: M.S. Hoss (Shell Creek), buried: McClain Cem., died: 23 Aug 1924, record (1924) #: 202.

Gene HAMBRICK, born: Mar 1924, parents: George Hambrick and Lena Glover, death cause: "colitis", buried: Jones Cemetery, died: 25 Aug 1924, record (1924) #: 203.

Arther Allen ARNETT, born: 2 Nov 1922 in Cenia, NC, parents: Echoid Arnett (Yancey Co., NC), and Dovie Burleson (Cenia, NC), death cause: "lobar pneumonia", informant: John Arnett (Hampton), buried: Arnett Cemetery, died: 30 Aug 1924, record (1924) #: 204.

Maude WEAVER, born: 4 Oct 1900, married, parents: (illegible Morris or Norris) and Patsie Glover (Sullivan County), death cause: "pulmonary tuberculosis", informant: Frank Guffy (Watauga Valley), buried: Buckles Cemetery, died: 30 Aug 1924, record (1924) #: 205.

Infant COLBAUGH, sex not stated, parents: Henry Colbaugh and Cresie Peters, death cause: "stillborn", informant: Ike Garland (Carter), buried: Colbaugh Cemetery, died: 13 Aug 1924, record (1924) #: 206.

Wesley JOHNSON, born: 18 Jun 1847, married, parents: Alford Johnson (NC) and Ellen Daniels (NC), death cause: not stated, informant: Herby Johnson (Roan Mountain), died: 3 Sep 1924, record (1924) #: 207.

John SHELL, born: 6 Feb 1865, widower, parents: father unknown and Honer Shell, death cause: "pneumonia fever", informant: Garfield Finney (Butler), buried: Elk Cemetery, died: 5 Sep 1924, record (1924) #: 208.

Delliah C. WEST, born: 6 Jul 1912, parents: W.H. West and Katie Whiteman, death cause: "acute nephritis", informant: W.H. West (Hampton), buried: West Cemetery, died: 10 Sep 1924, record (1924) #: 209.

Infant SHULL, female, parents: Steward Shull and Sarah Holden, death cause: not stated, informant: Steward Shull (Hampton), buried: Morten Cemetery, died: 10 Sep 1924, record (1924) #: 210.

Sarah MCCLOUD, born: 10 Jul 1872, married, parents: F. Lipford (NC) and mother unknown, death cause: "cerebral hemorrhage", informant: Clyde McEwen (Elizabethton), buried: Butler, died: 10 Sep 1924, record (1924) #: 211.

John M. SCOTT, age 74 years, single, parents: Marshall Scott and Sarah McKaney, death cause: "organic heart disease", informant: George Scott (Watauga), died: 12 Sep 1924, record (1924) #: 212.

Susan Agnes DOVE, born: 6 Dec 1858 in Hawkins County, married, parents: Wilson Large (NC) and Rachel Myers (VA), death cause: "diseased gall bladder, surgery", informant: J.D. Dove (Elizabethton), buried: Bountville, died: 12 Sep 1924, record (1924) #: 213.

Gladys Marie JOHNSON, born: 4 Sep 1924, parents: C.G. Johnson and Ethel Little, death cause: "deformity of mouth and throat", informant: C.G. Johnson (Valley Forge), died: 13 Sep 1924, record (1924) #: 214.

Edison GIBBS, age 15 months, parents: Gill Gibbs (NC) and Nettie McKinney, death cause: "bronchial pneumonia", informant: Dave Garland (Roan Mountain), died: 15 Sep 1924, record (1924) #: 215.

Dorothy Bell HOSS, born: 16 Mar 1924, parents: Andrew B. Hoss and Dellie Miller, death cause: "diptheria", informant: Dellie Hoss (Butler), buried: Elk Mills, died: 16 Sep 1924, record (1924) #: 216.

Bernice LOWE, born: 21 Feb 1923, parents: Ray Lowe and Lottie Paters, death cause: "bronchial pneumonia", buried: Grindstaff Cemetery, died: 17 Sep 1924, record (1924) #: 217.

Infant LEONARD, female, born: 20 Aug 1921, parents: James Leonard and Rhoda Leonard, death cause: not stated, buried: Lyons Cemetery, died: 20 Sep 1924, record (1924) #: 218.

Nat INGRAM, born: 15 Nov 1852, married, parents: Charley Ingram and Ollie Hill, death cause: "mitral regurgitation of heart", informant: Rosco Ingram, buried: Miller Cemetery, died: 22 Sep 1924, record (1924) #: 219.

Lillie M. HOLLY, born: 19 Feb 1876, married, parents: William G. Meredith and Elizabeth February, death cause: "cancer of uterus", inforamnt: W.R. Meredith (Valley Forge), buried: Williams Cemetery, died: 29 Sep 1924, record (1924) #: 221.

Martha Emma COLDWELL, born: 10 Sep 1862, widow, parents: William Moreland and Phoeba Richardson, death cause: "mitral regurgitation", informant: Nora Freeman (Roan Mountain), buried: Moreland Cemetery, died: 22 Sep 1924, record (1924) #: 220.

James E. CARVER, parents: Elijah Carver and Hulda Moore, death cause: "stillborn", died: 23 Sep 1924, record (1924) #: 222.

Infant GARLAND, male, parents: Joe Garland and Dora Elliott, death cause: "stillborn", buried: Garland Cemetery, died: 30 Sep 1924, record (1924) #: 223.

Infant HERRELL, parents: Rex Herrel and Bessie Crowder, death cause: "stillborn", died: 30 SEp 1924, record (1924) #: 224.

Julia LINKES, born: 1 Apr 1852 in Watauga County, NC, married, parents: H. Hicks (NC) and Jennie Tester (NC), death cause: "cancer of uterus", buried: Butler, died: 1 Oct 1924, record (1924) #: 225.

Infant LARGE, female, born: 27 Sep 1924, parents: Earl Large and Ora Miller, death cause: "unknown", buried: Colbaugh Cem., died: 1 Oct 1924, record (1924) #: 226.

Leonard Eugene RANGE, born: 14 Sep 1923, parents: Hugh Range and Myrtle Hart, death cause: "diptheria", informant: John Hart (Watauga), died: 2 Oct 1924, record (1924) #: 228.

Margaret P. WILCOX, born: 1 Mar 1847, widow, parents: Skidmon Barker (VA) and mother's name illegible (NC), death cause: "cardiac delatation", buried: Highland Cemetery, died: 2 Oct 1924, record (1924) #: 227.

Hannah MILLER, age about 75 years, single, parents: father not stated and Sallie Miller, death cause: "apoplexy", informant: J.D. Miller (Elizabethton), buried: Humphreys Cemetery, died: 3 Oct 1924, record (1924) #: 229.

Infant TAYLOR, black, male, born: 1 Oct 1924, parents: C.J. Taylor and Grace McGee, death cause: "immature" buried: Gap Creek Cemetery, died: 3 Oct 1924, record (1924) #: 230.

Lois HINKLE, age 1 year, 1 month and 3 days, parents: father not stated and Bessie Hinkle, death cause: not stated, informant: Charles Oliver (Watauga Valley), died: 3 Oct 1924, record (1924) #: 231.

Sarah Elizabeth RANGE, born: 5 Feb 1845, widow, parents: Wiley McKeehan and Nancy Douglas, death cause: "myocarditis", informant: Hollie Snodgrass (Watauga), buried: Range Cemetery, died: 5 Oct 1924, record (1924) #: 232.

William G. PAYNE, born: 8 Oct 1855, widower, parents: "unknown", death cause: "organic heart disease", informant: Luther Morrell (Johnson City), buried: Patton Cem., died: 7 Oct 1924, record (1924) #: 233.

J.L. MARTON, born: 13 Jul 1922, parents: James Marton and Vicie Pate, death cause: "croup", informant: Elyie Morton (Elizabethton), buried: Oak Grove Cemetery, died: 8 Oct 1924, record (1924) #: 234.

Worley BOYD, age 9 years, parents: Ike Boyd and Rettie Elliott, death cause: "spinal meningitis", informant: Bill Elliott (Carter), buried: Ensor Cemetery, died: 10 Oct 1924, record (1924) #: 235.

Sarah BOWLING, born: 12 Dec 1857, widow, parents: Gordon Oaks and Sinda Perry, death cause: "cancer of stomach", informant: Bob Bowling (Johnson City), buried: Crabtree, died: 14 Oct 1924, record #: 237.

Lilian SUESS, born: 15 Jun 1922, parents: Charles P. Suess and Laura Chambers, death cause: "brights disease", buried: Chambers Cemetery, died: 13 Oct 1924, record (1924) #: 236.

Trusel STRICKLAND, born: 23 Mar 1924, parents: Clarence Strickland and Lucy Winters, death cause: "colitis", informant: James Winters (Elk Park, NC), buried: State Line, NC, died: 17 Oct 1924, record (1924) #: 238.

Mania WOODBY, born: 28 May 1920, parents: Lee Woodby and Lottie Clark, death cause: "croup", born: 17 Oct 1924, record (1924) #: 239.

Walter Allen MYERS, born: 26 Jul 1924, parents: Silas Myers and Virgie Coply (Johnson City), death cause: "marasmus", informant: S.J. Myers (Elizabethton), buried: Highland Cemetery, died: 19 Oct 1924, record (1924) #: 240.

Amanda Jane HEATON, born: 26 Jul 1924, parents: Silas Myers and Virgie Coply (Johnson City), death cause: "marasmus", informant: S.J. Myers, buried: Highland Cem., died: 23 Oct 1924, record (1924) #: 241.

George SIMERLY, born: 12 Aug 1842, married, pensioner, parents: Henry Simerly and Polly Chambers (NC), death cause: "gastritis and nephritis, drank kerosene by mistake", informant: S.S. Hodge (Valley Forge), buried: Hodge Cemetery, died: 24 Oct 1924, record (1924) #: 242.

Claud TOWNSEND, age 4 years and 21 days, parents: Taylor Townsend and Bertha Glover, death cause: "tuberculosis of bowels", informant: John Townsend (Elizabethton), buried: Hyder Cemetery, died: 25 Oct 1924, record (1924) #: 243.

James P. ELLIOTT, born: 27 Oct 1847, married, parents: Joseph Elliott and Pegga Hopkins (Sullivan County), death cause: "Brights disease", informant: Mack Elliott (Elizabethton), died: 26 Oct 1924, record (1924) #: 244.

Jule CANON, male, age 57 years, parents: Elbert Canon and ___ Lowe, death cause: "pelegry", died: 27 Oct 1924, record (1924) #: 245.

L.L. PIERCE, born: 29 Mar 1860, married, parents: Richard Pierce and Rbecca Venable, death cause: "infected finger, septicemia", informant: Robert H. Pierce (Carter), buried: Carter, died: 28 Oct 1924, record (1924) #: 246.

Cora ESTEP, age 21 years, single, parents: Joe Estep and Moley Taylor, death cause: not stated, buried: Garland Cem., died: 28 Oct 1924, record (1924) #: 247.

Carcililie BEARD, female, age 77 years, widow, parents: John Stout and Jane Clauson, death cause: "typhoid fever", informant: William Beard (Dark Ridge, NC), buried: Church Cemetery, died: 29 Oct 1924, record (1924) #: 248.

Nancy POWELL, born: 1 May 1851, widow, parents: Elijah Smith and Lonna Moreland, death cause: "mitral regurgitation", informant: W.B. Powell (Roan Mountain), died: 31 Oct 1924, record (1924) #: 249.

Mildred CLARK, parents: Arther Clark and Nolia Tolley, death cause: "stillborn", informant: Arther Clark (Hampton), buried: Berry Cemetery, died: 3 Oct 1924, record (1924) #: 250.

Infant CABLE, female, parents: W.M. Cable and Elen Davis (NC), death cause: "abortion", informant: W.M. Cable (Butler), buried: Cable Cemetery, died: 5 Oct 1924, record (1924) #: 251.

Infant LOVELESS, male, parents: Herman Loveless and Allie Ellis, death cause: "stillborn", informant: S.E. Reynolds (Elizabethton), buried: Ellis Cemetery, died: 16 Oct 1924, record (1924) #: 252.

Infant WILSON, female, parents: Jack Wilson and Joda Johnson (Avery Co., NC), death cause: "stillborn", informant: Jack McClain (Shell Creek), buried: Markland Cemetery, died: 23 Oct 1924, record (1924) #: 253. (twin below)

Infant WILSON, female, parents: Jack Wilson and Joda Johnson (Avery Co., NC), death cause: "stillborn", informant: Jack McClain (Shell Creek), buried: Markland Cem, died: 23 Oct 1924, record (1924) #: 254.
Wilson STOVER, black, age 95 years, widower, parents: Dave Stover and mother unknown, death cause: "chronin brights", informant: Lane Stover (Elizabethton), buried: Drake Cemetery, died: 1 Nov 1924, record (1924) #: 255.
Nora SHULL, age 34 years, 4 months and 18 days, married, parents: James Holder and Mary L. Norris, death cause: not stated, informant: S.H. Shull (Hampton), buried: Morton Cemetery, died: 2 Nov 1924, record (1924) #: 256.
Gasta SCALF, female, born: 3 Oct 1910 in Sullivan County, parents: Charles Scalf and Netta Carr, death cause: "tuberculosis", informant: Charles Scalf (Elizabethton), buried: Colbaugh Cemetery, died: 3 Nov 1924, record (1924) #: 257.
Laurence Master FRERGE, age 70 years, born in Pennsylvania, married, parents: "unknown", death cause: "brights, dropsy", buried: Potter Cemetery, died: date not recorded, record (1924) #: 258.
Warren HARDIN, born: 7 Jan 1924, parents: Charles Hardin and Vern Canon, death cause: "infantile paralysis", died: 6 Nov 1924, record (1924) #: 259.
Martha CARAWAY, born: 8 Mar 1847, widow, parents: Dan Stout and Eliza Wilson, death cause: "unknown", informant: Nat Ingram (Shell Creek), buried: Caraway Cemetery, died: 7 Nov 1924, record (1924) #: 260.
Sarah SWANNER, age 40 years, married, parents: John Price and mother's name unknown, death cause: "pulmonary tuberculosis", buried: Taylor Chappell, died: 7 Nov 1924, record (1924) #: 261.
Hobert GRINDSTAFF, age 19 years, single, parents: Ezekiel Grindstaff and Lettie Brummitt, death cause: "acute lobar pneumonia", informant: G.W. Brumett (Johnson City), buried: Douglas Cemetery, died: 9 Nov 1924, record (1924) #: 262.
Arthur Guy CARRIER, age 9 years, parents: J.W. Carrier and Emma Williams, death cause: "rhumatism from infancy", died: 10 Nov 1924, record (1924) #: 263.
Waits A. HODGE, born: 12 Oct 1845, married, parents: "unknown", death cause: "bright disease", informant: G.W. Brummit (Johnson City), buried: Simmons Cemetery, died: 14 Nov 1924, record (1924) #: 264.

Ruth CASEY, born: 20 Jun 1924, parents: Fred Casey and Glada Bailey, death cause: "cattarhal debility", informant: G.F. Bailey (Hampton), buried: Hall Cemetery, died: 12 Nov 1924, record (1924) #: 265.

Matt GRINDSTAFF, age 14 years, parents: David Grindstaff and mother not stated, death cause: "pneumonia", informant: George Brumit (Johnson City), died: 17 Nov 1924, record (1924) #: 266.

Thomas Justa SHOUN, born: 17 Apr 1922, parents: D.R. Shoun (Johnson County) and Maggie Poe, death cause: "croup", informant: R.D. Shoun (Hunter), died: 19 Nov 1924, record (1924) #: 267.

Ora CAMPBELL, born: 25 Nov 1905, single, parents: Nick Campbell and Lula Lewis, death cause: "typhoid", informant: Nick Campbell (Elizabethton), buried: Academy Cem., died: 20 Nov 1924, record (1924) #: 268.

Gladys Marie VANCE, born: 29 May 1920, parents: W.B. Vance and Dealie Richardson, death cause: "clothes caught fire, burned to death", informant: Henry Vance (Shell Creek), buried: Richardson Cemetery, died: 22 Nov 1924, record (1924) #: 269.

Oma STREET, born: 10 Feb 1877 at Magnetic City, NC, married, parents: father not stated and ____ Garland (NC), death cause: "carcinoma of cervix and uterus", informant: A.L. Street (Hampton), buried: Hall Cemetery, died: 25 Nov 1924, record (1924) #: 270.

Robert LAMBERT, born: 31 Jan 1918, parents: William Lambert (NC) and Bessie Stout (NC), death cause: "heart nethatics", informant: Rad Morgan (Dark Ridge, NC), buried: Church Cemetery, died: 26 Nov 1924, record (1924) #: 271.

Elijah B. MCKINNEY, age about 32 years, married, parents: Henry McKinney and Ellen Woodby, death cause: "tuberculosis of right kidney", informant: Henry McKinney (Hampton), buried: McKinney Cemetery, died: 26 Nov 1924, record (1924) #: 272.

Mollie CARTER, black, born: 28 Sep 1861, married, parents: Alexander Lovie and Betsy Stover, death cause: "consumption", informant: John Carter (Elizabethton), buried: Watauga Cemetery, died: 29 Nov 1924, record (1924) #: 273.

William Henry CAMPBELL, born: 5 Feb 1856, married, parents: Alex Campbell and Nancy Simerly, death cause: "brights disease", informant: J.A. Campbell (Butler), buried: Smith Cemetey, died: 1 Dec 1924, record (1924) #: 274.

Afric REDRICK, black, born: 24 Dec 1862 in North Carolina, parents: John Rederick (NC) and mother's name illegible, death cause: "paralysis, brights, high blood pressure, ", informant: Cora Rederick (Elizabethton), died: 1 Dec 1924, record (1924) #: 275.

Marcellas LITTLE, age 65 years, married, parents: James Little and mother not stated, death cause: "organic heart trouble", informant: J.L. Persinger (Johnson City), buried: Little Cemetery, died: 2 Dec 1924, record (1924) #: 276.

George Brown DUGGER, single, born: 28 Oct 1907, parents: Robert Dugger and Nancy Sheets, death cause: "gun shot wound in stomach and bowels", informant: Tempie Dugger (Butler), buried: Elk Mills, died: 2 Dec 1924, record (1924) #: 277.

Robert COX, born: 19 Aug 1859 in Sullivan County, parents: father unknown and ____ Powell, death cause: "angina pectoris", buried: Taylor Chappell, died: 2 Dec 1924, record (1924) #: 278.

Mable Virginia GREEN, born: 20 Apr 1906 in North Carolina, parents: Newton Green (NC) and Tildie Green (NC), death cause: "bed sores complicated with infected meningitis", informant: Earl Merritt (Elizabethton), buried: Montezuma, NC, died: 4 Dec 1924, record (1924) #: 279.

Claud BRISTOL, age 5 months and 20 days, parents: Elbert Oney Bristol and Binnia Jane Williams, death cause: "broncho pneumonia", informant: Claud Williams (Hampton), buried: Hall Cemetery, died: 6 Dec 1924, record (1924) #: 280.

Rosa Caroline MORTON, age 70 years, married, parents: "unknown", death cause: "myocarditis", informant: J.H. Hyder (Elizabethton), buried: Stevens Cemetery, died: 7 Dec 1924, record (1924) #: 281.

Alice HEATON, born: 13 Aug 1862, widow, parents: Philip Lipford and Alice L. Whaley, death cause: "typhoid fever", informant: J.C. Collins (Elizabethton), buried: Heaton Cemetery, died: 8 Dec 1924, record (1924) #: 282.

Mary Lee CLARK, born: 12 Oct 1924, parents: Harry Campbell and Perly Clark, death cause: "supposed, bowl hives", informant: Wesley Willis (Roan Mountain), buried: Clark Cemetery, died: 10 Dec 1924, record (1924) #: 283.

Isaac B. BOWERS, age 76 years, parents: Daniel S. Bowers and Emeline Brown, death cause: "suicide, cut throat with razor", informant: S.J. Crumley, coroner (Watauga Valley), died: 11 Dec 1924, record #: 284.

Martha A. ELLIS, born: 15 Dec 1833, pensioner, widow, parents: John May (VA) and Elizabeth Underwood (VA), death cause: "senility", informant: Daniel Ellis (Valley Forge), buried: Ellis Cemetery, died: 11 Dec 1924, record (1924) #: 285.

Infant RICHARDS, born: 10 Nov 1924, parents: Ramam Richars and Biler Warde, death cause: not stated, informant: Ramon Richards (Carter), buried: Cole Cemetery, died: 15 Dec 1924, record (1924) #: 286.

Emma PETERS, born: 18 Feb 1875, married, parents: Ben Ferguson and Julia A. Lewis, death cause: "pulmonary tuberculosis", informant: W.J. Ferguson (Elizabethton), buried: Highland Cemetery, died: 17 Dec 1924, record (1924) #: 287.

Cordelia GRAHAM, born: 12 Nov 1853 in North Carolina, married, parents: John Jackson (NC) and mother's name illegible, death cause: "old age, general breakdown", informant: Ben Graham (Roan Mountain), died: 17 Dec 1924, record (1924) #: 288.

Michael S. HOSS, born: 1 Jul 1856, married, parents: William Hoss (NC) and Darkus Hughes (NC), death cause: "cerebral hemorrhage", informant: George W. Hoss (Shell Creek), buried: McClain Cemetery, died: 21 Dec 1924, record (1924) #: 289.

Jeme RICHARDSON, male, born: 13 Jun 1921, parents: John Richardson and Anna Cornett, death cause: "diptheria", informant: John Richardson (Hampton), buried: Campbell Cem, died: 24 Dec 1924, record (1924) #: 290.

Infant BAKER, male, parents: W.M. Baker and Dollie (illegible), death cause: not stated, informant: W.M. Baker (Hampton), buried: Campbell Cemetery, born/died: 25 Dec 1924, record (1924) #: 291.

Robert L. LAMBERT, age 6 years, born in Dark Ridge, NC, parents: Bill Lambert (NC) and Bessie Stout (NC), death cause: "heart failure", informant: Bill Lambert (Dark Ridge, NC), died: 27 Dec 1924, record #: 292.

Princess Irene JOHNSON, born: 10 Mar 1922, parents: Fred Johnson and Laura Shell (NC), death cause: "burns over body from clothes catching fire", buried: Valley Forge, died: 27 Dec 1924, record (1924) #: 293.

Effie Louise STANLEY, born: 16 Feb 1924, parents: Fred Stanley and Julie Arwood, death cause: "diptheria", informant: F.M. Stanley (Roan Mountain), buried: Burbank Cem., died: 28 Dec 1924, record (1924) #: 294.

Edith M. PIERCE, born: 17 Dec 1924, parents: G.C. Pierce and Catherine Buckles, death cause: unknown, informant: A.C. Pierce (Watauga Valley), buried: Buckles Cem., died: 29 Dec 1924, record (1924) #: 295.

Infant HYDER, female, born: 6 Dec 1924, parents: Sam J. Hyder and Mary Thomas (Sullivan County), death cause: "flu, broncho pneumonia", informant: W.C. Hyder (Milligan), buried: Oak Grove, died: 30 Dec 1924, record (1924) #: 296.
Infant HUGHS, male, parents: W.C. Hughs (NC) and Annie Slaggle, death cause: "stillborn", informant: Webb Oxendine (Elizabethton), buried: Shell Creek, died: 9 Dec 1924, record (1924) #: 297.
Mrs. George W. HYDER, born: Feb 1857, married, parents: Ples Williams (Johnson County) and Sarah S. Peters (Johnson County), death cause: "pellagra", informant: George W. Hyder (Elizabethton), died: 2 Jan 1925, record (1925) #: 1.
Lenna Myron FAIR, born: 23 Dec 1924, parents: J.D. Fair and Della Price, death cause: "influenza", informant: J.D. Fair (Elizabethton), buried: Highland Cemetery, died: 2 Jan 1925, record (1925) #: 2.
Ruth Elizabeth SIMS, born: 1 Jan 1924, parents: Wilson Sims and Margaret Minton, death cause: "influenza, pneumonia", buried: Highland Cemetery, died: 4 Jan 1925, record (1925) #: 3.
William Hugh POTTER, age 3 years, parents: Millard Potter and Bessie Church (Whaley, NC), death cause: "croup", informant: Frank Dugger (Dark Ridge, NC), buried: Potter Cemetery, died: 9 Jan 1925, record (1925) #: 4.
Wilson MCKINNEY, born: 10 Mar 1841, widower, parents: Joseph McKinney and mother unknown, death cause: "apoplexy", informant: A.J. Sims (Elizabethton), buried: McKinney Cemetery, died: 9 Jan 1925, record (1925) #: 5.
Infant OLIVER, male, age 1 year, parents: William Oliver and Abigail Williams, death cause: "poliomyrlets", died: 9 Jan 1925, record (1925) #: 6.
Absom B. BRUMIT, born: 2 Feb 1853, married, parents: not stated, death cause: "serious leakage of heart", informant: Lockett Brumit (Elizabethton), died: 11 Jan 1925, record (1925) #: 7.
Francis MARKLAND, born: Jun 1845 in Virginia, parents: Henry Harrison and Edith Baker, death cause: "dropsy and brights", informant: Yande Markland (Shell Creek), buried: Markland Cemetery, died: 14 Jan 1925, record (1925) #: 8.
Margaret Lee MEDIARIS, born: 13 Jan 1925, parents: W.E. Medearis and Ada Lee Partin, death cause: "premature birth", buried: Parsons, TN, died: 15 Jan 1925, record (1925) #: 9.

Lytha Mae GEISLER, born: 14 Feb 1902, married, parents: Joe Lipford and Mary McCloud, death cause: "purfural septicema", informant: Hebert Geisler (Elizabethton), buried: Highland Cemetery, died: 16 Jan 1925, record (1925) #: 10.

William NOEL, born: 15 May 1849 in North Carolina, married, parents: Jonithia Noel (NC) and Sallie Honeycutt (NC), death cause: "organic heart disease", informant J.T. Range (Elizabethton), buried: Highland Cemetery, died: 17 Jan 1925, record (1925) #: 11.

A.J. LITTLE, born: 6 May 1857, married, parents: Henry Little and Matilda Mottern, death cause: "organic heart disease", informant: George F. Little (Watauga), died: 19 Jan 1925, record (1925) #: 12.

Infant ADAMS, male, parents: Guy Adams and Carey Little, death cause: "premature birth", informant: Guy Adams (Johnson City), buried: Farrell Cemetery, died: 19 Jan 1925, record (1925) #: 13.

Oninnie WILSON, colored, age: not stated, married, parents: Bill Brady and Susana Molard, death cause: "pellagra", buried: Smith Cemetery, died: 21 Jan 1925, record (1925) #: 14.

Maggie Nunan WILSON, born: 24 Jul 1871 in Georgia, parents: Thomas Nunan (GA) and Sue Agatha (GA), death cause: "anemia", informant: B.P. Curtis (Elizabethton), buried: Atlanta, GA, died: 23 Jan 1925, record (1925) #: 15.

Carter WHITEHEAD, age: about 92 years, married, parents: James Whitehead (NC) and Jennie Garland, death cause: "brights disease", informant: Marven Whitehead (Hopson), buried: Hampton, died: 29 Jan 1925, record (1925) #: 16,

Infant GRINDSTAFF, female, parents: not stated, death cause: "stillborn", died: 4 Jan 1925, record #: 17.

Sarah CAMPBELL, born: 17 Aug 1844, married, parents: Henderson Smith and Ellen Wilson, death cause: "paralysis", informant: John Campbell (Milligan), buried: Cardens Bluff, died: 1 Feb 1925, record #: 18.

Laura Marie STOVER, black, born: 3 Aug 1924, parents: James Stover and Elmont Bailey, death cause: "bronchial pneumonia", buried: Elizabethton, died: 2 Feb 1925, record (1925) #: 19.

Edward HOPSON, born: 21 Jul 1923, parents: Charles Hopson and Rachel Harris, death cause: "diptheria", informant: Charles Hopson (Roan Mountain), died: 4 Feb 1925, record (1925) #: 20.

W.M. COLBOCK, age 68 years, parents: Henry Colbock and Nancy Nave, death cause: "brights disease", informant: Dan Colbock (Carter), buried: Grindstaff Cemetery, died: 7 Feb 1925, record (1925) #: 21.

Lillie Beth Sadie POTTER, born: 17 Apr 1918, parents: Soloman Potter and Julia Owens, death cause: "tonsilitis", informant: Soloman Potter (Shell Creek), buried: Potter Cem., died: 9 Feb 1925, record #: 22.

Worley BRITT, age 84 years, married, parents: Danel Britt and Mary Britt, death cause: "broncho pneumonia", informant: T.B. Arnett (Elizabethton), buried: Hyder Cemetery, died: 9 Feb 1925, record (1925) #: 23.

Crandell Jack RICE, born: 14 Nov 1924, parents: John Rice (Unicoi County) and Myrtle Snodgrass, death cause: "organic heart leakage", informant: John Rice (Johnson City), buried: Hughes Cemetery, died: 10 Feb 1925, record (1925) #: 24.

Keren H. WARD, born: 2 Mar 1831 in Wilkes County, NC, widow, parents: William Brown (NC) and mother not stated, death cause: "legripp and old age", informant: T.T. Ward (Fish Springs), buried: Hamby Cemetery, died: 11 Feb 1925, record (1925) #: 25.

Mary LOVELESS, age 72 years, married, parents: Preacly Wilson and Sarah Wilson, death cause: "pulmonary tuberculosis", informant: Ross Loveless (Elizabethton), buried: Williams Cemetery, died: 11 Feb 1925, record (1925) #: 26.

John W. DOVE, born: 2 Feb 1849 in Virginia, parents: James Dove (VA) and Ellmyra Murphy (VA), death cause: "leakage of heart, paralysis", buried: Bluntville Cemetery, died: 11 Feb 1925, record (1925) #: 27.

Ely JARRETT, born: 28 Mar 1823 in Lincoln County, NC, widower, parents: Lige Jarrett (NC) and mother unknown, death cause: "vlavulor heart disease", informant: Jacob Shepherd (Johnson City), buried: Peebles Cem., died: 13 Feb 1925, record (1925) #: 28.

Harrill WOODS, born: 16 Mar 1922, parents: Fred Lyon and Darkie Woods, death cause: "accidental burns from open heater", informant: Frank Woods (Hampton), buried: Tiger Creek Cemetery, died: 14 Feb 1925, record (1925) #: 29.

Mrs. Elsie M. HEATON, born: 22 Oct 1887, married, parents: George Larkin and Catherine Bradshaw, death cause: "tuberculosis", informant: John Landon Heaton (Elizabethton), buried: Heaton Cemetery, died: 14 Feb 1925, record (1925) #: 30.

Charly TAYLOR, age 50 years, married, parents: Alvin Taylor and Sara Markland, death cause: "mitral sanosis", informant: G.W. Ensor (Carter), buried: Markling Cem., died: 14 Feb 1925, record (1925) #: 31.
Sarah BYERS, born: 7 Mar 1841 in North Carolina, widow, parents: Jim Minton (NC) and Rennia Broyhill (NC), death cause: "Brights disease", informant: H.V. Byers (Elizabethton), buried in North Carolina, died: 14 Feb 1925, record (1925) #: 32.
Landon WILSON, age about 60 years, parents: James Wilson and Mary Jane Pierce, death cause: "pellagra", buried: Wilson Cem., died: 15 Feb 1925, record #: 33.
Eishe CAMEL, age 42 years, parents: James Camel and Ise Garland, death cause: "Brights diesese", informant: Jess Camel (Carter), buried: Garland Cemetery, died: 16 Feb 1925, record (1925) #: 34.
Mary Luvenia BRISTOL, born: 16 Nov 1897, married, parents: James T. Lunceford and Eliza C. Montgomery, death cause: "pelegra", informant: Daniel Montgomery (Shell Creek), buried: Walnut Mountain, died: 17 Feb 1925, record (1925) #: 35.
Earnest USARY, Jr., born: 15 Apr 1924, parents: Earnest Usary and Hattie Butler, death cause: "diptheria", informant: Earnest Usary (Milligan), died: 19 Feb 1925, record (1925) #: 36.
Mrs. (first name not stated) GENTRY, age 80 years, widow, parents: not known, death cause: "clothing caught fire, accidental burns on entire body", informant: J. Hampton Hyder (Elizabethton), died: 20 Feb 1925, record (1925) #: 37.
Eliza Jane WILSON, born: 16 May 1867, widow, parents: John R. Garland and Lettie Garland, death cause: "cirrhosis of liver", informant: J.D. Campbell (Elizabethton), buried: Garland Cemetery, died: 21 Feb 1925, record (1925) #: 38.
William Bingman ALLEN, born: 30 Dec 1863, married, parents: Robert James Allen and Mary Ferguson, death cause: "sudden heart failure", informant: John Allen (Elizabethton), died: 24 Feb 1925, record #: 39.
Erlina COLLINS, age 89 years, widow, parents: unknonn, death cause: not stated, informant: A.C. Collins (Watauga Valley), died: 28 Feb 1925, record #: 40.
Ellen WILLIAMS, age 2 months, parents: L.D. Williams and Lena Crumley, death cause: "croup", died: 2 Mar 1925, record (1925) #: 41.
Infant BERRY, male, parents: Alf Berry and Lottie Oliver, death cause: "unknown", buried: Buckles Cemetery, born/died: 5 Mar 1925, record (1925) #: 42.

June Haseltine SIMERLY, born: 8 Feb 1925, parents: Paul Simerly and Mayme Lewis, death cause: "bronchial pneumonia", informant: L.G. Lewis (Cardins Bluff), buried: Lewis Cemetery, died: 6 Mar 1925, record (1925) #: 43.

Roy CARVER, born: 16 Feb 1915, parents: John Carver and Betty More, death cause: "pulmonary tuberculosis", informant: Arthur Clark (Hampton), buried: Cochran Cemetery, died: 10 Mar 1925, record (1925) #: 44.

George Washington MILLER, born: 22 Feb 1925, parents: James J. Miller and Sarah South (North Fork, NC), death cause: "croup or hives", informant: James L. Miller (Shell Creek), buried: Walnut Mountain, died: 14 Mar 1925, record (1925) #: 45. (twin below, record # 48)

Isaac LEONARD, born: 10 Nov 1864 in Washington County, TN, married, parents: "unknown", death cause: "bronchial pneumonia", informant: F.S. Patton (Johnson City), buried: Patton Cemetery, died: 16 Mar 1925, record (1925) #: 46.

Callie EASTEPP, age 24 years, 5 months and 17 days, parents: Andy Eastepp and Eliza Campbell, death cause: "lobar pneumonia", informant: Dewey Eastepp (Carter), buried: Garland Cemetery, died: 17 Mar 1925, record (1925) #: 47.

Martha Washington MILLER, born: 22 Feb 1925, parents: James Miller and Sarah South, death cause: "bold hives", informant: James Miller (Shell Creek), buried: Walnut Mtn., died: 19 Mar 1925, record (1925) #: 48.

Fred MARTON, age 7 months, parents: Oliver Marton and Mary Marton, death cause: "croup", informant: Oliver Marton (Elizabethton), buried: Lyons Cemetery, died: 19 Mar 1925, record (1925) #: 47.

Pearl HUGHES, born: 8 Mar 1908, parents: Wash Hughes and Maggie Gouge (Mitchell Co., NC), death cause: not stated, informant: J.L. Gray (Roan Mountain), buried: Burbank Cem., died: 20 Mar 1925, record (1925) #: 50.

Marjorie Dimple BLEVINS, born: 16 Feb 1924, parents: S.L. Blevins (Johnson County) and Nonnie Hulse (Green County), death cause: "lagrippe", informant: S.L. Blevins (Elizabethton), died: 21 Mar 1925, record (1925) #: 51.

Delcenia PIERCE, born: 1 Oct 1837, widow, parents: David Campbell and J..(illegible) Campbell, death cause: "mitral regurgitation of heart", informant: Julia Pierce (Hampton), buried: Gouge Cemetery, died: 22 Mar 1925, record (1925) #: 52.

Infant MORRELL, male, parents: Roy Morrell and Elinor Forrester, death cause: "pneumonia", born/died: 24 Mar 1925, record (1925) #: 53.

Velna Gay HARVEY, born: 20 Mar 1925, parents: John Harvey and Irene Lacy, death cause: "premature", informant: John Harvey (Watauga), buried: Lacy Cemetery, died: 24 Mar 1925, record (1925) #: 54.

Gibson LINKUS, age 74 years, born in North Carolina, parents: John Linkus (NC) and Mary Housewright (NC), death cause: "apoplexy", informant: J.H. Linkus (Elizabethton), buried: Butler, TN, died: 27 Mar 1925, record (1925) #: 55.

Sarah F. WHITEHEAD, age 54 years, widow, parents: Ham Potter and Sarah Stout, death cause: illegible, informant: Caison Whitehead (Butler), buried: Butler, died: 28 Mar 1925, record (1925) #: 56.

William HUGHES, age 36 years, born in North Carolina, married, parents: Garrett Hughes (NC) and Ollie Forbes (NC), death cause: "gangrenous appendix", informant: William Forbes (Milligan), buried: Roan Mountain, died: 30 Mar 1925, record (1925) #: 57.

Emma Peters TAYLOR, born: 6 May 1901, married, parents: T.N. Peters and Martha Frazier, death cause: "mis-carriage, gangrenous appendix", informant: John W. Peters (Carter), died: 31 Mar 1925, record (1925) #: 58.

Ralph DULANEY, black, born: 9 Oct 1919, parents: Clarence Dulaney and Georgia Bradley, death cause: "pneumonia and meningitis", resided at Watauga, died: 31 Mar 1925, record (1925) #: 59.

Infant HUTSON, male, parents: John Huston (Washington Co., TN) and Geneva Humphrey, death cause: "stillborn", resided at Watauga, died: 9 Mar 1925, record (1925) #: 60.

Infant BLEVINS, sex not stated, parents: Jemison Blevins and Gurty Hurley, death cause: not stated, informant: Jenen Blevins (Carter), buried: Garland Cemetery, born/died: 31 Mar 1925, record (1925) #: 61.

Earl MINTON, age 23 years, single, parents: G.H. Minton (NC) and ____ Richard, death cause: "tuberculosis", buried: Minton Cemetery, died: 1 Apr 1925, record (1925) #: 62.

Scott HOWELL, age 58 years, born: Apr 6, in North Carolina, married, parents: Tom Howell (NC) and mother's name unknown, death cause: "lobar pneumonia", informant: Frank Patton (Rt 6, Johnson City), buried: Patton Cem., died: 1 Apr 1925, record (1925) #: 63.

Crete GARLAND, female, age 43 years, 3 months and 2 days, parents: Valentine Garland and Aney Estep, death cause: not stated, buried: Garland Cemetery, died: 1 Apr 1925, record (1925) #: 64.

Mary Louise DUNCAN, born: 15 Jun 1916, parents: W.L. Duncan and May Holt (GA), death cause: "diptheria", informant: W.L. Duncan (Elizabethton), died: 1 Apr 1925, record (1925) #: 65.

Eliza BOWERS, black, born: 6 Mar 1854 in North Carolina, widow, parents: father unknown and Deina Gordon (NC), death cause: "paralysis", buried: Bowers Cemetery, died: 1 Apr 1925, record (1925) #: 66.

Bell LEWIS, born: 13 Nov 1901, single, parents: J.S. Lewis and ____ Combs, death cause: "tuberculosis", buried: Kite-Miller Cemetery, died: 2 Apr 1925, record (1925) #: 67.

Emma Josephine BRUMET, born: 26 Mar 1925, parents: Joe Brumett and Mary S.(illegible), death cause: "premature birth", buried: Highland Cemtery, died: 3 Apr 1925, record (1925) #: 68.

James Polk WHITEHEAD, age about 85 years, widower, parents: William Whitehead and Susan Chambers, death cause: "accidental death, hit by a locomotive, killed instantly", informant: Tom Whitehead (Valley Forge), died: 6 Apr 1925, record (1925) #: 69.

Gladys STAFFORD, born: 25 Jan 1925, parents: T.H. Stafford and Gracie Stafford, death cause: "pneumonia", informant: T.H. Stafford (Hampton), buried: Crabtree, died: 7 Apr 1925, record (1925) #: 70.

Nat K. RANGE, born: 12 Dec 1868, married, parents: J.M. Range and Joanna McKeehan, death cause: "fractured skull, killed in auto wreck", informant: C.J. Range (Elizabethton), buried: Highland Cemetery, died: 7 Apr 1925, record (1925) #: 71.

James B. MCKINNEY, born: 19 Feb 1893, single, parents: T.C. McKinney and Martha Hyder, death cause: "killed in auto wreck, crushed breast and lung", informant: Claude Meredith (Elizabethton), died: 7 Apr 1925, record (1925) #: 72.

Ham S. MCKINNEY, born: 30 Jul 1982, married, parents: T.C. McKinney and Martha Hyder, death cause: "fractured skull from auto wreck", died: 7 Apr 1923, record (1925) #: 73.

William Elbert BRADSHAW, born: 6 Apr 1925, parents: George Bradshaw and Virgie Bowers, death cause: "premature", informant: George Bradshaw (Elizabethton), buried: Hyder Cemetery, died: 7 Apr 1925, record (1925) #: 74.

Pauline DANNER, born: 2 Jun 1906 in Johnson County, single, parents: C.L. Danner (NC) and Eva Hodges (NC), death cause: "tuberculosis", informant: C.L. Danner (Watauga Valley), buried: Highland Cemetery, died: 8 Apr 1925, record (1925) #: 75.

Mary Jane HICKS, born: 19 Jul 1842, widow, parents: Philip Davis (Washington County) and Axie Mariah Roberson (NC), death cause: "organic disease of heart", informant: W.J. Hicks (Elizabethton), buried: Lyons Cemetery, died: 9 Apr 1925, record (1925) #: 76.

Maggie CAMPBELL, born: 20 Jan 1870, widow, parents: William Shull and Cinda Campbell, death cause: "pulmonary tuberculosis", informant: Nat Campbell (Hampton), buried: Campbell Cemetery, died: 14 Apr 1925, record (1925) #: 77.

Winnie HODGE, parents: George Hodge and Sarah Hodge, death cause: "premature", informant: George Hodge (Butler), buried: Smith Cemetery, born/died: 15 Apr 1925, record (1925) #: 78.

Winnie HODGE, parents: George Hodge and Sarah Courtner (Doeville), death cause: "premature", informant: George Hodge (Butler), buried: Smith Cemetery, born/died: 15 Apr 1925, record (1925) #: 79. (duplicate of record 78)

John F. HATELY, born: 9 Jan 1831 in Watauga County, NC, married, parents: William Hately (Watauga Co., NC) and Annie Ford (Watauga Co., NC), death cause: "asthma, mitral regurgitation", informant: Mrs. John F. Hately (Butler), buried: Hately Cemetery, died: 10 Apr 1925, record (1925) #: 80.

Cande GARLAND, age 75 years, single, parents: Mader Garland and Honer Wilson, death cause: not stated, buried: Garland Cemetery, died: 16 Apr 1925, record (1925) #: 81.

Jake GRINDSTAFF, age 60 years, married, parents: William Grindstaff and Sarah Lowe, death cause: not stated, buried: Grindstaff Cemetery, died: 16 Apr 1925, record (1925) #: 82.

Canada GARLAND, male, age 75 years, widower, parents: Mad Garland and Hannah Wilson, death cause: not stated, buried: Carter, died: 16 Apr 1925, record (1925) #: 83.

Elizabeth PEATERS, born: 24 Dec 1832 in Virginia, widow, parents: Nick Miller and Kitty Blevins, death cause: "flu", informant: Ed Peaters (Elizabethton), buried: Ritchie Cemetery, died: 18 Apr 1925, record (1925) #: 84.

Roby ELLIOTT, born: 24 Jan 1893, single, parents: John Elliott and Cornelia Blevins, death cause: "pulmonary tuberculosis", informant: Landon Elliott (Elizabethton), buried: Highland Cemetery, died: 20 Apr 1925, record (1925) #: 85.

Mrs. Millie MCVAY, age 65 years, born in Memphis, widow, parents: "unknown", death cause: "broncho pneumonia", informant: Mrs. Charley Rogers (Elizabethton), died: 25 Apr 1925, record (1925) #: 86.

Infant DUGGER, male, parents: Monroe Dugger and Tilde Clauson, death cause: not stated, informant: Monroe Dugger (Dark Ridge, NC), buried: Clauson Cemetery, born/died: 27 Apr 1925, record (1925) #: 87.

John WILSON, age 70 years, married, parents: John Wilson, Sr., and Elln McKinney, death cause: "paralysis", informant: Sol Wilson (Carter), died: 29 Apr 1925, record (1925) #: 88.

Mary Alice WARD, parents: Gene Ward and Amanda Gregg, death cause: "stillborn", parents: James W. Robinson (Butler), died: 13 Apr 1925, record (1925) #: 89.

Infant ROBERTS, male, parents: Ernest Roberts and Beulah West, death cause: "stillborn, premature", informant: W.H. West (Hampton), born/died: 30 Apr 1925, record (1925) #: 90.

Luster A. BARBER, female, born: Dec 1848, married, parents: James A. Perry and Martha Smith, death cause: "cystitis, pneumonia", informant: H.F. Perry (Elizabethton), buried: Highland Cemetery, died: 1 May 1925, record (1925) #: 91.

Cameron Dayton COMBS, born: 19 Oct 1908, parents: Tom Combs (Sullivan County) and Armetta B. Smith, death cause: "mitral stenosis", informant: Roscoe Morrell (Elizabethton), buried: Ellis Cemetery, died: 1 May 1925, record (1925) #: 92.

Ralph MERRITT, born: 11 Jan 1925, parents: Charlie Merritt and Vernie Jenkins, death cause: "supposed to have choked on flame", informant: Charlie Merritt (Valley Forge), died: 4 May 1925, record (1925) #: 93.

T.C. MCCLOUD, age 79 years, widower, parents: Ishah McCloud (NC) and Polly Fair (NC), death cause: "decompensation of heart", informant: John F. McCloud, buried: Gap Creek, died: 7 May 1925, record #: 94.

L.K. EGGERS, age 77 years, 9 months and 4 days, born in Watauga County, NC, married, parents: T.K. Eggers (Watauga Co., NC) and Sarah Hagons (Watauga Co., NC), death cause: illegible, informant: Job Eggers (Butler), buried: Whitehead Cemetery, died: 4 May 1925, record (1925) #: 95.

Ray VINES, parents: Monroe Vines and Arie Black, death cause: "unknown", informant: J.C. Cook (Butler), born/died: 11 May 1925, record (1925) #: 96.

Della Mae HARDIN, born: 15 Jun 1924, parents: Cleveland Hardin and Celia Loveless, death cause: "uremia, intestinal nephritis", informant: John Hardin (Valley Forge), died: 12 May 1925, record #: 97.

Willie Maxine WHITAMORE, born: 16 Apr 1923, parents: W.F. Whitamore and Millie Markland, death cause: "spinal meningitis", informant: W.F. Whitamore (Braemar), buried: Hall Cemetery, died: 15 May 1925, record (1925) #: 98.

Emma SNODGRASS, born: 7 Nov 1856, widow, parents: Wiley McKeehan and Nancy Douglas, death cause: "hemiplegra left side", informant: Jim Brumitt (Elizabethton), buried: Oak Grove Cemetery, died: 16 May 1925, record (1925) #: 99.

Elijah WILLIAMS, born: 26 Mar 1871, married, parents: Bellie Williams and Phoeba Loveless, death cause: "valvulor heart disease", informant: J.L. Persinger (Rt 2, Johnson City), died: 24 May 1925, record (1925) #: 100.

Infant MASSENGILL, male, parents: J.B. Massengill and Nellie Shipley, death cause: "spina bifida", informant: J.B. Massengill (Watauga), died: 25 May 1925, record (1925) #: 101.

Ellen SCALF, born: 7 Mar 1845 in South Carolina, widow, parents: "unknown", death cause: "pulmonary tuberculosis", informant: C.M. Scalf (Elizabethton), buried: Highland Cemetery, died: 29 May 1925, record (1925) #: 102.

Robert A. FRANCIS, born: 10 Jan 1848, widower, parents: Ruce Francis and Elizabeth Marr (NC), death cause: "organic heart disease, rhumatism", informant: Sam Hart (Elizabethton), buried: Mottern Cemetery, died: 31 May 1925, record (1925) #: 103.

Infant STEPHENS, female, parents: Mike Stephens and Bettie Morton, death cause: "stillborn", informant: J.D. Markland (Elizabethton), died: 2 May 1925, record (1925) #: 104.

Infant OXENDINE, male, parents: W.E. Oxidine (Watauga Co., NC) and Emma Douglas, death cause: "stillborn", informant: W.E. Oxidine (Watauga), died: 9 May 1925, record (1925) #: 105.

Infant POTTER, male, parents: Millard Potter and Bessie Church, death cause: "born dead", informant: V.V. McGuire (Dark Ridge, NC), buried: Potter Cemetery, died: 11 May 1925, record (1925) #: 106.

Lucreesie WYETTE, age 79 years, married, parents: Dick Wyette and mother unknown, death cause: "heart trouble", informant: J.N. Young (Johnson City), buried: Simmons Cemetery, died: 1 Jun 1925, record (1925) #: 107.

Roy MALONE, age 22 years, married, parents: Robert Malone and Nora Massengill, death cause: "infection from tonsilitis", informant: Robert Malone (Watauga), died: 2 Jun 1925, record (1925) #: 108.

Jerry CAMPBELL, age about 72 years, widower, parents: not stated, death cause: "abscess on hip", informant: Charlie Campbell (Fish Springs), died: 2 Jun 1925, record (1925) #: 109.

Mrs. Bonnie Florence HOSS, born: 12 Sep 1904, parents: James B. Little and Mollie Holly, death cause: "mitral heart lesion and pneumonia", informant: George D. Little (Hopson), buried: Holly Cemetery, died: 4 Jun 1925, record (1925) #: 110.

James Martin PRESNELL, age 7 months, parents: Brownlow Potter and Imogene Heaton, death cause: "cholarine information", informant: Robert Jones (Shell Creek), buried: Jones Cemetery, died: 13 Jun 1925, record (1925) #: 111.

Dellie ELLIS, born: 16 May 1899, parents: S.F. Perkins and Mary Miller, death cause: "child birth", informant: S.F. Perkins (Shell Creek), buried: Perkins Cemetery, died: 14 Jun 1925, record (1925) #: 112.

Floyd Jasper OLLIVER, born: 25 Oct 1921, parents: Taylor Olliver and Mamie Hicks, death cause: "fractured skull from fall", informant: Taylor Oliver, buried: Crow Cemetery, died: 15 Jun 1925, record: 113.

Raymon PRESNELL, age 2 years, 1 months and 29 days, parents: Nathan Presnell and Susan Hix, death cause: "cholitis", informant: R.M. Presnell (Butler), buried: Elk River, died: 15 Jun 1925, record (1925) #: 114.

Fred WAMPLER, born: 8 Mar 1925, parents: Ottie Wampler and Oretta Wallace, death cause: "cholera", informant: William Snodgrass (Elizabethton), buried: Colbaugh Cemetery, died: 19 Jun 1925, record (1925) #: 115.

Elsie TOWNSEND, born: 25 Jun 1923, parents: John Townsend and Hattie Miller, death cause: "whooping cough and measles", informant: Jerd Townsend (Hampton), buried: Tiger Creek Cemetery, died: 20 Jun 1925, record (1925) #: 116.

Verlin Donley SMITH, born: 16 May 1925, parents: Grant Smith and Lula Morton, death cause: "cholera", informant: Grant Smith (Hampton), buried: Cardens Bluff, died: 22 Jun 1925, record (1925) #: 118.

Annie GRIMSLEY, born: 22 Jan 1842 in North Carolina, widow, parents: Palmar Baird (NC) and Besty McBride (NC), death cause: "kidney trouble and old age", informant: Ross Markland (Shell Creek), died: 20 Jun 1925, record (1925) #: 117.
Elizabeth Easlearling WILLIAMS, born: 4 Feb 1867 in Georgia, married, parents: John Easlearling (GA) and Emily Surancy (GA), death cause: "cardio nephritis", buried: Highland Cemetery, died: 22 Jun 1925, record (1925) #: 119.
Nellie MATTISON, age 48 years, born in North Carolina, married, parents: Joseph Huntly (NC) and Martha Turner (NC), death cause: "cancer of uterus", informant: G.W. Matherson (Butler), buried: Hamby Cemetery, died: 23 Jun 1925, record (1925) #: 120.
Infant HEATON, male, parents: Bob Heaton and Callie Hodge, death cause: "premature birth", informant: N.H. Hodge (Elizabethton), born/died: 24 Jun 1925, record (1925) #: 121.
Beatrice SHOUN, born: 24 May 1925, parents: J. Malcolm Shoun and Ethel Shuffield, death cause: "asphixia, congenital stenosis", informant: Sol Wilson (Carter), buried: Johnson County, died: 24 Jun 1925, record (1925) #: 122.
Sally HEATON, age about 45 years, married, parents: Dave Stout and ____ Hammons, death cause: "influenza", informant: J.C. Markland (Elizabethton), died: 25 Jun 1925, record (1925) #: 123.
Donley Hardin RICHARDSON, born: 6 Sep 1924, parents: Donley Richardson (NC) and Mabel Cooper (NC), death cause: "diarrhea", informant: Abe Cooper (Shell Creek), buried: Taylor Cemetery, died: 26 Jun 1925, record (1925) #: 124.
Edith WHITEHEAD, born: 10 Jul 1910, parents: John Whitehead and mother's name not known, death cause: "appendisitis", informant: Nat Whitehead (Elizabethton), buried: Whitehead Cemetery, died: 27 Jun 1925, record (1925) #: 125.
James Wilson SMITH, born: 12 Sep 1881, married, parents: George Smith and Lexia Malone, death cause: "tuberculosis", informant: Mrs. Selma Wilson (Knoxville), buried: Colbaugh Cemetery, died: 29 Jun 1925, record (1925) #: 126.
Prudie Miller TWIGGS, born: 1 Sep 1918, parents: Burnie Green (NC) and Daisy Twiggs, death cause: "tubeculosis and pneumonia", informant: Augustus Twiggs (Raon Mountain), died: 30 Jun 1925, record (1925) #: 127.

Louis CROW, colored, parents: John Crow and Magnolia Brown (West Virginia), death cause: "born dead", informant: John Crow (Elizabethton), died: 12 Jun 1925, record (1925) #: 128.

Opal Ivalee BOWERS, born: 1 Jun 1925, parents: father not stated and Kate Bowers, death cause: "cholera", informant: John Bowers (Elizabethton), died: 1 Jul 1925, record (1925) #: 129.

Richard WOOLVERTON, born: 4 Oct 1839, married, parents: "unknown", death cause: illegible, informant: Mrs. Jane Woolverton (Hampton), buried: Holly Cemetery, died: 4 Jul 1925, record (1925) #: 130.

Mrs. Emma OLIVER, age 36 years, married, parents: A.A. Williams and Sarah Buckles, death cause: "cancer of uterus", died: 5 Jul 1925, record (1925) #: 131.

Catherine TWIGGS, age 69 years, born in Catawba County, NC, married, parents: Henry Miller (NC) and Katey Woods (NC), death cause: "chronic nephritis", informant: Guss Twiggs (Roan Mountain), buried: Heaton Creek, died: 5 Jul 1925, record (1925) #: 132.

Catherine INGRAM, born: 29 SEp 1867, married, parents: Thomas Whitehead and Hannah Whitehead, death cause: "diabetes", informant: W.R. Ingram, buried: Blevins Cemetery, died: 7 Jul 1925, record (1925) #: 133.

Lizzie NAVE, born: 9 Jun 1865, married, parents: Isaac Nave and Minny Bowers, death cause: "carcinoma of stomach", informant: J.J. West (Hampton), buried: Campbell Cem., died: 9 Jul 1925, record (1925) #: 134.

Evaline JACKSON, colored, born: 10 Jul 1855 in North Carolina, married, parents: Brash Hampil (NC) and Katie Hampil (NC), death cause: "gall stone and chronic gastritis", informant: Milton Jackson, buried: Jackson Cem., died: 10 Jul 1925, record (1925) #: 135.

Carlis CARVER, born: 2 Apr 1925, parents: Bob Carver and Lockey Byrd, death cause: "fluks", informant: Henry Ellison (Hampton), buried: Fair View Cemetery, died: 13 Jul 1925, record (1925) #: 136.

Mrs. Ella LITTLE, born: 1 Dec 1876, married, parents: William M. Bishop and Mary Newton, death cause: "carcinoma of breast", inforamnt: Mrs. D.P. Little (Watauga), buried: Mottern Cemetery, died: 13 Jul 1925, record (1925) #: 137.

Cynthia LOGAN, born: 26 Dec 1886 in Allegheny County, NC, married, parents: George Krouse (Allegheny Co., NC) and Frankie Cordell (Allegheny Co., NC), death cause: "pulmonary tuberculosis", informant: George Logan (Hampton), buried: Hall Cemetery, died: 15 Jul 1925, record (1925) #: 138.

Earl SNEED, born: 11 Feb 1925, parents: Albert Sneed and Myrtle Pritchard, death cause: "marasmus and colitis", informant: Albert Sneed (Elizabethton), buried: Highland Cemetery, died: 16 Jul 1925, record (1925) #: 139.

Scarlottie CLAUSON, age 72 years, born in Watauga County, NC, married, parents: David Hix (Watauga Co., NC) and Betty Hix (Watauga Co., NC), death cause: "old age", informant: H.C. Clauson (Dark Ridge, NC), buried: Hix Cemetery, died: 16 Jul 1925, record (1925) #: 140.

James WILSON, age 98 years, born in North Carolina, widower, parents: "not known", death cause: not stated, informant: Robert Johnson (Hampton), buried: Wilson Cem., died: 16 Jul 1925, record (1925) #: 141.

Charles B. CLARK, born: 23 Feb 1874, married, lawyer, parents: "unknown", death cause: "auto accident, hemorrhage of lungs", informant: Walter B. Brumit (Elizabethton), buried: Highland Cemetery, died: 18 Jul 1925, record (1925) #: 142.

Inna FOUST, born: 1 Feb 1886, married, pareents: T.A. Crow and Sarah Colbaugh, death cause: "pulmonary tuberculosis", informant: Charles Foust (Elizabethton), died: 19 Jul 1925, record (1925) #: 143.

Harry C. LOWE, born: 9 Sep 1901, single, parents: Kitte Lowe and Mary Elliott, death cause: "pulmonary tuberculosis", informant: Steve Lowe (Carter), buried: Carter, died: 22 Jul 1925, record (1925) #: 144.

Hazle Marie HART, age 6 months, parents: Ralph Hart and Hattie Sims, death cause: "chronic colitis", informant: Ralph Hart (Elizabethton), buried: Highland Cemetery, died: 20 Jul 1925, record (1925) #: 145.

James Russell STOUT, born: 15 Jan 1841, married, parents: John R. Stout and Bettie Bunton, death cause: "think, lock of bowels", informant: W.M. Stout (Butler), buried: Cable Cemetery, died: 23 Jul 1925, record (1925) #: 146.

Lillian May CARR, born: 25 Jun 1903, married, parents: N.D. Bowen (NC) and mother not stated, death cause: "pulmonary tuberculisis", informant: James N. Carr (Watauga), buried: Rogersville, died: 25 Jul 1925, record (1925) #: 147.

Jane STILE, born: 19 Jan 1902 in North Carolina, married, parents: Samuel McKinney (NC) and Rebecca Knight (NC), death cause: "puerpoarl septichemia", informant: S.S. McKinney (Roan Mountain), buried: Heaton Creek, died: 25 Jul 1925, record (1925) #: 148.

Manda NAVE, born: 30 Sep 1917, parents: Camel Nave and Kate Estep, death cause: "flux", informant: Joe Estep (Elizabethton), buried: Wilbur, died: 26 Jul 1925, record (1925) #: 149.

Helen SHEPPARD, born: 13 Apr 1903 in Kentucky, married, parents: "unknown", death cause: "nephritis, eclampsia", informant: Clarence N. Sheppard (Elizabethton), buried: Colbaugh Cemetery, died: 26 Jul 1925, record (1925) #: 150.

Mrs. Mahala TOWNSEND, born: 15 Jul 1835 in North Carolina, widow, parents: Lewis Townsend (NC) and mother's name unknown, death cause: "cerebral heomorrhage", informant: R.L. Hodges (Elizabethton), buried: Elk Park, NC, died: 26 Jul 1926, record (1925) #: 151.

Caroline MANN, born: 11 Jul 1861 in Watauga County, NC, married, parents: Edmon Keller (Watauga Co., NC) and Bertha Bishop (Watauga Co., NC), death cause: "inaigestion of stomach", informant: W.P. Mann (Whaley, NC), buried: Whaley, NC, died: 27 Jul 1925, record (1925) #: 152.

(illegible) POTTER, female, born: 30 Sep 1914, parents: Clayton Potter and Gracie Edwards, death cause: "typhoid and abscess of jaw", informant: Clayton Potter (Shell Creek), died: 30 Jul 1925, record (1925) #: 153.

Duffie WHITEHEAD, born: 29 Oct 1923, parents: Earl Whitehead and Ruthie McKintos, death cause: "flux", informant: Earl Whitehead (Roan Mountain), buried: Nelson Cem., died: 30 Jul 1925, record (1925) #: 154.

Infant JOHNSON, male, parents: Robert Johnson anmd Derona McKeehan, death cause: "stillborn", informant: Ben Livingston (Johnson City), buried: McKeehan Cemetery, died: 6 Jul 1925, record (1925) #: 155.

Infant KISER, male, parents: Ezra M. Kiser (West Virginia) and Synthia O'Quinn (VA), death cause: "stillborn", informant: Mrs. Ezra Kiser (Watauga), died: 15 Jul 1915, record (1925) #: 156.

Infant LARIMER, male, parents: Bob Larimer and Cora Holly, death cause: "stillborn", parents lived at Watauga, died: 21 Jul 1925, record (1925) #: 157.

Infant SHEPPARD, female, parents: Clarence Sheppard (Indiana) and Helen Jackson (Kentucky), death cause: "stillborn", informant: Clarence Sheppard (Elizabethton), buried: Colbaugh Cemetery, died: 24 Jul 1925, record (1925) #: 158.

Infant HATHAWAY, male, parents: Harry Hathaway and Sarah Wilcox, death cause: "stilborn", informant: H.G. Hathaway (Elizabethton), died: 26 Jul 1925, record (1925) #: 159.

Willie Forbes PAYNE, female, age about 35 years, widow, parents: David Forbes (NC) and Sallie Bowman (Unicoi County), death cause: "pulmonary tuberculosis", informant: J.S. Williams (Elizabethton), buried: Milligan, died: 1 Aug 1925, record #: 160.

George W. HAYNES, Jr., born: 26 Jun 1924, parents: George W. Haynes and Vilon Laught, death cause: "colitis", informant: George W. Haynes (Rt 2, Johnson City), buried: Williams Cemetery, died: 4 Aug 1925, record (1925) #: 161.

Nora OLIVER, age 19 months, parents: Burgie Oliver and ____ Nidiffer, death cause: "cholera", died: 7 Aug 1925, record (1925) #: 162.

Rhoda HUMPHREY, born: 28 Feb 1855, parents: Roda Campbell and Rebecca Hyder, death cause: "Brights disease", informant: Mike Campbell (Elizabethton), buried: Oak Grove, died: 11 Aug 1925, record #: 163.

Luther STOUT, born: 29 Jun 1903 in Johnson County, single, parents: Grant Stout (Johnson County) and Violet (illegible), death cause: illegible, informant: Violet Stout (Elizabethton), buried: Highland Cemetery, died: 11 Aug 1925, record (1925) #: 164.

Indiana Virginia HENDERICKSON, born: 9 May 1842 in Craig County, VA, widow, parents: Jonathon Givens (Craig Co., VA) and Leathey Leffel (Craig Co., VA), death cause: "dilatation of heart", informant: D.L. Stout (Hampton), buried: Roan Mountain, died: 13 Aug 1925, record (1925) #: 165.

Mrs. Eddie JENKINS, age 51 years, married, parents: James Oliver and ____ Jenkins, death cause: "blood poisoning", died: 14 Aug 1925, record (1925) #: 166.

Dan Landon ESTEP, born: 6 Apr 1922, parents: Mallek Estep (NC) and Zora Campbell (NC), death cause: illegible, informant: Henry Church (Dark Ridge, NC) died: 16 Aug 1925, record (1925) #: 167.

John Clifton GIBSON, born: 21 May 1923, parents: Pierce Gibson (Washington County) and Sallie Carr, death cause: "ilio colitis", informant: Pierce Gibson (Watauga), died: 19 Aug 1925, record (1925) #: 168.

Lafayette JULIAN, born: 6 Jun 1849, widower, parents: James Julian and Deliah Hampton, death cause: "chronic nephritis", informant: Nathan Garland (Roan Mountain), buried: Heaton Creek, died: 21 Aug 1925, record: 169.

Alf SHUFFIELD, born: 24 Sep 1846, married, parents: George Shuffield and Elizabeth Sneed, death cause: "mitral regurgitation of heart", informant: Jass Robinson (Butler), buried: Big Elk Cemetery, died: 23 Aug 1925, record (1925) #: 170.

Calvin MATHIS, born: 2 Apr 1847 in North Carolina, Confederate pensioner, married, parents: William Mathis (NC) and Mollie Staples (VA), death cause: "paralysis", informant: Rena Mathis (Valley Forge), buried: Miller Cemetery, died: 24 Aug 1925, record (1925) #: 171.

Sallie TAYLOR, black, born: 25 Aug 1845, widow, parents: "unknown", death cause: "accident, fall from a cliff, 45 feet", resided at Watauga, died: 25 Aug 1925, record (1925) #: 175.

George M. BLEVINS, born: 6 Sep 1873, married, parents: Jerry Blevins (Johnson County) and Sarah Finey, death cause: "cancer of bladder", informant: George Blevins (Elizabethton), buried: Lacy Cemetery, died: 26 Aug 1925, record (1925) #: 173.

Wilburn TOLLEY, age 58 years, widower, parents: W.M. Tolley (NC) and Nancy Willis (NC), death cause: "appendecites", informant: Dock Tolley (Hampton), buried: Tolley Cemetery, died: 26 Aug 1925, record (1925) #: 174.

Infant BROYLES, female, parents: Robert Lee Broyles and Anna Mae Morse, death cause: "premature birth", buried: Colbaugh Cemetery, born/died: 27 Aug 1925, record (1925) #: 175.

Edith Kate NAVE, born: 30 May 1924, parents: McKinley Nave and Laura Nidiffer, death cause: "disentary", informant: John Nave (Watauga Valley), buried: Buckles Cemetery, died: 30 Aug 1925, record (1925) #: 176.

Hannah WHISENHUNT, born: 16 Dec 1923, parents: Wiley Whisenhunt and May McClelan, death cause: not stated, buried: Blevins Cemetery, died: 3 Aug 1925, record (1925) #: 177.

Infant HEATON, male, parents: Rudy Heaton and Resa Deloach, death cause: "stillborn", informant: Redy Heaton (Elizabethton), died: 7 Aug 1925, record (1925) #: 178.

Infant CRUMLEY, male, parents: Earl Crumley and Emma Myers, death cause: "stillborn", died: 9 Aug 1925, record (1925) #: 179.

Infant CAMPBELL, male, parents: Melvin Campbell and Louisa Glover, death cause: "stillborn", informant: M.D. Campbell (Cardens Bluff), buried: Campbell Cemetery, died: 14 Aug 1925, record (1925) #: 180.

Infant CARVER, female, parents: Nat Carver and Nola Cochran, death cause: "stillborn", informant: John Cochran (Hampton), buried: Cochran Cemetery, died: 20 Aug 1925, record (1925) #: 181.

Jennie Lee Elizabeth WATERS, born: 1 Apr 1916 in Washington County, VA, parents: Henry Waters (Ashe County, NC) and Martha Rouse (Johnson County), death cause: "pulmonary tuberculosis", informant: Henry Waters (Watauga), died: 3 Sep 1925, record #: 182.

Edgar SHULL, born: 25 Nov 1908, parents: Steward Shull and Nora Holden, death cause: "invalid from birth", informant: Steward Shull (Hampton), buried: Morten Cemetery, died: 4 Sep 1925, record (1925) #: 183.

Hubert Allen MCKEEHAN, born: 13 Dec 1919, born in Michigan, parents: Frank McKeehan and Pearl Pate (Unicoi County), death cause: "croup", informant: Frank O. McKeehan (Elizabethton), buried: McKeehan Cemetery, died: 5 Sep 1925, record (1925) #: 184.

Bessie Rosalee BAILEY, born: 9 Nov 1880 at Neva, TN, married, parents: U.G. Bailey (Neva) and Eva Ward (Neva), death cause: "pulmonary tuberculosis", informant: Fred Casey (Hampton), buried: Hall Cemetery, died: 5 Sep 1925, record (1925) #: 185.

Lon Hendrickson WILSON, born: 21 Oct 1894 in Johnson County, married, parents: James Wilson (Johnson County) and Sallie Lowe (Johnson County), death cause: "accidentally poisoned by potassium cyanide", informant: Mrs. Sallie Wilson (Elizabethton), buried: Highland Cem., died: 6 Sep 1925, record (1925) #: 186.

Nola C. Webb BROWN, Negro, born: 27 Aug 1903, married, parents: Duben Webb (NC) and Mary Long, death cause: "pulmonary tuberculosis", informant: Dubben Webb (Roan Mountain), died: 8 Sep 1925, record (1925) #: 187.

Evalyn WOODS, born: 27 Nov 1921, parents: R.F. Woods and Ollie Shell, death cause: "croup", informant: Henry Shell (Shell Creek), buried: Perkins Cemetery, died: 9 Sep 1925, record (1925) #: 188.

James Stacy WILSON, born: 8 Oct 1870 in Johnson County, parents: Abriam Wilson (Johnson County) and Elizabeth Wilcox (Johnson County), death cause: "lobar pneumonia", informant: Mrs. J.S. Wilson (Elizabethton), buried: Highland Cemetery, died: 9 Sep 1925, record (1925) #: 189.

Isaac ESTEP, age 75 years, married, parents: Tensu Estep and Susey Lose (Johnson County), death cause: "dropsy", informant: W.W. Estep, brother (Carter), buried: Richardson Cemetery, died: 12 Sep 1925, record (1925) #: 190.

Mrs. Mae COMBS, born: 25 Apr 1907 in Unicoi County, parents: George Smith (Roane County) and Jane Fair, death cause: "meningitis", informant: George Smith (Elizabethton), buried: Thomas Cemetery, died: 12 Sep 1925, record (1925) #: 191.
Delma Eugene OLIVER, born: 24 Apr 1924 in Virginia, parents: Taylor Oliver and Mamie Hicks, death cause: "typhoid fever", informant: Taylor Oliver (Elizabethton), died: 14 Sep 1925, record (1925) #: 192.
Martha DOUGLAS, born: 22 Sep 1901, single, parents: John Douglas and Rhodie Britt, death cause: "pellagra", informant: Hugh Patton (Rt 6, Johnson City), buried: Simmons Cemetery, died: 15 Sep 1925, record (1925) #: 193.
Lillie RAINES, age 22 years, single, parents: James Raines and Eliza Archer, death cause: "pulmonary tuberculosis", informant: R.H. Pierce (Carter), buried: Grindstaff Cemetery, died: 20 Sep 1925, record (1925) #: 194.
John Henry PERRY, born: 21 Aug 1925, parents: father not stated and Trixie Perry, death cause: not stated, informant: John Perry (Elizabethton), buried: Deloach Cemetery, died: 21 Sep 1925, record (1925) #: 195.
Calvin Coolidge LONG, born: 26 Sep 1924, parents: George Long (Knoxville) and Missouri Catherine Johnson, death cause: "typhoid fever", informant: D.O. Johnson (Hampton), died: 22 Sep 1925, record #: 196.
Charley PHIPPS, age 50 years, married, parents: Peter Phipps and mother's name illegible, death cause: not stated, informant: Login Phipps (Carter), buried: Ensor Cem., died: 24 Sep 1925, record (1925) #: 197.
Martha J. CAMPBELL, born: 13 Apr 1849, widow, parents: Eli Fletcher and Vinie Nave, death cause: "internal cancer", informant: J.B. Fletcher (Hampton), buried: Hall Cem., died: 25 Sep 1925, record (1925) #: 198.
Ellen TAYLOR, born: 24 Jan 1882, married, parents: M.F. Moreland and Martha Greenwell, death cause: "pulmonary tuberculosis", informant: Lee Taylor (Carter), died: 26 Sep 1925, record (1925) #: 199.
William CLOSSON, born: 27 Sep 1850, widower, parents: James Clauson and Ellen Potter, death cause: "dropsy", informant: T.J. Clauson (Butler), died: 27 Sep 1925, record (1925) #: 200.
William A. OAKS, born: 2 Jul 1849 in North Carolina, married, parents: (illegible) Oaks (NC) and Martha Franklin (NC), death cause: "double lobar pneumonia", informant: Mrs. J.M. Oaks (Hampton), buried: Cross Nore, NC, died: 28 Sep 1925, record (1925) #: 201.

Mrs. Lady BERRY, age 35 years, married, parents: Vince Cardin and Cas Campbell, death cause: "influenza and diabetes", informant: William Berry (Elizabethton), died: 30 Sep 1925, record (1925) #: 202.

Hildred NAVE, born: 25 Apr 1925, parents: Coy Nave and Mamie Hyder, death cause: illegible, buried: McKinney Cemetery, Valley Forge, died: 30 Sep 1925, record (1925) #: 203.

Infant SHELL, male, parents: William L. Shell and Bell Cook (Ashe County, NC), death cause: "stilborn", buried: Highland Cemetery, died: 6 Sep 1925, record (1925) #: 204.

Infant RANGE, female, parents: Arnold Range and Delia Leonard (Washington County), death cause: "stillborn", informant: Jake Range (Elizabethton), buried: Mottern Cemetery, died: 12 Sep 1925, record (1925) #: 205.

Herman CARR, born: 5 Nov 1924, parents: Odd Carr and Corintha Shipley (Sullivan County), death cause: "colitis", informant: Odd Carr (Elizabethton), died: 2 Oct 1925, record (1925) #: 206.

Flora WILSON, age 54 years, married, parents: father not stated and Pettie Hinkle, death cause: not stated, died: 11 Oct 1925, record (1925) #: 207.

H. Neer OAKS, male, born: 14 Mar 1846, married, parents: H.N. Oaks and Mary A. Hatten, death cause: "appendicitis, no operation", informant: W.C. Oaks (Shell Creek), buried: Buck Mountain, died: 5 Oct 1925, record (1925) #: 208.

Clarence STOUT, born: 27 Mar 1925, parents: George Stout and Nancy Howell, death cause: "rachitis, malnutrition", informant: E.G. Stout (Hampton), buried: Morton Cemetery, died: 5 Oct 1925, record (1925) #: 209.

Jack COLLINS, age 2 years and 6 months, parents: Harmon Collins and Maggie Crow, death cause: "colitis", informant: Fletcher Collins (Elizabethton), died: 5 Oct 1925, record (1925) #: 210.

Dr. Andrew W. CAMPBELL, born: 10 Oct 1856, physician, married, parents: Joseph Campbell and Mary Looney, death cause: "carcinoma of stomach", informant: Mrs. Campbell (Elizabethton), died: 5 Oct 1925, record (1925) #: 211.

Mrs. Fern HARDIN, age 20 years, married, parents: Isaac C.. (illegible) and Laura Hinkle, death cause: "influenza and nephritis", died: 6 Oct 1925, record (1925) #: 212.

Harry PLEASANT, age 8 years, born in Johnson County, parents: Garl Pleasant (Johnson County) and ____ Treadway, death cause: "meningitis", died: 8 Oct 1925, record (1925) #: 213.

J.J. SHEPPARD, age 52 years, born in Mitchell Court, NC, married, parents: Cruin Sheppard (McDowell Co., NC) and Mary Roberts (Rutherford Co., NC), death cause: "accident, fell from a tree", informant: W.M. Sheppard (Rt 2, Johnson City), buried: Peebles Cemetery, died: 11 Oct 1925, record (1925) #: 214.

Hazle Lee CANTER, born: 23 Apr 1921, parents: Will Canter (VA) and None Ledwell (Washington Co., TN), death cause: "infection, injury from being run over by automobile", informant: Will Canter (Elizabethton), buried: Hyder Cemetery, died: 11 Oct 1925, record (1925) #: 215.

Melica DUNMORE, age 47 years, married, parents: Godfrey Heatherly and mother's name illegible, death cause: "broncho pneumonia", informant: Enoch Dingmore (Carter), buried: Garland Cemetery, died: 12 Oct 1925, record (1925) #: 216.

Infant FRAZIER, male, parents: David Frazier and Rose Bradshaw, death cause: "premature birth", buried: Watauga Valley, born/died: 13 Oct 1925, record (1925) #: 217.

Sam DELOACH, born: 11 Sep 1913, parents: Dave Deloach and (illegible) Collins, death cause: "collitis", buried: Deloach Cem., died: 13 Oct 1925, record: 218.

Mrs. Charles C. MCCLAIN, born: 29 Sep 1897, married, parents: Fate Banner and Disa Briggs, death cause: "septicemia caused by childbirth", informant: Charles C. McClain (Shell Creek), died: 13 Oct 1925, record (1925) #: 219.

Carl Edward MERRITT, born: 5 Sep 1920, parents: Lwnis Merritt and Martha Simerly, death cause: "mumps and diptheria", informant: Lenis Merritt (Raon Mountain), buried: Hampton Creek Cemetery, died: 14 Oct 1925, record (1925) #: 220.

Andrew J. JOHNSON, born: 6 Oct 1855, married, parents: Nick Johnson (NC) and Mary Jenkins, death cause: "Bright disease", informant: Sam Johnson (Hampton), buried: Johnson Cemetery, died: 14 Oct 1925, record (1925) #: 221.

Tilda PERS (Pierce ?), born: 5 Oct 1873, married, parents: Denny Ensor and mother's name illegible (possibly, Blevins), death cause: "pulmonary tuberculosis", informant: D.B. Ensor (Carter), buried: Ensor Cem., died: 15 Oct 1925, record (1925) #: 222.

Norma CARR, born: 26 Jul 1922, parents: Odd Carr and Corrintha Shipley (Sullivan County), death cause: "croup", buried: Morrell Cemetery, died: 16 Oct 1925, record (1925) #: 223.

James CORNETT, born: 9 Nov 1869, married, parents: John Cornett and mother's name unknown, death cause: "gun shot wound to left arm and chest, homicide", Resided: 15th District, died: 17 Oct 1925, record (1925) #: 224.

Murrell HARDIN, female, born: 28 Aug 1925, parents: Chris Hardin and F.. (illegible) Cannon, death cause: illegible, informant: Chris Hardin (Watauga Valley), died: 18 Oct 1925, record (1925) #: 225.

Joel CLEMMONS, born: 7 Oct 1852, widower, parents: Jacob L. Clemmons (Germany) and mother unknown, death cause: "rupture of brain causing paralysis", informant: Will Clemons (Elizabethton), buried: Highland Cemetery, died: 19 Oct 1925, record (1925) #: 226.

Charles ELLIOTT, Jr., age 6 years, parents: Charles Elliott and Bell Crow, death cause: "colitis", informant: Charles Elliott (Elizabethton), died: 21 Oct 1925, record (1925) #: 227.

Jackson PIERCE, born: 1 Nov 1858, married, parents: Tennessee Pierce and mother's name unknown, death cause: "mitral regurgitation", informant: P. Clark (Watauga Valley), buried: Buckles Cemetery, died: 24 Oct 1925, record (1925) #: 228.

John Henry MILLER, born: 21 Jul 1925, parents: John Henry Miller and Millie Smith, death cause: "enlarged liver", died: 25 Oct 1925, record (1925) #: 229.

William Byron ALBERTSON, born: 10 Nov 1896, married, parents: Webb Albertson (NC) and Mollie Odom (or Adam) (Johnson County), death cause: "tuberculosis of chest", informant: Walter Albertson (Elizabethton), buried: Highland Cemetery, died: 26 Oct 1925, record (1925) #: 230.

Clara RUSSELL, born: 5 Feb 1848 in Johnson County, widow, parents: John Heaton and Adaline Shelley (NC), death cause: "cancer of nose", informant: C.P. Hardin (Elizabethton), buried: Stoney Creek, died: 26 Oct 1925, record (1925) #: 231.

Henry MERRITT, parents: John Merritt and Emma Merritt, death cause: "unknown", informant: John Merritt, buried: Carter Cem., died: 26 Oct 1925, record #: 232.

Jackson OLIVER, Jr., born: 10 Apr 1925, parents: Jackson Oliver and Pardie Bowers, death cause: "cholera". informant: D.C. Rominger (Watauga), died: 28 Oct 1925, record (1925) #: 233.

Joseph OLIVER, age 70 years, married, parents: William Oliver and mother not stated, death cause: "intestinal tuberculosis", informant: Robert Hardin (Carter), buried: Grindstaff Cemetery, died: 30 Oct 1925.

Infant HART, female, parents: A.F. Hart and Pearl Persinger, death cause: "born dead", informant: A.F. Hart (Elizabethton), buried: G.W. Mottern Cemetery, died: 7 Oct 1925, record (1925) #: 235.

John Wesley NORMAN, parents: Julius Casper Norman and Pernnie Ethel Vaught (Virginia), death cause: "stillborn", parents resided at Watauga, died: 11 Oct 1925, record (1925) #: 236.

Calvin GOUGE, born: 1 Nov 1855 in North Carolina, married, parents: Calvin Gouge and mother unknown, death cause: "hyper (illegible) of heart", informant: Chester Gouge (Roan Mountain), buried: Heaton Creek Cemetery, died: 1 Nov 1925, record (1925) #: 237.

Hubert CLAUSON, born: 11 Jul 1924, parents: Henry Clauson and Birthy Walsh (Johnson County), death cause: "hart dropsy", informant: Dewey Potter (Dark Ridge, NC), buried: Clauson Cemetery, died: 2 Nov 1925, record (1925) #: 238.

Mammie SIMERLY, born: 5 Nov 1923, parents: Milt Simerly and Ester Cole, death cause: "croup", informant: Dill Birchfield (Roan Mountain), buried: Blevins Cem., died: 3 Nov 1925, record (1925) #: 239.

A.G. CARR, male, parents: Alvin L, Carr (Washington Co., TN) and Bell Feathers, death cause: "failure of circulation at birth", informant: G.W. Feathers (Watauga), born/died: 5 Nov 1925, record #: 240.

Infant POTTER, female, parents: Frank Ray Potter (Elk Park, NC) and May February, death cause: "hydro cephalus", informant: Frank Potter (Hampton), buried: Hall Cemetery, died: 7 Nov 1925, record (1925) #: 241.

Nancy HOSS, born: 25 Feb 1846 in Avery County, NC, widow, parents: Thomas Persy and Nancy Ellis, death cause: "heart failure, brights disease", buried: Perry Cemetery, Shell Creek, died: 9 Nov 1925, record: 242.

Rebecca OAKS, age about 80 years, widow, parents: Peter Potter and Mary Bunton, death cause: "influenza, imphosima", informant: James Oaks (Shell Creek), buried: Oaks Cemetery, died: 12 Nov 1925, record (1925) #: 243 (numbered 244).

H.L. BROWNING, born: 18 Apr 1875 in Virginia, married, parents: John M. Browning (VA) and Nebraca Gibson (VA), death cause: "killed, cut by knife by Ike Blevins", informant: H.W. Browning (VA), died: 14 Nov 1925, record (1925) #: 244.

Dicie GARLAND, born: 17 Jan 1840 in Johnson County, widow, parents: Daniel M. Stout and mother not stated, death cause: illegible, informant: N.E. Garland (Elizabethton), buried: Grindstaff Cemetery, died: 20 Nov 1925, record (1925) #: 245.

Ruth LITTLE, born: 5 Aug 1855, widow, parents: Jacob Hicks and Elizabeth Hicks, death cause: "icterus", informant: Mrs. G.F. Little (Watauga), died: 22 Nov 1925, record (1925) #: 246.

Evelyn May GRAY, born: 18 Nov 1921, parents: Thomas Gray and Bertha Archer, death cause: "broncho pneumonia", informant: Thomas Gray (Roan Mountain), died: 23 Nov 1925, record (1925) #: 247.

Willie Maye GRINDSTAFF, born: 29 Jul 1894 in Pulaski, VA, married, parents: William H. Helvey (Montgomery Co., VA) and Sarah Jane Helvey (Pulaski, VA), death cause: "Brights disease", informant: Mrs. Frank J. Keller (Radford, VA), buried: Oak Grove Cemetery, died: 24 Nov 1925, record (1925) #: 248.

Ray VINES, born: 20 Nov 1925, parents: Dan Vines and Jannie Potter, death cause: "unknown", informant: Robert Potter (Dark Ridge, NC), buried: Clauson Cemetery, died: 25 Nov 1925, record (1925) #: 249.

Dellie SMITH, born: 3 Sep 1925, parents: Carl Smith and Reathia Harmon, death cause: "hives", informant: Grant Harmon (Dark Ridge, NC), buried: Stout Cemetery, died: 25 Nov 1925, record (1925) #: 250.

Infant GLENN, male, born: 27 Mar 1925, parents: Ault Glenn (NC) and Ludalla Ward (NC), death cause: "tuberculosis of bowels", informant: Ault Glenn (Hampton), buried: Hall Cemetery, died: 25 Nov 1925, record (1925) #: 251.

Lizzie BUCKLES, age 52 years, married, parents; William Buckles and Eliza Williams, death cause: "tuberculosis", informant: F.D. Nave (Watauga Valley), buried: Buckles Cem., died: 26 Nov 1925, record: 252.

Infant GLOVER, female, parents: Paul Glover and Mamie Carr, death cause: "premature birth", born/died: 27 Nov 1925, record (1925) #: 253.

Lawrence GARLAND, born: 3 Jun 1922, parents: E. Garland and Lottie Williams, death cause: "double tonsilitis", informant: Lee Williams (Roan Mountain), died: 28 Nov 1925, record (1925) #: 254.

Nancy ELLISON, age 73 years, born in Johnson County, parents: Joel Shoemaker (NC) and Polly Shoemaker (NC), death cause: "cardiac dropsy", informant: Henry Ellison (Roan Mountain), buried: Lacy Cemetery, died: 30 Nov 1925, record (1925) #: 255.

Infant LITTLE, female, parents: Charlie Little and Anna Clark, death cause: "stillborn", informant: Robert Little (Valley Forge), buried: Little Cemetery, died: 22 Nov 1925, record (1925) #: 256.

Bob TAYLOR, age 43 years, married, parents: Lank Taylor and Marthy Cass, death cause: "spos fevr", informant: Jack Taylor (Carter), buried: Cass Cemetery, died: 3 Dec 1925, record (1925) #: 257.

Willoughby O'QUINN, born: 15 May 1862 in Virginia, parents: Andy O'Quinn and Lonthia Deal, death cause: "mitral stenosis", informant: Oliver O'Quinn (Watauga), buried: Virginia, died: 3 Dec 1925, record (1925) #: 258.

Mary A. KITZMILLER, born: 31 Oct 1839, widow, parents: John Bowman and mother not stated, death cause: "cerebral (illegible)", informant: C.H. Price (Milligan), died: 4 Dec 1925, record (1925) #: 259.

James Newton WAGNER, born: 25 Jun 1888 in Johnson County, married, parents: George W. Wagner (Johnson County) and Sara Ellen Reece (Jonson County), death cause: "flu", informant: Mrs. Coy Wagner (Elizabethton), buried: Highland Cemetery, died: 4 Dec 1925, record (1925) #: 260.

Mrs. Bell TREADWAY, born: 8 May 1885, married, parents: Joe Ellis and Jessie Hamilton, death cause: "pneumonia", informant: Joe Treadway, buried: Hunter Cemetery, died: 5 Dec 1925, record (1925) #: 261.

John W. ARNETT, born: 4 Oct 1882 in North Carolina, married, minister, parents: Hyram Arnett (NC) and Tebitha Bryant (NC), death cause: "pulmonary tuberculosis", informant: Eckard Arnett (Plumtree, NC), buried: McKinney Cemetery, died: 6 Dec 1925, record (1925) #: 262.

Minerva HARRISON, born: 22 Jun 1840, widow, parents: Josire Ernest and ____ Patton, death cause: "organic heart disease", informant: Clyde Duncan (Watauga), buried: Telford, TN, died: 7 Dec 1925, record (1925) #: 263.

Elmer WHITE, born: 19 Nov 1910, parents: W.E. White and Bertha Edmonson (NC), death cause: "typhoid fever", informant: W.E. White (Elizabethton), buried: Highland Cem., died: 7 Dec 1925, record (1925) #: 264.

W.E. YOUNCE, born: 25 Aug 1876 in North Carolina, married, parents: Soloman Younce and Mollie Greer (NC), death cause: "typhoid fever", informant: N.J. Younce (Elizabethton), buried: Boone, NC, died: 7 Dec 1925, record (1925) #: 265.

Susie BOWERS, age 50 years, single, parents: F.N. Bowers and Mary Anderson, death cause: "tuberculosis", informant: Petibone Bowers, brother (Watauga Valley), died: 10 Dec 1925, record (1925) #: 266.

Larinda GOODWIN, born: 26 Sep 1834 in North Carolina, widow, parents: Andrew Goss (NC) and Rachel Perkins (NC), death cause: "acute gastro anteritis", informant: L.H. Goodwin (Butler), died: 12 Dec 1925, record (1925) #: 267.

Christine DAVIS, born: 20 Apr 1922, parents: Frank Davis and Mary (illegible), death cause: "diptheria", informant: Frank Davis (Elizabethton), buried: Highland Cem, died: 17 Dec 1925, record (1925) #: 268.

Infant DELOACH, male, parents: John Frank Deloach and Jina Fair, death cause: "premature labor", informant: Thomas Fair (Elizabethton), buried: Carter Cemetery, born/died: 18 Dec 1925, record (1925) #: 269.

William Marion CLARK, born: 1 Jul 1862, married, parents: Thomas Clark and Louise Williams, death cause: "gangrene of foot", informant: Mrs. William Clark (Gap Creek), buried: Jones Cemetery, died: 18 Dec 1925, record (1925) #: 270.

Muffey ARNOL, male, age 72 years, parents: father not known and Margaret Arnol, death cause: not stated, informant: Jess Arnol (Carter), buried: Richardson Cemetery, died: 19 Dec 1925, record (1925) #: 271.

Carl L. YOUNCE, born: 15 May 1900 in North Carolina, married, parents: W.C. Younce (NC) and Eliza Reece (NC), death cause: "typhoid", informant: Ed Younce (Elizabethton), buried: Highland Cemetery, died: 21 Dec 1925, record (1925) #: 272.

Godfrey STOUT, age 43 years, parents: Joa Stout and Sara Ann Blevins, death cause: "spos weakness", buried: Stout Cem., died: 20 Dec 1925, record #: 273.

Mrs. Mary Ann JONES, born: 17 May 1853, widow, parents: James Edens (England) and Elizabeth Berry, death cause: "heart leakage", informant: J.S. Jones (Elizabethton), buried: Jones Cemetery, died: 22 Dec 1925, record (1925) #: 274.

George Edwin BOREN, born: 25 Nov 1860, married, lawyer, parents: Wiley Boren and Arzilla Jane Williams, death cause: "alcoholism", informant: E. Shell (Elizabethton), buried: Highland Cemetery, died: 23 Dec 1925, record (1925) #: 275.

Henry Clay MORRIS, born: 2 Jun 1849, married, parents: "unknown", death cause: "unknown", informant: Miss Fannie Morris (Elizabethton), buried: Morris Cemetery, died: 23 Dec 1925, record (1925) #: 276.

Emmitt MILLER, born: 29 Apr 1904, single, parents: Ross Miller (Watauga Co., NC) and Lillie Goodwin, death cause: "uremia", informant: Ross Miller (Butler), buried: Elk Mills, died: 28 Dec 1925, record (1925) #: 277.

Sarah E. GLOVER, born: 3 Apr 1861, widow, parents: William H. Shell and Lucinda Campbell, death cause: "pneumonia, mitral regurgitation", informant: John Glover (Hampton), buried: Campbell Cemetery, died: 29 Dec 1925, record (1925) #: 278.

Name	Page	Name	Page
Absher, Della	192	Alford, James	288
Absher, Nannie	138	Alford, John	100
Achen, Bettie	228	Alford, John H.	126
Adam, Mollie	363	Alford, J.A.	100
Adams, Alice Tildon	228	Alford, Lucresia	256
Adams, Billy	52	Alford, Polly	288
Adams, Franie	123	Alfred, John	84
Adams, Guy	343	Alfred, Rebecca	84
Adams, Infant	343	Alfred, R.R.	126
Adams, Mande	329	Allen, Anna	207
Adams, Martha	167	Allen, Dilha	42
Adams, Mary A.	241	Allen, Gloria	84
Adams, Maud	95,126	Allen, John	345
Adams, May	52	Allen, John F.	247
Adams, Pollie	97	Allen, Mary	11,58,256
Adams, Rebeca	33	Allen, Mary Ann	290
Adams, Virgie	236	Allen, Nannie A.E.	247
Adams, William	97	Allen, Robert James	345
Adkins, Alice	89	Allen, William B.	345
Adkins, B.	210	Allen, W.R.	207
Adkins, Diana	299	Anderson, Alfred	17,223
Adkins, Emma	197	Anderson, Ben	330
Adkins, Infant	166	Anderson, Charlie	319
Adkins, John	89	Anderson, C.M.	118
Adkins, Nora	296	Anderson, Dewey	223
Adkins, Sam	166	Anderson, Elizabeth	222
Adkins, Samuel	197	Anderson, F.A.	118
Adkins, William Henry	82	Anderson, Grant	130
Adkinson, Lila	92	Anderson, Infant	319
Agitha, Sue	343	Anderson, John Henry	118
Albertson, Andrew	42	Anderson, J.R.	122
Albertson, Andrew C.	65	Anderson, Margaret	118
Albertson, Bruce	65	Anderson, Martha	253
Albertson, E.S.	99	Anderson, Mary	367
Albertson, Henry W.	99	Anderson, M.A.	75
Albertson, H.W. (Mrs)	99	Anderson, Nora	130
Albertson, Walter	363	Anderson, Pearl	263
Albertson, Webb	363	Anderson, Richard	122,204
Albertson, William B.	363	236,320	<
Aldredge, Jane	234	Anderson, Richard	320
Aldridge, Alma	296	Anderson, Sam	133
Alen, Gloria	84	Anderson, Samuel	223
Alexander, Julian	86	Anderson, Shelby	133
Alexander, Magnolia	86	Anderson, William G.	330
Alexander, William	298	Anderson, Willie	10
Alexander, Wm (Mrs)	298	Andes, Infant	218
Alford, Cresie	216	Andes, Joseph W.	131
Alford, Dara	132	Andes, Nicie	218

Andes, Peter	131	Arnett, Hyram	366
Andise, Charlie	298	Arnett, John	224,333
Andise, Ida	269	Arnett, John A.	286
Andise, Janit Litta	269	Arnett, John Wilson	203
Andrews, Cliff	267	Arnett, John W.	200,366
Andrews, D.C.	138,153	Arnett, J.S.	237
Andrews, Ellman	267	Arnett, Lena Mae	203
Andrews, Hattie	138	Arnett, Monroe	12
Andrews, Hessie	324	Arnett, Nannie	157
Andrews, James Davis	153	Arnett, Nora	286
Andrews, J.W.	153	Arnett, Phillip	284
Angel, Charles F.	247	Arnett, Rebecca	95
Angel, Folsome	103	Arnett, Sarah Anna	224
Angel, George	247	Arnett, T.A.	249
Angel, Mollie (Mrs)	37	Arnett, T.B.	344
Angel, Nora	103	Arnett, U.S.G.	208
Angel, Samuel	165	Arnol, Jess	367
An..., Sarah	140	Arnol, Margaret	367
Arants, Elizabeth	163	Arnol, Muffey	367
Archer, Allen	150	Arnold, Bethean	300
Archer, Bertha	365	Arnold, Calrey	226
Archer, Eliza	320,360	Arnold, Claude	118
Archer, Joan	327	Arnold, Connie	3
Archer, John	295	Arnold, Daniel	100
Archer, Lorettie	150	Arnold, David	100
Archer, Lucy	125	Arnold, Dovie Leota	187
Archer, Rena	326	Arnold, Eliza Ellen	67
Archer, Sarah	296	Arnold, Eller	28
Archer, William	237	Arnold, George	140
Archer, W.T.	237	Arnold, Hannah	8,307
Arlington, Nancy	163	Arnold, Hazel	118
Arnet, Andy	172	Arnold, H.M.	67
Arnet, A.J.	173	Arnold, James	140
Arnet, Dan	250	Arnold, James Thomas	67
Arnet, Infant	250,265	Arnold, Jess	300,367
Arnet, Nell	265	Arnold, John	128,187
Arnet, Rachel	148	Arnold, J.P.	158
Arnet, William	148	Arnold, Margaret	367
Arnet, William H.	148	Arnold, Minnie	188
Arnett, Andy J.	286	Arnold, Mollie	304
Arnett, Arther Allen	333	Arnold, Muffey	367
Arnett, A.J.	160,322,329	Arnold, Paul Raymon	128
Arnett, Bessie	175	Arnold, Susan	100
Arnett, Carl	284	Arrants, N.M.	78
Arnett, Dollie	119	Arrnats, James B.	78
Arnett, Echoid	333	Arrowood, Hettie B.	231
Arnett, Eckard	366	Arrowood, Liddie E.	79
Arnett, Ellen	222	Arrowood, Lydia	279

Arrowood, Nina	77		Bailey, Harm	257
Arrowood, William	79		Bailey, John	287
Arwood, Arlon C.	174		Bailey, U.G.	359
Arwood, Dela	269		Baily, Auston	202
Arwood, Dewey	174		Baird, Palmar	353
Arwood, Hattie	207,316		Baker, Callie	152
Arwood, John	323		Baker, David	56
Arwood, John W.	174		Baker, Dollie	341
Arwood, Julie	341		Baker, Edith	342
Arwood, Liddie	76		Baker, Ella	315
Arwood, Lillie	144		Baker, Helen	257
Arwood, Manuel	174		Baker, Henry	8
Arwood, Nina	79		Baker, Hettie	190
Arwood, Rosa Lee	323		Baker, Infant	341
Arwood, Sam	77		Baker, Janie	332
Arwood, William	77		Baker, Jessie B. (Mrs)	270
Asher, Nancy E.	67		Baker, John	234
Asher, Pearl	67		Baker, J.C.	162
Asher, Roy	124		Baker, Lee	56
Asher, Will	135		Baker, Lula	121
Asher, William E.	67		Baker, Margaret E.	66
Asher, W.E.	66,67,114		Baker, Mary Bell	332
185,188	<		Baker, Nancy	172
Ashley, Amanda	107		Baker, William	66
Ashley, Charlie	171		Baker, William Wilson	66
Ashley, Dallas	49		Baker, W.B.	115
Ashley, Harriett	282		Baker, W.M.	341
Ashley, Infant	282		Baker, _____	147
Ashley, James	171		Baliff, Abner	146
Ashley, Mattie	165		Baliff, Daniel	85
Ashley, Nora	282		Baliff, T.A.	85
Ashley, _____	238		Band, Nanie	105
Audes, Danlia	53		Bange, Clarence	186
Austin, Columbus	218		Bange, Dan	186
Avery, Martha	127		Banks, Katie	216
Avery, Tom	127		Banks, Mary	96
Bacon, Elizabeth	144		Banks, Moses	139
Badgett, Thomas	61		Banks, Nancy	139,192,201
Bailey, A.C.	257		253	<
Bailey, Bessie Rosa	258		Banner, Annie	284
Bailey, Bessie R.	359		Banner, Blanch	256
Bailey, Burnie	315		Banner, Cordelia A.	306
Bailey, Clyde William	258		Banner, C.E.	256
Bailey, C.F.	339		Banner, Fate	362
Bailey, Elmont	343		Banner, H.H.	306
Bailey, Floyd C.	258		Banner, Mannia	282
Bailey, Glada	339		Barber, Luster A.	350
Bailey, Gracey	315		Barder, Winnie	23

Barker, Callie	120	Beard, Sarah Jane		231
Barker, Moxie	289	Beard, S.J.		106
Barker, Skidmon	335	Beard, William		63,69,337
Barnes, Avery	129	Beard, _____		59
Barnes, Bonnie Dell	129	Beasley, C.G.		77
Barnett, Alice	299	Beasley, Henry Clay		77
Barnett, Bert	151	Beasley, Shadrack		77
Barnett, Birtha	16	Beaver, Hobart		182
Barnett, Carolina	156	Beaver, Rosevelt		182
Barnett, Carter	48	Beaver, Steven		182
Barnett, Criss	240	Beavers, Chase M.		252
Barnett, C.	204	Beavers, M____		252
Barnett, David	299	Beck, Joel		96,192
Barnett, Dolly	94	Beck, John		96
Barnett, Erby	151	Beckner, Eliza		319
Barnett, Erley	150	Bedemyer, Janice M.		49
Barnett, Ezekel	219	Beeler, Mary		66
Barnett, Harman	150	Benfield, Amos		239
Barnett, Hazel	212	Benfield, Amy		85
Barnett, Herby	212	Benfield, J.C.		239
Barnett, Infant	49	Benfield, Matthew		90
Barnett, Jane	74	Benfield, Merion		45
Barnett, J.G.	81,117	Benfield, Sarah L.		239
Barnett, Lenard	50	Benfield, Warner Gay		90
Barnett, Mary	184,238	Bennett, Clarissa		291
Barnett, Sara	237	Bennett, Claude D.		165
Barnett, Spencer	299	Bennett, Clause B.		226
Barnett, Stephen	240	Bennett, C.D. (Mrs)		226
Barnett, Steve	147	Bennett, Darkei		113
Barnett, Swin	297	Bennett, Francis N.		165
Barnett, S.B.	74	Bennett, James A.		226
Barnett, Will	297	Bently, Marry		297
Barr, Adline	71	Berry, Alf		345
Barry, Mary	299	Berry, Alford J.		91
Bartie, Delcinia	82	Berry, Alfred		214,293
Bartie, Joseph	82	Berry, Alvin		98
Bartie, Mollie	82	Berry, Arther		313
Basentine, Joanah	164	Berry, Arthur		293,294,298
Basket, Mary	144	Berry, Bernie		292
Bayler, _____	178	Berry, Bert		300
Bays, Willie	107	Berry, Bert Stewart		238
Beadly, Kyle	174	Berry, Bertie Lee		25
Beadly, Wat	174	Berry, B.S.		224
Bean, John	213	Berry, Carrie		166
Beard, Carcililie	337	Berry, Clo		78
Beard, Cata	142	Berry, C.R.		64
Beard, John Reubin	69	Berry, David Spencer		4
Beard, John Ruben	63	Berry, Earl		98

Berry, Earl D.	214	Billings, Mollie J.	119
Berry, Edd	221	Billings, R.C.	119
Berry, Elbert C.	224	Billings, William D.	226
Berry, Elizabeth	222,367	Bingham, Dr.	173
Berry, Ernistine	139	Bingham, Myrtle	265
Berry, Ethel	124,221,268	Birchett, Cora	103
Berry, Griffin	252	Birchett, Lillie	248
Berry, Hamilton	250	Birchfield, Addie	125
Berry, Hassie	294	Birchfield, Bertha	280
Berry, Infant	300,345	Birchfield, Bessie	72
Berry, James	64,91,181 218 <	Birchfield, Charles	313
Berry, James Haskel	181	Birchfield, Cinda	283
Berry, Jane	207,325	Birchfield, Dave	184,246
Berry, Jim	224,313	Birchfield, David	184,246
Berry, John	248,269,292 294,306 <	Birchfield, Dill	364
Berry, J.F.M.	91	Birchfield, Effie	62
Berry, J.M.	200	Birchfield, James	246
Berry, J.W.	248	Birchfield, James N.	231
Berry, Lady	361	Birchfield, John	147
Berry, Mary	35	Birchfield, John	215
Berry, Myrtle	77	Birchfield, Kinzie	184
Berry, Myrtle J.	252	Birchfield, Lila	206
Berry, Nancy	235	Birchfield, Nat	313
Berry, Paul	183	Birchfield, Nathan	62
Berry, Polly	91	Birchfield, Nathaniel	215
Berry, Rebecca	222	Birchfield, Pollie	212
Berry, Robert	268	Birchfield, Rheuben	156
Berry, Robert G.	293	Birchfield, Roy	332
Berry, Ruby Kate	224	Birchfield, Ruben	212
Berry, R.G.	293	Birchfield, Rubin	231
Berry, Samuel	183	Birchfield, Sam	156,304
Berry, Samuel P.	224	Birchfield, Samuel	304
Berry, Sarah	113	Birchfield, Sarah	287
Berry, S.M.	78	Birchfield, Tommy	20
Berry, Will	238	Birchfield, Vadie	45
Berry, William	361	Birchfield, Virgil	304
Berry, _____	200,293	Birchfield, William	332
Bery, Addala	35	Birchfield, William C.	313
Bery, Mary	35	Birchfield, W.L.	212,231
Bess, Alice A.	180	Biris, Flora	312
Bick, Ida	148	Bishop, Bertha	356
Biddie, Sarah	297	Bishop, David A.	83
Biddix, S.M.	132	Bishop, David Porter	205
Biddix, Ura	149	Bishop, Harlow	231
Bierd, Susie	314	Bishop, John	228
Billings, J.A.	226	Bishop, Margaret	209
		Bishop, Walter	205
		Bishop, William M.	228

Bishop, William M.	354	Blevins, Bonnie	275
Bishop, W. Edward	228	Blevins, Bonua	117
Bishop, W.E.	83	Blevins, Callie	284
Bishop, W.M.	7,83	Blevins, Cecil L.	45
Black, Arie	351	Blevins, Charles	174
Black, Cay	317	Blevins, Charley	221
Black, Dora M.	206	Blevins, Charlie	119,120
Black, Henry	206	150,194	<
Black, James M.	97	Blevins, Cilie	32
Black, John J.	97	Blevins, Cinda	215
Black, Lula Janne	133	Blevins, Clark	256
Black, Pearlie M.	198	Blevins, Claud	164
Black, Peggy	211	Blevins, Clemie	119
Black, Susan Bell	133	Blevins, Clemmie	39
Black, William H.	97	Blevins, Cornelia	350
Blackburn, Ida	233	Blevins, C.V.	251
Blackburn, May	122	Blevins, Dan	134
Blackburn, Nina Bell	274	Blevins, Dave	221
Blackburn, Una Bell	123	Blevins, David	66,164
Blackburn, Walter	122	Blevins, Dillard	141
Blackwell, Fred	20	Blevins, D.C.	240
Blackwell, George W.	240	Blevins, D.M.	211
Blackwell, James L.	240	Blevins, Earmon	28
Blackwell, William P.	240	Blevins, Eliza	12
Blair, Allie	276	Blevins, Elizabeth	217
Blair, Catherine	26	Blevins, Eva Kate	278
Blair, I.	26	Blevins, George	231
Blair, Jefferson Dale	176	Blevins, George M.	358
Blair, Job	176	Blevins, George W.	86
Blair, Julia	26	Blevins, Glenn	194
Blair, Lillie	312	Blevins, Golda	174
Blair, Lillie A.	308	Blevins, Grace	39
Blessing, Freelove	294	Blevins, Harry	250
Blevins, Addie	25	Blevins, H.A.	232
Blevins, Albert	9	Blevins, Ida	238
Blevins, Alfred	275	Blevins, Ike	364
Blevins, Alice B.	188	Blevins, Infant	8,29,96
Blevins, Allen	39,96,150	134,164,254,347	<
Blevins, Anna	82	Blevins, Isaac	66,67,306
Blevins, Arthur	236	Blevins, I.S.	86
Blevins, Aurge Earl	221	Blevins, James	238,250
Blevins, A.J.	161	317	<
Blevins, Bell	97	Blevins, James F.	278
Blevins, Belle	96	Blevins, Jemison	347
Blevins, Bessie	11	Blevins, Jenen	347
Blevins, Bettie	30	Blevins, Jerry	358
Blevins, Betty	197	Blevins, John	97,194,205
Blevins, Bill	306	217,250,254,321	<

Blevins,	John B.	211	Blevins,	William G.	219
Blevins,	John H.	34	Blevins,	W.C.	288
Blevins,	Josa	254	Blevins,	W.M.	34
Blevins,	Joseph Kint	236	Blevins,	_____	236,362
Blevins,	Josie	262	Boather,	W.H	94
Blevins,	Julia	99	Boathr,	Rachel T.	94
Blevins,	J.P.	278	Bolen,	Frank	234
Blevins,	Kittie	133	Bolen,	Jesse Lorance	234
Blevins,	Kitty	349	Boling,	Abe	106
Blevins,	Lillie	119,120	Boling,	Anna Blanch	213
Blevins,	Loon	61,256	Boling,	Edith	106
Blevins,	Loone	100,110 191 <	Boling,	Henry	84
			Boling,	James L.	213
Blevins,	Loreta	205	Boling,	Laura	106
Blevins,	Mable	277	Boling,	Sallie	84
Blevins,	Maggie	11	Boman,	Infant	214
Blevins,	Margarette	308	Boman,	Linea	214
Blevins,	Marjorie D.	346	Boman,	Linnie	242
Blevins,	Mary	4,39,74 164 <	Bontregie,	Anna J.	143
			Booker,	N.C.	78
Blevins,	Minnie	62	Booker,	Polly	111
Blevins,	M.A.	121	Boone,	Abraham Lincoln	18
Blevins,	Nancy	306	Boone,	David	147
Blevins,	Nannie	218	Boone,	Herman	49
Blevins,	Nat	223,277	Boone,	I.P.	49
Blevins,	Nerva	317	Boone,	James	147
Blevins,	Neta	320	Boone,	Mary	49
Blevins,	Nicolas D.	100	Boone,	Maxie	316
Blevins,	N.P.	141	Borden,	Winnie	22
Blevins,	Ralph Hyder	315	Borders,	Harrison	320
Blevins,	Robert	70	Borders,	Lockie	320,333
Blevins,	Romley	315	Borders,	Robert	333
Blevins,	R.L.	290	Borders,	Walter	320,333
Blevins,	Sallie	302	Boren,	Arzella Jane	94
Blevins,	Samuel E.	141	Boren,	George Edwin	367
Blevins,	Sara	249	Boren,	Wiley	367
Blevins,	Sarah Ann	367	Borogus,	James M.	82
Blevins,	Sarah C.	290	Borogus,	W.M.	82
Blevins,	Sherman	188	Bougus,	Sarah	305
Blevins,	Sissy	29	Boures,	May	200
Blevins,	Steward T.	223	Bowen,	N.D.	355
Blevins,	S.L.	346	Bower,	Monroe	6
Blevins,	Tennessee	277	Bowers,	Alice Loretta	137
Blevins,	Wailey Ray	232	Bowers,	Allen	290
Blevins,	Walter	110,284	Bowers,	Arnold	205
Blevins,	Widlow	236	Bowers,	A.B.	222
Blevins,	William	67,308	Bowers,	A.B., Jr.	226
Blevins,	William A.	96	Bowers,	A.J.	210

Bowers, Barbara E.	142
Bowers, Bell	133,321
Bowers, Bertha	303
Bowers, Bessie	114,260
Bowers, Blanche	159
Bowers, Brown Lowe	307
Bowers, B.D.	10
Bowers, Callie	161
Bowers, Cardia	223
Bowers, Carl A.	176
Bowers, Carolina	191
Bowers, Charles	66,153
Bowers, Charlie	143
Bowers, Christian C.	197
Bowers, Cordia	133,145
Bowers, Cordie	196
Bowers, C.B.	109.228
Bowers, C.F.	331
Bowers, C.S.	294
Bowers, Daniel S.	275,340
Bowers, David	66
Bowers, David B.	220
Bowers, Earl	226
Bowers, Elisa	29
Bowers, Eliza	218,348
Bowers, Elizabeth	251
Bowers, Emmaline	42
Bowers, Emmert	322
Bowers, Ernest	137
Bowers, Eugene	210
Bowers, E.H. (Mrs)	311
Bowers, Francis M.	257
Bowers, F.N.	367
Bowers, Gail	254
Bowers, George	78
Bowers, George F.	261
Bowers, Grace	137
Bowers, Haskell B.	155
Bowers, Henry	143,193
Bowers, Hester	274
Bowers, H. Taylor	109
Bowers, Infant	78,322
Bowers, Isaac B.	340
Bowers, I.N.	77
Bowers, Joe	269,307
Bowers, Joe (Dr)	307
Bowers, John	73,309,322 354 <
Bowers, John Henry	185
Bowers, John H.	251
Bowers, John N.	137
Bowers, Joseph P.	176
Bowers, Josie	98
Bowers, Josie	307
Bowers, J.C.	228
Bowers, J.H.	174,197
Bowers, Kate	74,354
Bowers, Landon	289
Bowers, Laura	75
Bowers, Lela	77,78,143
Bowers, Lelia	66
Bowers, Lena Ruth	331
Bowers, Lillie	260,305
Bowers, Lizzie	117
Bowers, Lucinda	246
Bowers, Maggie	134
Bowers, Mahalie	197
Bowers, Marjorie L.	309
Bowers, Martha	252,289
Bowers, Mary	98,155,224 257,275,293 <
Bowers, Mary E.	236
Bowers, May	200
Bowers, May Malissie	189
Bowers, Millard F.	155 220,307 <
Bowers, Minnie	354
Bowers, Mollie	129,188
Bowers, Murray	73
Bowers, Nora	142
Bowers, Opal Ivalee	354
Bowers, Pardie	363
Bowers, Petibone	367
Bowers, Polina	197
Bowers, Reba	233
Bowers, Rebecca	152,162
Bowers, Rita	290
Bowers, Rob	254
Bowers, Robert Randall	25
Bowers, Rosco	205
Bowers, Ruth	135
Bowers, Sal	98
Bowers, Sallie	155,307
Bowers, Sarah H.	241
Bowers, Susan	109,289
Bowers, Susie	367

Bowers, S.M.	77,78	Bowman, Mary	147,260
Bowers, Teter	155	Bowman, Matt	306
Bowers, Teter N.	197	Bowman, Nicie	200
Bowers, Ula	98	Bowman, Ollie	115,149,204
Bowers, Valentine B.	116	Bowman, Peter	109
Bowers, Virgie	348	Bowman, Rana	289
Bowers, Virginia	185	Bowman, Roy	192,200,306
Bowers, William	116,261	Bowman, Sallie	357
331	<	Bowman, S.M.	129
Bowers, W.A.	257	Bowman, Thomas	147
Bowers, _____	65,126,134	Bowman, William	160
135,150,153	<	Bowman, Willie	129
Bowgas, Marshall	110	Bowman, Willim Mina	262
Bowgus, Infant	110	Bowman, W.F.	37
Bowline, Annie	194	Bowman, _____	219
Bowling, Bill	197	Boyd, Ike	336
Bowling, Bob	336	boyd, Worley	336
Bowling, Charles	195	Bradley, Berte	328
Bowling, Dora	150	Bradley, Campbell	85
Bowling, Frank	155	Bradley, Frank	130
Bowling, Henry	155	Bradley, Frank L.	154
Bowling, Hildred P.	197	Bradley, Frank L. Jr.	154
Bowling, Jacob	261	Bradley, Georgia	130,347
Bowling, Jake	155	Bradley, G.M. Mrs.	138
Bowling, Luther	65	Bradley, James	128
Bowling, Mary E.	195	Bradley, John P.	217
Bowling, Melvin	65,322	Bradley, Julie	44
Bowling, Nannie	211	Bradley, J.C.	154
Bowling, Nell	322	Bradley, Lola M.	57
Bowling, Robert	197	Bradley, Minnie	262
Bowling, R.L.	111	Bradley, Nancy	91
Bowling, Sarah	247,336	Bradley, Nat T.	85,128
Bowman, Caleb	227	Bradley, S.T.	85,128
Bowman, Christopher	160	Bradley, William	252
Bowman, David	117	Bradley, William, Jr.	252
Bowman, Delila	147	Bradley, W.T.	130
Bowman, D.A.	160	Bradshaw, Catherine	344
Bowman, Emma	157	Bradshaw, Clara	212
Bowman, Floyd	157	Bradshaw, George	348
Bowman, Ford	306	Bradshaw, Haven	225
Bowman, Harris	147	Bradshaw, Infant	64,94
Bowman, Henry	94,192	Bradshaw, Jamk	240
Bowman, Isaac	109	Bradshaw, Jennie (Mrs)	18
Bowman, John	157,366	Bradshaw, John	68,94,202
Bowman, John P.	157	225,240	<
Bowman, Joseph	94	Bradshaw, John F.	136
Bowman, Junie	34	Bradshaw, Laura May	136
Bowman, Linnie	242	Bradshaw, Lydie	94

Bradshaw, Maggie	142	Briggs, Harrison	149	
Bradshaw, Mandy Catie	202	Briggs, James	149	
Bradshaw, Mary	194	Briggs, Lida	332	
Bradshaw, Mattie	128,221	Briggs, Lorrie	287	
Bradshaw, Mattie B.	300	Briggs, Lottie	184	
Bradshaw, Nancy	162	Briggs, Pollie	298	
Bradshaw, Rose	362	Briggs, Polly	277	
Bradshaw, Samuel P.	41	Briggs, Rufus	149	
Bradshaw, Selma	18	Briggs, ___	239	
Bradshaw, S.P.	295	Brinkley, Bonnie Lyde	219	
Bradshaw, William E.	348	Brinkley, Dallas Jr.	12	
Bradshaw, W.F.	142	Brinkley, D.F.	47	
Brady, Bill	343	Brinkley, J.W.	219	
Brady, Minnie	111	Bristol, Carrie	330	
Branch, Amy	37	Bristol, Claud	340	
Branch, Joe	291	Bristol, Elbert Oney	340	
Branch, Nathan	262	Bristol, Mary Luvenia	345	
Branch, Sarah	291	Britt, Adeline	60	
Branch, Sidney	85	Britt, Annie	85	
Branch, Stanley	291	Britt, Danel	344	
Braswell, S.B.	77	Britt, David	85	
Braswell, Tom	292	Britt, Frank	143	
Braswell, William	77	Britt, Franklin	235	
Braswell, W.M.	77	Britt, Henderson	296	
Brck, Jim	120	Britt, John	209,211	
Breedlove, George A.	253	Britt, Mary	344	
Breedlove, George W.	76	Britt, Mary A.	39	
Breedlove, Robert S.	76	Britt, Minerve	211	
Breedlove, W.A.C.	253	Britt, Oscar	296	
Brewer, Beatrice Mae	330	Britt, Rhodie	360	
Brewer, Birgin	47	Britt, Worley	344	
Brewer, Dan	330	Brooks, David	268	
Brewer, Hampton	247	Brooks, Decova	111	
Brewer, James	170,247	Brooks, James	38	
Brewer, Jim	115	Brooks, J.C.	69	
Brewer, Joseph	247	Brooks, Mary H.	259	
Brewer, Mabel G.	48	Brooks, Nannie	303	
Brewer, McDowell	170	Brooks, Rhodisa	13	
Brewer, Nancy	313	Brooks, R. Kemp	259	
Brewer, Olivia	304	Brooks, Stella	111	
Brewer, Ora	152	Brooks, ___	160	
Brewer, Wesley	152	Brookshire, Connie	161	
Bridges, Lillie	183,184	Brookshire, Minnie	87	
Bridges, Mathew	183	Brookshire, M.J.	87	
Bridges, Ossie	203	Brown, Benson	229,245,246	
Bridges, Sarah	183	Brown, Charles Thomas	245	
Briggs, A.W.	287	Brown, Dannis	314	
Briggs, Disa	362	Brown, Emeline	340	

Brown, Emma		270	Brumit, Infant	189,228
Brown, Flora		174	Brumit, Jacob	189
Brown, Hattie		251	Brumit, J.D.	189,292
Brown, Heague		101	Brumit, Lettie	338
Brown, Hickman		236	Brumit, Lockett	342
Brown, Infant		230,246	Brumit, Lorena	171
Brown, James		89,230	Brumit, Lucy	328
Brown, Lee		144,234	Brumit, L.W.	182
Brown, Leutitia		259	Brumit, Phillip F.	140
Brown, Lillie		230	Brumit, Roy	32
Brown, Lilly		144	Brumit, Sarah	140
Brown, Lutice		114	Brumit, Smith	167
Brown, L.W.		222	Brumit, Walter B.	355
Brown, Magnolia		306,354	Brumit, _____	136,140
Brown, Mildred		111	Brumitt, I.P.	73
Brown, Nola C. Webb		359	Brumitt, Jim	351
Brown, Rebecca		309	Brumitt, Mary	348
Brown, Rena		137,322	Brummett, Andy	330
Brown, Rosa		324	Brummit, Beckie	330
Brown, Ruth		154	Brummit, G.W.	338
Brown, Samuel		309	Brummit, Mattie	108
Brown, Sarah Ruby		229	Brummitt, A.B.	270
Brown, Thomas		234	Brummitt, E.M.	207
Brown, Tissie		73	Brummitt, James	270
Brown, Titia		73,267	Brummitt, J.W.	85
Brown, Tom		314	Brummitt, Lettie	338
Brown, William		344	Brummitt, Linda	195
Brown, _____		220,275	Brummitt, Mary Martha	85
Browning, H.L.		364	Bryant, Barney	133,331
Browning, H.W.		364	Bryant, Franklin	235
Browning, John M.		364	Bryant, H.A.	235
Broyhill, Rennia		345	Bryant, Infant	60,91,279
Broyles, Infant		358	Bryant, J.A.	133
Broyles, Robert Lee		358	Bryant, Kattie	331
Bruer, Call		131	Bryant, Lewis G.	60
Brumet, Emma J.		348	Bryant, Louis	91
Brumett, Joe		348	Bryant, Luisia	100
Brumett. G.W.		338	Bryant, Nat	279
Brumit, Absom B.		342	Bryant, Rosie A.	245
Brumit, Allen		12	Bryant, Sallie	85,133
Brumit, A.B.		167	Bryant, Tebitha	366
Brumit, Charles H.		228	Bryant, W.R.	235
Brumit, Charlie		222,230	Bryon, Nathaniel	203
Brumit, Clarie		25	Buchan, Birdie	223
Brumit, C.H.		171	Buchanan, Birdie	223
Brumit, Elizabeth R.		292	Buchanan, Dave	206
Brumit, Emma		152,236	Buchanan, David A.	206
Brumit, George		339	Buchanan, Deney	225

Buchanan, Dewey		192	Buckles, Joe		114
Buchanan, Duer		192	Buckles, Julia		188
Buchanan, Elizabeth		126	Buckles, J.		74
Buchanan, Fred		307	Buckles, Katherine		294
Buchanan, James		126,269 307 <	Buckles, Lee		74
Buchanan, Jim		192	Buckles, Lizzie		365
Buchanan, John		307,331	Buckles, Maggie		284
Buchanan, Nellie		269	Buckles, Margaret		219
Buchanan, Nora		289	Buckles, Mary		101,160,327
Buck, Beull Stokes		136	Buckles, Myrtle		219
Buck, Charles		120	Buckles, N.G.		261
Buck, Charlie		120,152	Buckles, Rebecca		132
Buck, Clemmie Jane		219	Buckles, Ruth		31
Buck, David C.		91	Buckles, R.C.		160
Buck, D.E. (Mrs)		91	Buckles, Sarah		354
Buck, D.M.		113	Buckles, Suda		329
Buck, Edna		329	Buckles, Thomas		101,324
Buck, George W.		91	Buckles, Toy		103
Buck, Harry Lee		152	Buckles, T.J.		188
Buck, Infant		211	Buckles, Vena		166
Buck, Isaac		211	Buckles, Venie		323
Buck, John E.		136	Buckles, William		74,103 133,365 <
Buck, Nathaniel E.D.		113	Buckles, _____		189
Buck, N.T.		113	Buckner, Alfred A.		84
Buck, O.D.		55	Buckner, A.S.		247
Buck, Ruth		120	Bullard, ...		93
Buck, Ruthie		151	Bullock, George W.		96
Buck, Sallie		23	Bullock, Grace		103
Buck, Will		329	Bullock, Infant		21
Buckles, Abe		144,188	Bullock, John H.		96
Buckles, Alf		166,313	Bullock, Margaret		103
Buckles, Alfred		325	Bullock, Sam		21
Buckles, A.F.		324	Bullock, S.T.		96,103
Buckles, Callie		153	Bullock, Thelma		103
Buckles, Catherine		264 341 <	Bullock, Will		103
Buckles, Clyde Sexton		324	Bullock, W.M.		103
Buckles, Dave		221	Bulock, Maud		292
Buckles, Delia		144	Bulson, Emma		332
Buckles, D.C.		283	Bumgardner, B.J.		255
Buckles, D.S.		98	Bumgardner, Ruben		258
Buckles, Eliza		283	Bunton, Adalade		161
Buckles, Ella May		313	Bunton, Alex		199
Buckles, F.D.		108	Bunton, Bettie		355
Buckles, Infant		188,221 325 <	Bunton, Betty		256
			Bunton, Coy		142
			Bunton, Eliza		308
Buckles, James		160	Bunton, Elizabeth		139

Bunton, Etta	199	Burrow, Sam	36
Bunton, Flora	17	Burty, Delcenia	112
Bunton, G.H.	175	Butler, Ben	268
Bunton, Harrison	142	Butler, Clint	185
Bunton, Marton	327	Butler, Emelyn	59
Bunton, Mary	364	Butler, E.S.	185
Bunton, Rosie	199	Butler, Hattie	345
Bunton, Sabra	212	Butler, Henry	270
Bunton, Sarafina	158	Butler, Hester	24
Bunton, Silva	175	Butler, Infant	263
Bunton, Ulysses G.	19	Butler, John	171,180
Burchett, Clide	19	Butler, Lewis	263
Burchett, Edward	330	Butler, M.	314
Burchett, Elmer	330	Butler, Tlitha	179,181
Burchett, John	103	Butler, Vestley	171
Burchfield, Cinda	166	Butler, ____ Dyer	270
Burchfield, Vadie	45	Byers, Essie	9
Burger, ____	167	Byers, Harrison V.	314
Burgie, Harry	290	Byers, H.V.	345
Burgie, Joseph	290	Byers, Infant	314
Burgie, T.R.	290	Byers, Sarah	345
Burleson, Dovie	333	Byrd, Albert	313
Burleson, Jane	164	Byrd, Delphia	242
Burleson, Joe	293	Byrd, George	253
Burleson, Lula	283	Byrd, Geroge W.	242
Burleson, L.W.	175	Byrd, Harvey Elmer	253
Burleson, Mary Jane	175	Byrd, Hutson	86
Burleson, ____	183	Byrd, John	253
Burlie, ____	5	Byrd, J.L.	326
Burnett, Bercice	270	Byrd, Katherine	144
Burow, Infant	41	Byrd, Lockey	354
Burow, Oscar	41	Byrd, Lou	294
Burrough, H.M.	291	Byrd, Minie	86
Burrough, William C.	291	Byrd, Robert	185
Burrow, Cathaline	186	Byrd, William	313
Burrow, Emily	295	Byre, Blake	166
Burrow, Frank	190	Byrum, Addie	142
Burrow, Fred	120	B____, J.V.	197
Burrow, Hellen Kate	74	B____, Rod Butler	27
Burrow, Infant	187	Cable, Calven	189
Burrow, Jake	186	Cable, Clad	238
Burrow, John	186	Cable, Daniel	158
Burrow, John F.	57	Cable, Dayton	267
Burrow, Josie	307	Cable, F. Dewey	115
Burrow, Martha	165	Cable, Hettie	293
Burrow, Nannie	185,187	Cable, Ina	131
Burrow, Oscar	41,74,187	Cable, Infant	267,337
Burrow, R.B.	120	Cable, James	100

Cable, J.J.	185,195,198 279 <		Campbell, Anna F.	108
			Campbell, Annie	207
Cable, J.S.		267	Campbell, Annis P.	147
Cable, Lafayette		115	Campbell, Arvy	100
Cable, Maggie		292	Campbell, Bell	309
Cable, Mary E.		197,198	Campbell, Bentley	270
Cable, McKinley		279	Campbell, Bertie	5
Cable, Patsy		164	Campbell, Bettie	66,75
Cable, Peter B.		279	Campbell, Buledene	139
Cable, Sarah Emaline		185	Campbell, Callie P.	224
Cable, Susan		133	Campbell, Calvin	237
Cable, Thomas		238,256	Campbell, Caroline	270
Cable, Will		314	Campbell, Carrie V.	261
Cable, W.M.		337	Campbell, Carter	216
Cain, Susan E.		296	Campbell, Cas	361
Caldwell, Bryan		84	Campbell, Charles	121,262
Caldwell, Clarence		49	Campbell, Charlie	352
Caldwell, Ida		49	Campbell, Cinda	349
Caldwell, John		84	Campbell, Clide	287
Caldwell, Leon		84	Campbell, Creta	305
Caldwell, Nellie		49	Campbell, Crisley	148
Caldwell, S.J.		251	Campbell, C.N.	319
Calhoun, David		156	Campbell, Daniel	154
Calhoun, Ida		240	Campbell, David	346
Calhoun, James Lester		156	Campbell, Davis	245
Calhoun, Joe		109	Campbell, Dayton	75,240
Calhoun, Margaret		238	Campbell, Derkis	271
Calhoun, Phebia		173	Campbell, Dortha	121
Calloway, Hiram		306	Campbell, Dudley	8
Calloway, _____		11	Campbell, D.C.	100,105
Caloway, Agnes Hays		240	Campbell, D.D.	195
Caloway, Dock		240	Campbell, Earl	191
Calton, Emeline		192	Campbell, Ed	158
Calton, Lottie		309	Campbell, Edward	92
Cambell, Letta		243	Campbell, Eishe	345
Cambll, Isaac		302	Campbell, Elijah	173
Cambll, Siley		302	Campbell, Eliza	75,214 346
Camel, Eishe		345		
Camel, James		345	Campbell, Elizabeth	253 277 <
Camel, Jess		345		
Camel, Walter		23	Campbell, Ellen	283
Cameron, Sarah		213	Campbell, Ethel	298
Campbell, Adalade		149	Campbell, E.A.	293
Campbell, Adalin		258	Campbell, E.K.	265
Campbell, Adeline		96,271	Campbell, E.M.	59
Campbell, Alex		339	Campbell, Foster	89
Campbell, Alexander		163	Campbell, Frank	270
Campbell, Andrew W.		361	Campbell, Fred	268

Campbell, F.C. (Mrs) 229 234 <	Campbell, J.E. 273
	Campbell, J.I. 271
Campbell, Galle 177	Campbell, J.R. 181,209
Campbell, George 50	Campbell, J.S. 152
Campbell, George P. 65 192 <	Campbell, Kate 264
	Campbell, Laura 76
Campbell, Grace 51	Campbell, Lavina 232
Campbell, Gracie B. 158	Campbell, Lawson 76,284
Campbell, Grant 2	Campbell, Lawton 59
Campbell, Gwnley 328	Campbell, Letta 243
Campbell, G.E. 59	Campbell, Lizzie 68,79 105,163,248 <
Campbell, Hampton 166	
Campbell, Harry 340	Campbell, Lola 176,319
Campbell, Hattie 187,303	Campbell, Lona E. 319
Campbell, Hellen 152	Campbell, Lucinda 368
Campbell, Horace 173	Campbell, Lucresia 67
Campbell, Ida 97	Campbell, L.W. 215
Campbell, Ike 89	Campbell, Maggie 349
Campbell, Ina 5	Campbell, Mamie 97
Campbell, Infant 75,76 96,100,117,296,358 <	Campbell, Martha 179,244 289 <
Campbell, Isaac 66,176 177,302 <	Campbell, Martha Bell 306
	Campbell, Martha J. 360
Campbell, Isabel 273	Campbell, Mary 171
Campbell, Isabell 174	Campbell, Mary E. 156
Campbell, Jack 89,125	Campbell, Mary Grace 301
Campbell, James 148,159 207,298,345 <	Campbell, Matilda 73
	Campbell, Melvin 177,358
Campbell, James G. 191	Campbell, Melvin C. 284
Campbell, James S. 231	Campbell, Mike 284,306 357 <
Campbell, Jan 256	
Campbell, Jane 47,65,236	Campbell, Milburn 236
Campbell, Jenne 268	Campbell, Minnie 186
Campbell, Jerry 270,352	Campbell, Mollie 100,105 110 <
Campbell, Jess 345	
Campbell, Jim 268	Campbell, M.D. 284,305 358 <
Campbell, John 76,96,103 148,343 <	
	Campbell, M.T. 306
Campbell, John D. 207	Campbell, Nancy 210,213
Campbell, John S. 152	Campbell, Nancy Ann 240
Campbell, John T. 190	Campbell, Nancy Jane 245
Campbell, Johnie 166	Campbell, Nannie 157
Campbell, Joseph 361	Campbell, Nat 287,301,349
Campbell, Julia 208	Campbell, Naten 236
Campbell, J. 346	Campbell, Nick 300,339
Campbell, J.A. 339	Campbell, Nola 47
Campbell, J.C. 124	Campbell, N.H. 174
Campbell, J.D. 345	Campbell, N.R. 139

Campbell,	Ocran	177	Campbell,	Z.C.	231
Campbell,	Ora	339	Campbell,	____	100,108
Campbell,	Parlie	181		153,315	<
Campbell,	Paul	121	Cannon,	Dewey	233
Campbell,	Pearl	49,327	Cannon,	D.C.	233
Campbell,	Pearlie	148	Cannon,	F____	363
Campbell,	Powell	147	Cannon,	Martha	266
Campbell,	Ralph	296	Cannon,	M.S.	124
Campbell,	Rebecca	232	Canon,	Annie	272
Campbell,	Rettie	109	Canon,	Elbert	337
Campbell,	Robert	117	Canon,	Hunter	6
Campbell,	Roda	357	Canon,	Jule	337
Campbell,	Rosa	181	Canon,	Martha	241
Campbell,	Roy	181	Canon,	Nelson	125
Campbell,	Roy B.	192	Canon,	Vern	338
Campbell,	Roy M.	173	Canter,	Hazle Lee	362
Campbell,	R.J.	135	Canter,	Jessie	276
Campbell,	Sallie	61,155	Canter,	Mary	276
Campbell,	Sam	319	Canter,	Rebecca	76,290
Campbell,	Sarah	188,227	Canter,	Ruby	87
	343	<	Canter,	Will	87,362
Campbell,	Sarah Ann	209	Caraway,	Altha	249
Campbell,	Sarah E.	100	Caraway,	Darvin	26
Campbell,	Sis	177	Caraway,	Martha	338
Campbell,	Stella	296	Caraway,	Nancy J.	11
Campbell,	Susan	300	Carden,	Alfred	88
Campbell,	Thomas G.	261	Carden,	Charles	181
Campbell,	Thomas R.	44	Carden,	Daniel	181
Campbell,	T.C.	301	Carden,	Eliza	131
Campbell,	Vara	97	Carden,	Infant	50
Campbell,	Vina	112	Carden,	Ladie	238
Campbell,	Vistie	171	Carden,	Presto	289
Campbell,	Walter	9,23	Carden,	Sam J.	273
Campbell,	Wilbern G.	231	Carden,	Susan	148
Campbell,	Wilburn	173,174	Carden,	Vince	361
Campbell,	Wilburn G.	173	Carden,	____	296
Campbell,	Will	181,283	Cardin,	Annie	136
Campbell,	William	20,262	Cardin,	A.G.	136
Campbell,	William C.	92	Cardin,	Dan	109
Campbell,	William G.	190	Cardin,	Dorothy L.	88
Campbell,	William H.	339	Cardin,	Emily C.	91
Campbell,	William R.	65	Cardin,	Grant	104
Campbell,	W.C.	215	Cardin,	Harry	109,196
Campbell,	W.G.	158,216	Cardin,	Hester	196
Campbell,	W.H.	173	Cardin,	Infant	32
Campbell,	W.M.	213	Cardin,	Leslie G.	104
Campbell,	Zachary	65	Cardin,	Loyd	104
Campbell,	Zora	357	Cardin,	Mintie	83

Cardin, N.J.	91	Carroll, Charlie	168
Cardin, Vince	361	Carroll, Emma E.	206
Carender, Ina Dorris	195	Carroll, Julia	210,282
Carender, Joseph L.	195	Carroll, Matilda	168
Carion, Laura	193	Carroll, Robert	125
Carlton, Ambrose	233	Carroll, Will	212
Caroway, Finly	253	Carrou, Anna	310
Caroway, William	253	Carson, Elise	104
Carper, Julia Ann	126	Carson, Willy	104
Carr, Alice	35	Carter, Blannie Edith	191
Carr, Alvin L.	364	Carter, Clarence	110
Carr, Anderson	125	Carter, C.C.	218
Carr, A.G.	364	Carter, C.D.	149
Carr, Edward	240	Carter, D.E.	307
Carr, Ella M.	35	Carter, Elizabeth B.	314
Carr, E.R.	168	Carter, Ella Burl	149
Carr, Gusta	38	Carter, Emma	235
Carr, Herman	361	Carter, Frank	110
Carr, James N.	355	Carter, F.L.	314
Carr, Johnson	168	Carter, James Gibson	307
Carr, Joseph	168	Carter, John	185,339
Carr, Lillian May	355	Carter, J.C.	221
Carr, Mahalia	94	Carter, Landon	82,110,307
Carr, Mamie	365	Carter, Landon (Capt)	223
Carr, Martha Ann	120	Carter, Loura	175
Carr, Mattie	165	Carter, Mollie	339
Carr, Nannie	110,292	Carter, Tessie	71
Carr, Netta	338	Carter, William J.	82
Carr, Norma	363	Carter, _____	249
Carr, Odd	361,363	Carver, Aden	253
Carr, Prescilla	206	Carver, Aderi	201
Carr, Sallie	357	Carver, Adin	192
Carrier, Alex	72	Carver, Aiden	139
Carrier, Arthur Guy	338	Carver, Arthur	232
Carrier, Biddie	126	Carver, Benjamin	253
Carrier, Charles F.	233	Carver, Bob	354
Carrier, Fannie	189	Carver, Carlis	354
Carrier, Gorda	3	Carver, Charlie	297
Carrier, Isaac	233	Carver, Cloyd	295
Carrier, Joana	100	Carver, David	232
Carrier, J.W.	160,338	Carver, Elijah	113,335
Carrier, Robert T.	72	Carver, Ellen	232
Carriger, David	15,286	Carver, Ernest	287
Carriger, Edna G.	134	Carver, Frank	139,253
Carriger, J.L.	250	Carver, George	169,297,313
Carriger, Roy	228	Carver, Grace	113
Carriger, Samuel J.	199	Carver, Infant	88,359
Carriger, William	258		

Carver, James 140,160,192	
248,295 <	
Carver, James E. 335	
Carver, James Robert 262	
Carver, Joe 192,304	
Carver, John 88,139,192	
287,294,346 <	
Carver, J.H. 31	
Carver, Lizzie 104	
Carver, Lon 192	
Carver, Martha 248	
Carver, Mary 150,292	
Carver, Mary Ann 148	
Carver, Mary Ellen 313	
Carver, Mollie 132	
Carver, Nancy 94,295,297	
304 <	
Carver, Nat 150,359	
Carver, Polly 303	
Carver, Rachel 255	
Carver, Roy 346	
Carver, Sarah M. 151	
Carver, Thomas Dayton 160	
Carver, Vere 50	
Carver, Vicy 304	
Carver, Will 201	
Carver, W.M. 201	
Carver, _____ 192	
Case, Martha 240	
Casey, Ernest William 66	
Casey, Fred 298,339,359	
Casey, George 103,154	
Casey, G.W. 225	
Casey, Ida May 66	
Casey, Ivan Eugene 298	
Casey, Lillie 154	
Casey, Mary 103	
Casey, Ruth 339	
Cass, Donald 63	
Cass, Edward C. 63	
Cass, Marthy 366	
Cass, Sam 253	
Cassida, Julia 327	
Casteel, Martha 202	
Cates, A.L. 97	
Cates, Carrie 97	
Cates, Edna Christine 181	
Cates, George Dewey 15	

Cates, Infant 96,101
Cates, James Howard 200
Cates, Laura Belle 200
Cates, Millard 96
Cates, Rhoda 180
Cates, Robert 101,179,181
Cates, Savina 282
Cates, Tempie 168
Cates, Willard 200
Cates, _____ 179
Cathern, Eliza 179
Cave, Elizabeth 186
Chambers, A.L. 21
Chambers, Bettie 330
Chambers, Charlie 192
Chambers, C.L. 319
Chambers, Dan 192
Chambers, Daniel 134
Chambers, David 176
Chambers, Delia 228
Chambers, Dellia 26
Chambers, D. 314
Chambers, D.J. 131
Chambers, D.T. 38
Chambers, Elijah 62
Chambers, Evline 277
Chambers, Hobart F. 159
Chambers, Infant 21,62
319 <
Chambers, James 310
Chambers, John 30
Chambers, Laura 336
Chambers, Mamie 291
Chambers, Marry 240
Chambers, Mary 154,225
257 <
Chambers, Nettie May 172
Chambers, O.L. 172
Chambers, Polly 336
Chambers, Robert M. 24
Chambers, Rose Anah 127
Chambers, Sallie 79,150
273 <
Chambers, Susan 90,286
348 <
Chambers, Susie 318
Chambers, William 54
Chambers, W.A. 159

Chambers, W.H. (Mrs)	279
Chance, Chrisly	128
Chappell, Glenn	291
Chappell, Walt	291
Chase, Mary A.	26
Chase, Thomas R.	105
Chase, William Dainey	105
Chatman, Arch	179
Chatman, Herbet	179
Cheek, David	63
Cheek, Mary	63
Cheek, Nancy	4
Chesser, Andrew W.	325
Chesser, Frank	222
Chesser, Henry	222
Chesser, Wilson	325
Chester, Cal	79
Chester, Helen	180
Chester, John	180
Childers, Ettie	94
Childs, Ada	294
Church, Bessie	342
Church, Bessie	351
Church, Caroline	158
Church, Elizabeth	220
Church, Garal	313
Church, Henry	357
Church, Mary Ann	226
Church, Phillip	313
Church, Sallie	219
Church, Walter F.	158
Church, William F.	219
Clamon, _____	145
Clark, Anna	366
Clark, Arther	337
Clark, Arthur	346
Clark, Bert	183
Clark, Bill	139
Clark, Caroline	319
Clark, Catherine	213
Clark, Charlie	292
Clark, Clara Jenette	248
Clark, Clarence	113
Clark, Dave	258,322
Clark, David	207
Clark, Elbert	35
Clark, Elizabeth	233
Clark, Elmer	324
Clark, Flora Ossie	95
Clark, Frank	89,207
Clark, George W.	277
Clark, Henry	160
Clark, Hettie	160
Clark, Infant	252
Clark, James	164,269
Clark, James B.	355
Clark, James L.	281
Clark, Jane	306
Clark, Jasper	181,183,183
Clark, John	144
Clark, Julia	127,144
Clark, Lillie	313
Clark, Lizzie	181,182
Clark, Lottie	336
Clark, Louize P.	45
Clark, Love	181
Clark, Lyda	181,183
Clark, Mary Lee	340
Clark, Mildred	337
Clark, Nalie	90
Clark, Nancy	315
Clark, Nat	306,324
Clark, Nola	171
Clark, N.B.	171
Clark, N.H.	113,127
Clark, Perly	340
Clark, P.	363
Clark, Rebecca E.	281
Clark, Roxie	292
Clark, Samuel	164
Clark, Savannah	136
Clark, Susan	298
Clark, Thomas	277,367
Clark, Tlitha	180
Clark, William	89
Clark, William C.	252
Clark, William J.	144
Clark, William Marion	367
Clark, William (Mrs)	367
Clark, W.M.	207
Clarke, Bessie	87
Clarke, Charles Ray	124
Clarke, O.W.	124
Clauson, Henry	277,278 364 <
Clauson, Hubert	364

Clauson, H.C.	355
Clauson, James	360
Clauson, Jane	337
Clauson, Maris	308
Clauson, Scarlottie	355
Clauson, Tilde	350
Clauson, William	360
Clauson, W.A.	308
Clausson, Lafayett	102
Clawson, Henry	277
Claymon, Jane	107
Clemens, Callie	21
Clemens, Garfield	1
Clemens, John	21
Clemmons, Jacob L.	363
Clemmons, Joel	363
Clemmons, Sarah	58
Clemmons, Will	363
Clemons, Benjamin	215
Clemons, Bill	58
Clemons, Callie	198,210
Clemons, Carl Haynes	193
Clemons, Carrie	85
Clemons, Cynthia	210,271
Clemons, David	193,215
Clemons, Emma	21
Clemons, Infant	21
Clemons, Jennie	35
Clemons, Liddy M.	91
Clemons, Lillie	85
Clemons, Martha	138
Clemons, Synthie	328
Clemons, William	215
Clemons, Willie Dean	42
Clossom, Robert	79
Clossom, Sarah	79
Closson, Dave	69
Closson, Elen	130
Closson, George	156
Closson, Homer R.	197
Closson, James	156
Closson, James E.	198
Closson, Lilly	183
Closson, Lonia C.	198
Closson, Nancy Jane	102
Closson, Roy	156
Closson, Sarah A.	198
Closson, T.C.	197,198
Closson, Will	182
Closson, William	360
Closson, William V.	198
Closson, W.M.	102,177
Cochoran, Nora	54
Cochran, Adda	38
Cochran, Allen	150
Cochran, Ernie	292
Cochran, Jame	292
Cochran, James	150
Cochran, Jane	164,269
Cochran, Jim	326
Cochran, Joe	313
Cochran, John	326,359
Cochran, Martha Jane	35
Cochran, Nola	359
Cochran, Roy	313
Cochran, William R.	27
Coffee, Ada	109
Coffee, Smith H.	109
Coffee, S.	109
Coffer, Clide	308
Coffer, _____	308
Cogswell, Mary Ann	167
Colback, Henry	344
Colbaugh, Ellen	312
Colbaugh, Ester	175
Colbaugh, Evelyn	176
Colbaugh, Fred	176,239
Colbaugh, George	239
Colbaugh, George Jr.	90
Colbaugh, Glenn	239
Colbaugh, Henry	202,293 333,344 <
Colbaugh, Infant	90,333
Colbaugh, James	175,211
Colbaugh, Jane	325
Colbaugh, J.N., Sr	133
Colbaugh, Maggie	74,126
Colbaugh, Nan	218
Colbaugh, Nola	231
Colbaugh, Sarah	355
Colbaugh, Vena	234,266 315 <
Colbaugh, William	211
Colbaugh, W.M.	100,178 344 <
Colbock, W.M.	344

Coldwell, Clarence	49	Cole, S.S.	208,276
Coldwell, James Fred	238	Cole, Walter	146
Coldwell, Martha E.	335	Cole, William	85
Coldwell, Nellie	49	Cole, William G.	169
Coldwell, Walter H.	238	Cole, Winnie	302
Cole, A.J.	69,146	Cole, W.J.	255,280
Cole, Benjamin	280	Cole, ____	243,304
Cole, Carrie	68	Coleman, C.C.	30
Cole, Clera	69	Coleman, John	254
Cole, Clide	322	Coleman, Maggie	198
Cole, Cony	69	Coleman, Mollie	267
Cole, C.G.	8	Coleman, Nat	195
Cole, C.W.	250	Coleman, Ruth	195
Cole, D.C.	287, 303	Coleman, Steward F.	27
Cole, Eliza	3,13	Collins, Andy Gilbert	292
Cole, Ellie	98	Collins, A.C.	345
Cole, Emma Celeste	276	Collins, A.R.	106,269,296
Cole, Ester	99,364	Collins, Bethwin	320
Cole, Estes	328	Collins, Charles	235
Cole, Ethel	169	Collins, Cordie	124
Cole, Eva A.	276	Collins, Dock	130
Cole, Flora J.	72	Collins, Elisah	125
Cole, Floyd	264	Collins, Emerly B.	77
Cole, George	85	Collins, Erlina	345
Cole, Harret	2	Collins, Fletcher	361
Cole, Infant	69,98,264 322 <	Collins, Grant	130
		Collins, Granville	130
Cole, James	98	Collins, G.O.	65
Cole, Jessie H.	56	Collins, Harmon	361
Cole, Joanna	85	Collins, Isaac	178
Cole, John	303	Collins, Jack	166,361
Cole, John S.	263	Collins, John	106,148
Cole, Julia	7	Collins, John Jr.	148
Cole, J.J.	280	Collins, Jospehine M.	262
Cole, Lina	282	Collins, J.C.	340
Cole, Lonnie	263	Collins, Katherine	117
Cole, Lucy Irene	311	Collins, Lena	269
Cole, Margaret	157	Collins, Lisey	104
Cole, Mary	205	Collins, Lusie	106
Cole, Mary A.	205	Collins, Maggie	321
Cole, Mattie	132	Collins, Nannie	294
Cole, Nancy Lillian	250	Collins, Ollie	316
Cole, Rebecca	99	Collins, Ollie Jr.	320
Cole, Robinson	89	Collins, R.C.	235
Cole, Ruby Pearl	138	Collins, Sam Newton	178
Cole, Sallie M.	255	Collins, Samuel P.	65
Cole, Steve	302	Collins, Tilson, O.	65
Cole, Susie	125	Collins, Wat	209

Collins, Will	119
Collins, W.G.	84
Collins, _____	362
Colts, Kathern	306
Combs, Anna Mae	256
Combs, Ben	6
Combs, Ben	16
Combs, Bruce	49
Combs, Cameron Dayton	350
Combs, Catherin	291
Combs, Crawford	231
Combs, Dora	296
Combs, Harrett	201
Combs, Harrette	186
Combs, Infant	6,16
Combs, Kel	231
Combs, Mae	360
Combs, Neva	173
Combs, Robert	179
Combs, Robert L.	269
Combs, Sarah	268
Combs, Tom	350
Combs, Vicey	181
Combs, William	17,219,269
Combs, _____	143,348
Conelly, _____	227
Conley, Wheeler	128,325
Connelly, Harriett	87
Connelly, Wheeler	128
Constable, Caroline	129
Constable, J.H.	129
Cook, Alma	325
Cook, Bell	361
Cook, Carley	317
Cook, Charlie	133
Cook, Claten	317
Cook, David C.	64
Cook, Dillie	325
Cook, Ethel	257
Cook, Ida C.	54
Cook, John	27
Cook, J.C.	351
Cook, J.M.	325
Cook, Manila	140
Cook, Patsey	64
Cook, Thomas	112
Cook, Thomas	140
Cook, Vernia	19
Cook, W.M.	325
Cook, _____	112
Cooper, Abe	317
Cooper, Abe	353
Cooper, George	47
Cooper, Hazy E.	317
Cooper, Jesse	132
Cooper, Joel	64
Cooper, Mabel	353
Cooper, M.B.	296
Cooper, Sarah Jane	64
Cooper, William	296
Copley, Dicy	121
Coply, Virgie	336
Cordell, Bessie	12
Cordell, Charles E.	46
Cordell, Darris	283
Cordell, Frankie	354
Cordell, Nat	283
Cordell, Raymond	283
Cordell, _____	255
Cornett, Anna	341
Cornett, Dan	200,323
Cornett, Daniel	200
Cornett, Edath	30
Cornett, Fannie	157
Cornett, Frank	90
Cornett, Infant	90
Cornett, James	363
Cornett, Jennettie	216
Cornett, John	363
Cornett, J.A.	157
Cornett, Mary Alice	323
Cornett, Myrtle	30
Cornett, Oscar Howard	200
Couley, Rufus	137
Courtner, Sarah	349
Cowe, Martha	232
Cox, Biddie Jane	181
Cox, Clifford	15
Cox, Eliza	113
Cox, Hugh (Mrs)	171
Cox, Jaunita	332
Cox, Jim	127
Cox, Margaret	153,329
Cox, Mary	222
Cox, Richard	208

Cox, Riley	332	Crow, D.S.	70
Cox, Robert	340	Crow, Elizabeth	273
Cox, Susan	269	Crow, Elva	59
Cox, S.M.	181,208	Crow, Emily	7
Craig, George	298	Crow, Ethel Bill	251
Craig, Harriett	298	Crow, Fervis D.	216
Craig, Hiram	298	Crow, Flora	151
Craig, William Robert	298	Crow, Frank	171,326
Crawford, Andrew	71	Crow, F.D.	102,215
Crawford, Manda	125	Crow, F.W.	289
Crawford, Sara	71	Crow, George	84
Creasman, Dave	249	Crow, Gladys Marie	244
Creasman, John Andrew	249	Crow, Godfrey	252
Creasman, J.A. (Mrs)	249	Crow, H.T.	252
Creed, Delia B. Payne	223	Crow, Infant	171
Creed, James	223	Crow, Isaac	179
Creed, Jane	246	Crow, Isaac	252,273
Creed, Jane	276	Crow, Jack	57
Creed, N.B.	118	Crow, Jennie	315
Creed, Rebecca	82	Crow, John	257,306,354
Creed, U.B.	220	Crow, Julia	326
Creed, William	82,220	Crow, J.B.	239
Creed, William C.	203	Crow, Lee	273,297,315
Creede, Clyde	128	Crow, Leslie B.	239
Creede, G.W.	128	Crow, Levi	273
Creger, Ethel Goss	255	Crow, Levisa	260,321
Cress, Debby M.	65	Crow, Lottie	188,308
Cress, James	70,89,131	Crow, Louis	354
Cress, Mary	89	Crow, Lucy	63
Cretsinger, Geroge W.	227	Crow, Maggie	57,59,361
Cretsinger, ____	251	Crow, Martin	7,238,263
Crisp, Delia	295	Crow, Mary	252
Crisp, Sallie	87	Crow, Mary L.	239
Crosswhite, J.B.	161	Crow, Mattie Mays	278
Crosswhite, Lonzo	190	Crow, Molly	53
Crosswhite, Mary A.	163	Crow, Overtte	244
Crosswhite, Webster	190	Crow, Ruby Roy	216
Crosswhite, W.B. (Mrs)	190	Crow, Ruth May	215
Crow, Alexander	297	Crow, Sam	238
Crow, Alvin Bertie	302	Crow, Samuel	251
Crow, Bell	363	Crow, Soloman A.	263
Crow, Blanch	320,322	Crow, Tennessee	65,274
Crow, Campbell	70,257	Crow, Thomas	42,84
Crow, Celia	304	Crow, T.A.	355
Crow, Clyde Owens	102	Crow, T.C.	70
Crow, Della	298	Crow, Vicey	280
Crow, D.	302	Crow, Virginia	306
Crow, D.B.	102,252	Crow, William	274

Crow, _____	229,268
Crowder, Bessie	335
Crowder, George	48
Crowder, Robert	240
Crowder, Stephen M.	27
Crowe, George	84
Crowe, Thomas	84
Crowell, Dora	323
Crowell, Will	323
Crowlie, Pollie	191
Croy, Bessie	79
Croy, J.D.	136
Croy, Udem	119
Croy, Z.J.	119
Crumley, Augustus	138
Crumley, Blanch	41
Crumley, Earl	358
Crumley, Emma	43
Crumley, Evelyn	138
Crumley, E.Y.	5
Crumley, G.A.	17
Crumley, Infant	5,17,42 358 <
Crumley, Jane	61
Crumley, Lena	345
Crumley, Luther H.	17
Crumley, Matilda	152
Crumley, Minnie	160
Crumley, Ray	9
Crumley, Robert	97
Crumley, S.J.	340
Crumley, Tessie	19
Crumley, ...	124
Crwe, Phebe	205
Culbert, Barbara	302,307
Culbert, Bessie	231
Culbert, Birtie	38
Culbert, Bud	323
Culbert, Elizabeth	147
Culbert, Floyd	302
Culbert, Hannah	284
Culbert, James	155
Culbert, Leta	307
Culbert, Luveina	1
Culbert, Robert	302,303
Culbert, Robert Jr.	303
Culbert, W.F.	226,227
Culbertson, Mary	239
Culbert. Elizabeth	214
Culver, Charles	193
Curd, Celia Dunn	78
Curd, Ezekiel	80
Curd, Infant	297
Curd, James	80
Curd, S.H.	297
Curd, Vernie	237
Curd, Wesley	80
Curd, _____	175
Curry, Clyde	78
Curry, George Albert	86
Curry, Jennie	86
Curry, Ralph	43
Curry, Thomas	86
Curtis, Arna S.	294
Curtis, B.P.	343
Curtis, Hila	159
Curtis, Howard	131
Curtis, J.A.	2
Curtis, J.G. (Mrs)	298
Curtis, Lawerenc E.	191
Curtis, Will	294
Curtis, William	131
Curtis, William T.	191
Curtis, W.E.	294
Curtis, _____	184
C___ Otta	196
Dalton, Minnie E.	128
Dalton, Willie	128
Daniel, H.T.	58,98,223
Daniel, Martha	252
Daniels, Alice	125
Daniels, Ellen	333
Daniels, Francis	260
Daniels, George W.	153
Daniels, H.T.	67,72,179 180,193,228 <
Daniels, Jessie	1
Daniels, Livcy	144
Daniels, Luta	199
Daniels, Lutie B.	223
Daniels, Riley	72
Danielson, C. Edward	56
Danner, C.L.	316,332,349
Danner, C.S.	332
Danner, Eva Sarah M.	316
Danner, John Jr.	332

Danner, Pauline	349
Daugherty, Clarence	322
Daugherty, Donna	194
Daugherty, Henry	194
Daugherty, Roy	322
Davenport, Amos	19
Davenport, Annie	235
Davenport, Desky	50
Davenport, Elizabeth	141
Davenport, Fannie	117
Davenport, Hilda	210
Davenport, Howard	87
Davenport, Monroe	201
Davenport, M.A.	87
Davenport, Sam	222
Davidson, Bessie	329
Davidson, Carl	277
Davidson, C.E.	221
Davidson, Infant	221
Davidson, James	29
Davidson, Lottie	221
Davidson, Lottie P.	277
Davis, Adda	105
Davis, Addie	143
Davis, Annie	194,267
Davis, Arthur	94,282
Davis, Aubry	180
Davis, Bessie	4,74
Davis, Bonnie May	67
Davis, Burtie	94
Davis, Christine	367
Davis, C.	283
Davis, Dan	1
Davis, Ellen	337
Davis, Ettie	282
Davis, Eveline	257
Davis, Frank	367
Davis, Hannah	166
Davis, Hickey R.	114
Davis, Hicks	221
Davis, Ina	73
Davis, Infant	14,282
Davis, J.E.	129
Davis, J.H.	194,225
Davis, Lank	3
Davis, Lettie	21
Davis, Lidy	136
Davis, Linc	267
Davis, Lincoln	73,236,267
Davis, Linda	180
Davis, Link	14,59,114
Davis, Link E.	259
Davis, Louisa	86
Davis, Lula	59
Davis, Luther	90
Davis, L.K.	73
Davis, Malissa	124
Davis, Mammie	257
Davis, Mark Allen	213
Davis, Martha J.	238
Davis, Martha Nave	307
Davis, Mary	367
Davis, Mattie	297
Davis, Mattie E.	259
Davis, Miller	73
Davis, M.C. (Mrs.)	1
Davis, Philip	349
Davis, Phillip	60,307
Davis, Rheuben	136,180
Davis, Rhuben	136
Davis, Robert Kennith	221
Davis, Rollie A.E.	194
Davis, R.B.	169
Davis, Sallie	169
Davis, Sam	303
Davis, Sanford	303
Davis, S.C.	67
Davis, Tessie	236
Davis, Thomas	235
Davis, Unice	171
Davis, Will	74
Davis, William	90,171
Davis, William A.	213
Davis, William B.	138
Davis, William D.	303
Davis, William L.	59
Davis, _____	139,146,248
Dawson, Susie	117
Deal, Lonthia	366
Dean, Archer	237
Dean, Gerald	237
Deaton, Sarah	257
Deffenbough, Lela	130
Delaney, Clarence	166
Delaney, Infant	166
Delaney, Matisie	166

Delanie, Oxie	250
Delaoch, Grace	267
Deloach, Belle	175
Deloach, Bessie	321
Deloach, Charlie	127
Deloach, Dave	321,362
Deloach, D.	93
Deloach, Eliza	210
Deloach, Eliza E.	95
Deloach, Emeline	320
Deloach, Eugene	317
Deloach, Henry	95,124,127
Deloach, Howard	56
Deloach, Ike	93
Deloach, Infant	233,367
Deloach, James	18,142,158, 268,320
Deloach, John	66,242,310, 313
Deloach, John Frank	367
Deloach, Joseph	89
Deloach, Maggie	290
Deloach, Margaret	268
Deloach, Mattie	218
Deloach, Mollie	192
Deloach, Nancy	92
Deloach, Robert	89,124
Deloach, Rosa	191
Deloach, Sam	192,362
Deloach, Thomas	158,320
Deloach, Tom	93
Deloach, Walter	191
Deloach, William M.	233
Dempsey, Florence	64
Dempsey, H.A.	64
Dempsey, _____	322
Dempseys, Infant	43
Dempseys, Milton	43
Dempsy, Fred Carr	120
Dempsy, Infant	142
Dempsy, Jack	142
Dempsy, John A.	120
Dempsy, John R.	167
Dempsy, Lilian	142
Dempsy, Mary K.	132
Dempsy, Nathan	80
Dempsy, Susan E.	291
Dempsy, William H.H.	80
Dennis, Frank	234,278
Dennis, Lillie	278
Dennis, Ray	234
Denny, John H.	94
Denny, Leo	94
Denton, Maggie	182
Denton, Mattie Cox	127
Deny, John H.	94
Denzamore, Nancy	28
Devalt, Abbigail	213
Dials, Dalie	192
Dials, Ples	17
Dicken, Elbert	293
Dicken, James Cuarley	288
Dicken, Thomas	288,293
Dickens, Clark	257
Dickens, Edgar Jr.	203
Dickens, Rossie Alice	124
Dickerson, Marabelle	194
Dickison, May B.	122
Dickison, William H.	122
Dickson, Edgar	203
Dickson, Henry	109,125
Dickson, Julia C.	150
Dickson, Mary Belle	108
Dickson, Mary V.	109
Dickson, William H.	150
Dier, Drret	229
Dikens, Edgar	203
Dingar, William	255
Dingmore, Enoch	362
Dison, Frank	208
Dison, George W.	208
Dixon, James	108
Dixon, Lee	108
Doby, Isham	107
Dockery, Pollie	274
Dodge, Sallie	272
Dolan, Caroline	134
Dolan, Nancy	318
Dolan, Sam	134
Dolen, J.H.	264
Dolen, Nels	264
Dolen, Paul	47
Dolen, Samuel Paxton	264
Donlson, _____	295
Donnell, Martha Carr	240
Donnell, W.H.	240

Donsil, Abe	22	Dugger, Hubert Ray	307
Dotson, E.A.	117	Dugger, Ida	331
Dotson, James A.	117	Dugger, Infant	142,175
Dotson, Rebecca Jane	122	282,288,350	<
Dougherty, M.	71	Dugger, James	46,111,146
Dougherty, Sarah	56,167	Dugger, Jane	285
Douglas, Daisy L.	34	Dugger, Joe E.	242
Douglas, Debbie	105,116	Dugger, John	18,177,288
Douglas, Emma	312,351	Dugger, John F.	256,307
Douglas, James	101,144	Dugger, J.W.	224
Douglas, John	360	Dugger, Liddie	321
Douglas, Martha	360	Dugger, Lidia	211
Douglas, Mary	229	Dugger, Maggie	297
Douglas, Nancy	336	Dugger, Margaret	315
Douglas, Nancy	351	Dugger, Martha	268
Douglas, Polly	23	Dugger, Melvina	111
Douglas, Rachel	127	Dugger, Mirida	307
Douglas, Susan	144	Dugger, Monroe	350
Douglas, Walter	101	Dugger, Robert	291,340
Douglas, William	101	Dugger, R.M.	285
Dove, James	344	Dugger, Samuel	134
Dove, John W.	344	Dugger, Sarah	291
Dove, J.D.	334	Dugger, Sarah E.	291
Dove, Susan Agnes	334	Dugger, Sarah J.	147
Drake, Louie	157	Dugger, Smith	192,242
Duffield, Nannie	69	Dugger, Susan	154,313
Duffield, Nelson	261	Dugger, S.B.	247
Duffield, Samuel L.	69	Dugger, S.E.	307
Dugan, William P.	242	Dugger, S____	211
Dugger, Ann	194	Dugger, Tempie	340
Dugger, Clara	302	Dugger, Thomas	53,171
Dugger, C.B.	282	Dugger, Tom	278
Dugger, David	177	Dugger, Tuck	171
Dugger, David A.	256	Dugger, T.	192
Dugger, Dora	142	Dugger, T.A.	175,266
Dugger, Easter	71	Dugr, Infant	288
Dugger, Eliza	142,225	Dugr, John	288
Dugger, Elizabeth	65,278	Dulaney, Clarence	347
Dugger, Frank	342	Dulaney, Ralph	347
Dugger, Frank E.	331	Duncan, Andrew J.	293
Dugger, George	65,224,266	Duncan, Clyde	366
Dugger, George Brown	340	Duncan, Mary Louise	348
Dugger, George F. Jr.	266	Duncan, Nancy	275
Dugger, Grace	212,246	Duncan, Sexton	290
Dugger, G.L.	142	Duncan, William P.	290
Dugger, G.W.	225	Duncan, W.L.	348
Dugger, Hanah M.	224	Dunkin, Mary	279
Dugger, Henry	331	Dunlap, Jasper	44

Dunlop, Arthur Blaine	155	Edmonson, Bertha	366
Dunlop, Infant	26	Edmonson, Hassie	306
Dunlop, James	189	Edmonson, Millard	248
Dunlop, Walter	155	Edmonson, Ruby	211
Dunlop, Walter D.	188	Edmonson, T.L.	10
Dunlop, W.D.	189	Edmonson, Willard	211
Dunmore, Melica	362	Edney, John	275
Dunn, G.M.	169	Edney, Nora	275
Dunn, Wesley	78	Edny, John	138
Dyer, Nancy	323	Edny, Selvia	138
Dyson, ____	112	Edwards, Bertha	244
Eadens, Sam	222	Edwards, Fannie	47
Eakin, John	167	Edwards, Gracie	356
Earvin, Alfred	33	Edwards, Levi C.	330
Easlearling, John	353	Edwards, Obe	330
Eastepp, Andy	346	Edwards, Richard G.	330
Eastepp, Callie	346	Eggers, Alexander	163
Eastepp, Dewey	346	Eggers, Allie	193
Eastridge, Barnabus	290	Eggers, Annie	305
Eastridge, Pleas	290	Eggers, E. Lorena	295
Eaton, Calvin	246	Eggers, Fahe	295
Echols, Cora	178	Eggers, Frank	9
Echols, John B.	178,211	Eggers, Job	350
Echols, Maggie	211	Eggers, John (Mrs)	146
Echols, Pearl	211	Eggers, J.F. (Mrs)	85
Edan, D.F.	83	Eggers, L.K.	350
Edens, Arther N. (Mrs)	272	Eggers, Martha	263
Edens, A.W.	132	Eggers, Maude	146
Edens, Benie	212	Eggers, M.C.	295
Edens, Dave	235	Eggers, Sarah	163
Edens, Edwin Vernon	78	Eggers, T.K.	350
Edens, E.L.	78	Elison, Celia	54
Edens, Helen Margaret	132	Elison, Henry	62
Edens, Hubert	37	Elkins, Katie	317
Edens, Infant	246	Eller, Lorina	248
Edens, James	367	Eller, Mose	249
Edens, John J.	71	Ellie, R.A.	92
Edens, J.N.	71	Elliott, Alexander	161
Edens, Laura	93	Elliott, Anis	306
Edens, Mary	57,235	Elliott, Barbara	233
Edens, Nat	212,246	Elliott, Belle	315
Edens, Nathaniel T.	71	Elliott, Bill	80,308,336
Edens, Sam	212	Elliott, Bonnie	310
Edens, Sarah E.	45	Elliott, Boyle	309
Edens, Visa	116	Elliott, B.M.	199
Edens, Will	93	Elliott, Charles	158,165 363
Edens, ____	238		<
Edmondson, Delphia	248	Elliott, Charles Jr.	363

Elliott, Charlie 71	Elliott, Thomas J. 171
Elliott, Cora Dickens 257	Elliott, Verdie 270
Elliott, Dan 93,171	Elliott, Violet 143
Elliott, David 68,143,171	Elliott, Will 164
Elliott, Dora 68,95,335	Elliott, William 91
Elliott, Easter 158	Elliott, W.D. 309
Elliott, Eva 209	Elliott, _____ 302,306
Elliott, Evvie 28	Ellis, Allie 296,337
Elliott, Floyd 80	Ellis, Arnold 157
Elliott, George W. 164	Ellis, Beatrice 43
Elliott, Goldy 161	Ellis, Blanch 227
Elliott, Harsin 302	Ellis, Carrie 139
Elliott, Hattie 183	Ellis, Carry 154
Elliott, Herman 31	Ellis, Claud 320
Elliott, Hurmen Daton 22	Ellis, Claude 308
Elliott, Infant 71	Ellis, C.E. 92
Elliott, James 135	Ellis, Dan 292
Elliott, James P. 337	Ellis, Daniel 61,209,341
Elliott, Jane 302	Ellis, David 227
Elliott, Joe 93	Ellis, Debbie 82,307
Elliott, John 80,287,350	Ellis, Dellie 352
Elliott, John A. 166	Ellis, D.G. 157
Elliott, Joseph 287,337	Ellis, Eliza 209,257,258
Elliott, J.J. 257	Ellis, Elizabeth 105
Elliott, Landon 350	Ellis, Emma 61
Elliott, Lessie 273	Ellis, Frank 216
Elliott, Lillie 250	Ellis, Harriett 85
Elliott, Lucy 91	Ellis, Haynes 171
Elliott, Mack 337	Ellis, Infant 216,241,320
Elliott, Maggie 327	Ellis, Jack 226
Elliott, Mandie 327	Ellis, James 241
Elliott, Mara 305	Ellis, James T. 331
Elliott, Martha 253	Ellis, Jim 184
Elliott, Mary 355	Ellis, Joe 366
Elliott, Mary E. 124	Ellis, John 292
Elliott, Mary Lewis 186	Ellis, Joseph Hooker 61
Elliott, Michael 253	Ellis, J.T. 61
Elliott, M.D. 209	Ellis, Lillie 149
Elliott, None 22	Ellis, Lizzie 263
Elliott, Nora 91,225	Ellis, Lola 176
Elliott, Pete 300,326	Ellis, Louise 241
Elliott, P.H. 309	Ellis, Lousia 292
Elliott, Raymond 135	Ellis, L.C. (Mrs) 311
Elliott, Rettie 336	Ellis, Martha 116
Elliott, Robert Hobert 22	Ellis, Martha A. 341
Elliott, Roby 287,350	Ellis, Minnie 308
Elliott, Samuel L. 253	Ellis, Nancey 111
Elliott, Thom 93	Ellis, Nancy 161,164,364

Ellis, Rad	331		Ensor, Robert	83
Ellis, Radford	157		Ensor, Sallie	89
Ellis, Rhoda	110		Epperson, Infant	71
Ellis, Richard	311		Epperson, J.B.	71
Ellis, Rosa	243		Ernest, Josire	366
Ellis, R.	61		Ervin, Bettie	226
Ellis, R.H.	61		Ervin, Mary	134
Ellis, R.J.	331		Erwin, Cain	240
Ellis, R.M.	35		Erwin, Charlie	214
Ellis, R.T.	224		Erwin, Clint	68
Ellis, Sarah	60		Erwin, George	214
Ellis, W.C.	89		Erwin, Harritte	325
Ellison, Charles	210		Erwin, Infant	240
Ellison, Charlie	262		Erwin, Julia	66,128
Ellison, Henry	175,354		Erwin, Margaret	133
	365 <		Erwin, Nellie	68
Ellison, John	31		Erwin, Sallie	66
Ellison, Nancy	365		Erwin, Thomas	3
Ellison, Pearl	109		Est, Infant	134
Ellison, Samuel	109		Est, Isaac	134
Ellison, Thomas J.	27		Estep, Addison	25
Emert, Caroline	80		Estep, Alen	283
Emmert, Catherine	283		Estep, Andrew	75
Emmert, C.M.	116		Estep, Andy	322,346
Emmert, George W.	190		Estep, Aney	348
Emmert, G.W.	58		Estep, Annie	186
Emmert, Jacob B.	116		Estep, A.D.	293
Emmert, Jeremiah	301		Estep, A.J.	293
Emmert, Katie	79		Estep, Betsy	255
Emmitt, Bate	268		Estep, Bob	305
Emmitt, Bill	268		Estep, Bruce	131
Endrus, Dave	83		Estep, Bruit	331
Endrus, Hubert	83		Estep, Butler	161
Endy, Eulia	72		Estep, Callie	346
Endy, John	72		Estep, Catherine	75
Enson, R.M.	197		Estep, Charles	75
Ensor, Amelia	323		Estep, Clarence	9,11,28
Ensor, Clara	134		Estep, Cora	305,337
Ensor, Creta	289		Estep, Cornelia T.	188
Ensor, C.W.	89		Estep, C.T.	193,257
Ensor, Denny	362		Estep, Dan Landon	357
Ensor, D.B.	362		Estep, Delila	76
Ensor, E.D.	84		Estep, Dewey	346
Ensor, G.W.	345		Estep, Dora	82
Ensor, John K.	83		Estep, Doris C.	302
Ensor, Matilda	84		Estep, Dorthia	3
Ensor, R.M.	136,146,177		Estep, Edia	253
	201 <		Estep, Elizabeth	170,320

Estep, Eveline	255	
Estep, Evline	214	
Estep, Freelove	299	
Estep, George	135,156	
Estep, Glen	5	
Estep, Glenn Jobe	258	
Estep, Grace	174	
Estep, Hazel	125	
Estep, Henry	77,321	
Estep, Heril	290	
Estep, H.D.	302	
Estep, Infant	13,28,77,93 135,226,302 <	
Estep, Isaac	70,214,283 290,359 <	
Estep, Jacob	125	
Estep, James	310	
Estep, James Franklin	184	
Estep, Joe	337	
Estep, John	136,265	
Estep, John Robertson	214	
Estep, Johnson	322	
Estep, Julia Ann	305	
Estep, Kate	356	
Estep, Lawrence E.	57	
Estep, Levi	70,277	
Estep, Low	161	
Estep, Luckey	61	
Estep, Lucy	314	
Estep, L.T.	258	
Estep, Malisey	240	
Estep, Mallek	357	
Estep, Martin	310	
Estep, Mary Blevins	191	
Estep, Mose	75	
Estep, Moses	176,265	
Estep, M.A.	28	
Estep, Nancy	176,177	
Estep, Nelly	82	
Estep, Raymond	321	
Estep, Rebecca	134,208	
Estep, Ruthey	268	
Estep, Sam	319	
Estep, Samuel	93	
Estep, Samuel M.	24	
Estep, Shaderic	193	
Estep, Susan	158,183	
Estep, Susay	28	

Estep, S.R.	61,191,305 322 <	
Estep, Tempie	326	
Estep, Tensu	359	
Estep, Tishie	103	
Estep, Tulva Grace	257	
Estep, Vergie	292	
Estep, Viola	131	
Estep, Virda	8	
Estep, Wanatie	277	
Estep, Wesley	302	
Estep, Widlow	236	
Estep, Wiley	226,302	
Estep, Will	175,188	
Estep, William	310	
Estep, W.R.	34	
Estep, W.W.	359	
Estep, Zak	331	
Estep, _____	236	
Estep. Lillie	165	
Estes, Millaoy	87	
Estes, Robert A.	87	
Estis, Eveline	3	
Faidley, Myrtle	259	
Faigen, Nanie	228	
Fair, A.B.	118	
Fair, Bennick	158	
Fair, Bessie	273,300	
Fair, Bill	253,274	
Fair, Bishop	56	
Fair, Charles S.	230	
Fair, Conley Phill	187	
Fair, C.D.	158	
Fair, David	187	
Fair, David A.	163	
Fair, Effie	64	
Fair, Elizabeth	138,157	
Fair, Eric Garton	84	
Fair, Fannie	122	
Fair, Franklin E.	230	
Fair, George	260	
Fair, George W.	84	
Fair, Gladys	274	
Fair, Grace	300,321,322	
Fair, Hannah	296	
Fair, Harry William	194	
Fair, Hattie	214	
Fair, Hazel	23	

Fair, Howard		154	Faitley, Clarence		182
Fair, Ida Grace		328	Faitley, Hobart J.		182
Fair, Infant	123,128,221		Farney, Lena		66
300		<	Farrance, Anthony		224
Fair, James H.		123,242	Farthing, Julia E.		281
274		<	Feather, Blonde		297
Fair, Jane		298,360	Feathers, Andrew J.		307
Fair, Jennie		175	Feathers, Bell		364
Fair, Jerry		123	Feathers, Christina A.		142
Fair, Jina		367	Feathers, Decia		127
Fair, John		328	Feathers, Elbert E.		282
Fair, John H.	123,138,274		Feathers, G.W.		364
Fair, J.D.		342	Feathers, Lillie		232
Fair, J.G.		287	Feathers, Margaret		168
Fair, Lena		163	Feathers, Nannie		122
Fair, Lenna Myron		342	Feathers, Viola B.		297
Fair, Lester		273	Feathers, William	124,282	
Fair, Linda		64	February, Elizabeth		335
Fair, Liza		171	February, May		364
Fair, Lizzie		274	February, ___		176
Fair, Maggie		277	Feer, Cassie		294
Fair, Mandy		169	Feinney, Catherine		317
Fair, Martha		118	Ferches, Sindy		299
Fair, Mary		326	Ferguson, Andrew		107
Fair, Mary Jane		242	Ferguson, Anthony M.		107
Fair, Mary J.		45	Ferguson, A.A.		107
Fair, Matilda E.		163	Ferguson, Ben		341
Fair, Mattie		185	Ferguson, Blanch	243,277	
FAir, May		190	Ferguson, B.B.		290
Fair, Minnie		106	Ferguson, Clarence B.		173
Fair, Mollie E.		315	Ferguson, Eliza		69
Fair, Non		273	Ferguson, Emma	60,277	
Fair, Ollie		216	Ferguson, Everett		173
Fair, Oscar M.		287	Ferguson, Joel C.		290
Fair, Pauline		123	Ferguson, Mary		345
Fair, Polly		350	Ferguson, William		290
Fair, Rebecca		276	Ferguson, W.J.		341
Fair, R.F.		138	Fields, Jeff		223
Fair, Sam H.		154	Fields, John	70,223	
Fair, Sheriff		162	Fields, J.H.		313
Fair, Shird		118	Fields, Oliver R.		223
Fair, S.S.	128,221,300		Fields, Sussin		11
Fair, Thomas	162,194,367		Fields, W.H.		313
Fair, Thomas Samuel		162	Fife, R.S.		194
Fair, William C.		7	Filars, John G. (Col)		42
Fair, W.F.	158,163,214		Fine, David A. (Mrs)		281
253		<	Fine, David R.		281
Fairclaw, Jennie		190	Fine, Nina		281

Finey, Sarah	358	Fletcher, Nannie Nave	254
Finiher, Cassie	94	Fletcher, Polina	311
Finley, Frank Sr.	184	Fletcher, Rena	258
Finley, Frank W. Jr.	184	Fletcher, Sarah	316
Finney, Garfield	333	Fletcher, Sesil	311
Finney, R.A.	317	Fletcher, Walter	199
Fipps, Alvin	189	Floyd, Lieda	121
Fipps, Daniel	137,139,196	Foister, _____	189
	197 <	Folsom, Anna	263
Fipps, Infant	137,139,196	Folsom, Benjamin F.	321
Fipps, Peter	197	Folsom, Elizabeth	41
Fipps, William	295	Folsom, George Lee	18
Fips, Bety	330	Folsom, Kittie	272
Fips, Manley	330	Folsom, Malcolm N.	321
Fips, Pete	330	Folsom, M.N.	165
Fisher, Infant	212	Folsom, Ruth	321
Fisher, John	212	Folsom, Sallie	41
Fisher, Joseph	274	Folsom, Shepard A.	329
Fisher, Joseph (Mrs)	274	Folsom, W.N.	329
Fisher, Thomas	274	Fonderant, Thomas	129
Fitzsimmons, C.H.	195	Fondren, Crocha J.	292
Fitzsimmons, Robert	317	Fondren, Crochia	129
Fitzsimmons, Sallie	160	Fondren, George	302
Fitzsimmons, William	317	Fondren, Lizzie	302
Fitzsimmons, W.R.	160	Fondren, S.A.	129
Fletcher, A.J.	157,199	Fondren, William	129,302
Fletcher, Cordelia	241	Forbes, Bert	258
Fletcher, Eli	124,360	Forbes, Caroline	46
Fletcher, Elizabeth	108	Forbes, Daniel	13
138,306	<	Forbes, Daniel R.	138
Fletcher, Ernest E.	149	Forbes, David	357
Fletcher, E.E.	149	Forbes, Earl	76
Fletcher, Infant	149	Forbes, E.F.	175,181
Fletcher, Jennie	111	Forbes, Frank	258
Fletcher, John W.	229	Forbes, George	303
Fletcher, Josie M	176	Forbes, Ismael	181
Fletcher, J.B.	209,315	Forbes, Jesse	279
360	<	Forbes, John	76,256,279
Fletcher, Lillie	145	Forbes, Kate	177,324
Fletcher, Lilly	70	Forbes, Lydia	251,289
Fletcher, Loss	229	Forbes, M.S.	138
Fletcher, Lucinda	79,313	Forbes, Nancy	322
Fletcher, Mark	229	Forbes, Ollie	347
Fletcher, Mary	271	Forbes, Rachel	238
Fletcher, Mary C.	75	Forbes, Ricklas	256
Fletcher, Mary E.	75	Forbes, Robert	279
Fletcher, M.N.	254	Forbes, Simon	138
Fletcher, Nancy	66	Forbes, William	256,347

Forbes, Willie	272		Frasier, Laura	266	
Forbes, W.M.	137		Frasier, Rettie	230	
Forbes, _____	289,333		Frasier, W.O.	151	
Forbs, George	303		Frasser, _____	232	
Forbs, Ida May	83		Frazier, Benjamin B.	196	
Forbs, Kate	177,324		Frazier, Creston	167	
Forbs, Larance	303		Frazier, David	362	
Ford, Adalade	215		Frazier, Edna M.	280	
Ford, Ana	201		Frazier, Ettie	178	
Ford, Annie	349		Frazier, Infant	362	
Ford, A.S.	215		Frazier, Julia	207	
Forney, Dewey William	257		Frazier, Martha	347	
Forney, William	257		Frazier, U.O.	196	
Forrester, Elinor	347		Frazier, William	233	
Foster, Hary	248		Frazier, W.A.	167	
Foster, Lucy	233		Frazier, W.O.	152,178	
Foster, Lula	330		Freeman, Carl	40	
Foster, Lula J.	130		Freeman, Chester	256	
Foster, Polly	253		Freeman, Desmond	40	
Foster, _____	96		Freeman, Elik	122	
Foust, Charles	355		Freeman, Frank	48	
Foust, Inna	355		Freeman, Fred	246	
Foust, Polly	266		Freeman, F.N.	265	
Foust, _____	266		Freeman, Henry	119	
Fox, Ham	241		Freeman, Infant	48,122	
France, Mary	191		Freeman, Jack, Jr.	251	
Francis, J.C.	207		Freeman, James W.	246	
Francis, Lucinda	250		Freeman, Jeter	265,288	
Francis, Robert A.	351		Freeman, J.F.	256	
Francis, Ruce	351		Freeman, Monroe	251	
Francis, William	207		Freeman, Nancy	265	
Franklin, A.C.	238		Freeman, Nora	335	
Franklin, A.E.	168		Freeman, Raleigh Ruth	265	
Franklin, Columbus	238		Freeman, Ralph	288	
Franklin, General H.	313		Freeman, Ranigh Ruth	288	
Franklin, G.A.	113		Freeman, Roy	55	
Franklin, G.F	229		Freeman, Sam	58	
Franklin, G.H.	139		Freeman, Sarah	122	
Franklin, Hattie	267		Freeman, Sarah Netie	119	
Franklin, Infant	168		Freeman, Stoker	58	
Franklin, Josie	293		Freeman, Taxana	148	
Franklin, Levi	313		Freeman, Will	148	
Franklin, Martha	360		French, Bryan	127	
Franklin, Minnie C.	238		French, Jane	127	
Franklin, Roby	168		Frerge, Laurence M.	338	
Franklin, R.E.	313		Frinklin, G.F.	229	
Frasier, Infant	151		Fritts, Andy	288	
Frasier, J.L.	17		Fry, Julie	267	

Fugate, Calvin	59,140		Garland, Frances	324
Fugate, Mary	59		Garland, Frank	210
Fugate, Thomas Hart	25		Garland, Garland	133
Fulkerson, Abe	20		Garland, George W.	120
Fullwalers, John	62		Garland, G.H.	237
Fulton, Earl	157		Garland, G.W.	55
Fulton, Sam	157		Garland, Haret	285
Gallaher, Ella	78		Garland, Henry	131
Gambell, Mattie	328		Garland, Hila Curtis	159
Gardener, John	66		Garland, Ida	270
Gardiner, _____	181		Garland, Ike	92,299,333
Gardner, Carrie	86		Garland, Infant	299,335
Gardner, Corrie	107		Garland, Isaac	186,218
Gardner, George	154,329		274	<
Gardner, James	154		Garland, Isah	305
Gardner, Jane	208		Garland, Ise	345
Gardner, John	154,315,329		Garland, James	140,210
Gardner, Julius	66		304	<
Gardner, Lillie	268		Garland, Jennie	87,173
Gardner, Ophelia	66		249,343	<
Gardner, Sallie	315		Garland, Joe	68,95,335
Gardner, Sarah	68,69,247		Garland, John	94,97,179
Garland, Aney	232		186,211,228,270	<
Garland, Annie	232		Garland, John R.	345
Garland, Bertha	290		Garland, Juda	201
Garland, Bettie	214		Garland, J.C.	131
Garland, Camel	210		Garland, Kate	76
Garland, Can	211		Garland, Lawrence	365
Garland, Canada	349		Garland, Lee Ann	96
Garland, Cande	349		Garland, Lettie	345
Garland, Crete	348		Garland, Lillie	184
Garland, Dave	120,302,332		Garland, Lish	97
334	<		Garland, Lizzie	95
Garland, David	70,75,88		Garland, Lucy	159
159,299,325	<		Garland, Lula	170
Garland, Davie	95		Garland, Lunna	204
Garland, Dealie	88		Garland, Luvenia	3
Garland, Delia	184		Garland, Mad	349
Garland, Dicie	365		Garland, Mader	349
Garland, D.C.	2		Garland, Margaret H.	163
Garland, Earv;an	75		Garland, Martha	8,61,322
Garland, Elisha	94		Garland, Mary	101,164
Garland, Eliza	118,156		221,283,293	<
Garland, Elizabeth	77,263		Garland, Mary Jane	138
Garland, Ellen	76		Garland, Mary J.	69
Garland, Elsie	237		Garland, Monte	120
Garland, Ethel	97,320		Garland, M.	103
Garland, E.	365		Garland, Nathan	357

Garland, Nancy	92,156 268,287,325,332 <		Geisler, Gladys P.	256
Garland, N.E.	365		Geisler, Hal	105
Garland, Patsy	191,240		Geisler, Hebert	343
Garland, Pettibone	320		Geisler, Henry	230
Garland, Pussie	67		Geisler, Hick	182
Garland, Rebecca	175,223		Geisler, Hubert	230
Garland, Robinson	170		Geisler, Hugh E.	230
Garland, Rosa	158		Geisler, Lytha Mae	343
Garland, Rosa Lee	95		Geisler, Mary	182
Garland, Salina	28		Geisler, S.G.	256
Garland, Salley	81		Gentry, John (Mrs)	333
Garland, Sam	332		Gentry, J.	10
Garland, Sara	325		Gentry, Noah (Mrs)	333
Garland, Sarah	96,150		Gentry, Oka	281
Garland, Sarah Jane	114		Gentry, Phillip	293
Garland, Smith	133,211		Gentry, P.D.	293
Garland, Susan	277		Gentry, _____	285,345
Garland, Thomas	304		Gibbs, Dora	112
Garland, Titia	133		Gibbs, Edison	334
Garland, Tribble	179		Gibbs, Fain	77,112
Garland, Valentine	348		Gibbs, Gill	334
Garland, Voltin	249		Gibbs, Infant	77
Garland, Wesley	285		Gibbs, James	324,332
Garland, Will	324		Gibbs, Jane	324
Garland, William	285		Gibbs, Rosa	324
Garland, William H.	68		Gibbs, _____	164
Garland, Willie	28		Gibson, John Clifton	357
Garland, Zella	66,67		Gibson, Mary	178,186
Garland, _____	175,239 303,314,339 <		Gibson, Neas	36
Garrison, Diza Ann	93		Gibson, Nebraca	364
Garrison, Eliza	258		Gibson, Pierce	357
Garrison, Elsie Pearl	145		Giesler, Mary Sue	97
Garrison, Hattie	170		Gilbert, Ed	79
Garrison, James	284		Gilbert, Edward	314
Garrison, James Hall	48		Gilbert, James	314
Garrison, Lizzie	292		Gilbert, James Jr.	127
Garrison, W.C.	145		Gilbert, James Sr.	127
Garson, Lizzie	292		Gilbert, Julia	117
Garvin, Flora	77		Gilbert, Lucinda	246
Garvin, J.A. (Mrs)	77		Gilbert, William	79
Garvin, Racr	77		Giles, Dunbar	84
Gastiger, Infant	83		Giles, Maggie E.	122
Gastiger, L.D.	83		Giles, William H.	84
Gastiger, Margaret	83		Giles, W.H.	84
Geisler, Albert	182		Gilland, Erma	97
Geisler, D.E.	105		Gillen, Emmaline	317
			Gilley, Bunch	15
			Gilliam, Bettie	116

Gilliam, Walter	116		Glover, Patsy	305
Gillim, Alberta	109		Glover, Paul	365
Gillim, James M.	109		Glover, Paul Edgar	257
Gills, Ethel	128		Glover, Rachel	67
Givens, Jonathon	357		Glover, Richard	78,124
Glen, Henry	213		303	<
Glenn, Ault	365		Glover, Rosa Edith	154
Glenn, Elizabeth	55		Glover, Sarah E.	368
Glenn, Infant	365		Glover, Stephen	233
Glenn, James	39		Glover, Steven	124
Glover, A.M.	314		Glover, Will	169
Glover, Bertha	202,203		Glover, William A.	78
337	<		Glover, Willie	43
Glover, Bessie	79,99		Glover, W.A.	78,93,154
Glover, Cinda	171		257	<
Glover, Daniel	100		Glover, _____	154
Glover, Edward	108		Gobble, Nannie	148
Glover, Elizabeth	69		Gobble, Roy	298
Glover, Eva	251		Gobble, William F.	298
Glover, Fran M.	251		Gobly, Thomas J.	332
Glover, Frank	112		Godsey, M.J.	331
Glover, Granville V.	322		Good, George	22
Glover, Harrison	251		Goode, C.J.	129
Glover, Howard	169		Goode, D.	120,129
Glover, Infant	314,365		Goode, Emana	120
Glover, James	156,168,171		Goode, George	129
Glover, Jane	108		Goode, Othie Mae	129
Glover, John	78,171,368		Goodman, Clarence	319
Glover, John A.	108		Goodman, Infant	319
Glover, John Edward	108		Goodman, Rosetta	90
Glover, Joseph	156,248		Goodsen, Georgia	238
Glover, Joseph A.	100		Goodsen, W.J.	238
Glover, Josie	70		Goodsen, W.J.	240
Glover, Josie Louise	177		Goodson, Matilda	332
Glover, J.A. (Mrs)	100		Goodson, Paul	240
Glover, Lena	260,333		Goodson, W.T.	332
Glover, Lizzie	43		Goodwin, Bell	267
Glover, Louisa	358		Goodwin, Clarence A.	293
Glover, Luby B.	225		Goodwin, Elsie	76,284
Glover, Lucy	93		Goodwin, Elsie Mae	293
Glover, Malissa	148		Goodwin, Henry C.	236
Glover, Marion	322		Goodwin, Isabell	104
Glover, Mary	124,210		Goodwin, James	53,259
Glover, Milton	314		Goodwin, Jean	301
Glover, Nancy	137		Goodwin, Julia	115,129
Glover, Nancy Jane	171		Goodwin, LaFayette	301
Glover, Nora	182		Goodwin, Larinda	367
Glover, Patsis	333		Goodwin, Lillie	368

Goodwin, L.H.	195,367	Gouge, Oscar		204
Goodwin, Melve	50	Gouge, Paris		199
Goodwin, Melvin	91	Gouge, Robert Avery		304
Goodwin, Minnie	125	Gouge, Robert C.		238
Goodwin, Polly	252	Gouge, Roderick B.		166
Goodwin, Raymond	42	Gouge, Ruby		125
Goodwin, Rhoda	292	Gouge, Ruth		289
Goodwin, R.E.	236	Gouge, R.		214
Goodwin, Sallie	236	gouge, R.F.		215
Goodwin, S.L.	115	Gouge, R.H.		105
Gorden, Ladima	4	Gouge, R.J.		212
Gordon, Deina	348	Gouge, R.P.		54
Gordon, Eliza	143	Gouge, Sallie		126
Goss, Andrew	367	Gouge, Thelma Marie		304
Goss, Andy	195	Gouge, Thomas		126
Goss, Estal	195	Gouge, William		318
Goss, Marion	255	Gouge, W.M.		227
Gouge, Allen	48	Gourley, Annie		80,186
Gouge, Arthur	289	Gourley, Annie L.		88
Gouge, Bettie	227	Gourley, A.F.		262
Gouge, Biddie	146	Gourley, Cad		83
Gouge, Calvin	364	Gourley, Charles		204
Gouge, Charles W.	238	Gourley, Charles M.		204
Gouge, Chester	364	Gourley, David		206
Gouge, Clarrie	200	Gourley, Eliz		135
Gouge, Dollie	125,206	Gourley, Eliza		206
Gouge, Edmon	190	Gourley, Frankie J.		83
Gouge, Elijah	284	Gourley, Haley		53
Gouge, Eva C.	90	Gourley, Infant		243
Gouge, E.	284	Gourley, James		204
Gouge, Fletcher	281	Gourley, Jenie		154
Gouge, Frank	156	Gourley, Jennie		103
Gouge, George	281	Gourley, Manda A.		104
Gouge, Hannah	92	Gourley, Martha		279
Gouge, H.	190	Gourley, Martha C.		277
Gouge, Infant	102,156,284	Gourley, Mollie		102
Gouge, James	102	Gourley, R.H.		243
Gouge, James H.	190	Gourley, R.N.		80,83,277
Gouge, Jane	225	Gourley, Sam S.		53
Gouge, John	102,110,237	Gourley, Thomas		78,141
Gouge, John Manley	125	Gourley, William R.		53
Gouge, John W.	238	Gourley, _____		133,291
Gouge, J.N.	102	Grace, John		124
Gouge, Lesley C.	105	Grace, Maggie Maud		124
Gouge, L.T.	204,206	Gragan, Sarah Jane		241
Gouge, Maggie	346	Gragg, Mary		265
Gouge, Marion	166,199	Gragg, Tilda		22
Gouge, Mary J.	318	Gragin, Isaac		241

Graham, Ben	341	Greer, Eligah	143
Graham, Cordelia	341	Greer, Franklin D.	101
Grant, E.C.	268	Greer, Harrison	164
Grant, James	262	Greer, Hety	153
Grant, Jaunita Grace	110	Greer, Lucy	106
Grant, Robert E.	110	Greer, Mickey	123
Gray, Alice	81	Greer, Mollie	366
Gray, Evelyn May	365	Greer, Polly	162
Gray, J.L.	312,346	Greer, Sallie	143
Gray, Thomas	365	Greer, Samuel	164
GraybeaL, David	238	Greer, Thomas	101
Graybeal, Florence	238	Greer, _____	123
Graybeal, Margaret	156	Gregg, Addie	153
Graybeal, Ruce	23	Gregg, Amanda	350
Graybill, _____	173,290	Gregg, Beatrice	43
Grayson, Crocket	204	Gregg, Delie	242
Grayson, Harry	204	Gregg, Edith	230
Grayson, James H.	204	Gregg, Edward Scalf	116
Grayson, William	42	Gregg, James	156
Green, Ada	277	Gregg, James L.	116
Green, Burnie	353	Gregg, John	296
Green, David William	267	Gregg, Mandy	233
Green, Emma	236	Gregg, Rosa	236,301
Green, Enoch	111	Gregg, Stanley	65
Green, Mable Virginia	340	Gregg, Tilda	141
Green, Newton	340	Gregg, William	141
Green, Peggy	124	Griff, Nancy	107
Green, Polly	215	Griffin, Bonnie K.	114
Green, Spincor	46	Griffin, Frank	203
Green, Tildie	340	Griffin, Handy	120
Green, W.H.	267	Griffin, Mary	120
Greenlee, Ellar	278	Griffin, Nina	79
Greenlee, Hanck	22	Griffith, Celia	161,211
Greenlee, John	278	269,272	<
Greenlye, Sarah F.	306	Griffith, C.N.	89
Greenway, Addie	274	Griffith, Elizabeth	137
Greenway, Carrie	320	Griffith, Ella	52
Greenway, Georgia	200	Griffith, Frank	89,114
Greenway, Sallie	317	225	<
Greenway, Susie	2	Griffith, F.M.	258
Greenway, T.H.	200	Griffith, Infant	65,225
Greenway, Wilson	317	Griffith, Mary	109
Greenwell, A.	80	Griffith, Pleasant	65
Greenwell, Ida	298	Griffith, Susan	258
Greenwell, Martha	242,360	Griffith, William	111
Greenwell, Zillie	266	Grifine, _____	247
Greer, Andy	138	Grimsley, Annie	353
Greer, Clarence	48	Grimsley, M.L.	256

Grindstaff, Alexander	14
211	<
Grindstaff, Annis	329
Grindstaff, A.J.	158
Grindstaff, Bate	79
Grindstaff, Bertie	29
Grindstaff, Bessie	78,206
Grindstaff, Bula	312
Grindstaff, Charles	245
Grindstaff, Charlie	46
Grindstaff, Clara	177
Grindstaff, Claud	194
Grindstaff, Claude	157
Grindstaff, C.L.	180
Grindstaff, Dan	263
Grindstaff, David	54,262
339	<
Grindstaff, Dworn M.	13
Grindstaff, D.H.	328
Grindstaff, D.J.	107
Grindstaff, D.L.	79,99
223	<
Grindstaff, D.M.	32
Grindstaff, Eidy	253
Grindstaff, Elbert	92
Grindstaff, Elicate	312
Grindstaff, Elick	313
Grindstaff, Eliza	170,200
Grindstaff, Ella May	67
Grindstaff, Ellen	262
Grindstaff, Elva	223
Grindstaff, Ezekiel	338
Grindstaff, Floid	37
Grindstaff, George	154
Grindstaff, Grace	308
Grindstaff, Gusta	24
Grindstaff, Guy	31
Grindstaff, Hamp	79
Grindstaff, Harriett	171
282	<
Grindstaff, Hasel R.	166
Grindstaff, Hattie	275
Grindstaff, Hila	156
Grindstaff, Hobert	338
Grindstaff, Houston	172
Grindstaff, H.H.	279
Grindstaff, H.R.	266
Grindstaff, Ida	211
Grindstaff, Infant	31,80
197,296,343	<
Grindstaff, Iona	157
Grindstaff, Ira	312
Grindstaff, Jack	330
Grindstaff, Jake	349
Grindstaff, Jarvice	19
Grindstaff, Joe	103
Grindstaff, John	84,107
217	<
Grindstaff, John H.	146
Grindstaff, J.B.	245
Grindstaff, J.H.	229
Grindstaff, J.L.	301
Grindstaff, Katie	228
Grindstaff, Lassie	107
Grindstaff, Linda	110
Grindstaff, Lindy	82
Grindstaff, Lorettie	146
Grindstaff, Louisa	180
Grindstaff, Lusely	262
Grindstaff, Luthrin	304
Grindstaff, L.L.	78
Grindstaff, Maggie	39
Grindstaff, Mandie	5
Grindstaff, Marry	225
Grindstaff, Martha	308
Grindstaff, Mary Ann	154
Grindstaff, Mary E.	279
Grindstaff, Matt	339
Grindstaff, Michael	79
225	<
Grindstaff, Mike	135,150
273	<
Grindstaff, Millie	313
Grindstaff, Nancy	154,173
254	<
Grindstaff, Narva	33
Grindstaff, Neomah	33
Grindstaff, Nicholas	80
Grindstaff, Nick	302
Grindstaff, Nola	39
Grindstaff, N...	129
Grindstaff, Ottis	266
Grindstaff, Pat D.	266
Grindstaff, Paul	296
Grindstaff, Robert	31,177
Grindstaff, Rod D.	266

Grindstaff, R.D.	166,197		Guinn, Ellen		267
Grindstaff, Sallie		135	Guinn, E.		274
Grindstaff, Sarah		279	Guinn, George		304
Grindstaff, Sarah Ann		92	Guinn, Hattie		88
Grindstaff, Sarah J.		103	Guinn, Ida Lou		267
Grindstaff, Stella		328	Guinn, Isaac	160,182,222	
Grindstaff, Susan		194	Guinn, Jake	182,185,310	
Grindstaff, Thomas		146	Guinn, J.B.		259,306
Grindstaff, Tom		254	Guinn, Lanier		160
Grindstaff, Tressie		17	Guinn, Luther		285
Grindstaff, U.R.		266	Guinn, Mary		234,259
Grindstaff, Vadie		92	Guinn, Maud		259
Grindstaff, Walter	103		Guinn, Nancy		180,286
146		<	Guinn, Pearl		306
Grindstaff, Wilburn		67	Guinn, Rebecca		160
Grindstaff, Will		238	Guinn, Robie		27
Grindstaff, William		146	Guinn, Sarah		329
349		<	Guinn, Tennessee		27
Grindstaff, William H.	103		Guinn, Warney		267
Grindstaff, Willie M.		365	Guinn, Warnie		304
Grindstaff, Worley S.		99	Guinn, Worley		274
Grindstaff, W.F.		301	Guy, Euretha		141
Grindstaff, W.J.		92	Guy, Infant		187
Grindstaff, W.R.		306	Guy, Lee		145
Grindstaff, Zeke		158	Guy, Lowery		187
Grmsley, Roxie		222	Guy, O.C.		147
Grogan, Sarah J.		149	Guy, Rebecca		201
Guenlie, William W.		210	Guy, Uretha		147
Guess, Charles		121	Gwyn, Ida Lou		267
Guess, Edgar		18	Gwyn, Warney		267
Guess, Henry		121	Hacker, C.C.		73,76,270
Guess, Mary		121	Hagan, Georgia M.		130
Guffie, Sarah E.		208	Hagie, Daniel		242
Guffy, Frank		333	Hagie, James Vounum		242
Guin, Jacob		325	Hagie, Julian		322
Guin, Liluriana		59	Hagie, J. (Mrs)		242
Guin, Nancy R.		102	Hagons, Sarah		350
Guin, Patty		130	Hale, Sarah		227
Guin, Susie		8	Hale, Sindy		137
Guin, ____		161	Hall, Elijah S.		143
Guinn, Adam		182	Hall, Emina		101
Guinn, Alex		160	Hall, E.S.		281
Guinn, Allie		285	Hall, James Spencer		143
Guinn, Arthur		185	Hall, J.M.		132
Guinn, Blake		285	Hall, Lizzie		79
Guinn, David		160	Hall, Merrian Arnold		167
Guinn, D.H.		234	Hall, Mike		143
Guinn, Eliza		323	Hall, Mikl		79

Hall, Ruth	281
Hall, _____	192
Hambric, Lena	174
Hambrick, Albert	260
Hambrick, Gene	333
Hambrick, George	260,333
Hambrick, Mollie	174
Hambrick, Polly J.	45
Hamby, Allen	123,174
Hamby, Dennuel	174
Hamby, D.M.	146
Hamby, J.L.	174
Hamby, Lawson	270
Hamby, Lester Carmuel	174
Hamby, Loss	144
Hamby, Minnie	63
Hamby, Molle	185,234
Hamby, Nancy	123,174
Hamby, Oscar	144
Hamer, A.C.	35
Hamilton, Jessie	366
Hamilton, John W.	74
Hamilton, Joshua	89
Hamilton, Joshua C.	89
Hamilton, J.C.	74
Hamilton, Nancie M.	262
Hamit, Ollie	206
Hamit, W.M.	67
Hamitt, Andy	74
Hamitt, Fannie	74
Hammit, Nola	141
Hammons, _____	353
Hampil, Brash	354
Hampil, Katie	354
Hampton, Annie	187
Hampton, Bertha	70,201
Hampton, Berthie	125
Hampton, Bessie	31
Hampton, Clark	49
Hampton, Cora Belle	235
Hampton, Daniel Henry	127
Hampton, David	254
Hampton, Deliah	204,357
Hampton, D.C.	152
Hampton, Elizabeth S.	117
Hampton, Henry	235
Hampton, Infant	153
Hampton, James	61
Hampton, Joe	148
Hampton, John A.	254
Hampton, Leonard	153
Hampton, Lizzie	78,118
Hampton, Losson	127
Hampton, Martha M.	286
Hampton, Mary E.	125
Hampton, May	138
Hampton, Morton	97
Hampton, Sallie	205
Hampton, Stewart	125
Hampton, W.H. (Mrs)	295
Hampton, W.L.	127,160,286
Hampton, W.P.	138
Hampton, _____	207
Hankal, Margaret	196
Hany, Lina	180
Harden, Sara	297
Hardie, George	315
Hardie, Isabell	174
Hardie, John	174,315
Hardie, Malinda	119
Hardil, Lester	48
Hardil, Willie	48
Hardin, Adiline	66
Hardin, Albert	178
Hardin, Allen	213
Hardin, Allen F.	309
Hardin, Alvin	114
Hardin, Alvin P.	271
Hardin, Arimility	139
Hardin, Ben	246
Hardin, Blannie	35,41
Hardin, Bob	114,304
Hardin, Cardie	89
Hardin, Caroline	32
Hardin, Catherine	206
Hardin, Cathern	219
Hardin, Charles	338
Hardin, Charles P.	242
Hardin, Chris	363
Hardin, Christian C.	32
Hardin, Christian J.	147
Hardin, Cleveland	309,351
Hardin, Cornelia	219
Hardin, C.P.	363
Hardin, Darsie	120
Hardin, Dayton	80

Hardin, Della Mae	351	
Hardin, Dock	182,183,246	
Hardin, D.C.	218	
Hardin, Eli	333	
Hardin, Elija	218,259,251	
289	<	
Hardin, Elijah	196	
Hardin, Elijah D.	242	
Hardin, Eliza	290	
Hardin, Elizabeth	91,134	
Hardin, Elizah	196	
Hardin, Ella	213	
Hardin, Ellen	92	
Hardin, Emily	299	
Hardin, Ercle	182	
Hardin, Ethel Kate	233	
Hardin, Evaline	316	
Hardin, E.H.	251	
Hardin, Fern (Mrs)	361	
Hardin, Frank	271	
Hardin, F.L.	228,316	
Hardin, George	164	
Hardin, Georgia	12	
Hardin, G.W.	66	
Hardin, Ham	89	
Hardin, Harriett	115	
Hardin, Harrison	120,129	
Hardin, Hatey Edith	44	
Hardin, Henry W.	158	
Hardin, Infant	14,92,152	
Hardin, Isaac	134,164	
Hardin, James	120,182	
Hardin, James T.	92	
Hardin, Jamie Owen	312	
Hardin, Jamima	140	
Hardin, Jane	265	
Hardin, Jennie	182,301	
Hardin, Joel	143	
Hardin, John	134,140,147	
152,242,309,351	<	
Hardin, John M.	271	
Hardin, John R.	178	
Hardin, Johnie	164	
Hardin, J.A.	182	
Hardin, J.N.	233	
Hardin, Leonard H.	114	
Hardin, Lige	297	
Hardin, Lizzie	60	
Hardin, Lonnie R.	111	
Hardin, Lottie	80	
Hardin, Lottie	316	
Hardin, Lovina	211	
Hardin, Margaret	70	
Hardin, Martha	32	
Hardin, Mary	193,260	
Hardin, Mattie	34,40	
Hardin, Millie	183	
Hardin, Minnie	181	
Hardin, Murrell	363	
Hardin, Nancy	288	
Hardin, Naoma	17	
Hardin, Phebe	265	
Hardin, Pherba	100	
Hardin, Robert	80,333,364	
Hardin, Rosa	178,211	
Hardin, Rosevelt	14	
Hardin, R.H.	111	
Hardin, Sallie	34,72	
Hardin, Sallie G.	14	
Hardin, Sara	305	
Hardin, Sarah	287	
Hardin, Sarah J.	89	
Hardin, Thomas	213	
Hardin, T.A.	137,280	
Hardin, Warren	338	
Hardin, Will	312	
Hardin, William D.	56	
Hardin, W.H.	111	
Hardin, W.R.	182	
Harels, Kathern	237	
Harkleroad, Geroge W.	145	
Harkleroad, Jacob	145	
Harkleroad, Lamlon C.	42	
Harless, Malinda	269	
Harmon, Barnet	216	
Harmon, Cassie	277	
Harmon, Elaurau	261	
Harmon, Ellen	308	
Harmon, Fesodo	283	
Harmon, Galher	277	
Harmon, Grant	302,308,365	
Harmon, J.C.	265	
Harmon, Mearing	216	
Harmon, Reathia	365	
Harmon, Urath	302	
Harmon, Virgle	261	

Harr, James L.	43	Hart, Infant	64,76,203
Harr, Willie Claud	43	364	<
Harrell, Cinday	312	Hart, John	335
Harris, Elisa	24	Hart, J.N.	166
Harris, Ellen	233	Hart, Leonard	157
Harris, Frank	35	Hart, Leonard Sr.	179
Harris, John	104	Hart, Lydia	108
Harris, Lula	246	Hart, Maggie T.	64
Harris, Patsy	77	Hart, Margaret	159
Harris, Rachel	343	Hart, Margaret Lillie	64
Harris, Rosa	237	Hart, Mary	187
Harrison, Anderson	323	Hart, Matilda	2
Harrison, Arthur	87	Hart, Mattie	172
Harrison, Arthur W.	87	Hart, Myrtle	335
Harrison, A.	294	Hart, M.E.	203
Harrison, Debora	291	Hart, Nellie E.	199
Harrison, Dora	310	Hart, Ollie	159
Harrison, Eave	111	Hart, Pheba	237
Harrison, George	87,111	Hart, Ralph	355
315	<	Hart, Riley	108,157
Harrison, Henry	342	Hart, Robert H.	57
Harrison, Mandie B.	323	Hart, Sam	351
Harrison, Minerva	366	Hart, Sarah A.	79
Harrison, Sallie	323	Hart, Stella	64,136,144
Harrold, Ellen	73	Hart, Thomas Allen	265
Hart, Abe	145	Hart, Walter	76
Hart, A.F.	364	Hartley, Albert	218
Hart, Bruce Edward	244	Hartley, Almetta R.	276
Hart, Callie	42	Hartley, Benjamin	220
Hart, C.H.	329	Hartley, Benjamin W.	323
Hart, C.W.	64,159	Hartley, Caloway	218
Hart, Dora Ruth	329	Hartley, Calvin	218
Hart, Dorothy May	106	Hartley, Jessie	323
Hart, Edgar	106	Hartley, Sallie	243
Hart, Eliza M.	165	Harvey, John	347
Hart, Elizabeth	179,273	Harvey, Lina	136
Hart, Ella J.	332	Harvey, Tessie	273
Hart, E.M.	79	Harvey, Velna Gay	347
Hart, Fantha Maud	136	Harvsin, Jessy	100
Hart, Feby	132,201	Hash, R.J.C.	151
Hart, Frank	244	Hatcher, Alf	201
Hart, Fred	332	Hatcher, Bill	160
Hart, F.S.	64,76,144,199	Hatcher, Elvie	240
Hart, George L.	264,265	Hatcher, Eva	68,94,136
Hart, Harmon P.	145	202,225	<
Hart, Hary Butler	264	Hatcher, Frankie	107
Hart, Hazle Marie	355	Hatcher, James	201
Hart, Ira	2	Hatcher, Lea	201

Hatcher, Lee	160	Hawkins, Lottie Kate		295
Hatcher, Mary	71	Hawkins, Loyd E.		282
Hatcher, Sam	202	Hawkins, Maggie		164
Hatcher, Will	107	Hawkins, Nancy		318
Hately, John F.	349	Hawkins, Pharaba		196
Hately, John F. (Mrs)	349	Hawkins, S.H.		210,282
Hathaway, Abe	2	Hawkins, S.N.		84
Hathaway, Alice D.	208	Hawkins, Thomas H.		280
Hathaway, Amelia	62,92	Hayes, Ethel		46
Hathaway, Charles	169	Hayes, Frank		199
Hathaway, Charles L.	62	Hayes, Harriet		236
Hathaway, Clarence	219	Hayes, Infant		20,298
Hathaway, C.L.	264	Hayes, James		85
Hathaway, Edward E.	98	Hayes, James C.		170
Hathaway, Finley	169	Hayes, James Wesley		167
Hathaway, Harry	98,357	Hayes, John		63,68,199
Hathaway, Harry Jr.	268	Hayes, J.E.		20
Hathaway, H.G.	357	Hayes, J.S.		88,298
Hathaway, Infant	357	Hayes, J.W.		167
Hathaway, Martha Jane	318	Hayes, Martha		145
Hathaway, Mary Rose	264	Hayes, Mary		20,84
Hathaway, Ruby	153	Hayes, Nellie		88
Hathaway, W.C.	153	Hayes, Okie		81
Hathaway, ____	229	Hayes, Orval		199
Hather, Mag	281	Hayes, Rebecca		122
Hatley, Alvin	188	Hayes, Roy		63,68
Hatley, Amanda	188	Hayes, R.L.		34
Hatley, Gath	225	Hayes, Samuel A.		20
Hatley, Infant	225	Hayes, Sina		263
Hatley, John F.	198	Hayes, William		298
Hatley, Martha L.	198	Haynes, George		172
Hatley, Pearl	206	Haynes, George W.		357
Hatley, Ray Blain	117	Haynes, George W., Jr		357
Hatley, Skiles	117	Haynes, Habakkuh		172
Hatley, William	201,349	Haynes, Nat		327
Hatley, W.S.	102,201,291	Haynes, ...		112
Hatly, W.S.	291	Hays, Dale		265
Hatten, Mary A.	361	Hays, Eliza		321
Haun, Elizabeth	244	Hays, George		228
Hawkins, Charles	295,313,318	Hays, James L.		228
Hawkins, C.R.	37	Hays, Martha C.		228
Hawkins, Eliza	313	Hays, Minnie		223
Hawkins, Ella	109	Hays, Phinia		231
Hawkins, George E.	280	Hays, Susan		221
Hawkins, Jessimine	210	Hays, ____		240
Hawkins, John	65	Hayse, Mary		84
Hawkins, Julia A.	212	Hayton, Julia		304
		Hazlewood, Gaines		4

Hazlewood, Hi	4	Heaton, Dollie	150
Hazlewood, Lidia	73	Heaton, Elijah Frank	84
Hazlewood, Richard	75	Heaton, Eliza	72
Hazlewood, Rose	9	Heaton, Ellen	92
Head, Hazel	113	Heaton, Elsie M.	344
Head, J.H.	164	Heaton, Emily	310
Head, Mandy	52	Heaton, E.F.	138
Head, Martha	30	Heaton, Gaston	131
Head, Mollie	252,331	Heaton, Grace	191
Head, Roy	164	Heaton, G.	170
Head, Sarah	193	Heaton, Harrold	178
Head, T.H.	113	Heaton, Imogene	352
Headrick, Alice	140	Heaton, Infant	84,150
Headrick, Bessie	145	353,358	<
Headrick, Charles	127	Heaton, Isaac M.	162
Headrick, John W.	241	Heaton, Jim	178,180
Headrick, J.W.	241,276	Heaton, John	241,363
Headrick, Kate	105	Heaton, John Landon	344
Headrick, Katie	115	Heaton, John W.	14,162
Headrick, Kattie	143	Heaton, J.A.	211
Headrick, Mary J.	151	Heaton, J.L.	162
Heagan, Wheeler	150	Heaton, Lucy	180
Heagen, William	150	Heaton, Margaret	45
Heartley, Albert	217	Heaton, Marry	218
Heartley, Calvin	217	Heaton, Martha	241
Heartly, Caloway	217	Heaton, Martha C.	170
Heatherly, Alice	311	Heaton, Mollie	223,274
Heatherly, Dicy	189	Heaton, Nellie	72
Heatherly, Evaline	186	Heaton, Peallie	199
246	<	Heaton, Pearl Edith	63,68
Heatherly, Godfrey	362	Heaton, Pearlie	167
Heatherly, Jesse	159	Heaton, Rachel	146
Heatherly, Jude	311	Heaton, Rebecca	196,197
Heatherly, Rebecca	203	299,303	<
220	<	Heaton, Resa	358
Heatherly, Thomas	157	Heaton, Rhudy	191
Heatherly, Tom	255	Heaton, Roder	166
Heatherly, _____	224	Heaton, Rudy	358
Heaton, Alice	340	Heaton, Sally	353
Heaton, Amanda Jane	336	Heaton, Tom	191
Heaton, A.R.	260	Heaton, Walter	260
Heaton, A.W.	216	Heaton, W.F.	61,70,150
Heaton, Bertha	130,178	Heaton, _____	80
Heaton, Blaine	241	Hednick, Bert	189
Heaton, Bob	353	Helvey, Sarah Jane	365
Heaton, Bulah	131	Helvey, William H.	365
Heaton, Cain	223	Hemphill, Judia	295
Heaton, Clara	242	Henderickson, Indiana	357

Henderlien, Liddy	144
Henderliter, D.C.	90
Henderliter, Milford	90
Hendricks, Hannah	83
Hendrickson, Edward	160
Hendrickson, Elisha	248
Hendrickson, George	248
Hendrickson, Robert L.	160
Hendrix, Anna	64
Hendrix, C.T.	124
Hendrix, Delcenia	279
Hendrix, J.R.	75
Hendrix, Mary	190
Hendrix, Mary C.	124
Hendrix, S.H.	6
Heniger, James W.	24
Heniger, Mandie	2
Henniger, Diza Allen	286
Henniger, John	182, 206
Henniger, May	206
Henniger, Sallie	182
Henry, Bowman	212
Henry, Carrie L.	186
Henry, Evelyn	268
Henry, James	186, 212
Henry, Lillie	117, 329
Henry, Maggie	66
Henry, Robert	13
Hensley, Bestie	90
Hensley, Mary	90
Henson, Alice	71, 268
Henson, Julia	215
Henson, William	306
Herman, Condon	153
Herman, Infant	153
Herrel, Rex	335
Herrell, Infant	335
Herrill, Rosa	209
Hethely, ____	224
Hetherly, Evaline	311
Hicks, Alfonso	102
Hicks, Andrew	258
Hicks, Calvin	93
Hicks, Charley L.	71
Hicks, Charlie	173, 248, 268 <
Hicks, Charlotte	177
Hicks, Clerie	244
Hicks, C.L.	71
Hicks, David	185
Hicks, Edith	248
Hicks, Elfnza	286
Hicks, Elizabeth	185, 222, 365 <
Hicks, Eveline	70
Hicks, Flosy Ann	102
Hicks, Gertrude	331
Hicks, Hahnie	248
Hicks, Harmon	258
Hicks, Henry	71
Hicks, H.	335
Hicks, Ina	260
Hicks, Inen	19
Hicks, Infant	87, 221, 268
Hicks, Jacob	365
Hicks, Joe	70
Hicks, John	93
Hicks, Jordan	87
Hicks, Joseph	244
Hicks, J.P.	244
Hicks, Lizzie	182
Hicks, Lottie	70, 308
Hicks, Low	83
Hicks, Mamie	352, 360
Hicks, Marsh	173
Hicks, Mary Jane	349
Hicks, Mollie	58
Hicks, Morris	221
Hicks, Nancy	51, 222
Hicks, Sarah	70
Hicks, Wallas Roe	286
Hicks, William	138, 183
Hicks, W.J.	349
Hicks, ____	230
Higgins, Emily	98
Higgins, Gengie	85
Higgins, Isaac	98
Hileman, John	317
Hileman, Nancy A.	94
Hileman, Thomas	94
Hilimon, Dovie	30
Hill, Alexander	173
Hill, Anderson	20
Hill, Bettie	146, 147, 194
Hill, Biddie	173
Hill, Bill	202

Hill, Clarie	202
Hill, Clarsey	102
Hill, David	206
Hill, Edie	135
Hill, Eligah	251
Hill, Emma	198
Hill, Ezekiel	170,252
Hill, Hattie	245
Hill, Hazel	30
Hill, Infant	206,251
Hill, James	216,260
Hill, James Jr.	181
Hill, John	135,200,202
Hill, Mandy	206
Hill, Margaret	219,243
Hill, Maria	92
Hill, Martha	46
Hill, Mary	181
Hill, Ollie	334
Hill, Ollie Belle	252
Hill, Oullie	86
Hill, Porter	331
Hill, Sallie	69,110
Hill, Sherman	260
Hill, Vina	251
Hill, W.C.	249
Hill, Zeke	331
Hill, ...	81
Hille, K.M.	87
Hilliard, Martha	214
Hillman, Julia	227
Hilman, Emmie	94
Hilman, Thomas	94
Hilton, Ina Pearl	284
Hilton, Lilian	312
Hinkle, Anderson	74
Hinkle, Annie Lee	99
Hinkle, Bessie	240,335
Hinkle, Birdie	184
Hinkle, David	271
Hinkle, Dora	173
Hinkle, Edward C.	77
Hinkle, Eliza	193
Hinkle, Elizabeth	13
Hinkle, Elsie	5
Hinkle, E.C.	77
Hinkle, Franklin	74
Hinkle, George	173
Hinkle, Hubert	77
Hinkle, Ina Vaneda	131
Hinkle, Jessie	106
Hinkle, John	271
Hinkle, John B.	77
Hinkle, Josie	99
Hinkle, Laura	280,361
Hinkle, Lois	335
Hinkle, L. Smith	173
Hinkle, L.S.	233
Hinkle, Mable B.	77
Hinkle, Margaret	152,196
Hinkle, Nancy	133
Hinkle, Pansy E.	4
Hinkle, Pettie	361
Hinkle, Ruth	329
Hinkle, Sallie	233
Hinkle, Smith	99
Hinkle, Stacy	271
Hinkle, T.S.	329
Hinkle, Will	184
Hinkle, William	106
Hinkle, _____	288
Hinly, George	157
Hirds, Oscar	44
Hix, Betty	355
Hix, Dave	105
Hix, David	355
Hix, J.J.	105
Hix, Kate	105
Hix, Nancy	162
Hix, Rachel	11
Hix, Susan	352
Hobson, Caney	222
Hobson, Charlie	222,321
Hobson, George	71
Hobson, George W.	129
Hobson, Herbert	71
Hobson, Jack	321
Hobson, Jackson	129,320
Hobson, John H.	320
Hobson, Madge	222
Hobson, Mary Etta J.	83
Hobson, William	83
Hodge, Abe	99,285,328
Hodge, Arlena	324
Hodge, Callie	353
Hodge, Camron	132

Hodge, Carter		158	Hodge, Winnie		349
Hodge, Charley		114	Hodge, Zora		124
Hodge, Dorcia		103	Hodge, _____		181
Hodge, Edey		290	Hodges, Eva		349
Hodge, Edith		70	Hodges, F.M.		74
Hodge, Eliza		187	Hodges, R.L.		356
Hodge, Ethel		28	Hodges, Thomas		148
Hodge, Eva		332	Hoge, Ollie		261
Hodge, Findly		239	Holbough, _____		89
Hodge, Flora		328	Holden, David		316
Hodge, F.M.		132	Holden, Eloise		95
Hodge, George		114,349	Holden, Evaline		293
Hodge, Hampton		114	Holden, Lou		214
Hodge, H...		104	Holden, Lula		259
Hodge, Infant		285	Holden, Nora		309
Hodge, John A.		217	Holden, Sarah		334
Hodge, John Finley		217	Holden Nora		359
Hodge, J.C.		139	Holder, Blanche		82
Hodge, Littleton		218,239	Holder, Charles		124
Hodge, Lizzie		139,188	Holder, Clytie		189
Hodge, Lucy		104	Holder, Curtis		189
Hodge, Luther		7	Holder, E.D.		28
Hodge, L.G.		316	Holder, Harley		28
Hodge, Martha		100,264	Holder, James		82,338
Hodge, Minnie		110	Holder, Nick		82
Hodge, Nancy	112,163,218 274,305	<	Holder, N.R. Holder, Silia		189 331
Hodge, Nathan		218	Holder, _____		125
Hodge, N.H.		288,353	Holland, C.P.		207
Hodge, N.H. (Mrs)		288	Holley, Mary Ruth		201
Hodge, Oney		328	Holley, Noah Taylor		132
Hodge, Pearl		234	Holley, Walter		132,201
Hodge, R.L.		275	Hollifield, Elizabeth		102
Hodge, Samuel		152	Holloway, Daniel		305
Hodge, Sarah		349	Holloway, Dicy A.		4
Hodge, Sarh		152	Holloway, Ellen		200
Hodge, Sarrah Edna		279	Holloway, George A.		95
Hodge, Scott		324	Holloway, George W.		305
Hodge, Siamon		158	Holloway, Paul		270
Hodge, Sidney		99	Holloway, William		305
Hodge, Simon		274	Holloway, ...		52
Hodge, S.S.		336	Holly, Caroline		73
Hodge, Thomas		152	Holly, Cora		356
Hodge, Vadie		43	Holly, Dave		232
Hodge, Waits A.		338	Holly, David		24
Hodge, Will		124	Holly, Ella Grace		304
Hodge, William		239	Holly, Fred		79
Hodge, William R.		20	Holly, Fred M.		25

Holly, G.H.	299	Honeycutt, Maggie	125
Holly, G.W.	162	Honeycutt, Manuel	252,283
Holly, Herman Zachary	79	Honeycutt, M.B.	298
Holly, Ina Mae	162	Honeycutt, M.C.	106
Holly, James	168,299	Honeycutt, M.R.	81
Holly, John	299	Honeycutt, Nancy	143
Holly, Lillie M.	335	Honeycutt, Nat	76,124
Holly, Margaret	226,232 236 <	Honeycutt, Nathan	81,219
Holly, Mary E.	203	Honeycutt, Polly	59
Holly, Millie	168	Honeycutt, Reuben	215,219
Holly, Mollie	352	Honeycutt, Robert	124
Holly, M.L.	123	Honeycutt, Sallie	343
Holly, Noah Taylor	132	Honeycutt, Sam	125
Holly, Robert	182	Honeycutt, Samuel	70,201
Holly, Sarah E.	138	Honeycutt, Walter	45
Holly, Tempie	179,282	Honeycutt, William	58,81 206 <
Holly, Walter	132,201	Honeycutt, W.M.	128,206
Holly, ____	174	Honeycutt, Zeb	215
Hollyfield, Bentley	315	Hopkins, Margaret	287
Hollyfield, Eligah	317	Hopkins, Ostland	44
Hollyfield, Hannah J.	315	Hopkins, Pegga	337
Holmes, Hunter	37	Hopkins, Sarah A.	176
Holoway, D.E.	270	Hopson, Archie	124
Holoway, Erven H.	270	Hopson, Charles	343
Holoway, George Allen	95	Hopson, Edward	343
Holoway, Infant	113	Hopson, Emmer	273
Holoway, John H.	270	Hopson, George	205,269 269 <
Holoway, Nancy A.	140	Hopson, Harris	273
Holoway, Oda	113	Hopson, Henry Jr.	21
Holoway, ____	120	Hopson, Jason	246
Holsclaw, Elizabeth	278	Hopson, J.P.	157
Holsclaw, Janie	55	Hopson, Manda Adams	205
Holsclaw, J.W.	272	Hopson, Marian	124,130
Holsclaw, William	272	Hopson, Martha	246
Holsclaw, William L.	272	Hopson, Mary	130,246
Holt, Mary	348	Hopson, Mary Jane	164
Hombrick, Gertie	38	Hopson, Massy	135
Honeycutt, Bertie	48	Hopson, Nellie	269
Honeycutt, Bessie	212	Hopson, Paul	157
Honeycutt, Bettie	106,113	Hopson, Pollie	289
Honeycutt, Betty	88	Hopson, Polly	254
Honeycutt, Blanche	235 305 <	Hopson, Rex	299
Honeycutt, Byrd	256	Hopson, Rex Jr.	299
Honeycutt, Dollie	204	Hopson, Sallie	21,103,155
Honeycutt, Infant	58,70 201 <	Hopson, Sarah Jane	273
		Hopson, Thomas	249

Hopson, Tom	130
Hopson, W.B.	145
Hopson, Zell	16
Horton, Andy	115
Horton, A.H.	64
Horton, Harriett	115
Horton, Helley	111
Horton, Lucinda	158
Horton, Lula	64
Horton, Minnie	149
Horton, Nancy Taylor	244
Hoss, Andrew B.	334
Hoss, Annie	128
Hoss, Bonnie F.	352
Hoss, Claracy	333
Hoss, Clifton	99,128,200
Hoss, Dellie	334
Hoss, Dorothy Bell	334
Hoss, George	128
Hoss, George Elancy	297
Hoss, George E.	297
Hoss, George W.	341
Hoss, Gladys	200
Hoss, James	21
Hoss, James Henry	99
Hoss, James H.	297
Hoss, J.G.	297
Hoss, Lora	47
Hoss, Louisa	128
Hoss, Michael S.	341
Hoss, M.S.	333
Hoss, Nancy	297,364
Hoss, Nannie	84
Hoss, Ray	329
Hoss, Rebecca	174
Hoss, Sarah	314
Hoss, Ted	314
Hoss, William	341
Houges, Robert	234
Housewright, Mary	347
Houston, Callie	247
Houston, Clara	235
Houston, Grover	7
Houston, Minnie C.	307
Houston, R.S.	268,307
Howard, Florence	245
Howard, Infant	245
Howard, Jack Mariah	73
Howard, Laura	73
Howard, Miriah	73
Howel, Nancy	103
Howell, E.	119
Howell, James	220
Howell, Mary	182
Howell, M.	223
Howell, Nancy	212,361
Howell, Roda	220
Howell, Scott	347
Howell, Thomas	220
Howell, Tom	347
Hubard, Rhoda	28
Hubble, Henry	294
Hubble, Mary G.	115
Huffine, Daniel	250
Hughes, Albert	227
Hughes, Bill	74
Hughes, Bob	15
Hughes, Brother	156
Hughes, Cass	160
Hughes, Celia	156,231
Hughes, Celie	212
Hughes, Charles	88,214
Hughes, Charlie	263
Hughes, Darkus	341
Hughes, D.	38
Hughes, D.W.	122
Hughes, Edward	16
Hughes, Eli	149
Hughes, Elizabeth	296
Hughes, Ellen	7,96,97
Hughes, Emma Francis	166
Hughes, Ethel E.	166
Hughes, Eugene Taylor	148
Hughes, Garrett	347
Hughes, George	46
Hughes, Gertie	49
Hughes, G.W.	182
Hughes, Hannah	81
Hughes, H.	263
Hughes, Infant	7,96
Hughes, James	227
Hughes, James J.	182
Hughes, Jane	251
Hughes, Jennie	158
Hughes, Jessie	149
Hughes, Jim	199

Hughes, John	148,237	Humphreys, ___		195
Hughes, Jonas	113	Humphries, Henry J.		157
Hughes, J.C.	199	Humphries, Lucy V.		84
Hughes, J.M.	158	Hunt, M.A. (Mrs)		121
Hughes, Larua C.	169	Hunt, Robert		121
Hughes, Laura	298	Hunter, D.E.E.		126
Hughes, Lewis	263	Hunter, Edwin Eugene		178
Hughes, Lillie	149	Hunter, Joseph		178
Hughes, Louis	251	Hunter, Mollie Jobe		178
Hughes, Luckey	20	Hunter, W.E.		126
Hughes, Luna	156	Huntley, Martha		22
Hughes, Maggie	312	Huntley, S.P.		309
Hughes, Margaret	138	Huntly, Joseph		353
Hughes, Mary Belle	55	Hurdt, James		208
Hughes, Pearl	346	Hurdt, James W.		208
Hughes, Ray	122	Hurdt, Mast		208
Hughes, Rebecca M.	126	Hurley, Bess		253
Hughes, Reuben	44	Hurley, Bessie		151
Hughes, Robert L.	43	Hurley, Betsy		248
Hughes, Roscoe	199	Hurley, Calvin		112
Hughes, Sallie	212	Hurley, Dori		288
Hughes, Sam	156	Hurley, Ellen		34
Hughes, Susan M.	55	Hurley, Gordy		179
Hughes, Wash	346	Hurley, Gurty		347
Hughes, William	214,251	Hurley, Ham		179
347	<	Hurley, Hardin	34,112,163	
Hughes, W.C.	342	Hurley, Henry		300
Hughs, Elizabeth	296	Hurley, Howard		206
Hughs, Infant	342	Hurley, Infant	34,122,136	
Hughs, W.C.	342	290,301	<	
Hulse, Nonnie	346	Hurley, James	112,136,301	
Humphrey, Cassie	155	Hurley, Jessey		290
Humphrey, Eliza	122	Hurley, Jessie		170
Humphrey, F.W.	284	Hurley, John	206,237	
Humphrey, Geneva	347	Hurley, Lizzie		106
Humphrey, Mack	276	Hurley, Margaret		163
Humphrey, Martha	284	Hurley, Mary Cox		179
Humphrey, Rhoda	357	Hurley, Mary Jane		237
Humphreys, Autie	184	Hurley, Mufer		268
Humphreys, F.W.	175	Hurley, Nancy	75,133	
Humphreys, George	157	Hurley, Paul		170
Humphreys, John	175,325	Hurley, Sam		300
Humphreys, Lillie	154	Hurley, Tennessee		122
Humphreys, Marion	325	Hurley, William		131
Humphreys, Matilda	144	Hurley, Wright		131
Humphreys, Tilda Ann	144	Hurt, Dayton		321
Humphreys, W.H.K.	267	Hurt, Infant		275
Humphreys, W.J.	44	Hurt, Mary		208

Hurt, Polley	321
Hurt, Will	275
Hurts, Hiley	228
Huston, John	347
Huston, Ulara	215
Hutson, Bruce	251
Hutson, Infant	347
Hutson, Sam	251
Hyder, Alice	151
Hyder, Alice Emma	291
Hyder, Allace	55
Hyder, Alleen	154
Hyder, Arnold	55
Hyder, Beckie	166
Hyder, Benjamin	309
Hyder, Bennie	309
Hyder, Bessie	55
Hyder, B.G.	135,272
Hyder, Cad	241
Hyder, Carvil	235
Hyder, Caswell	215
Hyder, Catherine	12
Hyder, Cecil	102
Hyder, Charlotte	233
Hyder, Cinda	27
Hyder, C.H.	149,230,235
Hyder, Daniel	117
Hyder, Daniel L.	154
Hyder, D.S.	117
Hyder, Ed	235
Hyder, Edith	23
Hyder, Edna	241
Hyder, Eliza Jane	286
Hyder, Eliza J.	316
Hyder, Elizabeth F.	108
Hyder, Ernest	39
Hyder, Francis M.	198
Hyder, Frank	327
Hyder, Frank M.	116
Hyder, Geneva	285,322
Hyder, George W.	342
Hyder, George W. (Mrs)	342
Hyder, Gretchen	316
Hyder, G.W.	291
Hyder, Harrison	257
Hyder, Henry	27,235
Hyder, Henry R.	116
Hyder, Hilda	327
Hyder, H.K.	148
Hyder, Ida	9,123
Hyder, Infant	102,144,243, 277,342 <
Hyder, James	53,102
Hyder, Jane	288
Hyder, Jesse N.	117
Hyder, Jessie	114
Hyder, Johathon	306
Hyder, John	141,230
Hyder, John W.	255
Hyder, Joseph	53
Hyder, Joseph D.	198
Hyder, J. Hampton	345
Hyder, J.C.	286
Hyder, J.H.	108,228,309, 340 <
Hyder, J.N.	75
Hyder, J.W.	141
Hyder, Lela	235
Hyder, Lena	257
Hyder, Lersnia	71
Hyder, Lon T.	277
Hyder, Lula	114
Hyder, L.F. (Dr)	10
Hyder, Mamie	361
Hyder, Marion	279
Hyder, Mark	243
Hyder, Mark Maynard	108
Hyder, Martha	198,204, 348 <
Hyder, Martha J.	255
Hyder, Martin	241
Hyder, Mary Bell	244
Hyder, Mary Jane	75
Hyder, Mintta	141
Hyder, Myrtle	215,228,316
Hyder, Nancy	247
Hyder, Nannie	134
Hyder, Nat	144,314
Hyder, Nat T.	84
Hyder, Ora	244
Hyder, Pearl	9,315
Hyder, Randal Jack	23
Hyder, Rebecca	162,357
Hyder, Rhoda J.	45
Hyder, Robert D.	108
Hyder, Roy	296

Hyder, R. Bennick	88	Ingrum. Hubert	23
Hyder, R. Brooks	243	Inscoe, Sallie A.	295
Hyder, R.B.	77,87,154,237 246 <	Irick, Jane	270
		Irick, John	134
Hyder, R.O.	204	Irvin, Mary	106
Hyder, Sam J.	342	Irwin, Clint	68
Hyder, Samuel	228,233	Irwin, Julia	66
Hyder, Samuel L.	215	Irwin, Nellie	68
Hyder, Samuel W.	116	Irwin, Sallie	66
Hyder, Sarah	159,207	Isaacs, Aaron	165
Hyder, Sexton	55	Isaacs, Anner	165
Hyder, Susie	298	Isaacs, Clint	326
Hyder, Taft	84	Isaacs, Emsley	234
Hyder, Thomas	235	Isaacs, Emsley Jr.	234
Hyder, Tobitha	210	Isaacs, J.B.	234
Hyder, Wid	230	Isaacs, Thelma	326
Hyder, William A.	114	Jackson, A.C.	151,160
Hyder, W.C.	342	Jackson, Bedie	232
Hyett, E.	251	Jackson, C.A.	273
H____, Waits	184	Jackson, Evaline	354
Icenhour, John	274	Jackson, Helen	356
Icenhour, Margaret	274	Jackson, Ida	59
Infgram, Lorance	229	Jackson, James	295
Ingle, Cordie	174	Jackson, John	341
Ingram, Bessie Mara	312	Jackson, Lida	295
Ingram, Cash	264	Jackson, Loftis	303
Ingram, Cash	312	Jackson, Mary	115
Ingram, Catherine	354	Jackson, Milton	354
Ingram, Charles	103	Jackson, Nona	309
Ingram, Charles	166	Jackson, Rebecca	332
Ingram, Charley	334	Jackson, Robert	209,232
Ingram, Emma	103	Jagan, Will	138
Ingram, Genia	31	James, Pleasant	95
Ingram, George	229	James, William	95
Ingram, Hattie	58,229,283	Jarredd, Rhoeba	196
Ingram, Julia	161	Jarrett, Ely	344
Ingram, Lener	155	Jarrett, Lige	344
Ingram, Lillie	90	Jarrett, ____	113
Ingram, Martha	226	Jenkins, Abraham	151
Ingram, Mollie	158	Jenkins, Belle	220
Ingram, Nat	334,338	Jenkins, Clarinda	162
Ingram, N.G.	253	Jenkins, C.R.	72
Ingram, N.J.	90	Jenkins, Dick	272
Ingram, Ray	103	Jenkins, Ed	246
Ingram, Rosco	334	Jenkins, Eddie (Mrs)	357
Ingram, Sam	166,283	Jenkins, Elijah	229
Ingram, W.R.	354	Jenkins, Fannie	179
Ingrum, Emma	23	Jenkins, Frank	6

Jenkins, Harold	26		Jobe, Jane	271
Jenkins, Harve	307		Jobe, Mary Eva	112
Jenkins, Hugh	162,276		Jobe, Mollie	126,178
Jenkins, Infant	6,72,246 310 <		Jobe, Sarafina	56
Jenkins, James D.	115		Johnson, Alford	333
Jenkins, James Edward	72		Johnson, Alice	259
Jenkins, Jennie	88		Johnson, Andrew J.	362
Jenkins, Jennie	88,220 291 <		Johnson, Annie	205
			Johnson, Arnold	203
			Johnson, Bernice	319
Jenkins, Jess W.	307		Johnson, Bessie	141,264
Jenkins, Jesse	276		Johnson, Bettie	135,202 208 <
Jenkins, Jessie	209			
Jenkins, Lizie	157		Johnson, Bill	146
Jenkins, Lizzie Pearl	272		Johnson, Carrick	165
Jenkins, Mary	205,362		Johnson, Carrier	276
Jenkins, Mary A.	255		Johnson, Charles	81
Jenkins, Mat	67,196		Johnson, Charles C.	231
Jenkins, May	214		Johnson, Charlie	316
Jenkins, Minnie	239		Johnson, Charlie J.	207
Jenkins, Mollie	318		Johnson, Cinda	307
Jenkins, Neah	229		Johnson, C.G.	213,242,334
Jenkins, Nellie	180		Johnson, Delphia	220
Jenkins, Ora	188		Johnson, Dorie	11
Jenkins, Ottie	231		Johnson, D.O.	360
Jenkins, Pearl	100,255		Johnson, Elizabeth	193 262 <
Jenkins, Richard	269			
Jenkins, Samuel	264		Johnson, Ellen	276
Jenkins, Thomas H.	179		Johnson, Esther	118
Jenkins, Vance	310		Johnson, Ettie	150,151
Jenkins, Vanie	272		Johnson, Eula E.	207
Jenkins, Venie	191		Johnson, Frank	207,316
Jenkins, Vernie	350		Johnson, Fred	155,341
Jenkins, Will	179		Johnson, Gladys Marie	334
Jenkins, William	67,151		Johnson, Goldman	319
Jenkins, _____	211,254,357		Johnson, Herby	333
Jennings, Mary	78		Johnson, Ida	256
Jennings, Mattie	120		Johnson, Infant	130,165 231,316,356 <
Jennings, Nancy	153			
Jerdin, Nannie	74		Johnson, I. Ester	59
Jerritt, Rosa	106		Johnson, Jacob Alford	59
Jett, Anna	280		Johnson, James	144,213 256 <
Jett, Shelly Searcy	280			
Jett, Stephen	280		Johnson, Joda	319,337,338
Jinkins, Neah	229		Johnson, John	165,203,276
Jobe, Bob	271		Johnson, John B.	205
Jobe, G.C.	296		Johnson, John Henry	155
Jobe, Infant	296		Johnson, John W.	262

Johnson, Josephine E.	108	
Johnson, J.A.	59	
Johnson, J.M.	52	
Johnson, Landon	266	
Johnson, Lula	12	
Johnson, Maree	178	
Johnson, Margie R.	38	
Johnson, Martha	244	
Johnson, Martha A.	264	
Johnson, Martina R.	309	
Johnson, Mary	52,100,234	
Johnson, Mary E.	113	
Johnson, Miriah	261	
Johnson, Missouri C.	360	
Johnson, Nancy	289	
Johnson, Nancy A.	98	
Johnson, Nelia	185	
Johnson, Nick	362	
Johnson, Oka	11	
Johnson, Oma	266	
Johnson, Polly	110	
Johnson, Princess I.	341	
Johnson, Rena	216	
Johnson, Robert	355,356	
Johnson, Robert, Jr.	77	
Johnson, Ruth A.	242	
Johnson, Sallie	220	
Johnson, Sallie	328	
Johnson, Sam	261,362	
Johnson, Sandy	266	
Johnson, Sondia	286	
Johnson, Stewart	178	
Johnson, Stuart	130	
Johnson, Susan	51	
Johnson, S.A.	328	
Johnson, Vick	310	
Johnson, Wesley	333	
Johnson, W.C.	81,113,205	
Johnson, W.R.	254	
Johnson, W.T.	243	
Johnson, W.V.	216	
Johnson, _____	138	
Johnston, J.L.	118	
Jolly, Milas	179	
Jones, Alex	244	
Jones, Alice Malissa	67	
Jones, Ambrose	25	
Jones, Andy	72	
Jones, Anna Belle	276	
Jones, Austin	121	
Jones, Belva	216	
Jones, Bob	165	
Jones, Charles H.	248	
Jones, Charles R.	248	
Jones, Clyde	48	
Jones, Clyde Henry	274	
Jones, David	59	
Jones, David, Jr.	63	
Jones, Elbert	40	
Jones, Elizabeth	255	
Jones, Elizabeth J.	93	
Jones, Ella	179	
Jones, Florence	236	
Jones, Ford	301	
Jones, Freddie	105	
Jones, Georgia	153	
Jones, Golda	216	
Jones, Hardin	22	
Jones, Howard	50	
Jones, Ida	244	
Jones, Infant	151.248	
Jones, Jackson	169	
Jones, John	15,248	
Jones, Johnie	68,105	
Jones, Josephine	165	
Jones, Josie	180	
Jones, J.H.	91	
Jones, J.P.	22	
Jones, J.S.	367	
Jones, Kate	74	
Jones, Lester	91	
Jones, Littleton	153	
Jones, Lizzie	236	
Jones, Maggie	195	
Jones, Marian	93	
Jones, Martha E.	242	
Jones, Mary Ann	253	
Jones, Mary Ann	367	
Jones, May Mary	63	
Jones, Minnie	240	
Jones, Nancy	116,123	
Jones, Ray Earl	68	
Jones, Robert	301,352	
Jones, Robert Jr.	274	
Jones, Robert J.	236	
Jones, Rosa	265	

Jones, Ruley	121	Julian, Myrtle	274
Jones, Russell N.	216	Julian, Peggy	51
Jones, R.J.	265	Julian, Rader	51
Jones, R.T.	168	Julian, William M.	207
Jones, Sam	192,292	Julian, W.D.	250
Jones, Sarah	134	Justice, F. Ross	133
Jones, Walter	274	Justice, Madge	248
Jones, Wes	192	Justice, Mary	205
Jones, Wesley	238	Justice, Roy	64
Jones, William	68,105,151	Justice, Samuel	64
Jones, Wriley	20	Justice, William	133
Jones, W.H.	124	Justis, Celia	284
Jordan, Bertha	243	Justis, Josephine	170
Jordan, C.H.	185	Justis, Sam	328
Jordan, C.H.	210	Keen, Caroline	247
Jordan, Herman	129	Keen, Ellen Coleman	170
Jordan, Infant	130	Keen, Enoch	101,260
Jordan, John	129,130,179	Keen, Hannah	153
Jordan, J.V.	164,170,174	Keen, John W.	101
Jordan, Katie M.	179	Keen, Mandy	190
Jordan, Sela	323	Keen, Nancy	93,258
Jordan, Sula	200	Keller, Cora	175
Jordan, William D. Jr.	210	Keller, Edmon	356
Jordan, William R.C.	210	Keller, Frank J. (Mrs)	365
Julian, Arthur	155	Keller, G.W.	224
Julian, Bessie	16	Keller, Loflin A.	177
Julian, Cain	155	Keller, Maggie	202
Julian, Clara	62,70	Keller, Zeb Theodore	177
Julian, C.M.	207	Kelley, Ettie	105
Julian, C.W.	270	Kelley, James	165
Julian, Effie C.	215	Kelley, James A.	250
Julian, Ellen	250	Kelley, Nannie	310
Julian, Etta	208	Kelley, Preston E.	250
Julian, Francis	208	Kelley, William A.	165
Julian, Hacker	155	Kelly, J.K.	23
Julian, Ida	324	Kelly, Margaret	107
Julian, Infant	261	Kemmick, H.H.	47
Julian, James	357	Kemp, Elizabeth	167
Julian, James J.	215	Kent, Alice Lee	194
Julian, James N.	72	Kent, James	194
Julian, James Sr.	207	Kent, Mary S.	194
Julian, Jane	51	Kidd, Jona	226
Julian, J.	261	Kidwell, Helen	131
Julian, J.F.	238,261,269	Kidwell, Lue Hellen	191
Julian, Lafayette	357	Kilog, Haynes	123
Julian, Lou	258	Kimick, Hiley	136
Julian, Luther	238	Kines, Preston	44
Julian, Mollie	237	King, Eliza H.	195

King, Joanna	247
King, J.A.	262
King, Robert H.	290
Kinnes, Ramon	33
Kinnick, Eliza	174
Kinnick, John	179
Kinnie, Virdie Lee	331
Kinnis, Ira Annie E.	60
Kinnis, John	60
Kipping, W.F.	82
Kirkpatrick, Jasper	205
Kirkpatrick, Joseph T.	205
Kirkpatrick, Taylor	205
Kiser, Ezra M.	356
Kiser, Ezra (Mrs)	356
Kiser, Infant	356
Kite, Adline	107
Kite, Alvin	300
Kite, Anderson	108
Kite, Anne Lee	194
Kite, A.N.D.	108
Kite, Christine	294
Kite, Dora	95
Kite, F.D.	300
Kite, Harmon Sales	14
Kite, Joseph B.	34
Kite, J.R.	90,108,172,186 194 <
Kite, Lissie	91
Kite, Marion B.	301
Kite, Marion Leon	301
Kite, Paul	172
Kite, Rena	68
Kite, Walter	16
Kitzmiller, Mary A.	366
Knight, A.K.	269
Knight, Elakander	310
Knight, Lydia	238,261
Knight, Marion	283
Knight, Rebecca	271,355
Knight, Ruby	283
Knight, Susie	310
Knight, William	310
Krouse, George	354
Krouse, Rhoda	209
Kuhn, Christine	297
Kuhn, Ollie Mae	271
Kuhn, Sam	297
Kun, Ollie Mae	271
Kyte, Infant	275
Kyte, William	275
Lacey, Charles T.	304
Lacey, John L.	304
Lacey, R.S.	280,304
Lacy, Alice	268
Lacy, Alice D.	98
Lacy, A.K.	184
Lacy, A.S.	81
Lacy, Caroline	73
Lacy, Catherine	182
Lacy, Dishmonia	81
Lacy, D. Porter	267
Lacy, D.P.	150
Lacy, Eliza	317
Lacy, Elizabeth	104
Lacy, Ellis	96
Lacy, Evaline	37
Lacy, Frank L.	73
Lacy, George	267
Lacy, Infant	36
Lacy, Irene	347
Lacy, James Phillips	288
Lacy, John M.	208
Lacy, John W.	247
Lacy, Joseph Mark	244
Lacy, Josie	248
Lacy, J.M.	98,179
Lacy, J.M. (Mrs)	208
Lacy, J.W.	36,288
Lacy, Lillie	244
Lacy, Lucinda Dempsy	167
Lacy, L.C.	73
Lacy, Martha A.	179
Lacy, Mary Jane	179
Lacy, Nanie	10
Lacy, Nellie	25
Lacy, Roy	17
Lacy, R.S.	179
Lacy, Samuel M.	33
Lacy, S.C.	64
Lacy, Vernia	327
Lacy, William S.	244
Lacy, W.B.	104
Lacy, W.S.	267
Lambert, Bill	341
Lambert, Ella	195

Lambert, Isac	286	Laws, G.J.	12
Lambert, John	172	Laws, Henry	202
Lambert, Myrtle	129	Laws, Hildred	87
Lambert, Robert	339	Laws, Infant	243
Lambert, Robert L.	341	Laws, J.C. (Mrs)	123
Lambert, Ruth J.	268	Laws, J.E. (Mrs)	172
Lambert, Sarah Jane	172	Laws, K.W.	87
Lambert, William	268,339	Laws, Martha	284
Lambert, William W.	268	Laws, Mary	264
Landown, Peggy	108	Laws, Milda	57
Landy, George	76	Laws, Minnie A.	177
Landy, Infant	76	Laws, Nancy P.	111
Lane, Clarence	41	Laws, Robert	243
Lane, Cleveland	137	Laws, Robert E.	222
Lane, J.T.	1	Laws, Roxil May	172
Laramer, Roady	33	Laws, R.B.	321
Large, Earl	335	Laws, R.D.	264
Large, Elizabeth	69	Lawson, Caroline	99
Large, Infant	335	Lawson, James	39
Large, Isaac	167	Lawson, Minnie	55
Large, James	305	Lawson, Mollie	318
Large, James Jr.	305	Leadford, Clyde	210
Large, Jess	167	Leadford, C.K.	210
Large, Jessie	69	Leadford, Vinney	168
Large, Rachel	41	Leadwell, Robert	76
Large, Thomas	41,58	Ledford, B.C.	249
Large, Tilla Bell	196	Ledford, David	168
Large, Wilson	167,334	Ledford, H.H.	249
Largen, Land	194	Ledford, Isaac	289
Largen, Thomas	194	Ledford, John	183
Largent, Nat	330	Ledford, Maggie	289
Largent, Thomas	330	Ledford, Mary Ann	249
Larger, John	88	Ledford, Nannie	87
Larger, Marion Allen	88	Ledford, Rosa	317
Larimer, Bob	356	Ledford, Sester	186
Larimer, Infant	356	Ledmire, Hubert E.	143
Larkin, George	344	Ledmire, Liza	143
Larkins, Walter	40	Ledwell, Eddie Harmon	36
Larrimer, E.W.	283	Ledwell, None	362
Latham, Tish	273	Ledwell, Robert	290
Lathern, Bell	152	Ledwell, Will	76
Lathom, Alexander	95	Lee, John	308
Laught, Vilon	357	Lee, Lottie Ann	188
Lawhorn, Sam	208	Lee, Soloman	294
Laws, Alzy	229	Lee, W.T.	308
Laws, Bertha	222	Leffel, Leathey	357
Laws, Delia	220	Lendwell, A.	319
Laws, Earl Haskel	202	Lendwell, Infant	319

Lenear, Emma		117	Lewis, Josephine		241
Leonard, Bob		312	Lewis, Julia		290
Leonard, Charlie		213	Lewis, Julia A.		341
Leonard, Delia		361	Lewis, J.F.M.		205,255
Leonard, Della		319	Lewis, J.M.		186
Leonard, George		259	Lewis, J.S.		232,348
Leonard, Infant		312,334	Lewis, Katie		62
Leonard, Isaac		346	Lewis, Lafayette		218,252
Leonard, Jacob		309	Lewis, Landon		301
Leonard, James		9,334	Lewis, Lawson		161,218,273
Leonard, John		259,312	Lewis, Lee		31
Leonard, Rhoda		334	Lewis, Lena		152
Lesis, May		303	Lewis, Lewis D.		134
Lewis, Addie		326	Lewis, Liddie		226
Lewis, Albert		46	Lewis, Lizzie		67,201,202
Lewis, Alfred		267	Lewis, Lou		139
Lewis, Anna		330	Lewis, Lula		339
Lewis, Annetha		317	Lewis, L.G.		241,252,346
Lewis, Annie		268	Lewis, Mag		246
Lewis, Bell		348	Lewis, Maggie		137,139,196
Lewis, Brownlow		176	Lewis, Manuel		49
Lewis, Catherine		246	Lewis, Margaret		165,254
Lewis, Celia Ann		116	Lewis, Martha		17,299,311
Lewis, C.C.		327,328	Lewis, Mary		78,186,306
Lewis, C.L.		327	Lewis, Mary Jane		328
Lewis, Dollie		10	Lewis, Matilda		99,128,200
Lewis, Dora		288	Lewis, Mattie		169,219
Lewis, Elie		21	Lewis, May		328
Lewis, Elila		272	Lewis, Mayme		346
Lewis, Eliza		134	Lewis, Milborn		232
Lewis, Ellen		299	Lewis, Murey		232
Lewis, Ephrem		147	Lewis, Murray		134,186,311
Lewis, Evaline		86	Lewis, Nancy Jane		327
Lewis, Fred		175	Lewis, Nancy Taylor		189
Lewis, Fuson		232	Lewis, Neal		216
Lewis, Gidwon		252	Lewis, Nettie		7,301
Lewis, G.M.		161	Lewis, Nola		312
Lewis, Hampton		116	Lewis, N.R.		134
Lewis, Hastin		196	Lewis, Pearl		327
Lewis, Hattie Mottern		257	Lewis, P.P.		330
Lewis, Hildred		272	Lewis, Raymond		328
Lewis, Houston		257	Lewis, Rile		312
Lewis, H.C.		82	Lewis, Robert		216
Lewis, Infant		161,312	Lewis, Rosa Christine		327
Lewis, Isaac		135	Lewis, Ruby		328
Lewis, Jennie		239	Lewis, Sallie		96,230
Lewis, John		147	Lewis, Sarah		215
Lewis, Johnnie		109	Lewis, Sarrina		223

Name	Page	Name	Page
Lewis, Shelby	330	Lipps, Infant	238
Lewis, Stephen	189	Lipps, James	184
Lewis, Tina	116	Lipps, Maggie	304
Lewis, Tobias	210,267	Lipps, Martha	297,321
Lewis, U.R.	176	Lipps, Martha W.	210
Lewis, Will	272	Lipps, Raymond	238
Lewis, William H.	205	Lipps, Roby M.	8
Lewis, William Smith	273	Lipps, Stella	184
Lewis, Willis	139	Little, A.J.	343
Lewis, W.D.	109	Little, A.R.	281
Lewis, W.M.	186	Little, Bessie Ann	277
Lewis, _____	145,217	Little, Bonnie	314
Lifton, Bud	70	Little, Callie	188
Lilley, Belle	250	Little, Carey	343
Lilley, J.J.	132	Little, Charlie	366
Lilley, Perlina	157	Little, Christine A.	307
Lilly, Belle	194	Little, D.P. (Mrs)	354
Lilly, Mary A.	322	Little, Ella	354
Lindawood, Francis	268	Little, Ethel	242,334
Lindawood, John	268	Little, E.H.	148
Lindsey, George	286	Little, Fanny	111
Lindsey, John	286	Little, Frank N.	3
Lindvill, Jane	227	Little, George D.	352
Lindy, Eliza J.	234	Little, George F.	343
Lindy, Mary E.	201	Little, G.F. (Mrs)	365
Lineback, Charlotie	80	Little, Henry	142,343
Lineback, Emma	255	Little, H. Clay	213
Lineback, H.	80	Little, Infant	128,366
Liner, Bluah	288	Little, James	340
Lines, Bulah	265	Little, James B.	230
Linkes, Hiram	106	Little, James B.	352
Linkes, Infant	106	Little, James R.	213
Linkes, Julia	335	Little, Katherine	145
Linkess, J.H.	231	Little, Kattie	30
Linkess, Ruby Ray	231	Little, Maggie	203
Linkus, Gibson	347	Little, Marcellas	340
Linkus, John	347	Little, Martin	230
Linkus, J.H.	347	Little, Mollie	282
Linville, Brocen	171	Little, Mollie B.	230
Linville, Worley	171	Little, Nola	96
Lions, Callie	183	Little, Nola Lee	200
Lions, E.L.	183	Little, Phoebe	269
Lipford, F.	334	Little, Robert	366
lipford, Joe	343	Little, Ruth	365
Lipford, Maggie	154	Little, Sallie	154
Lipford, May	152	Little, Thomas	281
Lipford, Philip	340	Little, Thurman M.	281
Lipps, D.W.	184	Little, Walter	128

Little, Wanaeta	7	Long, William	86
Little, _____	201	Looney, Nancy	361
Livingston, Alfred	159	Lord, Manda	188
Livingston, Bat	159,183	Lose, Susie	359
188	<	Loudy, Bill	133
Livingston, Ben	261,356	Loudy, Bob	133
Livingston, Edith	267	Loudy, Hobert L.	44
Livingston, Francis	14	Louerson, Mollie	113
Livingston, Frankie P.	202	Louis, Landon	299
Livingston, George	115	Louis, L.D.	299
143,188	<	Loury, Nancy Ann	221
Livingston, George P.	183	Loury, Peter Nick	221
Livingston, Georgie M.	158	Love, Belle	74
Livingston, G.A.	105	Love, Mollie	245
Livingston, Haskell	15	Loveles, A.F.	299
Livingston, Infant	105	Loveless, Addie Bell	105
143,331	<	Loveless, Allen	197
Livingston, James F.	115	Loveless, Allen F.	196
Livingston, John	1,122	Loveless, A.F.	303
Livingston, J.B.	202	Loveless, Belle	129
Livingston, Lizzie B.	122	Loveless, Celia	309,351
Livingston, Louisa	61	Loveless, Clarence E.	236
Livingston, Mae	84	Loveless, Daisy	196
Livingston, Mary	158	Loveless, David K.	152
Livingston, Maxel	202	236	<
Livingston, May	144	Loveless, D.K.	152,236
Livingston, Pauline	183	Loveless, Eligia A.	260
331	<	Loveless, Elijah	100
Livingston, Pettibone	158	Loveless, Eliza Jane	260
Livingston, Samuel	306	Loveless, Ellen	100
Livingston, Sheeley	261	Loveless, Evelyn	56
Livingston, S.B. (Mrs)	15	Loveless, Frank	202
Livingston, W.M.	331	Loveless, Glenn	200
Lofton, Delia Stout	255	Loveless, Herman	296,337
Logan, Albert	79	Loveless, Infant	296,303
Logan, Cynthia	354	337	<
Logan, Eugene	79	Loveless, James H.	116
Logan, George	354	Loveless, Joseph H.	152
Londy, W.M.	201	Loveless, Laura	197
Long, Calvin Coolidge	360	Loveless, Mary	344
Long, Charles P.	57	Loveless, Othello	56
Long, George	360	Loveless, Phoeba	351
Long, Infant	86,107	Loveless, Raymond	299
Long, Lonie (Mrs)	307	Loveless, Rosa Belle	202
Long, Mary	359	Loveless, Ross	260,344
Long, Polly	97	Loveless, Thomas	196
Long, R.A.	37	Loveless, Tom	100,200,299
Long, Will	107	Loveless, Waita	196

Loveless, William H.	14
Loveless, W.B.	202
Loveless, W.D.	262
Loveless, W.M.	165
Loveless, W.P.	105,116 117,188,254,261
Lovie, Alexander	339
Low, Cori	299
Low, Marthy	311
Low, Steve	299,311
Lowe, Bernice	334
Lowe, Casie	168
Lowe, Charles D.	310
Lowe, Cori	299
Lowe, Dan	332
Lowe, Daniel	169
Lowe, David	84
Lowe, Eliza J.	325
Lowe, Ethel	8
Lowe, Eva	149
Lowe, Eveline	293
Lowe, Foyst Delmer	310
Lowe, George	183
Lowe, George J.	325
Lowe, George S.	297
Lowe, Harry C.	355
Lowe, Henry	84
Lowe, H.D.	84,168,210,297
Lowe, H.W.	62
Lowe, Infant	62,169
Lowe, Jacob	332
Lowe, Jacob R.	210
Lowe, Jamima J.	202
Lowe, Jerry	97
Lowe, John	321
Lowe, John A.	210
Lowe, John A.	297
Lowe, Kitte	355
Lowe, Letha	261
Lowe, Maggie	141
Lowe, Mahala	146
Lowe, Martha	168,231
Lowe, Mary	100
Lowe, Mollie	89
Lowe, Noah	149,230,293
Lowe, Ray	334
Lowe, Roy	325
Lowe, Roy B.	202,261
Lowe, Sallie	359
Lowe, Sarah	146,349
Lowe, Steve	299,355
Lowe, Steve, Jr.	230
Lowe, S.J.	141
Lowe, S.L.	332
Lowe, Tissie	176
Lowe, William H.	321
Lowe, W.H.	112
Lowe, _____	337
Loy, Elsey	302
Lucus, Lucy	71
Luis, D.	232
Luis, Landon	299,301
Luis, L.D.	299
Luis, Martha	299
Luis, Mary	306
Luis, Milbon	232
Luis, Murey	232
Luis, Murry	311
Luis, M.	299
Luis, Netty	301
Lunceford, Andy	217
Lunceford, A.E.	232
Lunceford, Carter	146,164
Lunceford, Clementine	115
Lunceford, C.	239
Lunceford, Daniel L.	59
Lunceford, D.E.	146
Lunceford, Enoch	54
Lunceford, Ephraim	232
Lunceford, E.M.	115
Lunceford, Hobbert	54
Lunceford, Ida	128,187
Lunceford, James	217
Lunceford, James E.	59
Lunceford, James T.	345
Lunceford, Jody B.	146
Lunceford, J.A.	304
Lunceford, L.M.	59
Lunceford, Noah	217
Lunceford, Robert	217
Lunceford, R.M.A.	19
Lunceford, Sarah A.	101
Lundy, Denny	55
Lundy, Thomas Leonard	229
Lunsford, A.J.	12
Luther, William	17

Lutrell, Laura	150
Luttrell, Eliza	330
Luttrell, James	163
Luttrell, John M.	312
Luttrell, Laura	312
Luttrell, Loura E.	330
Lyle, Allen	112
Lyle, George W.	112
Lynn, Hattie	143
Lynn, Robert C.	143
Lynn, William	143
Lyon, Alvin	190
Lyon, Estel	154
Lyon, Florence	38
Lyon, Fred	344
Lyon, Henry	58
Lyon, Jackson	58
Lyon, John	108,154
Lyon, Rebecca	85
Lyon, Samuel B.	108
Lyon, William S.	179
Lyons, Alf	230
Lyons, Clarence	291
Lyons, Dasie	201
Lyons, Dock	201
Lyons, Edward	18
Lyons, Eva	143
Lyons, George	264
Lyons, Gernie	53
Lyons, Grace	236
Lyons, G.T.H.	168
Lyons, G.W.	324
Lyons, Hettie	50
Lyons, Infant	230,237
Lyons, Jane	244
Lyons, John	291
Lyons, J.T.	236
Lyons, Kate	237
Lyons, Mary	115,206
Lyons, Nancy	116
Lyons, Patsy	168
Lyons, Rosa Nell	324
Lyons, Rosie	50
Lyons, Sallie	131
Lyons, Thomas	206
Lyons, Will	305
Lyons, William	115,235 305
Lyons, William Jr.	235
Lyons, William Paul	305
Lyons, W.A.	131
Mackley, John	234
Madron, E.M. (Mrs)	173
Mahaffey, Ida Francis	213
Main, Emma H.	257
Main, Julia	326
Main, W.K.	257
Maine, Nallie	72
Maise, Annie	271
Maleon, Alf	113
Malone, Alfred	265
Malone, A.L.	113
Malone, Edith	265
Malone, Geroge M.	229
Malone, Hazel	113
Malone, Jake	229
Malone, Jane	229
Malone, Lexia	353
Malone, Robert	352
Malone, Roy	352
Malone, Willie	265
Malone, Willie Alford	265
Mann, Caroline	356
Mann, W.P.	356
Manning, D.C.	110
Manning, Ebb	273
Manning, Emmert	248
Manning, H.H.	204
Manning, Kittie	110
Manning, Nola	92,173
Manning, Sam	231
Manning, Sue Pauline	231
Manning, Sylva Alice	248
Manning, W.S.	315
Maples, Dempsy	132
Maples, L.L.	132
Markland, Alice	141,217
Markland, Allen	200,231 232
Markland, Amanda	164
Markland, Anga	197
Markland, Angie	121,162
Markland, A.C.	111,141
Markland, Charlie	243
Markland, Ellen	3
Markland, Francis	342

Markland, Frank	126,127 193 <	
Markland, George M.	200	
Markland, Helen O.	193	
Markland, Henry	29,193 256 <	
Markland, Infant	82	
Markland, James	82	
Markland, James E.	74	
Markland, J.C.	353	
Markland, J.D.	351	
Markland, Lizzie	123	
Markland, Martha L.	12	
Markland, Millie	351	
Markland, Mollie	112	
Markland, Myrtle	111	
Markland, Parrot	164	
Markland, Ross	353	
Markland, Roy	32	
Markland, Sarah	189,297 345 <	
Markland, Thelma	243	
Markland, Wilbon	305	
Markland, Wilburn	193	
Markland, Will	74,193	
Markland, Yande	342	
Markland, ____	155	
Marklin, Josie	62	
Marklin, Lelia	175	
Marklin, William	175	
Marklin, ____	155	
Markling, Barbara	305	
Markling, Hanry	256	
Markling, Mary Jane	256	
Markling, Wilbon	305	
Marler, Mollie	4	
Marley, Wiley J.	121	
Marlow, Eula May	176	
Marlow, William	176	
Marr, Elizabeth	351	
Marsh, Ella	318	
Marsh, Maggie	137	
Marshall, Jane	325	
Marshall, Mary	312	
Marshall, ...	94	
Martin, Charles	89	
Martin, C.L.	169	
Martin, Emma	195	
Martin, Fred Deforest	169	
Martin, Hamp	89	
Martin, Mandy	260	
Martin, Mary E.	53	
Marton, Cora	298	
Marton, Coy	292	
Marton, David	284	
Marton, Fred	346	
Marton, James	336	
Marton, Jennie	179	
Marton, John L.	285	
Marton, J.L.	336	
Marton, J.S.	284	
Marton, Mary	346	
Marton, Myrtle	312	
Marton, Oliver	346	
Marton, Rina	300	
Marton, W.C.	292	
Masingill, C.D.	104	
Masingill, Nellie G.	104	
Massengill, Infant	263 282,351 <	
Massengill, J.B.	351	
Massengill, Nora	352	
Massengill, Sallie	278	
Massengill, William	227 263,282 <	
Massingill, John	132	
Massingill, Lawrence	132	
Massingill, William	227	
Mast, Andrew J.	247	
Mast, D.P. (Mrs)	227	
Mast, Gilbert S.M.	227	
Mast, James Patterson	247	
Mast, J.D.	227	
Masters, Levina	330	
Maston, Junior Etta	172	
Maston, J.F.	172	
Matherly, Alex	269	
Matherly, Dayton	306	
Matherly, D.C.	154	
Matherly, D.M.	286	
Matherly, Infant	66,86,87 112,185 <	
Matherly, James	66,86,87 112,185 <	
Matherly, Maud	259	
Matherly, Susanah	220,286	

Matherly, Susannah	110	McAllister, Randolph	122
Matherly, W.M.	306	McArver, Susan	230
Matherson, Charles K.	195	McBride, Betsy	353
Matherson, G.W.	94,353	McCathern, William	92
Matherson, Lillie	94	McCauley, Thomas	136
Matherson, Nellie	353	McClain, Alex	159
Matherson, N.D. (Mrs)	195	McClain, Charles C.	362
Matherson, William T.	195	McClain, Charles (Mrs)	362
Matheson, Addie	304	McClain, Dolf	174
Matheson, Ruby Ellen	183	McClain, Florence	235
Matheson, Will	304	McClain, Infant	159
Matheson, W.C.	51	McClain, Jack	337,338
Mathis, Calvin	358	McClain, Mary	137
Mathis, John	183	McClean, Cora B.	156
Mathis, Marrion	295	McClean, Hanner	280
Mathis, Rena	358	McClelan, May	358
Mathis, William	358	McClellan, Frank	83
Mathison, Mangla	155	McClellan, Mary	117
Mattison, Nellie	353	McClellan, Willie	83
Maupin, Bonnie	41,42	McClenen, Maggie	314
Maupin, Bonnie Bell	37	McCloud, Elbert	42
Maupin, Helen	25	McCloud, Hannah M.	293
May, David E.	141	McCloud, Harold	57
May, John	341	McCloud, Infant	137
May, Julia	78	McCloud, Ira	26
May, Julie E.	21	McCloud, Ishah	350
May, Lila Hattie	141	McCloud, Isham	326
May, Lovey	287	McCloud, James	275
May, Martha	61	McCloud, John	137
May, Mary	217	McCloud, John F.	350
May, Pearl	16	McCloud, Joseph	326
May, William	195	McCloud, J.F.	293
Maynard, E.B.	220	McCloud, Kathrine	230
Mayrnes, Sarah	11	McCloud, Mary	343
Mays, Albert D.	139	McCloud, Mollie	326
Mays, Annie	271	McCloud, Nora	63,69
Mays, Disey Ellen	285	McCloud, Robert	275
Mays, Frank	278	McCloud, Sarah	334
Mays, John Wesley	285	McCloud, T.C.	350
Mays, J.W.	285	McClure, Addie	110
Mays, Matilda	314	McConnaheay, Mattie E.	18
Maze, Alice	218	McCurry, Earnest	78
Maze, Susan	217	McCury, J.E.	63
McAdams, Henry	106	McEllen, Frank	221
McAdams, Thomas	106	McEllen, Nancy	221
McAdams, T.J.	106	McElyea, Mary	208
McAlister, Crosha	302	McElyea, Roy	278
McAllister, Lillie	208	McElyea, Thomas	278

McEwen, Bennie	36		McKeehan, Walter	263
McEwen, Clyde	252,334		McKeehan, Wiley	263,351
McFall, Jim	168		McKeehan, _____	231
McFarland, Elizabeth	140		McKehan, Jim	129
McFarland, Lidia	140		McKhin, Frank	80
McFarland, Moses	140		McKhin, Infant	80
McFarland, ...	94		McKilhine, A.M.	15
McGee, Arther	226		McKinis, George	247
McGee, Charles M.	160		McKinner, Cassie	46
McGee, Dan	215		McKinney, Anney	53
McGee, Daniel	113,160		McKinney, Bate	118
McGee, Evelyn	211		McKinney, Becky	122
McGee, Grace	335		McKinney, Bessie	245
McGee, Luened	139		McKinney, Bettie	221
McGee, Sallie	195		McKinney, Bruce	163,301
McGuire, V.V.	351		McKinney, Cam	92
McHaney, _____	262		McKinney, Cassie	46
McIntire, Cinda	105		McKinney, Celia	332
McIntosh, Hester	245		McKinney, Celie	148
McIntosh, Minnie Bell	73		McKinney, Clingman	291
McIntosh, Ruth	231		McKinney, Cloyd	245
McIntosh, Sallie	121		McKinney, Corda	284
McIntosh, Sarah A.	292		McKinney, C.C.	281
McIntosh, Thomas	73		McKinney, David	126,185
McInturf, Wilson	287		McKinney, David M.	73
McInturf, W.K.	287		McKinney, Drucilla	45
McInturff, W.R.	93		McKinney, D.M.	92
McKaney, Sarah	334		McKinney, Edgar	317
McKanny, Sallie	321		McKinney, Elijah B.	339
McKay, Elsie	34		McKinney, Eliza	317
McKeehan, Caroline	129		McKinney, Elizabeth	149
McKeehan, Charles R.	165		McKinney, Elln	350
McKeehan, David F.	95		McKinney, E.E.	97
McKeehan, Derona	356		McKinney, Fannie	149
McKeehan, Frank	131,165		McKinney, Flosa	24
186,359	<		McKinney, Frank	208
McKeehan, Frank O.	359		McKinney, General	265
McKeehan, Frankie	186		McKinney, Gurney	26
McKeehan, Helen L.	141		McKinney, Gustava	119
McKeehan, Hubert A.	359		McKinney, G.A.	105
McKeehan, Infant	263		McKinney, Ham S.	348
McKeehan, Joanna	348		McKinney, Harrison	105
McKeehan, Josie	284		McKinney, Henry	92,224
McKeehan, Lee	141		339	<
McKeehan, May	314		McKinney, Infant	271,329
McKeehan, Ossa May	131		McKinney, James	221,245
McKeehan, Victoria	202		259,291	<
McKeehan, Violet	261		McKinney, James B.	348

McKinney, Jennie	219	McKinney, Wilson	301,332
McKinney, Jessie Loyd	73		342 <
McKinney, John	81,221,265	McKinney, W.C.	206
McKinney, John P.	61	McKinney, ___	112,155,239
McKinney, Joseph	76,210	Mckinneys, Anney	53
	342 <	McKinnie, Peggie	291
McKinney, Julia Ann	327	McKinnies, M.W.	53
McKinney, J.B.	243	McKinnis, John	247
McKinney, J.B. (Mrs)	210	McKinnis, Thomas N.	247
McKinney, Kate	317	McKintos, Ruthie	356
McKinney, Katie	210	McLain, Annie	213
McKinney, Lucy	105	McLane, Charles	282
McKinney, Margaret	248	McLane, Charles Jr.	282
McKinney, Mary	259,266	McLaughlin, Bessie	246
	320 <	McLean, O.L.	186
McKinney, Mary E.	129	McLemore, Floyd	208
McKinney, Mollie	87	McLemore, F.C.	174
Mckinney, M.W.	53	McLeod, Mary	252
McKinney, Nancey	265	McMan, Rachel	132
McKinney, Nettie	334	McNeal, Albert	316
McKinney, Nola	66,185	McNeal, Gemmima	220
McKinney, Nolie	86	McNeal, John	316
McKinney, N.N.	76	McNeal, J.A.	256
McKinney, O.J.	148	McNeal, Laura Lee	230
McKinney, Partive	163	McNeal, Robert	220
McKinney, Peggie	221	McNeeley, Nerue	146
McKinney, Pollie	126	McNeely, Anna	252
McKinney, Polly	163	McNeely, Esq	50,94
McKinney, Puckney	259	McNeely, Martha L.	198
McKinney, Roy	169,329	McNeely, Nancy	294
McKinney, R.C.	144	McNeely, R.F.	294
McKinney, Sallie	281	McNeese, Alice	196
McKinney, Sam S.	271	McNeese, Eli	271
McKinney, Samuel	355	McNeese, William	196
McKinney, Sarah Ann	203	McNeese, W.R.	196
McKinney, Sincler	155	McNeil, Enoch	119
McKinney, S.S.	216,355	McNess, Rebecca	102
McKinney, Tenie	30	McPherson, Annie	248
McKinney, Thomas	156	McQueen, Alfred S.	241
McKinney, Thomas C.	76	McQueen, David L.	74
McKinney, T.C.	148,163	McQueen, Ed	92
	301,348 <	McQueen, Elias	205
McKinney, Vana	152	McQueen, E.D.	320
McKinney, Walter	119	McQueen, Finley	165
McKinney, Will	169	McQueen, Herman	92
McKinney, William	156,169	McQueen, Infant	104
	317 <	McQueen, Kattie	117
McKinney, William C.	243	McQueen, Lorattie	141

McQueen, Loretta	205		Merritt, Earl	340
McQueen, Paul A.	74		Merritt, Emma	363
McQueen, Ransom	104		Merritt, George	70
McQueen, Sarah	143		Merritt, Harry	36
McQueen, Sarah A.	319		Merritt, Henry	363
McQueen, Wade	300		Merritt, Infant	106,256
McQueen, Wheeler	254		Merritt, James	221
McQueen, William L.	254		Merritt, John	106,221,363
McQueen, _____	59,167,169		Merritt, Laura	331
McRafts, Infant	14		Merritt, Lenis	362
McRafts, Peter	14		Merritt, Lwnis	362
McRath, Georgia	134		Merritt, Ralph	350
McRath, Henry	134		Merritt, Thomas	152
McRath, Infant	14		Merritt, Thomas	162
McRath, Pete	99,134,247		Merritt, Wheeler H.	70
McRath, Peter	14		Merritt, W.H.	191
McRath, Robert	99		Messer, Deliah	222
McRath, Sarah	247		Messimer, Abraham	290
McReynolds, Mary	137		Messimer, Deina	291
McVay, Millie	350		Messimer, Harvie Jr.	153
McYea, Mary	100		Messimer, H.E.	153
Medearis, W.E.	342		Messimer, James A.	97
Mediaris, Margaret	342		Messimer, James H.	290
Meeker, James A.	72		Messimer, Laura	172
Melim, Malinda	277		Messimer, Victoria	290
Meramer, Nancy	123		Messiner, L.W.	52
Meredith, Calvin L.	322		Micals, Sallie	251
Meredith, Carl G.	331		Michaels, Abbigail	178
Meredith, Claude	285,348		180	<
Meredith, C.E.	322		Michaels, Alford	109
Meredith, Daniel M.	260		Michaels, Jane	274
Meredith, Elizabeth	176		Michaels, Sallie	251
Meredith, Infant	285		Michals, Alford	329
Meredith, J.A.	322		Michals, Gus	329
Meredith, Minnie	331		Michals, Sallie	15
Meredith, William G.	335		Michiels, Guss	274
Meredith, Willie	306,315		Milam, Joe	241
Meredith, W.R.	331,335		Milam, T.L.	241
Meredith, _____	260		Milams, George	97
Meritt, James	221		Milams, Paul	97
Merrit, Harry	36		Milans, Bill	97
Merritt, Alpha	257		Miller, Absolom	208
Merritt, Arthur	191		Miller, Adam	295
Merritt, Carl Edward	362		Miller, Annie	246
Merritt, Charles	191		Miller, Apsy	322
Merritt, Charley	350		Miller, A.J.	140,228
Merritt, Charlie	256		Miller, A.M.	316
Merritt, Dan	256		Miller, Bayless	69

Miller, Bill	119,295
Miller, Bob	27
Miller, Caline Donald	87
Miller, Carmen Robert	193
Miller, Catherine	139
Miller, Charlie	16,315
Miller, Clarence	131,135
Miller, Clarence C.	16
Miller, Crystal Jane	154
Miller, C.T.	77
Miller, Dara O.	107
Miller, David	222
Miller, David H.	322
Miller, Dellie	334
Miller, Dollie Mae	297
Miller, Don	224
Miller, Earl	46
Miller, Edne	212
Miller, Edwin Ellis	105
Miller, Elbert	153
Miller, Elizabeth	65,119
Miller, Ella	222,249,311
Miller, Emily	240
Miller, Emma	103
Miller, Emma B.	254
Miller, Emmitt	368
Miller, Ernest	24,49
Miller, Evelyn	153
Miller, E. Dudley	87
Miller, E.M.	68
Miller, Florence	213
Miller, Floyd	46,225
Miller, George W.	346
Miller, Hannah	51,77,335
Miller, Harmon Tipton	82
Miller, Hattie	352
Miller, Henry	354
Miller, Infant	60,194,195
Miller, Jake	20,204
Miller, James	204,208
Miller, James J.	346
Miller, James L.	346
Miller, Jane	261
Miller, Jennie Ann	170
Miller, Joe	254
Miller, John	209,273
Miller, John Henry	363
Miller, Junie	20
Miller, J.D.	193,213,335
Miller, J.G.	316
Miller, J.O.	297
Miller, J.T.	87,170
Miller, J.W.	264
Miller, Katherine	289
Miller, Lee F.	82
Miller, Lee F. (Mrs)	294
Miller, Liza	320
Miller, Losson	295
Miller, Maggie	289
Miller, Martha	294
Miller, Martha W.	346
Miller, Mary	83,254,352
Miller, Maud	35,220
Miller, Miner	110
Miller, M.C.	40,137
Miller, M.D.L.	69
Miller, M.F. (Mrs)	274
Miller, M.M.	309
Miller, M.M. (Mrs)	309
Miller, M.T.	118
Miller, Nancy	60,124,175 262,306,313 <
Miller, Nat	84
Miller, Nervie	237
Miller, Nicholas	133
Miller, Nick	349
Miller, Ora	335
Miller, Orville	194,195
Miller, Paul	175
Miller, Pheby	269,307
Miller, Philmore O.	327
Miller, Pollie	274
Miller, Rebecca J.	68
Miller, Richard	135
Miller, Robert	105,193
Miller, Ross	368
Miller, Ruby	222
Miller, R.L.	65
Miller, Sallie	335
Miller, Sam	204,289
Miller, Samuel	154,170
Miller, Sanford	295
Miller, Sarah	61,171,306
Miller, S.	264
Miller, S.A.	195
Miller, S.J.	269

Miller, S____	209	Moland, Susana	343
Miller, Taylor	315	Monda, Cinda	245
Miller, Ulie	84	Monda, Robert	245
Miller, Viola	46	Monda, Sarah	245
Miller, Virgo	11	Monday, Laura	316
Miller, Wesley	154,327	Montgomery, Caroline	259
Miller, Willard	135	Montgomery, Daniel	345
Miller, William	225	Montgomery, D.E.	111
Miller, William H.	208	Montgomery, Elbert	327
Miller, W.M.	289	Montgomery, Elbert Jr.	327
Millhorn, Eliza	236	Montgomery, Eliza C.	345
Millhorn, Ida	103	Montgomery, Hannah C.	217
Mills, Joe	245	Montgomery, Infant	223
Milton, A.M.	318	326	<
Milton, Carl	318	Montgomery, Jeff	153
Milton, Minnie Lee	304	Montgomery, L.E.	317
Minnich, Edna M.	296	Montgomery, Mary	18
Minton, Annie	20	Montgomery, McKinley	326
Minton, Bessie	199	Montgomery, Samuel	111
Minton, Earl	347	223	<
Minton, Elizabeth B.	231	Montgomery, Tilda	153
Minton, E.H. (Mrs)	312	Moody, Altia	319
Minton, Griff	119	Moody, Claud	170
Minton, Griff H.	130	Moody, Dana	279
Minton, G.H.	347	Moody, Dana Jr.	279
Minton, Hewbert	62	Moody, Fanny	301
Minton, Ira	279	Moody, George	298
Minton, Jim	345	Moody, Joe H.	170
Minton, L.L. (Mrs)	71,317	Moody, Joseph H.	161
Minton, Margaret	342	Moody, Julia	276
Minton, Minnie	280	Moody, Lee	161
Minton, Roscoe	62	Moody, Naome	109,181
Minton, R.G.	20	Moor, Bill	174
Mitchell, Bessie	197	Moor, Henry	97
Mitchell, Betsy	213	Moor, Infant	97
Mitchell, Bob	197	Moor, Mollie	174
Mitchell, Hattie	101	Moor, Polly	128
Mitchell, Minnie	134	Moore, Annie	64
Mitchell, Rhoda	60	Moore, Bettie	88,287
Mitchell, Robert	134	Moore, Betty	346
Mitchell, Sallie	275	Moore, Celia	54
Mitchell, Tom	134	Moore, David	27
Mockely, John	269	Moore, Ed	203
Mody, Pollie	139	Moore, George	59
Moffate, J.M.	90	Moore, Henry	88,97,113
Moffett, Gertrude	263	287,303	<
Moffett, Hettie L.	230	Moore, Hulda	113,335
Moffett, James	230	Moore, Ike	325

Moore, Infant	203	Morgan, J.C.		79
Moore, Isaac	87	Morgan, J.G.		133
Moore, John	9	Morgan, Lasson		119
Moore, Lee	102	Morgan, Linda		271,276
Moore, Lee	303	Morgan, Logan		133
Moore, Mary	54	Morgan, Lowell		251
Moore, Mary E.	109	Morgan, Malinda		222
Moore, Polly	128	Morgan, Marian		215
Moore, Rhoda	200	Morgan, Marsha Ellen		287
Moore, Thedore	87	Morgan, M.C.		177
Moore, Will	325	Morgan, Nora		167
Moore, ____	303	Morgan, Paul S.		235
More, Betty	346	Morgan, Rad		339
More, George	59	Morgan, Robert David		250
Morefield, Jefferson	245	Morgan, Temperance		314
Morefield, Walter A.	245	Morgan, Thomas		119,251
Moreland, John	182	Morgan, Wilby		273
Moreland, Lonna	337	Morgan, William L.		251
Moreland, Lucinda J.	243	Morgan, ____		204,250
Moreland, Mary A.	149	Morley, Bonnie		262
Moreland, M.F.	360	Morley, Dicey		68
Moreland, Nancy	120	Morley, Letta M.		265
Moreland, Ruth	133	Morley, Retta M.		264
Moreland, R.B.	243	Morley, Sarah		224
Moreland, Sarah	131	Morrell, Abigail		72
Moreland, Susana	343	Morrell, Alice		98
Moreland, William	335	Morrell, Alzenia		228
Moreland, Wright	154	Morrell, Anna Grace		129
Moreland, ____	160,206	Morrell, Bessie		76
Moreley, Infant	168	Morrell, B.T.F.		86
Moreley, W.B.	168	Morrell, Caleb		260,268
Morely, Rena	196	280,321		<
Morgan, Alice	91,107,313	Morrell, Catherine		116
Morgan, Arlie M.	107	Morrell, Catherine M.		187
Morgan, Asley	329	Morrell, Charles		155
Morgan, Charles	287,289	Morrell, Dora		115
Morgan, Charlie	119	Morrell, Earl		159
Morgan, Creesie	222	Morrell, Ellis		321
Morgan, David M.	235	Morrell, E.A.		159
Morgan, Dellis	255	Morrell, Hattie		73
Morgan, Frank	250	Morrell, Infant		347
Morgan, Frank Edward	99	Morrell, Isaac		162
Morgan, Idas	223	Morrell, Joe		132
Morgan, Infant	220,276	Morrell, John		86,280
Morgan, James	99,107,220	Morrell, John J.		321
251	<	Morrell, John S.		132
Morgan, Jane	180	Morrell, Joseph E.		260
Morgan, John	59,289	Morrell, J.A.		330

Morrell, J.D.	233	Morris, Will	219
Morrell, J.J.	139	Morris, W.A.	225
Morrell, J.M.	252	Morris, ____	333
Morrell, J.P. (Mrs)	132	Morrow, Elizabeth	207
Morrell, Lee	187	Morse, Anna Mae	358
Morrell, Louise	138	Morse, George	192
Morrell, Luther	336	Morton, Bettie	351
Morrell, L.T.	129,187	Morton, Bionett	15
Morrell, L____	252	Morton, David	285
Morrell, Maggie	6	Morton, D.S.	144
Morrell, Ottie	32	Morton, Easter	144
Morrell, Rebecca	326	Morton, Elyie	336
Morrell, Roscoe	350	Morton, Everett	125
Morrell, Roy	347	Morton, E.E.	125,226
Morrell, Sarah Ann	218	Morton, Florence	188
Morrell, Thomas M.	280	Morton, George	96,149
Morrell, William E.	280	Morton, George F.	108
Morrell, ____	219,226	Morton, Hannah	17
Morris, Alice	221	Morton, Harmon	10
Morris, Anna Mae	358	Morton, Hurd	207
Morris, Beckey	1	Morton, James	299
Morris, Cleo	108	Morton, Jennie	179
Morris, David	155	Morton, Lottie	216
Morris, Ella	254	Morton, Lottie P.	215
Morris, Ernest	260	Morton, Lula	352
Morris, Essie Ellen	218	Morton, Mary D.	92
Morris, Eva May	61	Morton, M.Y.	144
Morris, E.E.	150,278	Morton, Rosa Caroline	340
Morris, Fannie	367	Morton, R.D.	207
Morris, Florence	150	Morton, Sam	203
Morris, Geneva	225	Morton, Samuel	148
Morris, George	219	Morton, Velia	318
Morris, Grocen	30	Mosler, Sallie	62
Morris, Henry	155,206	Mottern, Anna	98
Morris, Henry Clay	367	Mottern, Carrie	280
Morris, Infant	260	Mottern, Cecil R.	44
Morris, James	305	Mottern, D.S.	282
Morris, Jefa	219	Mottern, Elizabeth	86,132 280 <
Morris, Jefferson	61		
Morris, John Sr.	189	Mottern, Fate	257
Morris, Joshua	75	Mottern, Harold	234
Morris, Katy	161	Mottern, Ida	106
Morris, Lavonia	155	Mottern, Infant	280
Morris, Martha	1	Mottern, John	132
Morris, Mary	305	Mottern, Lafayette	257
Morris, Mollie	295	Mottern, Matilda	142,343
Morris, Susan	153	Mottern, Rebecca C.	163
Morris, Walter	108	Mottern, Robert	234

Mottern, Samuel	7	Myers, Lucy		170
Mottern, Susan	244	Myers, Marian		128
Mottern, Susanna	102	Myers, Mattie		40
Mottern, William J.	280	Myers, May		40
Mueter, Mollie	317	Myers, Mollie		75,100
Mullens, Ethel	282	Myers, Myrtle		38
Mumpower, Nell	40	Myers, Rachel		334
Murklin, John Paul	36	Myers, Rebecca		285
Murphey, Charles	26	Myers, Silas		308
Murphey, Charlie	172	Myers, Silas		336
Murphey, Harriett	26	Myers, S.J.		336
Murphy, Betsy	208	Myers, Thomas		303
Murphy, Ellmyra	344	Myers, Virgie		332
Murphy, George	208	Myers, Walter Allen		336
Murphy, Liddie	30	Myers, _____		105,218
Murphy, Will	172	Myhrs, Lottie		20
Murray, Belle	225	Nance, J.F.		37
Murray, Charles Ben	240	Nave, Abba		166
Murray, C.E.	240	Nave, Abbie		313
Murray, Elbert	282	Nave, Andy		70
Murray, Frank	240	Nave, A.J.		145
Murray, Hobert	310	Nave, Bennie		145
Murray, Infant	310	Nave, Bessie		181
Murray, Joseph	226	Nave, Brownlow C.		266
Murray, Lidia	226	Nave, Camel		356
Murray, Margaret C.	282	Nave, Claud		266
Murray, Mat S.	139	Nave, Coy		361
Murray, Thomas Clay	326	Nave, Coy E.		134
Murray, T.C.	141	Nave, Daisy		32
Murray, William	139	Nave, Dan		221
Murry, Belle	225	Nave, David		145,155,207
Musgrove, Margaret	206	Nave, Dessie		320
Myers, Annie	128	Nave, D.E.		124
Myers, Bruce	40	Nave, D.F.		120
Myers, Byon	128	Nave, Earl		114
Myers, C.C.	329	Nave, Edith Kate		358
Myers, Elizabeth	124	Nave, Eliza		209,276
Myers, Ellen	139,185,188	Nave, Elizabeth		57
Myers, Emma	358	Nave, Emma		107
Myers, Eugene	308	Nave, Eugin		124
Myers, Eva	184	Nave, Evelyn		223
Myers, George Albert	303	Nave, Forrest		266
Myers, Henry	37	Nave, F.D.		74,365
Myers, Hiram	185	Nave, Gay		287
Myers, Houston	128	Nave, George		32
Myers, Kennie Anyies	29	Nave, George		32,114,293
Myers, Lizzie	184	Nave, Grant		153,192
Myers, Lottie	20	Nave, Haynes		6

Nave, Henry	116,133
Nave, Henry L.	319
Nave, Herman	75
Nave, Hildred	259,361
Nave, Infant	11,13,221 300 <
Nave, Isaac	197,354
Nave, Isaac S.	259
Nave, James A.	143
Nave, James D.	256,326
Nave, James D. (Mrs)	326
Nave, James S.	31
Nave, Joe	266
Nave, Joel	143,187
Nave, Joel D.	319
Nave, John	358
Nave, John D.	272
Nave, John Folsom	272
Nave, Josie	162
Nave, Judson	114
Nave, Julian	155
Nave, J.B.	256
Nave, J.G.	197
Nave, J.T.	299
Nave, Lizzie	354
Nave, Luther Blane	129
Nave, Mack	166
Nave, Maggie	12,134
Nave, Manda	356
Nave, Marcella	32
Nave, Mary	56,120
Nave, Mary A.	319
Nave, Mary E.	153
Nave, McKinley	358
Nave, Minnie	261
Nave, Mollie	199
Nave, Nancy	344
Nave, Nat C., Jr.	265
Nave, N.C.	265
Nave, Pauline	70
Nave, Porter	143
Nave, Raman	31
Nave, Red	316
Nave, Robert	300
Nave, Roy Earl	316
Nave, Ruth	80,210
Nave, R.W.	129
Nave, Sallie	165
Nave, Sallie A.	313
Nave, Shelby	6
Nave, S.G.	117
Nave, Victoria	123
Nave, Vicy	202,293
Nave, Vina	124
Nave, Vinie	360
Nave, Wilbur Toney	187
Nave, William	75,145,254
Nave, W.E.	313
Nave, W.E. (Mrs)	211
Nave, W.J.	70,80
Nave, W.T.	60,114
Nave, ____	67
NcNeese, Susan	141
NcNeily, C.L.	63
Nead, Mathias	279
Neal, Infant	189
Neal, Roy A.	189
Neal, R.A.	203
Neal, ____	203
Nealy, Alva	123
Neatherly, Lillie	195
Nelson, Eliza A.	198
Nelson, Ellen	184
Nelson, Ezekiel	142
Nelson, Nancy	243
Netherlen, Nellie	218
Netherly, Lillie	304
Newton, Cale Emmert	222
Newton, Clifton	283
Newton, C.M.	249,257,258 311 <
Newton, David	222
Newton, David A.	283
Newton, David Thomas	249
Newton, D.A.	311
Newton, James	79,165
Newton, James Matison	283
Newton, Katie	165
Newton, Mary	83,354
Newton, ____	249
Nichols, John	231
Nichols, Samuel P.	231
Nidiffer, Alf	286,302
Nidiffer, Amanda	102
Nidiffer, Arthur	135
Nidiffer, Bessie	258

Nidiffer, Cecil	267,323	
Nidiffer, Cephas G.	184	
Nidiffer, Cordia	308	
Nidiffer, Elizabeth	26	
Nidiffer, Gracey Mae	310	
Nidiffer, Hattie	205	
Nidiffer, Heck	37	
Nidiffer, Hellen	184	
Nidiffer, Henry	135	
Nidiffer, Howard	323	
Nidiffer, Ina	161	
Nidiffer, Infant	6,191 267,286 <	
Nidiffer, James	255	
Nidiffer, Jennie	65	
Nidiffer, John	217	
Nidiffer, J.C.	225	
Nidiffer, Laura	358	
Nidiffer, Levi	67,122	
Nidiffer, Lizzie	303	
Nidiffer, Lowrence	225	
Nidiffer, Milisey	240	
Nidiffer, Mollie	76	
Nidiffer, Nancy	318	
Nidiffer, Nannie	85	
Nidiffer, Nelie	331	
Nidiffer, Nora	250	
Nidiffer, Robert	2,240	
Nidiffer, Robert L.	241	
Nidiffer, Roy	323	
Nidiffer, Ruby	230	
Nidiffer, Superb	286	
Nidiffer, S.T.	65	
Nidiffer, Will	191	
Nidiffer, William	135,241	
Nidiffer, William D.	217	
Nidiffer, W.G.	163	
Nidiffer, W.L.	164,184 268,331 <	
Nidiffer, ____	172,357	
Nififfer, Mary	6	
Nilson, John	130	
Noel, Jonithia	343	
Noel, William	343	
Noland, C.W.	144	
Noris, Clementine	187	
Noris, Hobart	228	
Noris, Infant	228	
Noris, Julie	187	
Norman, Elizabeth	257	
Norman, Henry T.	123	
Norman, John Wesley	364	
Norman, Julius Casper	364	
Norris, Abby	128	
Norris, Ailace	204	
Norris, Argeline L.	175	
Norris, Carline	330	
Norris, Hobart	228	
Norris, James	285	
Norris, Mary L.	338	
Norris, Rutha	285	
Norris, Washington F.	75	
Norris, Will	204	
Norris, W.A.	143	
Norris, ____	333	
Nunan, Thomas	343	
Nush, Carl	268	
Nush, Infant	268	
Oaks, Alice	47	
Oaks, Aubre Geneva	229	
Oaks, Berry	47	
Oaks, Bertha A.	95	
Oaks, Charlie	229	
Oaks, C.G.	284	
Oaks, Daniel	133	
Oaks, David	63,146	
Oaks, Edith	56	
Oaks, Elizabeth	63	
Oaks, Ethel	300	
Oaks, Finly	242	
Oaks, Gordon	336	
Oaks, H. Neer	361	
Oaks, H.N.	361	
Oaks, James	364	
Oaks, James R.	308	
Oaks, James S.	284	
Oaks, John	242	
Oaks, Julis	308	
Oaks, Julus	91	
Oaks, J.M. (Mrs)	360	
Oaks, J.S.	164	
Oaks, Lilian	235	
Oaks, Lucinda	164	
Oaks, Mamie	274	
Oaks, Mary	47	
Oaks, Mary Alice	20	

Oaks, Rebecca	364	
Oaks, Ruth A.	262	
Oaks, Sarah	308	
Oaks, Sarah Allen	63	
Oaks, Tessie G.	284	
Oaks, William A.	360	
Oaks, William Garman	91	
Oaks, W.C.	361	
Oaks, ____	216	
Odem, Hensley	48	
Odom, Ancil	161	
Odom, A.C.	149	
Odom, Biddie	109	
Odom, B.J.	82	
Odom, Custer	251	
Odom, Edkar	81	
Odom, Gerrett	212	
Odom, Hensley	48	
Odom, Infant	86	
Odom, Infant	110	
Odom, Infant	161	
Odom, Jessie	45	
Odom, Martha	212	
Odom, Mollie	363	
Odom, Rosie Estel	242	
Odom, Serhie	81	
Odom, Soloman	214,242	
Odom, Tempa	9	
Odom, Vici	160	
Odom, Vicie	69	
Odom, Vicy	83	
Odom, Waits	86,110	
Odum, Katie	323	
Oliver, Amy	10	
Oliver, Andy	6	
Oliver, Annie	179	
Oliver, Bertha L.	214	
Oliver, Betsy	265	
Oliver, Burgie	139,331 357 <	
Oliver, Charles	2,6,17 86,317,335 <	
Oliver, Daniel	202	
Oliver, Dave	241	
Oliver, Delma Eugene	360	
Oliver, Elijah D.	250	
Oliver, Eliza	106,288	
Oliver, Eliza Jane	146	
Oliver, Emma	354	
Oliver, Emmit	271	
Oliver, Eva	201	
Oliver, Flora	151	
Oliver, Floyd	126	
Oliver, Floyd Jasper	352	
Oliver, George	86	
Oliver, Grant	16	
Oliver, Hazel Bulah	157	
Oliver, Hooker	262	
Oliver, Hula	135	
Oliver, H.A.	155	
Oliver, Infant	6,16,17 66,67,253,342 <	
Oliver, Jackson	363	
Oliver, Jackson Jr.	363	
Oliver, James	128,157,241 250,289,357 <	
Oliver, James Allen	289	
Oliver, James H.	289	
Oliver, James Thomas	66	
Oliver, Jane	50,121	
Oliver, John	214,257	
Oliver, Joseph	364	
Oliver, Judson	145,196	
Oliver, J.M.	179	
Oliver, Laura	112	
Oliver, Lee	258,271	
Oliver, Lottie	18,214,345	
Oliver, Mary	254	
Oliver, Mary Jane	331	
Oliver, Mollie	289	
Oliver, Morrell	289	
Oliver, Nancy	86,245	
Oliver, Nannie	155	
Oliver, Nora	357	
Oliver, Oscar	16	
Oliver, Pat	112,126,241	
Oliver, Paulina	158	
Oliver, Pearl	36,145,196	
Oliver, Pollie	223	
Oliver, Rosa	17	
Oliver, Roy	253,257	
Oliver, Sallie	164	
Oliver, Selma	127	
Oliver, Shelby	139	
Oliver, Susan	66,86,225 236 <	

Oliver, Susie	114,242	Oxendine, Infant	351
Oliver, Taylor	352,360	Oxendine, James	91
Oliver, Tenie	62	Oxendine, Larkin	249
Oliver, Vice	268	Oxendine, Sarah J.	234
Oliver, Walter	127	Oxendine, Webb	342
Oliver, Warren	262	Oxendine, W.E.	312,351
Oliver, Will	165	O'Brien, Mary A.	73
Oliver, William	67	O'Donnell, John J.	264
Oliver, William	67,200	O'Donnell, Thomas A.	264
201,202,205,342,364 <		O'Neal, Cassie	288,293
Oliver, Winfield	128	O'Quinn, Andy	366
Oliver, ____	29,122,134	O'Quinn, Oliver	366
228,269,320	<	O'Quinn, Synthia	356
Olliver, Floyd Jasper	352	O'Quinn, Willoughby	366
Olliver, Taylor	352	Pain, Delie	128
Orr, Elizabeth	214	Pain, ____	128
Orr, Flora	61	Palmer, Joseph Felix	95
Orr, Infant	223	Palmer, Mary Rebecca	95
Orr, Jackson	228	Pardin, Vada	31
Orr, James	114	Pardue, Florence	275
Orr, James W.	298	Pardue, Jane	327
Orr, Mary	260	Pardue, J.M.	200
Orr, Polly	101	Pardue, Pearl	327,328
Orr, P.D.	228	Parham, Ezry	158
Orr, P.S.	214	Parham, Infant	158
Orr, Rebecca	286	Parker, Cora	146
Orr, Robert	114,223	Parker, Tina	176
Orr, William Howard	214	Parlier, Anthony	107
Orr, W.A.	114	Parlier, Arthur	107
Orr, W.B.	61	Parlier, Loyd Monroe	107
Orr, ____	145	Parmer, Catherine	213
Osborn, John	58	Parmer, N.C.	213
Osborn, Mae	294	Parrott, H.R. (Mrs)	245
Osborn, Mary	170	Parson, Elenor	97
Osborn, May	190	Parsons, Sarah	95
Osborn, Rosa	121	Partin, Ada Lee	342
Osborn, Samuel	58	Pate, Pearl	131,165,359
Osborne, Beckie	310	Pate, Vicie	336
Osborne, Catherine	107	Paters, Jim	307
Osborne, Hannah E.	52	Patterson, Infant	60
Osborne, John Alvin	263	Patterson, Margaret	286
Osborne, Walter Ray	263	Patterson, W.C.	60
Overholser, Polly	206	Patton, Bulia C.	294
Overland, Jane	329	Patton, Dave	314
Owens, Julia	344	Patton, Floy Veina	309
Owens, Rhoda	272	Patton, Frank	347
Oxendine, Edward	234	Patton, F.S.	85,309,346
Oxendine, Francis	312	Patton, Hugh	294,360

Patton, Joshua M.	209	Peoples, Rachel		136
Patton, Susan C.	34	Peoples, R.W.		172
Patton, S.E.	314	Peoples, Sam		206
Patton, Thomas Young	314	Percy, C.O.		37
Patton, T.Y.	209	Percy, Infant		37
Patton, _____	366	Perkins, Annis		114
Payne, Charity	68	Perkins, Charles		22
Payne, Delie	128	Perkins, Crede		333
Payne, Evaline	90	Perkins, Creet		269
Payne, Frank	231,272	Perkins, C.B.		298
Payne, James D.	223	Perkins, Dallas Earl		90
Payne, Luvenia	212	Perkins, Della		227
Payne, Mary	250,289	Perkins, Era Milling		177
Payne, Myrtle	272	Perkins, Florence		287
Payne, Nat	263	Perkins, G.		275
Payne, Nathaniel G.	231	Perkins, Jacob	63,168	
Payne, William G.	336	Perkins, James		80
Payne, Willie Forbes	272	Perkins, Joseph	168,177	
357	<	Perkins, Joseph C.		249
Payne, Zebulon	68	Perkins, J.C.	90,177	
Payne, _____	128	Perkins, Lula	175,176	
Peaks, Alfred	224	Perkins, Nancy		298
Peaks, J.T.	172	Perkins, Oscar		90
Pearce, Armstead P.	239	Perkins, Other		309
Pearce, C.C.	239	Perkins, Rachel	195,367	
Pearce, James M.	210	Perkins, Ruth		333
Pearce, Mae	159	Perkins, Sam		249
Pearce, Ollie	72	Perkins, Sarah Orr		298
Pearce, W.L.	210	Perkins, S.A.	62,63,237	
Peaters, Ed	349	Perkins, S.F.		352
Peaters, Elizabeth	349	Perkins, S.J.		80
Peebles, Andrew J.	159	Perkins, Wallace		25
Peebles, Clarissa H.	136	Perkins, William J,		62
Peebles, William	159	Perkins, William Rily		62
Peeks, Jerry	58	Perkins, William R.		63
Peeks, J.T.	176	Perkins, Wrily R.		249
Peeks, Presley	176	Perry, Andrew J.		89
Peeples, John	109	Perry, A.J.		63
Penington, Lula	310	Perry, Cora		1
Penix, John	249	Perry, David		131
Penix, Martha	249	Perry, Debby		224
Penland, Louise	86	Perry, Eliza		178
Penland, Monthia	86	Perry, Flora		210
Penland, W.M.	86	Perry, George		118
Peoples, Ervena	212	Perry, George M.		64
Peoples, John W.	159	Perry, George Sr.		78
Peoples, J.W.	136	Perry, Harrison		214
Peoples, Margaret	172	Perry, Homer		48

Perry, Homie	21	Persinger, R.T.	144,148
Perry, H.F.	350	Persy, Thomas	364
Perry, India	38	Peters, Alf	129,283
Perry, Infant	78,118	Peters, Alfred	235
Perry, Irelene	48	Peters, Angie	121
Perry, Isaac	62	Peters, Anna	166,197
Perry, James	64	Peters, Ben	96
Perry, James A.	350	Peters, Benjamin H.	327
Perry, John	360	Peters, Bill	121
Perry, John Henry	360	Peters, Blach	283
Perry, J.E.	131	Peters, Bula	98
Perry, J.T.	89	Peters, B.H.	301
Perry, Landon C.	111	Peters, Callie E.	304
Perry, Lester	259	Peters, Catherine	103
Perry, Lizzie	1	Peters, Charlotte	82
Perry, Margaret	324	Peters, Christopher C.	235
Perry, Marie	292	Peters, Clarence	33
Perry, Mary Anne	89	Peters, Cora	262
Perry, Nancy	69,297	Peters, Cordelia	169
Perry, Nat T.	64,178	Peters, Cresie	333
Perry, O.E.	182	Peters, C.C.	98,245,299
Perry, Pearl	182	Peters, Dan	283,301
Perry, Reta	214	Peters, Daniel	209
Perry, Rhoda	58,155	Peters, Ed	349
Perry, Sinda	336	Peters, Eliza	226
Perry, Thomas	111,161,164 214,259 <	Peters, Elizabeth	349
		Peters, Emily	251
Perry, Trixie	360	Peters, Emma	92,166,341
Perry, T.	324	Peters, E.L.	326
Perry, William	131,145 189 <	Peters, Fannie	134
		Peters, Fender	176,215
Perry, W.	145	Peters, Frank	292,311,327
Pers, Tilda	362	Peters, F.N.	70
Persinger, C.W.	292	Peters, Grace	326
Persinger, George	126	Peters, Green	217
Persinger, George A.	232	Peters, Henry	299
Persinger, G.H.	126,204	Peters, Ida	261
Persinger, Infant	15	Peters, Ike	209
Persinger, James L.	59	Peters, Infant	114,218
Persinger, John H.	126	Peters, Jack	307
Persinger, Julia	232	Peters, James	218
Persinger, Julia May	292	Peters, James C.	301
Persinger, Julia P.	145	Peters, Joan	327
Persinger, J.L.	351	Peters, John	180
Persinger, J.R.	340	Peters, John Gilbert	129
Persinger, Lewis	277	Peters, John W.	234,315 347 <
Persinger, Margaret	199		
Persinger, Pearl	364	Peters, J.N.	302

Peters, J.W.	215,217,266	Phillips, John Wesley	36
Peters, Lorina	226	Phillips, Matilda	25
Peters, Lorrie	61	Phillips, William	104
Peters, Lottie	334	Phillips, W.O.	63,112
Peters, Louisa	331	Phipps, Betty	330
Peters, Lyddia	92	Phipps, Charley	360
Peters, Lydia	145	Phipps, Daniel	137,139
Peters, Maggie	32	Phipps, Elizabeth	217
Peters, Mary Ann	301	Phipps, Infant	137,139
Peters, Matilda	288	Phipps, Logan	217,360
Peters, Mike	261	Phipps, Manley	330
Peters, Mort	235	Phipps, Pete	330
Peters, Nancy	96	Phipps, Peter	360
Peters, Nora C.	266	Pierce, Ada	179
Peters, Pausy	180	Pierce, Adas	130
Peters, Pearl	162	Pierce, Ader	129
Peters, Pheba	180	Pierce, Allen	254
Peters, Powell	98,114	Pierce, Amstead	99
Peters, Rebecca	209,228	Pierce, A.C.	264,294,341
Peters, Reubin	245	Pierce, Charles	121
Peters, Robert G.	275	Pierce, C. Arthur	285
Peters, Robert H.	304	Pierce, Dan	224,329
Peters, Rosa	69,303	Pierce, Delcenia	346
Peters, R.G. Jr.	275	Pierce, Dicie	69
Peters, R.H.	234,245,304	Pierce, D.T.	227
Peters, Sarah Frazier	233	Pierce, Edith	329
Peters, Sarah S.	342	Pierce, Edith M.	341
Peters, Stant	315	Pierce, Edna	261
Peters, Thomas	311	Pierce, Edward	12
Peters, Thomas Wilson	121	Pierce, Eliz	135
Peters, T.M.	179	Pierce, Eliza	118
Peters, T.N.	347	Pierce, Ethel	191,268
Peters, Wiley	215	Pierce, E.M.	163
Peters, Will	277	Pierce, E.S.	285
Peters, William	160,162	Pierce, Flora Annice	102
197	<	Pierce, Franklin M.	112
Peters, William H.	234	Pierce, George M.	112,232
Peters, W.C.	217,221	268	<
Peters, W.M.	180	Pierce, Grant	75,85
Philips, Sindie	185	Pierce, Griffin	191
Philips, W.O.	224	Pierce, Guy Buteir	4
Phillips, Alice	99,251	Pierce, G.C.	341
Phillips, Assa	130	Pierce, Henry	87,146,205
Phillips, A.A.	25	224,254,261	<
Phillips, Blaine (Mrs)	318	Pierce, Hobert	321
Phillips, George	56	Pierce, Hubert	6
Phillips, G.W.	245	Pierce, H.S.	117
Phillips, Isaac	130,318	Pierce, Ida May	293

Pierce, Ina		264	Pierce, T.		162
Pierce, Infant		3,84,178	Pierce, Vadie		50
Pierce, Iva		168,294	Pierce, Vica		98
Pierce, Jackson		363	Pierce, Victoria		275
Pierce, James		61	Pierce, Wilburn		135
Pierce, James Claude		61	Pierce, Wilburn Paul		135
Pierce, Joe		303	Pierce, William		68,116
Pierce, John		178	226		<
Pierce, John R. (Mrs)		206	Pierce, William A.D.		52
Pierce, Joseph		285	Pierce, William C.		147
Pierce, Julia		95,346	Pierce, Willie Mae		87
Pierce, Julia C.		227	Pierce, W.B.		130
Pierce, J.A.		206	Pierce, W.C.		64,99,147
Pierce, J.C.		100,226	191		<
Pierce, J.F.M.		293	Pierce, Zoh		2
Pierce, J.G.		75	Pierce, _____		296,318
Pierce, J.H.		219,221	Pierson, Alex		125
Pierce, Kate		162	Pierson, Walter		125
Pierce, Lettie		230	Pilkerson, Christine		202
Pierce, Lewis		29	Pilkerson, Enick		187
Pierce, Lillie		149	Pilkerson, Filmore		202
Pierce, L.L.		337	Pilkerton, Dora		102
Pierce, Martha		116	Pilkerton, Infant		102
Pierce, Mary		185	Pilketon, E.P.		225
Pierce, Mary Anner		117	Pilketon, Lizzie		225
Pierce, Mary Ellen		226	Pilks, Julia		204
Pierce, Mary Jane		345	Pilktson, Clemtine		285
Pierce, Minnie		99	Pippin, A.J.		315
Pierce, Mollie		198,199	Pippin, Frank		81
Pierce, Nancy L.		147	Pippin, Franklin		235
Pierce, Nathaniel		13	Pippin, Henry		119
Pierce, Nick		321	Pippin, Infant		81,235
Pierce, Phoba J.		254	Pippin, John Wesley		119
Pierce, Rebecca		99,147	Pippin, J.W.		59
Pierce, Rena		303	Pippin, Okie		235
Pierce, Rhoda		64	Pippin, Patsy		83
Pierce, Richard		118,337	Pippin, S.B.		119
Pierce, Rina		105	Pircy, H.F.		160
Pierce, Robert H.		102,337	Pitts, Nancy		299
Pierce, R.H. (Mrs)		207	Pitts, Vina		285
Pierce, R.M.		61,84,110	Plaster, James Auston		292
Pierce, Sallie		261	Plaster, Newton		292
Pierce, Sarah		296	Platt, Leander		174
Pierce, Sarah E.		217	Pleasant, Andy J.		114
Pierce, Selina		189	Pleasant, Carl		362
Pierce, Tennessee		363	Pleasant, Harry		362
Pierce, Tilda		362	Pleasant, Joseph		100
Pierce, Tina		108	Pleasant, Samuel J.		100

Plott, Leander	173	Potter, Mirfie		17
Poe, Maggie	339	Potter, Mollie		123
Pope, George	172	Potter, Murphey		234
Porch, Susie	288	Potter, Murphy		17,185
Poston, M.E.	63	Potter, Noah		53,194,271
Potter, Alfred Taylor	222	Potter, Paul		298
Potter, Brownlow	352	Potter, Peter		130,161,364
Potter, Caric	276	Potter, Peter H.		161
Potter, Catherine	129,320	Potter, Robert		365
Potter, Clayton	356	Potter, Rosa A.		245
Potter, Dan	269,304	Potter, Rosalee		133
Potter, Daniel	81,203,298	Potter, Roxie		250
Potter, Dave	185	Potter, Sam		123
Potter, David	234	Potter, Samuel		234
Potter, Delia	280	Potter, Sarah E.		262
Potter, Dewey	364	Potter, Soloman		344
Potter, Dick	81	Potter, Sylvania		19
Potter, Dillie May	47	Potter, Will		133
Potter, Dorothy	46	Potter, William		29,245
Potter, D.D.	296	Potter, William Hugh		342
Potter, D.H.	222,271	Potter, ____		92,131,356
Potter, Eliza	211	Powel, Nancy		62
Potter, Ellen	34,92,360	Powell, Eliza Jane		255
Potter, E.A.	100,222	Powell, Infant		63
Potter, E.B.	19	Powell, Jacob		63
Potter, E.J.	79	Powell, Johnie		46
Potter, Frank Ray	364	Powell, Nancy		63,168,337
Potter, George	185,219	Powell, Stewart		63
Potter, Gracie	19	Powell, W.B.		337
Potter, Gurney	219	Powell, ____		340
Potter, Ham	324,347	Powers, Hazel		41
Potter, Hannah	134	Powlard, Clarence		33
Potter, Hester	203	Presnell, Catherine		142
Potter, Infant	296,324	Presnell, Florence		190
351,364	<	Presnell, Garfield		55
Potter, Isabel	18	Presnell, Henry		281
Potter, Jackson	262	Presnell, Infant		308,310
Potter, Jannie	365	Presnell, James M.		352
Potter, John	161,285,287	Presnell, Joyce E.		312
Potter, Josie	54	Presnell, Link		310
Potter, J.M.	18	Presnell, Nathan		352
Potter, Lillie	81	Presnell, Ramon		352
Potter, Lillie Beth	344	Presnell, Roy Hill		190
Potter, Lon	280	Presnell, Ruth		143
Potter, Lucy	285	Presnell, R.J.		308,312
Potter, Martha	289	Presnell, R.M.		352
Potter, Mary	17	Presnell, Sam		190
Potter, Millard	342,351	Presnell, Sincon		142

Preston, Annie M.	184		Prichet, John	248
Preston, J.W.	184		Prichet, Louise	158
Preston, Pleasant	3,4,19		Prichet, Mave	248
Price, Albert	191		Prichett, Annie	148
Price, Allen	275		Pridghead, T.S.	157
Price, Amos	234,270		Pritchard, Annie	243
Price, Andy	151		Pritchard, Bessie	151
Price, Charles L.	153,260		Pritchard, James	170
Price, C.H.	366		Pritchard, Jim	149
Price, Della	342		Pritchard, John	151
Price, Emaline	37		Pritchard, Myrtle	355
Price, Fred	39		Pritchard, Patsy	91
Price, James Taylor	60		Pritchard, Thomas L.	243
Price, Joe	221		Pritchard, Willie	151
Price, John	270,338		Pritchell, Lorrie	147
Price, John C.	275		Proffitt, Juritta	260
Price, Leona G.	275		Proffitt, Thomas J.	175
Price, Lowisie	213		Proffitt, Thomas J.	210
Price, Mary	250		Profit, ___	235
Price, Mary Jane	275		Pugart, Milfred (Mrs)	63
Price, Mordci	60		Pugh, Elmer	247
Price, Rosa	191,278		Pugh, May	278
Price, Rosanna	191,234		Pugh, Rachel	323
Price, R.R.	323		Pugh, William	206
Price, Sam	60		Pugh, W.T.	247
Price, Sarah	112,192		Pugh, Zachary	247
Price, Thomas	213,221		Raberts, Mary	180
Price, Thomas C., Sr.	323		Radford, Austin	120
Price, T.C., Jr.	323		Radford, Cordia	223
Price, Wiley	270		Radford, Vera	120
Price, William	151		Rainbolt, Anna C.	332
Prichard, Cordie	180		Rainbolt, Caroline	192
Prichard, Edmond	16		Rainbolt, Dana	252
Prichard, Eik	253		Rainbolt, Dugger	247
Prichard, Hester	180		Rainbolt, Ethel	176
Prichard, James	120		Rainbolt, James T.	247
Prichard, Jerry	239		Rainbolt, John	192
Prichard, John	139,253		Rainbolt, Mattie	210
Prichard, M.F.	139		Rainbolt, Novella	252
Prichard, Nellie	239		Rainbolt, Ola	270
Prichard, Rosan	275		Rainbolt, William B.	252
Prichard, Sarah	84		Raines, James	360
Prichard, Sidney	63		Raines, Lillie	360
Prichard, Thomas	139		Rains, Amanda M.	164
Prichard, Tomas	63		Rains, Annie	102
Prichell, Alf	147		Rains, Bessie	172
Prichet, Annie	96		Rains, Charlie	207
Prichet, Cresie	74		Rains, Clyde	123

Rains, Dortha	330
Rains, D.K.	123
Rains, Eliza	320
Rains, James	176,320
Rains, Jess	330
Rains, Lucy	172
Rains, Presley	172,176
Rains, Will	176
Rambo, J.W.	277
Rambo, N.D.	277
Ramsey, Clyde	97
Ramsey, Hellen	181
Ramsey, H.R.	109
Ramsey, Infant	327
Ramsey, Joe E.	181
Ramsey, Joseph	327
Ramsey, Laura	109
Ramsey, Mirah	61
Randolf, Thomas	136
Randolph, Ruben	236
Range, Arnold	319,361
Range, Charles	235
Range, C.J.	348
Range, Ettie	93
Range, Grant	318
Range, G.M.	235
Range, Hanry	106
Range, Hascal	93
Range, Henry	215
Range, Hettie	200
Range, Hugh	335
Range, H.H.	23
Range, Infant	319,361
Range, Jacob	171
Range, Jake	319,361
Range, James	7
Range, Jerry B.	43
Range, J.M.	348
Range, J.S.E.	124,130,135
Range, J.T.	343
Range, Kate	200
Range, Leonard Eugene	335
Range, Lidia Ann	145
Range, Louisa	309
Range, Manna	21
Range, Mary Jane	171
Range, Maude	207,285
Range, Myrtle	285,286
Range, Nat K.	348
Range, Peter	141,306
Range, P.G.	104
Range, Robert	78
Range, Robert A.	24
Range, R.A.	62,69,78,118
	291,320 <
Range, R.A. (Mrs)	190
Range, Sarah E.	336
Range, Sarah F.	78
Range, W.A.	93
Range, Zena	56
Rasar, Ana Pearl	12
Rash, Callie	259
Rash, Daniel	216
Rash, Infant	5,6,16
Rash, Johnie	16
Rash, L.R.	5,6,16
Rasor, Barsheba	293
Rasor, Infant	235
Rasor, I.W.	263
Rasor, Margaret	263
Rasor, Snyder	235
Ratler, ____	225
Ratterman, Mary	271
Ray, Henry	136
Razor, J.N. (Mrs)	255
Reagan, Calvin	85
Red, Rena	269
Red, Walter	269
Rederick, Cora	340
Rederick, John	340
Rednick, Cheny	59
Redrick, Afric	340
Redrick, Cora	315
Reece, Daniel L.	305
Reece, Dora	278
Reece, Eliza	367
Reece, Isaac V.	260
Reece, James F.	305
Reece, M.B.	132
Reece, Sarah Ellen	366
Reed, Elliot S.	138
Reed, Robert E.	195
Reed, Thomas	311
Reed, Wesley	195
Reese, Valentine	276
Reeves, Rhoda E.	112

Renfro, D.S.	69	Richardson, Angy	325
Renfro, Ganus W.	270	Richardson, Annie	253
Renfro, H.M.	302	254	<
Renfro, James	270	Richardson, A.J.	15, 173
Renfro, James W.	73	Richardson, Bob	99
Renfro, Joseph C.	73	Richardson, Butler	332
Renfro, W.H.	291	Richardson, Carrie	189
Reynolds, Andrew	152	Richardson, Cass	101
Reynolds, Beulah E.	98	Richardson, Dan	6
Reynolds, Elizabeth	152	Richardson, Daniel	188
Reynolds, Eva	61	Richardson, Darriel	227
Reynolds, James	98	Richardson, Dealie	339
Reynolds, J.A.	38	Richardson, Dela	67
Reynolds, Lannie	152	Richardson, Delaney	16
Reynolds, S.E.	152,337	Richardson, Delany	285
Rhea, Charles Jessie	218	Richardson, Docia	215
Rhea, William	218	217	<
Rhes, Francis	48	Richardson, Donley	353
Rhodi, Barbara	279	Richardson, Donley H.	353
Rhudy, Carrie Dungur	255	Richardson, Dora	177
Rhudy, L.M.	255	Richardson, Eliza	59,93
Rhymer, Leuse	50	216	<
Ribbs, Bob	155	Richardson, Elizabeth	261
Ricahrs, Raman	341	Richardson, Ellen M.	185
Ricardson, Earnest	330	Richardson, Ellie	16
Rice, Crandell Jack	344	Richardson, Ernest	112
Rice, John	344	140	<
Rice, W.A.	119	Richardson, George	309
Rich, Boon	101	Richardson, G.W.	287,299
Rich, May	101	Richardson, Hannah	140
Richard, Susan	114	Richardson, Herman A.	148
Richard, Susan	117	Richardson, H.P.	299
Richard, ____	347	Richardson, H.T.	66
Richards, Ben	137	Richardson, Infant	6,16
Richards, Carrie	153	33,101,139	<
Richards, Cinda	119	Richardson, James	287
Richards, F.W. (Mrs)	227	Richardson, Jane	33
Richards, Griff	119	Richardson, Jeme	341
Richards, Herman	178	Richardson, Jesse	139
Richards, Infant	341	Richardson, John	341
Richards, Jane E.	227	Richardson, John W.	289
Richards, Jim	178	Richardson, Joseph	95
Richards, Lola Maud	281	Richardson, Joseph T.	140
Richards, Pearl	119	Richardson, J. Alford	299
Richards, Raymond	341	Richardson, J.J.	70,167
Richards, Susy	309	Richardson, Kate	5
Richardson, Alf	148	Richardson, Larance	285
Richardson, Alice	67	Richardson, Lizzie	33,131

Richardson, Loss	76,314	
Richardson, Ludley	314	
Richardson, Lutishia	76	
Richardson, Marthy	323	
Richardson, Mary	323	
Richardson, Mary L.	309	
Richardson, Miley	277	
Richardson, Milton	239	
Richardson, Moriah	66	
Richardson, Nancy	63,70	
Richardson, Noa	323	
Richardson, Noah	67	
Richardson, Other	287	
Richardson, Phoebe	335	
Richardson, Rachel	138	
Richardson, Saley	323	
Richardson, Sam	76,177	
Richardson, Samuel	177	
Richardson, Susie	309	
Richardson, Thomas	139	
188,239,287,289,309 <		
Richardson, Will	332	
Richardson, William H.	112	
Richardson, William W.	299	
Richarson, Ganes W.	332	
Richarson, Thomas	309	
Riddle, George	329	
Riddle, J.A.	329	
Riddle, M.D.	329	
Riggins, Nancy	220	
Riggs, Bertha	297	
Riggs, Bob	188,189	
Riggs, James Harmon	151	
Riggs, Julia	305	
Riggs, Mollie	155,189	
Riggs, Robert	151	
Riggs, R.G.	279	
Riggs, Sarra Taylor	279	
Riley, James	218	
Riley, Rosane	145	
Riley, William	94	
Ritchie, Alvin	220,256	
Ritchie, Andrew	88,291	
308	<	
Ritchie, A.B.	276	
Ritchie, A.P.	216	
Ritchie, A.S.	220	
Ritchie, David	276	
Ritchie, David C.	246	
Ritchie, David E.	225	
Ritchie, Dora	100,126	
Ritchie, D.E.	132	
Ritchie, Elbert	88	
Ritchie, Elizabeth	118	
Ritchie, Esther	118	
Ritchie, Frona	209,283	
Ritchie, Infant	5,74,118	
216,225,256,308	<	
Ritchie, James	14	
Ritchie, J.P.	220	
Ritchie, Lester	13	
Ritchie, Mamie	13	
Ritchie, Marie Jane	203	
Ritchie, Mollie	5	
Ritchie, Sarah	146	
Ritchie, Thomas	118	
Ritchie, T.J.	246	
Ritchie, Will	74	
Ritchie, William	29	
Ritchie, W.B.	246	
Ritchie, W.B.	329	
Ritchie, W.C.	132,291	
Ritchie, ___	217	
Roark, Emmett	157	
Roark, Ora	50	
Roark, Timothy	333	
Roarks, Susan	333	
Roarks, Timothy	333	
Robers, Mary	178	
Roberson, Axie	307	
Roberson, Axie M.	349	
Roberson, Clarence	259	
Roberson, Clyde	250	
Roberson, C.S.	131	
Roberson, Infant	131,250	
259	<	
Roberson, T.H.	250	
Robert, Allen	100	
Roberts, Allen	208	
Roberts, Arthur	181,182	
Roberts, A.R.	167	
Roberts, Bill	234	
Roberts, Burt	183,322	
Roberts, Calloway	90	
Roberts, Calloway (Ms)	90	
Roberts, Cinda	167	

Roberts, Coon (Mrs)	9	Roberts, Sarah F.	237
Roberts, Dewey	155	Roberts, Sarah Jane	169
Roberts, Dick	258	Roberts, Tina	9
Roberts, Dudley	320	Roberts, Vestal	181
Roberts, D.J.	322	Roberts, Walter	26
Roberts, Earl	182	Roberts, Will	196
Roberts, Edd	62	Roberts, Will W.	83
Roberts, Edgar	7	Roberts, William	115
Roberts, Eliza	297	Roberts, William C.	258
Roberts, Ellen	122,304	Roberts, William E.	310
Roberts, Ernest	350	Roberts, Willie	62
Roberts, Fletcher P.	316	Roberts, Willis H.	320
Roberts, George	83	Roberts, W.C.	93,102,310
Roberts, George D.	93,295	Roberts, W.W.	206,304
332	<	Robertson, Callie	6
Roberts, Ham	146	Robertson, George W.	213
Roberts, Harry D.	322	Robertson, Joseph	163
Roberts, Hattie	179	Robertson, J.T.	218
Roberts, Henderson	93	Robertson, Lena	203
Roberts, Hildred J.	310	Robertson, Mary A.	163
Roberts, Hutchins	75	Robertson, Myrtle	27
Roberts, Infant	9,350	Robertson, Roy Edward	218
Roberts, Isaac	183	Robertson, Virginia	213
Roberts, Jennie	206,258	Robinson, Chris	323
Roberts, John	75,90,179	Robinson, James D.	232
180,304,316	<	Robinson, James Frank	178
Roberts, John H.	94	Robinson, James W.	350
Roberts, Johnie	196	Robinson, Jess	358
Roberts, Josie	62	Robinson, Joseph	112
Roberts, Joyce	322	Robinson, Julia	135
Roberts, Julia	102	Robinson, J.C.	178
Roberts, J.H.	239	Robinson, Mary	190
Roberts, Kate King	316	Robinson, M.P.	41
Roberts, Lillian E.	295	Robinson, Nancy	23
Roberts, Loyd	332	Robinson, Nannie J.	85
Roberts, Lydia	88,284	Robinson, N.D.	209
Roberts, L.	115	Robinson, Sampson	180
Roberts, Mary	101,180,180	Robinson, Zillie	277
201,283,362	<	Robison, Charles	266
Roberts, Nancy	75	Robson, N.D.	265
Roberts, Rebecca	61	Rockhard, ...	64
Roberts, Rebecca M.	271	Rockholds, Sallie	60
Roberts, Rhoda	94	Roe, Etta	273
Roberts, Riley	239	Roe, Linnie	173
Roberts, Robert Elmer	310	Rogers, Carry Stella	213
Roberts, Rose M.	159	Rogers, Charley (Mrs)	350
Roberts, Russell	148,155	Rogers, Mary	186,193
332	<	Rogers, Mary Virginia	178

Rogers, William	178
Rogers, William W.	193
Rogers, W.G.	213
Rogers, W.W.	186
Rogers, Yetta	186
Roiston, Johua	324
Roiston, Mary	324
Rominger, Bessie	195
Rominger, D.C.	363
Rosenbalm, Frank	331
Rosenbalm, Mandie	25
Rosenbalm, Sam	331
Rosenbaum, Jasper	177
Rosenbaum, M.L.	177
Rosenbaum. C.B.	107
Roten, Hannah	135
Roten, Mary	224
Rotler, Eliza	224
Roton, Elizabeth	249
Roton, Hannah	135
Rouse, J.W.	162
Rouse, Martha	359
Rowe, Basmath Emaline	136
Rowe, Elizabeth	40
Rowe, Elizabeth Clark	281
Rowe, John L.	136
Rowe, Linnie	173
Rowe, L.D.	227
Rowe, L.L.	136,281
Rowe, Robert R.	134
Rowe, R.W.	134
Rowton, Hannah	135
Royal, Carrie	69
Royal, Clyde	58
Royal, Jim	272
Royal, Lillie	310
Royal, Lilly	140
Royal, Mary	137
Royal, Rebecca	232
Royal, Vance	58,190,272
Royal, Willie	190
Royal, ____	190
Royston, Isaac	250
Royston, J.M.	250
Royston, Mary E.	250
Royston, Polly	250
Ruble, Mary	60
Rumbly, J.E. (Mrs)	296
Rumley, Bessie	213
Rush, Sam	298
Rusle, Alfred	40
Russel, James H.	52
Russell, Cassie	196
Russell, Clara	363
Russell, Eliza	259
Russell, Infant	140
Russell, James H.	57
Russell, Jeff	229
Russell, Jim	81
Russell, Maggie	81
Russell, M.	95,127
Russell, Nancy Ann	140
Russell, Rhoda	191
Russell, T.D.	39
Russell, Walter	259
Russell, William	140
Russle, Alfred	40
Rutledge, John	223
Rutledge, William	223
Rutlidge, William D.	191
Ryan, Annie Grace	187
Ryan, Elizabeth	98
Ryan, Eva Margaret	188
Ryan, Frank M. (Mrs)	295
Ryan, George W.	98
Ryan, John	188
Ryan, John F.	129
Ryan, Sallie	321
Sadler, Betty	107
Sallings, Polly	311
Salor, J.W.	306
Salts, Alice	213
Salts, Carrie	134
Salts, Catherine	124
Salts, John	117
Salts, Susan	117
Sames, J.	321
Sammons, Alice	318
Sampson, Joe	127
Sams, Berry	149,178
Sams, Carrie	282
Sams, Evert	165
Sams, Infant	153,300,322
Sams, Johney	149
Sams, Katie	168
Sams, Lee	153,165,316

Sams, Owen E.	316	Scott, Bersha	204
Sams, R.M.	153	Scott, Betty	155
Sams, Sallie	117	Scott, David	97
Sams, Silas	300,322	Scott, E.E.	322
Sams, W.S.	315	Scott, Frank Jr.	234
Sanders, Edith	317	Scott, Franklin	142,234
Sanders, Floyd	130		321 <
Sanders, Julia	239	Scott, George	334
Sanders, Louil	208	Scott, Gerogia Marion	222
Sanders, Mollie	190	Scott, Harriett	261
Sanders, Richard H.	130	Scott, Hazel Viloa	210
Sat..., Nat	4	Scott, Howard B.	222
Saylor, Flanders	118	Scott, Ida	191
Saylor, Hupert	44	Scott, John M.	334
Saylor, James O.	118	Scott, K.A.B.	191
Saylor, May A.	219	Scott, Lilian	142
Saylor, Noah	44	Scott, Love	87
Scalf, Angeline	267	Scott, Marshall	321,334
Scalf, Bert	77	Scott, Mary	70
Scalf, Bessie	197	Scott, Ray	322
Scalf, Charles	338	Scott, Ross R.	234
Scalf, C.M.	351	Scott, Roy Dexter	144
Scalf, Dave	93	Scott, Thurman	317
Scalf, David	60,309	Scott, Tom	210
Scalf, Dunie	267	Scott, William	44,144
Scalf, Elizabeth	266	Scott, Willie	317
Scalf, Ellen	351	Scott, W.F.	222
Scalf, Gasta	338	Sdipery, Margaret	118
Scalf, Infant	134	Seabock, Infant	191
Scalf, James	134	Seabock, Roy	191
Scalf, James M.	60	Seanner, Eva	280
Scalf, John Eddie	307	Searcy, Anna	280
Scalf, Maggie	149	Seigle, James Edward	262
Scalf, Margarie A.	267	Seigler, John M.	239
Scalf, Mary Elizabeth	309	Seigler, Mary Alice	239
Scalf, Myrtle E.M.	261	Seiney, Mary E.	253
Scalf, Nannie	116	Sellars, J.M.	230
Scalf, Ruby	174	Sellars, Sallie	292
Scalf, S.D.	106	Sellars, Soloman	259
Scalf, Tissue	307	Shade, Minnie	147,174
Scalf, William	266	Shade, Susa	127
Scalf, _____	174	Shankel, Frank	114
Schnider, Nancy	262	Shankle, Eunice	114
Scoggins, Annie E.	311	Sharp, Adellia	133
Scoggins, Arthor	311	Sharp, Deborah	227
Scoggins, Charlie	199	Sharp, Dora	5
Scoggins, Edith	199	Sharp, Lena	139
Scoggins, Emry	51	Sharp, W.H.	133

Shaw, Albert	186	Shell, Fletcher	237
Shaw, Callie	152	Shell, Florence Ettie	115
Shaw, D.M.	186	Shell, George Henry	267
Shaw, Franklin (Mrs)	143	Shell, George H.	198
Shaw, John	121	Shell, Grace	198
Shaw, Katie	200	Shell, Hannah A.	283
Shaw, Marie Catherine	121	Shell, Harrett E.	80
Shaw, Thomas	186	Shell, Harrison	100,324
Shea, Amanda	13	Shell, Henry	161,199,359
Shea, Elizabeth	13	Shell, Honer	333
Shea, George	13	Shell, Hubert	93,119,205
Shea, Infant	13	229	<
Shear, John	111	Shell, Hurbert	119
Shear, Stella	111	Shell, H.F.	274
Sheets, Mary E.	211	Shell, Infant	91,93,115
Sheets, Nancy	291,340	199,244,267,285,	>
Sheets, Young	19,211	286,294,361	<
Sheetz, Elizabeth	159	Shell, James	95,207
Sheffield, C.J.	314	Shell, James A.	33
Shell, Allen P.	150	Shell, James B.	41
Shell, Alvin	110	Shell, James S.	100
Shell, Andrew Allen	229	Shell, Jane E.	64
Shell, Andy	141,158,291	Shell, Joe E.	110
Shell, A.J.	207	Shell, John	91,180,241
Shell, Belle	2	273,333	<
Shell, Bernon	45	Shell, John A.	213
Shell, Bertha	131	Shell, John L.	241
Shell, Bob	64	Shell, Laura	341
Shell, Bula	213	Shell, Linda	187
Shell, Calie Mildred	11	Shell, Lydie E.	292
Shell, Canan	32	Shell, Maggie	78,301
Shell, Carle Thomas	205	Shell, Martha	325
Shell, Cerie	324	Shell, Mary Ann	158
Shell, Charles	244	Shell, Mattie	275
Shell, Cruss	267	Shell, Mollie	95,235
Shell, Dalice	324	Shell, Monta E.	110
Shell, Danil	237	Shell, Montie	223
Shell, David	274	Shell, Nancy J.	273
Shell, Debbie	141	Shell, Nannie Leona	292
Shell, Ed	292,294	Shell, Nathaniel C.	34
Shell, Edna	108	Shell, Noah T.	115
Shell, Effie	62	Shell, Ollie	72,359
Shell, Essie Mable	119	Shell, Polly	147
Shell, E.	367	Shell, Revel	47
Shell, Faitha	229	Shell, Rody	193
Shell, Farthey	205	Shell, Sam	267
Shell, Fathie	205	Shell, Sinda	33
Shell, Fitzhue	273	Shell, Stella	169

Shell, Suda	185	Shortt, ____		249
Shell, Tine	23	Shoun, A. Lincoln		70
Shell, T.	203	Shoun, Beatrice		353
Shell, Walter	18	Shoun, Clyde R.		300
Shell, Walter (Mrs)	207	Shoun, D.R.		339
Shell, William	158	Shoun, Elizabeth		141
Shell, William H.	274,368	Shoun, Fred		70
Shell, William L.	361	Shoun, George		141,265
Shell, William M.	158	Shoun, Harry		141
Shell, Willie	285,286	Shoun, J. Malcolm		353
Shell, W.D.	147,207,241	Shoun, J.B.		160,169,222
Shell, ____	77	Shoun, Landon		300
Shell, ____ Ann	215	Shoun, Margaret		289
Shelley, Adaline	363	Shoun, Martha		208
Shelton, John F.	268	Shoun, Nan		218
Shepard, Jacob	196	Shoun, Powell		141,181,289
Shepard, Rexter	196	Shoun, Robert Earl		265
Shepard, Woodfin	22	Shoun, R.D.		339
Shepherd, Frankie	113	Shoun, Thomas Justa		339
Shepherd, Jacob	344	Shuffield, Alf		358
Shepherd, J.A.	113	Shuffield, Alice		209,233
Sheppard, Clarence	356	Shuffield, Bertha		311
Sheppard, Clarence N.	356	Shuffield, Clary		88
Sheppard, Cruin	362	Shuffield, Coose		88
Sheppard, Hele	356	Shuffield, Corley		17
Sheppard, Infant	356	Shuffield, Dora		19
Sheppard, J.B.	362	Shuffield, Elizabeth		158
Sheppard, Phil	238	Shuffield, Ethel		353
Sheppard, Richmond	107	Shuffield, George		136,358
Sheppard, Rosa	269	Shuffield, G.G.		136
Sheppard, W.M.	362	Shuffield, James		18
Shepperd, Rosa	71	Shuffield, John G.		137
Shipley, Corintha	361	Shuffield, L.C.		32,208
Shipley, Corrintha	363	Shuffield, Mary		179,302
Shipley, Fred	123	Shuffield, May		208,303
Shipley, J.M.L.	123	Shuffield, Nancy Jane		179
Shipley, J.M.	123	Shuffield, William E.		136
Shipley, Maggie	114	Shuffield, ____		88
Shipley, Nellie	351	Shuler, Fred		117
Shipley, Ollie	227,263	Shuler, Hank		117
	282 <	Shuler, Houk		117
Shoemaker, Ella	193	Shull, Alice		215
Shoemaker, Joel	365	Shull, Caroline		108
Shoemaker, Polly	365	Shull, Edgar		359
Short, Catherine	321	Shull, Erest		309
Short, E.S.	168	Shull, Infant		334
Short, John H.	168	Shull, Joe		277
Short, Mary	237	Shull, John		108

Shull, Nora		338	Simerly, John Hande		90
Shull, Steward		334,359	Simerly, June H.		346
Shull, S.H.		309,338	Simerly, J.B.		278
Shull, William		349	Simerly, J.C.		180
Shupe, Emma Love		315	Simerly, J.H.		174
Shupe, Gay		108	Simerly, J.L.		286
Shupe, Infant		122	Simerly, J.S.		105
Shupe, Isaac		108,122,194	Simerly, Lena Helen		151
Shupe, Virginia A.		194	Simerly, Lillie		21
Sigla, John M.		262	Simerly, Lou		245
Sigler, Lillie E.		120	Simerly, Mammie		364
Simerly, Annie Evley		131	Simerly, Maney M.		224
Simerly, Arvel Scott		104	Simerly, Martha		362
Simerly, Bertie		219	Simerly, Martin		104
Simerly, Bettie		140,295	Simerly, Mary		229
Simerly, Carl		157	Simerly, Mary F.		255
Simerly, Charlie		131	Simerly, Mary Jane		266
Simerly, Clayton		305	Simerly, Mattie		1
Simerly, Clyde		27	Simerly, Maud		246
Simerly, Cordie		322	Simerly, Millie		168
Simerly, Crisley		21	Simerly, Millie Holly		168
Simerly, C.R.		301	Simerly, Milt		364
Simerly, Dan		126	Simerly, Nancy		339
Simerly, Daniel		1	Simerly, Nat		16,243
Simerly, Dautan		96	Simerly, Onie		92
Simerly, David A.		224	Simerly, Paul		346
Simerly, David C.		286	Simerly, Polly		324
Simerly, David H.		151	Simerly, Ray		57
Simerly, Dora		323	Simerly, Rhoda		101,181
Simerly, D.H.		151	Simerly, Robert L.		160
Simerly, Elizabeth		144	Simerly, Rossie		104
Simerly, Elmer		69	Simerly, R.S.		280
Simerly, Emeline		133	Simerly, Sam		83
Simerly, Emma		123	Simerly, Sam E.		168
Simerly, Ethel		307	Simerly, Samuel		69
Simerly, Floe		280	Simerly, Sarah		326
Simerly, Flora		10	Simerly, Stella		174,323
Simerly, Francis Jane		305	Simerly, Susan		78,204
Simerly, Francis R.		180	Simerly, Theodore R.		140
Simerly, George		180,336	Simerly, Toy		160
Simerly, Hazel Marie		100	Simerly, Walter		100,255
Simerly, Henry		245,336	Simerly, William (Mrs)		255
Simerly, Infant		49,83,90 126 <	Simerly, W.A.		266
Simerly, Jacob		92	Simerly, W.H.		96
Simerly, John		278,286,318	Simerly, W.M.		123
Simerly, John B.		123	Simerly, W.N.		278
Simerly, John F.		140	Simerly, _____		97
			Simes, Eliza		192

Simmons, Maggie	172	Slagle, Lona	99
Simmons, Maggie Mae	194	Slagle, Maggie	1
Simpson, Alice Della	99	Slagle, Mollie	21,226
Simpson, James	99	Slagle, Nellie	200
Sims, Alice	67	Slagle, Noah	99
Sims, Andrew	233	Slagle, Peter	107
Sims, Andy	88	Slemp, John	170
Sims, A.J.	342	Slimp, Elizabeth	80
Sims, Benie	10	Slimp, Nancy	111,146
Sims, Dan	324	Slimp, Peter	80
Sims, Daniel	177	Sluder, Neiley	173
Sims, Della	306	Sluder, R.B.	185
Sims, Hannah	14	Smalling, Alfred Boyd	80
Sims, Harvie	10	Smalling, Ann	122
Sims, Hattie	233	Smalling, Annie	125
Sims, Infant	257	Smalling, Cora	262
Sims, Jackson	67	Smalling, Duke	172
Sims, Jamie	233	Smalling, Evalyn L.	264
Sims, Jane	269	Smalling, George	264
Sims, John	67	Smalling, Nancy A.	150
Sims, Julia	160	Smalling, Nancy J.	109
Sims, Mary	177	Smalling, Robert W.	80
Sims, Rachel	233	Smalling, R.W.	7
Sims, Rosie	88	Smalling, Samuel M.	273
Sims, Ruth Elizabeth	342	Smalling, Sison	309
Sims, Sara	147	Smart, Calline	28
Sims, Thomas	257	Smatt, Gibe	242
Sims, Wilson	342	Smierly, W.M.	126
Sims. Hattie	355	Smith, Alfred	217
Sims. Rosa	324	Smith, Alice	167
Singletary, John	98	Smith, Annie	186,254
Singleton, Jinia	156	Smith, Armetta B.	350
Sizemore, Beckey	63	Smith, Bessie	244
Sizemore, D____	206	Smith, Bettie	102,286
Sizemore, E.W.	96	Smith, Bruce	161,211,272
Sizemore, George	63	Smith, Bruce A.	192
Slage, Roy A.	107	Smith, Bunch	301
Slagle, Annie	342	Smith, Burl	244
Slagle, Annis	154	Smith, Burl W.	101
Slagle, A.C.	250	Smith, Butler	167
Slagle, A.P.	172	Smith, Carl	49,151,302
Slagle, Charles (Mrs)	76	365	<
Slagle, Eliza	206	Smith, Cart	151
Slagle, Eliza E.	190	Smith, Celia	224
Slagle, Elizabeth	38	Smith, China	302
Slagle, Hattie	132	Smith, Clinton Ellis	243
Slagle, James Peter	107	Smith, Columbus	327
Slagle, Levi	226,236	Smith, C.C.	154,196

Smith, C.E.		108	Smith, Lee		94
Smith, Daisy		116	Smith, Lee (Dr)		311
Smith, David C.		255	Smith, Lillie		163
Smith, David F.		276	Smith, Linda		101
Smith, Dellie		365	Smith, Lizzie		108
Smith, Dorothy		320	Smith, Lois		318
Smith, D.J.		196	Smith, Loss		320
Smith, Ed		186,187,271	Smith, Lottie		95
Smith, Edith C.		196	Smith, Louisa		311
Smith, Edward		272	Smith, Luster		186,285
Smith, Elbert		149	Smith, L.L.		63,96
Smith, Elijah		337	Smith, Maggie		112
Smith, Elizabeth		119	Smith, Mandie		199
Smith, Ethel		317	Smith, Margaret		58,203
Smith, Evelyn Inez		192	Smith, Marry		1
Smith, Fred		176	Smith, Martha		58,350
Smith, George		353,360	Smith, Martha E.		216
Smith, George W.		332	Smith, Mary		102,131,187
Smith, Grant		318,352	190,239,300,325		<
Smith, G.F.L.		1	Smith, Mary Elizabeth		104
Smith, Hattie		234	Smith, Mattie		141
Smith, Henderson		343	Smith, Maudie		174
Smith, Hobart		281	Smith, Minnie		224,363
Smith, Houston		281	Smith, Morah		64
Smith, H.C.		292	Smith, Nancy C.		96
Smith, Ida		264	Smith, Nathaniel		271
Smith, Infant		101,161,211	Smith, Nicholas		332
281,300		<	Smith, Nick		271
Smith, Iva (Mrs)		24	Smith, Nittie		300
Smith, James		189,332	Smith, Ollie		288
Smith, James C.		198,199	Smith, Oma Marton		299
Smith, James Richard		244	Smith, Oscar		300
Smith, James Wilson		353	Smith, Otis		63
Smith, Jane		281	Smith, Polly		58
Smith, Janie		113	Smith, Rebecca		241
Smith, Jaunita		311	Smith, Rob B.		198
Smith, Jim		184	Smith, Robert A.		43,243
Smith, John		102,142,229	Smith, Rosa		169
288,290		<	Smith, Ruby		154
Smith, John K.		217	Smith, R.W.		262
Smith, John W.		142	Smith, Sallie		207,271,332
Smith, Julia		327	Smith, Sarah Ann		315
Smith, Julie		328	Smith, Saral		216
Smith, J.A.		125	Smith, Susan		46,272
Smith, J.A.B.		299,300,327	Smith, Tassie Lee		167
328		<	Smith, Verlin Donley		352
Smith, J.R.E.		216	Smith, Virgie		132
Smith, J.W.		220	Smith, Wiley Stacy		125

Smith, Willard	327	Sorrell, Sterling P.	56
Smith, William	39,251	Sorrell, W.A.	129,241
Smith, William (Mrs)	251	Soules, Cora	159
Smith, W.G.B.	10	Soules, Thomas	156
Smith, W.K.	287	South, Catherine	219
Smith, W.T.	276	South, Jessie	188
Smith, _____	173	South, Mary	89
Smith, _____ Bell	189	South, Sarah	346
Smithpeters, Sarah	104	South, _____	235,325
Smith. Catherine	7	Sparks, Finley Winton	173
Sneed, Albert	355	Sparks, J.A.	173
Sneed, A.J.	137	Sparks, Rebecca	228
Sneed, David	257	Sparks, Sam	173
Sneed, Delia	303	Sparks, Suckie	237
Sneed, Delsa Virginia	137	Sparks, Susan	110
Sneed, Earl	355	Spears, Sarah	295
Sneed, Elizabeth	358	Speer, Edwin	116
Sneed, Nancy	136	Speer, Infant	116
Sneyd, Elbert	24	Spivia, A.P.	314
Sneyd, Launza	24	Spoon, Charles	151
Snider, George Hardin	72	Spoon, Ruby	151
Snider, G.W.	72	Spraks, Susie	102
Snider, J.H. (Mrs)	72	Stafford, Albert	91
Snider, Lula Cornelia	158	Stafford, Gladys	348
Snodgrass, Ann	303	Stafford, Gracie	348
Snodgrass, Bob Taylor	270	Stafford, Thomas	91
Snodgrass, Cad	157	Stafford, T.H.	348
Snodgrass, Cornelius	328	Stalcup, C.C.	279
Snodgrass, Emma	351	Stallings, W.P.	52
Snodgrass, G.W.	157,200	Stanfield, Rebecca	179
Snodgrass, Hollie	336	Stanley, Effie Louise	341
Snodgrass, John	303,328	Stanley, Fred	341
Snodgrass, John C.	169	Stanley, F.M.	341
Snodgrass, J.S.	157	Stanley, Sallie	181
Snodgrass, Myrtle	344	Stanley, Sissie	318
Snodgrass, Nat	133	Stanley, Stacie	256
Snodgrass, Robert	270	Stanly, Lila	205
Snodgrass, Sarah C.	169	Staples, Mollie	358
Snodgrass, William	352	Starling, Rebecca	187
Snodgrass, W. Emery	169	Starnes, Daniel	60
Snow, Honor	228	Starnes, J.H.	107
Snyder, Daniel	253	Steen, Morgan	162
Snyder, Geneva	260	Steen, Nancy	244
Snyder, Infant	5	Steer, B. Caroline	123
Snyder, Noah	5	Step, Clementine M.	115
Sorrell, Eliza L.	241	Stephens, C.M.	232
Sorrell, M.E.	129	Stephens, Dovie	90
Sorrell, Ned Leon	129	Stephens, Florida	281

Stephens, Harriett	86		Stout, Amanda	120
Stephens, Infant	351		Stout, Anna	184
Stephens, Joshua	243		Stout, Annie	130
Stephens, Julia	225		Stout, Arthur	327
Stephens, J.K.	243		Stout, A.G. (Grant)	120
Stephens, Lillie	281		163,220	<
Stephens, Michael	243		Stout, A.K.	327
Stephens, Mike	351		Stout, Bessie	339,341
Stephens, Susie Ann	110		Stout, Cenia	241
Stephens, Taylor	86		Stout, Clarence	361
Stephens, Texie	216		Stout, C.E.	286
Stephens, Thelma	281		Stout, Dan	338
Stephens, Willie	281		Stout, Daniel	164
Stephens, W.T.	110		Stout, Daniel M.	365
Stepp, Bessie	317		Stout, Dave	353
Stepp, Jane	140		Stout, David	75,156,269
Stepp, Mary C.	202		308	<
Stepp, Silas Hagy	11		Stout, D.L.	357
Stepp, ____	217		Stout, D.S.	248
Stevens, Bell	273		Stout, Edward	161,166,170
Stevens, Conley	86		Stout, Eliza	103
Stevens, Ellie	121		Stout, Eva	228
Stevens, Ethel	281		Stout, E.G.	361
Stevens, E.S.	227		Stout, Fanny L.	92
Stevens, Frank	227		Stout, Fred	286
Stevens, G.S.	225		Stout, Geneva	103
Stevens, Henry	248		Stout, George	212,329,361
Stevens, Hester	156		Stout, George W.	126
Stevens, Hester	301		Stout, Godfrey	367
Stevens, John	219		Stout, Grant	194,245,357
Stevens, Johsua	219		Stout, G.W.	95,149,164
Stevens, Maude	119		Stout, Hanner	285
Stevens, Myrtle	90		Stout, Hettie	315
Stevens, M.J.	278		Stout, Infant	3,33,75,92
Stevens, Nannie	85		95,122,126,152,166,>	
Stevens, William	266		212	<
Stevens, W.T.	219		Stout, James	163
Steward, Ethel	6		Stout, James Russell	355
Steward, Manda	330		Stout, James R.	175
Stile, Jane	355		Stout, Joe	367
Stockner, ____	146		Stout, John	337
Stockton, Rubin	46		Stout, John L.	88
Stocton, Rubin	46		Stout, John M.	279
Stone, Minnie F.	19		Stout, John R.	139,308
Stornes, Dewey	310		355	<
Stornes, Drewey	310		Stout, Julia	203
Stornes, Infant	310		Stout, J.A.	92,201
Story, Rufus	187		Stout, Kittie	150

Stout,	Leolia	8	Stover,	Laura Marie	343
Stout,	Lillie	163	Stover,	Maggie	326
Stout,	Lum	255	Stover,	Mattie	60
Stout,	Luther	357	Stover,	Moriah	119
Stout,	Martha	253	Stover,	Patsey	110
Stout,	Mary	314	Stover,	Rhoda	38
Stout,	Maude	194,195	Stover,	Shanon	333
Stout,	Millard	199,202	Stover,	Susan	276
Stout,	Minnie	261	Stover,	Thursday	238
Stout,	M.E.	175	Stover,	Will	183,184,271
Stout,	Nathan	152	Stover,	Wilson	338
Stout,	Nettie	24	Street,	A.L.	339
Stout,	Omar	286	Street,	Beckie	272
Stout,	Ornie Sanford	311	Street,	Bekie	177
Stout,	Polly	256	Street,	Bettie	106,128
Stout,	P.W.	215	Street,	Birdie Lee	144
Stout,	Rachel	171	Street,	Bud	123
Stout,	Rex	329	Street,	Charley	36
Stout,	Robert	169,311	Street,	Clingmon C.	204
Stout,	Salina	156	Street,	C.C.	159
Stout,	Samuel	184	Street,	Daunt	83
Stout,	Sarah	347	Street,	Doak	39
Stout,	Thomas	308	Street,	Ed	316
Stout,	T.J.	139	Street,	Edith	240
Stout,	Violet	357	Street,	Emily	135
Stout,	Virginia	199,202	Street,	Etta	128
Stout,	Wilkie S.	327	Street,	Gomer	123
Stout,	Will	122	Street,	Harrison	144,230
Stout,	William R.	224	Street,	Henry	177
Stout,	W.M.	355	Street,	H.	270,272
Stover,	Alex	68,69	Street,	H.M.	128
Stover,	Alice	73	Street,	Ike	272
Stover,	Andrew J.	289	Street,	Infant	83,230
Stover,	Andy	14	Street,	Jane	39
Stover,	Beatrice	69	Street,	Jossie	272
Stover,	Betsy	339	Street,	Lillie Brown	234
Stover,	Bob	71,333	Street,	Lucy	274
Stover,	Clyde	193	Street,	Nancy	204
Stover,	Daniel	289	Street,	Nettie	166,199
Stover,	Dave	338	Street,	Oma	339
Stover,	David	110	Street,	Peter	77
Stover,	Ellen	271	Street,	Rhoda	256
Stover,	Ethel	68	Street,	Rosa Etta	185
Stover,	James	71,343	Street,	Rosa K.	269
Stover,	John	73,193	Street,	Ruth	316
Stover,	John L.	326,327	Street,	Samuel	77,177
Stover,	J.P.	327	Street,	Simon	51
Stover,	Lane	338	Street,	Stephen	72

Street, Steven Capt	204	Sweeney, Nancy Anne	71
Street, Verlean	201	Sweeney, Tena	212
Street, Wesley	209	Sweeney, Tennie	148
Street, William	201	Swenny, Baker	318
Strickland, Catherine	316	Swift, Lizzie	234
Strickland, Clarence	336	Swift, W.F.	290
Strickland, Trusel	336	Swingle, Eva E.	75
Stuart, James	130	Swingle, Margaret H.	209
Sudwick, Mildred	265	Syren, Ellen M.	175,266
Suess, Charles P.	336	Taler, Buck	214
Suess, Lilian	336	Tate, Florie	230
Sumerlin, M.f.	305	Taylor, Alice	144
Summerland, M.F.	278	Taylor, Allen	150
Summerland, Wilford M.	278	Taylor, Alvin	8,76,189
Surancy, Emily	353	345	<
Susong, Agnes	65	Taylor, Amanda	205
Susong, George	104,237	Taylor, Andrew	186
Susong, Infant	163	Taylor, Andrew J.	173
Susong, James	163	Taylor, Angeline	326
Susong, Joe L.	237	Taylor, Anna	126
Swain, Charly	43	Taylor, Annie	244
Swaner, Barney	81	Taylor, Arthur S.	180
Swaner, Gourley	127	Taylor, A.B.	261
Swaner, Luther	127	Taylor, A.J.	278
Swaner, Mary	159	Taylor, Barah	234
Swaner, Taylor	81	Taylor, Barbary	313
Swaner, Thomas	159	Taylor, Berdie	288
Swaner, Verness	159	Taylor, Bessie	136,261
Swanner, Alice	216	Taylor, Betsy	300,301
Swanner, Alonzo	217	Taylor, Billy	173
Swanner, Amon	216	Taylor, Bob	291,304,366
Swanner, Denie	247	Taylor, Buck	214
Swanner, Floid	112	Taylor, Carley	345
Swanner, G.W.	190	Taylor, Caroline	14
Swanner, Joe	282	Taylor, Carrie Jane	236
Swanner, Joshua (Mrs)	264	Taylor, Cas	279
Swanner, J.P.	192	Taylor, Catherine	124,181
Swanner, Mary	217	Taylor, Charity	204
Swanner, Mary E.	281	Taylor, Clayton	31
Swanner, Nellie	192	Taylor, Clementine	113
Swanner, R.F.	112	Taylor, C.C.	275
Swanner, Sarah	338	Taylor, C.J.	335
Swanner, Taylor	282,284	Taylor, Dora	245
Swanner, Thomas	217	Taylor, Elijah	85
Swanson, _____	111	Taylor, Eliza	261
Sweeney, Jim	62	Taylor, Elizabeth	13,92
Sweeney, Maggie	318	106,215	<
Sweeney, Mary	62	Taylor, Ellen	13,360

Taylor, Emma	288	Taylor, J.L.	231
Taylor, Emma Peters	347	Taylor, J.T.	180,201
Taylor, Esteline	231	Taylor, J.V.	201
Taylor, Eva	86,134,214	Taylor, J.W.	115
Taylor, E.E.	158	Taylor, Kallie	300
Taylor, E.H.	90	Taylor, Lank	366
Taylor, Finer	159	Taylor, Laura	76
Taylor, Flora	151	Taylor, Lee	147,360
Taylor, Frank	85	Taylor, Leevi	155
Taylor, General	76,82	Taylor, Lena	277
Taylor, General J.	201	Taylor, Levice	3
Taylor, George	101,180	Taylor, Lillie	193
180,181,201	<	Taylor, Lizzie	99,250
Taylor, George D.	44	Taylor, Lizzie C,	155
Taylor, George W.	288	Taylor, Lola	195
Taylor, Grace	75,137	Taylor, Losson	188
Taylor, Grant	67	Taylor, Luther	227
Taylor, Henry	227	Taylor, L.D.	118
Taylor, H.	219	Taylor, Maggie	158,185
Taylor, H.L.	232	283,309	<
Taylor, Infant 75,101,105		Taylor, Manuel	125
115,137,149,183,	>	Taylor, Mariah	110
232,250,335	<	Taylor, Martha	242
Taylor, I.C.	185	Taylor, Martin J.	202
Taylor, Jack	291,366	Taylor, Mary	57
Taylor, Jacob	168	Taylor, Mary E.	35
Taylor, Jake	226	Taylor, Michael	96,186
Taylor, James	74,126	Taylor, Mike	118,300
Taylor, James C.	219	Taylor, Moley	337
Taylor, Jane	64,267	Taylor, Mollie	88
Taylor, Jasper	277	Taylor, Mont	64
Taylor, Jefferson	96	Taylor, M.C.	250
Taylor, Jennie	128	Taylor, Nancy	163
Taylor, Joe 75,95,137,186		Taylor, Nannie	29
205,283,	<	Taylor, Nat	195
Taylor, John 105,143,144		Taylor, Nathaniel	112,201
149,150,158,202,	>	Taylor, Noth R.	64
204,226,238,244,	>	Taylor, N.M.	40
245	<	Taylor, Pearl	91
Taylor, John H.	180	Taylor, Pheba	300
Taylor, John J.	185	Taylor, Rufus	119
Taylor, John M.	204	Taylor, R.C.	261
Taylor, John W. Jr.	204	Taylor, Sallie	220,358
Taylor, Julie	219	Taylor, Sam	164
Taylor, J.E.	278	Taylor, Samuel	75,254
Taylor, J.E.	288	Taylor, Sarah	121
Taylor, J.H.	180	Taylor, Sarah C.	34
Taylor, J.J. Jr.	92	Taylor, Sherman	8

Taylor, Snide	304
Taylor, Stella	131
Taylor, Susan	226,276
Taylor, Susis	278
Taylor, S.C.	88
Taylor, Teener	175
Taylor, Thomas	29,254
Taylor, Tinka	168
Taylor, Victoria	275
Taylor, Vila	300
Taylor, Will	86,125,175 226 <
Taylor, Will Jr.	119
Taylor, William	64,110 119,184,226,278 <
Taylor, William R.	147
Taylor, William T.	74
Taylor, W.S.	105,126
Taylor, W.S. (Mrs)	212
Taylor, W.T.	13,147
Taylor, Zella	185
Taylor, _____	33,142,201 240 <
Teague, Anniebell	217
Teague, Disey	308
Teague, Ella	319
Teague, Franie	308
Teague, Herment	141
Teague, Logan	275,308
Teague, Robert	308
Teague, R.A.	275
Teague, Thomas	141,217
Teague, William W.	275
Teaster, Pearl	22
Tenner, Susan	331
Terry, Nancy	247
Tester, B.G.	82
Tester, Carl	267
Tester, Dannia	54
Tester, Infant	112
Tester, Jennie	267,335
Tester, John	82
Tester, L.A.	112,229
Tester, Nellie	193
Tester, Robert	142
Tester, Susan	229
Tester, William H.	82
Tester, William P.	82
Thatney, Matilda	234
Thomas, Charles U.	187
Thomas, Hazel	225
Thomas, Henderson F.	175
Thomas, Henry	225
Thomas, Jennie	326
Thomas, John V.	187
Thomas, Mandy	108
Thomas, Mary	342
Thomas, Susan	124
Thomas, W.S.	175
Thompson, Charles	19,331
Thompson, E.M.	62
Thompson, Infant	19
Thompson, Isam G.	331
Thompson, John	322
Thompson, Larkin	283
Thompson, Maritia	319
Thompson, Mary E.	106
Thompson, Melvina	80
Thompson, Rhoda	60
Thompson, Samuel	239
Thompson, Samuel Jacob	2
Thompson, William	68,205
Thompson, W.N.	116
Tickles, Infant	9
Tillison, James	69
Tilson, Letitia	165
Timbs, Abbie	176
Timbs, Crosley	176
Timbs, Crumley	233
Timbs, Danna	300
Timbs, Dock	198,210,300
Timbs, Gertie	50
Timbs, Mae	198
Timbs, Offie	233
Timbs, Ora Ruth	210
Timbs, Stella	318
Tinner, Alexander	47
Tinner, George W.	119
Tinner, Infant	121
Tinner, James A.	121
Tiptin, John H.	115
Tipton, Aught	258
Tipton, Bud	62
Tipton, Clara A.	72
Tipton, Flora K.	82
Tipton, Infant	53

Tipton, John W.	26	Tolley, Nolia	337
Tipton, J.W.	115	Tolley, Robert T.	252
Tipton, Lockey	62	Tolley, Ruth	227
Tipton, Martha	160	Tolley, Sampson	182,183
Tipton, Mary C.	201	186	<
Tipton, Mary Grace	294	Tolley, Samson	123
Tipton, Pierce	258	Tolley, Sester	183
Tipton, Rachel Brown	115	Tolley, Susan	182
Tipton, Ret	147	Tolley, Swin	232
Tipton, Sidney	258	Tolley, Vista	35
Tipton, Virginia Ray	271	Tolley, Wilburn	186,358
Tipton, Walter P.	271	Tolley, William D.	224
Toler, Rosa M.	159	Tolley, W.M.	232,358
Toler, ____	238	Tolliver, D.C.	223
Toliver, Clinton E.	223	Tolly, John	23
Tolley, Avery	182	Tolly, J.M.	9
Tolley, Brownlow	90	Tonchay, Charles P.	18
Tolley, Castine	182	Toncray, Annie	243
Tolley, Charlie	166,281	Toncray, Caroline	43
Tolley, Dan	223	Toncray, Margaret	42
Tolley, Daniel	113,271	Toncray, William J.	58
Tolley, David	227	Tounsel, Finley	51
Tolley, Dock	90,358	Townsell, Katie	325
Tolley, Dora	281	Townsell, Lee Etta	310
Tolley, Emma	166	Townsell, Will	310
Tolley, France	102	Townsend, Callie	28
Tolley, France R.	102	Townsend, Claud	337
Tolley, Frances	113	Townsend, Ed.	330,204
Tolley, Fred	35	Townsend, Elsie	352
Tolley, Hartie	90	Townsend, Emma	294
Tolley, Hobart	294	Townsend, Emma	328
Tolley, Hosa	123	Townsend, Galilie	216
Tolley, Howard	294	Townsend, George	203
Tolley, Infant	252	Townsend, Georgia	219
Tolley, Jackson	273	Townsend, Ida	210
Tolley, John	113,186	Townsend, Infant	9,328
Tolley, J.H.	259	Townsend, Isaac	9
Tolley, Lace	273	Townsend, James	101,198
Tolley, Larkie E.	102	219	<
Tolley, Lodinia	281	Townsend, Jerd	352
Tolley, Lurly	273	Townsend, John	202,203
Tolley, L.M.	281	219,337,352	<
Tolley, Mack	232	Townsend, J___	198
Tolley, Martha	27,54	Townsend, Larkin	275
Tolley, Mirah	259	Townsend, Lewis	356
Tolley, Mollie	252	Townsend, Louise	221
Tolley, Nancy	35,58,223	Townsend, Nahala	356
Tolley, Nancy An	271	Townsend, Nola	294

Townsend, Pearl	330	
Townsend, Peter	213,275	
Townsend, Sallie	87	
Townsend, Sarah	101,148	
Townsend, Taylor	198,202, 203,337,	<
Townsend, Walter	294,328	
Townsend, Will	244	
Townsend, ____	298	
Treadway, A.J.	140	
Treadway, Bell	366	
Treadway, Ben	265	
Treadway, Benjamin	204	
Treadway, Bessie	65	
Treadway, Bulah	32	
Treadway, Charles	287	
Treadway, C.E.	170,287	
Treadway, Euna	114	
Treadway, Eveline	324	
Treadway, G.H.	141	
Treadway, Hicks	324	
Treadway, Infant	161,170	
Treadway, Jacob	2,117	
Treadway, James S.	189	
Treadway, John	161	
Treadway, John L.	15	
Treadway, Julie	166	
Treadway, J.H.	140	
Treadway, Lettie	186	
Treadway, Lillie	212	
Treadway, Lina	275	
Treadway, Liza	2	
Treadway, Maggie	89	
Treadway, Margie	87	
Treadway, Martha	178	
Treadway, Mary Ann	284	
Treadway, Monroe	186,189, 212	<
Treadway, Morgan	278,316	
Treadway, Nannie A.	277	
Treadway, Nathaniel	189	
Treadway, Ray Elmer	141	
Treadway, Roderick R.	199	
Treadway, Roy Jr.	287	
Treadway, Sarah E.	206	
Treadway, William	206	
Treadway, William Q.	199	
Treadway, W.B.	140	
Treadway, W.R.	199	
Treadway, ____	362	
Trent, Andrew	71	
Trent, James Cecil	71	
Triplett, Abe	314	
Triplett, Charlie	300	
Triplett, Dealie	300	
Triplett, Ernest	69	
Triplett, G.	300	
Triplett, Jessie	123,124	
Triplett, Joel	314	
Triplett, Lillie	295	
Triplett, Love	296	
Triplett, Martha	69	
Triplett, Mary	69	
Triplett, Nannie	259	
Triplett, Rebecca	314	
Triplett, Ruth	259	
Triplett, Samuel	314	
Trivett, Abe	246	
Trivett, Dovie	183	
Trivett, Ellen	216	
Trivett, Infant	72	
Trivett, Jake	133	
Trivett, Kelly	72	
Trivett, Mary A.	187	
Trivett, Nannie	115	
Trivett, Vicy	192	
Trivett, ____	182,183,246	
Troutman, Wash	312	
Troxell, David	70	
Troxell, Infant	26	
Troxell, Jim	295	
Troxell, Joe	295	
Troxell, Mollie	61	
Troxell, Samuel	70	
Trusler, George	76,172	
Trusler, Mary	125	
Trusler, Mollie	73	
Trusler, W.M.	71	
Trussler, George	71	
Trussler, Maggie	71	
Tucker, A.J.	106	
Tucker, Bud (Mrs)	199	
Tucker, Dolly	164	
Tucker, Infant	106	
Tucker, Joseph	164	
Tucker, Malcolm M.	164	

Turbyfield, Infant	122
Turbyfield, Jane	138
Turbyfield, John	122
Turner, Anna	174
Turner, Dan	282
Turner, Hazel	37
Turner, Herald	282
Turner, Infant	70
Turner, James	57
Turner, John F.	282
Turner, John S.	23
Turner, Julia	70
Turner, Martha	353
Turner, Mary E.	165
Turner, Milda	57
Turner, Nellie Cleo	150
Turner, Ralph	70
Turner, Ruth	191,310
Turner, Sam	150
Turner, Susan	133
Turner, Will	79
Twiggs, Augustus	353
Twiggs, Catherine	354
Twiggs, Daisy	353
Twiggs, Guss	354
Twiggs, Prudie Miller	353
Umpris, Lillie	154
Underwood, Elizabeth	341
Underwood, John	111,136,215
Underwood, Pearl	215
Underwood, Sally	136
Underwood, Sarah Bula	111
Usary, David	104
Usary, Earnest	345
Usary, Earnest Jr.	345
Usary, Edna	105
Usary, Samuel	105
Usary, Sarah	104
Vance, Birdie Alma	141
Vance, Don	274
Vance, Gladys Marie	339
Vance, Henry	339
Vance, John	141,264
Vance, Julia	98,114
Vance, J.P.	264
Vance, Polly	127
Vance, Samuel	306
Vance, Verna	288
Vance, Walter	288
Vance, Winnie	264
Vance, W.B.	339
Vandeventer, Barbara	142
Vandeventer, Carrie	169
Vandeventer, Celil	167
Vandeventer, Jacob	142,217
Vandeventer, John	123
Vandeventer, John T.	71
Vandeventer, J.P.	115
Vandeventer, Kate	80
Vandeventer, Lorena	115
Vandeventer, Marion	167,169
Vandike, Clyde	68
Vandike, Julie	324
Vandike, Marques	139
Vandike, P.M.	68
Vandike, R.M.	68
VanHook, Grace	199
Vanhoy, Lesetta J.	311
Vanhoy, L.J. (Mrs)	94
Vanhoy, Nancy (Mrs)	36
Vanhuss, D.B.	258
Vanhuss, Effie	219
Vanhuss, Elizabeth	65
Vanhuss, Infant	258
Vanhuss, J.F.	258
Vanhuss, Katie	162
Vanhuss, Minnie	162
Vanhuss, Myrtle	221
Vanhuss, Rebecca	279
Vanhuss, Tom	219
Vanover, Delia	72
Vanover, Roby	72
Vanoy, Martha Preston	242
Vaughn, Anna	202
Vaughn, Charles	38
Vaughn, Lottie	1
Vaught, Lillie	111,136
Vaught, Mary	255
Vaught, Pernnie Ethel	364
Vaught, W.M.	134
Vaun, Anna	199
Venable, Rebecca	337
Veniable, Lucinda	247

Vest, Arch	309	Wagner, Elizabeth		293
Vest, Arch J.	244	Wagner, E.J.		115
Vest, Elizabeth	222	Wagner, Frankie		189
Vest, John	244	Wagner, George W.	255,	366
Vest, Katahrine	301	Wagner, G. Edward		311
Vest, Lottie	244	Wagner, G.E.		204
Vest, Lula	325	Wagner, Infant	137,	326
Vest, Mary	282	Wagner, I.G.		142
Vestie, ____	270	Wagner, James Newton		366
Viall, Dodge	272	Wagner, Joe	253,255,	326
Viall, Frank	272	Wagner, Joseph	247,	311
Vials, William H.	57	Wagner, Joseph W.		247
Vilis, Maude	132	Wagner, J.W.		243
Vines, Addie E.	220	Wagner, Mary	50,	122
Vines, Beuna	140	Wagner, Mary Louise		138
Vines, Dan	365	Wagner, Nancy		247
Vines, Edward	11	Wagner, Nora Ethel		142
Vines, Grover	318	Wagner, Rachel		121
Vines, Harry	220	Wagner, Rebecca		204
Vines, Hattie	328	Wagner, Richell		137
Vines, Hobart	269	Wagner, Sarah		228
Vines, Infant	19,108	Wagner, Sofia		138
Vines, Jane	156	Wagner, T.S.		238
Vines, Jose	170	Wagner, Wilson		137
Vines, Josey	161	Wagner, ____		189
Vines, Josie	140	Waldren, Rebecca		116
Vines, L.M.	270	Walforn, Pauline		87
Vines, Margaret	166	Walker, Canada		276
Vines, Monroe	351	Walker, Carr		116
Vines, N.W.	10	Walker, Chester		258
Vines, Ray	351,365	Walker, C.		116
Vines, William	108,130, 166	Walker, Elbert		303
	<	Walker, Emaline		45
Vines, ____	269	Walker, Grace		116
Voncanan, A.F.	269	Walker, Jesse		303
Voncanan, Glades M.	269	Walker, J.B.		242
Voncanon, C.A.	179	Walker, Lola		258
Wagner, Adam	121	Walker, Mary		275
Wagner, Annie Austin	12	Walker, Millard A.		41
Wagner, A.C.	257	Walker, Nat		276
Wagner, A.R.	138	Walker, Yansal		104
Wagner, Bertha	320	Wallace, Luther		281
Wagner, Catherine	140	Wallace, Nancy		167
Wagner, Coy (Mrs)	366	Wallace, Oretta		352
Wagner, C.E.	247	Wallace, Warren		281
Wagner, Deliah	142	Wallis, Lottie		193
Wagner, D.S.	140,311	Wallis, Sherman		193
Wagner, Elis	121	Walsh, Berthy		364

Walsh, James	274	Warren, Sabina	305
Walsh, Sarah	97	Warrick, Alice	151
Walsh, W.R.	97	Waters, Henry	359
Wampler, Fred	352	Waters, Jennie Lee	359
Wampler, Ottie	352	Waters, Laura	184
Ward, Ace	288	Waters, Martha Lucy	162
Ward, A.L.	52	Watson, Cordie Eva	149
Ward, A.S.	209,244	Watson, Daniel S.	314
Ward, Bertha	265	Watson, Elizie	199
Ward, Biner	341	Watson, Flora	47
Ward, Butler	209	Watson, Hattie	134
Ward, Carolina	124	Watson, Hubert	54
Ward, Clate	318	Watson, Infant	14,101
Ward, Cretie	148	Watson, Ira	312
Ward, Daniel	120	Watson, Kate	232
Ward, Dottie	256	Watson, Kattie	209
Ward, Eugene	233	Watson, Luna	22
Ward, Eva	359	Watson, Mama	3
Ward, Gene	350	Watson, Mollie	68,189
Ward, Howard	244	Watson, Ralph	312
Ward, Infant	320	Watson, Ray	314
Ward, Isaac	304	Watson, Rosa	149
Ward, Jane	148	Watson, Rosie	199
Ward, Jennie	267	Watson, Roy	149,199,312
Ward, John	197	Watson, Thomas	3
Ward, Keren H.	344	Watson, Wiley	272
Ward, Laura	301	Watson, Will	101
Ward, Lona	282	Watson, Willie	14
Ward, Ludalla	365	Watson, W.W.	197
Ward, Lula	81	Waycaster, Albert O.	11
Ward, Mandy	163,220	Waycaster, Allen	132
Ward, Marrie	287	Waycaster, Benson H.	81
Ward, Mary	51	Waycaster, Caroline	168
Ward, Mary Alice	350	Waycaster, Charcie	120
Ward, Mattie	209,284	Waycaster, Elija	297
Ward, Minnie	318	Waycaster, E.B.	132
Ward, Mollie	82	Waycaster, George W.	297
Ward, Rhody	88	Waycaster, Goldie	142
Ward, Thomas F.	81	Waycaster, Gracie	91
Ward, Tobetha	204	Waycaster, Isaac	81
Ward, T.T.	344	Waycaster, I.G.	297
Ward, Will	328	Waycaster, Mary	315
Ward, William C.	197	Waycaster, O.C.	132
Ward, William S.	233	Waycaster, Sarah C.	81
Ward, W.G.	320	Waycaster, S.	22
Wardeck, Jim	160	Waycaster, William	142
Wards, Biner	341	Weaver, David G.	163
Warren, Roe	305	Weaver, E.B.	103

Name	Page	Name	Page
Weaver, Henry	111	Whaley, Benjamin B.	91
Weaver, Huston	225	Whaley, Bula D.	96
Weaver, Maude	333	Whaley, Harrison	91
Weaver, Russell	111	Whaley, James	198
Weaver, Susan	290	Whaley, Myrtle	316
Webb, Albert	154	Whaley, Nathan W.	96
Webb, Bessie	99	Whaley, Rachael	50
Webb, Charles	237	Whaley, Roy	318
Webb, Cinda	208	Whaley, William	318
Webb, Duben	359	Wheeler, Gades	250
Webb, Elbert	154	Whieenhunt, Laura	140
Webb, Gussie	291	Whipple, William	72
Webb, Henry	123	Whipple, William G.	72
Webb, John	187	Whisenhunt, Amanda	211
Webb, Julia	237	Whisenhunt, Hannah	358
Webb, L.W.	70	Whisenhunt, Infant	280
Webb, Myrtle	264	Whisenhunt, Isaac	140,310
Webb, Orris Willard	154	Whisenhunt, Joe	280,282
Webb, Sallie	229	Whisenhunt, Lena	310
Webster, Lottie	7	Whisenhunt, Nola	282
Weeks, _____	209	Whisenhunt, Wiley	358
Welch, Joanna	253	Whisenhut, A.B.	53
Wells, Infant	2	Whitaker, I.N.	259
Welsh, Joe	252	Whitaker, Laura A.	259
Welsh, Sara	252	Whitamore, R.B.	162
Wesley, John	318	Whitamore, Willie M.	351
West, Annie	190	Whitamore, W.F.	351
West, Betsy	198	White, Abraham	153
West, Beulah	350	White, Alexander	95
West, Delliah C.	334	White, Anna	178
West, Jane	197	White, Ben	145,290
West, John	330	White, Bettie	159
West, Johnson James	170	White, Catherine	176
190	<	White, Cora	259
West, Joseph B.	190	White, David M.	146
West, J.	294	White, D.F.	158
West, J.B.	330	White, D.L.	317
West, J.J.	354	White, Ed	26,307
West, Rosy Kate	170	White, Elizabeth	254
West, Walter Wallace	294	White, Elmer	366
West, William	198	White, Fannie	67
West, W.H.	334,350	White, Flossie	302
Wetzel, Fred Eugene	143	White, George	31,153,327
Wetzel, Fred L.	143	White, Grace	52
Whailey, C.C.	156	White, Hattie	217
Whailey, Legrand	156	White, Ida Bell	244
Whaley, Alice L.	340	White, Infant	282
Whaley, A.C.	316	White, James Harry	307

White, Jane	5	
White, Joe	37	
White, John V.	233	
White, J.J.	153	
White, J.W.	212	
White, Lawson	233	
White, Lawson W.	146	
White, Leeaner	192	
White, Lewis	95	
White, Lottie	43	
White, Lou	193	
White, Lula	74	
White, Martha	212	
White, Mildred	290	
White, M.J. Mrs.	137	
White, Nona	317	
White, Ottie	282	
White, Robert	233	
White, Roy	254	
White, Sabrie	52	
White, Sallie	266	
White, Samuel C.	145	
White, Thomas	69,176,327	
White, Ursal	145	
White, Washington	175	
White, W.E.	366	
Whitehead, Albert	237	
Whitehead, Anna	58	
Whitehead, Bell	156	
Whitehead, Bessie	231	
Whitehead, Bettie	329	
Whitehead, Biddie	170	
Whitehead, Caison	347	
Whitehead, Carry	315	
Whitehead, Carter	343	
Whitehead, Celia	280	
Whitehead, Claud	265	
Whitehead, Clementine	59	
Whitehead, C.V.	150,248 324	<
Whitehead, Dan	265,266	
Whitehead, Daniel	115	
Whitehead, Dauson	238	
Whitehead, David	249	
Whitehead, Duffie	356	
Whitehead, Earl	231,356	
Whitehead, Edith	353	
Whitehead, Emma	228	
Whitehead, Frank	330	
Whitehead, George	132,169	
Whitehead, Grace	266	
Whitehead, G.L.	265	
Whitehead, G.W.	238	
Whitehead, Hannah	354	
Whitehead, Hattie	62,319	
Whitehead, Henry E.	262	
Whitehead, Herbert	194	
Whitehead, Infant	318	
Whitehead, Jackson	81	
Whitehead, James	87,173 249,343	<
Whitehead, James Polk	348	
Whitehead, Jerdson	287	
Whitehead, John	87,262 353,266	<
Whitehead, John L.	262	
Whitehead, Larkin	147,194	
Whitehead, Larkin L.	81	
Whitehead, Lass	254	
Whitehead, Lelia	159	
Whitehead, Liza	330	
Whitehead, Loos	132	
Whitehead, Loss	318	
Whitehead, L.L.	228	
Whitehead, Margaret	23 194	<
Whitehead, Marvel	147	
Whitehead, Marven	343	
Whitehead, Mary Jane	248	
Whitehead, Mollie	169	
Whitehead, Nat	353	
Whitehead, Ora Bell	318	
Whitehead, Oscar	315	
Whitehead, Pearl	312	
Whitehead, Ralph R.	254	
Whitehead, Sallie	54,185 306	<
Whitehead, Samuel	273	
Whitehead, Sarah Ann	147	
Whitehead, Sarah F.	347	
Whitehead, Suda	181,260	
Whitehead, Susan	259	
Whitehead, Thomas	354	
Whitehead, Tom	348	
Whitehead, T.H.	228	

Whitehead, William	153
273,348	<
Whitehead, ___	237
Whiteman, Katie	334
Whitemore, Kate	198
Whitlow, James L.	291
Whitson, Abe	135
Whitson, Isabelle	82
Whitson, Mary	124
Whitson, Sally	135
Whitson, Sarah	206
Widener, Joe	110
Widener, Violet	110
Widener, Willis	212
Widener, Wilma	212
Widner, Annie F.	148
Widner, Mary Ellen	253
Widner, Mollie	71
Widner, Willis	148,196
Widner, Willis M.	253
Wilbird, Roxie	233
Wilbrd, A.S.	233
Wilburn, Dora	77
Wilburn, Landon	232
Wilburn, Sam	112
Wilburn, Sarah E.	187
Wilcox, David	264
Wilcox, David Powell	165
Wilcox, Elizabeth	359
Wilcox, Jennie	148,152
Wilcox, John	165
Wilcox, Margaret P.	335
Wilcox, Nancy	326
Wilcox, O.A.	165
Wilcox, Rebecca	180,241
Wilcox, Sarah	357
Wilkens, Jims	207
Willey, J.T.	65
Willey, Leo T.	65
Williamd, P.	318
Williams, Abigail	257,342
Williams, Addie B.	15
Williams, Albert	321
Williams, Alfred	283
Williams, Allen	170
Williams, Althia	5
Williams, Andy	146
Williams, Anna B.	103
Williams, Annie Jean	127
Williams, Arzilla J.	367
Williams, A. Julian	94
Williams, A.A.	354
Williams, A.B.	225
Williams, A.C.	98,222
Williams, A.G.	230
Williams, A.J.	93
Williams, Bellie	351
Williams, Bessie	316
Williams, Betsie	226
Williams, Binnia Jane	340
Williams, Bryan	126
Williams, Callie	228
Williams, Carline	150
Williams, Caroline	81
Williams, Cass	60
Williams, Celia	188,324
Williams, Charles	61
Williams, Charlotte A.	148
Williams, Claud	340
Williams, C.B.	117
Williams, Daisy	157
Williams, Daniel	317
Williams, Dora	155
Williams, Elihu	214
Williams, Elijah	351
Williams, Eliza	283,295
307,365	<
Williams, Elizabeth	191
Williams, Ellen	345
Williams, Emma	44,254,338
Williams, Eva	321
Williams, Eva Kate	61
Williams, Eveline	209
Williams, E.B.	254
Williams, E.J.	103,145
155,296	<
Williams, Feb	292
Williams, F.A.	161
Williams, F.P.	296
Williams, George	112
Williams, Gertie	317
Williams, Godfrey	146
Williams, Grace	5,319
Williams, Grace Mae	293
Williams, Harvey	98
Williams, Hazel	115

Williams, Hence		284	Williams, Minnie		104
Williams, Henry		64,85	Williams, Mollie		249
Williams, H.C.		98	Williams, M.C.		260,305
Williams, Infant		29,59,64	Williams, Nancy		313
68,85,98,126,161,272 <			Williams, N.T.		252
Williams, Isaac		41	Williams, Odis		112
Williams, Issack		35	Williams, Paul		170
Williams, Ivel		29	Williams, Paul Alfred		249
Williams, Jack		244	Williams, Pleasant		98
Williams, James H.T.		319	Williams, Ples		342
Williams, Jess		272	Williams, P.M.		104
Williams, Joe		171	Williams, Redding		319
Williams, John		110,220	Williams, Rhoda A. T.		68
268,292		<	Williams, Robert		80
Williams, John B.		319	Williams, Rosa		95,151
Williams, John C.		146,153	Williams, Rube		175
Williams, Josephine		60	Williams, Ruby		225
Williams, Josie		5	Williams, R.J.		61
Williams, June		260	Williams, R.L.		288,319
Williams, J.C.		155,258	Williams, R.R.		32
Williams, J.F.		73,85	Williams, Sallie		65,130
Williams, J.G.		191	145,176		<
Williams, J.H.		219	Williams, Sallie R.		24
Williams, J.S.		357	Williams, Sam		98
Williams, J.T.		148	Williams, Samuel		153,161
Williams, Lavina		255	212		<
Williams, Lee		289,365	Williams, Sarah		328
Williams, Leon		254	Williams, Sarance		29
Williams, Lloyd Q.		321	Williams, Shapp A.		258
Williams, Lonnie		157	Williams, Sidney G.		107
Williams, Lottie		365	Williams, Sinda		104
Williams, Louise		367	Williams, Susanah		269
Williams, Louise H.		279	Williams, S.A. (Mrs)		145
Williams, Lourie		258	Williams, S.H.		203
Williams, Lucindy		205	Williams, S.W.		115
Williams, Lucy		78,313	Williams, Thomas		303,313
Williams, L.C.		107	Williams, Thomas J.		42
Williams, L.D.		345	Williams, Tom		68
Williams, L.S.		232,279	Williams, Trephoria		83
Williams, L.T.		214	Williams, T.E.		238
Williams, Maggie		142,193	Williams, Viola		214
Williams, Margaret		303	Williams, Virgil		6
Williams, Martha		68,205	Williams, Warren G.		305
Williams, Mary		31,50	Williams, William S.		80
Williams, Matilda		127,155	Williams, Winnie		24
Williams, Mattie V.		167	Williams, Worley		292
Williams, Mike C.(Dr)		249	Williams, W.G.		59
Williams, Mike G.		275	Williams, W.I.		82

Williams, W.J.	60	Wilson, G.A.	229
Williams, W.L.	127	Wilson, G.W.	317
Williams, Zilla	267	Wilson, Hannah	99,120,349
Williams, Zillie	304	Wilson, Harriett	127
Williams, ____	70,257 277,329 <	Wilson, Henry	226
Williamsm W.C.	170	Wilson, Hester	25
Williamson, Lottie	61	Wilson, Honer	349
Williams. Celia	101	Wilson, Howard K.	121
Willis, Charlie	102	Wilson, H. Ellen	279
Willis, James	223	Wilson, Ida	183
Willis, James Lace	271	Wilson, Infant	111,337 338 <
Willis, J.P.	58	Wilson, Jack	337,338
Willis, Laura	123	Wilson, Jackson	135
Willis, Leneer	281	Wilson, James	121,127,345 355,359 <
Willis, Wesley	340		
Willis, W.M.R.	271	Wilson, James P.	195
Wills, Jennie	319	Wilson, James R.	135
Willson, Jim	159	Wilson, James Stacy	359
Willson, Susan	24	Wilson, Jane	99,162
Wilson, Abraham	359	Wilson, Janes	310
Wilson, Alec	287	Wilson, Janes E.	310
Wilson, Alexander	80	Wilson, Jim	183
Wilson, Alice	189	Wilson, John	66,80,93,130 203,246,350 <
Wilson, Andrew	293		
Wilson, Andson	28	Wilson, John A.	195
Wilson, Andy	127,156,215	Wilson, John Sr.	350
Wilson, Anna	243	Wilson, Jordan	127
Wilson, Betsy	70	Wilson, Joseph	8
Wilson, Bettie	302	Wilson, J. Richard	226
Wilson, Clarence	51	Wilson, J.R.	226
Wilson, Closson	162	Wilson, J.S. (Mrs)	359
Wilson, Cornelia	305	Wilson, Katie	324
Wilson, David	99,162,265	Wilson, Landon	125,227 345 <
Wilson, Donnie	280		
Wilson, Eldrith	135	Wilson, Laura	165,183,276
Wilson, Eliza	338	Wilson, Lefler	159
Wilson, Eliza C.	106	Wilson, Lemuel	305
Wilson, Eliza Jane	345	Wilson, Leonard	292
Wilson, Elizabeth	136,306	Wilson, Leonard C.	281
Wilson, Ellen	343	Wilson, Lizzie	211
Wilson, Emily	229	Wilson, Loftus	262
Wilson, Ester	28	Wilson, Lon H.	359
Wilson, Flora	361	Wilson, Lucy Jane	163
Wilson, Frankie	258	Wilson, Maggie	272
Wilson, George	66,292	Wilson, Maggie Nunan	343
Wilson, Gilbert	88,111 262 <	Wilson, Mara	215
		Wilson, Margarette	320

Wilson, Mary	12,66,100	
325	<	
Wilson, Maud	246	
Wilson, Michel	159	
Wilson, Mollie	301	
Wilson, Mordica	99	
Wilson, Nancy	3,130,197	
Wilson, Neiley	88	
Wilson, Neita	312	
Wilson, Oninnie	343	
Wilson, Pansy Pearl	12	
Wilson, Poe	156,325	
Wilson, Polly	135	
Wilson, Preacly	344	
Wilson, Ray	159	
Wilson, Red	293	
Wilson, Richard	151	
Wilson, Robert	93	
Wilson, Sallie	36,195,236	
359	<	
Wilson, Samuel	18	
Wilson, Sarah	29,122,190	
344	<	
Wilson, Sarah J.	302	
Wilson, Selma (Mrs)	353	
Wilson, Smith	118	
Wilson, Sol	303,350,353	
Wilson, Susan	91	
Wilson, Tapley	197	
Wilson, Thomas H.	279	
Wilson, Toke	312	
Wilson, Troy	183	
Wilson, Wash	175	
Wilson, William B.	183	
Wilson, William D.	62	
Wilson, William N.	183	
Wilson, William R.	258	
Wilson, William Smith	293	
Wilson, Worley Ernest	151	
Wilson, Worlie	118	
Wilson, W.M.	159	
Wilson, Z.N.	280	
Wilson, ____	101	
Winter, Augusta A.	127	
Winter, Henry	127	
Winter, Mary B.	127	
Winters, Bessie	93,161	
212	<	
Winters, Bessie Lee	302	
Winters, Carrirk	109	
Winters, Cinda	173	
Winters, Cora	258	
Winters, Cynthia	258	
Winters, Ellen	77	
Winters, Fred	109	
Winters, Infant	93,175	
212,243	<	
Winters, Inma	25	
Winters, James	212,336	
Winters, John	273	
Winters, John H.	316	
Winters, Lucinda	221	
Winters, Lucy	336	
Winters, Mack	243	
Winters, Mary C.	123	
Winters, Monroe	175	
Winters, Odell	302	
Winters, Rosa	331	
Winters, Tesh	95	
Winters, Tine	161	
Winters, Vista	55	
Winters, Wilford	273	
Winters, William	93,161	
212	<	
Winters, William M.	302	
Winters, W.M.	302,316	
Wisenhunt, Infant	117	
Wisenhunt, Willy	117	
Wisenhut, Arthur	9	
Wisenhut, Infant	27	
Witherspoon, Kennith	101	
Witherspoon, Sam	101	
Wood, Delia	246	
Wood, Infant	72	
Wood, R.F.	72	
Wood, Samuel Burnett	211	
Wood, Theodore	69	
Wood, Thomas	69	
Wood, W.B.	211	
Woodby, Annie	188	
Woodby, Ellen	339	
Woodby, Jerry	211	
Woodby, Jerry	284	
Woodby, Jessie	294	
Woodby, Lee	336	
Woodby, Mania	336	

Woodby, Rhoda	294	Younce, Ed.			367
Woodby, ____	188	Younce, Ettie			224
Woodfin, Lucinda	319	Younce, F.F.			224
Woodley, Ellen	224	Younce, J.W. (Mrs)			15
Woodley, Martha	86	Younce, N.J.			366
Woodley, Winnie	55	Younce, Phillip			206
Woodruff, E.M.	126,104	Younce, Soloman			366
Woodruff, Nancy	104	Younce, S.S.			224
Woods, Darkie	344	Younce, W.C.			367
Woods, Emanuel	232	Younce, W.E.			366
Woods, Evalyn	359	Young, Clay			149
Woods, Frank	344	Young, Clifford			51
Woods, Harrill	344	Young, C.T.			230
Woods, Infant	232	Young, Daniel			47
Woods, James Madison	82	Young, Foy			38
Woods, Katey	354	Young, Garrett			149
Woods, Mary	253	Young, H.P.			59
Woods, Paul	284	Young, Ida	229,	245,	246
Woods, Ruben	82,284	Young, Jermima			236
Woods, R.F.	359	Young, Joe			133
Woods, R____	209	Young, John W.			59
Woods, William T.	209	Young, J.N.			352
Woods, ____	27	Young, Kate			47
Woodward, ____	72	Young, Martha			113
Woolverton, Jane	354	Young, Melvin			86
Woolverton, Richard	354	Young, Milt			81
Worley, Thomas E.	66	Young, Patterson			296
Wright, Aaron	277,297,298	Young, Sarah			133
Wright, Bonnie	20	Young, Sukie			133
Wright, Gracie	58	Young, S.S.			113
Wright, Infant	69	Young, Vida			241
Wright, Jane	297	Young, Wilson			296
Wright, Kirk	256	Young, Wilson (Mrs)			296
Wright, Lourance	254	Young, ____			90
Wright, Margaret M.	126				
Wright, Mary Margaret	138				
Wright, Plato	69,138,254				
Wright, Samuel	60,298				
Wright, Samuel S.	126				
Wright, Thomas	209				
Wright, Thomas M.	209				
Wright, Wesley	254				
Wright, ____	272				
Wyette, Dick	352				
Wyette, Lucreesie	352				
Yates, Gemima	104				
Yokley, Mary Ann	105				
Younce, Carl L.	367				

www.ingramcontent.com/pod-product-compliance
Lightning Source LLC
Chambersburg PA
CBHW050241230426
43664CB00012B/1782